T0314099

Rethinking Expectations

Rethinking Expectations

THE WAY FORWARD FOR MACROECONOMICS

Edited by

Roman Frydman *and* Edmund S. Phelps

PRINCETON UNIVERSITY PRESS

Princeton and Oxford

Published by Princeton University Press, 41 William Street, Princeton, New Jersey 08540
In the United Kingdom: Princeton University Press, 6 Oxford Street, Woodstock,
Oxfordshire OX20 1TW
press.princeton.edu

Library of Congress Cataloging-in-Publication Data

Rethinking expectations : the way forward for macroeconomics / edited by Roman Frydman
and Edmund S. Phelps.
   p.   cm.
  Includes bibliographical references and index.
  ISBN 978-0-691-15523-4 (hardcover : alk. paper)
  1. Macroeconomics.   2. Rational expectations (Economic theory)   I. Frydman, Roman,
1948– II. Phelps, Edmund S.
HB172.5.R48   2013
339—dc23   2012030492

British Library Cataloging-in-Publication Data is available

This book has been composed in Sabon using ZzTEX
by Princeton Editorial Associates Inc., Scottsdale, Arizona

Printed on acid-free paper. ∞

Printed in the United States of America

10 9 8 7 6 5 4 3 2 1

CONTENTS

Rethinking Expectations

Which Way Forward for Macroeconomics and Policy Analysis?

Roman Frydman and Edmund S. Phelps

There was a palpable sense of excitement among the economists who met in Philadelphia in 1969 at the conference organized by Edmund Phelps. Their research over the preceding years had coalesced into a new approach to macroeconomic analysis, one that based macrorelationships on explicit microfoundations. These foundations' distinctive feature was to accord market participants' expectations an autonomous role in economists' models of aggregate outcomes. The conference contributions, published in what came to be known as "the Phelps microfoundations volume" (Phelps et al. 1970), provided radically new accounts of the comovements of macroeconomic aggregates—notably, inflation and unemployment. They also cast serious doubt on the validity of policy analysis based on then-popular Keynesian macroeconometric models.

The Phelps volume is often credited with pioneering the currently dominant approach to macroeconomic analysis. Indeed, it is easy to see why today's prevailing models of aggregate outcomes might seem to share much with their counterparts in the Phelps volume. Like their predecessors in the late 1960s, economists today often point to their models' "microfoundations" as their essential feature. Moreover, in modeling decisionmaking, these microfoundations include a representation of market participants' expectations. However, on closer inspection, the similarities between today's models and those included in the Phelps volume are purely linguistic.

The authors thank the Alfred P. Sloan Foundation for its support of the Center on Capitalism and Society's 8th Annual Conference, at which the papers published in this volume were originally presented. Ned Phelps acknowledges the Ewing Marion Kauffman Foundation's support for his research, and Roman Frydman is grateful to the Institute for New Economic Thinking (INET) for its support of his work on Imperfect Knowledge Economics. The authors are indebted to Michael Goldberg for his invaluable comments on a previous draft of this chapter.

In the early 1970s, just a few years after the Phelps volume was published, economists began to embrace the Rational Expectations Hypothesis (REH), according to which market participants' expectations are "essentially the same as the predictions of the relevant economic theory" (Muth 1961: 316). What has been largely overlooked is that, in contrast to the contributors to the Phelps volume, REH theorists presume that the role of market participants' expectations in driving outcomes is *not* autonomous from the other components of the model. As one of the pioneers of the REH approach succinctly put it: "in rational expectations models, people's beliefs are among the outcomes of [economists'] theorizing. They are not inputs" (Evans and Honkapohja 2005: 566). Because REH models, by design, rule out an autonomous role for expectations, they are best viewed as derailing, rather than developing, the microfoundations approach.

Early critics pointed out REH's fundamental epistemological flaws (see Frydman 1982, 1983; Frydman and Phelps 1983; Phelps 1983). They argued that REH, even if viewed as a bold abstraction or approximation, is grossly inadequate for representing how even minimally reasonable profit-seeking participants forecast the future in real-world markets. Nevertheless, for various reasons (some of them discussed in this volume), an overwhelming majority of economists has embraced REH as *the* way to represent how rational individuals think about the future.

The epistemological flaws inherent in REH models have, not surprisingly, resulted in serious empirical difficulties, despite decades of "fine-tuning." As one of us recently commented, "the stampede toward 'rational expectations,' widely called a 'revolution,' though it was only a generalization of the neoclassical idea of equilibrium . . . has not illuminated how the world economy works" (Phelps 2007: xv).

Nowhere have REH's epistemological flaws and empirical disappointments been more apparent than in efforts to model financial market outcomes, which are largely driven by participants' expectations. Beginning with Robert Shiller's (1981) pathbreaking paper, research has shown that REH models are unable to explain the basic features of fluctuations and risk in stock markets. Likewise, in their magisterial work on the current state of international macroeconomics, Maurice Obstfeld and Kenneth Rogoff (1996: 625) concluded that "the undeniable difficulties that international economists encounter in empirically explaining nominal exchange-rate movements are an embarrassment, but one shared with virtually any other field that attempts to explain asset price data."

The failures of REH explanations of aggregate outcomes gave rise to alternative approaches, most notably behavioral finance models. However, sober assessments even by the likes of Obstfeld and Rogoff did not dispel the faith of most economists that REH models would one day be able to explain financial market outcomes and macroeconomic performance.

Indeed, in the wake of the crisis that began in 2007, most economists continue to seek modifications of REH models that would remedy their empirical failures. However, by highlighting the irredeemable shortcomings of so-called rational market models, the crisis has led many researchers to join the quest to develop alternatives to REH.

So, what comes next? Although many more researchers now seem to agree that we need new approaches to macroeconomics and finance theory, the way forward has not been easy to discern. This is to be expected during a time of transition away from an approach that for decades has virtually monopolized the education and thinking of professional economists.

To be sure, the proposed alternatives differ in important respects from the approach promoted in the Phelps volume. But the recent flurry of theoretical efforts has been notable for approaches that in one way or another bring us back to the major theme of the original Phelps conference: non-REH modeling of market participants' expectations and their active role in driving aggregate outcomes. The new models have led to reconsideration of some of the main applied problems that occupied the participants in the Phelps conference and subsequent REH researchers: explaining employment fluctuations, modeling the natural rate of unemployment, and investigating the consequences of economic policy.

In view of the financial crisis, recent research efforts have also been focused on closely related themes: understanding the role of expectations in modeling fluctuations in asset prices and risk, and representing the two-way interdependence between asset markets and the real economy. The crisis has also demanded reconsideration of the theory and practice of economic policy.

With that in mind, in the fall of 2010, the Center on Capitalism and Society invited researchers engaged in developing alternatives to REH to a conference commemorating the fortieth anniversary of the Phelps volume. In this introductory chapter, we provide a brief, admittedly idiosyncratic discussion of the papers presented, the historical background, and the various efforts to reinvent macroeconomics that were discussed at the conference. In view of the central role played by autonomous expectations in the contributions to the Phelps volume, this overview devotes attention particularly to non-REH alternatives—many of which are represented in this volume—and their implications for economic analysis.

A Research Program Derailed

Even cursory observation indicates that how market participants in a modern economy think about the future and revise their forecasts is one of the crucial factors driving their decisionmaking (and thus outcomes) in many markets. Implementing a formal approach to macroeconomic analysis that is based on individual decisionmaking requires, therefore, that an economist represent participants' forecasting behavior mathematically. In discussing his vision for the microfoundations approach, Phelps et al. (1970: 22) underscored the fundamental difficulty in portraying individuals' expectations: "isolated and apprehensive, these Pinteresque figures construct expectations of the state of the economy . . . and maximize relative to that imagined world."

The papers presented at the Phelps conference did not attempt to formalize market participants' "imagined world." Instead, relying on the so-called adaptive expectations rule, they modeled the forecasting process as an automatic response to forecast errors: participants were assumed to revise up or down their one-period-ahead forecast of, say, inflation by a fixed proportion of the error between the realization of inflation in the current period and the previous period's inflation forecast.

Nearly a decade prior to the Phelps conference, John Muth (1961) criticized such error-correcting rules. He argued that they assume away an important consideration: in forming expectations, market participants take into account their understanding of the causal process driving the outcomes that they are attempting to forecast. He proposed REH as a way to represent market participants' "imagined world"—their understanding of the economy and how they use this understanding in forecasting outcomes.

Attendees at the 1969 conference were aware of REH. However, the models that they developed for the Phelps volume did not make use of it; indeed, REH did not even appear in the index. This was consistent with Muth's caveat that, despite its name, the hypothesis was not intended to represent how participants should forecast the future. As he put it: "At the risk of confusing this purely descriptive hypothesis with a pronouncement as to what firms ought to do, we call such expectations 'rational'" (Muth 1961: 316).

To implement REH, an economist must find an economic model to represent participants' understanding of how market outcomes unfold over time. For Muth, whenever an economist formulates a model of the causal process driving outcomes, his own model is "the relevant economic theory." Muth embedded REH in a model of an agricultural market that characterized change with an overarching probability distribution: conditional on its structure, as well as on realizations of the causal variables at any point in time, the model implied a unique probability distribution of participants' forecasts and outcomes at any other point in time.

Over the past four decades, economists have come to agree that only models that generate such "sharp" predictions of change should be considered "the relevant economic theory." As Roman Frydman and Michael Goldberg argue in Chapter 4 of this volume, it is this conception of economic science that led economists to embrace REH as the only valid way to model how rational, profit-seeking market participants forecast the future.

"Rational Expectations" versus Nonroutine Change

To construct a model that generates sharp predictions of change, an economist must fully and simultaneously specify how participants' forecasting strategies and the causal process driving market outcomes unfold between any two points in time—past, present, and future. This requires that an economist assume that nonroutine change—change that cannot be specified in advance with mechanical rules and procedures that are programmable on a computer—is unimportant for understanding outcomes.

Muth's model provides a particularly simple example of such *fully predetermined* models. He constrained his model's structure—its functional form and the properties of the causal variables, as well as the parameters relating them to outcomes—to be unchanging over time. Such a time-invariant structure in effect assumes that market participants do not change the way that they make decisions, and that the process driving prices and other market outcomes also remains unchanged over time.

Economists subsequently recognized that, as time passes, participants do indeed revise their forecasting strategies and alter the way in which they make decisions. Moreover, the social context and the causal process underpinning market outcomes also change over time. Nevertheless, economists' insistence that their models generate sharp predictions trumped the importance of nonroutine change, leading them to represent decisionmaking and the process underpinning the causal variables with mechanical rules and procedures.

A particularly influential class of such models uses several time-invariant structures to characterize forecasting strategies and market outcomes during different time periods. These models represent change with a probabilistic Markov rule that governs switches between the assumed structures, or "regimes." But, because they fully specify both the process governing change and the post-change representation of outcomes in advance, these models share a key property with their time-invariant counterparts: they describe change with an overarching probability distribution in which the set of outcomes and their associated probabilities are fully predetermined in all time periods—past, present, and future.

Rationality as Model Consistency

By the 1980s, the vast majority of the economics profession embraced the belief that any fully predetermined model could be used to represent how rational market participants forecast the future: an economist had only to impose consistency between his model's predictions on the individual and aggregate levels.

This belief seems puzzling: why would the predictions of a particular economist's overarching account have any connection with how profit-seeking participants forecast outcomes in real-world markets?

There are no doubt complex reasons for why a group of thinkers or scientists comes to embrace a common belief. But such a coalescence of views around a controlling idea—in this case, the idea that economic analysis can provide a universal procedure for representing how rational individuals forecast the future—often involves tacit acceptance of one or more false premises. In Chapter 4 of this volume, Frydman and Goldberg trace the profession's belief in the efficacy of REH representations to the assumption (and presumption) that economists can discover an overarching account of change in capitalist economies.

Lucas (2001) articulates a story that has been invoked time and again during the past four decades to support the claim that, by imposing consistency on his model, an economist can adequately capture how rational market participants understand the economy. He observed that when an economist formulates an overarching model of market prices, he supposes that it provides an adequate account of real-world outcomes, and that, if it did, profit-seeking market participants would discern what the economist already knew. He then observed that in the context of his model, non-REH forecasting rules generate systematic forecast errors. The key to the REH narrative, therefore, was the belief that such errors pointed to obvious, yet unrealized, profit opportunities in real-world markets. As Lucas later emphatically put it, "if your theory reveals profit opportunities, you have the wrong theory" (Lucas 2001: 13) of how "actual prices" unfold over a longer run.[1]

In a leap of faith that transformed macroeconomics and finance for generations, Lucas presumed that the right theory of capitalist economies, which arguably thrive on nonroutine change, is a fully predetermined model that assumes that such change is unimportant. He then argued that, to represent rational forecasting in real-world markets, an economist must remove the systematic forecast errors—unrealized "profit opportunities"—from his model by imposing consistency between its individual and aggregate levels.

From the early 1970s on, Lucas's story gained wide acceptance among macroeconomists and finance theorists, spanning all major schools of

---

1. Lucas (1986) did acknowledge that non-REH "adaptive theory" might be useful in accounting for shorter run behavior in some contexts. In Lucas (2004: 23), he acknowledged that REH does not "let us think about the US experience in the 1930s or about financial crises and their consequences. . . . We may be disillusioned with the Keynesian apparatus for thinking about these things, but it doesn't mean that this replacement [REH] apparatus can do it either. It can't."

thought. Chicago free-market adherents, New Keynesians, asymmetric-information theorists, and behavioral finance modelers all took the same leap.

The Diversion of Microfoundations Research

The models presented in the Phelps volume all relied on a time-invariant structure, with an adaptive-expectations rule to portray market participants' forecasting behavior.[2] By design, these models presumed that participants at least partly ignore systematic forecast errors. As a result, there was substantial tension between these formalizations and Phelps's vision of a microfoundations research program that would portray how, in making decisions, market participants maximize relative to their "imagined world."

This was the state of economic model-building at the time. A modeling strategy that would both preserve an autonomous role for market participants' expectations and approach Phelps's vision had to await further development of the theory and better empirical knowledge of how participants form forecasts in real-world markets.

However, the widely accepted REH narrative suggested a different direction for further development. Because most economists did not question the premise that overarching accounts of outcomes are within reach of economic analysis, inconsistent models—those that made use of non-REH representations of expectations—became "the wrong theory" and were jettisoned. Furthermore, the vast majority of economists, captivated by Lucas's narrative, embraced REH as the right theory.

Part One: Back to the Foundations

As the epistemological flaws of REH became recognized, and as evidence of REH models' inconsistency with empirical evidence accumulated, some economists returned to modeling expectations as autonomous—as an input rather than an output of their models. But developing a way to represent participants' expectations that could replace REH has remained a daunting problem, which may be why the alternatives have largely adhered to the core tenet of the contemporary approach to modeling, namely, that fully predetermined accounts of outcomes are within reach of economic analysis. This has enabled critics to move forward while avoiding the question of whether the epistemological and empirical difficulties of REH's portrayals of forecasting reveal a fatal flaw in the fundamental precept on which contemporary macroeconomics and finance models rest.

---

2. The Phelps paper in the conference volume is, strictly speaking, not time invariant, but it does share the property of the time-invariant papers in that it fully determines the consequences of the disturbance for the time-path of employment and inflation.

From Immanent Critique of REH to Mechanical Learning Models

In Chapter 1 of this volume, Roger Guesnerie discusses one line of criticism of REH: "the failure of economic theory stressed here concerns expectational coordination" (Chapter 1: 51).

REH presumes a special form of expectational coordination, often called the "rational expectations equilibrium" (REE): except for random errors that average to zero, an economist's model—"the relevant economic theory"—adequately characterizes each and every participant's forecasting strategy. Guesnerie's immanent critique is that decentralized markets, in general, will not produce the uniformity among participants' forecasting strategies that REE takes for granted, even in the context of an overarching model.

Eductive Games and Stability Analysis

Guesnerie formalizes the problem by examining whether each market participant would forecast according to an economist's REH model in the context of what he calls an "eductive game." The game assumes that every market participant knows perfectly the structure of the model—its functional form, the causal variables, and the values of the parameters attached to them.

The game starts with the observation that even if a market participant believes that an economist's overarching model adequately represents how outcomes unfold over time, she also understands that it is the aggregate of others' decisions that will determine the price. Because she cannot be sure about others' beliefs, she may think that it is not in her interest to forecast according to an economist's REH model. In deciding whether to do so, she begins a mental eductive process by attempting to guess other participants' price forecasts. She assumes that everyone knows the demand-and-supply specification of the economist's model: "All objective characteristics of the situations (cost function, demand function, and individual payoffs) are assumed to be public information" (Guesnerie 2005: 8).

In this game, participants understand that if their initial guesses differ in the aggregate from the REH forecast, their decisions will result in a market price that differs from the price forecasts that individuals attributed to others. This leads them to contemplate revising their guesses before they make any actual trading decision. Guesnerie examines whether this a priori process might be eductively stable—that is, every market participant comes to the conclusion that she should forecast according to an economist's REH model. He finds that there are parameter values for which the eductive game converges to uniformity among participants' forecasting strategies, just as standard REH models assume.[3]

---

3. Guesnerie points out that the question of whether REH models with multiple equilibria are eductively stable involves additional considerations.

In drawing implications for developing alternatives to the REH approach, Guesnerie (Chapter 1: 62) argues that if an economist's model is eductively stable, "the rational expectations equilibrium coordination is a priori robust . . . [and] the eductive approach . . . provides the basis [for replacing REE with] . . . the set of rationalizable equilibria."[4] He then suggests that representations of outcomes in such equilibria provide an alternative view of plausible economic outcomes.

Guesnerie recognizes the problematic nature of the assumption that an economist's model adequately represents each and every market participant's forecasting strategy. However, he argues that "eductive learning may be justified as a kind of shortcut to evolutive learning" (Chapter 1: 56)—an adaptive learning and forecasting algorithm that takes into account the co-evolution (two-way interdependence) between participants' forecasting and the model's aggregate outcomes. The connection between eductive and evolutive learning leads from Guesnerie's analysis of REE expectational coordination to the adaptive learning models that George Evans and Seppo Honkapohja present in Chapter 2.

Expectations as Algorithmic Learning
The learning approach recognizes that market participants do not have complete knowledge of the causal process driving outcomes while maintaining the core assumption of contemporary economic analysis. It thus represents participants' learning with mechanical rules.

The adaptive learning models on which Evans and Honkapohja focus in Chapter 2 have emerged as one of the main approaches for portraying participants' expectations when participants are assumed to have incomplete knowledge of an economist's model. These models are based on least squares (LS) regressions.[5] They represent learning about the process driving a payoff-relevant outcome, such as the market price, with so-called adaptive rules that entail regressing price on a set of causal variables. This regression is reestimated at each point in time as the economist's model generates new prices. The predictions implied by these regressions are used to represent the unfolding of participants' expectations over time.

In contemplating how to justify reliance on LS regressions to portray learning, Evans and Honkapohja (Chapter 2: 101) propose what they call "the 'cognitive consistency principle': economic agents should be assumed to be about as smart as (good) economists." Noting that economists use econometric techniques to learn about the causal process driving outcomes,

---

4. The eductive-stability approach builds on attempts by game theorists to "rationalize" Nash equilibria (which are equivalent to standard REE in macroeconomics) by appealing to an a priori mental process. For seminal papers, see Bernheim (1984) and Pearce (1984).

5. Chapter 2 contains an extensive list of references concerning the development of econometric learning and various applications.

Evans and Honkapohja argue that the cognitive consistency principle rationalizes the use of such techniques in modeling participants' expectations.

The early motivation for choosing LS regressions as the basis for econometric learning models, given that many other techniques were available, was to "obtain an understanding of how agents might come to have rational expectations" (Chapter 2: 73).[6] This early literature assumed that "agents have a correctly specified model with unknown parameters" (Branch and Evans 2003: 2): each market participant knows the "correct" set of causal variables and functional forms, which are assumed to be those chosen by an economist in constructing his model. But they do not know the specific parameter values that they should attach to these variables. They attempt to "learn" these values by running LS regressions.

Learning models based on LS regressions have been used to provide "a test of the plausibility of rational expectations in a particular model" (Chapter 2: 73). Rational expectations were considered plausible if the LS algorithm converged on REE.[7] Evans and Honkapohja show that whether a model does so depends on the parameter representing the impact of participants' expectations on market outcomes.

In proposing the cognitive consistency principle to justify adaptive learning algorithms, Evans and Honkapohja are aware of Lucas's argument that in the context of their model, non-REH representations of forecasting point to irrationality on the part of market participants. They emphasize that REE is "the natural benchmark" (Chapter 2: 70) for LS learning rules, and they refer to participants' use of such rules as "only boundedly rational in that [participants'] forecasts have systematic forecast errors during the learning process" (Chapter 2: 73).

According to Lucas's story, however, even if LS learning does eventually converge, models that generate forecast errors are the "wrong theory" of *transition* to REE: such errors would thus lead profit-seeking participants to abandon the LS learning rule attributed to them.[8] But Evans and Honkapohja argue that these errors are too subtle to be detectable, and that if LS rules converge on REE, they "vanish asymptotically." They conclude that the convergence of a "correctly specified" LS learning rule would provide "a rational foundation for rational expectations" (Chapter 2: 73).

As the econometric adaptive learning approach developed, researchers began to consider learning on the basis of "incorrectly" specified models. They examined models in which participants run regressions on the basis of

---

6. For a seminal formulation of how LS "learning" can rationalize REH, see Bray (1982) and Evans (1983).

7. LS learning algorithms have also been used as a criterion for selecting the most "plausible" equilibrium in models with multiple equilibria.

8. Frydman (1982) builds on this argument in his critique of efforts to rationalize REH with LS learning rules.

a restricted set of causal variables or have heterogeneous expectations based on several LS-related learning rules. In Chapter 2, Evans and Honkapohja present macroeconomic applications of such learning models. They focus on what they call "persistent learning dynamics" in which there is not full convergence to REE. Though the limit of the learning process may be close to REE constantly or occasionally, or very far from REE, Evans and Honkapohja argue that such learning dynamics may be consistent with bounded rationality on the part of market participants.

This interpretation of adaptive learning rules that do not converge on REE differs from Guesnerie's interpretation of models in which the eductive game fails to converge. Guesnerie (Chapter 1: 51) focuses on important examples of macroeconomic and finance models in which REE is not eductively stable: "the failure of economic theory stressed here concerns expectational coordination." He points out that these cases are, in general, characterized by the absence of stationarity in the data and suggests that we may need to reconsider the "philosophical determinism that has shaped the development of . . . economics as a social science" (Chapter 1: 64). Guesnerie concludes that "to be more relevant, our knowledge claims might have to become more modest."

This conclusion, with its concern about the soundness of contemporary models' philosophical underpinnings, sets the stage for the more radical departures from REH that are presented by Sheila Dow in Chapter 3 and by Roman Frydman and Michael Goldberg in Chapter 4. But, before we discuss these contributions, we briefly sketch how the emergence of behavioral finance, despite its reliance on fully predetermined models, helped to pave the way for an alternative approach that jettisons the search for such accounts of change.

Incorporating Psychological and Social Factors into Behavioral Finance Models

The learning approach attributes to each individual a learning rule that is based on observable time-series data. It supposes that available data and computation (e.g., LS estimation) alone can adequately represent market participants' forecasting strategies, thereby disregarding evidence that psychological and social factors play an important role in how market participants forecast outcomes and make decisions. In contrast, behavioral theorists have incorporated such factors into their macroeconomic and finance models.[9] Although they emphasize "realism" as the hallmark of their approach, behavioral theorists nonetheless believe that REH models

---

9. Seminal behavioral models include Frankel and Froot (1987) and DeLong et al. (1990). For more recent examples, see Shleifer (2000), Abreu and Brunnermaier (2003), De Grauwe and Grimaldi (2006), and references therein.

represent how rational participants *should* forecast the future. Consequently, they have described the departures from REH that they have observed in real-world markets as a symptom of participants' "irrationality" or "bounded rationality."

Nevertheless, because they base their portrayals of expectations on context-specific empirical evidence, behavioral models represent a significant advance over REH's reliance on a priori, supposedly universal, constraints on how market participants should behave.[10]

Of course, behavioral economists' use of mechanical models to formalize their empirical findings means that their representations of forecasting behavior are associated with systematic, easily detectable forecast errors. That, according to Lucas's REH narrative, makes these models "the wrong theory" of longer term regularities in the movements of aggregate variables over time.

To be sure, Lucas did not deny that an inconsistent overarching model might adequately represent the relationship between the causal variables and aggregate outcomes in a certain historical period—all that was needed was insightful selection of the causal variables and a stretch of time that did not involve much change. Indeed, in his widely cited critique of policy analysis based on non-REH models, Lucas (1976) acknowledged the good short-term forecasting performance of the so-called Keynesian econometric models that were developed in the 1960s. But he argued that "'the long-run' implications of . . . [these] models are without content" (Lucas 1976: 24).

The reason for this striking claim is rooted in his account of REH: as time passes, market participants would begin to see their forecasting errors and would thus alter the non-REH forecasting rules attributed to them by a behavioral economist. Such revisions of forecasting strategies would render the structure of the behavioral model inadequate as a representation of both individual decisionmaking and market outcomes over the longer term.

Recognizing the Limits of Economists' Knowledge

Once an economist embraces the core assumption that overarching accounts of change are within his reach, he must choose between two types of models: consistent REH models that, by design, rule out an active role for participants' expectations in driving outcomes, and inconsistent behavioral models that allow for such a role. But this dualism is problematic. On one hand, the fundamental considerations—the causal factors in an economist's model—

---

10. Behavioral models' explicit appeal to actual empirical findings also contrasts with the cognitive consistency principle's claim that economists' use of econometrics rationalizes basing representations of learning solely on econometric procedures. Leaving aside the observation that econometric methods are only one of many ways in which economists attempt to learn about the world, the principle provides no guidance to economists in selecting a particular econometric procedure, such as LS regression.

on which REH models focus are likely to be important for understanding outcomes on the individual and aggregate levels. On the other hand, the psychological and social factors that underpin non-REH behavioral representations are clearly relevant for modeling individual decisionmaking and its implications for outcomes in many markets.

In discussing John Maynard Keynes's approach to understanding individual decisionmaking, Dow argues in Chapter 3 that this duality disappears once we acknowledge the inherent imperfection of knowledge on the part of both market participants and economists. Building on Keynes's (1921) critique of the standard (so-called frequentist) approach to quantifying uncertainty, she points to nonroutine change as the primary source of contemporary models' epistemological flaws and empirical failures:

> If the system's internal structure is evolving in a nondeterministic manner, and the influences to which it is subject in the future are *not known (or are not fully knowable) in advance*, then there is no scope for using frequency distributions to quantify a probabilistic or stochastic expectation. [Chapter 3: 114, emphasis added]

This acknowledgment of the limits of economists' and market participants' knowledge implies that fundamental considerations and computations based on them cannot by themselves account for how participants make decisions. Individual decisionmaking is also influenced by social and psychological factors. As Dow emphasizes,

> Individuality or agency allows for individual choice as to whether to follow social convention. But sociality means that social-conventional judgment provides the norm, such that expectations are formed *interdependently* with expectations in the market. This nondeterministic social interactionism is a key ingredient of Keynes's . . . view of the economic system. [Chapter 3: 117, emphasis added]

Discussing how the "framework of social conventions and institutions . . . supports decisionmaking under uncertainty" (Chapter 3: 118), Dow argues that the dualism between rationality and irrationality/emotion, which is a hallmark of the contemporary approach to modeling individual behavior, disappears once we acknowledge the limits of our knowledge. She points out that Keynes came to think that human behavior arises from the combination of reason and emotion—that they are complementary rather than contradictory.[11] "What is rational for agents therefore is not separable from what is emotional" (Chapter 3: 121).

---

11. Dow cites influential research by Damasio (1994) that points to the role of emotions in motivating human behavior.

Dow's critique of the a priori notion of rationality as an artifact of what Guesnerie calls "philosophical determinism" raises a key question: How can economists represent individual decisionmaking in a way that incorporates both fundamental and psychological or social factors without presuming that individuals forgo obvious profit opportunities? Building on Keynes, Dow (Chapter 3: 122) sets out what any answer must assume: "An open system is not the opposite of a closed system, because there is a range of possibilities for openness, depending on which conditions are not met and to what degree. . . . Deviating from a closed system . . . does not mean abandoning theory or formal models."

Moving beyond Fully Predetermined Models of Expectations

How can economic analysis jettison mechanical representations, and thereby be opened to nonroutine change and imperfect knowledge, while continuing to portray individual and aggregate behavior in mathematical terms? How would this conceptual shift enable economists to accord market participants' expectations an autonomous role and yet avoid presuming that they forgo profit opportunities systematically?

Imperfect Knowledge Economics (IKE), which Frydman and Goldberg introduce in Chapter 4, proposes answers to these essential questions. In modeling market participants' expectations, IKE enables economists to incorporate both fundamental considerations, on which REH theorists focus, and the psychological and social considerations that behavioral economists emphasize. Moreover, despite their recognition of market participants' and economists' ever-imperfect knowledge about the process driving change, IKE macroeconomic and finance models generate empirically testable implications.

IKE stakes out an intermediate position between unrestricted open models, which have no empirical content, and contemporary models, which are based on the premise that change and its consequences can be adequately prespecified with mechanical rules. As in overarching models, the key set of assumptions that impute empirical content to IKE models are those that restrict change. Although IKE stops short of fully prespecifying change, it recognizes that economic behavior must display some regularity if formal economic theory is to generate empirically testable implications. Thus, IKE explores the possibility that individuals' decisionmaking, particularly how they revise their forecasting strategies, exhibits qualitative, context-dependent regularities.

In searching for such regularities to replace REH's a priori constraints, IKE relies in part on findings by behavioral economists and other social scientists concerning individual behavior. Like behavioral finance theorists, Frydman and Goldberg cite the empirical relevance of such evidence to justify its use in modeling participants' expectations. However, unlike the behavioral finance approach, IKE formalizes these empirical regularities with qualitative conditions. Moreover, Frydman and Goldberg argue that, in general, one should not expect even qualitative regularities on the individual level to persist indefinitely. That is, they become manifest—or cease to be relevant—at moments that no one can fully predict. Consequently, the conditions that underpin an IKE model's microfoundations—and thus the aggregate outcomes that it implies—are not only qualitative and context dependent but are also contingent.

By acknowledging economists' and market participants' imperfect knowledge, the microfoundations of IKE models abandon the dualism between reason and emotion that divides "rationality" from "irrationality" in contemporary models. As Keynes put it:

> We are merely reminding ourselves that human decisions affecting the future, whether personal or political or economic, cannot depend on strict mathematical expectation, since the basis for making such calculations does not exist; and . . . that our *rational* selves [are] choosing between alternatives as best as we are able, calculating where we can, but often falling back for our motive on whim or sentiment or chance. [Keynes 1936: 162, emphasis added]

For Keynes, unlike for behavioral economists, reliance on psychological factors in decisionmaking is not a symptom of irrationality. Rational individuals in the real world use knowledge of facts; but because knowledge is imperfect, calculation alone is insufficient for decisionmaking.

Although Keynes (1936: 162) emphasizes that psychological considerations, such as confidence, play an important role in individual decisionmaking, "we should *not* conclude from this that everything depends on waves of irrational psychology." Likewise, Frydman and Goldberg argue that psychological considerations themselves could not sustain the recurrent long swings that we observe in asset prices. Indeed, comprehending changes in fundamental factors is crucial for understanding how confidence and other sentiments are influenced over time.[12]

There is a more extreme view, which many economists and nonacademic commentators associate with Knight (1921), that uncertainty is so radical as to preclude economists from saying anything useful about how market outcomes unfold over time. Thus, the evidence that psychology alone cannot drive asset price movements is good news for the possibility of empirically relevant formal economic theory. After all, fundamental considerations are, for the most part, the only tangible factors that economists can use to

---

12. For an extensive discussion of this point, see Chapters 7 and 9 in Frydman and Goldberg (2011: 117–148, 163–174).

develop models that might enable them to distinguish between alternative explanations of outcomes.

Departing from the positions of Knight and Keynes, Frydman and Goldberg make nonstandard use of probabilistic formalism: they represent outcomes at every point in time with myriad probability distributions.[13] The qualitative and contingent conditions on which IKE models rely place restrictions on how the conditional moments of these distributions unfold over time—restrictions that are sufficient to generate empirically testable implications for aggregate outcomes.

In Chapter 6, Frydman and Goldberg show how such probabilistic formalism can be used to model market participants' revisions of autonomous forecasting strategies and the fundamental and psychological factors that underlie them. They then examine the implications of such revisions and find that trends in fundamentals play a central role in driving asset price swings away from and back toward benchmark values. In this sense, an IKE model of such swings differs from its behavioral finance counterparts, which imply that swings away from benchmark values are largely driven by nonfundamental factors. Blake LeBaron explores the implications of such a model in Chapter 5.

Part Two: Autonomous Expectations in Long Swings in Asset Prices

Instability is an inherent feature of capitalist economies, perhaps nowhere more markedly than in modern financial markets. Asset prices and risk tend to undergo long swings around commonly used benchmark values—for example, the price-dividend (P/D) ratio in equity markets or purchasing power parity values in currency markets—which can persist for years. REH theorists have encountered much difficulty in accounting for such fluctuations.

In REH models, market participants' expectations are tightly connected to the benchmark, which precludes the possibility that their forecasts might actively push the asset price away from benchmark values. Consequently, although these models can rationalize a slow-moving benchmark, they cannot account for the pronounced persistence that characterizes swings away from and back toward such values.[14] This failure suggests that according par-

---

13. For a mathematical exposition, see Frydman and Goldberg (2007) and Chapter 6 of this volume.

14. Frydman et al. (2011) find that currency fluctuations are even more persistent—and thus that REH models' inability to explain them is even more pronounced—than the literature suggests.

ticipants' expectations an autonomous role in driving outcomes—the role that they actually play in real-world settings—is essential to understanding aggregate outcomes.

Divorcing Asset Price Swings from Fundamentals

Agent-based computational economics (ACE) has become an influential way to model an active role for expectations in asset markets and individual decisionmaking more broadly.[15]

In Chapter 5, LeBaron develops an ACE model of price swings in the equity market. The model supposes that there are two assets: a "safe" asset that pays a fixed rate of return each period and a risky asset (equity) whose one-period return depends on the market price in the next period, $t + 1$, and a dividend that is paid at the beginning of the next period.

The market for the risky asset consists of many participants, each allocating their wealth across the two assets according to a standard mean-variance optimization rule. In making their portfolio decisions, participants are assumed to rely on one of four types of forecasting rules, which are either time invariant or subject to parameter updates using recursive least-squares algorithms.

Two of the forecasting rules play a particularly important role in the model's ability to generate equity-price swings away from the constant P/D ratio that REH would imply.[16] One is a standard adaptive-expectations rule that assumes that participants revise their one-period-ahead forecast of the mean rate of return on equity by a fixed proportion of their one-period forecasting error. The proportion is a critical parameter in the model, for it determines the weight that participants put on the recent return when forming their expectations, which plays a role in producing persistence in the model.

The other forecasting rule is a "fundamentalist strategy" that relates the forecast of the next period's return to the 52-week average return and the difference between the P/D ratio's value in the current period and its longer run (52-week) average. The fundamentalist strategy always predicts the P/D ratio's reversion in the coming period toward its constant REH benchmark value.

Two factors in the model are important in determining how the equity price unfolds over time: revisions of forecasting rules,[17] which may include switching from one rule to another, and reallocation of wealth

---

15. For a broad overview of ACE modeling, see Borrill and Tesfatsion (2011).

16. The dividend process is assumed to follow a random walk with drift.

17. The adaptive forecast involves only fixed forecast parameters, so its updates are trivial, requiring only the most recent return. However, the forecasts generated by other rules are updated in each period using recursive least squares.

across forecasting rules. This reallocation plays a key role in sustaining a price swing, which is triggered by a shock to the dividend process, by determining whether the aggregate wealth-weighted forecast of return moves persistently away from the benchmark P/D value or reverts relatively quickly to it.

For example, a positive shock to dividends will lead current users of the adaptive rule to bet on the continuation of the incipient trend by allocating a greater proportion of their wealth to equities, which will push the P/D ratio away from the benchmark. However, unless additional participants switch to the adaptive rule, the effect of the initial dividend shock on the movement of the P/D ratio will fizzle out. As time passes, the magnitude of upward forecast adjustments implied by the adaptive rule diminishes, thereby reducing participants' desire to bet additional wealth on further increases in the P/D ratio above its longer run average.

LeBaron simulates the evolution of forecasting rules, wealth shares, and equity prices. Each simulation is based on a particular set of parameters, forecasting rules, and their revisions. His simulations generate a rich variety of patterns, some of which mimic the long-swings pattern that one observes in the P/D ratio for the S&P 500 price index.

As LeBaron acknowledges, it remains entirely unclear how well his simulated series match the P/D ratio's characteristics (such as persistence) in real-world equity markets. He cautions that "this series [simulated P/D ratio] is not easy to characterize, and it is possible that visual analysis may be the best that can be done" (Chapter 5: 183–184).

Nevertheless, LeBaron's framework sheds light on the mechanisms underlying the simulated patterns. He traces the simulated pattern of persistent price swings to the set of parameters that drive the reallocation of wealth toward adaptive-expectations strategies: "Throughout the simulation the adaptive types control nearly 30% of wealth, compared with 15% for the fundamental types" (Chapter 5: 190). His results indicate that price swings away from the REH benchmark occur because market participants' forecasting strategies increasingly abandon fundamental factors in favor of extrapolating past trends.

LeBaron's account of equity prices is part of a large class of behavioral finance models, a hallmark of which is that long swings away from benchmark values are largely unrelated to fundamental considerations. Some of these models rely on "technical trading" rules, which, like LeBaron's adaptive rule, extrapolate past price trends, while others assume that purely psychological factors can sustain the swing.

To be sure, technical trading and psychological factors play a role in asset price movements. But, again, as Keynes argued, "we should not conclude from this that everything depends on waves of irrational psychology" (Keynes 1936: 162–163).

Returning Economic Fundamentals to Models of Expectations

Behavioral finance theorists have assumed that REH is *the* way to represent how rational participants understand the effect of fundamental factors on asset prices. This has led them to seek accounts of price swings that make "less than full rationality" and nonfundamental considerations the primary factors driving market participants' expectations of payoff-relevant outcomes.

But, as Goldberg and Frydman point out in Chapter 6, models that attribute asset price movements largely to nonfundamental factors are inconsistent with the growing empirical evidence that such variables as interest rates and income growth are the main drivers of fluctuations in currency, equity, and other asset markets.[18] At the same time, the composition of the relevant set of fundamental factors changes over time in ways that no one can foresee. This suggests that we should not expect that an overarching model would adequately characterize, in terms of fundamental factors, how expectations and asset prices unfold over time.

IKE models of asset markets rest on a core premise: market participants and economists have ever-imperfect knowledge of the relationship between assets' actual prospects—the values of their future earnings and the probabilities with which these values might be realized—and fundamental factors. It is this premise that enables IKE models to incorporate psychological considerations, and yet, in contrast to most behavioral finance models, still accord to fundamental factors the primary role in explaining the persistence of long swings in asset prices and risk. Paradoxically, by abandoning the REH-motivated search for fully predetermined relationships between asset prices and fundamental factors—that is, by conceiving of expectations as being autonomous—IKE can accord such factors a central role in its models of expectations.

In formulating the foundations of their model of asset price swings in Chapter 6, Frydman and Goldberg point out that no a priori universal standard can adequately characterize (as REH purports to do) how rational participants would forecast the future in all contexts and time periods. To model individual decisionmaking, therefore, economists must draw on empirical findings from psychology and other social sciences. They may also use their understanding of the historical record, social norms, conventions, and institutions.

---

18. Goldberg and Frydman (1996a,b) find that short-term currency fluctuations depend on fundamentals, but that this relationship is temporally unstable. See also Rogoff and Stavrakeva (2008). For evidence that fundamental considerations are the main drivers of equity prices, but in temporally unstable ways, see Mangee (2011).

In this sense, IKE reframes the relationship between the individual and aggregate levels of analysis: its models' microfoundations incorporate the influence that the broader social and historical context, together with actual aggregate outcomes, has on market participants' decisionmaking process. Even if market participants are purely self-interested, how they deploy their resources depends as much on such social factors as it does on their individual motivations.[19] Chapter 6 shows how this feature of capitalist economies can be represented in the context of modeling swings in prices and risk in equity markets.

As in LeBaron's model, Frydman and Goldberg assume that the market consists of many participants who hold their wealth in either a risky asset (equity shares) or a safe asset. An IKE model, like standard REH models, represents a participant's forecasting strategy by relating her forecast of a stock's future price and riskiness to a set of fundamental factors. However, in contrast to extant models, an IKE model assumes that market participants revise their forecasting strategies at times and in ways that they themselves, let alone an economist, cannot fully foresee.[20] Consequently, IKE models stop short of fully prespecifying participants' forecasts at each point in time, as well as their revisions over time. Instead, such models represent forecasting behavior by relying on empirically based conditions that formalize qualitative and contingent regularities.

In Chapter 6, Frydman and Goldberg formalize one such qualitative behavioral observation: regardless of whether participants in financial markets are bulls or bears, they tend to assume that the "existing state of affairs will continue indefinitely, except in so far as [they] have specific reasons to expect a change" (Keynes 1936: 152).[21] Even when a market participant does "have specific reasons to expect a change," it is entirely unclear which new forecasting strategy, if any, she should adopt. Faced with this uncertainty, participants tend to revise their thinking about how fundamentals matter in what one of us has called "guardedly moderate ways": there are stretches of time during which they either maintain their current strategies or revise them gradually.

But, like price swings themselves, the tendency toward guardedly moderate revisions is not only qualitative but is also contingent. A participant's

---

19. In this way, IKE's approach to microfoundations of aggregate models contrasts sharply with REH's reliance on methodological individualism.

20. The IKE model in Chapter 6 also differs from extant models in relying on a new specification of preferences, which Frydman and Goldberg call "endogenous prospect theory." This approach adapts the prospect theory of Kahneman and Tversky (1979) to conditions of imperfect knowledge.

21. This regularity is also related to behavioral economists' observation that individuals tend to revise their assessments of probabilities in a way that is much more conservative than the standard Bayesian updating formulas would suggest. See Shleifer (2000).

decision to revise her forecasting strategy depends on many considerations, including her current strategy's performance, whether she has "specific reasons to expect a change" in fundamental trends or how they are influencing prices, and the "*confidence* with which we . . . forecast" (Keynes 1936: 148). Moreover, using data from media coverage of financial markets, Frydman and Goldberg argue that psychological factors like confidence are partly related to movements in fundamental factors. For example, the exuberance that appeared to sustain the equity price boom of the 1990s quickly evaporated when positive trends in earnings and other fundamental factors began to reverse at the end of that decade.

Frydman and Goldberg show that a price swing arises during periods in which market participants on the whole revise their forecasting strategies in guardedly moderate ways and fundamentals trend in unchanging directions. By relating asset price swings to fundamental factors, an IKE model can be tested on the basis of time-series evidence using econometric procedures.[22]

Part Three: Rethinking Unemployment-Inflation Trade-offs and the Natural Rate Theory

As different as they are on both theoretical and empirical grounds, the foregoing models of asset price movements bring us back to the Phelps volume's central message: ascribing an autonomous role to market participants' expectations substantially alters our understanding of the processes driving aggregate outcomes. Indeed, a common theme running through the papers presented at the 1969 conference was that the then-prevailing view of monetary policy ignored the role of participants' expectations, and that the belief that expansionary policy could permanently lower unemployment by spurring higher inflation was misguided. Monetary expansion could lower the unemployment rate in the short run, but its effects fizzle out over time: in the long run, nonmonetary factors determine unemployment.

The embrace of REH in the early 1970s led to revisions of these conclusions, particularly concerning the short-run effectiveness of monetary policy. But, as the chapters in Part Three argue, standard REH models obfuscated comprehension of the dynamics of unemployment and thus how changes in monetary policy might affect these dynamics in both the short and long run.

The arguments developed in this part of the volume grapple with the problem of unemployment by exploring alternative approaches to modeling the role of participants' expectations in driving outcomes. As in Parts One

---

22. Behavioral models typically rely on so-called calibration exercises, rather than attempting to explain the actual time path on the basis of time-series data. For a forceful argument that calibration procedures should not be considered a test of how well models match the actual time path of the data, see Sims (1996).

and Two, some of the authors move beyond REH and fully predetermined models. This leads them to rethink the natural rate theory and how it has been tested empirically. Indeed, the empirical results that they report raise important questions about the dualism between the short-run (cyclical) and long-run (steady state) movements of real output and unemployment—a distinction that plays a key role in contemporary macroeconomic analysis.

From the 1969 Conference to New Keynesian Models

Friedman (1968) and Phelps (1968, 1970) argued that Phillips's (1958) claim of a permanent trade-off between inflation and unemployment was flawed, because market participants would revise their inflation expectations as the actual inflation rate increased in the wake of expansionary monetary policy. This would render the Phillips curve unstable over time. As Phelps put it in the introduction to the 1969 conference volume:

> The crucial role that the new theory assigns to expectations . . . of wage and price change, together with the notion of adaptive expectations, ha[s] led most of the authors here to the hypothesis that the momentary Phillips curve will shift according to the point chosen on it. Today's Phillips curve may be quite stable, but tomorrow's curve will depend upon how the economy behaves today. In particular, it may be that an increase in the steady rate of inflation will have only a vanishing effect on the unemployment rate. [Phelps et al. 1970: 4]

In the models in the Phelps volume, the unstable short-run trade-off between inflation and unemployment, together with the long-run "vanishing" of this trade-off, is deduced from an economic system characterized by adaptive expectations. This forecasting rule assumes that for some time—the short run—market participants' assessments of inflation lag behind the actual economywide inflation rate. In the long run, the adaptive rule leads participants' expectations to catch up with the actual inflation rate, while unemployment converges to its natural rate.

Replacing adaptive with "rational" expectations, REH models retained the Phelps volume's conclusion that monetary policy has no effect on the natural rate of unemployment. However, reliance on REH dramatically altered the conclusion concerning inflation-unemployment trade-offs in the short run. As Sargent and Wallace (1975) argued in the context of an REH model, as long as changes in monetary policy are publicly announced, expansionary policy that permanently raises the inflation rate would not be effective in lowering unemployment in either the short or the long run (Sargent and Wallace 1975). Their so-called policy ineffectiveness proposition implied that the only changes in monetary policy that affect unemployment in the short run arise from either purely random shocks or policymakers' attempts to fool the public by not openly announcing changes in monetary policy. As such, monetary policy's effect on unemployment is ephemeral.

To persuade the broader public that such REH-based models should inform public policy, their proponents have invoked Abraham Lincoln's famous adage: the policymaker "can fool all the people some of the time, and some of the people all the time, but [he] cannot fool all the people all the time." But that bit of common sense is inapplicable in this context, because the policy ineffectiveness proposition is an artifact of REH and thus shares its epistemological flaws and poor empirical track record.[23]

Indeed, as Milton Friedman (1960: 87) pointed out, contrary to the ineffectiveness proposition's claim that a permanent increase in the rate of monetary growth would raise the actual and expected inflation rate with little delay, "there is much evidence that monetary changes have their effect only after a considerable lag and over a long period, and that the lag is rather variable." That lag implies that a policy-induced increase in the monetary growth rate, though unpredictable in terms of the timing and magnitude of its impact, would lead to a lower unemployment rate in the short run.[24]

Despite Friedman's findings of long and variable lags, which called into question the mechanical link between inflation and unemployment implied by fully predetermined models, economists' subsequent embrace of REH solidified their adherence to such models. To maintain REH while attempting to account for the short-run effects of monetary policy on unemployment, macroeconomists had to freight their models with additional constraints— so-called frictions that would prevent wages and prices from rising in lock-step with monetary expansion.

Phelps and Taylor (1977) and Fischer (1977) pointed out that the existence of various contractual arrangements in the economy, such as staggered wage agreements, would preclude a nearly synchronous effect of expansionary monetary policy on actual and expected inflation. They formalized "wage stickiness" in an REH model and concluded that monetary policy had a short-run effect on unemployment. In the long run, unemployment converged to its natural rate.

---

23. Nevertheless, reliance on such rhetoric has turned out to be remarkably successful in persuading the public that REH-based models' implications, such as the policy ineffectiveness proposition, are relevant for understanding the consequences of monetary policy. For a recent example of the use of the Lincoln adage quoted here, in a popular discussion of REH models, see Sargent (2008).

24. Phelps's (1969) so-called island model rationalized the lagged effect of monetary policy on the inflation rate by appealing to heterogeneous information on the part of each wage- or price-setting firm concerning its competitors' price responses to monetary expansion and the resulting changes in nominal demand.

Over the past four decades, formalizations of the short-run Phillips curve using various representations of wage and price stickiness have been developed extensively, becoming the cornerstone of the New Keynesian macroeconomic models.[25] Beyond their use in academic research, these models serve as the core of the dynamic stochastic general equilibrium models that underpin central banks' analyses of the consequences of alternative policies.[26]

In Chapter 7, Roger Farmer constructs an REH model of business cycle fluctuations in aggregate outcomes that jettisons the New Keynesian Phillips curve. A key implication of the model that sets it apart from New Keynesian models is that real output does not converge to its natural level in the long run.

Business Cycles without Frictions

The canonical New Keynesian model consists of three equations. The investment-saving (IS) curve relates the growth rate of real GDP to the real interest rate and a "demand shock." The so-called Taylor rule characterizes how the central bank adjusts the interest rate to deviations of the inflation rate and real output from their steady state values. Finally, the New Keynesian Phillips curve relates the current-period inflation rate to the expected next-period rate and the gap between real output and its natural steady state level, which in turn depends on a "supply shock."

Because the model uses REH to represent participants' expectations, it precludes the possibility that these expectations might autonomously drive aggregate outcomes, such as the inflation rate and real output, away from their steady state values. Thus, to produce business cycle fluctuations around steady state values, New Keynesian models rely on demand and/or supply shocks and at least partly exogenous (often institutional) frictions, which amplify these shocks' purely random and short-lived effects into longer-lasting departures of aggregate outcomes from steady state values. As the effects of these frictions wane over time, inflation and real output converge to their REH-implied steady state values.

Farmer (Chapter 7: 256) argues that "price stickiness at the micro level is not large enough for the New Keynesian model to explain the aggregate data." Empirical evidence shows that, though sticky, wages and prices are not sluggish enough for New Keynesian models to generate the persistence that we observe in actual inflation and real output.

25. For a formulation of price stickiness that has been widely used in New Keynesian models, see Calvo (1983).

26. For a seminal development and extensive overview of New Keynesian models, with particular focus on their use in policy analysis, see Woodford (2003). For a recent survey of such models and further references, see Gali (2008).

Farmer supposes that this persistence stems from market participants' forecasting behavior. To represent this behavior, he uses REH to portray how market participants forecast nominal GDP. Moreover, he constrains these forecasts to take a particular form: they are based on the belief "that the growth rate of nominal GDP follows a random walk" (Chapter 7: 263). Imposing this belief together with REH in effect assumes that nominal GDP growth actually follows a random walk; that is, the level of nominal GDP follows a highly persistent pattern, called an "integrated of order two," or $I(2)$, process.[27] This specification of nominal GDP replaces the New Keynesian Phillips curve. The rest of the model consists of the other two canonical New Keynesian equations: the IS curve and the Taylor policy rule.

Farmer shows that his model has only two steady state equations to determine the three steady state values for the deviation of real output from trend and the inflation and interest rates. In contrast to its behavior in the New Keynesian model, therefore, the deviation of real output from trend in Farmer's monetary model does not converge to zero: although the central bank "can decide how movements in nominal GDP are divided between movements in real output and inflation, . . . it cannot stabilize all . . . variables at the same time" (Chapter 7: 265).

Beyond implying a long-run gap between actual unemployment and its natural rate, Farmer's model differs from the New Keynesian model in its analysis of fiscal policy in combating recessions. He argues that "to explain the data, the New Keynesian model must attribute much of the persistence in the unemployment rate to movements in the natural rate of unemployment" (Chapter 7: 269). Because the New Keynesian model represents movements in the natural rate as being driven by supply shocks, this "is a problem for New Keynesians who favor policy activism" (Chapter 7: 269). In contrast, Farmer's model can rationalize the use of government expenditures or taxes by treating such policies as a mean shift in the IS curve's demand shock. "If fiscal policy *is* effective, then [the Farmer] model provides support for its use in times of high unemployment to increase aggregate demand" (Chapter 7: 270).

The differences in the implications of the Farmer and New Keynesian models arise from replacing the New Keynesian Phillips curve with the assumption that nominal income follows an $I(2)$ process. With REH, then, market participants' expectations are characterized by this belief. Farmer interprets this key assumption as a representation of Keynes's notion of "animal spirits."

But, as Dow discusses at length in Chapter 3, animal spirits compel profit-seeking market participants to make investment decisions despite "the

---

27. In Chapter 10, Katarina Juselius provides an extensive discussion of $I(2)$ processes and further references.

extreme precariousness of the basis of knowledge on which our estimates of prospective yield have to be made" (Keynes 1936: 149). Keynes invoked the notion of animal spirits to characterize situations in which standard probabilistic representations, which underpin REH, cannot adequately capture participants' beliefs concerning future outcomes.

In Chapter 8, Phelps explores how moving away from REH and recognizing the "precariousness of our knowledge" concerning assets' future prospects substantially changes the meaning of the natural rate. He argues "that the term 'natural' is obviously inappropriate once we recognize that the unemployment rate to which the economy tends is contingent on the market's guesses about the future—that is, future prices of capital goods and labor" (Chapter 8: 291).

Moving beyond Fully Predetermined Models of the Natural Rate

The contributors to the Phelps 1969 conference supposed that the natural rate of unemployment is a constant that corresponds to steady output growth.[28] Consequently, they modeled the observed swings in real output and unemployment as business cycle fluctuations around their respective steady state values. These fluctuations were thought to be triggered primarily by shocks, real or monetary, that were propagated through monetary channels.

In *Structural Slumps* (1994), Phelps argued that the comovements of inflation and unemployment during the final four decades of the twentieth century did not seem consistent with these models' implications. Although inflation rates were relatively low and stable, economic activity fluctuated widely. In the 1960s, unemployment nearly vanished in several European countries, without fueling high inflation. Symmetrically, unemployment was high in the 1980s in nearly all OECD economies, but there was little or no disinflation—and even considerable inflation in France and some other economies. Then, in the 1990s, unemployment in several OECD economies fell sharply, with little inflation, or even some disinflation. Such observations led Phelps to develop a theory that attributes swings in unemployment to nonmonetary shocks and developments operating through nonmonetary channels. In Chapter 8, he sketches the key steps in the development of his theory of "structural" booms and slumps.

The early structuralist models in Phelps (1994) have the property that the equilibrium path of unemployment always approaches the natural rate, as do the monetary models in the Phelps et al. (1970) volume and New

---

28. Phelps did not require the "equilibrium," or "warranted" unemployment rate, in his terminology of that time, to be invariant to real interest rates, real wealth, or, for that matter, real exchange rates. As a result, structural shifts that changed those determinants would alter the "natural" unemployment rate.

Keynesian models. In *Structural Slumps,* "something has been added. The natural rate moves!" (Phelps 1994: vii). Moreover, econometric analysis finds that the historical fluctuations in the actual rate arise largely from the structural forces driving the natural rate.

The structuralist approach regards investment—and thus expectations of its profitability and the unanticipated events that raise or lower those expectations—as the key force driving long swings in real output and unemployment. In the models developed by Hoon and Phelps (1992), Phelps (1994), and Phelps and Zoega (1998), firms undertake investment in a business asset (fixed capital, the stock of customers, or job-ready employees). The asset's per-unit valuation has a positive impact on the pace of investment: it boosts construction (which is labor intensive), competition for customers (which shrinks markups), or workers' preparation to be functioning employees. Increased investment, in turn, has a positive impact on labor demand, lowering unemployment and raising wages.

Movements of investment and employment are determined in these models alongside those of the real interest rate, the real exchange rate, and wealth. These movements unfold along a "conditional" equilibrium path that assumes that *absent* any significant and unforeseeable structural shift, participants have "correct" expectations about assets' prospects, *whatever they might be.* But, rather than study the movements along the equilibrium path, Phelps and Zoega examine how that path would change when one of the structural parameters shifts. In particular, they examine the consequences of shifts in productivity growth and expectations concerning prospects for profitable new investment opportunities.[29]

According to structuralist models, "the sudden expectation of a *future surge* of *productivity* creates an expected simultaneous surge of profits; this at once prompts a speculative lift in the asset valuation, which will look unjustified to uninformed observers; the increased valuation sets in motion an upswing in employment; when the productivity surge is realized, employment subsides." These models claim that "such expectations are *potentially* important: that an unusually large shift of this sort in the valuation of business assets would cause an unusually wide structural expansion or contraction" (Phelps and Zoega 2001: 3).

Phelps and Zoega emphasize that the shift in valuations is not purely a result of psychological factors, as supposed by Pigou (1927) and by more recent behavioral models. "In this account, the boom is *not* sparked by the 'optimism' and *not* doomed by the 'miscalculations'" (Phelps and Zoega

---

29. The 1994 volume postulated punctuated expectational equilibrium, so that, after an unanticipated structural shift, expectations are corrected. The aim was only to put the focus on how very differently the model behaves from the Keynesian and classical models it bid to replace.

2001: 3).[30] In contrast to Pigou's thesis that "the response of investments to a class of future prospects exceeded what 'rational' calculation would suggest ('errors in optimism'), . . . [structuralist theory relied] on the effects of future prospects that it is *'rational'* for investments of various kinds to respond to" (Phelps 2006: 69, emphasis added).

In considering how to model "rational" market participants' expectations of assets' future prospects, Phelps (Chapter 8: 285) points out that the structuralist model "is not inherently yoked to perfect knowledge . . . or to [its] offspring, rational expectations . . . the Hoon-Phelps papers of 2002–2006 on 'structural booms'—handle the arbitrariness in valuations at least as naturally as Keynes's 'marginal efficiency' did."

Opening the way for accounts of unemployment that move beyond REH and fully predetermined models, Phelps (Chapter 8: 285) emphasizes that expectations of assets' prospects, which determine their market valuations, do "not have to be 'solved out' by supposing perfect understanding of the working of the economy—as I was driven to do in *Structural Slumps* to minimize the complexity of the models and the themes." These expectations—influenced by participants' own understanding of the future, as well as by their autonomous intuitions, instincts, and emotional needs—may be taken as given, much as Keynes did. A downward shift in these expectations leads to a drop in observed valuations, which in turn leads to a shift from one equilibrium unemployment path, with its supposed destination, to another. This approach treats participants' expectations as a structural parameter and thus sidesteps the problem of how market participants settle on particular expectations, and how they might revise them. Nonetheless, it moves beyond REH, which regards expectations as an endogenous factor determined by an economist's own model, because treating expectations as a structural parameter recognizes that they play an autonomous role in driving outcomes. It also recognizes that the future is inherently open, and that how it unfolds depends crucially on participants' revisions of *their* expectations; thus, these models' predictions are necessarily contingent on how we represent these expectations.[31]

Such considerations lead Phelps (Chapter 8: 291) to the key question: "Does this . . . mean that the 'natural' level of (un)employment no longer exists?" Phelps recognizes the importance of "radical uncertainty," in the sense of Knight and Keynes: the economy's structure is always changing in ways that cannot be modeled in standard probabilistic terms, and, "with

---

30. This argument echoes Keynes's view that psychological factors alone cannot sustain asset price swings if fundamental considerations suggest that investment prospects have substantially worsened (Frydman and Goldberg 2011).

31. IKE is based on the same premise. See Chapters 4 and 6 and Frydman et al. (2011) for a discussion of the concept of contingent predictions and how IKE models, despite their openness with respect to forecast revisions, generate empirically testable implications.

it, the unemployment rate to which the system may—or may not—tend." For Phelps (Chapter 8: 291), "the 'contingent equilibrium' rate would be a better term than 'natural' for that conception of the homing tendency." In his chapter, he works out the valuations that participants place on a unit of capital and on a unit of labor in the present, given their expectations of future productivity levels for each of these factors of production, and given their understanding of how the economy works, an understanding that the analyst's model is assumed to represent.

Phelps then sharply contrasts his position to what has become known as Keynesian macroeconomics:

> It is ironic that the originators of models of the natural rate, whose formulations did not explicitly exclude that background expectations of future capital goods prices and future wages might be quite wrong, stand accused of not appreciating that any sort of economic equilibrium is to some extent a social phenomenon—a creature of beliefs, optimism, the policy climate, and so forth—while today's crude Keynesians, despite their mechanical deterministic approach, wrap themselves in the mantle of Keynes, who, with his profound sense of indeterminacy and, consequently, radical uncertainty, was worlds away from their thinking. [Chapter 8: 291]

Phelps and Zoega (2001) argue that, despite this contingency, structuralist models generate an empirically testable implication concerning the shifting relationship between average valuations of assets and the average unemployment level: during stretches of time in which valuations tend to be relatively high (low), the unemployment rate should be relatively low (high). In Chapter 9, Gylfi Zoega presents empirical evidence about this relationship that uses asset prices as a proxy for autonomous expectations concerning their prospects (and thus their valuations).

Unemployment, Share Prices, and Investment
The key premise of the first structuralist models was that actual unemployment primarily reflects movements in the natural rate. This premise implied "that asset valuations belong in the employment growth equation or unemployment equation" (Phelps and Zoega 2001: 20). Hoon and Phelps (1992) and Phelps and Zoega (2001) worked out the dynamics of business assets' shadow price (equivalently, the share price) as they enter a trajectory approaching the expected resting point. If the shadow price is rising to meet this point, the rate of investment in the business asset is rising, too.

In Chapter 9, Zoega examines empirical evidence concerning such a relationship, using share prices in 16 OECD countries from 1960 to 2009 as proxies for market participants' expectations of business assets' prospects—their future profitability—and their assessments of the current state of real business activity.

Prior to undertaking an econometric investigation, Zoega examines descriptive evidence concerning six countries with sharply different historical employment rates. Although mean unemployment in three of the countries (Belgium, Italy, and Spain) tended to shift upward throughout the period, in the Netherlands, the United Kingdom, and the United States, unemployment reverted to its earlier mean following recessions.

To capture the observation that hiring decisions do not have an instantaneous effect on the employment level, the share-price variable is set to its average for the first 3 years of each half-decade of the period, whereas the employment rate is set to its average for the last 3 years of each half-decade. Zoega (Chapter 9: 310) observes that a "clear upward-sloping relationship [between the employment rate and share prices] is apparent for each of the countries." Estimates of a pooled cross-section time-series regression for the 16 OECD countries "confirm a robust relationship between share prices and unemployment . . . [and thus] suggest . . . that changes in the level of share prices precede changes in the rate of employment" (Chapter 9: 312).

The structuralist view also suggests that business investment is one of the principal factors underlying employment movements. To examine this channel, Zoega, noting that employment and investment are related, replaces share prices with gross capital formation (as a share of GDP) in his employment equation.

Beyond examining bivariate correlations, Zoega explores whether changes in share prices "cause" changes in employment. To this end, he converts the data to annual averages and applies Granger causality tests. The null hypothesis that changes in average share prices do not cause changes in average employment "can be rejected for 14 of the 16 countries. . . . [Moreover,] the alternative hypothesis of changes in employment not . . . causing changes in share prices can only be rejected for two countries" (Chapter 9: 313).

Zoega's empirical methodology reflects the comparative statics approach to analyzing the implications of structuralist models. This approach assumes that, "*absent* any significant and unforeseeable structural shift," the configuration of the macroeconomic relationships does not change very much, and that structural shifts "are very infrequent" (Phelps and Zoega 2001: 93). The reliance on averages is supposed to capture the unchanging processes driving macroeconomic variables, such as share prices and employment, during the period in which a conditional equilibrium prevails. Each such equilibrium path is supposed to last for only a limited time; it shifts when one of the structural parameters shifts. The regression analysis relating the half-decade averages of, say, employment rates and share prices aims to capture how the average employment rate, moving along an equilibrium path, would change in response to occasional shifts in participants' expectations concerning assets' prospects.

The IKE approach (Chapters 4 and 6) provides a way to model revisions of exogenous expectations of asset prices, which, in Phelps (1999) and ensuing studies, underpin shifts in the structuralist equilibrium path. Katarina Juselius pursues this line of research in Chapter 10. In her account, expectations drive the real exchange rate and the real interest rate, which, in turn, are among the key variables underlying unemployment movements in the structuralist model. Juselius confronts the structuralist account of unemployment with empirical evidence by embedding it in the multivariate cointegrated vector autoregressive (CVAR) model (Johansen 1996; Juselius 2006).

Unemployment Fluctuations and Swings in Asset Markets
According to the structuralist theory, three variables—the real exchange rate, the real interest rate, and markups of prices over costs—are the main determinants of the unemployment rate. As these variables tend to undergo protracted swings around their benchmark values, the unemployment rate also undergoes swings. In Chapter 10, Juselius examines whether the theoretical implications of combining the IKE approach to asset price swings with the structuralist model of unemployment are consistent with the empirical evidence. She surveys previous empirical studies concerning comovements among the unemployment rate, the real exchange rate, and the real interest rate, as well as markups of prices over costs (which, according to the structuralist model, is a principal channel through which asset market outcomes are transmitted to the real economy).

These studies share a common econometric framework: the CVAR model. Juselius argues that one of the CVAR model's main advantages over other approaches stems from its ability to represent covariances among "persistent" variables, that is, variables characterized by nonstationary processes, such as random walks in levels or first differences (referred to as $I(1)$ or $I(2)$ models, respectively). Such nonstationarity is typical in macroeconomic time series. The CVAR econometric model summarizes the covariance structure of such nonstationary time series by expressing comovements among the model's variables in terms of cointegrating relationships involving their values, as well as first- and higher order differences.

To confront theoretical representations, such as the structuralist models of unemployment in Phelps (1994), with time-series evidence, Juselius translates their testable implications into a set of hypotheses about the parameters of the CVAR model describing long-run relationships, adjustment dynamics, driving trends, and their effects on the model's variables.[32] The

32. Juselius contrasts the CVAR approach with extant approaches to testing REH models, which often involve the imposition of restrictions—"the use of mild force to make [the data] tell . . . [the] story" (Chapter 10: 346) that is consistent with a particular model. Estimation of contemporary models typically disregards the possibility of structural change. Moreover, in many cases (including REH and behavioral finance models), the "testing" dispenses with statistical analysis altogether, relying instead on calibration and computer simulations. In contrast, the CVAR methodology starts by estimating the data's largely unrestricted covariance structure, including their temporal breaks, and then asks whether the implications of one or more theoretical models are consistent with the estimated statistical model.

analysis of the CVAR model also generates estimated empirical regularities concerning the comovements of macroeconomic aggregates. In Chapter 10, Juselius discusses several such tests and empirical regularities. In doing so, she draws on the results of previous CVAR-based studies of asset markets, the real economy, and their two-way interdependence.

To set the stage for empirical testing of the structuralist model, Juselius analyzes the persistence of the real exchange and real interest rates in the context of the IKE model elaborated in Chapter 6. She observes that for this model of asset price swings to be useful in testing whether structuralist theories can help account for the fluctuations in the unemployment rate, the IKE model must imply that both real exchange rates and real interest rates are persistent.

Frydman et al. (2012) show that this is the case. Even though its restrictions on individual behavior are qualitative and contingent, the IKE model yields testable implications for time-series data: highly persistent real exchange rate and real interest rate differentials that can be characterized as near $I(2)$. Juselius shows that this characterization is consistent with empirical evidence.[33]

Having examined persistence, Juselius reports empirical evidence suggesting that real exchange rates and real interest rates comove: they tend to undergo parallel swings away from and toward their respective benchmark values. This comovement, which is implied by the IKE model, plays a key role in confronting the implications of Phelps's (1994) theory with time-series data on relevant macroeconomic aggregates.

One of the main implications of the structuralist theory is that real exchange rate appreciation, by lowering the price of competing foreign goods, reduces firms' markups of prices over costs. This implies that the real exchange rate and the economy's profit share, which proxies for an aggregate of markups, comove: profit share would decline (rise) during the periods of persistent appreciation (depreciation) of the real exchange rate. This implication is consistent with the "evidence of a non-stationary profit share co-moving with the real exchange rate" (Juselius 2006: 378–379).

Taken together, the negative comovement of the profit share and the real exchange rate and the positive comovement of the real exchange rate and the real interest rate imply that unemployment would, according to

---

33. Juselius argues that, beyond providing a summary of the covariance structure of the data that is superior to those provided by other econometric approaches, the multivariate CVAR framework is crucial for uncovering the $I(2)$ persistence displayed by asset prices and other macroeconomic time series. Although the literature has reported results consistent with such persistence (e.g., see Engel and Hamilton 1990), the vast majority of studies, which have relied on univariate procedures, have rejected $I(2)$ in favor of $I(1)$ persistence. Juselius (2012) shows that such tests lack sufficient power to detect the $I(2)$ nonstationarity that arises from the slowly unfolding trends that underlie persistence in asset prices.

the structuralist model, persistently rise during periods in which the real interest rate undergoes a persistent upswing. Juselius (2006) found that unemployment comoves positively with the real interest rate.

Thus, reliance on the structuralist model to represent the transmission process by which asset markets influence the real economy generates an important implication: given persistent movements in real interest rates, the natural rate of unemployment is nonstationary. Juselius (2006) and Juselius and Ordonez (2009) provide empirical evidence for such a transmission process and, with it, for the nonstationarity of the natural rate.

The empirical analyses of Zoega and Juselius focus on nonmonetary factors that, according to the structuralist theory, influence the natural rate of unemployment. As the natural rate is not observable, they rely on the assumption that swings in the actual unemployment rate largely reflect the movements of the natural rate. However, as Phelps (1994: 314) pointed out, "the data on the actual rate of unemployment in any country unquestionably reflect . . . the influence of monetary [factors]." This opens the possibility that monetary policy, as well as other macroeconomic policies aiming to attenuate cyclical fluctuations in economic activity in the short run, may influence the trend growth of real output and the movement of the long-run "natural" unemployment rate that is associated with such changes. In Chapter 11, Philippe Aghion and Enisse Kharroubi argue that such a connection between short-run stabilization policies and the long-run behavior of real output and unemployment is empirically significant.

Stabilization Policies and Economic Growth

The conventional wisdom among economists and nonacademic commentators is that there is no connection between short-run macroeconomic policies and an economy's trend growth rate. The findings of Juselius in Chapter 10, which connect fluctuations in currency markets to movements in the natural rate of unemployment, suggest otherwise.

In Chapter 11, Aghion and Kharroubi present further evidence that challenges the conventional view. Their empirical analysis appeals to the argument advanced by Aghion et al. (2008) that growth-enhancing investments (in skills, research and development, or structural capital) need to be maintained over the long run. Business cycle fluctuations, they argue, tend to be detrimental to innovation and growth, particularly for firms facing credit constraints that prevent them from investing more than some multiple of their cash flow. As cash flows decline during recessions, such firms are forced to cut productivity-enhancing investments, thereby contributing to a reduction in the long-run growth rate.

Aghion and Kharroubi therefore argue that active countercyclical stabilization policies "may have [significant] implications for long-term growth. For instance, if monetary policy reduces the cost of short-term refinancing in downturns . . . that should help firms go through downturns without having to cut . . . [growth-]enhancing investments" (Chapter 11: 352). To test this hypothesis empirically, they compare the size and effects of active fiscal and monetary policies on growth across industries in countries that differ in the degree to which they pursue active stabilization policies.

Using panel regressions based on data from 15 OECD countries, Aghion and Kharroubi examine whether industries that faced tighter financial constraints tended to grow faster in countries with active fiscal and monetary policies. To proxy the degree of financial dependence on external credit markets, they use industry measures of borrowing or liquidity constraints. They estimate the degree of countercyclicality of a country's stabilization policy (fiscal or monetary) according to the sensitivity with which the policy responds to the output gap (departures of real output from its long-run trend).

For fiscal policy, they use two alternative measures of fiscal balance. Because these indicators are available only annually, they estimate their effects on industry growth across countries over a relatively long period, 1980–2005. Their regression results show that "increased sensitivity of fiscal balance . . . to the output gap raises . . . real value added growth disproportionately for industries with [higher financial dependence]" (Chapter 11: 357).

Aghion and Kharroubi also investigate the relationship between industry growth and countercyclicality of monetary policy across countries, using the short-term real interest rate as a proxy for the monetary policy stance. Relying on quarterly observations, the analysis spans 1995–2005. As is true of active fiscal policy, their empirical results show that a degree of countercyclicality of a country's monetary policy "tends to raise . . . real value added growth disproportionately for industries with higher financial dependence" (Chapter 11: 362). They conclude that "the effect of countercyclical fiscal or monetary policy is economically significant [in the long run] and cannot be discarded as being of second-order importance" (Chapter 11: 353).

Aghion et al. (2008: 3) emphasize that, "while [such effects] provide some justification for stimulus packages during recessions, this justification is quite distinct from the argument based on Keynesian multipliers." Although the standard multiplier analysis relies on the short-run demand-side effects of active stabilization policies, the results reported in Aghion and Kharroubi call attention to the way in which such policies affect long-run growth, primarily through the supply side of the economy.

Short-Run (Cyclical) versus Long-Run Unemployment?

The empirical results obtained by Aghion and Kharroubi point to a connection between cyclical fluctuations in real output and its long-run growth. However, the structuralist approach to unemployment fluctuations does not model short-run behavior; its account of unemployment relies on the factors that drive the long-run natural rate.

Indeed, the empirical analyses of the structuralist theory of unemployment, in Phelps (1994), Phelps and Zoega (2001), and Chapters 9 and 10 of this volume, come close to jettisoning altogether the distinction between cyclical movements in unemployment and its long-run behavior.[34] These studies assume that observed quarterly unemployment fluctuations, which are typically referred to as short-run or cyclical, largely reflect the movements of long-run natural rate unemployment.

As we have discussed, share prices, real interest rates, and real exchange rates tend to undergo persistent upswings and downswings that do not converge or abate. According to structuralist models, therefore, unemployment also tends to fluctuate without settling down in the long run. Indeed, Juselius finds that unemployment follows a persistent $I(2)$ process and that its fluctuations stem largely from persistent swings in the real interest rate and the real exchange rate.

This characterization of the unemployment rate as a highly persistent process accords well with the view of Phelps (1994, 2006) and Phelps and Zoega (2001) that market participants' expectations of assets' prospects are among the main drivers of unemployment. The IKE model in Chapter 6 lends further support to this claim by showing that the $I(2)$ trends found in asset prices reflect market participants' (as well as economists') imperfect knowledge (see Frydman et al. 2011).

Beyond raising doubts about the dualism of cyclical and long-run unemployment, the finding of near-$I(2)$ persistence points to fundamental difficulties in using mechanical rules to understand how to conduct monetary and other macroeconomic policies. For example, Taylor rules relate the interest rate to the gap between the current and long-run unemployment rate. But the unemployment rate's persistent character raises fundamental questions concerning the definition and measurement of this gap.

Advocating that macroeconomic policy be conducted according to rules presupposes that its sole role is to offset any "shocks" that buffet the system. Absent such shocks, the economy would be growing at its "normal" steady pace, with unemployment at its natural rate. These representations of the

---

34. Phelps (1994) includes the inflation rate in the unemployment equation to control for cyclical influences. But he does not model short-run movement, and his account of unemployment relies on the factors that drive the movements of the natural rate. His reliance on expectational shifts to model macroeconomic fluctuations stands in sharp contrast to the so-called real business cycle approach. Because these models rely on REH, they rule out the possibility that participants' expectations play an autonomous role in understanding movements in unemployment; instead, cyclical fluctuations supposedly arise solely from various "shocks" and ad hoc "frictions." For a survey of various attempts to identify these shocks, see Rebelo (2005). For the seminal exposition of the real business cycle approach, see Kydland and Prescott (1982).

economy underpin the view that policymakers should have virtually no scope for discretion. In Chapter 12, John Taylor discusses how the debate over reliance on rules versus discretion has unfolded over time.

Part Four: Policymaking after "Rational Expectations"

The finding of nonstationary and highly persistent $I(2)$ unemployment rates suggests that fluctuations, rather than steady output growth, are the "normal" behavior of such macroeconomic aggregates in modern capitalist economies. These economies thrive on nonroutine change, which leads to shifts in the processes driving outcomes, engenders imperfect knowledge about these processes, and thus is among the primary causes of instability.

Friedrich Hayek and Milton Friedman argued that the economic rationale for constraining officials to follow fully predetermined rules stems from inherently imperfect knowledge about how economic policies affect individual behavior and aggregate outcomes over time. In contrast, contemporary arguments for rule-based policymaking appeal to REH, which assumes away imperfect knowledge on the part of policymakers and market participants. In Chapter 12, Taylor documents the profound impact of the REH approach on how economic policy has come to be conducted.

Shifts in the Rules-Discretion Balance

For Hayek (1978: 34), the claim that state intervention could not improve on outcomes produced by unfettered markets stemmed from his "recognition of the insuperable limits of our knowledge." He pointed out that markets' essential role in allocating society's resources to alternative uses, particularly its savings to diverse investment projects, stems from nonroutine change and imperfect knowledge. This was the essence of his prescient argument that central planning is impossible in principle.[35]

To be sure, policymakers, too, face ever-imperfect knowledge, and active intervention in markets is fraught with difficulty. Echoing Hayek, Friedman (1968) invoked the imperfection of knowledge—the inability to know when and how a discretionary change in monetary policy might affect the economy—to argue that central banks should be constrained by fixed rules. But, as influential as Friedman's empirical findings of "long and variable lags" have been, they lacked a rigorous theoretical underpinning, for the simple reason that prevailing economic theory, then as now, has assumed

---

35. See Hayek (1948). The inherent tension between contemporary theory's disregard of imperfect knowledge and the appeal to Hayek's arguments in support of markets has again become apparent in debates about public policy in the wake of the global financial crisis. See Cochrane (2009) and Frydman and Goldberg (2011).

away economists' ever-imperfect knowledge about how alternative policies influence market participants' expectations and aggregate outcomes.

As Taylor points out in Chapter 12, Hayek's arguments for policy rules have primarily appealed to political and normative considerations; for example, that the state, beyond enforcing the rule of law, has no authority to interfere with individuals' freedom to act as they choose. "Stripped of all technicalities, this means that government in all its actions is bound by rules *fixed and announced beforehand*—rules which make it possible to foresee with fair certainty how the authority will use its coercive powers in given circumstances and to plan one's individual affairs on the basis of this knowledge" (Hayek 1944: 112, emphasis added).

However, such arguments cannot provide an *economic* rationale for rules. In particular, they cannot support the claim that allowing policy-makers discretion would necessarily result in inferior economic performance. REH models were widely seen as providing the missing "scientific" rationale for banning discretion in all circumstances.[36] As we have noted, early REH-based models assumed that monetary policy could influence unemployment only by fooling market participants, and that, left to themselves, financial markets populated by so-called rational participants would allocate resources nearly perfectly. As Taylor (Chapter 12: 374) notes, "the [REH] macro policy evaluation by Lucas (1976) . . . reinforced the economic rationale for rules."

Lucas's critique examined the validity of policy analysis based on large-scale Keynesian econometric models. These models typically included a number of policy variables, such as interest rates, money supply growth, or tax rates. Policy analysis involved the use of these models' estimates, based on historical data, to simulate the paths of macroeconomic outcomes, such as inflation or unemployment, under alternative trajectories for selected policy variables. Lucas pointed out that "for [Keynesian policy analysis] to have any meaning, it is essential that the structure [of the model] not vary systematically with the choice of the sequence of [a policy variable]" (Lucas 1976: 25).

The main point of Lucas's critique was the untenability of the premise that models with the same structure could adequately represent the causal process driving outcomes both before and after a change in policy. Lucas argued that changes in policy variables would alter the way that market

---

36. The belief in the scientific status of REH-based conclusions was so strong that leading economists advocated far-reaching institutional changes to eliminate discretion on the part of policymakers. In a seminal paper, for example, Kydland and Prescott (1977: 487) advocate

> institutional arrangements which make it difficult and time-consuming to change the policy rules in all but emergency situations. One possible institutional arrangement is for Congress to legislate monetary and fiscal policy rules and these rules to become effective only after a 2-year delay. This would make discretionary policy all but impossible.

participants forecast the future and hence their decisionmaking. In general, this change on the individual level would also alter the causal process driving aggregate outcomes, thereby rendering policy analysis based on Keynesian models "invalid."

Lucas offered a straightforward solution to this daunting problem: REH would enable policymakers to represent exactly the change in the structure of their models that would result from market participants' revisions of their forecasting strategies following the contemplated change in policy.

Taylor (Chapter 12: 376) acknowledges that "though I and many others have favored rules over discretion for economic reasons, when it comes to explaining shifts in the balance between rules and discretion over time, . . . political factors must also be considered." He therefore invokes such considerations to explain the shifts in the rules-discretion balance during the closing decades of the twentieth century. For example, he points out that "there was clearly a political change in the 1980s in the United States and in the United Kingdom in which attitudes favoring more limited government and corresponding encouragement of free markets were on the rise" (Chapter 12: 385).

This shift was maintained—and extended—even after President Bill Clinton and Prime Minister Tony Blair succeeded putatively more conservative governments. Such bipartisan political support for unfettered markets highlights the remarkably broad resonance of the belief that REH-based models' implications for the balance between state and market are based on sound scientific foundations. REH also suggested that policymakers could influence market participants' expectations to a far greater degree than was actually possible, given that policy instruments might work quite differently than expected in real-world markets (in which nonroutine change is an ever-present possibility).

Drawing on Federal Open Market Committee transcripts that contain "a large number of references to policy rules and related developments" (Chapter 12: 377), Taylor documents the profound impact of rules on the conduct and instruments of U.S. monetary policy. For example, in considering how its policies should be communicated to the public, the Federal Reserve has implicitly adopted REH models' premise that imperfect knowledge is unimportant for understanding outcomes. Consequently, policymakers focus on transparency of information and disregard altogether their own, as well as market participants', inherent difficulties in interpreting how changes in economic policy would affect outcomes.

Although REH's flaws imply that its models cannot provide the rationale for rule-based policymaking, this does not necessarily mean that other constraints, such as qualitative guidelines, have no place in thinking about the objectives, design, and implementation of economic policies. What REH's flaws do suggest is that the question of rules versus discretion needs to be reexamined using models that recognize that nonroutine change and imperfect knowledge are essential to understanding the consequences of economic policies in real-world markets. The crisis that erupted in 2008 has, if nothing else, made starkly clear the need for such a reexamination.

Rules versus Discretion after "Rational Expectations"

Echoing Hayek and Friedman, Lucas (1976: 46) asserted that constraining policymakers to follow fully predetermined rules "accord[s] well with a preference for democratic decision-making." However, in sharp contrast to Hayek's and Friedman's appeal to imperfect knowledge, Lucas and his followers have claimed that REH models provide an explicitly economic rationale for rule-based policymaking.

As they do with all their other components, REH models represent economic policies with fully predetermined rules. Consequently, that is how a typical macroeconomist nowadays represents alternative policies. Lucas takes for granted that "the only *scientific* quantitative policy evaluations available to us are comparisons of the consequences of alternative policy rules" (Lucas 1976: 41, emphasis in the original) in the context of his own REH model.[37]

In Chapter 13, Michael Woodford acknowledges that nonroutine change undermines the desirability of standard REH-based policy rules. However, he emphasizes that

> the reconsideration of macroeconomic theory and policy that is necessary in the wake of the global financial crisis . . . does not eliminate the need to assess policy strategies, . . . even if such strategies cannot realistically be supposed to represent complete specifications of behavior in all possible circumstances. Nor does it eliminate the potential benefits from requiring policy decisions to be based on general principles, rather than making an ad hoc decision about what will achieve the best outcome under current circumstances. [Chapter 13: 392]

In an attempt to reconcile rules with recognition that nonroutine change may create circumstances in which policymakers must exercise discretion, Woodford proposes to reframe the rules-versus-discretion debate. He observes that "there are different levels at which it is possible to describe the process through which policy decisions are to be made" (Chapter 13: 385). He then argues that "the levels of description differ in the degree to which it is useful to imagine specifying a rule for policy in advance" (Chapter 13: 398).

Woodford discusses how the instruments and conduct of monetary policy could follow from such policy design and implementation. He illustrates his approach, which he calls "principled policymaking," by discussing how the

---

37. For an early example of REH policy analysis in the context of unemployment-inflation trade-offs, see Lucas (1973).

specificity and degree of monetary policy's precommitment already depends in some respects on how important nonroutine change is likely to be for the different levels on which policy is implemented.

Specifically, he argues that at the lowest level, where policy decisions pertain to largely routine situations, they could be specified in advance with mechanical rules. For example, such a rule would specify a decision about the quantity of bank reserves to inject or withdraw each day, typically through open-market purchases or repo transactions, as a function of some observable conditions.

Policy decisions on the higher, "instrument" level pertain to largely routine circumstances as well, according to Woodford, and they also can be fully prespecified with a mechanical rule. Such decisions involve, for example, the choice of an operating target for a particular overnight interest rate—the federal funds rate.

Moving to the highest level of description, Woodford considers policy decisions that involve various forms of so-called inflation targeting. For example, "many central banks now have explicit quantitative targets for some measure of medium-run inflation; a few have also been fairly explicit about the criteria used to judge whether near-term economic projections are acceptable" (Chapter 13: 397).

Notwithstanding the central bank's supposedly firm precommitment, Woodford acknowledges that nonroutine change might lead it to revise its pre-announced target. He points out that "one would specify the principles on which policy targets are chosen, given a particular model of the way that monetary policy affects the economy." As a result, "a commitment to specified principles at this level could be maintained in the face of a change in either the structure of the economy or policymakers' understanding of that structure." However, he notes that "it might well be appropriate to modify a central bank's policy targets in light of such change" (Chapter 13: 397).[38]

It seems to us that the inherent ambiguity about the appropriate response to nonroutine change underscores the key reason policymaking should *not* be fully rule based: whether and how the central bank should revise the way in which it conducts monetary policy cannot be fully specified in advance. Not only is there no way to prespecify how monetary policy should adapt when the economy's structure eventually changes; the assessment that such change has occurred also necessarily involves nonquantifiable judgment.[39]

---

38. This may also lead to revision of procedures and instruments on the lower levels of policy design and implementation.

39. For example, even if one uses strictly statistical criteria to detect change, the assessment of whether and when structural change has occurred depends on the choice of tests and their significance levels. Moreover, after the change has been detected, the decision concerning what the new structure might be also necessarily involves nonquantifiable judgment. For an example of such a revision process involving structural change, see Frydman and Goldberg (2007).

Recognition of nonroutine change necessarily blurs the putatively sharp distinction between rules and discretion. As desirable as precommitment to specific targets, such as "explicit quantitative targets for some measure of medium-run inflation," might appear to be in REH models, such targets are credible for limited periods at best. Sooner or later, nonroutine change renders the monetary authority's model obsolete and thus necessitates revisions of at least some aspects of policy design.

Expectations in Policy Analysis

The 1970 Phelps volume pioneered modern macroeconomics by constructing models of aggregate outcomes on the basis of mathematical representations of individual decisionmaking. Individuals' forecasts play a key role in how they make decisions and in how markets aggregate those decisions into prices. The causal processes behind both individual decisions and aggregate outcomes, therefore, depend on market participants' understanding of the economy and how they use this knowledge to forecast the future. In the context of such models, representing how market participants might revise their forecasts in response to new policies or other changes lies at the heart of evaluating economic policies.

REH presumes that participants' forecasts of revisions following a change in policy can be adequately represented by the change in the structure of an economist's REH model. By design, REH-based policy analysis can compare only the consequences of alternative overarching rules that specify how policy is conducted in all time periods, past, present, and future.

As we noted above, Woodford argues that constraining the central bank to pre-announce commitments remains important even if one departs from REH. Seeking to provide theoretical support for this point, he discusses, in the context of the eductive and adaptive learning models of Chapters 1 and 2, the implications of the claim that market participants' expectations take into account such commitments. Woodford concludes that, for "these approaches, a comparative evaluation of alternative monetary policies will require a specification of the entire (state-contingent) future path of policy, and not simply a current action, just as in the case of REE analysis. Similarly, there will be potential benefits from commitment relative to the outcome under discretionary policy" (Chapter 13: 395).[40]

Although eductive and adaptive learning approaches depart from REH, they assume away nonroutine change by fully prespecifying how market participants revise their forecasting strategies and how aggregate outcomes

---

40. Woodford also examines the implications of policy commitments in his models with so-called near-rational expectations (Woodford 2010). In these models, the actual probability distribution of outcomes in all periods is presumed to be generated by an economist's REH model. Participants' "subjective beliefs [are assumed] not [to] be grossly out of line with [those] probabilities [of outcomes]" (Chapter 13: 394).

unfold over time. In fact, even if it were feasible for officials to specify "the *entire* (state-contingent) future path of policy," market participants in capitalist economies are strongly motivated to search for genuinely new ways to forecast the future and deploy their resources.

The social context, including the institutions within which individuals make decisions, also changes in unforeseeable ways. But when the social context or how market participants forecast aggregate outcomes changes, so, too, does the causal process underpinning these outcomes. Policymakers and market participants understand that, even if economic policy were somehow to remain constrained to a fully predetermined path, they would face ever-imperfect knowledge of the processes driving outcomes.

Thus, even if prespecification of the entire future policy path was feasible and desirable, models that rely on mechanical rules to represent the consequences of policy changes for participants' forecasts and aggregate outcomes cannot serve as a guide for real-world policy analysis; assuming away nonroutine change does not magically eliminate its importance. Nevertheless, Woodford (Chapter 13: 395) maintains that "the argument that rule-based policymaking is necessarily foolhardy in a world where nonroutine change occurs depends on too narrow a conception of what is involved in following a rule."

By opening macroeconomic analysis to nonroutine change and ever-imperfect knowledge, the IKE approach presented in Chapters 4 and 6 aims to provide a theoretical underpinning for an intermediate position on rules versus discretion. In the context of financial markets, IKE suggests a policy framework that constrains officials in a qualitative way, while allowing them to exercise judgment in confronting infrequent but recurring episodes in which imperfect knowledge leads market participants to make decisions that, though individually rational, carry potentially high social costs (see Frydman and Goldberg 2009, 2011). The extent to which such suggestions may be applicable to the design and implementation of macroeconomic policy more broadly requires empirically relevant and testable models that do not fully prespecify how policymakers and market participants revise their expectations in response to nonroutine change—the hallmark of modern capitalist economies.

References

Abreu, Dilip, and Markus K. Brunnermeier. (2003) "Bubbles and Crashes," *Econometrica* 71: 173–204.

Aghion, Philippe, George-Marios Angelotos, Abhijit Banerjee, and Kalina Manova. (2008) "Volatility and Growth: Credit Constraints and Productivity-Enhancing Investment," NBER Working Paper 11349, National Bureau of Economic Research, Cambridge, MA.

Bernheim, Douglas. (1984) "Rationalizable Strategic Behavior," *Econometrica* 52: 1007–1028.

Borrill, Paul L., and Leigh Tesfatsion. (2011) "Agent-Based Modeling: The Right Mathematics for the Social Sciences?" in J. B. Davis and D. W. Hands (eds.), *Elgar Recent Economic Modeling Methodology Companion.* Cheltenham, UK: Edward Elgar, pp. 228–258.

Branch, Bill, and George W. Evans. (2003) "Intrinsic Heterogeneity in Expectation Formation." Working Paper 2003-32, Economics Department, University of Oregon, Eugene. Revised October 4, 2004.

Bray, Margaret. (1982) "Learning, Estimation and the Stability of Rational Expectations Equilibria," *Journal of Economic Theory* 26: 318–339.

Calvo, Guillermo A. (1983) "Staggered Prices in a Utility-Maximizing Framework," *Journal of Monetary Economics* 12: 383–398.

Cochrane, John H. (2009) "How Did Paul Krugman Get It So Wrong?" Mimeo. Available at: http://faculty.chicagobooth.edu/john.cochrane/research/Papers/krugman_response.htm.

Damasio, Antonio R. (1994) *Descartes' Error: Emotion, Reason, and the Human Brain.* New York: Avon Books.

De Grauwe, Paul, and Marianna Grimaldi. (2006) *The Exchange Rate in a Behavioral Finance Framework.* Princeton, NJ: Princeton University Press.

DeLong, Bradford J., Andrei Shleifer, Lawrence H. Summers, and Robert J. Waldman. (1990) "Positive Feedback Investment Strategies and Destabilizing Rational Speculation," *Journal of Finance* 45: 375–395.

Engel, Charles, and James D. Hamilton. (1990) "Long Swings in the Dollar: Are They in the Data and Do Markets Know It?" *American Economic Review* 80: 689–713.

Evans, George W. (1983) "The Stability of Rational Expectations in Macroeconomic Models," in Roman Frydman and Edmund S. Phelps (eds.), *Individual Forecasting and Aggregate Outcomes: "Rational Expectations" Examined.* New York: Cambridge University Press, pp. 63–94.

Evans, George W., and Seppo Honkapohja. (2005) "An Interview with Thomas J. Sargent," *Macroeconomic Dynamics* 9: 561–583.

Fischer, Stanley. (1977) "Long-Term Contracts, Rational Expectations, and the Optimal Money Supply Rule," *Journal of Political Economy* 85: 191–205.

Frankel, Jeffrey, and Kenneth Froot. (1987) "Understanding the U.S. Dollar in the Eighties: The Expectations of Chartists and Fundamentalists," *Economic Record* 62: 24–38.

Friedman, Milton. (1960) *A Program for Monetary Stability.* New York: Fordham University Press.

———. (1968) "The Role of Monetary Policy," *American Economic Review* 58: 1–17.

Frydman, Roman. (1982) "Towards an Understanding of Market Processes: Individual Expectations, Learning and Convergence to Rational Expectations Equilibrium," *American Economic Review* 72: 652–668.

———. (1983) "Individual Rationality, Decentralization and the Rational Expectations Hypothesis," in Roman Frydman and Edmund S. Phelps (eds.), *Individual Forecasting and Aggregate Outcomes: "Rational Expectations" Examined.* New York: Cambridge University Press, pp. 97–122.

Frydman, Roman, and Michael D. Goldberg. (2007) *Imperfect Knowledge Economics: Exchange Rates and Risk*. Princeton, NJ: Princeton University Press.

———. (2009) "Financial Markets and the State: Price Swings, Risk, and the Scope of Regulation," *Capitalism and Society* 4(2): Article 2, available at: http://www.bepress.com/cas/vol4/iss2/art2/.

———. (2011) *Beyond Mechanical Markets: Asset Price Swings, Risk, and the Role of the State*. Princeton, NJ: Princeton University Press.

Frydman, Roman, and Edmund S. Phelps. (1983) "Introduction," in Roman Frydman and Edmund S. Phelps (eds.), *Individual Forecasting and Aggregate Outcomes: "Rational Expectations" Examined*. New York: Cambridge University Press, pp. 1–30.

Frydman, Roman, Katarina Juselius, Soren Johansen, and Michael D. Goldberg. (2011) "Long Swings in Currency Markets: $I(2)$ Trends and Imperfect Knowledge." Mimeo, New York University, New York.

Frydman, Roman, Michael D. Goldberg, Soren Johansen, and Katarina Juselius. (2012) "Why REH Bubble Models Do Not Adequately Account for Swings." Mimeo, New York University, New York.

Gali, Jordi. (2008) *Monetary Policy, Inflation, and the Business Cycle: An Introduction to the New Keynesian Framework*. Princeton, NJ: Princeton University Press.

Goldberg, Michael D., and Roman Frydman. (1996a) "Imperfect Knowledge and Behavior in the Foreign Exchange Market," *Economic Journal* 106: 869–893.

———. (1996b) "Empirical Exchange Rate Models and Shifts in the Co-Integrating Vector," *Journal of Structural Change and Economic Dynamics* 7: 55–78.

Guesnerie, Roger. (2005) *Assessing Rational Expectations: "Eductive" Stability in Economics*. Cambridge, MA: MIT Press.

Hayek, Friedrich A. (1944) *The Road to Serfdom*. Chicago: University of Chicago Press.

———. (1948) *Individualism and Economic Order*. Chicago: University of Chicago Press.

———. (1978) "The Pretence of Knowledge," 1974 Nobel lecture, in *New Studies in Philosophy, Politics, Economics and the History of Ideas*. Chicago: University of Chicago Press, pp. 23–34.

Hoon, Hian Teck, and Edmund S. Phelps. (1992) "Macroeconomic Shocks in a Dynamized Model of the Natural Rate of Unemployment," *American Economic Review* 82: 889–900.

Johansen, Soren. (1996) *Likelihood Based Inference on Cointegration in the Vector Autoregressive Model*. Oxford: Oxford University Press.

Juselius, Katarina. (2006) *The Cointegrated VAR Model: Methodology and Applications*. Oxford: Oxford University Press.

———. (2012) "The Haavelmo Probability Approach and the Cointegrated VAR." Discussion paper, Economics Department, University of Copenhagen.

Juselius, Katarina, and Javier Ordonez. (2009) "The Balassa-Samuelson Effect and the Wage, Price, and Unemployment Dynamics in Spain." Working Paper 0529, Department of Economics, University of Copenhagen.

Kahneman, Daniel, and Amos Tversky. (1979) "Prospect Theory: An Analysis of Decision Under Risk," *Econometrica* 47: 263–291.

Keynes, John Maynard. (1921) *A Treatise on Probability.* London: Macmillan.

———. (1936) *The General Theory of Employment, Interest and Money.* London: Harcourt, Brace and World.

Knight, Frank H. (1921) *Risk, Uncertainty and Profit.* New York: Harper.

Kydland, Finn E., and Edward C. Prescott. (1977) "Rules Rather than Discretion: The Inconsistency of Optimal Plans," *Journal of Political Economy* 85: 473–491.

———. (1982) "Time to Build and Aggregate Fluctuations," *Econometrica* 50: 1345–1370.

Lucas, Robert E., Jr. (1973) "Some International Evidence on Output-Inflation Trade-Offs," *American Economic Review* 63: 326–334.

———. (1976) "Econometric Policy Evaluation: A Critique," in Karl Brunner and Allan H. Meltzer (eds.), *The Phillips Curve and Labor Markets.* Carnegie-Rochester Conference Series on Public Policy. Amsterdam: North-Holland, pp. 19–46. Reprinted in Robert E. Lucas, Jr. (1981) *Studies in Business-Cycle Theory.* Cambridge, MA: MIT Press, pp. 104–130.

———. (1986) "Adaptive Behavior and Economic Theory," *Journal of Business* 59: S401–S426.

———. (1995) "The Monetary Neutrality," 1995 Nobel lecture. Available at: http://www.nobelprize.org/nobel_prizes/economics/laureates/1995/lucas-lecture.html.

———. (2001) "Professional Memoir." Mimeo. Available at: http://home.uchicago.edu.

———. (2004) "My Keynesian Education," in Michael De Vroey and Kevin D. Hoover (eds.), *The IS-LM Model: Its Rise, Fall, and Strange Persistence.* Annual Supplement to volume 36 of *History of Political Economy.* Durham, NC: Duke University Press, pp. 12–24.

Mangee, Nicholas. (2011) "Long Swings in Stock Prices: Market Fundamentals and Psychology." PhD dissertation, University of New Hampshire, Durham.

Muth, John F. (1961) "Rational Expectations and the Theory of Price Movements," *Econometrica* 29: 315–335.

Obstfeld, Maurice, and Kenneth Rogoff. (1996) *Foundations of International Macroeconomics.* Cambridge, MA: MIT Press.

Pearce, David G. (1984) "Rationalizable Strategic Behavior and the Problem of Perfection," *Econometrica* 52: 1029–1050.

Phelps, Edmund S. (1968) "Money-Wage Dynamics and Labor Market Equilibrium," *Journal of Political Economy* 76: 678–711.

———. (1969) "The New Microeconomics in Inflation and Employment Theory," *American Economic Review* 59(Papers and Proceedings): 147–160.

———. (1983) "The Trouble with 'Rational Expectations' and the Problem of Inflation Stabilization," in Roman Frydman and Edmund S. Phelps (eds.), *Individual Forecasting and Aggregate Outcomes: "Rational Expectations" Examined.* New York: Cambridge University Press.

———. (1994) *Structural Slumps: The Modern Equilibrium Theory of Unemployment, Interest and Assets.* Cambridge, MA: Harvard University Press.

———. (1999) "Behind This Structural Boom: The Role of Asset Valuations," *American Economic Review* 89(Papers and Proceedings): 63–68.

——. (2006) "Prospective Shifts, Speculative Swings: 'Macro' for the Twenty-First Century in the Tradition Championed by Paul Samuelson," in M. Szenberg, L. Ramrattan, and A. A. Gottesman (eds.), *Samuelsonian Economics*. Oxford: Oxford University Press, pp. 66–87.

——. (2007) "Foreword," in Roman Frydman and Michael D. Goldberg, *Imperfect Knowledge Economics: Exchange Rates and Risk*. Princeton, NJ: Princeton University Press.

Phelps, Edmund S., and John B. Taylor. (1977) "Stabilizing Powers of Monetary Policy under Rational Expectations," *Journal of Political Economy* 85: 163–190.

Phelps, Edmund S., and Gylfi Zoega. (1998) "Natural-Rate Theory and OECD Unemployment," *Economic Journal* 108: 782–801.

——. (2001) "Structural Booms: Productivity Explanations and Asset Valuations," *Economic Policy* 16: 85–126.

Phelps, Edmund S., G. C. Archibald, and Armen A. Alchian (eds.). (1970) *Microeconomic Foundations of Employment and Inflation Theory*. New York: W. W. Norton.

Phillips, A. W. (1958) "The Relation between Unemployment and the Rate of Change of Money Wage Rates in the United Kingdom, 1861–1957," *Economica* 25: 283–299.

Pigou, Arthur C. 1927. *Industrial Fluctuations*. London: Macmillan.

Rebelo, Sergio. (2005) "Real Business Cycle Models: Past, Present, and Future," *Scandinavian Journal of Economics* 107: 217–238.

Rogoff, Kenneth, and Vania Stavrakeva. (2008) "The Continuing Puzzle of Short Horizon Exchange Rate Forecasting." NBER Working Paper 14701, National Bureau of Economic Research, Cambridge, MA.

Sargent, Thomas J. (2008) "Rational Expectations," *The Concise Encyclopedia of Economics*. Library of Economics and Liberty. Available at: http://www.econlib.org/library/Enc/RationalExpectations.html.

Sargent, Thomas J., and Neil Wallace. (1975) " 'Rational' Expectations, the Optimal Monetary Instrument, and the Optimal Money Supply Rule," *Journal of Political Economy* 83: 241–254.

Shiller, Robert J. (1981) "Do Stock Prices Move Too Much to be Justified by Subsequent Changes in Dividends?" *American Economic Review* 71: 421–436.

Shleifer, Andrei. (2000) *Inefficient Markets*. Oxford: Oxford University Press.

Sims, Christopher A. (1996) "Macroeconomics and Methodology," *Journal of Economic Perspectives* 10(1): 105–120.

Woodford, Michael. (2003) *Interest Rates and Prices: Foundations of a Theory of Monetary Policy*. Princeton, NJ: Princeton University Press.

——. (2010) "Robustly Optimal Monetary Policy with Near-Rational Expectations," *American Economic Review* 100: 274–303.

PART ONE

Back to the Foundations

CHAPTER ONE

Expectational Coordination Failures and Market Volatility

Roger Guesnerie

1.1 Introduction

The stability of market economies has been a recurrent subject of debate since the beginning of the nineteenth century, which is usually viewed as the starting point of economics as a scientific field. "L'offre crée sa propre demande" ("supply creates its own demand"): this formula, a remarkable digest of the argument, is supposed to capture the essence of Jean Baptiste Say's analysis (1803). It expressed the basis for some of the early protagonists' strong confidence in the systemic stability of markets. But others strongly disagreed: Jean Baptiste Sismondi and the "catastrophist school"— and its most famous adept, Karl Marx—awaited the next crisis (possibly the final crisis) of the capitalist system. In the middle, Léon Walras thought that Say's argument was unconvincing but developed an alternative analysis that has long been viewed as supporting the optimists. The skepticism about market economies' systemic stability reappeared after the 1929 crisis, and Keynes forcefully argued for government intervention to counter markets' instability.

This chapter develops ideas that have been presented on several occasions, including at the "Conférence Jean Jacques Laffont" of the 2010 Congress of the Association Française de Science Economique (published in 2011 as "Défaillances de coordination et volatilité des marchés" in *La Revue Economique* 62: 395–408) and at invited lectures (e.g., in the series "Food for Thought: On a Post Mortem of the Financial Crisis" of the European Investment Bank and at the Columbia University conference "Micro-Foundations for Macroeconomics"). Related ideas have been presented and discussed in many seminars and workshops in Marseille, Stanford, New Delhi, Bombay, Aix-en-Provence, and Warwick. I thank participants for their comments and suggestions and in particular thank Ken Binmore, Massimo Cingolani, and Partha Sen. I am especially grateful to Alan Kirman for his careful critical reading of a previous version, which contributed to improving both the English and the content. I remain responsible for any shortcomings.

At the beginning of the current millennium, mainstream economic theory had apparently rallied to Say's optimism. Even if markets may not be fully self-regulating, our knowledge had improved, so that, according to Robert Lucas (2003), the "central problem of depression prevention has been solved." Was not the "great moderation" (see Bernanke 2008) proof of the adequacy and efficiency of the prevailing macroeconomic and monetary policies? But the argument reflected an appraisal of the facts that was intellectually and geographically biased (see Reinhardt and Rogoff 2008). Facts, such as crises and bubbles, are stubborn, and their stubbornness challenges the system of explanations that dominate contemporary economics. Neither the volatility of financial markets nor the logic of crises is satisfactorily explained by the best of our existing models.

Many economists, though not all, would agree that the recent crisis has raised questions about the state of economic theory; a subset would probably agree that reading the crisis through the standard lenses of the dominant approaches signals an outright failure of economic theory. Going somewhat further, I am among those who believe that economic theory has a key responsibility in the financial crisis that triggered recent economic events. The bottom line is that economists have provided an overly optimistic view of the workings of financial markets (many specialists' emphasis on the Efficient Market Hypothesis is a spectacular illustration of this bias). Such an overly optimistic view in the group of financial practitioners—a group already prone to self-satisfaction and reluctant to submit to regulation—triggered the deployment of uncontrolled imagination. Exaggeratedly sanguine conclusions, whether in finance or macroeconomics, reflected uncritical acceptance of modeling principles that, without justification, had become axioms. The question of what went wrong with standard economic theory in general and with its modeling principles in particular is, however, likely to suggest a variety of answers. Let me sketch three.

1. The first answer does not refer so much to modeling principles as to the diversification of modeling. There has been a multiplication of fronts in modern economic research, but progress on each front is increasingly obscure to outsiders, even those from neighboring subfields. I have argued elsewhere that the balkanization of knowledge is more of a problem in the study of economics (or social science more broadly), where social action must rely on all dimensions of understanding, than in a field like physics, where applications depend significantly on specifics. From my teaching experience, I have been struck by the fact that, in the field of finance, the communication between, say, the subfields of standard asset pricing, mathematical finance, "informational" finance, corporate finance, the econometrics of finance, and so forth, is surprisingly limited. Moreover, the difficulty of constructing a synthetic view of the different fronts is

exacerbated by the question of systemic stability—not only of the financial system but also of the economy as a whole.

2. A second line of criticism concerns the rationality hypothesis, which has long been a quasi-obligatory ingredient of economic analysis. Real economic agents do not have the supposed rationality of *Homo economicus*. In fact, the rapid development of behavioral economics in the past 20 years has highlighted the limits of the standard concepts of rationality: behavior under uncertainty, time consistency, and symmetric treatment of losses and gains, to cite a few research themes, have been the subject of critical reconsideration. Hence the problem is not so much a failure to analyze the limits of the standard conception of rationality but rather a failure to focus on the consequences of this reconsideration in, say, finance and macroeconomics.[1]

3. The failure of economic theory stressed here concerns expectational coordination. The changing assessment of expectational coordination in our models reflects major trepidation: either, as in most of the period before the 1950s, expectations are modeled as exogenous (the approach taken until recently in temporary equilibrium modeling of dynamics), or from the mid-1960s they have increasingly become "right on average," the essence of the Rational Expectations Hypothesis (REH), which emerged in the 1960s. The first option, taking expectations as given, can be at best a preliminary step in a more complex analysis: market expectations have to be explained and not taken as exogenous data. But the ability of decentralized systems, such as markets, to produce good (in the sense of REH) coordination also has to be explained.[2] And it may or may not be possible to produce reasonable explanations. In the latter case, one must conclude that markets are likely to fail to coordinate expectations in a satisfactory way (satisfactory in the sense of REH but also in many other senses of the word).

Section 1.2 returns briefly to the history of economic thought after World War II. It recalls the rise of REH in the field of formalized economic theory. Section 1.3 reviews the critical assessments of REH that have developed, particularly since the beginning of the 1980s. Section 1.4 illustrates how a critical approach, and in particular the one associated with my own

---

1. With notable exceptions, such as Bolton et al. (2006).

2. There are two different senses in which rational expectations are good: first, agents are right on average and hence make decisions that are individually optimal; second, the social outcome is satisfactory, because, for example, the equilibrium of plans, prices, and price expectations (see Section 1.2) is Pareto optimal. In general, although rational expectations might not be second-best optimal expectations, the failure of REH signals an expectational coordination failure and, in a sense, a market failure in the usual sense of the word (see Section 1.4 for a brief discussion of such a market failure).

research, may trigger a dramatic change in our understanding of economic problems and in how we evaluate economic policies. I stress three examples: the economic role of speculation, the so-called informational efficiency of markets, and the ability of agents with long horizons to predict the future. Section 1.5 recapitulates the arguments and underscores future challenges.

1.2 The Rise of REH in Modern Theory

REH states that economic agents have a view of the future that is "basically right": this view may vary, depending on individual information, but it is not biased. That the hypothesis is distinct from the hypothesis of individual rationality is obvious but still worth emphasizing. The idea that REH is nothing else than an extension of the rationality hypothesis to expectations has been a misleading but (unfortunately) extremely popular argument in favor of REH. In fact, in a large economy,[3] it is "right" (individually rational) to adopt REH, but only if the other agents adopt it as well. Otherwise it is wrong. To put it in game-theoretical parlance, the rational expectations equilibrium is a Nash equilibrium, not a dominant strategy equilibrium.

The rise of the debate on expectations in economic theory can be traced to the 1950s and 1960s. Although Muth's (1961) pioneering article addressed a microeconomic problem, the polemics triggered by some so-called Keynesian macroeconomic policies resonated in the background: agents can be fooled once or twice (implicitly, by the government) but not endlessly: they will refer (or one has to model them as if they refer) to the "relevant economic theory." The Relevant Economic Theory Hypothesis then became the Rational Expectations Hypothesis, a more appealing, though misleading, label. Then REH progressively took over theoretical modeling, or, if one prefers, "formalized economic theory."

Start with the field of general equilibrium, which emphasized a formally static model (Debreu 1959) that nonetheless supported an atemporal implementation of intertemporal equilibrium. In a truly intertemporal framework, the economy consists of a succession of spot markets for goods and financial markets in each period (replacing the futures markets that existed at the beginning of time in the static theory). The equilibrium becomes an "equilibrium of plans, prices and price expectations" (Radner 1972), an equilibrium that may be interpreted either as involving perfect foresight or, in the broader sense stressed here, rational expectations. In this general framework, if markets are "essentially complete," the outcome is efficient and replicates the complete markets solution of the static model (see Arrow 1953; Guesnerie and Jaffray 1974). In this setting, both incompleteness and the inadequacy of price expectations are sources of markets failure.

---

3. I refer, for example, to the framework of a continuum of agents, which serves as a basis for the analysis presented by Guesnerie and Jara-Moroni (2011).

Moreover, since Walras, economists are aware that the market, to deliver the prices that solve the equilibrium equations, has to substitute for a computing machine. According to Walras, the virtues of the market-computing algorithm are not obvious and have to be demonstrated (this is the purpose of tâtonnement theory). In the intertemporal context, the "equilibrium of plans, prices and price expectations" possibly hides two dei ex machina: spot markets clear at a given time (one of the algorithmic virtues of the market, which normally is subject to verification), but this process relies on an understanding of the clearing of the next period's spot markets, the equations of which are implicitly supposed to be resolved in people's minds. Hence, part of the market "equilibrations," in the sense of Perroux (1973), can be viewed as the product of agents' collective thinking. Such a collective thought process helps to resolve the Walrasian auctioneer's problem: the mental activity of the agents mimicking the calculation of tomorrow's market algorithm.

General equilibrium provides a good reference for the development of contemporary economics. Most intertemporal modeling in most subfields—whether with a general equilibrium flavor (as in trade) or with a partial equilibrium focus (labor markets, insurance, etc.)—routinely adopts REH.

Modern finance is partially rooted in general equilibrium, and REH has a clear hegemonic position in the field and underlies its influential theoretical models, for example, those stressing the informational efficiency of markets, even in its most critical versions (Grossman and Stiglitz 1980).

Last but not least, REH has acquired a hegemonic position in modern macroeconomics. Lucas's (1972) dismissal of voluntarist policies takes place in a rational expectations world. The Real Business Cycles (RBC) models, sometimes presented as "Walrasian," describe long-lived (identical) agents who anticipate the entire future correctly (in the sense of REH). In this world, there are few spot market adjustments, most adjustments come from expectations, and agents are as good as the best theorist at computing complex equilibria. New Keynesian models echo some of the Walrasian preoccupation with the implementation of the equilibrium. Prices are quoted, not tentatively by the auctioneer, but irrevocably in each round of quotation by firms with market power. The procedure introduces frictions, which indeed have a Keynesian flavor, but the announcement of prices, which provides a non-Walrasian response to the Walras problem, relies on REH: firms have a correct understanding of the future, particularly of the future flows of bids by rival firms. "Good" expectational coordination is also taken for granted.[4]

---

4. However, modern macroeconomic theory does not rule out a critical assessment of REH. For example, the Taylor rule leads to choosing a monetary policy, along the lines of its standard theoretical justifications, that triggers a "determinate" equilibrium, a requirement that casts suspicion on other intertemporal solutions, even those that satisfy REH (see the next section).

1.3 Directions for a Critical Assessment

If REH has gained a hegemonic position in formal economic theory, paralleling the rise of the Nash equilibrium in game theory, it has not been unchallenged. I review three avenues of criticism.

1.3.1 Internal Challenges

In economic theory as well as in game theory, an internal challenge (internal in the sense that it arises even if you find the theory's assumptions impeccable) arises from multiplicity. In a game setting, the challenges take the form of a question: what happens if there are several Nash equilibria? Rephrased in Muth's defense of REH, the question becomes: what is the relevant economic theory when there are several candidates?

In economic models, the multiplicity challenge is particularly acute in infinite-horizon models. For example, consider the simplest model of this sort, a one-dimensional, one-step-forward-looking model, where the state at time t obtains as a function of the expectation of the state at time $t + 1$. Typically, such a model has at least a steady state (x^* such that $x^* = f(x^*)$) but also a continuum of perfect-foresight equilibria, which may (or may not) remain close to the steady state (in the former case, the steady state is referred to as "indeterminate"; in the latter, it is said to be "determinate"). Also, it has been understood that, besides the "focal solution" (the perfect-foresight steady state equilibrium), there could also be well-behaved (stationary) stochastic rational expectations equilibria: indeed, the stochastic stationary beliefs governing sunspot equilibria look arbitrary but are self-fulfilling (see Azariadis 1981; Azariadis and Guesnerie 1982, 1986; Benhabib and Farmer 1994; Farmer and Woodford 1997; for a broader approach and an attempt at synthesis, see Chiappori and Guesnerie 1991; Guesnerie and Woodford 1992; Guesnerie 2001). The lessons drawn from the sunspot literature are fairly general. For example, in a slightly more complicated framework than the one just introduced (one-dimensional, memory one, one-step-forward-looking models), the focal solution switches to a saddle-path trajectory, although the logic of multiplicity (whether sunspot or nonsunspot) remains the same, so that the investigation triggers analogous results. Adding complexity (see Evans and Guesnerie 2005) and/or intrinsic noise does not change the flavor of the analysis.

Another line of research that falls under the heading of a critical assessment of REH is the line associated with the *global games* literature initiated by Carlsson and Van Damme (1993) and Morris and Shin (1998, 2003). This approach emphasizes the incompleteness of information held by the agents. The initial message (Morris and Shin 1998) is somewhat different from, and to some extent opposed to, the message of the sunspot literature. The simple theory of speculative currency attacks suggests the existence of multiple equilibria, whereas a better modeling of the noisy information used by the agents often leads to the restoration of uniqueness.[5] Taking into account the incomplete information faced by the agents is a key ingredient of global games analysis.

Finally, another line of critique is again internal (it accepts the hypothesis but emphasizes intrinsic difficulties). In the *herd behavior* literature, the rational expectations equilibrium exists, but the outcome depends on details of the starting conditions and is fragile in the sense that the information transmitted may be unreliable (see Banerjee 1992; Chamley 2002).[6]

1.3.2   External Criticisms

There are also lines of criticism that do not accept REH's assumptions and that imply a more basic reconsideration of REH. I start from more fundamental approaches, as opposed to those that are more informal or eclectic.

It is natural to interpret Muth's relevant economic theory as what would be called, in game-theoretic terms, a common knowledge (CK) "theory."[7] The rational expectations equilibrium is then known to everybody, and everybody knows that everybody knows it. The natural, somewhat fundamental, question to be raised is the following: Is it the case that CK of the world (the logic of interactions) and CK of rationality (the logic of decision) imply CK of the equilibrium? If the answer is yes, then in a sense there is a CK-relevant economic theory. In my terminology (Guesnerie 1992, 2005), the equilibrium is "strongly rational" and globally "eductively stable" ("eductively" because the assumptions trigger a collective learning process that takes place in people's minds). In a simple variant of Muth's original model (Guesnerie 1992), the answer to the question may be positive or negative, depending on the characteristics of supply and demand. Interestingly, the answer is closely connected to the convergence of the old-fashioned cobweb tâtonnement (a real-time process that the virtual collective learning process mimics). As global eductive stability along the lines sketched here is very demanding, it makes sense generally to define local eductive stability. This line of investigation has numerous applications, a subset of which is reported in Guesnerie (2005).

---

5. Furthermore, this unique equilibrium is eductively stable in the sense suggested below.

6. Part of the literature keeps REH but emphasizes agents' imperfect awareness of the state of the economy. Such imperfect information may occur even when all information is publicly available and agents have limited attention. See Reis (2006), Woodford (2009), and Sims (2011).

7. See Phelps (2007), on "equilibrium theory. . . . This in turn implies that everyone knows this understanding to be common knowledge" (Frydman and Goldberg 2007: 14).

The line of research conducted by M. Kurz and his co-authors can also be interpreted as a departure from some of the Muth implicit CK assumptions. In Muth, the exogenous processes generating intrinsic uncertainty have to be CK. Giving up this assumption implies drastic changes in how the dynamics of coordination are modeled, which involve so-called rational beliefs (or diverse beliefs; see Kurz 1994; Kurz and Motolese 2011)—that is, non-REH beliefs. More generally, the assumption of a common prior is dubious, which suggests bridges between criticism focusing on "rationality" and that focusing on rational expectations.

1.3.3   Criticism Based on Real-Time Learning

The third avenue of criticism is the one associated with the old line of research on real-time learning: here agents predict the future using inferences that rely on the past. As time passes, they adapt their forecasts, to the point that eventually learning is successful in the sense that forecasts and realizations become aligned (for a review of such a line of research with applications especially to macroeconomics, see Evans and Honkapohja 2001). As with the eductive learning approach, evolutive learning may be viewed as providing a robustness test for a given rational expectations equilibrium: the test is successful when the learning process converges and unsuccessful when it does not. And also as with the eductive approach, the test is only apparently binary; in fact, eductive as well as evolutive learning may be slow or fast, a fact that affects the plausibility of the equilibrium.

There are numerous connections between eductive and evolutive learning. Studies show that the success or failure of eductive or evolutive learning is affected by the same parameters describing the situation (the connections are particularly interesting and spectacular in the infinite-horizon models introduced above; see Gauthier 2002; Evans and Guesnerie 2003; Gauthier and Guesnerie 2005). And it has been argued that eductive learning may be justified as a kind of shortcut to evolutive learning (Guesnerie 2005).

This brief and subjective summary should suffice to show that critical assessments of REH have been numerous and have proceeded from different viewpoints. But have they modified our views of the problems under consideration and of related economic policy questions?

I argue in the next section that they have, or at least that they should have, if the profession had paid enough attention.

1.4   How a Critical Assessment of REH in Different Contexts Changes the Standard (REH-Based) Economic Intuition

I consider three examples that are related, although not exclusively, to the eductive learning viewpoint and to my own research. The first is concerned with the question of the value of new financial instruments, or the stabilizing virtues of speculation; the second deals with the informational efficiency of the market. Both raise key questions in finance. The third example reconsiders the "good" expectational coordination that RBC-like models assume. I argue that in this case a critical assessment of the rational expectations assumption suggests that it has weak foundations: indeed, there are convincing arguments that in the case under consideration, expectational coordination is likely to be "bad."

1.4.1 New Financial Instruments

Guesnerie and Rochet (1993) have developed a simple inventory model with two goods and no production, which is, however, in some respects, reminiscent of the Muth model. The initial organization of the economy rests on the existence of storage capacities allowing, through costly actions, the transfer of part of a crop from a period of abundance to the next period. One then considers opening a futures market for this storable good, allowing people who are unable to store to participate. In both settings, REH leads to a unique equilibrium. In a sense, the rational expectations equilibrium associated with the futures market is better: thanks to increased possibilities of insurance, the volatility of the crop price is decreased. This reflects an argument made by Friedman that has indeed some generality: speculation is stabilizing (Friedman's informal argument is that speculators sell when the price is high and buy when it is low). However, the point made in the paper is that the expectational robustness or plausibility of REH (evaluated from the viewpoint of eductive stability) decreases when the futures market opens.[8] In other words, the set of parameters of the model for which the rational expectations equilibrium is stable shrinks when the futures market is introduced. Then, speculation is destabilizing, in a different but legitimate sense: *it makes the rational expectations coordination less plausible.* Naturally, the specific (parameter-related) conclusions drawn are debatable. However, the model neatly stresses one important insight: the effect on the quality of expectational coordination of opening new markets should be a key issue in the discussion of their usefulness.

The same idea was illustrated recently in a different context, based on evolutive learning. Brock et al. (2009) consider a model in which the exchange of stocks at time t is based on the anticipation of the price at time $t + 1$. This anticipation is formed from a set of learning strategies whose distribution among players depends on their past success. The authors consider two versions of the conditions of exchange. In the first version, the stock market is backed by no other market. In the second, claims contingent

---

8. The same would likely be true with stability criteria based on evolutive learning, as suggested several times in this chapter.

on a number of considerations that determine the dividend stock can be traded. However, their number is insufficient for completing the markets. The robustness of the rational expectations equilibrium will be validated by the convergence of the learning process toward the equilibrium that is based on fundamental values. And convergence properties are summarized by thresholds in the parameters that determine the bifurcations of the dynamic system generated by learning. The conclusion of the article echoes that of Guesnerie and Rochet (1993): new markets, desirable from the standpoint of risk spreading, have a destabilizing effect (i.e., a dramatic negative effect on the convergence of learning).

Why wouldn't such analyses, although admittedly specialized, have significant policy implications? At the least, they suggest that instead of approving new financial products they do not understand, regulators should put the burden of proof (in particular, that the instruments will not destabilize market expectations) on those who want to introduce them. The studies cited above suggest that the current functioning of markets for primary goods and the role played by speculation raise questions to which standard REH analysis is likely to provide dubious answers.

1.4.2 Informational Efficiency: Prices and the Transmission of Information

That markets are informationally efficient (the Efficient Market Hypothesis) has been given different meanings in the literature. The classic work of Grossman and Stiglitz (1980) proposes a very moderate version of the property. I will argue that the critical assessment of REH permitted by the approach presented above shows that the Grossman-Stiglitz conclusions still provide an overly optimistic view of the ability of markets to transmit information. In their model, agents receive a private signal about the value of an asset, with the average of private signals providing a summary statistic of the total information available. Agents send a demand curve to the market organizer. The latter aggregates these individual curves and deduces, given the random and unexplained supply of noise traders, an equilibrium price that clears the transaction requests. In a rational expectations (Nash-Bayesian) equilibrium, agents combine their own information with the information that they optimally extract from the price, which reflects the other agents' information. Indeed, in this setting, the market transmits a substantial part of the total information available in society.

But is expectational coordination robust or fragile, for example, with regard to the criteria of eductive stability presented above? The answer given by Desgranges (2000) and Desgranges and Heinemann (2005) is clear. The equilibrium is expectationally stable (or strongly rational, in my terminology) only if it does not transmit too much information, "too much" being assessed against the individual's information. The intuition behind the logic of eductive coordination derives from a simple story. If the market provides too much information, the (out of equilibrium) actions of agents, who therefore have a high degree of confidence in the market, hardly reflect their personal information. But market information is simply the sum of the information individually transmitted and will not be reliable if the agents transmit it sparingly: *trusting the market too much leads you to dismiss your individual information, and if everybody does that, the market will receive little information.* (There is a contradiction between the incentives to transmit information and the confidence that it arouses: this is the source of the abovementioned expectational coordination fragility.)

This message has been echoed in other contexts (Desgranges et al. 2003) or on related subjects (Ben Porath and Heifetz 2006). Desgranges et al. (2003) have considered another model used in the literature of the 1970s and 1980s concerning the role of prices in the transmission of information. In this setting, there is a unique rational expectations equilibrium. Again, the aggressive search for information can kill eductive stability: one cannot trust the market too much if everybody else trusts it too much.

This differs from the argument of Grossman and Stiglitz (1980) that the strong form of the Efficient Market Hypothesis is impossible, because if markets were efficient in the sense that prices convey all present and future information, nobody would invest resources in acquiring information. Hence the weak form of the hypothesis, in line with the Grossman-Stiglitz views, looks, on the present grounds, much too optimistic.

Two more points should be emphasized:

• The set of possible outcomes of the interaction that can be rationalized (in the game-theoretic sense alluded to above) when the rational expectations equilibrium ceases to be (locally) stable, can be identified in the Grossman-Stiglitz framework. This set (a substitute for the set of equilibria) no longer consists of a single point or of locally isolated points. Instead, it is "thick": it follows that the quality of information that agents can infer from it is, in a sense, very poor. Yet in the context thus outlined, agents cannot, in any clear sense, beat the market. The analysis suggests that the retreat of the most notorious supporters of informational efficiency toward the position: "informational efficiency holds because agents cannot beat the market" is a real rout.

• In this setting, the Grossman-Stiglitz paradox that agents are not willing to pay for information because it will be provided freely by the market partly disappears. In parallel, the risk premium required for market participation is much higher than the one associated with the rational expectations equilibrium.

In terms of policy implications, these results cast doubt on the unquestioned faith of many in the preeminence of market prices of assets and liabilities in accounting and regulation.

1.4.3 Expectational Coordination: Long-Lived Agents and the Prediction of the Future

The design of RBC models is unlikely to support any Keynesian-like message: long-lived agents can transfer their intertemporal wealth without any constraints other than those relating to market conditions. Short-run income has little effect on permanent income, so that the Keynesian multiplier can, at best, be very modest. And, if the agents rationally anticipate that taxes will be raised tomorrow to offset the deficit today, the Keynesian stimulus can be relegated to oblivion. The modeling options, long horizon and rational expectations (leaving to one side the criticism bearing on the high aggregation level and possibly on price flexibility), rule out a Keynesian cure. In this context, however, the New Keynesian models introduced an interesting innovation: firms announce prices for their products, so that price adjustments are no longer the product of the dei ex machina of the market (again, an indirect homage to Walras, even if the solution does not rest on a process of trial and error). As noted above, such models inherit some Keynesian-like properties: activity is variable across periods, with corresponding alternations of inflationary or deflationary effects that can be associated with a Phillips curve. But here, as in RBC models, agents have long horizons that allow them to reallocate their intertemporal wealth as they wish, and they also have rational expectations. So firms announce prices, which is reasonable, but their decision is based on a statistically accurate view of the future decisions of their competitors. So, the central question addressed here is back on the agenda: what can we say about the quality of coordination of expectations in all the models just invoked?

I "advertise" here a discussion paper that I co-authored with G. Evans and B. McGough (Evans et al. 2010), in which we consider the simplest possible RBC model (i.e., one that is deterministic) and examine the steady state, characterized by a level of capital that is stable over time. Under what conditions is the equilibrium (locally) strongly rational or eductively stable in the sense described above? The surprising answer is never: in this model, viewed through the lenses advocated here, the infinite-horizon equilibrium has maximum fragility.

Let us indeed consider the neighborhood of the intertemporal equilibrium: it must be a neighborhood of the entire trajectory, say, for a simple example, a "tubular" neighborhood: everyone believes that the capital will remain indefinitely in an epsilon neighborhood of its equilibrium value. If all agents share such a belief (that the system will remain in the tubular neighborhood), then their individual plans are constrained, and the same is true, by aggregation, of the corresponding states of the system. For example, the hypothetical initial belief implies that during the first period capital will remain, at least for certain values of parameters, inside the tube (we call this property "weak stability"). The initial belief also puts bounds on the path of planned savings at each time by each agent, and thus on the capital stock that would result in each period. But the key to the difficulty is that within the bounds set by the beliefs, intertemporal aggregate plans can deviate as much as one wants from the initial tubular neighborhood, and this holds true regardless of the system's parameters. The reason is interesting: agents' decisions (either plans or immediate decisions) are sensitive to the expectations of interest rates not only in the short run but also in the long run. It follows that the long-term plans become increasingly sensitive to the forecast of interest rates over the entire trajectory and become more sensitive, the more distant the period under consideration is. The strong effect of the initial uncertainty on the long-term plans of the agents implies that the mental process of elimination of dominated strategies is blocked at the first iteration: the hypothetical common belief of the first stage cannot generate CK of the equilibrium; the equilibrium is necessarily eductively unstable.

This "high-tech" story has "low-tech" counterparts: beliefs in line with the initial tubular restriction will eventually lead the system to leave the tube, and the same is true if beliefs are adapted in conformity with standard learning rules. Without going into the details of the model, which later combines an evolutive dimension of learning together with an a priori tubular or nontubular restriction, the analysis brings Keynes back onto the stage: in this world a key role for government expenditures is to improve expectational coordination. But the policy discussion would be premature and clearly goes beyond the scope of this chapter.

1.5 Conclusion

Where do we go from here? Several lessons need to be learned—and learned quickly.

First, proponents of REH tend to view it as a modeling axiom that is equally reasonable for all problems and situations. But *the idea that REH is an equally reasonable modeling option in all contexts is manifestly unbelievable.* Does that mean, as some suggest, that REH is uniformly unreasonable and uninteresting?

One cannot seriously claim that it is uninteresting: for every problem, REH provides a reference description of economic evolution, free of serious expectational mistakes. Its lack of compatibility with observed facts, when it occurs, is an intellectual challenge, not a symptom of uniform unreasonableness. There are problems and situations (characterized by the values of the relevant parameters for the problem under consideration) in which REH provides a reasonable description of what may happen. And quiet times, when the hypothesis provides a reasonable modeling tool, may alternate with turbulent times, when it does not.

A critical view of REH does not necessarily mean uniform and complete dismissal of it. But, as the preceding section makes clear, a critical view of REH makes a huge difference in policy discussions. When REH holds, a policy change does not affect the quality of expectational coordination: the system goes from one rational expectations equilibrium to another.[9] Outside this REH world, policy changes will affect the quality of expectational coordination and the evaluation of this quality change is an unavoidable and potentially major dimension of economic policymaking.

Going beyond the present argument, let us return to the different research strategies for producing theories that truly grapple with the difficulty of explaining, across markets and situations, the quality of expectational coordination or the extent of expectational miscoordination.

A first strategy aims at checking the robustness of REH in a given context. The conclusion we may arrive at is that, in a given situation, the rational expectations equilibrium coordination is a priori robust. This is the point of view taken in part of the research presented here, which was labeled "eductive" and has two possible directions of application. The global eductive test relies on the high-tech analysis of a sophisticated mental process and is very demanding. The local eductive test, which in a sense is the local version of the global hyperrationalistic criterion, has a low-tech interpretation.[10] Local eductive stability essentially reflects the elasticity of realizations relative to expectations: low elasticity signals robustness, whereas a high elasticity signals fragility. The standard learning studies can be given similar interpretations; convergence of the learning processes signals the plausibility of coordination, whereas absence of convergence signals coordination difficulties. In both the eductive approach and the standard evolutive one, the test is in principle binary, but in both cases another, less radical, interpretation is available (e.g., convergence may be fast or slow).

A more demanding (although attractive) strategy is to search for a general alternative to REH modeling. Pursuing this approach does not necessarily mean rejecting the robustness line of investigation just sketched: the alternative might be close to REH in cases where the REH construct produces robust outcomes. But this approach is clearly much more ambitious: the objective is to stress outcomes that are not rational expectations equilibria but are, in a sense, generalized economic equilibria.[11]

---

9. The multiplicity issue raises expectational coordination considerations relating to equilibrium selection. These considerations are policy relevant and have received some attention in the literature.

10. For example, it does not even suppose, in its less sophisticated interpretation, that agents know the model.

11. Standard learning studies may stress the possibilities of different outcomes of learning processes, although it is difficult to view them as generalized economic equilibria.

Note that the eductive approach presented here provides the basis for such an alternative theory, where the generalized economic equilibria would be identified with the set of rationalizable equilibria. Indeed, in some cases, they have been identified and provide an alternative view of plausible economic outcomes.[12] Other alternatives that have been proposed include the diverse beliefs equilibria of Kurz (1994) or the Imperfect Knowledge Economics of Frydman and Goldberg (2011), which I cannot discuss in depth here.[13]

The task is formidable. Outside the ordered world of REH, a wilderness of non-REH worlds beckons (borrowing from Sims's metaphor of the "wilderness of bounded rationality"). Let me stress four reasons that make it such a wilderness.

First, one has to disentangle the difficulties of predicting, on the one hand, exogenous or intrinsic uncertainty (the states of the world, which are not affected by actions) and on the other hand, strategic or extrinsic uncertainty (the agents' actions). These two problems are not similar, although they may be connected. Note that in the basic models sketched in the previous section, there is no intrinsic uncertainty. The focus is on the difficulty of predicting other individuals' actions, a problem that REH axiomatically resolves. Note also that it has been argued convincingly that in our economies, some basic structural parameters change in ways that agents do not correctly assess. The consequent absence of stationarity in the data raises legitimate but different concerns about the difficulties of coordination. Naturally, the two difficulties may interact: if it is difficult to predict others' beliefs about changing intrinsic uncertainty, it will be difficult to predict their actions, even if predicting their actions conditional on beliefs is possible.

Second, the risk for theory is not emptiness but overflow. Once miscoordination (in the sense of the existence in the economy of a variety of views about the future) of expectations is allowed, one is forced to recognize that there are myriad ways for this to happen. Economic theory faces the challenge of assessing such diversity while putting plausible limits on it (otherwise, its models would have no predictive power).

Third, the theory under consideration must face the challenge of being, in some sense, a "relevant economic theory." This expression has various meanings, one of them being that if the theory becomes known by agents, and if the situation is sufficiently reproducible, it should remain true when reproduced. Many possible stories about the functioning of stock markets, which involve, for example, competition among learning schemes, cannot

---

12. See Guesnerie and Jara-Moroni (2011) for the characterization in models with strategic complementarities or substitutabilities.

13. See also Kirman (2010) for alternative approaches to reconsidering standard theory and Soros (2010) for an outsider's critique.

fit such a requirement; if the story convincingly shows that one of the learning schemes is superior, then why would the others still be competing in the future? Naturally, this question makes sense only if the future looks sufficiently like the past. The question of the degree of similarities of situations clearly operates behind the scene.[14]

Finally, many fascinating normative questions are triggered by the reconstruction of an alternative viable theory. For example, REH leads to the view that the market's coordination of expectations is good, in the sense of being unbiased, but also to some extent from the viewpoint of social welfare.[15] Outside REH territory, the question of the possible role of government for improving the coordination of expectations returns.[16] In any case, the question raised in Section 1.4 concerning the effect of policies on the quality of expectational coordination will remain unavoidable and more difficult to resolve.

In the background lies the question of the philosophical determinism that has shaped the development of the natural sciences but also of economics as a social science. Let me suggest, in conclusion, that to be more relevant, our knowledge claims might have to become more modest.[17]

References

Arrow, K. (1953) "Le rôle des Valeurs Boursières pour la Répartition la Meilleure des Risques," *Cahiers du Séminaire d'Econométrie* 40: 41–48.

Azariadis, C. (1981) "Self-Fulfilling Prophecies," *Journal of Economic Theory* 25: 380–396.

Azariadis, C., and R. Guesnerie. (1982) "Prophéties Créatrices et Persistance des Théories," *Revue Economique* 33: 787–806.

———. (1986) "Sunspots and Cycles," *Review of Economic Studies* 53: 725–737.

Banerjee, A. (1992) "A Simple Model of Herd Behavior," *Quarterly Journal of Economics* 107: 797–817.

Benhabib, J., and R. Farmer. (1994) "Indeterminacy and Increasing Returns," *Journal of Economic Theory* 63: 19–41.

Ben Porath, E., and A. Heifetz. (2006) "Rationalizable Expectations." Mimeo, Center for the Study of Rationality, Jerusalem.

---

14. I have discussed this problem (Guesnerie 2000) in my inaugural lecture at Collège de France. In a very different way, the black swan argument (Taleb 2007) raises the question of the recurrence of rare situations.

15. In the absence of completeness, what is socially good is not always clear.

16. Although I do not claim that there is an obvious answer, there may be a Hayekian line of argument claiming that the government cannot improve on market coordination even when the latter is bad. Market failures may go hand-in-hand with government failure. Note, however, that Pierre Massé's views of the merits of French planning stressed almost uniquely its expectational coordination virtues ("une ètude de marché généralisée"; Massé 1978: 144).

17. And it may be closer to the standards that some sociologists assign to their field (Passeron 1991).

Bernanke, B. (2008) "Origins of the Great Moderation," *New York Times,* January 23.

Bolton, P., J. Scheinkman, and Wei Xiong. (2006) "Executive Compensation and Short-Termist Behavior in Speculative Markets," *Review of Economic Studies* 73: 577–610.

Brock, W., C. Hommes, and F. Wagener. (2009) "More Hedging Instruments May Destabilize Markets," *Journal of Economic Dynamics and Control* 33: 1912–1928.

Carlsson, H., and E. Van Damme. (1993) "Global Games and Equilibrium Selection," *Econometrica* 61: 998–1018.

Chamley, C. (2002) *Rational Herds: Economic Models of Social Learning.* Cambridge: Cambridge University Press.

Chiappori, P. A., and R. Guesnerie. (1991) "Sunspot Equilibria in Sequential Markets Models," in W. Hildenbrand and H. Sonnenschein (eds.), *Handbook of Mathematical Economics,* volume IV. Amsterdam: North-Holland, pp. 1683–1762.

Debreu, G. (1959) *The Theory of Value: An Axiomatic Analysis of Economic Equilibrium.* New York: Wiley.

Desgranges, G. (2000) "CK-Equilibria and Informational Efficiency in a Competitive Economy." Mimeo, University of Cergy-Pontoise, France.

Desgranges, G., and M. Heinemann. (2005) "Strongly Rational Expectations Equilibria with Endogenous Acquisition of Information." Working Paper Series in Economics 9, University of Lüneburg, Institute of Economics, Lüneburg, Germany.

Desgranges, G., P. Y. Geoffard, and R. Guesnerie. (2003) "Do Prices Transmit Rationally Expected Information?" *Journal of the European Economic Association* 1: 124–153.

Evans, G., and S. Honkapohja. (2001) *Learning and Expectations in Macroeconomics.* Princeton, NJ: Princeton University Press.

Evans, G., and R. Guesnerie. (2003) "Coordination on Saddle-Path Solutions: The Eductive Viewpoint–Linear Univariate Models," *Macroeconomic Dynamics* 7: 42–62.

———. (2005) "Coordination on Saddle-Path Solutions: The Eductive Viewpoint–Linear Multivariate Models," *Journal of Economic Theory* 124: 202–229.

Evans, G., R. Guesnerie, and B. McGough. (2010) "Eductive Stability in RBC Models." Working paper, University of Oregon, Eugene.

Farmer, R., and M. Woodford. (1997) "Self-Fulfilling Prophecies and the Business Cycle," *Macroeconomics Dynamics* 1: 740–769.

Frydman, R., and M. Goldberg. (2007) *Imperfect Knowledge Economics: Exchange Rates and Risk.* Princeton, NJ: Princeton University Press.

———. (2011) *Beyond Mechanical Markets: Asset Price Swings, Risk, and the Role of the State.* Princeton, NJ: Princeton University Press.

Gauthier, S. (2002) "Determinacy and Stability under Learning of Rational Expectations Equilibria," *Journal of Economic Theory* 102: 354–374.

Gauthier, S., and R. Guesnerie. (2005) "Comparing Expectational Stability Criteria in Dynamical Models: A Preparatory Overview," in R. Guesnerie (ed.), *Assessing Rational Expectations 2: "Eductive" Stability in Economics.* Cambridge, MA: MIT Press, pp. 343–379.

Grossman, S., and J. Stiglitz. (1980) "On the Impossibility of Informationally Efficient Financial Markets," *American Economic Review* 70: 393–408.

Guesnerie, R. (1992) "An Exploration of the Eductive Justifications of the Rational-Expectations Hypothesis," *American Economic Review* 82: 1254–1278.

———. (2000) "L'Etat et le Marché, constructions savantes et pensée spontanée." Inaugural lecture, Collège de France, Paris. Reprinted in *Revue d'Economie Politique* 111: 797–814.

———. (2001) *Assessing Rational Expectations: 1—Sunspot Multiplicity and Economic Fluctuations.* Cambridge, MA: MIT Press.

———. (2005) *Assessing Rational Expectations: 2—Eductive Stability in Economics.* Cambridge, MA: MIT Press.

Guesnerie, R., and J. Y. Jaffray. (1974) "Optimality of Equilibrium of Plans, Prices and Price Expectations," in J. Dreze (ed.), *Allocation under Uncertainty, Equilibrium, Optimality.* London: Macmillan, pp. 70–86.

Guesnerie, R., and P. Jara-Moroni. (2011) "Expectational Coordination in Simple Economic Contexts: Concepts and Analysis with Emphasis on Strategic Substitutabilities," *Economic Theory* 47: 205–246.

Guesnerie, R., and J. C. Rochet. (1993) "(De)stabilizing Speculation on Futures Markets: An Alternative Viewpoint," *European Economic Review* 37: 1043–1063.

Guesnerie, R., and M. Woodford. (1992) "Endogenous Fluctuations," in J. J. Laffont (ed.), *Advances in Economic Theory.* Cambridge: Cambridge University Press, pp. 289–412.

Kirman, A. (2010) "The Crisis in Economic Theory." Greqam discussion paper, Marseille, France.

Kurz, M. (1994) "On the Structure and Diversity of Rational Beliefs," *Economic Theory* 4: 877–900.

Kurz, M., and M. Motolese. (2011) "Diverse Beliefs and Time Variability of Risk Premia," *Economic Theory* 47: 293–337.

Lucas, R. (1972) "Expectations and the Neutrality of Money," *Journal of Economic Theory* 4: 103–124.

———. (2003) "Macroeconomic Priorities." Working paper, University of Chicago.

Massé, P. (1978) *Le plan ou l'anti-hasard.* Paris: Dunod.

Morris, S., and H. S. Shin. (1998) "Unique Equilibrium in a Model of Self-Fulfilling Currency Attacks," *American Economic Review* 88: 587–597.

———. (2003) "Global Games: Theory and Applications," in M. Dewatripont, L. Hansen, and S. Turnovsky (eds.), *Advances in Economics and Econometrics,* volume 1. Cambridge: Cambridge University Press, pp. 57–114.

Muth, J. F. (1961) "Rational Expectations and the Theory of Price Movements," *Econometrica* 29: 315–335.

Passeron, J. C. (1991) *Le raisonnement sociologique, l'espace non-poppérien du raisonnement naturel.* Essais & Recherches. Paris: Nathan.

Perroux, F. (1973) Pouvoir et économie. Paris: Dunod.

Phelps, N. (2007) "Foreword," in R. Frydman and M. Goldberg, *Imperfect Knowledge Economics: Exchange Rates and Risk.* Princeton, NJ: Princeton University Press, pp. xiii–xx.

Radner, R. (1972) "'Existence of Equilibrium of Plans, Prices, and Price Expectations," *Econometrica* 40: 289–303.

Reinhardt, C., and K. Rogoff. (2008) "Banking Crises: An Equal Opportunity Menace." NBER Working Paper 14587, National Bureau of Economic Research, Cambridge, MA.

Reis, R. (2006) "Inattentive Consumers," *Journal of Monetary Economics* 53: 1761–1800.

Say, J. B. (1803) *Traité d'économie politique.* Paris: Economica, 2006 reprint.

Sims, C. (2011) "Rational Inattention and Monetary Economics," in B. M. Friedman and M. Woodford (eds.), *Handbook of Monetary Economics,* volume 3A. Amsterdam: Elsevier.

Soros, G. (2010) *Quelques Leçons tirées de la crise.* Paris: Denoel.

Taleb, N. (2007) *The Black Swan: The Impact of the Highly Improbable.* New York: Random House.

Woodford, M. (2009) "Information-Constrained State-Dependant Pricing," *Journal of Monetary Economy* 56S: 100–124.

CHAPTER TWO

Learning as a Rational Foundation for Macroeconomics and Finance

George W. Evans and Seppo Honkapohja

2.1 Introduction

Expectations play a central role in modern macroeconomics. Economic agents are assumed to be dynamic optimizers whose current economic decisions are the first stage of a dynamic plan. Thus, households must be concerned with expected future incomes, employment, inflation, and taxes, as well as the expected trajectory of the stock market and the housing market. Firms must forecast the level of future product demand, wage costs, productivity levels, and foreign exchange rates. Monetary and fiscal policymakers must forecast inflation and aggregate economic activity, and they must consider both the direct impact of their policies and the indirect effect of policy rules on private sector expectations.

The recent financial crisis has demonstrated that circumstances can suddenly change greatly, and in such situations information and understanding become very imperfect. Even in normal times one can expect that agents are at best boundedly rational, and in exceptional times there will be a particular need for agents to improve their knowledge of the situation, so that learning becomes central.

In this chapter we discuss the central ideas about learning and bounded rationality using several standard macroeconomic models and settings (though we do not focus on finance and banking problems). One basic message is that in standard macroeconomic models rational expectations can emerge in the longer run, provided the agents' environment remains stationary for a sufficiently long period. However, from a policy point of view,

Any views expressed are those of the authors and do not necessarily reflect the views of the Bank of Finland. Financial support from National Science Foundation Grant SES-1025011 is gratefully acknowledged.

it is important to take into account the learning process and periods when knowledge is quite imperfect and learning is a major driver of economic dynamics.

The structure of the chapter is as follows. In the next section we develop the main methodological issues concerning expectation formation and learning, and we discuss the circumstances in which rational expectations may arise. Section 2.3 reviews empirical work that applies learning to macroeconomic issues and asset pricing. In Section 2.4 we take up the implications of the use of structural information in learning and the form of the agents' decision rules, and, as an application, we discuss the scope of Ricardian equivalence. Section 2.5 develops three applications of the learning approach to monetary policy: the appropriate specification of interest rate rules; implementation of price-level targeting to achieve learning stability of the optimal rational expectations equilibrium; and whether under learning, commitment to price-level targeting can be sufficient to rule out the deflation trap of a zero interest rate lower bound and return the economy to the intended rational expectations steady state. Section 2.6 concludes.

2.2 Methodological Issues in Bounded Rationality and Learning

We develop the main ideas in an abstract setting. Macroeconomic models can often be summarized as a reduced-form multivariate dynamic system

$$y_t = \mathcal{F}(y_{t-1}, \{y^e_{t+j}\}_{j=0}^{\infty}, w_t, \eta_t) \tag{1}$$

where y_t is a vector of endogenous aggregate variables, w_t is a vector of observable stochastic exogenous variables, and η_t is an unobserved random shock. Typically, w_t is assumed to follow a stationary stochastic process, such as a finite-dimensional vector autoregression. The setting implicitly assumes that a representative-agent setup is adequate: the vector y_t (which, e.g., includes aggregate output, labor hours, consumption, inflation, and factor prices) is the result of individual decisions, and aggregation to means is assumed acceptable. The literature contains papers that allow for heterogeneity in agents' expectations or characteristics.

Crucially, y_t depends not only on the state of the system, captured by the exogenous variables and lagged endogenous variables, w_t, and y_{t-1}, but also on expectations of future endogenous variables, $\{y^e_{t+j}\}_{j=1}^{\infty}$, and possibly on forecasts of the current endogenous variables. The presence of expectations $\{y^e_{t+j}\}_{j=0}^{\infty}$ is a key feature of the system that makes economics distinct from natural sciences.

At a general level, a learning mechanism is, for each period t, a mapping from the time-t information set to the sequence of expectations of future (and possibly current) values of relevant variables together with an initial set of expectations of these variables. Some crucial aspects of the system to bear in mind are:

1. The horizon for decisions and expectations. In some models only one-step-ahead forecasts matter, whereas in others there is a long or infinite horizon.

2. Degree of structural information. Do agents know the whole structure or part of it, or do they forecast using a reduced form? In the latter case do they know the correct functional form?

3. The precise information set on which expectations are based. Expectations may be based on all observables dated at time $t - 1$ or at time t. In the latter case w_t is assumed known at t, and the current endogenous aggregate state y_t may or may not be known when agents make their decisions, so that y_t may depend also on "forecasts" of contemporaneous variables y_t^e. There may also be unobserved shocks η_t.

4. A learning rule describing how expectations are formed over time. One can think of various ways for updating expectations, and various standard statistical forecasting rules are special cases of this general formulation.

Since the work of Muth (1961), Lucas (1972), and Sargent (1973), the benchmark model of expectation formation in macroeconomics has been rational expectations. This hypothesis posits, for both private agents and policymakers, that expectations are equal to the true statistical conditional expectations of the unknown random variables. The "learning theory" approach in macroeconomics argues that although rational expectations is the natural benchmark, it is implausibly strong. We need a more realistic model of rationality, which may, however, be consistent with agents eventually learning to have rational expectations.

A natural criterion for a model of rationality is what we call the "cognitive consistency principle": economic agents should be assumed to be about as smart as (good) economists. This still leaves open various possibilities, because we could choose to model households and firms like economic theorists or, alternatively, model them like econometricians. The adaptive or econometric learning approach, which will be our principal focus here,[1] takes the latter viewpoint, arguing that economists, when they forecast future economic aggregates, usually do so using time-series econometric techniques. This seems particularly natural, because neither private agents nor economists at central banks or other institutions know the true model. Instead economists formulate and estimate models. These models are re-estimated and possibly reformulated as new data become

---

1. However, see also Section 2.4.2.1, where we discuss the eductive approach.

available. Economists themselves engage in processes of learning about the economy.

2.2.1 Least-Squares Learning and Expectational Stability

We introduce the econometric learning approach using a simple linear model

$$y_t = \mu + \alpha y_t^e + \delta' w_{t-1} + \eta_t \tag{2}$$

where μ and α are scalar parameters, δ is a column vector of parameters, and δ' denotes the transpose of δ. Throughout the chapter a prime will denote the transpose of a vector or matrix, and vectors will normally be written as column vectors. Here y_t is a scalar endogenous variable, w_{t-1} is a vector of exogenous observable variables, and η_t is an unobservable iid (independently and identically distributed) random shock with zero mean. The expectation variable $y_t^e = E_{t-1}^* y_t$ in this model is the expectation of y_t based on the set of observables dated $t - 1$ or earlier. The notation $E_{t-1}^* y_t$ here indicates the information set, and the use of E_{t-1}^* instead of E_{t-1} indicates that the expectations of economic agents are not (necessarily) fully rational (in the usual sense of "rational expectations"). This model is particularly simple: no expectations of future variables are included. For convenience in this example we also date the exogenous observable variables w_{t-1}, because the information set is taken to be variables at time $t - 1$.

The unique rational expectations equilibrium of this model is

$$y_t = \bar{a} + \bar{b}' w_{t-1} + \eta_t, \quad \bar{a} = (1 - \alpha)^{-1} \mu, \quad \bar{b} = (1 - \alpha)^{-1} \delta \tag{3}$$

as is easily verified by applying the method of undetermined coefficients to the functional form $y_t = a + b' w_{t-1} + \eta_t$. Two well-known economic examples lead to reduced-form model (2).

Example 1 (Lucas-type aggregate supply model) A simple version of the "Lucas islands" model presented in Lucas (1973) consists of the aggregate supply and demand equations

$$q_t = \bar{q} + \pi(p_t - p_t^e) + \zeta_t$$

$$m_t + v_t = p_t + q_t$$

where $\pi > 0$. Here q_t is aggregate output, p_t is the price level, v_t is a velocity shock, and m_t is the money supply. All variables are in log form, ζ_t is a white-noise random shock, and $\bar{q}$ denotes the natural rate of output. Here p_t^e denotes the expected price level. Assuming both v_t and the m_t rule depend in part on exogenous observables w_{t-1}, we have

$$v_t = \mu + \gamma' w_{t-1} + \xi_t$$

$$m_t = \bar{m} + \rho' w_{t-1} + u_t$$

where μ and $\overline{m}$ are fixed scalars, γ and ρ are column parameter vectors, and u_t and ξ_t are white-noise shocks. The reduced form of the model is of the form (2) with $y_t \equiv p_t$, $0 < \alpha = \pi(1+\pi)^{-1} < 1$, and $\eta_t = (1+\pi)^{-1}(u_t + \xi_t - \zeta_t)$.

Example 2 (Muth market model) In the classic "cobweb model" analyzed under rational expectations by Muth (1961), an isolated market has a one-period production lag with competitive and (for simplicity) identical supply decisions based on the expected price $p_t^e = E_{t-1}^* p_t$ formed at the end of $t - 1$. Demand d_t and supply s_t are

$$d_t = m_I - m_p p_t + v_{1t}$$

$$s_t = r_I + r_p p_t^e + r_w' w_{t-1} + v_{2t}$$

where m_I, m_P and r_I, r_P are the usual demand and supply parameters; r_w is a parameter vector for observable supply shocks w_{t-1}; and v_{1t} and v_{2t} are white noise. With market clearing, $d_t = s_t$, we obtain (2) as the reduced form with $y_t \equiv p_t$, $\eta_t = (v_{1t} - v_{2t})/m_p$, $\mu = (m_I - r_I)/m_p$, $\delta = -m_p^{-1} r_w$, and $\alpha = -r_p/m_p$. Note that $\alpha < 0$ for $r_p, m_p > 0$.

The rational expectations equilibrium (3) of the reduced form (2) implies the rational expectation

$$y_t^e = E_{t-1} y_t = \bar{a} + \bar{b}' w_{t-1}$$

How would agents come to have rational expectations? In the econometric approach to learning, agents are assumed, like econometricians, to use past data to estimate the parameters a and b in the perceived model

$$y_t = a + b' w_{t-1} + \eta_t \tag{4}$$

and to use the parameter estimates a_{t-1}, b_{t-1} to make forecasts

$$y_t^e = a_{t-1} + b_{t-1}' w_{t-1}$$

For simplicity, all agents are here assumed to have the same expectations.

The exogenous shocks w_{t-1} and η_t and the expectations y_t^e determine actual y_t according to the model (2). This is called the "temporary equilibrium" at time t. Under learning the parameters of the forecasting model are updated in t to (a_t, b_t), for example, by using least squares. The sequence of temporary equilibria under learning can thus be defined recursively. Agents are said to attain rational expectations asymptotically if $a_t, b_t \to \bar{a}, \bar{b}$ as $t \to \infty$.

For this setup Bray and Savin (1986), Fourgeaud et al. (1986), and Marcet and Sargent (1989b) demonstrated asymptotic convergence to rational expectations with probability one if $\alpha < 1$ and convergence with probability zero if $\alpha > 1$. Why is the condition $\alpha < 1$ required for rational expectations to be attained? The setup differs from the standard econometric assumptions in that the model is self-referential: because the actual price process y_t depends on y_t^e and because the coefficients of y_t^e evolve under learning, the system during the learning transition is actually nonstationary. Under least-squares learning agents neglect this nonstationarity and are thus making a subtle misspecification error. However, when $\alpha < 1$ the specification error vanishes asymptotically and the system converges to a stationary process: their estimates are econometrically consistent and in fact converge with probability one. When instead $\alpha > 1$ the self-referential feature of the system dominates, agents' parameter estimates diverge, and the rational expectations solution fails to be stable under learning.

Provided $\alpha < 1$, agents' expectations y_t^e converge to rational expectations asymptotically. Agents are only boundedly rational in that their forecasts have systematic forecast errors during the learning process, but we have a rational foundation for rational expectations in the sense that agents do not stick with incorrect parameters in the long run. By adjusting their estimated parameters in response to forecast errors using least squares, agents are eventually led to fully consistent expectations.

The econometric learning approach to expectation formation can thus be used to obtain an understanding of how agents might come to have rational expectations, thus providing a test of the plausibility of rational expectations in a particular model. The stability conditions are typically straightforward to obtain using the expectational stability (E-stability) technique, which examines the core dynamics of the differential equation approximation to the stochastic discrete-time system under learning. The E-stability technique looks at the actual law of motion generated by a given perceived law of motion. For the case at hand the actual law of motion is given by inserting the perceived law of motion expectations $y_t^e = a + b'w_{t-1}$ into (2), yielding the actual law of motion

$$y_t = \mu + \alpha a + (\delta + \alpha b)'w_{t-1} + \eta_t$$

and a corresponding mapping from the perceived law of motion to the actual one is given by $T(a, b) = (\mu + \alpha a, \delta + \alpha b)$. E-stability is defined as stability of $(\bar{a}, \bar{b})$ under the ordinary differential equation $d(a, b)/d\tau = T(a, b) - (a, b)$, which in the current case immediately yields the correct condition $\alpha < 1$. Here τ denotes virtual time.[2]

The general E-stability technique is described in detail in Evans and Honkapohja (2001) and is summarized in Evans and Honkapohja (2009b).

---

2. Virtual time can be related to calendar time measured in discrete periods. See, for example, Evans and Honkapohja (2009b).

Dynamic macroeconomic models, in which there are expectations of future endogenous variables, can have multiple equilibria, including in some cases sunspot equilibria or cycles, and E-stability can be used to select those rational expectations equilibria that are attainable under econometric learning (e.g., see Evans et al. 1998, 2007). Thus, in principle the cognitive consistency principle and the bounded-rationality econometric learning approach can provide a rational foundation for the rational expectations approach in macroeconomics, both in cases of "well-behaved" economies with a unique equilibrium and in some cases in which there are fully self-fulfilling, but inefficient, macroeconomic fluctuations.

However, the econometric learning approach can also generate new learning dynamics not found under the Rational Expectations Hypothesis, and recent research has focused on several issues that are at the heart of the question "are there rational foundations for macroeconomics?"

2.2.2 Structural Change and Misspecification

We argued above that the econometric learning approach could in some cases provide a rational foundation for the use of rational expectations in macroeconomics. But the approach also raises some natural questions that can undercut the Rational Expectations Hypothesis. Real-world econometricians do not know the correct specification of the data-generating process. Limitations on degrees of freedom imply that econometric forecasting models will typically be misspecified, for example, underparameterized in terms of explanatory variables or lags. If this is true for applied econometricians, then the cognitive consistency principle implies that it is also true for households, firms, and policymakers.

Furthermore, the economy continually undergoes structural change, whether incrementally or occasionally in sudden shifts, with the change taking an unknown form. If the structure of the economy does not remain stationary over time, the true data-generating process may never be known. Appealing again to the cognitive consistency principle, economic agents should be aware of the likelihood of structural change and take measures to deal with it. Finally, if economic agents cannot be expected to know the correct specification of the data-generating process, then agents are likely to disagree about the best forecasting model to use: heterogeneity of expectations can be expected to be widespread. We now outline approaches that incorporate these points.[3]

---

3. Frydman and Goldberg (Chapter 4, this volume) describe rational expectations models as "fully predetermined models" and also group the learning approach in the same camp. We feel this is misleading. Although learning as a stability theory for rational expectations was the main focus of the early literature on learning, there is an increasing focus on the dynamics introduced by learning. Learning models now focus on a wide variety of issues, many of which are described in this section. Topics like heterogeneity, misspecification, and structural change

2.2.2.1 Misspecification and Restricted Perceptions Equilibria

The reality that econometricians sometimes use misspecified models suggests we should consider implications of agents using misspecified econometric forecasting models. This can result in convergence to restricted perceptions equilibria, in which the agents use the best misspecified model.

As a simple example, consider (2), and suppose the perceived law of motion takes the form of omitting a subset of the variables w_t. Specifically, write $w_t' = (w_{1,t}', w_{2,t}')$, and assume that the agents' perceived law of motion takes the form

$$p_t = a + c'w_{1,t-1} + \varepsilon_t$$

where ε_t is believed to be white noise. This perceived law of motion gives an actual law of motion $p_t = (\mu + \alpha a) + (\gamma_1 + \alpha c)'w_{1,t-1} + \gamma_2'w_{2,t-1} + \eta_t$. For this actual law of motion the best model in the permitted class of perceived laws of motion is the "projected actual law of motion" obtained by computing the linear projection of p_t onto the information set $E(p_t|1, w_{1,t-1}) = \tilde{T}_a(a, c) + \tilde{T}_c(a, c)'w_{1,t-1}$. Here we use the notation $\tilde{T}$ to emphasize that we are considering restricted perceived laws of motion, and we use $\tilde{T}_a$ and $\tilde{T}_c$ to denote the intercept and slope coefficients, respectively, of this map. This gives a mapping $(a, c) \to \tilde{T}(a, c)$, but now $\tilde{T}(a, c) = (\tilde{T}_a(a, c), \tilde{T}_c(a, c))$ depends on the covariance matrix for (w_{1t}, w_{2t}). A fixed point of $\tilde{T}$ has the property that forecasts are optimal relative to the restricted information set used by agents, and we therefore call this solution a "restricted perceptions equilibrium." It can be shown that under least-squares learning there is convergence to the restricted perceptions equilibrium if $\alpha < 1$.[4]

2.2.2.2 Constant-Gain Learning and Escape Dynamics

Suppose now that agents are concerned about the structural change of an unknown form. A changing structure is tracked more effectively by weighting recent data more heavily. This can be conveniently done using a discounted (or constant-gain) version of least squares. Because constant-gain least squares weight recent data more heavily, convergence will be to a stochastic process near the rational expectations equilibrium rather than to the rational expectations equilibrium itself. As an example, consider again the model (2). Under standard least squares each data point receives the same weight $1/t$. The current data point thus has a declining weight as t increases. If agents instead use constant-gain least squares, the current datum receives a

show that the learning literature can account for aspects of "unknown unknowns" as well as "known unknowns." Furthermore, the set of adaptive learning rules currently being explored is quite broad and thus allows for a wide range of possible learning dynamics.

4. The idea of restricted perceptions equilibrium was introduced in Evans and Honkapohja (2001: 317–329). Related notions have been suggested by Marcet and Sargent (1989a), Sargent (1991), and Hommes and Sorger (1997).

fixed weight $0 < \gamma < 1$, and weights on past data points decline geometrically at the rate $1 - \gamma$. For the model (2) it can be shown that estimates (a_t, b_t) now fail to converge fully to the rational expectations values. Instead the estimates converge to a stochastic process centered on $(\bar{a}, \bar{b})$, with a finite variance scaled by the gain γ, so that learning remains imperfect.

In some cases this use of constant-gain least squares can have major implications for economic policy. For example, Cho et al. (2002) show the possibility of escape dynamics in inflation models, in which parameter estimates stray far from the rational expectations equilibrium for an extended period. As another example, Orphanides and Williams (2007) argue that monetary policy needs to take account of imperfect learning by private agents.

2.2.2.3 Heterogeneous Expectations

The preceding discussion has assumed homogeneous expectations for analytical convenience. In practice, heterogeneous expectations can be a major concern. In some models the presence of heterogeneous expectations does not have major effects on convergence conditions, as first suggested by Evans and Honkapohja (1996) and further studied by Evans et al. (2001) and Giannitsarou (2003). These papers assume that expectations are the only source of heterogeneity (i.e., agents' preferences and technologies are identical). Honkapohja and Mitra (2006) show that the interaction of structural and expectational heterogeneity can make the conditions for convergence of learning significantly more stringent than those obtained under homogeneous expectations. Agents' behavioral heterogeneity, their speed of learning, and the mixture of specific learning rules all affect the conditions for convergence to rational expectations equilibrium. There are also conditions on agents' characteristics that ensure convergence for all speeds of learning and mixtures of specific learning rules.

Heterogeneity of expectations can have other implications. For example, the papers just cited do not focus on multiple equilibria. Guse (2006) studies the stability of equilibria in a model with multiple solutions, emphasizing that the distribution of forecasting heterogeneity can play an important role in determining stability properties. Misspecification and heterogeneous expectations are combined in Berardi (2007, 2008) to yield models of heterogeneous expectations equilibria. Heterogeneity of beliefs among agents is clearly central in empirical and experimental research on expectations formation (see Section 2.3.5 for references).[5]

In many settings there is no difficulty incorporating heterogeneous expectations into adaptive learning models, and this heterogeneity can

---

5. An important approach to heterogeneous expectations, developed by M. Kurz in a number of papers, is the concept of rational beliefs equilibrium, which requires consistency of heterogeneous beliefs with the empirical distribution of past data. See, for example, Kurz (1997, 2009, 2011).

take various forms. For example, Evans et al. (2001) allow for stochastic heterogeneity across agents' expectations stemming from random gains and random inertia (updating frequency). In (mean) constant-gain versions of these rules this would lead to persistent heterogeneity. Expectation shocks can also be included, as in Evans and Honkapohja (2003a: 1059–1062) and Milani (2011), and it would be straightforward to allow for idiosyncratic components to these shocks.

2.2.2.4 Dynamic Predictor Selection

Once one accepts that forecasting models may be misspecified and that agents have heterogeneous expectations, one is driven toward the possibility that agents choose among competing models. If agents can alter their choices over time, then the dynamic predictor-selection approach may be warranted. Having multiple forecasting models in play is one way of obtaining heterogeneous expectations and can lead to a variety of learning dynamics, including regime-switching behavior and additional volatility.

Brock and Hommes (1997) postulate that agents have a finite set of predictors or expectation functions, and that each predictor has a fitness, i.e., an estimate based on past data of its profits net of the cost of using the predictor. The proportion of agents who select a predictor depends on this fitness. Brock and Hommes (1997) study in detail the resulting adaptively rational expectations dynamics for the standard cobweb model when there are two predictors: a costly rational predictor and a costless naive forecast. They show that cycles and even chaotic dynamics can arise in such a setting.

The dynamic predictor-selection framework is extended by Branch and Evans (2006a, 2007, 2010) to incorporate stochastic features and econometric learning. Noting pervasive degrees-of-freedom limitations, Branch and Evans appeal to the merits of parsimonious forecasting models and study the implications of agents choosing between (equally costly) underparameterized models. As a simple illustration, each of two competing models might omit one of the two exogenous shocks. In models with negative expectational feedback (e.g., model (2) with $\alpha < 0$ as in the cobweb model), there is the possibility of intrinsic heterogeneity, in which both forecasting models are in use in equilibrium. In models with positive feedback (e.g., (2) with $\alpha > 0$, as in the Lucas-type monetary model), two misspecification equilibria can exist, and agents may coordinate on either of the two forecasting models. Under real-time learning the stochastic process for inflation and output can then exhibit regime-switching or parameter drift, in line with much macroeconometric evidence.

The dynamic predictor-selection approach has been used in other applications. For example, Brazier et al. (2008) and De Grauwe (2011), who both emphasize switching between alternative forecasting models, look at the implications of regime switching for macroeconomic policy. Another approach to model specification is for agents to switch between model specifications over time, based on econometric criteria, as in Markiewicz (2012). A related approach, based on tests for misspecification, is developed in Cho and Kasa (2012).

Another natural approach when multiple models are in play would be for individual agents to do some form of averaging across forecasting models. A simple alternative would be to assume that agents have fixed weights between models, as in the natural expectations employed by Fuster et al. (2010), in which agents use a fixed weight to average between rational expectations and an "intuitive model."[6] A contrasting formulation is to assume that agents update model estimates using standard econometric tools and then use Bayesian model averaging (e.g., Slobodyan and Wouters 2012a). Evans et al. (2012b) consider the dynamics of Bayesian model averaging and learning in the basic model discussed in Section 2.2.1.

The central message of the modified learning procedures, discussed in this section, is that variations of econometric learning, which adhere to the cognitive consistency principle and reflect real-world concerns of applied econometricians, can lead to new learning dynamics that are qualitatively different from rational expectations dynamics. In these learning dynamics agents are boundedly rational, in that their perceived law of motion does not *fully* reflect the actual economic dynamics, but given their knowledge, they are forecasting in a nearly optimal way.

2.3 Learning and Empirical Research

There is an expanding literature that employs the learning approach to study empirical issues in macroeconomics and finance. We give an overview of the main topics that have been studied.

2.3.1 Rise and Fall of Inflation

Several recent papers have argued that learning plays a central role in the historical explanation of the rise and fall of U.S. inflation during 1960–1990. Sargent (1999) and Cho et al. (2002) emphasize the role of policymaker learning. They argue that if monetary policymakers attempt to implement optimal policy while estimating and updating the coefficients of a mis-specified Phillips curve, there will be both periods of inefficiently high inflation and occasional escapes to low inflation. Sargent et al. (2006) estimate a version of this model. They find that shocks in the 1970s led monetary authorities to perceive a trade-off between inflation and unemployment,

---

6. From the viewpoint of cognitive consistency both the weight between and the parameters of the forecasting models could be allowed to respond to data over time.

leading to high inflation, and subsequent changed beliefs about this trade-off account for the conquest of U.S. inflation during Volcker's tenure as chairman of the Federal Reserve.

Primiceri (2006) makes a related argument, emphasizing both policymaker learning about the Phillips curve parameters and the aggregate demand relationship, and uncertainty about the unobserved natural rate of unemployment. The great inflation of the 1970s initially resulted from a combination of underestimates of both the persistence of inflation and the natural rate of unemployment. This also led policymakers to underestimate the disinflationary impact of unemployment.

Other empirical accounts of the period that emphasize learning include Bullard and Eusepi (2005), which examines the implications of policymaker learning about the growth rate of potential output; Orphanides and Williams (2005a), which underscores both private-agent learning and policymaker misestimates of the natural rate of unemployment; Orphanides and Williams (2005c), which looks at estimated models that focus on the explanation of the large increase in inflation rates in the 1970s; and Cogley and Sargent (2005), which develops a historical account of inflation policy emphasizing Bayesian model averaging and learning by policymakers uncertain about the true economic model.

Recent papers include Ellison and Yates (2007) and Carboni and Ellison (2009), which emphasize the importance of policymaker model uncertainty and the role of central bank learning in explaining the historical evolution of inflation and unemployment in the post-1950 period.

2.3.2 Latin American Inflation

Marcet and Nicolini (2003) use an open-economy extension of the standard seigniorage model of inflation, in which government spending is financed by printing money. They present a calibrated learning model that aims to explain the central stylized facts about hyperinflation episodes during the 1980s in a number of South American countries: (1) hyperinflation episodes recur; (2) exchange rate rules stop hyperinflation episodes, though new hyperinflation events eventually occur; (3) during hyperinflation, seigniorage and inflation are not highly correlated; and (4) average inflation and seigniorage are strongly positively correlated across countries.

These facts are difficult to explain using the rational expectations assumption. Under learning there are occasional escapes from the low inflation steady state to an unstable hyperinflationary process that is eventually arrested by imposing an exchange rate rule. All four stylized facts listed above can be matched using this model. For example, under learning higher levels of deficits financed by seigniorage make average inflation higher and the frequency of hyperinflation episodes greater. Simulations of a calibrated model look very plausible.

2.3.3 Real Business Cycle Applications

Williams (2004) explores the real business cycle model dynamics under learning. Using simulations, he shows that the dynamics under rational expectations and learning are not very different unless agents need to estimate structural aspects as well as the parameters for the reduced-form perceived law of motion. Huang et al. (2009) focus on the role of misspecified beliefs and suggest that these can substantially amplify the fluctuations stemming from technology shocks in the standard real business cycle model. Eusepi and Preston (2011) incorporate infinite-horizon learning into the standard real business cycle model and find that the volatilities and persistence of output and employment are higher under learning than under rational expectations. Mitra et al. (2012) show that the government spending multiplier is substantially larger under learning than under rational expectations.

Other papers on learning and business cycle dynamics include Giannitsarou (2006) and Van Nieuwerburgh and Veldkamp (2006). The latter formulates a model of Bayesian learning about productivity and suggests that the resulting model can explain the sharp downturns that are an empirical characteristic of business cycles. The former extends the basic real business cycle model to include government spending financed by capital and labor taxes. It is shown that if a reduction of capital taxes is introduced following negative productivity shocks, the learning adjustment exhibits a delayed response in economic activity, in contrast to an immediate positive response under rational expectations.

2.3.4 Asset Pricing and Learning

The initial work by Timmermann (1993, 1996) studied the implications of learning in the standard risk-neutral asset pricing model. The main finding was that in both short- and long-horizon models learning increased the volatility of asset prices during learning.

In more recent literature on learning and stock prices Brock and Hommes (1998) introduce heterogeneous expectations using the dynamic predictor-selection methodology discussed earlier. Lansing (2010), Branch and Evans (2011), and Adam et al. (2012) present models in which stock market bubbles arise endogenously.

Branch and Evans (2011) examine learning in a portfolio model in which the demand for risky assets depends positively on the expected returns and negatively on expected conditional variance of returns. Under constant-gain learning there is a regime in which stock prices exhibit bubbles and crashes driven by changing estimates of risk. Adam et al. (2012) use the standard consumption-based model of stock prices modified to include learning. The model exhibits a number of salient features of the data, including mean reversion of returns, excess volatility, and persistence of price-dividend ratios. A calibrated version of the model is shown to match many aspects of U.S. data. Lansing (2010) shows that in Lucas-type asset pricing models, there are driftless near-rational solutions that are stable under learning; these solutions generate intermittent bubbles and dynamics qualitatively similar to long-run U.S. stock market data.

The model of LeBaron (this volume) focuses on the role of heterogeneous gains in learning rules for estimating the mean returns and conditional variances by risk-averse investors. He argues that agents putting relatively large weights on the recent past are important for magnification of asset price volatility and replication of long samples of U.S. financial data.

In summary, several recent papers are arguing that adaptive learning can play a key role in explaining asset price behavior. The issues of market completeness and the role of financial derivatives have also received some attention. Using the eductive approach, Guesnerie and Rochet (1993) demonstrate that opening futures markets can be destabilizing; using a dynamic predictor-selection approach, Brock et al. (2009) show that adding hedging instruments can destabilize markets and increase price volatility.

Exchange rate dynamics also exhibit some puzzles that learning models may resolve. For example, Kim (2009) shows that adaptive learning can generate the excess volatility, long swings, and persistence that appear in the data. Chakraborty and Evans (2008) focus on the forward-premium puzzle and argue that adaptive learning can explain this anomaly while simultaneously replicating other features of the data, such as positive serial correlation of the forward premium. Another, potentially complementary, approach to exchange rate modeling is based on dynamic predictor selection (see De Grauwe and Grimaldi 2006). Further applications of learning to exchange rates include Kasa (2004), Mark (2009), and Markiewicz (2012).[7]

2.3.5 Estimated Models with Learning

The rational expectations version of New Keynesian models needs to incorporate various sources of inertia arising from indexation and habit-formation in preferences to account for observed persistence in inflation and output data. These have been criticized as being ad hoc. Incorporating

---

7. In several publications Roman Frydman and Michael Goldberg have recently developed Imperfect Knowledge Economics as a model of nonroutine change in expectations formation. Frydman and Goldberg (Chapter 6, this volume) describe the application of this approach to account for persistence and long swings in asset prices and exchange rates. It is difficult to assess their approach (presented in their Section 6.2), because several key aspects are purposely only loosely specified. These include updating of forecasting strategy $\Delta\beta_t^i$, the bound δ_t for change in baseline drift, and some aspects of the stochastic structure. Juselius (this volume) finds that many empirical regularities in exchange rate dynamics under rational expectations are empirically violated and suggests that the Frydman-Goldberg approach works better. However, she does not relate her empirical regularities to those implied by other learning and related models that relax the rational expectations assumption.

learning provides an alternative to account for the observed persistence. This point was initially made in a simple calibrated model by Orphanides and Williams (2005b). Milani (2007) addresses this issue using an estimated dynamic stochastic general equilibrium (DSGE) model with learning and finds that both habit formation and indexation inertia play minor roles when estimation allows for adaptive learning. The implications of incorporating learning in applied DSGE models has most recently been explored by Slobodyan and Wouters (2012a,b).

There is also empirical work on forecasts, based on survey data, and indirect measures of expectations from asset markets that help to assess the alternative models of learning and expectations formation. For recent papers, see Branch (2004), Basdevant (2005), Orphanides and Williams (2005a), Branch and Evans (2006b), Pfajfar (2007), and Pfajfar and Santoro (2010). For research on expectations formation and learning in experimental settings, see Marimon and Sunder (1993, 1995), Evans et al. (2001), Adam (2007), and the new survey, Hommes (2011).

Recently, Milani (2011) has investigated the importance of expectations as a driving force for business cycles in the United States. In an estimated New Keynesian model with constant-gain first-order vector autoregressive learning, Milani (2011) uses survey data on expectations in conjunction with aggregate macro data both to estimate the structural parameters of the model and to identify expectation shocks, interpreted as arising from shifts in market sentiment. His provocative conclusion is that expectations shocks can account for roughly half of business cycle fluctuations.

We think that empirically oriented research on learning will continue to grow. As discussed above, adaptive learning has the potential to resolve a number of puzzles and difficulties that rational expectations models encounter when confronted with the data.

2.4 Further Issues in Modeling Learning

2.4.1 *The Planning Horizon*

In the Lucas-Muth model and in overlapping-generations models with two-period lifetimes, agents in the current period make forecasts for the values of aggregate variables in the next period. However, many modern macroeconomic models are set in a representative-agent framework with infinite-lived agents who solve infinite-horizon dynamic optimization problems. Typically, under rational expectations the reduced-form equations for these models can be stated in the form $y_t = \mathcal{F}(y_{t-1}, y_{t+1}^e, w_t, \eta_t)$, where $y_{t+1}^e = E_t y_{t+1}$. This reduction relies on the use of the Euler equations to describe the first-order optimality conditions.

There are alternative approaches to learning and bounded rationality in infinite-horizon settings. In Evans and Honkapohja (2001: 227–263), the learning framework was kept close to the rational expectations reduced-form setup, a procedure that can be justified if agents make decisions based directly on their Euler equations. This approach has been used, for example, in Bullard and Mitra (2002) and Evans and Honkapohja (2003b). An alternative approach, followed by Preston (2005, 2006), assumes that households use estimated models to forecast aggregate quantities infinitely far into the future to solve for their current decisions.[8] We now illustrate the two approaches using a simple endowment economy.[9]

A representative consumer makes consumption-saving decisions using the intertemporal utility function

$$E_t^* \sum_{s=t}^{\infty} \beta^{s-t} U(C_s) \tag{5}$$

where C_s is consumption at date s, and $0 < \beta \leq 1$. Each agent has a random endowment Y_t of the perishable good. There is a market in safe one-period loans with a gross rate of return R_t, known at t. Initial wealth for each agent is zero. Output Y_s follows an exogenous process given by

$$\log Y_s = \mu + \rho \log Y_{s-1} + v_s$$

where $|\rho| < 1$, and v_s is white noise. Expectations are not necessarily rational, indicated by the $*$ on the expectations operator. Defining $\mathcal{R}_{t+1,s}^{-1} = \prod_{j=t+1}^{s} R_{t+j}$, the household's intertemporal budget constraint is

$$C_t + \sum_{s=t+1}^{\infty} \mathcal{R}_{t+1,s} C_s = Y_t + \sum_{s=t+1}^{\infty} \mathcal{R}_{t+1,s} Y_s$$

Maximizing (5) subject to the intertemporal budget constraint yields the Euler necessary first-order condition, $U'(C_t) = \beta R_t E_t^* U'(C_{t+1})$. In the Euler-equation learning approach, the Euler equation is treated as a behavioral equation, determining for each agent their temporary equilibrium demand for C_t as a function of R_t and their forecast $E_t^* U'(C_{t+1})$. Imposing the market clearing condition $C_t = Y_t$ and using the representative agent setting, we obtain the temporary equilibrium interest rate $R_t^{-1} = \beta(E_t^* U'(C_{t+1}))/U'(Y_t)$.

Writing $y_t = \log(Y_t/\bar{Y})$ and so forth, and using log-linearizations around $\bar{Y} = \bar{C} = (1 - \rho)^{-1}\mu$, $\bar{R} = \beta^{-1}$ yields $y_t = \rho y_{t-1} + v_t$ and the consumption demand

$$c_t = E_t^* c_{t+1} - \sigma r_t \tag{6}$$

---

8. Infinite-horizon learning based on an iterated Euler equation was used by Sargent (1993: 122–125) in the "investment under uncertainty" model. See also the example in Marcet and Sargent (1989b).

9. This passage is based largely on Honkapohja et al. (2012), and we also draw on Evans et al. (2009).

where $\sigma = -U'(\bar{C})/(U''(\bar{C})\bar{C})$ is the intertemporal elasticity of substitution.[10] In the temporary equilibrium $c_t = y_t$ and $r_t = \sigma^{-1}(E_t^* c_{t+1} - y_t)$. The rational expectations equilibrium of the linearized model is given by

$$r_t = -(1-\rho)\sigma^{-1}y_t$$
$$E_t c_{t+1} = \rho y_t$$

To formulate Euler-equation learning based on (6), suppose agents have the perceived law of motion

$$E_t^* c_{t+1} = m + n y_t \tag{7}$$

with coefficient estimates (m_t, n_t) obtained using a regression of c_s on y_{s-1} supplied by data $s = 1, \ldots, t-1$. As usual, (m_t, n_t) are updated over time. Will agents learn to hold rational expectations over time? That is, will we have $(m_t, n_t) \to (0, \rho)$ as $t \to \infty$? This can be assessed using E-stability: the perceived law of motion (7) leads to the actual law of motion $r_t = -\sigma^{-1}[y_t(1-n) - m]$ and $c_t = y_t$. Because the actual law of motion forecasts are $E_t c_{t+1} = \rho y_t$, the T-map is simply $T(m, n) = (0, \rho)$. The E-stability differential equation $d(m, n)/d\tau = T(m, n) - (m, n)$ is stable, and there is convergence of least-squares learning to rational expectations in this model.

To summarize, under Euler-equation learning, agents choose their c_t using (6). This requires a forecast of the agent's own c_{t+1}. This forecast is made by means of (7), in which agents assume that their future consumption is related (as in the rational expectations equilibrium) to the key state variable y_t. Thinking one step ahead in this way appears to us to be a plausible and natural form of bounded rationality. Although this formulation does not explicitly impose the intertemporal budget constraint, it can be verified that along the learning path both the intertemporal budget constraint and the transversality condition are satisfied.[11]

An alternative approach treats consumption demand each period as based on forecasts over an infinite horizon.[12] We call this approach, presented for the New Keynesian model in Preston (2005), "infinite-horizon learning,"

---

10. Note that in Evans et al. (2009) σ denotes the inverse intertemporal elasticity of substitution. Our notation in this chapter is consistent with Honkapohja et al. (2012).

11. Euler-equation learning is a special case of shadow price learning, which can be shown to deliver asymptotically optimal decisionmaking in general settings. See Evans and McGough (2010).

12. Thus, infinite-horizon agents explicitly solve dynamic optimization problems, which can be viewed as a version of the "anticipated utility" approach formulated by Kreps (1998) and discussed in Sargent (1999) and Cogley and Sargent (2008).

and we describe it for the current context. Log-linearizing the intertemporal budget constraint yields

$$c_t + \sum_{s=t+1}^{\infty} \beta^{s-t} E_t^* c_s = y_t + \sum_{s=t+1}^{\infty} \beta^{s-t} E_t^* y_s$$

From the linearized Euler equation (6) we have

$$E_t^* c_s = c_t + \sigma \sum_{j=t}^{s-1} E_t^* r_j$$

for $s \geq t + 1$. Substituting into the linearized intertemporal budget constraint and solving for c_t leads to the behavioral equation

$$c_t = (1 - \beta)y_t - \sigma \beta r_t + \sum_{s=t+1}^{\infty} \beta^{s-t}[(1 - \beta)E_t^* y_s - \sigma \beta E_t^* r_s] \qquad (8)$$

where we have assumed that both y_t and r_t are known at t.

Under infinite-horizon learning, suppose agents do not know the rational expectations relationship between y_t and r_t but have the perceived law of motion

$$r_t = d + f y_t$$

where at time t the coefficients are estimated to be d_t and f_t. To determine E-stability, use $E_t^* r_s = d + f y_s$ and $E_t^* y_s = \rho^{s-t} y_t$ in (8), impose market clearing $c_t = y_t$, and solve for r_t to obtain the implied actual law of motion, given by

$$T(d, f) = \left(-\beta(1 - \beta)^{-1}d, -(1 - \beta\rho)^{-1}(\sigma^{-1}(1 - \rho) + \beta\rho f) \right)$$

The fixed point of T is the rational expectations equilibrium, and it is easily checked that the E-stability differential equation is stable. Thus, we have convergence of least-squares learning to rational expectations under infinite-horizon learning.

Although for this particular model learning stability holds for both Euler-equation and infinite-horizon learning, in more general models it is possible for stability to depend on the planning horizon of the agents. For example, in a real business cycle model with a mixture of rational and boundedly rational agents, Branch and McGough (2011) show that hump-shaped responses of consumption to productivity shocks can arise and are particularly strong when the boundedly rational agents have a long but finite planning horizon.[13] As another example, Eusepi and Preston (2011) show the

---

13. Learning with finite planning horizons is developed further in Branch et al. (2012).

implications for macroeconomic volatility of constant-gain infinite-horizon learning in a real business cycle setting.

2.4.2 Structural Knowledge

In Section 2.2.1 we assumed that agents estimated the correct perceived law of motion, that is, the form of the perceived law of motion corresponding to the rational expectations solution. Implicitly we assumed that they knew the list of observable variables driving the rational expectations equilibrium and that the solution was linear. However, we did not assume that they had the structural knowledge needed to compute the rational expectations equilibrium. Under (standard, i.e., decreasing gain) least-squares learning their expectations can converge to rational expectations (if $\alpha < 1$), even though they do not necessarily know the full economic structure. This is possible asymptotically, because to forecast optimally, all that is required in this setting is the linear projection of y_t onto the information set, and this can be consistently estimated by least squares. Of course, because the result is asymptotic, agents will not have rational expectations during the learning transition. This result raises the following question: If agents do have structural knowledge, will they be able to coordinate on rational expectations more quickly? Alternatively, if agents have incomplete structural knowledge, is there a natural way for them to incorporate this knowledge into econometric learning? We take up these two issues in turn.

2.4.2.1 Eductive Stability under Full Structural Knowledge
Consider again the reduced-form model (2). For convenience we now omit the observable stochastic shocks, so that we have

$$y_t = \mu + \alpha y_t^e + \eta_t \tag{9}$$

where η_t is a white-noise exogenous shock. We now suppose that all agents know the structure (9) and that this is common knowledge. We further suppose that all agents are fully rational and know that all other agents are fully rational. Thus, our cognitive consistency principle now takes a different form, in which we model economic agents like economic theorists. This form leads to the eductive learning approach.

We now take up the eductive viewpoint for model (9). The argument here was initially given by Guesnerie (1992) in the context of the cobweb model. See Evans and Guesnerie (1993) for the multivariate formulation and Guesnerie (2002) for a more general discussion using the eductive approach.

To focus the discussion, we use the cobweb example, which can be reformulated as a producers' game in which the strategy of each firm is its output, and the optimal choice of output depends on expected price.

We assume that firms have identical costs. We allow for heterogeneous expectations, however, so that the equilibrium market price is given by

$$y_t = \mu + \alpha \int E^*_{t-1} y_t(\omega) d\omega + \eta_t$$

where we now assume a continuum of agents indexed by ω, and $E^*_{t-1} y_t(\omega)$ is the expectation of the market price held by agent ω. The rational expectations equilibrium is $y_t = \bar{a} + \eta_t$, where $\bar{a} = (1 - \alpha)^{-1} \mu$, and expectations are $E_{t-1} y_t = \bar{a}$. We now ask whether rational agents would necessarily co-ordinate on rational expectations.

The eductive argument works as follows. Let $S(\bar{a})$ denote a neighborhood of $\bar{a}$. Suppose it is common knowledge that $E^*_{t-1} p_t(\omega) \in S(\bar{a})$ for all ω. Then it follows that it is common knowledge that $E p_t \in |\alpha| S(\bar{a})$. Hence, by individual rationality, it is common knowledge that $E^*_{t-1} p_t(\omega) \in |\alpha| S(\bar{a})$ for all ω. If $|\alpha| < 1$, then this reinforces and tightens the common knowledge. Iterating this argument, it follows that $E^*_{t-1} p_t(\omega) \in |\alpha|^N S(\bar{a})$ for all $N = 0, 1, 2, \ldots$, and hence, the rational expectations equilibrium $E p_t = \bar{a}$ is itself common knowledge. Guesnerie calls such a rational expectations equilibrium "strongly rational." We also use the equivalent terminology that the rational expectations equilibrium is "eductively stable" or "stable under eductive learning." We thus have the result: if $|\alpha| < 1$, then the rational expectations equilibrium is stable under eductive learning; if $|\alpha| > 1$, then the rational expectations equilibrium is not eductively stable.

Note two crucial differences from the least-squares adaptive learning results. First, the learning here takes place in mental time, not real time. Given the common knowledge assumptions and full power of reasoning ability, if $|\alpha| < 1$, then rational agents would coordinate instantaneously, through a process of reasoning, on the rational expectations equilibrium. For the Lucas supply model this condition is always satisfied, and for the cobweb model, with $\alpha < 0$, satisfaction of the stability condition depends on the relative slopes of the supply and demand curves and is satisfied when $\alpha > -1$. Second, when $\alpha < -1$ the rational expectations equilibrium is not eductively stable, but it is asymptotically stable under adaptive learning.

The finding that eductive stability can be more demanding than stability under adaptive learning appears to be general. In simple models the eductive stability condition reduces to iterative E-stability, that is, stability of the rational expectations equilibrium under iterations of the T-map, which itself is more demanding than E-stability. With structural heterogeneity and in dynamic models, the eductive stability conditions are even tighter (e.g., see Evans and Guesnerie 2003). A particularly striking example of this is the generic failure of strong eductive stability in infinite-horizon real business cycle models, established in Evans et al. (2010).

2.4.2.2 Partial Structural Knowledge

In practical policy situations a question that often arises concerns the impact of anticipated future changes in policy. For instance, it is well recognized that there are long lags involved in changing fiscal policy. The process of changing taxes involves legislative lags between when the new tax is proposed and when it is passed, and implementation lags between when the legislation is signed into law and when it actually takes effect. The bulk of the literature on adaptive learning has focused on situations where the environment is stationary, so that in particular the policy used by the authorities never changes. Some papers have studied the effect of policy changes, but under the assumption that the policy change is completely unanticipated and agents begin to learn the new equilibrium as data arrive after the policy change. Such changes are examined in Evans et al. (2001), Marcet and Nicolini (2003), and Giannitsarou (2006). However, the anticipation of policy changes is likely to influence economic decisions even before the actual implementation of the proposed policy change.[14]

Evans et al. (2009) propose a learning model in which agents combine limited structural knowledge about the economy with adaptive learning for other variables that they need to forecast. Under this approach agents use statistical knowledge to forecast many economic variables (e.g., GDP growth and inflation) while incorporating structural knowledge about specific variables (e.g., announced future changes in government spending or taxes).[15] In this setting, anticipated policy changes lead to immediate changes in the behavior of agents who are learning adaptively, even before the implementation of the proposed policy. Evans et al. (2009) show that the dynamic paths resulting from this framework can differ significantly from the corresponding rational expectations path. The assumption that private agents know the monetary policy rule in models by Eusepi and Preston (2010) and Evans and Honkapohja (2010) are two other examples in which agents have partial structural knowledge but need to learn about other aspects of the economy.

2.4.2.3 Application: Ricardian Equivalence When Expectations Are Not Rational

One of the most prominent theories in macroeconomics is the Ricardian Equivalence proposition that if taxes are nondistortionary, then the mix of tax and debt financing of government purchases has no impact on the equi-

---

14. One of the contributions of the rational expectations revolution was the idea that agents look forward and can anticipate the effects of an announced future shift in policy. Early examples are Sargent and Wallace (1973a,b). The rational expectations analysis of anticipated impacts is nowadays standard in textbooks.

15. An alternative, and potentially complementary, approach is the "active cognition" framework of Evans and Ramey (1992, 1998), in which agents employ a calculation algorithm based on a structural model but are impeded by calculation costs.

librium sequence of key real variables. Conditions for validity or failure of the Ricardian proposition have been examined in the voluminous theoretical and empirical literature (e.g., see the survey papers by Bernheim 1987; Barro 1989; Seater 1993; Ricciuti 2003).

A key assumption that has not been examined in this literature is the role of rational expectations. If expectations are made using adaptive (or statistical) learning rules, can Ricardian Equivalence still hold? Recently, Evans et al. (2012a) have argued that Ricardian Equivalence holds under the usual conditions when agents are dynamic optimizers but with nonrational forecasts. Two key assumption are that agents understand the government's budget constraint and that expectations are based on a suitable information set.

The main results of Evans et al. (2012a) are obtained in the context of a standard Ramsey model with government bonds and lump-sum taxes. Ricardian Equivalence is often analyzed using this framework. The model is assumed to be nonstochastic and is populated with a large number of identical households (but individual households do not know that they are identical). Taxes are assumed to be lump sum. At each time t the household maximizes its utility subject to a flow budget constraint and to no-Ponzi-game and transversality conditions. The model implies a consumption function for households, which depends on current asset values and present values of labor incomes and taxes.[16]

The model also has a standard production function with labor and capital as inputs. The government's flow budget constraint states that end-of-period debt equals current gross interest payments on beginning-of-period debt plus the difference between government spending and tax receipts. The model also includes a standard market clearing equation.

Given predetermined variables, current fiscal policy variables, and expectations, a temporary equilibrium at time t is defined by the consumption function, the wage rate, the interest rate, the government flow budget constraint, and market clearing. Two key assumptions concerning households' perceptions of the government budget constraint are: (1) households understand the flow budget constraint of the government, and (2) they believe that the expected limiting present value of government debt is zero.

These assumptions imply that the consumption function can be written as a function of the sum of current (gross) income from capital and the present values of wages and government spending. It follows that Ricardian Equivalence holds in the temporary equilibria under the additional assumption that neither government spending nor expectations depend on current government financing variables.

---

16. The present values are calculated using expected interest rates. All relevant expected present value sums are assumed to be finite.

The evolution of the economy over time is described as a sequence of temporary equilibria with learning. The economy starts with some initial capital stock, public debt, and beliefs about the future path of the economy and evolves along a path of temporary equilibria, given fiscal policy rules that determine government spending and taxes as well as debt dynamics. To close the dynamic model, a learning mechanism and its information set must be specified. The former is a mapping from the time t information set to the sequence of expectations over the infinite future, together with an initial set of expectations. The latter is assumed to consist of observable variables and past expectations. The key result of Evans et al. (2012a) is as follows.

Proposition 1   *Assume that neither government spending nor expectations depend on current government financing variables (taxes and end-of-period debt). The Ramsey model exhibits Ricardian Equivalence; that is, for all initial conditions, the sequence of consumption, capital, rates of return, and wages along the path of equilibria with learning is independent of the government financing policy.*

For the result, it is crucial that the expectations of agents do not depend on government financing variables in addition to the usual assumptions about government spending and taxes. Evans et al. (2012a) give simple examples illustrating the role played by the assumption about expectations when agents are learning.

2.5   Learning and Monetary Policy

In the analysis of economic policy the Rational Expectations Hypothesis should not be taken for granted, because expectations can be out of equilibrium at least for a period of time. Economic policies should in part be designed to avoid instabilities that can arise from expectational errors and the corrective behavior of economic agents in the face of such errors. We now consider aspects of these concerns for analysis of monetary policy in the widely used New Keynesian framework.[17]

We first look at the implications of requiring stability under learning for the choice of the optimal interest rate rule in the linearized New Keynesian model. We also consider price-level targeting from the learning viewpoint by deriving the optimal learnable policy rule. Second, we consider the performance of a Wicksellian price-level targeting rule in a global setting in which the zero lower bound can impose a constraint on setting the interest rate.

---

17. For surveys of the growing literature on learning and monetary policy, see Evans and Honkapohja (2003a, 2009a) and Bullard (2006).

2.5.1 Learning and the Choice of the Interest Rate Rule

2.5.1.1 The Basic Model

We use a linearized New Keynesian model that is very commonly employed in the literature. See Clarida et al. (1999) for this particular formulation and references to the literature. The original nonlinear framework is based on a representative consumer, a continuum of firms producing differentiated goods under monopolistic competition, and price stickiness.

The behavior of the private sector is described by two equations:

$$x_t = -\varphi(i_t - E_t^*\pi_{t+1}) + E_t^*x_{t+1} + g_t \tag{10}$$

which is the "IS" curve derived from the Euler equation for consumer optimization, and

$$\pi_t = \lambda x_t + \beta E_t^*\pi_{t+1} + u_t \tag{11}$$

which is the price-setting rule for the monopolistically competitive firms. Here x_t and π_t denote the output gap and inflation for period t, respectively; i_t is the nominal interest rate;[18] and $E_t^*x_{t+1}$ and $E_t^*\pi_{t+1}$ denote the private sector expectations, respectively, of the output gap and inflation for the next period. These expectations need not be rational (E_t without $*$ denotes rational expectations). The parameters φ and λ are positive, and β is the discount factor, so that $0 < \beta < 1$.

The shocks g_t and u_t are assumed to be observable and to follow

$$\begin{pmatrix} g_t \\ u_t \end{pmatrix} = F \begin{pmatrix} g_{t-1} \\ u_{t-1} \end{pmatrix} + \begin{pmatrix} \tilde{g}_t \\ \tilde{u}_t \end{pmatrix} \quad \text{where } F = \begin{pmatrix} \mu & 0 \\ 0 & \rho \end{pmatrix} \tag{12}$$

$0 < |\mu| < 1$, $0 < |\rho| < 1$, and $\tilde{g}_t \sim iid(0, \sigma_g^2)$, $\tilde{u}_t \sim iid(0, \sigma_u^2)$ are independent white noise. The u_t shock is important for the policy issues, because the g_t shock can be fully offset by appropriate setting of the interest rate. For simplicity, μ and ρ are assumed to be known (if not, they could be estimated).

One part of the literature focuses on simple policy rules. Under Euler-equation learning, $E_t^*\pi_{t+1}$ and $E_t^*x_{t+1}$ represent private sector forecasts, which need not be rational, and (10) and (11) are interpreted as behavioral equations resulting from Euler-equation-based decision rules. This setup has been studied by Bullard and Mitra (2002) and Evans and Honkapohja (2003b) for learning stability of the rational expectations equilibrium under alternative interest rate rules.

Bullard and Mitra (2002) examine stability under learning of the targeted rational expectations equilibrium when policymakers follow simple Taylor

---

18. Variables are expressed as deviations from their nonstochastic steady state values.

rules of various forms, including

$$i_t = k + \chi_\pi \pi_t + \chi_x x_t \tag{13}$$

$$i_t = k + \chi_\pi E^*_{t-1} \pi_t + \chi_x E^*_{t-1} x_t \quad \text{or} \tag{14}$$

$$i_t = k + \chi_\pi E^*_t \pi_{t+1} + \chi_x E^*_t x_{t+1} \tag{15}$$

where χ_π, $\chi_x \geq 0$ are policy parameters, and the constant k reflects the steady state real interest rate and the target inflation rate. Bullard and Mitra (2002) show that under (13) and (14) the targeted rational expectations equilibrium is stable under learning if and only if

$$\lambda(\chi_\pi - 1) + (1 - \beta)\chi_x > 0 \tag{16}$$

a condition that holds if the Taylor principle $\chi_\pi > 1$ is satisfied. Under the forward-looking rule (15) this condition is still necessary, but there are additional stability conditions that require that χ_x and χ_π not be too large.[19]

Next, assume rational expectations for the moment and consider optimal policy obtained from minimizing a quadratic loss function

$$E_t \sum_{s=0}^{\infty} \beta^s \left(\pi^2_{t+s} + \alpha x^2_{t+s} \right) \tag{17}$$

This type of optimal policy is often called "flexible inflation targeting" (e.g., see Svensson 1999, 2003). The parameter α is the relative weight on the output target and pure inflation targeting would be the case $\alpha = 0$. The target for output is set at its efficient level. Without loss of generality for our purposes, the inflation target is set at zero. We treat the policymaker's preferences as exogenously given.[20]

The full intertemporal optimum under rational expectations, usually called the "commitment solution," is obtained by maximizing (17) subject to (11) for all periods $t, t+1, t+2, \ldots$. This solution leads to time inconsistency, and Woodford (1999a,b) has suggested that monetary policy ought to be based on the *timeless perspective*. We refer to this as the "commitment solution" with the *commitment optimality condition*

$$\lambda \pi_t = -\alpha(x_t - x_{t-1}) \tag{18}$$

Assuming that agents are learning, Evans and Honkapohja (2003b, 2006) consider optimal policy. For the commitment case Evans and Honkapohja

---

19. Additional considerations arise when there are heterogeneous expectations. See, for example, Honkapohja and Mitra (2005), Branch and McGough (2010), and Kurz (2011).

20. It is well known that the quadratic loss function (17) can be viewed as an approximation of the utility function of the representative consumer (see Rotemberg and Woodford 1999).

(2006) show that an expectations-based rule of the form

$$i_t = k + \delta_L x_{t-1} + \delta_\pi E_t^* \pi_{t+1} + \delta_x E_t^* x_{t+1} + \delta_g g_t + \delta_u u_t \qquad (19)$$

with coefficients δ_L, δ_π, δ_x, δ_g, and δ_u, chosen based on the structural parameters and the policymaker loss function, can implement optimal policy (i.e., deliver an optimal rational expectations equilibrium that is stable under learning).

2.5.1.2 Policy and Infinite-Horizon Learning

The infinite-horizon learning approach to monetary policy has been analyzed by Preston (2005, 2006). When Euler-equation learning is replaced by infinite-horizon learning, the model becomes

$$x_t = E_t^* \sum_{T=t}^{\infty} \beta^{T-t}[(1-\beta)x_{T+1} - \varphi(i_T - \pi_{T+1}) + g_T] \qquad (20)$$

$$\pi_t = \lambda x_t + E_t^* \sum_{T=t}^{\infty} (\varpi\beta)^{T-t} [\lambda\varpi\beta x_{T+1} + (1-\varpi)\beta\pi_{T+1} + u_T] \quad (21)$$

where ϖ is the Calvo stickiness parameter. Under this approach the agents make fully optimal decisions, given their forecasts over the infinite future.

Both Euler-equation and infinite-horizon approaches are valid models of bounded rationality. The Euler-equation approach, which looks forward only one period, is clearly boundedly optimal in decisions and also boundedly rational in terms of forecasts because it does not explicitly incorporate long-term forecasts. In contrast, in the infinite-horizon approach agents' decisions depend on long-horizon forecasts, which will likely be modified by substantial amounts over time. As noted in Section 2.4.1, both types of learning can converge to the rational expectations equilibrium.

How does infinite-horizon learning affect the rational expectations equilibrium stability results for alternative interest rate rules? Under infinite-horizon learning and the Taylor rule, condition (16) remains necessary but is no longer sufficient for E-stability. Furthermore, Preston (2006) argues that as $\beta \to 1$, E-stability cannot hold under (14) and that it may not hold in calibrated models. The primary reason is that with long horizons, agents must forecast future interest rates as well as future inflation and the output gap. Indeed, if the private agents know the policy rule (14) and impose this relationship in their forecasts, then (16) is again necessary and sufficient for stability. As Preston points out, these results can be interpreted as an argument for central bank communication.

A related point arises in connection with optimal policy. Evans and Honkapohja (2003b, 2006) advocated expectations-based rules with coefficients chosen to implement the first-order conditions for optimal policy. To implement this in the model (10) and (11), they recommended an interest rate obtained by solving (10), (11), and (18) simultaneously to eliminate π_t and x_t and obtain i_t in terms of expectations and fundamental shocks. This yields the rule (19), where $\delta_L = \frac{-\alpha}{\varphi(\alpha+\lambda^2)}$, $\delta_\pi = 1 + \frac{\lambda\beta}{\varphi(\alpha+\lambda^2)}$, $\delta_x = \delta_g = \varphi^{-1}$, and $\delta_u = \frac{\lambda}{\varphi(\alpha+\lambda^2)}$. Evans and Honkapohja (2006) showed that this interest rate rule guarantees determinacy and stability under learning.

If instead agents use long-horizon forecasts, then (19) can lead to instability under learning. In this case the expectations-based approach advocated by Evans and Honkapohja (2003b, 2006) would have to be modified to use the behavioral equations (20) and (21). This is possible if observations of long-horizon expectations are available for the output gap, inflation, and interest rates:

$$E S_t^* z = E_t^* \sum_{T=t}^{\infty} \beta^{T-t} z_{T+1}, \quad \text{for } z = x, \pi, i$$

$$E \tilde{S}_t^* z = E_t^* \sum_{T=t}^{\infty} (\varpi\beta)^{T-t} z_{T+1}, \quad \text{for } z = x, \pi$$

The long-horizon version of the Evans-Honkapohja expectations-based rule would then solve i_t from long-horizon IS and Phillips curves and the optimality condition (18). This procedure yields a rule of the form

$$i_t = \psi_L x_{t-1} + \psi_\pi E S_t^* \pi + \psi_x E S_t^* x + \psi_i E S_t^* i + \tilde{\psi}_\pi E \tilde{S}_t^* \pi$$
$$+ \tilde{\psi}_x E \tilde{S}_t^* x + \psi_g g_t + \psi_u u_t$$

where the coefficients are straightforward to compute. This rule would yield an optimal rational expectations equilibrium that is both determinate and stable with infinite-horizon learning.

As is clear from these results, the evolution of the economy under learning depends in part on the planning horizon of the agents. The interest rate rule used to implement optimal policy must therefore reflect the planning horizon as well as the rest of the economic structure.

2.5.2 Application: Price-Level Targeting and Optimal Policy

The research on learning and monetary policy has so far mostly considered the performance of interest rate rules that implement inflation targeting under either discretion (when commitment to a rule is not feasible) or commitment. There has been only limited research on the performance of price-level targeting from the viewpoint of learning stability and equilibrium determinacy.[21]

The commitment optimality condition (18) can also be written in terms of the logarithm of the price level p_t as $\lambda(p_t - p_{t-1}) = -\alpha(x_t - x_{t-1})$. This expression will be satisfied if

---

21. Evans and Honkapohja (2006), Gaspar et al. (2007), and Preston (2008) consider aspects of price-level targeting under learning.

$$x_t = -\frac{\lambda}{\alpha} p_t + k \tag{22}$$

for any constant k. Under price-level targeting the model with Euler-equation learning is given by (10), (11), and (22), where we also specify that $\pi_t = p_t - p_{t-1}$.

We next compute the rational expectations equilibrium of interest using (11) and (22). Using the method of undetermined coefficients, the optimal rational expectations equilibrium can be expressed in the form

$$x_t = \bar{b}_p p_{t-1} + \bar{c}_x u_t + \bar{a}_x \tag{23}$$

$$p_t = \bar{b}_x p_{t-1} + \bar{c}_p u_t + \bar{a}_p \tag{24}$$

Here $\bar{b}_x = (2\beta)^{-1}[\gamma - (\gamma^2 - 4\beta)^{1/2}]$ is the root inside the unit circle of the quadratic equation $\beta b_x^2 - \gamma b_x + 1 = 0$, where $\gamma = 1 + \beta + \lambda^2/\alpha$, and $\bar{b}_p = -\frac{\lambda}{\alpha} \bar{b}_x$, and the other unknown coefficients depend on the model parameters and the value of k.[22]

2.5.2.1 A Fundamentals-Based Reaction Function

It is important to notice that the representation (23) and (24) of the optimal equilibrium does not indicate the form of the policy reaction function. Standard practice for rational expectations analysis is to calculate $E_t p_{t+1}$ and $E_t x_{t+1}$ and to insert these and the rational expectations equilibrium p_t equation into the IS curve (10). This leads to the interest rate reaction function

$$i_t = \eta_p p_{t-1} + \varphi^{-1} g_t + \eta_u u_t + \eta_0 \tag{25}$$

where $\eta_p = \bar{b}_x(1 - \bar{b}_x)(\frac{\lambda}{\alpha\varphi} - 1)$, $\eta_u = (1 - \bar{b}_x)(\frac{\lambda}{\alpha\varphi} - 1)\bar{c}_p$, and $\eta_0 = (\frac{\lambda}{\alpha\varphi} - 1)\bar{b}_x \bar{a}_p$. Equation (25) can be called a "fundamentals-based reaction function," as it indicates how to set optimally the policy instrument given the predetermined and exogenous variables p_{t-1}, g_t, and u_t.

We now examine the stability of both the fundamentals-based and an expectations-based interest rate rule under learning.[23] Substituting (25) into (10), the reduced form of the model can be written in the general form

$$y_t = A + M E_t^* y_{t+1} + Q E_t^* y_t + N y_{t-1} + P v_t \tag{26}$$

---

22. The precise expressions for other coefficients are not needed in the analysis below.

23. As noted above, we are here assuming short decision horizons based on the agents' Euler equations. Preston (2008) works out the analogous learning results for the model of price-level targeting with infinite-horizon decision rules.

where $y_t = (x_t, p_t)'$ and the coefficients are given in Appendix A. The analysis of learning stability for models of the general form (26) is developed in Appendix A.

For the fundamentals-based interest rate rule we have the following result.

Proposition 2 *Implementing price-level targeting using the fundamentals-based reaction function (25) does not guarantee local convergence of least-squares learning to the optimal rational expectations equilibrium. In particular, instability occurs if $\varphi > \frac{\lambda}{\alpha}$.*

It can be noted that, somewhat paradoxically, nearly strict inflation targeting (meaning that $\alpha \approx 0$) is very likely to lead to expectational instability.

2.5.2.2 An Expectations-Based Reaction Function

The above computation deriving the fundamentals-based reaction function (25) relied heavily on the assumption that the economy is in the optimal rational expectations equilibrium. We now obtain the expectations-based reaction function under price-level targeting optimal policy. The policy rule is obtained by combining the optimality condition, the price-setting equation, and the IS curve, for given private expectations.

Formally, we combine (10), (11), the optimality condition (22), and the definition of inflation in terms of current and past price levels, $\pi_t = p_t - p_{t-1}$, treating private expectations as given.[24] Solving for i_t, the expectations-based reaction function for price-level targeting is

$$i_t = \delta_L p_{t-1} + \delta_\pi E_t^* \pi_{t+1} + \delta_x E_t^* x_{t+1} + \delta_g g_t + \delta_u u_t \tag{27}$$

where $\delta_L = \frac{\lambda}{\varphi(\alpha+\lambda^2)}$, $\delta_\pi = 1 + \frac{\lambda\beta}{\varphi(\alpha+\lambda^2)}$, $\delta_x = \varphi^{-1}$, $\delta_g = \varphi^{-1}$, and $\delta_u = \frac{\lambda}{\varphi(\alpha+\lambda^2)}$.

Looking at the rule (27) it can be seen that its coefficients stipulate a relatively large response to expected inflation ($\delta_\pi > 1$) and that effects coming from the expected output gap and the aggregate demand shock are fully neutralized ($\delta_x = \delta_g = \varphi^{-1}$). The next proposition shows that our interest rate rule (27) performs well.

Proposition 3 *Implementing price-level targeting using the expectations-based reaction function (27), the optimal rational expectations equilibrium is stable under least-squares learning for all structural parameter values.*

Proposition 3 thus provides a remarkably strong result: Under the interest rate setting rule (27), learning is stable, and the economy is guided specifically to the optimal rational expectations equilibrium, and this result holds

---

24. Without loss of generality we set $k = 0$ in the formal analysis.

for all possible values of the structural parameters. Partial intuition for this result comes from the following (see also the reduced form (42) in Appendix A). An increase in inflation expectations now leads to an increase in actual inflation that is smaller than the change in expectations. This dampened effect arises from the interest rate reaction to changes in $E_t^* \pi_{t+1}$ and is a crucial element of the stability result.

2.5.3 Price-Level Targeting and the Zero Lower Bound

Discussions about the risk of deflation continue to be topical as the Western world is attempting to recover from its current financial crisis. For example, see Bullard (2010). The experiences of 2008 and 2009 in several countries, as well as the experience of Japan since the 1990s, have created a situation in which the monetary policy response is constrained by the zero lower bound on nominal interest rates, a phenomenon sometimes called a "liquidity trap." Furthermore, in a liquidity trap there is the potential for the economy to get stuck in a deflationary situation with declining or persistently low levels of output.

The possibility of the economy becoming trapped in a deflationary state, and the macroeconomic policies that might be able to avoid or extricate the economy from a liquidity trap, have been examined predominantly from the rational expectations perspective. Benhabib et al. (2001) and Eggertsson and Woodford (2003) show that besides the usual targeted steady state, there exists another steady state involving deflation. Eggertsson and Woodford (2003) argue that if the economy encounters a liquidity trap, monetary policy should commit to being expansionary for a considerable period of time, by keeping interest rates near zero even after the economy has emerged from deflation. Price-level targeting is, moreover, shown to be a nearly optimal policy response to the zero lower bound.[25]

In our opinion, the rational expectations assumption is particularly questionable in an episode of deflation, which is far away from the inflation target and the normal state of the economy, and presents a new environment for economic agents. Our own view, reflected in Evans and Honkapohja (2005, 2010) and Evans et al. (2008), is that the evolution of expectations plays a key role in the dynamics of the economy and that the tools from learning theory are needed for a realistic analysis of the zero lower bound issues.[26]

---

25. Eggertsson and Woodford (2003) show that under rational expectations optimal policy can be implemented using a modified form of price-level targeting.

26. Evans and Honkapohja (2005) and Evans et al. (2008) formulate short-horizon learning using Euler equations, whereas Evans and Honkapohja (2010) postulates that agents use infinite-horizon decision rules. A related paper is Reifschneider and Williams (2000), which uses a fully backward-looking model.

These papers argue that when monetary policy is conducted using a Taylor rule with an inflation target, the usual targeted steady state is locally but not globally stable for least-squares and related learning processes. Moreover, deflation arises as a possible outcome when the economy is subject to large shocks. The workability of price-level targeting has, however, not been examined from the learning viewpoint, and as an application we take up this issue here.

Consider the following standard price-level targeting rule. It is like a Taylor rule, but instead of the inflation rate, the interest rate reacts to deviations from the trend price-level target. These rules are sometimes called "Wicksellian rules." The rule also takes into account the zero lower bound on interest rates in a piecewise-linear way.

The gross interest rate R_t follows the equation

$$R_t = 1 + \max[\bar{R} - 1 + \psi(p_t - \bar{p}_t), 0]$$

where trend inflation is modeled by $\bar{p}_t/\bar{p}_{t-1} = \pi^*$, and π^* is the inflation target. A steady state that satisfies $p_t = \bar{p}_t$ for all t implies $R_t = \bar{R}$. If $\bar{R}$ is set at the value $\bar{R} = \beta^{-1}\pi^*$, then the steady state also satisfies the Fisher equation, and the usual targeted steady state obtains under price-level targeting.

However, there is also a second steady state in which the zero lower bound on interest rates is binding. If $p_t - \bar{p}_t \leq 0$ and $R_t = 1$, we can set

$$\pi_t = p_t/p_{t-1} = \beta$$

and obtain a second deflationary steady state due to a binding zero lower bound as the Fisher equation is also satisfied. It follows that, by itself, price-level targeting does not rule out a deflationary outcome.

Our objective is to consider the two steady states from the learning viewpoint. We employ a standard New Keynesian model with quadratic costs of price adjustment. For simplicity, we directly employ the model of Evans et al. (2008), in which agents have short decision horizons with decisions given by the Euler equations for consumption and price-setting decisions. The system is

$$\beta\frac{\alpha\gamma}{\nu}\left(\pi_{t+1}^e - 1\right)\pi_{t+1}^e = -(c_t + g)^{(1+\varepsilon)/\alpha} + \frac{\alpha\gamma}{\nu}\left(\pi_t - 1\right)\pi_t \qquad (28)$$

$$+ \alpha\left(1 - \frac{1}{\nu}\right)(c_t + g)c_t^{-\sigma_1}$$

$$c_t = c_{t+1}^e(\pi_{t+1}^e/\beta R_t)^{\sigma_1} \qquad (29)$$

$$R_t = 1 + \max[\beta^{-1}\pi^* - 1 + \psi(p_t - \bar{p}), 0] \qquad (30)$$

$$p_t = p_{t-1}\pi_t, \quad \bar{p}_t = \bar{p}_{t-1}\pi^* \qquad (31)$$

where the first equation is the nonlinear Phillips curve in implicit form, and γ indexes the degree of price stickiness. The second equation is the consumption Euler equation, while the third equation is the interest rate rule. The last two equations define the actual and target price levels. One also adds the adjustment of expectations, which are

$$\pi^e_{t+1} = \pi^e_t + \phi(\pi_{t-1} - \pi^e_t)$$

$$c^e_{t+1} = c^e_t + \phi(c_{t-1} - c^e_t)$$

assuming constant-gain steady state learning; ϕ is the gain parameter.

To simplify the analysis, assume that $\pi^* = 1$, so that $\bar{p}_t = \bar{p}$ for all t. Then the two steady states are the targeted steady state with a constant price level and the deflationary steady state $\pi_t = \beta$. We are interested in the possibility of local convergence of learning to each of the two steady states.

Consider the system near the targeted steady state $(c_t, \pi_t, p_t) = (c_H, 1, \bar{p})$. Here c_H is the steady state level of consumption that corresponds to $\pi^* = 1$. The analysis can be done using the nonlinear system (28)–(31) with point expectations.[27] Substituting the interest rate rule into the consumption function yields an implicit system of three equations for the temporary equilibrium. Write this symbolically as

$$\mathcal{F}(y_t, y^e_{t+1}, y_{t-1}) = 0$$

using vector notation $y_t = (c_t, \pi_t, p_t)'$. Linearizing around the targeted steady state yields

$$y_t = (-D\mathcal{F}_y)^{-1}(D\mathcal{F}_{y^e} y^e_{t+1} + D\mathcal{F}_{y_{t-1}} y_{t-1}) \tag{32}$$

$$\equiv M y^e_{t+1} + N y_{t-1} \tag{33}$$

where we have omitted constants and now interpret y_t as the deviation from its steady state value. For the formal results we assume that price stickiness $\gamma > 0$ is sufficiently small. Appendix B works out the analytical details and shows the following sufficient condition for E-stability.

Proposition 4 *An active price-level targeting rule with $\psi > \beta^{-1}$ implies E-stability of the targeted steady state.*

For the deflationary steady state $(c_t, \pi_t, p_t) = (c_L, \beta, p_0\beta^t)$, where c_L is the steady state level of consumption corresponding to deflation rate β, the system consists of two key equations: (28) and

$$c_t = c^e_{t+1}(\pi^e_{t+1}/\beta)^{\sigma_1}$$

27. Shocks have been dropped for brevity.

because $R_t = 1$ near the deflationary steady state, and p_t does not influence the dynamics of c_t and π_t. The system for $y_t' = (c_t, \pi_t)$ is purely forward looking, so that the linearized system (32)–(33) has the form

$$y_t = (-D\mathcal{F}_y)^{-1}(D\mathcal{F}_{y^e})y_{t+1}^e = My_{t+1}^e$$

and the perceived law of motion is just the intercept term. E-stability requires that the matrix $M - I$ be stable. Appendix B shows that we have the following result (specified there more precisely).

Proposition 5 *The deflationary steady state is usually not E-stable under price-level targeting.*

Moreover, because the interest rate is constant at $R = 1$ near the deflationary steady state, the model is locally approximately the same as in Evans et al. (2008). It follows that the deflationary steady state is a saddle point in (π^e, c^e) space, implying that there exists a deflationary trap for the economy, in which there is worsening deflation and falling output over time.

2.6 Conclusion

This chapter has addressed the question of whether there exist rational foundations for macroeconomics and finance models by focusing on the issue of how expectations are formed. This is a natural focus because of the centrality of rational expectations in modern macroeconomics, following the pioneering work of Muth (1961), Lucas (1972), and Sargent (1973). Expectations of future economic conditions are clearly a major determinant of current economic developments, and it can be argued that the role of expectations is the most fundamental way in which economics differs from the natural sciences.

How should we model how expectations are formed by households, firms, traders, and policymakers? The Rational Expectations Hypothesis has a natural appeal to economists, because it appears that optimizing agents would necessarily employ rational expectations—not to use rational expectations means that agents would be making systematic forecast errors, which must surely be to their disadvantage. For this reason rational expectations is necessarily the benchmark in macroeconomics.

But how can agents arrive at rational expectations? In the self-referential world of macroeconomics and finance, it is in fact rational to have rational expectations only if *other* agents have rational expectations. Rational expectations thus turns out to be an equilibrium concept. Once this is recognized, one is driven to consider the issue of stability: Can agents plausibly coordinate on rational expectations? If this is possible, then it involves a process of learning in which agents with limited and imperfect knowledge come to hold rational expectations.

At this point we invoke the cognitive consistency principle that the agents in the economy should be assumed to be about as smart as are we, the economists studying the economy. This principle provides strong guidance but leads to several paths. For example, should we model agents like economic theorists, who think strategically about the actions of other agents in the context of a known structure? Or is it more plausible to model agents as applied econometricians trying to determine the appropriate specification of a forecasting model in a world of structural change? There appear to be diverse ways to model human—bounded—rationality, and the appropriate choice presumably depends on the problem at hand. The range of plausible implementations can be regarded as a virtue, allowing for fruitful adaptation to a range of problems.

In this chapter we have emphasized adaptive learning approaches, in which agents revise their forecasting model, or their choice of models, over time as new data become available. This approach has been fruitful in providing new approaches for explaining a range of phenomena, including the rise and fall of inflation, business cycle fluctuations, recurrent hyper-inflation episodes, and asset-price volatility and bubbles, and for studying the appropriate way to design monetary and fiscal policies. Our presentation has been selective, and several important topics have been omitted. These include endogenous fluctuations and sunspot equilibria, analytical techniques, alternative learning algorithms, and escape dynamics. See Evans and Honkapohja (2009b) for a review of these topics.

To concretely illustrate the adaptive learning approach to expectation formation, we have focused on applications to monetary policy in New Keynesian models. The first application, in Section 2.5.1, to the choice of Taylor-type rules, stresses the potential importance, in models with private agent learning, of using monetary policies that do not simply react to the fundamental exogenous shocks but also explicitly react to private sector expectations. At the same time we find that it is important, when formulating the specific interest rate rule, for policymakers to understand the planning horizon used by private agents in making their decisions. In Section 2.5.2 we extend this analysis to interest rate rules aiming to implement optimal policy using a form of price-level targeting. We again find that to ensure stability of the equilibrium under learning, it is desirable to condition policy on private sector expectations.

Finally, in Section 2.5.3, we reexamine the zero lower bound constraint on interest rates. In previous work we have shown the possibility of a deflation-trap region that can lead to unstable trajectories if the economy is subject to a large negative expectation shock. Extending this earlier work, we consider whether a price-level targeting rule is sufficient to avoid this outcome. Our conclusion is that it is not, and in some cases fiscal policy is needed to return the economy to the targeted steady state. Further issues in monetary policy and learning are reviewed in Evans and Honkapohja (2009a).

We think these applications illustrate the potential for adaptive learning approaches to provide a rational foundation for modeling expectations in macroeconomics and finance.

Appendix 2.A   E-Stability Conditions in Multivariate Linear Models

Here we explain the main formal ideas for learning in the context of the general model (26). At each period t private agents have a perceived law of motion that they use to make forecasts about the future. The perceived law of motion takes the form

$$y_t = a_t + b_t y_{t-1} + c_t v_t \tag{34}$$

where we are using the vector notation $y_t' = (x_t, p_t)$ and $v_t' = (g_t, u_t)$. For the reduced form (26) the optimal rational expectations equilibrium can be written as

$$y_t = \bar{a} + \bar{b} y_{t-1} + \bar{c} v_t$$

where

$$\bar{a} = \begin{pmatrix} \bar{a}_x \\ \bar{a}_p \end{pmatrix}, \bar{b} = \begin{pmatrix} 0 & \bar{b}_x \\ 0 & \bar{b}_p \end{pmatrix} \quad \text{and} \quad \bar{c} = \begin{pmatrix} 0 & \bar{c}_x \\ 0 & \bar{c}_p \end{pmatrix}$$

Given the perceived law of motion and the current value of v_t, the forecast functions of the private agents are $E_t^* y_{t+1} = a_t + b_t E_t^* y_t + c_t E_t^* v_{t+1}$, or

$$E_t^* y_{t+1} = a_t + b_t(a_t + b_t y_{t-1} + c_t v_t) + c_t F v_t \tag{35}$$

where (a_t, b_t, c_t) are the parameter values of the forecast functions that agents have estimated on the basis of past data up to and including period $t - 1$. It is assumed that current exogenous variables, and lagged (but not current) endogenous variables, are in the information set when forecasts are made.

These forecasts are used in decisions for period t, which yields the actual law of motion for $y_t = (x_t, p_t)'$. The actual law of motion provides a new data point, and agents are then assumed to re-estimate by least squares the parameters (a_t, b_t, c_t) with data through period t and to use the updated forecast functions for period $t + 1$ decisions. Together with v_{t+1} these in turn yield the temporary equilibrium for period $t + 1$, and the learning dynamics continues with the same steps in subsequent periods. The rational expectations equilibrium $(\bar{a}, \bar{b}, \bar{c})$ is said to be *stable under least-squares learning* if the sequence (a_t, b_t, c_t) converges to $(0, \bar{b}, \bar{c})$ over time.

Convergence conditions for least-squares learning can be obtained from E-stability conditions. For any model of the form (26), E-stability conditions are obtained as follows. Consider a perceived law of motion of the form

$$y_t = a + b y_{t-1} + c v_t \qquad (36)$$

Computing expectations and inserting into (26) yields the actual law of motion

$$y_t = A + (Q + M(I + b))a + (Mb^2 + Qb + N)y_{t-1}$$
$$+ (Qc + M(bc + cF) + P)v_t \qquad (37)$$

Here I is the identity matrix. This equation defines the mapping of parameters from the perceived law of motion to the actual law of motion:

$$T(a, b, c) = (A + (Q + M(I + b))a, Mb^2 + Qb + N, Qc + M(bc + cF) + P)$$

A rational expectations equilibrium $(\bar{a}, \bar{b}, \bar{c})$ is a fixed point of this map. Next, compute the derivative matrices

$$DT_a = Q + M(I + \bar{b}) \qquad (38)$$

$$DT_b = \bar{b}' \otimes M + I \otimes M\bar{b} + I \otimes Q \qquad (39)$$

$$DT_c = F' \otimes M + I \otimes M\bar{b} + I \otimes Q \qquad (40)$$

where $\otimes$ denotes the Kronecker product, and $\bar{b}$ denotes the rational expectations equilibrium value of b. The necessary and sufficient condition for E-stability is that all eigenvalues of $DT_a - I$, $DT_b - I$, and $DT_c - I$ have negative real parts.[28]

Proof of Proposition 2   The coefficients of (26) are

$$A = \begin{pmatrix} -\varphi\eta_0 \\ -\lambda\varphi\eta_0 \end{pmatrix}, \quad M = \begin{pmatrix} 1 & \varphi \\ \lambda & \beta + \lambda\varphi \end{pmatrix}, \quad Q = \begin{pmatrix} 0 & -\varphi \\ 0 & -\beta - \lambda\varphi \end{pmatrix}, \quad (41)$$
$$N = \begin{pmatrix} 0 & -\varphi\eta_p \\ 0 & 1 - \lambda\varphi\eta_p \end{pmatrix}, \quad \text{and} \quad P = \begin{pmatrix} 0 & -\varphi\eta_u \\ 0 & 1 - \lambda\varphi\eta_u \end{pmatrix}$$

We now apply the general E-stability conditions given earlier in this Appendix to the specific form of (26) with coefficients (41). A sufficient condition for instability is that one of the eigenvalues of $DT_a - I = Q + M(I + \bar{b}) - I$ has a positive real part. Hence, a sufficient condition for instability is that $\det(DT_a - I) < 0$. It is easily computed that

$$Q + M(I + \bar{b}) - I = \begin{pmatrix} 0 & \bar{b}_p + \varphi\bar{b}_x \\ \lambda & \lambda\bar{b}_p + (\lambda\varphi + \beta)\bar{b}_x - 1 \end{pmatrix}$$

---

28. We are excluding the exceptional cases where at least one eigenvalue has a zero real part.

and $\det(DT_a - I) = -\lambda(\bar{b}_p + \varphi \bar{b}_x)$. Using $\bar{b}_p = -\frac{\lambda}{\alpha}\bar{b}_x$, we get $\det(DT_a - I) = -\lambda(\varphi - \frac{\lambda}{\alpha})\bar{b}_x$. Because $0 < \bar{b}_x < 1$, this determinant is negative when $\varphi > \frac{\lambda}{\alpha}$.

Q.E.D.

Proof of Proposition 3 The reduced form of the economy under (27) is given in the standard form (26) by

$$
\begin{pmatrix} x_t \\ \pi_t \\ p_t \end{pmatrix} = \begin{pmatrix} 0 & -\frac{\lambda\beta}{\alpha+\lambda^2} & 0 \\ 0 & \frac{\alpha\beta}{\alpha+\lambda^2} & 0 \\ 0 & 0 & 0 \end{pmatrix} \begin{pmatrix} E_t^* x_{t+1} \\ E_t^* \pi_{t+1} \\ E_t^* p_{t+1} \end{pmatrix} +
\tag{42}
$$

$$
\begin{pmatrix} \frac{\alpha}{\alpha+\lambda^2} & 0 & 0 \\ \frac{\alpha\lambda}{\alpha+\lambda^2} & 0 & 0 \\ 1 & 0 & 0 \end{pmatrix} \begin{pmatrix} x_{t-1} \\ \pi_{t-1} \\ p_{t-1} \end{pmatrix} + \begin{pmatrix} 0 & -\frac{\lambda}{\alpha+\lambda^2} \\ 0 & \frac{\alpha}{\alpha+\lambda^2} \\ 0 & 0 \end{pmatrix} u_t
$$

Using Mathematica,[29] it can be computed that the eigenvalues of $DT_a - I$ are two repeated roots of -1 and one root equal to $-1 + \frac{\alpha\beta}{\alpha+\lambda^2}$. Those of $DT_b - I$ are eight repeated roots of -1 and one root equal to $-1 + \frac{\alpha\beta}{\alpha+\lambda^2}$. Those of $DT_c - I$ are four roots of -1, $-1 + \frac{\alpha\beta\mu}{\alpha+\lambda^2}$, and $-1 + \frac{\alpha\beta\rho}{\alpha+\lambda^2}$. Thus, all eigenvalues are negative, so that learning stability obtains. Q.E.D.

Appendix 2.B   E-Stability in the Model of Section 2.5.3

The E-stability conditions in Appendix A require that all eigenvalues of the matrices $M(I + \bar{b})$ and $\bar{b}' \otimes M + I \otimes M\bar{b}$ have real parts less than one. The general case leads to complex expressions, but in the limit $\gamma \to 0$ we obtain, using Mathematica,

$$
M = \begin{pmatrix} 0 & 0 & 0 \\ \frac{\sigma_1}{c_H \bar{p}\beta\psi} & \frac{1}{\bar{p}\beta\psi} & 0 \\ \frac{\sigma_1}{c_H \beta\psi} & \frac{1}{\beta\psi} & 0 \end{pmatrix}, \qquad N = \begin{pmatrix} 0 & 0 & 0 \\ 0 & 0 & \frac{-1}{\bar{p}} \\ 0 & 0 & 0 \end{pmatrix}
$$

From now on, we normalize $\bar{p} = 1$.

Assuming that the solution takes the form $y_t = a + by_{t-1}$ and solving the equation $Mb^2 - b + N = 0$, we obtain

$$
a = 0, \qquad b = \begin{pmatrix} 0 & 0 & 0 \\ 0 & 0 & b_{23} \\ 0 & 0 & b_{33} \end{pmatrix}
$$

---

29. The Mathematica routines used in the chapter are available on request.

where $(\beta\psi)^{-1}b_{23}^2 - b_{23} - 1 = 0$, and $b_{33} = (\beta\psi)^{-1}b_{23}^2$. The quadratic for b_{23} has two roots, from which we pick the negative root:

$$b_{23} = \frac{1}{2}\left(\beta\psi - \sqrt{\beta\psi}\sqrt{4+\beta\psi}\right)$$

The E-stability conditions are that the matrices $DT_a - I = M(I+b) - I$ and $DT_b - I = \bar{b}' \otimes M + I \otimes M\bar{b} - I$ are stable (i.e., all their eigenvalues have real parts less than one). Two of the eigenvalues of $DT_a - I$ are -1, and the third one is

$$\frac{2 - \beta\psi - \sqrt{\beta\psi}\sqrt{4+\beta\psi}}{2\beta\psi}$$

The matrix $DT_b - I$ has six roots of -1, two roots equal to

$$-1 + \frac{\beta\psi - \sqrt{\beta\psi}\sqrt{4+\beta\psi}}{2\beta\psi}$$

and the remaining root equal to

$$\frac{1 - \beta\psi - \sqrt{\beta\psi}\sqrt{4+\beta\psi}}{\beta\psi}$$

Clearly, for stability it is sufficient that $\beta\psi > 1$, or $\psi > \beta^{-1}$.

For the deflationary steady state, the determinant of the E-stability system is equal to

$$\frac{-c_L^{1+\sigma_1}(c_L+g)^{\frac{1+\varepsilon}{\alpha}}(1+\varepsilon)v - g^2\alpha^2(v-1)\sigma_1 - c_L\alpha^2(v-1)[g(2\sigma_1-1)+c_L(\sigma_1-1)]}{c_L^{\sigma_1}(c_L+g)\alpha^2\beta(2\beta-1)\gamma\sigma_1}$$

It is certainly negative for $\sigma_1 \geq 1$ and even when a weaker (but cumbersome) condition is satisfied.

References

Adam, K. (2007) "Experimental Evidence on the Persistence of Output and Inflation," *Economic Journal* 117: 603–636.

Adam, K., A. Marcet, and J. P. Nicolini. (2012) "Stock Market Volatility and Learning." Working paper, Mannheim University, Germany.

Barro, R. J. (1989) "The Ricardian Approach to Budget Deficits," *Journal of Economic Perspectives* 3(2): 37–54.

Basdevant, O. (2005) "Learning Processes and Rational Expectations: An Analysis Using a Small Macro-Econometric Model for New Zealand," *Economic Modelling* 22: 1074–1089.

Benhabib, J., S. Schmitt-Grohe, and M. Uribe. (2001) "The Perils of Taylor Rules," *Journal of Economic Theory* 96: 40–69.

Berardi, M. (2007) "Heterogeneity and Misspecification in Learning," *Journal of Economic Dynamics and Control* 31: 3203–3227.

———. (2008) "Monetary Policy with Heterogeneous and Misspecified Expectations," *Journal of Money, Credit, and Banking* 41: 79–100.

Bernheim, B. D. (1987) "Ricardian Equivalence: An Evaluation of Theory and Evidence," *NBER Macroeconomics Annual* 2: 263–304.

Branch, W. A. (2004) "The Theory of Rationally Heterogeneous Expectations: Evidence from Survey Data on Inflation Expectations," *Economic Journal* 114: 592–621.

Branch, W. A., and G. W. Evans. (2006a) "Intrinsic Heterogeneity in Expectation Formation," *Journal of Economic Theory* 127: 264–295.

———. (2006b) "A Simple Recursive Forecasting Model," *Economic Letters* 91: 158–166.

———. (2007) "Model Uncertainty and Endogenous Volatility," *Review of Economic Dynamics* 10: 207–237.

———. (2010) "Asset Return Dynamics and Learning," *Review of Financial Studies* 23: 1651–1680.

———. (2011) "Learning about Risk and Return: A Simple Model of Bubbles and Crashes," *American Economic Journal: Macroeconomics* 3: 159–191.

Branch, W. A., and B. McGough. (2010) "Dynamic Predictor Selection in a New Keynesian Model with Heterogeneous Expectations," *Journal of Economic Dynamics and Control* 34: 1492–1508.

———. (2011) "Heterogeneous Expectations, Shock Amplification and Complex Dynamics in Competitive Business Cycle Models," *Economic Theory* 47: 395–422.

Branch, W. A., G. W. Evans, and B. McGough. (2012) "Finite Horizon Learning," in T. J. Sargent and J. Vilmunen (eds.), *Macroeconomics at the Service of Public Policy*. Oxford University Press, forthcoming.

Bray, M., and N. Savin. (1986) "Rational Expectations Equilibria, Learning, and Model Specification," *Econometrica* 54: 1129–1160.

Brazier, A., R. Harrison, M. King, and T. Yates. (2008) "The Danger of Inflating Expectations of Macroeconomic Stability: Heuristic Switching in an Overlapping Generations Monetary Model," *International Journal of Central Banking* 4: 219–254.

Brock, W. A., and C. H. Hommes. (1997) "A Rational Route to Randomness," *Econometrica* 65: 1059–1095.

———. (1998) "Heterogeneous Beliefs and Routes to Chaos in a Simple Asset Pricing Model," *Journal of Economic Dynamics and Control* 22: 1235–1274.

Brock, W., C. Hommes, and F. Wagener. (2009) "More Hedging Instruments May Destabilize Markets," *Journal of Economic Dynamics and Control* 33: 1912–1928.

Bullard, J. (2006) "The Learnability Criterion and Monetary Policy," *Federal Reserve Bank of St. Louis Review* 88: 203–217.

———. (2010) "Seven Faces of the Peril," *Federal Reserve Bank of St. Louis Review* 92: 339–352.

Bullard, J., and S. Eusepi. (2005) "Did the Great Inflation Occur Despite Policymaker Commitment to a Taylor Rule?" *Review of Economic Dynamics* 8: 324–359.

Bullard, J., and K. Mitra. (2002) "Learning about Monetary Policy Rules," *Journal of Monetary Economics* 49: 1105–1129.

Carboni, G., and M. Ellison. (2009) "The Great Inflation and the Greenbook," *Journal of Monetary Economics* 56: 831–841.

Chakraborty, A., and G. W. Evans. (2008) "Can Perpetual Learning Explain the Forward Premium Puzzle?" *Journal of Monetary Economics* 55: 477–490.

Cho, I.-K., and K. Kasa. (2012) "Learning and Model Validation: An Example," in T. J. Sargent and J. Vilmunen (eds.), *Macroeconomics at the Service of Public Policy*. Oxford: Oxford University Press, forthcoming.

Cho, I.-K., N. Williams, and T. J. Sargent. (2002) "Escaping Nash Inflation," *Review of Economic Studies* 69: 1–40.

Clarida, R., J. Gali, and M. Gertler. (1999) "The Science of Monetary Policy: A New Keynesian Perspective," *Journal of Economic Literature* 37: 1661–1707.

Cogley, T., and T. J. Sargent. (2005) "The Conquest of US Inflation: Learning and Robustness to Model Uncertainty," *Review of Economic Dynamics* 8: 528–563.

———. (2008) "Anticipated Utility and Rational Expectations as Approximations of Bayesian Decision Making," *International Economic Review* 49: 185–221.

De Grauwe, P. (2011) "Animal Spirits and Monetary Policy," *Economic Theory* 47: 423–457.

De Grauwe, P., and M. Grimaldi. (2006) *The Exchange Rate in a Behavioral Finance Framework*. Princeton, NJ: Princeton University Press.

Eggertsson, G. B., and M. Woodford. (2003) "The Zero Bound on Interest Rates and Optimal Monetary Policy," *Brookings Papers on Economic Activity* 1: 139–233.

Ellison, M., and T. Yates. (2007) "Escaping Volatile Inflation," *Journal of Money, Credit, and Banking* 39: 981–993.

Eusepi, S., and B. Preston. (2010) "Central Bank Communication and Expectations Stabilization," *American Economic Journal: Macroeconomics* 2: 235–271.

———. (2011) "Expectations, Learning and Business Cycle Fluctuations," *American Economic Review* 101: 2844–2872.

Evans, G. W., and R. Guesnerie. (1993) "Rationalizability, Strong Rationality, and Expectational Stability," *Games and Economic Behavior* 5(4): 632–646.

———. (2003) "Coordination on Saddle Path Solutions: The Eductive Viewpoint— Linear Univariate Models," *Macroeconomic Dynamics* 7: 42–62.

Evans, G. W., and S. Honkapohja. (1996) "Least Squares Learning with Heterogeneous Expectations," *Economics Letters* 53: 197–201.

———. (2001) *Learning and Expectations in Macroeconomics*. Princeton, NJ: Princeton University Press.

———. (2003a) "Adaptive Learning and Monetary Policy Design," *Journal of Money, Credit, and Banking* 35: 1045–1072.

———. (2003b) "Expectations and the Stability Problem for Optimal Monetary Policies," *Review of Economic Studies* 70: 807–824.

———. (2005) "Policy Interaction, Expectations and the Liquidity Trap," *Review of Economic Dynamics* 8: 303–323.

———. (2006) "Monetary Policy, Expectations and Commitment," *Scandinavian Journal of Economics* 108: 15–38.

———. (2009a) "Expectations, Learning and Monetary Policy: An Overview of Recent Research," in K. Schmidt-Hebbel and C. E. Walsh (eds.), *Monetary Policy under Uncertainty and Learning*. Santiago: Central Bank of Chile, pp. 27–76.

———. (2009b) "Learning and Macroeconomics," *Annual Review of Economics* 1: 421–451.

———. (2010) "Expectations, Deflation Traps and Macroeconomic Policy," in D. Cobham, Ø. Eitrheim, S. Gerlach, and J. F. Qvigstad (eds.), *Twenty Years of Inflation Targeting: Lessons Learned and Future Prospects.* Cambridge: Cambridge University Press, pp. 232–260.

Evans, G. W., and B. McGough. (2010) "Learning to Optimize." Mimeo, University of Oregon, Eugene.

Evans, G. W., and G. Ramey. (1992) "Expectation Calculation and Macroeconomic Dynamics," *American Economic Review* 82: 207–224.

———. (1998) "Calculation, Adaptation and Rational Expectations," *Macroeconomic Dynamics* 2: 156–182.

Evans, G. W., S. Honkapohja, and P. Romer. (1998) "Growth Cycles," *American Economic Review* 88: 495–515.

Evans, G. W., S. Honkapohja, and R. Marimon. (2001) "Convergence in Monetary Inflation Models with Heterogeneous Learning Rules," *Macroeconomic Dynamics* 5: 1–31.

———. (2007) "Stable Sunspot Equilibria in a Cash-in-Advance Economy," *B.E. Journal of Macroeconomics* (Advances) 7(1): Article 3.

Evans, G. W., E. Guse, and S. Honkapohja. (2008) "Liquidity Traps, Learning and Stagnation," *European Economic Review* 52: 1438–1463.

Evans, G. W., S. Honkapohja, and K. Mitra. (2009) "Anticipated Fiscal Policy and Learning," *Journal of Monetary Economics* 56: 930–953.

Evans, G. W., R. Guesnerie, and B. McGough. (2010) "Eductive Stability in Real Business Cycle Models." Mimeo, University of Oregon, Eugene.

Evans, G. W., S. Honkapohja, and K. Mitra. (2012a) "Does Ricardian Equivalence Hold When Expectations Are Not Rational?" *Journal of Money, Credit, and Banking,* forthcoming.

Evans, G. W., S. Honkapohja, T. J. Sargent, and N. Williams. (2012b) "Bayesian Model Averaging, Learning and Model Selection," in T. J. Sargent and J. Vilmunen (eds.), *Macroeconomics at the Service of Public Policy.* Oxford: Oxford University Press, forthcoming.

Fourgeaud, C., C. Gourieroux, and J. Pradel. (1986) "Learning Procedures and Convergence to Rationality," *Econometrica* 54: 845–868.

Fuster, A., D. Laibson, and B. Mendel. (2010) "Natural Expectations and Macroeconomic Fluctuations," *Journal of Economic Perspectives* 24: 67–84.

Gaspar, V., F. Smets, and D. Vestin. (2007) "Is Time Ripe for Price Level Path Stability?" Working Paper 818, European Central Bank, Frankfurt am Main, Germany.

Giannitsarou, C. (2003) "Heterogeneous Learning," *Review of Economic Dynamics* 6: 885–906.

———. (2006) "Supply-Side Reforms and Learning Dynamics," *Journal of Monetary Economics* 53: 291–309.

Guesnerie, R. (1992) "An Exploration of the Eductive Justifications of the Rational-Expectations Hypothesis," *American Economic Review* 82: 1254–1278.

———. (2002) "Anchoring Economic Predictions in Common Knowledge," *Econometrica* 70: 439–480.

Guesnerie, R., and J.-C. Rochet. (1993) "(De)stabilizing Speculation on Futures Markets: An Alternative Viewpoint," *European Economic Review* 37: 1043–1063.

Guse, E. (2006) "Stability Properties for Learning with Heterogeneous Expectations and Multiple Equilibria," *Journal of Economic Dynamics and Control* 29: 1623–1642.

Hommes, C. H. (2011) "The Heterogeneous Expectations Hypothesis: Some Evidence from the Lab," *Journal of Economic Dynamics and Control* 35: 1–24.

Hommes, C. H., and G. Sorger. (1997) "Consistent Expectations Equilibria," *Macroeconomic Dynamics* 2: 287–321.

Honkapohja, S., and K. Mitra. (2005) "Performance of Monetary Policy with Internal Central Bank Forecasting," *Journal of Economic Dynamics and Control* 29: 627–658.

———. (2006) "Learning Stability in Economies with Heterogeneous Agents," *Review of Economic Dynamics* 9: 284–309.

Honkapohja, S., K. Mitra, and G. W. Evans. (2012) "Notes on Agents' Behavioral Rules under Adaptive Learning and Recent Studies of Monetary Policy," in T. J. Sargent and J. Vilmunen (eds.), *Macroeconomics at the Service of Public Policy*. Oxford: Oxford University Press, forthcoming.

Huang, K., Z. Liu, and T. Zha. (2009) "Learning, Adaptive Expectations and Technology Shocks," *Economic Journal* 119: 377–405.

Kasa, K. (2004) "Learning, Large Deviations, and Recurrent Currency Crises," *International Economic Review* 45: 141–173.

Kim, Y. S. (2009) "Exchange Rates and Fundamentals under Adaptive Learning," *Journal of Economic Dynamics and Control* 33: 843–863.

Kreps, D. M. (1998) "Anticipated Utility and Dynamic Choice," in D. Jacobs, E. Kalai, and M. Kamien (eds.), *Frontiers of Research in Economic Theory*. Cambridge: Cambridge University Press, pp. 242–274.

Kurz, M. (ed.). (1997) *Endogenous Economic Fluctuations: Studies in the Theory of Rational Beliefs*. Berlin: Springer-Verlag.

———. (2009) "Rational Diverse Beliefs and Economic Volatility," in T. Hens and K. Shenk-Hoppé (eds.), *Handbook on Financial Markets: Dynamics and Evolution*. Amsterdam: North-Holland, pp. 439–506.

———. (2011) "A New Keynesian Model with Diverse Beliefs." Mimeo, Stanford University, Stanford, CA.

Lansing, K. (2010) "Rational and Near-Rational Bubbles without Drift," *Economic Journal* 120: 1149–1174.

Lucas, Jr., R. E. (1972) "Expectations and the Neutrality of Money," *Journal of Economic Theory* 4: 103–124.

———. (1973) "Some International Evidence on Output-Inflation Tradeoffs," *American Economic Review* 63: 326–334.

Marcet, A., and J. P. Nicolini. (2003) "Recurrent Hyperinflations and Learning," *American Economic Review* 93: 1476–1498.

Marcet, A., and T. J. Sargent. (1989a) "Convergence of Least-Squares Learning in Environments with Hidden State Variables and Private Information," *Journal of Political Economy* 97: 1306–1322.

———. (1989b) "Convergence of Least-Squares Learning Mechanisms in Self-Referential Linear Stochastic Models," *Journal of Economic Theory* 48: 337–368.

Marimon, R., and S. Sunder. (1993) "Indeterminacy of Equilibria in a Hyperinflationary World: Experimental Evidence," *Econometrica* 61: 1073–1107.

———. (1995) "Does a Constant Money Growth Rule Help Stabilize Inflation? Experimental Evidence," *Carnegie-Rochester Conference Series on Public Policy* 43: 111–156.

Mark, N. (2009) "Changing Monetary Rules, Learning, and Real Exchange Rate Dynamics," *Journal of Money, Credit, and Banking* 41: 1047–1070.

Markiewicz, A. (2012) "Model Uncertainty and Exchange Rate Volatility," *International Economic Review* 53: 815–844.

Milani, F. (2007) "Expectations, Learning and Macroeconomic Persistence," *Journal of Monetary Economics* 54: 2065–2082.

———. (2011) "Expectation Shocks and Learning as Drivers of the Business Cycle," *Economic Journal* 121: 379–401.

Mitra, K., G. W. Evans, and S. Honkapohja. (2012) "Fiscal Policy and Learning." Mimeo, University of St. Andrews, St. Andrews, Scotland.

Muth, J. F. (1961) "Rational Expectations and the Theory of Price Movements," *Econometrica* 29: 315–335.

Orphanides, A., and J. C. Williams. (2005a) "The Decline of Activist Stabilization Policy: Natural Rate Misperceptions, Learning and Expectations," *Journal of Economic Dynamics and Control* 29: 1927–1950.

———. (2005b) "Imperfect Knowledge, Inflation Expectations, and Monetary Policy," in B. Bernanke, and M. Woodford (eds.), *The Inflation-Targeting Debate*. Chicago: University of Chicago Press, pp. 201–234.

———. (2005c) "Inflation Scares and Forecast-Based Monetary Policy," *Review of Economic Dynamics* 8: 498–527.

———. (2007) "Robust Monetary Policy with Imperfect Knowledge," *Journal of Monetary Economics* 54: 1406–1435.

Pfajfar, D. (2007) "Formation of Rationally Heterogeneous Expectations." Mimeo, University of Tilburg, The Netherlands.

Pfajfar, D., and E. Santoro. (2010) "Heterogeneity, Learning and Information Stickiness in Inflation Expectations," *Journal of Economic Behavior and Organization* 75: 426–444.

Preston, B. (2005) "Learning about Monetary Policy Rules when Long-Horizon Expectations Matter," *International Journal of Central Banking* 1: 81–126.

———. (2006) "Adaptive Learning, Forecast-Based Instrument Rules and Monetary Policy," *Journal of Monetary Economics* 53: 507–535.

———. (2008) "Adaptive Learning and the Use of Forecasts in Monetary Policy," *Journal of Economic Dynamics and Control* 32: 3661–3681.

Primiceri, G. E. (2006) "Why Inflation Rose and Fell: Policy-Makers' Beliefs and U.S. Postwar Stabilization Policy," *Quarterly Journal of Economics* 121: 867–901.

Reifschneider, D., and J. C. Williams. (2000) "Three Lessons for Monetary Policy in a Low-Inflation Era," *Journal of Money, Credit, and Banking* 32: 936–966.

Ricciuti, R. (2003) "Assessing Ricardian Equivalence," *Journal of Economic Surveys* 17: 55–78.

Rotemberg, J. J., and M. Woodford. (1999) "Interest Rate Rules in an Estimated Sticky-Price Model," in J. Taylor (ed.), *Monetary Policy Rules*. Chicago: University of Chicago Press, pp. 57–119.

Sargent, T. J. (1973) "Rational Expectations, the Real Rate of Interest and the Natural Rate of Unemployment," *Brookings Papers on Economic Activity* 2: 429–472.

———. (1991) "Equilibrium with Signal Extraction from Endogenous Variables," *Journal of Economic Dynamics and Control* 15: 245–273.

———. (1993) *Bounded Rationality in Macroeconomics*. Oxford: Oxford University Press.

———. (1999) *The Conquest of American Inflation*. Princeton, NJ: Princeton University Press.

Sargent, T. J., and N. Wallace. (1973a) "Rational Expectations and the Dynamics of Hyperinflation," *International Economic Review* 14: 429–472.

———. (1973b) "The Stability of Models of Money and Growth with Perfect Foresight," *Econometrica* 41: 1043–1048.

Sargent, T. J., N. Williams, and T. Zha. (2006) "Shocks and Government Beliefs: The Rise and Fall of American Inflation," *American Economic Review* 96: 1193–1224.

Seater, J. J. (1993) "Ricardian Equivalence," *Journal of Economic Literature* 31: 142–190.

Slobodyan, S., and R. Wouters. (2012a) "Estimating a Medium-Scale DSGE Model with Expectations Based on Small Forecasting Models," *American Economic Journal: Macroeconomics* 4: 65–101.

———. (2012b) "Learning in an Estimated DSGE Model," *Journal of Economic Dynamics and Control* 36: 26–46.

Svensson, L. E. (1999) "Inflation Targeting as a Monetary Policy Rule," *Journal of Monetary Economics* 43: 607–654.

———. (2003) "What Is Wrong with Taylor Rules? Using Judgement in Monetary Policy through Targeting Rules," *Journal of Economic Literature* 41: 426–477.

Timmermann, A. G. (1993) "How Learning in Financial Markets Generates Excess Volatility and Predictability in Stock Prices," *Quarterly Journal of Economics* 108: 1135–1145.

———. (1996) "Excessive Volatility and Predictability of Stock Prices in Autoregressive Dividend Models with Learning," *Review of Economic Studies* 63: 523–557.

Van Nieuwerburgh, S., and L. Veldkamp. (2006) "Learning Asymmetries in Real Business Cycles," *Journal of Monetary Economics* 53: 753–772.

Williams, N. (2004) "Adaptive Learning and Business Cycles." Working paper, University of Wisconsin, Madison.

Woodford, M. (1999a) "Commentary: How Should Monetary Policy Be Conducted in an Era of Price Stability?" in Federal Reserve Bank of Kansas City (ed.), *New Challenges for Monetary Policy*. Kansas City: Federal Reserve Bank of Kansas City, pp. 277–316.

———. (1999b) "Optimal Monetary Policy Inertia," *Manchester School* 67(Supplement): 1–35.

CHAPTER THREE

Keynes on Knowledge, Expectations, and Rationality

Sheila Dow

3.1 Introduction

In his seminal 1968 article, and in the edited volume that followed in 1970 (Phelps et al. 1970), Phelps refocused economists' attention on expectations formed with incomplete information. In doing so, he referred back to Keynes's *General Theory*, particularly to Keynes's analysis of the labor market. The purpose here is to revisit Keynes's work with special emphasis on his treatment of knowledge, expectations, and rationality. The focus is not only on his ideas on expectations formation but also on the degree of confidence attached to those expectations (i.e., uncertainty) and what this means for macroeconomic theory. Specifically, because uncertainty stands in the way of the complete ordering of assets according to risk and return required for rational choice theory, Keynes's ideas have particular import for the discussion of microfoundations.

This aspect of Keynes's thinking also provides the basis for an explanation of the current financial and economic crisis. But it has been downplayed in current discussion, compared to his macroeconomic theory and policy as a potential cure for the crisis. Yet Keynes's macroeconomics developed on the foundation of his philosophy, and in particular on his theory of knowledge. Keynes (1937a) made it clear that he saw uncertainty as lying at the heart of the *General Theory*. Although a few scholars (dubbed by Coddington [1976] as "fundamentalist Keynesians") continued to keep Keynes's ideas on knowledge, uncertainty, and rationality alive, it was only in the 1970s, following the publication of Keynes's *Collected Writings,* that research on this topic expanded significantly. Over the subsequent decades, Keynes's ideas on knowledge, expectations, and rationality were explored, reinterpreted, and developed.

Here I provide a summary account of Keynes's philosophical ideas in relation to his economics rather than a history of Keynes's thought. There is a large history of thought literature on the subject, spearheaded by Carabelli (1988) and O'Donnell (1989), as well as an extensive literature on subsequent interpretations and developments, for example, as gathered in Runde and Mizuhara (2003). Inevitably, as for any great thinker, Keynes's ideas evolved over his lifetime, particularly as his economics both drew on and fed back into his philosophy. Further, his ideas have inspired a range of interpretations and developments. Keynes's thought is an open system. But this rich detail is downplayed in what follows in the interests of considering what we might draw from Keynes as we consider future developments in macroeconomics in the light of the crises in banking, the global economy, and economics itself.

I therefore start with a synthetic account of Keynes's ideas on knowledge and expectations, and his understanding of the source of uncertainty. I consider his emphasis on the role of conventional judgment, and of conventions more generally, and then focus on the implications of these ideas for how we may understand and use the concept of rationality in a Keynesian framework, alongside considerations of logic and consistency. Keynes's concern with the interplay between individuality and sociality sheds some light on Keynes in relation to the formulation of microfoundations. The chapter concludes with a consideration of the implications of Keynes's ideas on knowledge, expectations, and rationality for economic methodology.

3.2   Keynes on Knowledge and Expectations

For Keynes the general case was uncertainty, rather than certainty or certainty equivalence. His ideas on knowledge were developed in his first book, *A Treatise on Probability* (Keynes 1921), whose purpose was to explore how the grounds for belief in propositions are established as the basis for action. As we shall see, "action" involves more than the conventional mainstream notion of choice among an array of existing possibilities, because it also includes creative leaps.

By "probability" Keynes meant logical probability, "the various degrees of rational belief about a proposition which different amounts of knowledge authorise us to entertain" (Keynes 1921: 3). Scope for quantified probability based on frequency distributions was a special case; the general case was uncertainty, where even nonquantifiable (ordinal) probability may not be identifiable. Although probability might not be quantifiable due to lack of knowledge that is in principle available ("known unknowns"), he was more concerned with the more general case where there is no firm basis on which to quantify it (there are "unknown unknowns"). The focus on uncertain knowledge was general in its application to scientific argument as well as to argument in everyday life: "in metaphysics, in science, and in conduct, most of the arguments, upon which we habitually base our rational beliefs, are admitted to be inconclusive in a greater or less degree" (Keynes 1921: 3).

The source of this inconclusivity or uncertainty was the nature of the real world, which he understood to be organic rather than atomistic. As Keynes (1926: 262) put it in discussing the application of mathematics to economics:

> We are faced at every turn with the problems of organic unity, of discreteness, of discontinuity—the whole is not equal to the sum of the parts, comparisons of quantity fail us, small changes produce large effects, the assumptions of a uniform and homogeneous continuum are not satisfied.

Keynes notably applied one feature of an organic system, the fallacy of composition, in his macroeconomics. For example, the paradox of thrift arises when individual intentions to increase savings are thwarted by their macroeconomic consequences, something of concern in current circumstances. Similarly, there is a paradox of liquidity, whereby the attempt to make portfolios more liquid may reduce the liquidity in the system, as we experienced during the banking crisis. Such fallacies of composition provide just one reason individuals cannot be sure of their expectations being met, creating uncertainty.

More generally, an organic system involves complex and evolving interactions among heterogeneous and evolving elements. The result is the problem of induction explored by Hume (of whom Keynes was a scholar; see Carabelli 1988). If the system's internal structure is evolving in a nondeterministic manner, and the influences to which it is subject in the future are not known (or are not fully knowable) in advance, then there is no scope for using frequency distributions to quantify a probabilistic or stochastic expectation. Keynes believed that this was particularly the case for social systems.

Although probability might not be quantifiable, there may be scope for an ordinal notion of probability, such that one outcome is judged on the basis of the evidence to be more probable than another. But even then, there are cases that are incommensurate—for example, how do we compare the probability of a further banking crisis next year against the probability of nuclear war 10 years hence? There is an extensive literature on subjective quantitative valuations of probability around the subjective expected utility (SEU) approach, which implies that agents are nevertheless able to make subjective quantitative estimates of probability with respect to all variables. But Keynes (1931) pointed to the inadequacy of Ramsey's (1931) use of formal inductive logic as the basis for subjective probability (Gerrard 2003). In an organic system, we cannot logically be certain that the past is an adequate guide to the future. Indeed, in the context of SEU theory, Savage (1954: 16) himself warns that it is practical only in suitably limited domains to assume that agents are capable of a complete preference ordering of all possible choices. Carried to its logical extreme, such an assumption "is utterly ridiculous . . . because the task implied is not even remotely resembled by human possibility."

In particular, the SEU framework does not take account of uncertainty (the confidence with which these subjective valuations are regarded), so that agents may prefer to keep options open rather than commit to a choice (Davidson 2009: 108–109). In other words, there is the possibility that uncertainty may be so high as to preclude any bets at all (Runde 1995), as evidenced by the customary exclusions from insurance policies on a routine basis, or the refusal to enter a market under conditions of particular uncertainty. For example, the freezing of the interbank market during the recent banking crisis reflected such high uncertainty as to the riskiness of bank assets that banks were no longer prepared to lend to one another at any price. Similarly, when uncertainty is too high to justify commitment to capital investment, firms strongly prefer to keep assets liquid (and thus options open; Davidson 2003). The preference for high liquidity has been a notable feature of the current crisis, reflecting the high degree of uncertainty about future economic developments (Bibow 2009).

Although Keynes's theory of probability undermines the logical foundation for a general frequentist theory of probability itself, he also undermined any idea of a general frequentist theory of confidence or uncertainty. Keynes introduced the notion of weight of argument as the determinant of confidence, where weight increases with increasing amounts of relevant evidence brought to bear (relative to relevant ignorance). But of course, what is relevant is itself theoretically loaded, and theoretical understandings can change and themselves be the source of higher order uncertainty (Dow 1995). Therefore, it should not be assumed that weight inevitably increases with amount of evidence; in particular, more evidence may reveal new realms of ignorance (Runde 1990). Weight falls if new evidence reveals previously unrecognized unknown unknowns, as happened in the financial crisis. Finally, there is no direct correspondence between degree of confidence and degree of probability, so, for example, there may be high confidence that an outcome has low probability, and vice versa.

It is therefore not possible in general to order all possibilities according to risk and uncertainty in a reliable way. Even if it were feasible to contemplate an identification of all future possibilities and to establish complete orderings of these according to risk, the degree of uncertainty attached to these calculations is liable to discrete shifts according, not only to new information, but also to how that information feeds back into the subjective knowledge system that generated the risk estimates. Although the basis for decisionmaking (e.g., in portfolio choice) may be expressed formally in terms of probability and weight (Dequech 2005), the derivation of probability and weight cannot be derived deductively. In any case, the outcome depends on *attitude* to confidence (or uncertainty), which is also subject to shifts and is therefore also not a purely logical derivation.

Where aversion to uncertainty is low, then high uncertainty may be overridden, resulting in positive action; this is the exercise of animal spirits (Dequech 1999). For example, in analyzing the investment decision, Keynes (1936: 149) implied that a rational investor (in the Benthamite sense) would never invest at all, because expectations as to return were bound to be highly uncertain: "The outstanding fact is the extreme precariousness of the basis of knowledge on which our estimates of prospective yield have to be made." But entrepreneurs have the psychological capacity to act in spite of uncertainty (Dow and Dow 1985, 2011; Dow 1995). This involves not just optimistic expectations but also a willingness to ignore the uncertainty surrounding these expectations. This is Keynes's meaning of animal spirits, which implies that the build-up to the current crisis was characterized by animal spirits in the form of a widespread spontaneous optimism in spite of an insufficient basis for calculative rational choice. By the same token, decisions by firms to engage in the new investment needed to strengthen weak economies would require a beneficial exercise of animal spirits.

This understanding of animal spirits differs from the meaning now commonly employed, which is the (possibly subconscious) choice to substitute irrationality, or unsubstantiated beliefs, for rationality. Animal spirits in these terms are something to be discouraged. Although Akerlof and Shiller (2009) share this view of animal spirits in terms of irrationality, they also consider animal spirits as including noneconomic motives. Their discussion of such matters as fairness and trust is welcome, but it refers more to the kind of structural social convention that Keynes saw as evolving to allow decisionmaking under uncertainty than to the decisionmaking itself. In what follows, the term "animal spirits" is used instead in Keynes's sense of an "urge to action" (or willingness to act in spite of uncertainty); frameworks of conventions will be considered separately.

Animal spirits have an important role to play because, as Keynes argued, in an open organic system, reason and evidence alone are not sufficient for judgment to yield theoretical conclusions or to justify decisionmaking. Yet agents normally do manage to form a view when uncertainty is present but not prohibitive, even if they are engaging in routine behavior rather than in the exercise of individualistic animal spirits. Keynes argued that this was made possible by recourse to conventional judgment as an input to individual judgment:

> We do not know what the future holds. Nevertheless, as living and moving beings, we are forced to act. Peace and comfort of mind require that we should hide from ourselves how little we foresee. Yet we must

be guided by some hypothesis. We tend, therefore, to substitute for the knowledge which is unattainable certain conventions, the chief of which is to assume, contrary to all likelihood, that the future will resemble the past. [Keynes 1937b: 124]

In spite of the problem of induction, past evidence is the most reliable source of knowledge we have, adding weight to argument. Two other common conventions that Keynes (1937a: 114) identified are relying on expert opinion and following conventional expectations.

Conventional judgment in conditions of uncertainty cannot be based on demonstrable logic any more than individual judgment can. Yet it provides a more objective benchmark for individual judgment, as a point of reference (Davis 1994: 117, 133). Individuality or agency allows for individual choice as to whether to follow social convention. But sociality means that social-conventional judgment provides the norm, such that expectations are formed interdependently with expectations in the market. This nondeterministic social interactionism is a key ingredient of Keynes's organic view of the economic system (Park and Kayatekin 2002).

Conventional judgment is supported by a framework of social conventions, which may have a moral dimension. Incorporating moral principles into the analysis of behavior compounds the heterogeneity of the factors at work. For example, van Staveren (2001: 6–7) argues that the two incommensurate principles of liberty and justice are better understood as commitments rather than preferences, that they involve conflict and thus negotiation, and that their interpretation is specific to particular cultural contexts. Therefore, they cannot be homogenized within a general optimization framework.

Moral issues have attracted new attention in the wake of the crisis. The conventional level of executive pay in the financial sector and the procedure of rewarding staff with bonuses, for example, have come under public scrutiny on moral grounds. It is not just the apparent rewards for failure that have been questioned from the perspective of principles of social justice, but also what has been revealed of the growing disparities in compensation across different occupations. In the meantime, the literature on executive pay suggests that the system itself relies heavily on convention as to what is normal for such positions, on reciprocity relations, and on power relations (e.g., see O'Reilly and Main 2010). Similarly, the evidence suggests that relativities, rather than absolute levels, dominate the response to bonuses. This is heavily reminiscent of Keynes's (1936) analysis of the labor market more generally. Further, he observed the convention of relatively stable money wage levels as providing some stability alongside other conventions.

Keynes himself approached the subject of uncertainty from an ethical perspective: How do we as individuals determine the morally best action if we are uncertain of the consequences? The answer to that question was what divided Keynes and Hayek, who grappled with similar issues of reconciling individuality with sociality. For Hayek, knowledge difficulties were such that institutions, like government, could not justify intervention; individual judgment was more reliable. But for Keynes, public institutions provided a mechanism for actively promoting public-spirited behavior, which would address the consequences of uncertainty in the economy and in society, albeit on the basis of uncertain knowledge (O'Donnell 1989; Davis 1994).

The framework of social conventions, and institutions more generally, supports decisionmaking under uncertainty. As Hodgson (1988: 205) put it:

> The argument, in short, is that in a world of uncertainty, where the probabilistic calculus is ruled out, rules, norms and institutions play a functional role in providing a basis for decision-making, expectation and belief. Without these "rigidities", without social routine and habit to reproduce them, and without institutionally conditioned conceptual frameworks, an uncertain world would present a chaos of sense data in which it would be impossible for the agent to make sensible decisions and to act.

Insofar as most agents operate in a framework of social conventions, they normally act to stabilize markets. Indeed, markets in general function successfully only because participants observe social norms in trading, for example. Similarly, the institution of money has developed to provide liquidity in the face of uncertainty, and central banks have evolved to support that role.

Keynes argued that conventional judgment in this framework is particularly important for financial markets. Keynes (1936: 147–164) explored the juxtaposition of the long-term expectations of firms seeking to invest in capital projects and the short-term expectations of capital markets as the source of finance. For firms, as Shackle (1955) explained, capital projects are crucial experiments; it was clear to him that frequency distribution data are inadequate for projecting long-term yields, and animal spirits are vital. In contrast, for capital markets, where sociality dominates over individuality and the relevant variables are more clearly expectational than for producers, social conventions play a more important role. Both entrepreneurs and financial markets require conventional judgment and individualistic animal spirits to some degree, but arguably Keynes's analysis of conventions (and conventional attitudes toward uncertainty, i.e., nonindividualistic animal spirits) has more force for financial markets.

However, conventional judgment in financial markets may fuel instability, because it is prone to discrete shifts. One form of conventional judgment is market sentiment, which played a powerful role in the banking crisis. Conventional expectations that the long boom in asset prices would continue fueled the boom; these expectations were confidently shared by the banks, capital markets, and households, encouraging the credit creation and asset purchases that fueled the boom. Yet when awareness grew of the implications of structured products containing unknown elements of toxic debt, there was a massive turnaround in market sentiment, which created the crisis. Certainly, information was concealed, or willfully ignored, and incentives encouraged more risky behavior than otherwise. There is an extent to which we can talk about conventional valuations losing touch with the underlying reality (i.e., they were unreasonable). But the underlying reality for financial markets is in turn influenced by market valuations and the resulting decisions as to investment, production, and consumption.

Keynes's argument is that there is no basis on which to identify anything we might regard as a "true" market valuation of any asset, because any valuation is contingent on unknown and unknowable future developments. Markets require some conventional judgment by which to establish prices and to serve as a benchmark for opinion. We have seen that his analysis precludes the complete formal ordering of assets required by the rationality axioms of mainstream choice theory. We consider now where Keynes's analysis leaves us on the subject of rationality, and focus on the fact that understanding of rationality is contingent on the type of logic being applied.

3.3   Keynes on Rationality

"Rationality," in the sense the term is used in mainstream economics, is the application of calculative deductive logic (i.e., formal logic) to a set of premises taken as given (optimizing behavior with respect to a set of preferences, endowments, and technologies). It requires agents to make calculative choices among the array of all possible options (including contingent options) and these choices to be consistent. As long as deductive logic is correctly applied and contradiction avoided, the system itself will be internally consistent.

The formal logic view of rationality places huge knowledge demands on economic agents. But Keynes had argued that the scope for calculative rationality was very limited, given the relative shortage of knowledge that could be held with certainty (including certainty equivalence). If probabilistic expectations (even where they can be calculated) are held with varying degrees of confidence, and confidence may shift discretely with expert or conventional opinion (or may fail altogether), the rational optimum set of choices cannot be deduced.

In his response to Ramsey's subjective probability approach, Keynes pointed to Ramsey's reliance on induction as the "useful mental habit" we employ given the shortcomings of formal axiomatic logic under uncertainty. Ramsey identified recourse to convention as "human logic" (as opposed to formal logic), which conforms to the theory of knowledge Keynes developed in his economics (Gerrard 2003). As we have seen, Keynes's human logic draws on inductive logic, in the sense that evidence is brought to bear as far as possible. It was in this sense that Keynes referred to rational belief, as opposed to mere belief (Winslow 2003). But for Keynes, neither induction nor deduction is sufficient, given the organic nature of the economic system. So conventional knowledge and animal spirits are required to fill the gap, if action is to be taken. We can therefore understand rational judgment in human logic as "reasonable judgment"—employing evidence and reason as far as possible.

Of course, not all conventions are reasonable (just as not all conventions are moral). In particular, Keynes identified the conventional goal of financial accumulation as unreasonable, indeed, as pathological (Winslow 2003). However, in the absence of alternative knowledge, the convention of assuming the future to be like the past is not unreasonable:

> It would be foolish, in forming our expectations, to attach great weight to matters which are very uncertain. It is reasonable, therefore, to be guided to a considerable degree by the facts about which we feel somewhat confident, even though they may be less decisively relevant to the issue than other facts about which our knowledge is vague and scanty. [Keynes 1936: 148]

What is not reasonable, in this framework, is to focus on what we confidently know in one respect when it is contradicted by what we know we don't know. Thus, according to the well-known joke, a drunk insists on looking for his keys under a lamppost, because he can see better there, even though he knows he dropped his keys elsewhere. This is not reasonable behavior.

But rationality in the sense of formal logic can itself be a social convention, and it apparently came to dominate thinking in the financial sector, with its reliance on quantitative models to predict asset prices as if the data were drawn from an atomic system with a fixed structure. Given this convention, we are driven by the need to appear to others as rational. Thus, an investment decision may be presented as a comparison between the marginal efficiency of capital and the rate of interest as if the former were knowable. This is a useful procedure, "which saves our faces as rational economic men," even though it cannot generally provide a rational basis for decisions (Keynes 1937a: 114). But actual decisions are taken, reasonably and of necessity, on the basis of conventional judgments and ultimately on the basis of animal spirits (Carabelli 1988; Dow 1991). But it can also be reasonable for individual decisionmakers—with their own evidence, creative thinking, and animal spirits—to flout convention (Dequech 2003). In other words, some conventional judgments and animal spirits may well conflict.

Part of the conventional formal logic view in economics is a dualism between rationality and irrationality or emotion (Dow 1990). Discussion of social conventions—and even more so, of animal spirits—raises the issue of the relationship between psychology and economics, between emotion and rationality (with which the two disciplines were traditionally associated, respectively). Deductivist logic sees the two as distinct and mutually exclusive. But for Keynes, as for Hume, emotion was integral to his theory of human nature and thus of human decisionmaking. And indeed, the modern psychology literature points to the need for emotion, or "affect," to motivate behavior (e.g., see Damasio 1994). Keynes's evolving thinking on this subject was captured in his essay (Keynes 1949), where he presents his realization, during a talking-at-cross-purposes between Bertrand Russell on the one hand and D. H. Lawrence on the other (promoters of reason and emotion, respectively), that human behavior arose from a combination of reason and emotion. Keynes increasingly came to think of them as complements rather than opposites (Chick 1995). What is rational for agents therefore is not separable from what is emotional (for more on this topic, see Dow 2011).

Rationality is important—reasons are given to justify decisions. But these reasons can include support from social convention, or a dismissal of concerns about uncertainty, as well as a more conventional theoretical argument. Indeed, support from social convention and dismissal of concerns about uncertainty can be employed by economists as much as by business investors. The key is that formal deductivist logic yields definitive conclusions that can be classified as rational (even if they do not pertain to the economic system being studied), whereas human logic yields arguments involving reasoned judgment that is always open for discussion. There is no hard and fast divide between what is rational and what is irrational in human logic.

3.4   Implications for Methodology

I noted earlier that Keynes's theory of knowledge was intended to apply to economists as well as to agents. For economists, uncertainty means that certainty is in general beyond our grasp. Although researchers by definition push reason further and analyze more evidence than do other individuals, these efforts are not enough for forming judgments under uncertainty, and so we too draw on conventional knowledge and knowledge conventions. Theory then evolves when new connections are made on the basis of creative thinking, fueled by animal spirits.

One of the strongest conventions in mainstream economics is to employ general equilibrium analysis, based on rational optimizing individual behavior, to aim for the one best model of the economy. Lucas (1980) argued that Keynesian uncertainty was formalized and therefore operationalized by later technical advances in economics. For example, formal macro modeling techniques appeared to allow economists (and agents) to anticipate correctly the macroeconomic consequences of individual action and thus subvert any fallacy of composition. Similar analytical optimism is evident in current attempts to model the macroeconomic phenomenon of systemic risk. Inattention to systemic interdependencies among financial portfolios in decisionmaking at the micro level was a feature of the run-up to the crisis, causing a paradox of liquidity, as noted above.

A complete modeling system that yields definitive predictions (or at least multiple equilibria) requires the following conditions: structures with fixed (or at least predictably random) interrelations between separable parts (e.g., economic agents) and predictable (or at least predictably random) outside influences. Such a system is a "finite" system (Keynes 1921: 280), or in modern parlance, a closed system. Such a system, correctly applied, promotes internal consistency but risks inconsistency with the nature of the economic system, unless the latter is also closed. Arguably, an open, organic economic system can therefore be understood more consistently by means of an open theoretical system (Lawson 1997).

An open system is not the opposite of a closed system, because there is a range of possibilities for openness, depending on which conditions are not met and to what degree (Chick and Dow 2005). Indeed, it is an important feature of this view of knowledge that it is not dualistic. Deviating from a closed system, and thus from certainty or certainty equivalence, does not mean abandoning theory or formal models. On the contrary, Keynes was interested in identifying the logical grounds on which we habitually form beliefs, make judgments, and make decisions (both as economists and as economic agents) *in spite of* uncertainty. The question was what view of probability would be logically justified, in relation to the evidence, in an open system.

Economic agents are seen by Keynes as drawing on a range of incommensurate sources of knowledge, which, in combination with the exercise of judgment, provide the basis for decisionmaking. The weight of an argument increases as different lines of argument and sources of evidence support it. By the same token, economists also face uncertainty with respect to the future of an economy and can therefore also draw on a range of (incommensurate) sources of knowledge. By implication, sole reliance on a deductive chain of reasoning within mathematical formalism reduces the weight of the argument. One of the main attractions of mathematics is that it is capable of making different arguments commensurate. Thus, such variables as confidence and uncertainty aversion can be combined in a formal system (e.g., see Dequech 2000). But if these variables cannot be derived formally from a foundational account of behavior and in addition are not quantifiable, then such a model is not sufficient for prediction. Further, as Chick and Dow (2001) argue, the process of formalization is nonneutral in that it tends to change meanings. According to Keynes (1936: 297), formal modeling is therefore best used as an aid to thought, rather than something that alone yields definitive final answers:

> The object of our analysis is, not to provide a machine, or method of blind manipulation, which will furnish an infallible answer, but to provide ourselves with an organised and orderly method of thinking out particular problems; and, after we have reached a provisional conclusion by isolating the complicating factors one by one, we then have to go back on ourselves and allow, as well as we can, for the probable interactions of the factors amongst themselves. This is the nature of economic thinking. Any other way of applying our formal principles of thought (without which, however, we shall be lost in the wood) will lead us into error.

Any formal model is a closed system. Variables are specified and identified as endogenous or exogenous, and relations are specified among them. This is a mechanism for separating off some aspect of an open-system reality for analysis. But, for consistency with the subject matter, any analytical closure needs to be justified on the grounds that, for the purposes of the analysis, it is not unreasonable to treat the variables as having a stable identity, for them to have stable interrelations and not to be subject to unanticipated influences from outside. (To allow for random shocks is simply to assume certain knowledge of the randomness of outside influences.) But in applying such an analysis, it is important to consider what has been assumed away. Keynes's (1936: 297–298) own words, discussing formal theory that separates the effects of monetary expansion on output and prices, are appropriate:

> It is a great fault of symbolic pseudo-mathematical methods of formalising a system of economic analysis . . . that they expressly assume strict independence between the factors involved and lose all their cogency and authority if this hypothesis is disallowed; whereas, in ordinary discourse, where we are not blindly manipulating but know all the time what we are doing and what the words mean, we can keep "at the back of our heads" the necessary reserves and qualifications and the adjustments which we shall have to make later on, in a way in which we cannot keep complicated partial differentials "at the back" of several pages of algebra which assume that they all vanish. Too large a proportion of recent "mathematical" economics are merely concoctions, as imprecise as the initial assumptions they rest on, which allow the author to lose sight of the complexities and interdependencies of the real world in a maze of pretentious and unhelpful symbols.

Although general equilibrium analysis may be thought of as a mechanism for keeping hold of all relevant variables and interrelations among variables, Keynes's argument is that *any* formal model is bound to be an incomplete representation of an open-system reality. Any formal specification—in particular, any formal closure—abstracts from the complex interactions and evolution of interactions, as well as from unforeseen developments characterizing that reality. Models are inevitably partial representations, invoking closures that are both porous and provisional. They can only approximate reality, and even then cannot be presumed to persist. Therefore, from a Keynesian perspective, the better approach is simultaneously to segment off certain aspects of reality for partial formal modeling, keeping "at the back of our heads" as best we can what needs to be relaxed when applying the model's conclusions (in combination with the conclusions of other partial models) to policy recommendations. This approach is not the equivalent of rational expectations theory's assumption that the economist's expectations are formed with full knowledge of all interactions. The inconsistency of such an assumption with the real world is at the heart of Keynes's philosophy. Rather, it is more of a warning to bear in mind the assumptions made for modeling purposes and thus to take care not to leap directly from any one model to policy conclusions.

This methodology explains why Keynes's general theory did not take the form of a single large model with formal microfoundations. Macroeconomic relations in Keynes's view were separable as a partial analysis. It was not that Keynes lacked a microeconomic analysis, but rather that his study of individual behavior concluded that it was organic rather than atomistic. In particular, when facing uncertainty, individuals' sociality comes to the fore in their (rational) reliance on social conventional knowledge. Only if social conventions can be derived deductively from optimizing individual behavior can they be incorporated in a bottom-up microfoundation framework. And even then, changes in conventions and the choice to exercise animal spirits (or not) would have to be derivable from optimizing individual behavior. Indeed, it has been suggested that individual behavior instead needs to be expressed in relation to macrofoundations, to capture the macro influences on the individual (Nelson 1984). But from a Keynesian perspective, danger lies in retaining the idea of the macro and micro levels as conceptually distinct, with one foundational to the other. How the reality is segmented for analytical purposes in a pluralist framework is a matter of judgment, and different partial analyses can focus on different directions of influence between the micro and macro levels (for a full expression of this argument, see King 2012).

Thus, Keynesian analysis (of which there is a large body, mostly categorized as Post-Keynesian economics) employs a range of models and methods for gathering evidence, much of which will be incommensurate; were they commensurate, we would be back to general equilibrium theory as a complete system. There might be contradictions, in the sense that one variable might be endogenous to one chain of reasoning and exogenous to another (each chain being a provisional form of abstraction). The emphasis is rather on consistency with the organic nature of the subject matter and thus the uncertainty of knowledge about it. This is a pluralist strategy, in contrast to a monist strategy intent on generating a complete formal system (Salanti and Screpanti 1997; Dow 2004). It draws on ideas about robustness in systems of thought developed by Wimsatt (1981).

Such a methodology is intended to raise confidence in economists' judgment. Confidence increases with increasing weight of evidence (i.e., the number of partial chains of reasoning and types of evidence addressing a particular question). These partial analyses may not point in the same direction, but this may reflect the presence of a range of countervailing forces potentially acting simultaneously (Lawson 1997). Thus, it is unlikely that, putting together a range of analyses, it is possible to say with certainty that, say, inflation will rise to a certain level in the next 6 months. Rather, the economist can point to a range of potential forces and express some judgment as to where the balance lies in terms of the likely inflation outcome. Indeed, the balancing of a range of partial analyses normally characterizes the reasoning behind monetary policy (Downward and Mearman 2008). This is the case even though central banks still also use large formal macroeconomic models. Is the use of such formal models a reflection of convention in mainstream academic economics?

Finally, although partial formal models are important, we need to return to Keynes's theory of knowledge to recall that a major source of uncertainty is change in conventional judgment, especially that related to confidence in expectations, as well as to the exercise of agency under animal spirits, which may encourage discrete shifts in conventional judgment. Neither deductive logic nor inductive logic can predict such things with certainty. Therefore, Keynes's theory incorporates socio-psychological variables that cannot be explained and yet are not random; they can only be observed, and signs of impending changes noted by using alternative methods. Similarly, changes in practice and products can make the past a poor guide to the future; this observation has been an important element of Minsky's (1982) Keynesian theory of financial instability.

These sources of uncertainty have direct implications for policymakers. For example, although it is encouraging that systemic risk is now being modeled so that the interdependencies in the financial structure are better understood, the predictive power of such models is limited by their inability to explain or predict the state of confidence and changes in it (i.e., market sentiment). Methods to identify and observe market sentiment, as well as other aspects of conventional behavior, would therefore be part of a pluralist strategy for understanding financial markets. Similarly, when implementing macroprudential policy in response to knowledge about systemic risk, it would also be important for regulators to be vigilant at the micro level to pick up new practices and products, many of which may indeed be prompted by attempts to avoid macroregulation. In other words, the design of financial regulation itself could usefully reflect the micro-macro interactions identified by Keynes.

3.5   Conclusion

In considering rationality and the microfoundations issue in the light of Keynes's ideas, we have seen the centrality of uncertainty. For agents, uncertainty prevents a definitive complete ordering of assets (and of possibilities more generally), such that decisionmaking must rely on additional input from social convention and animal spirits. Because these are both liable to indeterminate discrete shifts, as well as to mutual conflict, there is scope for market behavior to be unstable in a way that is very difficult to anticipate (as to timing, direction, and degree). Such behavior by agents may well be reasonable, given existing knowledge, particularly given the internal logic of financial markets. At the same time, conventional understandings (e.g., with respect to the ability of a central bank to support a banking system) will reduce uncertainty and stabilize markets. But there may also be conflict with other social conventions (e.g., the sense of justice when considering remuneration across sectors), prompting individual responses and a political response in the form of regulation. The knowledge base for individual decisionmaking is not homogeneous.

The rationality implied for agents is more like something we might call "reasonableness," avoiding the strict conditions of the mainstream notion of rationality, which uncertainty precludes us from satisfying. This focus on possibilities for the individual to acquire knowledge has pointed us in the direction of the social, in the form of social conventions.

Uncertainty is also crucial for economists themselves when attempting to theorize about this inhomogeneous economic system, with its interplay between individuality and sociality. Given this subject matter, both deductive and inductive logic fall short, so that economists must also employ conventions as to how to proceed. Although a dominant convention has been to seek one best, formal, general equilibrium model, this approach has created inconsistencies with actual behavior, which is conditioned by uncertainty. The methodology emerging from Keynes's theory of knowledge is instead a pluralist one, mirroring the multipronged approach he suggested we take to knowledge as agents. This approach implies using a range of partial models, with provisional closures, together with a range of sources of evidence to build up a picture of the various forces at work in the economy. Forming a view on the basis of this plurality of knowledge in turn requires the exercise of judgment according to economists' human logic.

References

Akerlof, G. A., and R. J. Shiller. (2009) *Animal Spirits: How Human Psychology Drives the Economy, and Why It Matters for Global Capitalism*. Princeton, NJ: Princeton University Press.

Bibow, J. (2009) *Keynes on Monetary Policy, Finance and Uncertainty: Liquidity Preference Theory and the Global Financial Crisis*. London: Routledge.

Carabelli, A. (1988) *On Keynes's Method*. London: Macmillan.

Chick, V. (1995) "'Order out of Chaos' in Economics?" in S. C. Dow and J. Hillard (eds.), *Keynes, Knowledge and Uncertainty*. Cheltenham, UK: Edward Elgar, pp. 25–42.

Chick, V., and S. C. Dow. (2001) "Formalism, Logic and Reality: A Keynesian Analysis," *Cambridge Journal of Economics* 25: 705–722. Reprinted in S. C. Dow (ed.). (2012) *Foundations for New Economic Thinking: A Collection of Essays*. London: Palgrave Macmillan, pp. 140–161.

———. (2005) "The Meaning of Open Systems," *Journal of Economic Methodology* 12: 363–381. Reprinted under the title "The Non-Neutrality of Formalism," in S. C. Dow (ed.). (2012) *Foundations for New Economic Thinking: A Collection of Essays*. London: Palgrave Macmillan, pp. 178–196.

Coddington, A. (1976) "Keynesian Economics: The Search for First Principles," *Journal of Economic Literature* 14: 1258–1273.

Damasio, A. R. (1994) *Descartes' Error: Emotion, Reason, and the Human Brain*. New York: Avon Books.

Davidson, P. (2003) "The Terminology of Uncertainty in Economics and the Philosophy of an Active Role for Government Policies," in J. Runde and S. Mizuhara (eds.), *The Philosophy of Keynes's Economics: Probability, Uncertainty and Convention*. London: Routledge, pp. 229–238.

———. (2009) *John Maynard Keynes*. London: Palgrave Macmillan.

Davis, J. B. (1994) *Keynes's Philosophical Development*. Cambridge: Cambridge University Press.

Dequech, D. (1999) "Expectations and Confidence under Uncertainty," *Journal of Post Keynesian Economics* 21: 415–430.

———. (2000) "Asset Choice, Liquidity Preference and Rationality under Uncertainty," *Journal of Economic Issues* 34: 159–176.

———. (2003) "Conventional and Unconventional Behavior under Uncertainty," *Journal of Post Keynesian Economics* 26: 145–168.

———. (2005) "Confidence and Alternative Keynesian Methods of Asset Choice," *Review of Political Economy* 17: 533–547.

Dow, A. C., and S. C. Dow. (1985) "Animal Spirits and Rationality," in T. Lawson and H. Pesaran (eds.), *Keynes' Economics: Methodological Issues*. London: Croom Helm, pp. 46–65. Reprinted in S. C. Dow (ed.). (2012) *Foundations for New Economic Thinking: A Collection of Essays*. London: Palgrave Macmillan, pp. 33–51.

———. (2011) "Animal Spirits Revisited," *Capitalism and Society* 6: Article 1, available at: http://www.bepress.com/cas/vol6/iss2/art1/.

Dow, S. C. (1990) "Beyond Dualism," *Cambridge Journal of Economics* 14: 143–158. Reprinted in S. C. Dow (ed.). (2012) *Foundations for New Economic Thinking: A Collection of Essays*. London: Palgrave Macmillan, pp. 52–71.

———. (1991) "Keynes's Epistemology and Economic Methodology," in R. O'Donnell (ed.), *Keynes as Philosopher-Economist*. London: Macmillan, pp. 144–167.

———. (1995) "Uncertainty about Uncertainty," in S. C. Dow and J. Hillard (eds.), *Keynes, Knowledge and Uncertainty*. Cheltenham, UK: Edward Elgar, pp. 117–127. Reprinted in S. C. Dow (ed.). (2012) *Foundations for New Economic Thinking: A Collection of Essays*. London: Palgrave Macmillan, pp. 72–82.

———. (2004) "Structured Pluralism," *Journal of Economic Methodology* 11: 275–290. Reprinted in S. C. Dow (ed.). (2012) *Foundations for New Economic Thinking: A Collection of Essays*. London: Palgrave Macmillan, pp. 162–177.

———. (2011) "Cognition, Sentiment and Financial Instability: Psychology in a Minsky Framework," *Cambridge Journal of Economics* 35: 233–250.

Downward, P., and A. Mearman. (2008) "Decision-Making at the Bank of England: A Critical Appraisal," *Oxford Economic Papers* 60: 385–409.

Gerrard, B. (2003) "Keynesian Uncertainty: What Do We Know?" in J. Runde and S. Mizuhara (eds.), *The Philosophy of Keynes's Economics: Probability, Uncertainty and Convention*. London: Routledge, pp. 239–251.

Hodgson, G. (1988) *Economics and Institutions: A Manifesto for a Modern Institutional Economics*. Cambridge: Polity.

Keynes, J. M. (1921) *A Treatise on Probability*. London: Macmillan. Reprinted in *A Treatise on Probability. Collected Writings*, volume VIII. London: Macmillan, for the Royal Economic Society, 1973.

———. (1926) "Francis Ysidro Edgeworth 1845–1926," *Economic Journal* 36: 140–158. Reprinted in *Essays in Biography. Collected Writings*, volume X. London: Macmillan, for the Royal Economic Society, 1972, pp. 251–268.

———. (1931) "Ramsey as a Philosopher," *New Statesman and Nation*, October 3, pp. 153–154. Reprinted in *Essays in Biography. Collected Writings*, volume X. London: Macmillan, for the Royal Economic Society, 1972, pp. 335–346.

———. (1936) *The General Theory of Employment, Interest and Money*. London: Macmillan and Cambridge University Press. Reprinted in *The General Theory of Employment, Interest and Money. Collected Writings*, volume VII. London: Macmillan, for the Royal Economic Society, 1973.

———. (1937a) "The General Theory of Employment," *Quarterly Journal of Economics* 51: 209–223. Reprinted in *The General Theory and After: Defence and Development. Collected Writings*, volume XIV. London: Macmillan, for the Royal Economic Society, 1973, pp. 109–123.

———. (1937b) "Some Economic Consequences of a Declining Population," *Eugenics Review* 29: 13–17. Reprinted in *The General Theory and After: Defence and Development. Collected Writings*, volume XIV. London: Macmillan, for the Royal Economic Society, 1973, pp. 124–133.

———. (1949) "My Early Beliefs," in *Two Memoirs*. London: Rupert Hart Davis. Reprinted in *Essays in Biography. Collected Writings*, volume X. London: Macmillan, for the Royal Economic Society, 1972, pp. 433–451.

King, J. E. (2012) *The Microfoundations Delusion: Metaphor and Dogma in the History of Macroeconomics*. Cheltenham, UK: Edward Elgar.

Lawson, T. (1997) *Economics and Reality*. London: Routledge.

Lucas, R. E., Jr. (1980) "Methods and Problems in Business Cycle Theory," *Journal of Money, Credit, and Banking* 12: 696–715.

Minsky, H. P. (1982) *Can "It" Happen Again?* New York: ME Sharpe. Also published as *Inflation, Recession and Economic Policy.* Brighton, UK: Wheatsheaf.

Nelson, A. (1984) "Some Issues Surrounding the Reduction of Macroeconomics to Microeconomics," *Philosophy of Science* 51: 573–594.

O'Donnell, R. M. (1989) *Keynes: Philosophy, Economics and Politics.* London: Macmillan.

O'Reilly, C. A., III, and B. G. M. Main. (2010) "Economic and Psychological Perspectives on CEO Compensation: A Review and Synthesis," *Industrial and Corporate Change* 19: 675–712.

Park, M.-S., and S. Kayatekin. (2002) "Organicism, Uncertainty and 'Societal Interactionism': A Derridean Perspective," in S. C. Dow and J. Hillard (eds.), *Keynes, Uncertainty and the Global Economy.* Cheltenham, UK: Edward Elgar, pp. 106–127.

Phelps, E. S. (1968) "Money-Wage Dynamics and Labor Market Equilibrium," *Journal of Political Economy* 76: 678–711.

Phelps, E. S., G. C. Archibald, and A. A. Alchian (eds.). (1970) *Microeconomic Foundations of Employment and Inflation Theory.* New York: W. W. Norton.

Ramsey, F. P. (1931) *Foundations of Mathematics,* R. B. Braithwaite (ed.). London: Kegan Paul.

Runde, J. (1990) "Keynesian Uncertainty and the Weight of Argument," *Economics and Philosophy* 6: 275–292.

———. (1995) "Risk, Uncertainty and Bayesian Decision Theory: A Keynesian View," in S. C. Dow and J. Hillard (eds.), *Keynes, Knowledge and Uncertainty.* Cheltenham, UK: Edward Elgar, pp. 197–210.

Runde, J., and S. Mizuhara (eds.). (2003) *The Philosophy of Keynes's Economics: Probability, Uncertainty and Convention.* London: Routledge.

Salanti, A., and E. Screpanti (eds.). (1997) *Pluralism in Economics: Theory, History and Methodology.* Cheltenham, UK: Edward Elgar.

Savage, L. (1954) *The Foundations of Statistics.* New York: John Wiley.

Shackle, G. L. S. (1955) *Uncertainty in Economics.* Cambridge: Cambridge University Press.

Van Staveren, I. (2001) *The Values of Economics: An Aristotelian Perspective.* London: Routledge.

Wimsatt, W. C. (1981) "Robustness, Reliability and Overdetermination," in M. B. Brewer and B. E. Collins (eds.), *Scientific Inquiry and the Social Sciences.* San Fransisco: Jossey Bass.

Winslow, T. (2003) "The Foundation of Keynes's Economics," in J. Runde and S. Mizuhara (eds.), *The Philosophy of Keynes's Economics: Probability, Uncertainty and Convention.* London: Routledge, pp. 143–158.

CHAPTER FOUR

The Imperfect Knowledge Imperative in Modern Macroeconomics and Finance Theory

Roman Frydman and Michael D. Goldberg

> Quite apart from the fact that we do not know the future, the future is objectively not fixed. The future is open: objectively open.
>
> Karl R. Popper, *A World of Propensities* (1990)

> I confess that I prefer true but imperfect knowledge . . . to a pretense of exact knowledge that is likely to be false.
>
> Friedrich A. Hayek, *Nobel Lecture* (1974)

4.1   Introduction

Modern macroeconomics constructs models of aggregate outcomes on the basis of mathematical representations of individual decisionmaking, with market participants' forecasting behavior lying at the heart of the interaction between the two levels of analysis. Individuals' forecasts play a key role in how they make decisions, and markets aggregate those decisions into prices. The causal processes underlying both individual decisions and aggregate outcomes, therefore, depend on market participants' understanding of the economy and on how they use this knowledge to forecast the future.

Over the past four decades, economists have come to a nearly universal consensus that the Rational Expectations Hypothesis (REH) is the way to represent how rational, profit-seeking market participants forecast the future. Even behavioral economists, who have uncovered much evidence of REH's empirical failure, generally subscribe to this belief and have interpreted their findings as evidence that individuals fall short of "full rationality."

In this chapter, we argue that REH has no connection to how even minimally reasonable profit-seeking individuals forecast the future in real-world markets. We trace the root of REH's insurmountable epistemological difficulties and widespread empirical problems to a single, overarching premise that underpins contemporary macroeconomics and finance theory:

The authors are grateful to the Institute for New Economic Thinking for supporting the research on which this chapter is based.

nonroutine change—change that does not follow mechanical rules and procedures—is unimportant for understanding outcomes.

We also point out that contemporary behavioral finance models rest on the same core premise as their REH-based counterparts. Behavioral finance theorists claim that their portrayals of individual behavior are more "realistic." However, the assumption that nonroutine change is unimportant for understanding individual decisionmaking implies that their models, too, lack plausible microfoundations.

We also sketch an alternative approach to modeling individual behavior and aggregate outcomes: Imperfect Knowledge Economics (IKE). IKE opens macroeconomics and finance models to nonroutine change and the imperfect knowledge that it engenders, which is necessary to render their microfoundations both plausible and compatible with individual rationality.

4.2 The Pretense of Exact Knowledge

On the occasion of his 1974 Nobel lecture, Friedrich Hayek appealed to fellow economists to resist the "pretence of exact knowledge" in economic analysis. Drawing on his prescient analysis of the inevitable failure of central planning, Hayek warned against the lure of predetermination: no economist's model would ever render fully intelligible the causes of market outcomes or the consequences of government policies.

Ignoring Hayek's warning, contemporary macroeconomists and finance theorists have been much less circumspect about the ability of economic analysis to uncover the causal mechanism that underpins market outcomes. In fact, nearly all economists have come to believe that, to be worthy of scientific status, economic models should generate "sharp" predictions that account for the full range of possible market outcomes and their likelihoods.[1] But to construct such models, which we refer to as "fully predetermined," contemporary economists must fully specify in advance whether and how market participants alter their decisionmaking, and whether and how the social context—including economic policies, social and political factors, and institutions—unfolds over time. Contemporary models, therefore, rule out *by design* nonroutine change.

4.3 Assuming Away Nonroutine Change

In modeling the microfoundations of their models, economists relate an individual's preferences, forecasting strategy, and the constraints that she

---

1. For a comprehensive treatment of the concept of sharp prediction in the context of fully predetermined probabilistic models, see Sargent (1987) and Frydman and Goldberg (2007: chapters 3, 4, and 6).

faces to some set of causal variables. Assuming that an individual chooses the option that, according to her forecasting strategy, will maximize her well-being, an economist represents her decisionmaking in terms of the causal variables and parameters appearing in each of the components— preferences, forecasting strategy, and constraints. The functional form of such a representation of optimal decisions, its parameters, and the properties of the causal variables constitute the causal structure of the microfoundations of macroeconomic models.

An economist formalizes his assumptions about how an individual makes decisions with restrictions that constrain the structure of his model and how it might change over time. Alternative sets of restrictions permit economists to formalize alternative causal accounts of outcomes. Although contemporary macroeconomic and finance models differ in their specifications on both the individual and aggregate levels, they *all* share one core feature: restrictions that exactly relate the properties of the model's causal structure at all points in time, past and future, to the properties of the structure at some "initial" point in time.

4.3.1 The Causal Structure

At each point in time, the structure of an economist's representation is characterized by the following properties:

1. The composition of the set of causal variables.
2. The properties of the joint probability distribution of the causal variables.[2]
3. A functional form that relates outcomes to the causal variables, which typically includes the signs of partial derivatives. In cases such as the example we examine here, in which the functional form is explicit, economists often restrict the signs of some parameters.

Contemporary macroeconomists and finance theorists assume away nonroutine change by fully prespecifying how the structure of their models changes over time, which is illustrated by our simple algebraic example. Later, we use this example to show how assuming away nonroutine change led economists to the nearly universal, yet fundamentally misguided, belief that REH is the only scientific way to represent rational forecasting. We also make use of this simple model to show how IKE provides macroeconomic models with plausible individual foundations.

---

2. If the model includes additive error terms, the conditions imposed by an economist also specify the joint probability distribution between these terms and the causal variables.

4.3.2 A Fully Predetermined Model of an Asset Price

Our example is motivated by basic supply-and-demand analysis in financial markets. In modeling an individual's demand for and supply of an asset, economists typically relate these to her forecast of the asset's future price and a set of causal variables. Aggregating over individuals and equating aggregate demand and supply typically yields the following representation, in semi-reduced form, for the equilibrium market price at a point in time t:[3]

$$P_t = a_t + b_t X_t + c_t \hat{P}_{t|t+1},\tag{1}$$

where $\hat{P}_{t|t+1}$ is an aggregate of market participants' forecasts formed at t of the market price at $t + 1$, (a_t, b_t, c_t) is a vector of parameters, and X_t is a set of causal variables. These variables typically represent the unfolding of economic policies, including those affecting the money supply, interest rates, or tax rules. Sometimes the causal variables include factors that represent other aspects of the social context in which an individual makes decisions, such as institutional and regulatory changes.

Individual forecasts that comprise the aggregate forecast, $\hat{P}_{t|t+1}$, are formed on the basis of forecasting strategies at t. Economists model these strategies by relating them to a set of causal variables, which represents the information sets used by market participants. An aggregate of such representations can be written as

$$\hat{P}_{t|t+1} = \alpha_t + \beta_t Z_t\tag{2}$$

where Z_t is a vector of variables that characterizes the union of information sets used by market participants, and (α_t, β_t) is a vector of parameters.

4.3.3 Fully Predetermining Restrictions

In general, as time passes, individuals alter the way they make decisions. Institutions, economic policies, and other factors also change over time. These changes influence the way aggregate outcomes move over time. Thus, to model how market outcomes unfold over time, an economist will need different structures—different specifications of forecasting, preferences, constraints, decision and aggregation rules, or the processes driving the causal variables—at different points in time to represent individual behavior.

Remarkably, contemporary macroeconomists typically constrain the structure of their models to remain unchanging over time. As we shall discuss shortly, except for random deviations that average out to zero, these models rule out altogether the importance of change on the individual and

---

3. In Frydman and Goldberg (Chapter 6, this volume), we derive the aggregate representation for the movement of equity prices of the form in (1) from explicit microfoundations.

aggregate levels for understanding outcomes. In those relatively infrequent cases in which contemporary models do allow for change in their structure, they fully prespecify when it occurs. They also specify in advance the structure of the post-change representation of outcomes on the individual and aggregate levels.

To illustrate how this is done, we focus on revisions in forecasting strategies and constrain the structure of the other components of the model to be time invariant. The following constraints in (1) impose time invariance on the nonexpectational components of the model:

- The composition of the set of causal variables, X_t, and the properties of their joint probability distribution remain unchanged at all times, past and future.

- The parameters (a_t, b_t, c_t) are constants, that is, $(a_t, b_t, c_t) = (a, b, c)$ for all t.[4]

In general, the representation of revisions in forecasting strategies may involve a change in the composition of the set of causal variables, Z_t, or even different functional forms. Because these complications would not affect any of our conclusions, we suppose that an economist represents revisions of forecasting strategies with a parametric shift in his aggregate representation at $t+1$ and that he assumes that these strategies will remain unchanged thereafter:

$$\hat{P}_{t+\tau|t+\tau+1} = \alpha_{t+\tau} + \beta_{t+\tau} Z_{t+\tau} \tag{3}$$

where $\alpha_t \neq \alpha_{t+1}$, $\beta_t \neq \beta_{t+1}$, $\alpha_{t+\tau} = \alpha_{t+\tau+1}$, and $\beta_{t+\tau} = \beta_{t+\tau+1}$ for all $\tau = 1, 2, 3 \ldots$. In this example, revisions, which are set to occur only at $t+1$, are represented by two constants, $\alpha_{(t,t+1)}$ and $\beta_{(t,t+1)}$:[5]

$$\alpha_{(t,t+1)} = \alpha_{t+1} - \alpha_t \quad \text{and} \quad \beta_{(t,t+1)} = \beta_{t+1} - \beta_t \tag{4}$$

Contemporary economists fully prespecify revisions of forecasting strategies, which can be simply represented as constraining $\alpha_{(t,t+1)}$ and $\beta_{(t,t+1)}$ to

4. For the sake of simplicity, we display time-invariance constraints only on the aggregate level. However, the parameters and causal variables in (1) arise from the nonexpectational components on the individual level. Thus, the time-invariance constraints implicitly apply to these components of the model's microfoundations.

5. Except for purely formal complications, our conclusions in this section apply to nonlinear representations. For example, suppose that the representation of the aggregate forecasting strategy at $t+1$ is a nonlinear function of the causal variables. In such a case, $\alpha_{(t,t+1)}$ and $\beta_{(t,t+1)}$ would be nonlinear functions of the causal variables.

be equal to particular values, say, $\bar{\alpha}$ and $\bar{\beta}$, respectively:

$$\bar{\alpha} = \alpha_{t+1} - \alpha_t \quad \text{and} \quad \bar{\beta} = \beta_{t+1} - \beta_t \tag{5}$$

We refer to such constraints as "fully predetermining restrictions."[6]

Sometimes fully predetermining restrictions are probabilistic. For example, an influential class of contemporary models fully prespecifies the timing of all changes with a Markov switching process. At any point in time, t, this rule exactly relates the timing of future change and the switch to the fully prespecified post-change structure of (2) to the structure at t.[7] Frydman and Goldberg (2007: chapters 4 and 6) show that all our conclusions in this chapter, derived in the context of the simple model presented here, apply to models that use fully prespecified probabilistic rules to represent change.

To complete the full prespecification of change in their models, economists also prespecify how the social context in which individuals forecast the future and make decisions unfolds over time. This is typically done by representing the processes that govern the movements of the causal variables with standard time-series models. These movements are driven by stochastic "shocks," the probability distributions of which are also fully predetermined.

To simplify our presentation, assume that each set of causal factors in (1) and (2), X_t and Z_t, consists of only one causal variable, x_t and z_t, respectively.[8] We make use of the following simple representations of these variables:

$$x_t = \mu_x(1 - \rho_x) + \rho_x x_{t-1} + \epsilon_t^x \tag{6}$$

$$z_t = \mu_z(1 - \rho_z) + \rho_z z_{t-1} + \epsilon_t^z \tag{7}$$

where $\mu_x, \mu_z, \rho_x, \rho_z$ are constant parameters, $|\rho_x| < 1$, $|\rho_z| < 1$, and ϵ_t^x and ϵ_t^z are random shocks. As is customary in the literature, we refer to the causal variables appearing in the representation of forecasting strategies as "information" and to the shocks to these variables as "news."

Once an economist portrays causal factors as random variables, his representations become probabilistic. To render them fully predetermined, economists specify in advance the probability distribution governing the random shocks. We follow the usual practice and constrain these shocks

---

6. The imposition of time invariance, which is common in contemporary models, thus involves a particularly simple form of fully predetermining restrictions: $\bar{\alpha} = 0$ and $\bar{\beta} = 0$.

7. For the seminal formulation of such models, see Hamilton (1988, 1994).

8. The set Z_t often includes endogenous variables, such as the current asset price P_t. We omit such variables here, as allowing for them would complicate our analysis without affecting our general conclusions.

to be drawn from an unchanging distribution with a mean of zero and constant variances, $\sigma^2_{\epsilon^x}$ and $\sigma^2_{\epsilon^z}$, respectively. For the sake of simplicity, we also constrain these shocks to be uncorrelated over time and uncorrelated with each other at every point in time. Such invariant distributions of shocks are a special case of standard probabilistic representations of uncertainty, which we refer to as "fully predetermined probability distributions."

4.4 Sharp Predictions of Nothing New

The fully predetermined distribution of shocks and the fully predetermined —and time-invariant—processes governing the movements of the causal variables immediately imply that the joint probability distribution of x_t and z_t is also fully predetermined.

Thus, conditional on realizations of the shock, ϵ^z_t, from time t to $t+\tau$, and the structure of processes governing its movement over time, (7), the overarching probability distribution characterizes $z_{t+\tau}$ for all $\tau = 0, 1\ldots$:

$$z_{t+\tau} = \mu_z \left[1 - (\rho_z)^\tau\right] + (\rho_z)^\tau z_t + \varepsilon^z_{(t,t+\tau)} \tag{8}$$

where

$$\varepsilon^z_{(t,t+\tau)} = \sum_{j=1}^{\tau} (\rho^z)^j \epsilon^z_{t+\tau-j} \tag{9}$$

Similarly, $x_{t+\tau}$ can be written in terms of μ_z, ρ_z, and $\varepsilon^x_{(t,t+\tau)}$.

The representation in (8) shows that by specifying information to evolve according to a mechanical rule, an economist in effect presumes that he can fully prespecify changes in the social context. Once this presumption is combined with a fully prespecified representation of revisions in forecasting strategies, (5), an economist can produce a "sharp prediction" of the one-period-ahead forecasts and their probabilities at any time $t+\tau$, conditional on the structure of the model and the realization of the causal variable at t:

$$\hat{P}_{t+\tau|t+\tau+1} - \hat{P}_{t|t+1} = \hat{A} + \hat{B}z_t + (\beta_t + \overline{\beta})\varepsilon^z_{(t,t+\tau)} \quad \text{for } \tau = 1, 2\ldots \tag{10}$$

where $\hat{A} = \left\{\overline{\alpha} + (\beta_t + \overline{\beta})\mu_z \left[1 - (\rho_z)^\tau\right]\right\}$, and $\hat{B} = \overline{\beta} + (\beta_t + \overline{\beta})\left[(\rho_z)^\tau - 1\right]$.

Analogously to (8), the representation in (10) decomposes change in the one-period-ahead forecast formed at t and $t+\tau - \left(\hat{P}_{t+\tau|t+\tau+1} - \hat{P}_{t|t+1}\right)$ into two fully predetermined components. The first is the expectation of change

$\hat{A} + \hat{B}z_t$, which an economist presumes to know exactly, conditional on the structure of the parameters of the forecasting strategies at t; their change at $t + 1$, $(\overline{\alpha}, \overline{\beta})$; and current and past information, as summarized in z_t. As time passes, this fully predetermined path of forecast revisions varies with new realizations of information triggered by the second component of change: future news, $(\beta_t + \overline{\beta})\varepsilon^z_{(t,t+\tau)}$.

This second component represents the only uncertainty in an economist's model concerning future information that market participants might consider relevant in forming their forecasts. Contemporary models constrain news to evolve according to an overarching probability distribution that fully predetermines its possible realizations and their probabilities in all time periods.

Thus, contemporary representations of forecast revisions assume away the possibility that participants might revise their forecasting strategies, or that the social context might change, in ways that cannot be fully foreseen— that is, that an economist cannot characterize with a standard probability distribution. An analogous argument shows that contemporary models also assume away nonroutine change in other aspects of behavior on the individual and aggregate levels.

As they do for forecast revisions, these models represent change in aggregate outcomes with two fully predetermined components, each presuming that nothing genuinely new can ever happen:

$$P_{t+\tau} - P_t = \left[A + Bx_t + B^z z_t\right] + \left[b\varepsilon^x_{(t,t+\tau)} + c(\beta_t + \overline{\beta})\varepsilon^z_{(t,t+\tau)}\right] \quad (11)$$

where $A = b\mu_x\left[1 - (\rho_x)^\tau\right] + c\hat{A}$, $B = b\left[(\rho_x)^\tau - 1\right]$, $B^z = c\hat{B}$, and $\hat{A}$ and $\hat{B}$ are defined in (10).

4.5   Fully Predetermined Rationality

We have shown how insistence on sharp predictions requires an economist to embrace contemporary models' core premise that nonroutine change is unimportant for understanding outcomes. Moreover, this premise has led economists to believe that they have discovered a universal way to represent how rational individuals make decisions.

To select and justify the particular parametric functions that they use to represent "rational" preferences in the microfoundations of their models, economists appeal to a set of a priori assumptions, which postulate that an individual's choices among the available options follow a consistent pattern. The structure of such preference representations is typically constrained to remain unchanged over time.

Macroeconomists typically assume that the consequences of each option are uncertain. To rank such options, conventional economists have relied on the expected utility hypothesis (von Neumann and Morgenstern 1944). But, to represent expected utility, an economist must represent how a "rational" individual assesses the probabilities that she attaches to the consequences of choosing alternative options, as well as how she revises these assessments over time. Nearly all economists have come to believe that REH provides their models' fully predetermined microfoundations with the forecasting component needed to generate such assessments.

4.5.1 The Rational Expectations Hypothesis

Prior to REH, economists portrayed market participants' forecasting strategies with mechanical rules that made no explicit reference to the way the economy works or how the causal process underpinning outcomes might change over time.[9] In an attempt to incorporate such considerations into representations of forecasting, John Muth proposed the Rational Expectations Hypothesis: market participants' forecasts "are essentially the same as the predictions of the relevant economic theory" (Muth 1961: 316).

Muth's idea was that economists, by representing participants' forecasting strategies with a model that adequately described their understanding of the causal process underpinning outcomes, would be able to "make sensible predictions about the way expectations would change . . . when the structure of the system is changed" (Muth 1961: 315–316).

Muth was well aware that the term "rational expectations" suggests some notion of rationality. Indeed, he explicitly warned that REH should not be viewed as a normative hypothesis about how rational individuals should forecast the future. As he put it, "at the risk of confusing this *purely descriptive hypothesis* with a pronouncement as to what firms ought to do, we call such expectations 'rational' " (Muth 1961: 316, emphasis added).

Even viewed as a purely descriptive hypothesis, it is far from clear how REH should be used to describe market participants' forecasting strategies. To implement REH, economists had to take a stand on the question of "the relevant economic theory" to which the hypothesis refers.

Muth, in illustrating REH, implemented it in a time-invariant model of a market for an agricultural good that is produced with a production lag. This lag requires that farmers must form forecasts of its future market price to decide how much of the good to produce. Muth represented these forecasts by equating farmers' expectations regarding the market price at t to be equal to the prediction of that price, implied by his own model, at $t - 1$.

---

9. The most widely used rule was called "adaptive expectations," originally formulated by Cagan (1956), Friedman (1956), and Nerlove (1958).

Examining his model, Muth then observed that, were his representation of the aggregate of participants' forecasting strategies to differ from his model's sharp prediction—the conditional probability distribution—of the market price, his representation of participants' forecasting would result time and again in obvious and systematic forecast errors. Although Muth's model represented an aggregate outcome in a particularly simple market, it is easy to see that this implication holds in the context of any fully predetermined model. For example, the forecast errors, $\left(P_{t+1} - \hat{P}_{t|t+1}^{\mathrm{FP}}\right)$, resulting from a fully predetermined non-REH forecasting strategy, represented in our model with (2) and (5), are obviously and systematically correlated with the information at time t:

$$E_{\mathrm{M}}\left[\left(P_{t+1} - \hat{P}_{t|t+1}^{\mathrm{FP}}\right)|I_t\right] = C^{(1)} + b(\rho_x)^{\tau}x_t + C^{(2)}z_t \tag{12}$$

where E_{M} is the expectation of the fully predetermined conditional distribution produced by our example, I_t is the information available at t, (x_t, z_t), and $C^{(1)}$ and $C^{(2)}$ are constants that depend on the parameters of the model and its representation of forecasting strategies at t and $t + 1$.

Nevertheless, because the model is fully predetermined, its prediction error, $\left(P_{t+1} - E_{\mathrm{M}}[P_{t+1}|I_t]\right)$, is *by design* uncorrelated with I_t:

$$E_{\mathrm{M}}\left[\left(P_{t+1} - \hat{P}_{t|t+1}^{\mathrm{M}}\right)|I_t\right] = 0 \tag{13}$$

where $\hat{P}_{t|t+1}^{\mathrm{M}} = E_{\mathrm{M}}\left[P_{t+1}|I_t\right]$.

Comparing expressions analogous to (12) and (13) in the context of his model, Muth remarked that, were a fully predetermined model to impute non-REH forecasting strategies to participants, "there would be opportunities . . . to profit from the knowledge—by inventory speculation . . . or by selling a price forecasting service to the firms" (Muth 1961: 318). The "knowledge" that such a service would presumably sell is the superior price predictions produced by an economist's own fully predetermined model.

It also follows that the imposition of REH in any fully predetermined model eliminates the correlation between forecast errors and current information implied by fully predetermined non-REH representations of the aggregate of forecasting strategies. To illustrate this point and to display the structure of the REH representation, $\hat{P}_{t|t+1}^{\mathrm{RE}}$ (which will be useful in our later discussion), we note that because this representation is defined by

$$\hat{P}_{t|t+1}^{\mathrm{RE}} = E_{\mathrm{M}}\left[P_{t+1}|I_t\right] \tag{14}$$

it immediately follows that[10]

$$\hat{P}^{RE}_{t|t+1} = \alpha^{RE} + \beta^{RE} x_t \tag{15}$$

where

$$\alpha^{RE} = \frac{a}{(1-c)} + \frac{(1-\rho^x)\mu_x}{(1-c)(1-c\rho^x)} \quad \text{and} \quad \beta^{RE} = \frac{b\rho^x}{(1-c\rho^x)} \tag{16}$$

By design, one-period-ahead forecast errors, $\left(P_{t+1} - \hat{P}^{RE}_{t|t+1}\right)$, are represented with a linear combination of future news, $\left(\epsilon^x_{t+1}, \epsilon^z_{t+1}\right)$. Consequently, Muth (1961: 318) observed that, *in the context of his model*, "profit opportunities would no longer exist if the aggregate expectation of [market participants] is the same as the prediction of the theory."

Muth did not explicitly acknowledge that these implications crucially depend on his model's core premise that its fully predetermined specification adequately represents how the market price unfolds over time. Once an economist presumes that he has found a fully predetermined account of outcomes, it follows as a matter of straightforward logic that not making use of this "knowledge" would imply passing up obvious profit opportunities. Nevertheless, Muth was ambivalent about treating such "profit opportunities" as pointing to opportunities in real-world markets. Remarkably, he seemed to treat his observation that REH could somehow result from profit-seeking behavior as a purely theoretical artifact of his model's assumptions. Although his model suggested a connection between REH and rational forecasting, he did not alter his interpretation of REH as a "purely descriptive hypothesis,"[11] and he did not soften his warning that it should not be confused with "a pronouncement of what [market participants] ought to do."

4.5.2 The End of Ambivalence

Lacking a normative or other justification for using REH to represent individual forecasting, macroeconomists working in the 1960s largely ig-

---

10. In deriving the REH representation in (15), we follow standard practice and constrain the parameter c_t in (1) to be equal to or less than unity. We recall that for the sake of simplicity, each of the parameters a_t, b_t, and c_t in that specification is also assumed to be unchanging over time; that is, $a_t = a$, $b_t = b$, and $c_t = c$. Allowing for fully predetermined change would modify the REH representation, but it would not affect any of our conclusions.

11. As we shall argue shortly, REH is neither a descriptively nor a normatively adequate hypothesis concerning forecasting in real-world markets. In fact, the insurmountable flaws in both of these interpretations stem from the core premise of the contemporary approach. For an extensive discussion, see Frydman and Goldberg (2011: chapters 3 and 4).

nored it in modeling forecasting behavior.[12] However, many models developed at that time, particularly large-scale econometric models aimed at explaining time series of aggregate outcomes, were characterized by inconsistency between their representations of individual forecasting and their structure on the aggregate level. Robert Lucas focused on this inconsistency as these models' fundamental flaw. As he recounted in his Nobel lecture,

> The prevailing strategy for macroeconomic modeling in the early 1960s held that the individual or sectoral models . . . could . . . simply be combined in a single [macroeconomic] model. But models of individual decisions over time necessarily involve expected future prices. . . . However, . . . [aggregate] models assembled from such individual components implied behavior of actual prices . . . that bore no relation to, and were in general *grossly inconsistent* with, the price expectations that the theory imputed to individual agents. [Lucas 1995: 254–255, emphasis added]

Echoing Muth, Lucas observed that models involving such "gross inconsistency" imply that an economist imputes to market participants forecasting strategies that generate obvious and systematic forecast errors. But, because Lucas took for granted the premise that a fully predetermined model could provide an adequate account of how "actual prices" evolve over time, he interpreted the obvious forecast errors—implied by non-REH representations in such a model—as a symptom of irrationality on the part of participants in real-world markets. Thus, in contrast to Muth, he presumed that the ostensibly easily detectable, yet unexploited, correlations between these forecast errors and readily available information, which are an artifact of his model's assumptions, point to obvious, yet unrealized, profit opportunities in real-world markets. As he later emphatically put it, "if your theory reveals profit opportunities, you have the wrong theory" (Lucas 2001: 13) of "actual prices."

In a leap of faith that would change macroeconomics and finance for generations, Lucas brushed aside Muth's ambivalence and presumed that the "right theory" is a fully predetermined model in which REH characterizes how rational individuals forecast future market outcomes.

---

12. Indeed, when Phelps organized a milestone conference in 1969 on the role of expectations in modeling the microfoundations of macroeconomic theories, the papers collected in the conference volume (Phelps et al. 1970) made no use of REH, and it is not even listed in the index.

4.5.3 The REH Revolution: Model Consistency as a Standard of Rationality

Lucas's belief of what constitutes the "right theory" gained wide acceptance among macroeconomists and finance theorists. REH was embraced by a vast majority of economists, spanning the Chicago free-market and MIT's New Keynesian schools. REH's imposition of exact consistency between the predictions of market outcomes implied by an economist's own fully predetermined model and individuals' forecasting strategies quickly became the standard way to represent how rational individuals think about the future.

Because it could be applied in every fully predetermined model, the REH standard had much to recommend it to economists who believe that fully predetermined accounts of market outcomes are within reach of economic analysis. Faith in the divine apotheosis of economic theory led economists to hypothesize that every time one of them formulates a fully predetermined model, he has discovered such an account of market outcomes. Once an economist entertained such a hypothesis, it seemed reasonable to suppose that profit seeking would compel market participants to search for such a model, which they should be able to discover, because, after all, an economist already did.

4.5.4 The Misleading Narrative of REH

Lucas's (2001) informal account of why he found REH so compelling highlights the narrative that led so many economists to share his belief. Lucas considered a simple, fully predetermined model of a market that attributes to firms in each period the forecast that a market price will remain constant at its current level, whereas the model predicts that the market price nonetheless rises period after period. According to Lucas (2001: 13), "in such a model, you could see profit opportunities that firms were passing up. Why couldn't they see these opportunities, too?"

Such informal arguments have underpinned the widespread belief that REH somehow follows from the assumption of profit maximization—that it simply represents the idea that market participants optimally use the information available to them.

However, even before REH reached its ascendancy in macroeconomics, critics pointed out that this narrative has no foundations. Contrary to Lucas's presumption, the early critics of REH showed that, even under the fanciful assumption that an economist has discovered a fully predetermined account of market outcomes, profit seeking would, in general, neither compel nor lead market participants to forecast according to a particular economist's model.[13]

---

13. See Frydman (1982, 1983) for a rigorous demonstration of this point in the context of a widely used class of REH models with decentralized information, such as those developed by

Thomas Sargent, one of the most forceful early advocates of REH, acknowledged these critical arguments and recognized that treating REH as a descriptively or normatively plausible hypothesis about how market participants forecast the future is "misleading":

> The idea of rational expectations is sometimes explained informally by saying that it reflects a process in which individuals are inspecting and altering their forecasting records. . . . It is also sometimes said that [REH embodies] the idea that economists and the agents they are modeling should be placed on equal footing: the agents in the model should be able to forecast and profit-maximize and utility-maximize as well as . . . the econometrician who constructed the model. [Sargent 1993: 21]

He then pointed out that

> these ways of explaining things are suggestive, but *misleading*, because they make [REH] sound less restrictive and more behavioral than it really is. [Sargent 1993: 21, emphasis added]

4.6   The Orwellian World of "Rational" Microfoundations

Despite such seemingly incisive criticisms, nearly all economists, including Sargent himself, have continued to use REH to model "rational" microfoundations. Because REH, by design, imposes exact consistency between the sharp prediction—a single probability distribution of outcomes—implied by an economist's aggregate model and the probability distribution representing participants' forecasting strategies, REH forces an economist to represent forecasting on the individual level with a single overarching probability distribution.[14]

Thus, REH determines forecasting on its models' aggregate and individual levels jointly. And, because in "rational expectations models, people's beliefs are the outcomes of our theorizing,"[15] these models lack genuine microfoundations. After all, they rule out the possibility that "people's beliefs" could affect outcomes in a way that an economist cannot fully prespecify.

Lucas (1973) and Stiglitz (2001). For an extensive discussion of REH's epistemological flaws, see Frydman and Phelps (1983) and Phelps (1983).

14. Sometimes economists allow for more than one way for an individual to alter her decisionmaking strategy. As in other contemporary models, however, such "multiple-equilibrium" models fully prespecify the set of decisionmaking strategies to which an individual may switch from an initial strategy. Indeed, these models typically use REH to predetermine fully each of the forecasting strategies to which an individual may switch. For a formal demonstration of how such models disregard nonroutine change, see Frydman and Goldberg (2007: chapter 6).

15. Sargent in an interview with Evans and Honkapohja (2005: 566).

Economists have interpreted REH-based models' microfoundations in one of two ways. The REH forecasting strategy is thought to represent either how market participants forecast the future in the aggregate, or how every one of them does so individually. Both interpretations suffer from insurmountable difficulties, owing to flaws that can be traced to the contemporary approach's core premise.

4.6.1   The Market Renamed

In proposing REH, Muth thought of it as a "purely descriptive hypothesis" about "the market's" forecasting strategy. Moreover, he did not claim that REH presupposes that every market participant must forecast according to "the relevant economic theory": REH "does not assert that the scratch work of entrepreneurs resembles the system of equations [in an economist's model] in any way" (Muth 1961: 317). Moreover, REH did not imply "that predictions of [individuals] are perfect or that their expectations are all the same" (Muth 1961: 317).

Although Muth's formulation of REH as a hypothesis about the market sidestepped the diversity of forecasting strategies, he did suggest that REH is compatible with it. This belief seems to be widely shared. Many economists view REH as an approximation that enables them to capture in a parsimonious way the complexities that the diversity of forecasts, and market participants' revisions of their forecasting strategies, pose for understanding outcomes.

However, the interpretation that REH approximates the market's— rather than an individual's—forecasting strategy somehow had to be reconciled with REH's use in modeling the microfoundations of aggregate models. Because REH, by design, obscures the distinction between individual forecasting and aggregate prediction, the separation between the two levels was accomplished by renaming "the market," which was henceforth known as a "representative agent." Soon, the purely definitional aggregate of market participants' strategies began to be viewed as the way a single "representative" individual thinks about the future.[16] Because, after Phelps's

---

16. The contemporary models' presumption that the aggregate of market participants' forecasting strategies adequately approximates how a single representative agent thinks about the future disregards the key distinction between an individual's and the market's allocation of resources. As Hayek (1945, 1948) argued in his prescient analysis of the inevitable failure of socialist planning, helping society cope with and take advantage of the diversity of knowledge, "which is not given to anyone in its totality" (Hayek 1945: 520), is the key to understanding what markets do. For a rigorous demonstration of how Hayek's critique of socialist planning implies the incoherence of contemporary models of the market, see Frydman (1983). For an extensive discussion of the close affinity of these models to the ideas underlying central planning, see Frydman and Rapaczynski (1993, 1994) and Frydman and Goldberg (2011: chapter 2).

milestone 1969 conference, macroeconomists began to take their models' microfoundations seriously, this obfuscation became an important component of REH's misleading narrative, opening the way to its widespread use in modeling "rational" foundations of contemporary macroeconomic and finance models.[17]

4.6.2 The Pseudodiversity of Rational Expectations

Calling the market's forecasting strategy that of a "representative agent" was supposed to sidestep the problem caused by constraining representations of individual forecasting to a single probability distribution; namely, that REH could not explicitly model the diversity of market participants' forecasting strategies.[18] The belief, shared by many economists, that the rational representative agent's forecasting strategy adequately captures this diversity stood reality—forecasting in real-world markets—on its head: the rational representative agent neither represents how participants' diversity unfolds over time, nor is it compatible with individual rationality.

The claim that the representative agent's forecasting strategy approximates micro-level diversity overlooks REH's requirement that the proportions of participants holding particular views of the future, together with their forecasting strategies, must unfold over time in a fully predetermined way. The same mechanical rules are presumed to characterize the pseudodiversity of participants' forecasting strategies, so that any change in the proportion of market participants holding different views, or any revisions in their views, must be mechanically tied to each other to ensure that REH holds in the aggregate at all points in time—past, present, and future.

To illustrate this point, we allow for a minimal degree of diversity in our simple example of the REH model in (1), (14), and (15). In accordance

---

17. The belief of Lucas and most other economists that the representative agent's forecasting strategy adequately captures such diversity has underpinned macroeconomic and policy analysis around the world. For example, a representative agent's forecasting strategy plays a key role in Lucas's (1976) famous crititique of Keynesian macroeconometric models. Moreover, even the most prominent critics of orthodox theory use REH as a "matter of convenience" in modeling microfoundations. See, for example, Stiglitz (2010). For an extensive discussion of this point, see Frydman and Goldberg (2008, 2011).

18. Although REH models by design rule out explicit representation of the diversity of forecasting strategies, they have been used to represent heterogeneity of market participants' forecasts. Such representations suppose that every participant forecasts according to REH, and that differences in their forecasts arise solely from participants' access to, or their choosing to rely on, different information. Such formulations include Lucas's (1973) model with decentralized information and Stiglitz's (2001) models with asymmetric information. As Frydman (1982, 1983) showed rigorously and Frydman and Goldberg (2011: chapter 1) discuss extensively, our critique of the standard REH models that ignore decentralized information also applies to models that allow for heterogeneity of information used by market participants in forming their forecasts.

with the contemporary approach, we represent forecasting strategies of two groups of participants—say, bulls and bears in an equity market—with two *distinct* fully predetermined analogues to (2):

$$\hat{P}^{(i)}_{t|t+1} = \alpha^{(i)} + \beta^{(i)} Z^{(i)}_t, \quad i = 1, 2 \tag{17}$$

where $(\alpha^{(i)}, \beta^{(i)})$ are parameters and $Z^{(i)}_t$ denotes the two causal variables appearing in the representation of the forecasting strategies, $i = 1, 2$. Consequently, the market's—the representative agent's (RA's)—forecasting strategy can be written as:

$$\hat{P}^{RA}_{t|t+1} = w \hat{P}^{(1)}_{t|t+1} + (1 - w) \hat{P}^{(2)}_{t|t+1} \tag{18}$$

where w and $(1 - w)$ are the aggregation weights that sum up to unity.[19]

We suppose that the causal factors in (17) follow the same kind of autoregressive process as in (7):

$$z^{(i)}_t = \mu_{z^{(i)}}(1 - \rho_{z^{(i)}}) + \rho_{z^{(i)}} z^{(i)}_{t-1} + \epsilon^{z^{(i)}}_t, \quad i = 1, 2 \tag{19}$$

To simplify our presentation, we specify explicitly the relationships between $z^{(i)}_t$ and the causal factor appearing in the economists' aggregate model, x_t in (1). To this end, we suppose that the vector of shocks $(\epsilon^x_t, \epsilon^{z^{(1)}}_t, \epsilon^{z^{(2)}}_t)$ is normally distributed and uncorrelated over time. Using standard formulas enables us to express the causal factors in terms of x_t as follows:

$$z^{(i)}_t = \gamma^{(i)}_0 + \gamma^{(i)}_1 x_t + \eta^{(i)}_t, \quad i = 1, 2 \tag{20}$$

where

$$\gamma^{(i)}_0 = \mu_{z^{(i)}}(1 - \rho_{z^{(i)}}), \qquad \gamma^{(i)}_1 = \frac{Cov\left(\epsilon^x_t, \epsilon^{z^{(i)}}_t\right)(1 - \rho_x)}{\sigma^2_{\epsilon^x}(1 - \rho_x \rho_{z^{(i)}})}$$

$Cov(\cdot)$ denotes the covariance operator, and, by construction, $E[\eta^{(i)}_t | x_t] = 0$, $i = 1, 2$.

We are now ready to illustrate the pseudodiversity that underpins the belief that REH approximates the diversity of market participants' forecasting strategies. Substituting (20) into (18) yields the following expression for the market's—representative agent's—forecast:

$$\hat{P}^{RA}_{t|t+1} = \alpha^{RA} + \beta^{RA} x_t + \eta_t \tag{21}$$

---

19. These weights are typically wealth shares of each group as a percentage of the total wealth of all market participants.

where α^{RA} and β^{RA} are functions of w, $\alpha^{(i)}$, $\beta^{(i)}$, and $\gamma_1^{(i)}$ (which we explicitly write out in (22) and (23)); and $\eta_t = \left[w\beta^{(1)}\eta_t^{(1)} + (1-w)\beta^{(2)}\eta_t^{(2)} \right]$. Because $E[\eta_t|x_t] = 0$, a comparison of (15) with (21) shows that for $\hat{P}_{t|t+1}^{RE}$ to approximate $\hat{P}_{t|t+1}^{RA}$ up to a random shock, η_t, which is uncorrelated with the causal variable in an economist's model, x_t, the parameters of the bulls' and bears' forecasting strategies must satisfy the following constraints:

$$\alpha^{RE} = \alpha^{RA} = w(\alpha^{(1)} + \beta^{(1)}\gamma_0^{(1)}) + (1-w)(\alpha^{(2)} + \beta^{(2)}\gamma_0^{(2)}) \qquad (22)$$

and

$$\beta^{RE} = \beta^{RA} = w\beta^{(1)}\gamma_1^{(1)} + (1-w)\beta^{(2)}\gamma_1^{(2)} \qquad (23)$$

Thus, the claim that REH "*does not* assert that expectations are all the same" (Muth 1961: 317) requires that participants' forecasting strategies are tied to each other and to the economist's REH model according to fully predetermined rules, such as those in (22) and (23) in all time periods. Consequently, when any group of participants alters their forecasting strategies, the strategies of the others must change to ensure that REH holds in the aggregate.

By focusing on the market and renaming it a representative agent, REH does abstract from the differences among participants' forecasting strategies. But, in presuming that an economist's fully predetermined model adequately approximates the predictions of the aggregate forecast, REH does not approximate the diversity underpinning outcomes in real-world markets. Rather, it abstracts from its models' already constructed pseudo-diversity, which evolves according to rigid, prespecified mechanical rules and has no connection with how differences of views in real-world markets unfold over time.[20]

4.6.3 The Incoherence of the "Rational" Representative Agent

Beyond its inherent incompatibility with how participants revise their forecasting strategies in real-world markets, fully predetermined pseudo-diversity renders incoherent the very notion of rational microfoundations

20. Some contemporary economists interpret Muth's claim that REH is compatible with diversity as hypothesizing that market participants' forecasting strategies differ from some common aggregate—the market's strategy—by a random error term that averages to zero. However, this definition of diversity is just another, slightly weaker, version of the assumption of unanimity: on average, each market participant's forecasting strategy conforms to the same mechanical rule. Under this interpretation, the way in which the diversity unfolds over time is represented with a random shock around this common rule (as illustrated by η in (21)). Because contemporary models fully prespecify the probability distribution of such shocks, this specification is just another representation of how REH's pseudodiversity unfolds over time.

based on REH's representative agent. If the representative agent indeed stood for the views of market participants who make use of different forecasting strategies, every one of them would obviously be irrational, in the sense that they ignore systematic forecast errors and thereby forgo obvious profit opportunities endlessly. This conclusion follows immediately from the observation that in the context of a fully predetermined model, $\left(\hat{P}_{t|t+1}^{(i)} - \hat{P}_{t|t+1}^{RA}\right)$ is systematically correlated with $z_t^{(i)}$. Because, under REH, $\hat{P}_{t|t+1}^{RA} = E_M\left[P_{t+1}|I_t\right]$, the forecast errors $\left(\hat{P}_{t|t+1}^{(i)} - \hat{P}_{t|t+1}^{RA}\right)$ implied by each of the diverse forecasting strategies are systematically correlated with the information that an economist supposes underpins each of these strategies. Thus, microfoundations of contemporary macroeconomic and finance models that are based on a "rational" representative agent construct could hardly be called "rational," whatever this term might mean.

4.6.4 *The Distorted Language of Economic Discourse*

Distorting or inverting the meaning of notions like "rationality" or "the representative agent" in contemporary macroeconomics and finance has had a profound impact on public debate. When economists invoke rationality to justify their public-policy recommendations, noneconomists interpret such statements to mean that the recommendations are based on scientific representations of how reasonable people behave in the real world. In addition, because economists claim that their conclusions follow as a matter of straightforward logic,[21] those who doubt their claims have often been portrayed as being akin to creationists or flat-earthers.

To understand the assumptions that underpin the language of these constructions is to comprehend that the standard of rational forecasting purportedly provided by REH turns the very notion of rationality on its head. What economists imagine to be rational forecasting would be considered obviously irrational by anyone in the real world who is minimally rational. After all, a rational profit-seeking individual understands that the world around her will change in nonroutine ways. She simply cannot afford to believe that, contrary to her experience, she has found a true overarching forecasting strategy, let alone that everyone else has found it as well.

The distorted language of economic discourse has also had a profound impact on the development of economics itself. Behavioral economics provides a case in point. After uncovering massive evidence that contemporary economics' standard of rationality fails to capture adequately how individuals actually make decisions, the only sensible conclusion to draw was that

---

21. For a recent example, see Cochrane (2009). For further discussion, see Frydman and Goldberg (2011: chapter 1).

this standard was utterly wrong. Instead, behavioral economists concluded that individuals are less than fully rational or are irrational.

To justify such a conclusion, behavioral economists and nonacademic commentators argued that the REH-based standard of rationality works—but only for truly intelligent investors.[22] Most individuals lack the abilities needed to understand the future and compute correctly the consequences of their decisions.[23]

In fact, REH requires no assumptions about the intelligence of market participants whatsoever.[24] Rather than imputing to individuals superhuman cognitive and computational abilities, REH presumes just the opposite: market participants forgo using whatever cognitive abilities they do have. REH supposes that individuals do not engage actively and creatively in revising the way they think about the future. Instead, they are presumed to adhere steadfastly to a single mechanical forecasting strategy at all times and under all circumstances. Thus, contrary to widespread belief, in the context of real-world markets, REH presumes that participants are obviously irrational. When new relationships begin driving asset prices, they supposedly look the other way, and thus either abjure profit-seeking behavior altogether or forgo profit opportunities that are in plain sight.

4.7 The Predictable Empirical Difficulties of Fully Predetermined Rationality

In real-world markets, participants must rely on their own imperfect understanding of which variables are important for forecasting and how those variables are related to future outcomes. No participant, let alone an economist, knows in advance how she will revise her forecasting strategies or how the social context will change as the future unfolds.

Thus, even if a fully predetermined model might adequately represent the past relationship between causal variables and aggregate outcomes in a selected historical period, its structure would cease to be adequate

---

22. Having embraced the fully predetermined notion of rationality, behavioral economists proceeded to search for reasons, mostly in psychological research and brain studies, to explain why individual behavior is so grossly inconsistent with it.

23. For example, an important class of models in the behavioral finance literature, originated by Delong et al. (1990a,b), contrasts the behavior of "fully rational" participants, whom they refer to as "smart" investors, with those who are "less-than-fully rational." Even Simon (1971), a forceful early critic of economists' notion of rationality, regarded it as an appropriate standard of decisionmaking, though he believed that, for various cognitive and other reasons, it was unattainable for most people. To underscore this view, he coined the term "bounded rationality" to refer to departures from the supposedly normative benchmark.

24. For an extensive discussion, see Frydman and Goldberg (2011: chapters 2, 3, and 4).

at moments that no one can fully prespecify.[25] Such contingent change implies that the statistical estimates generated by fully predetermined models of asset prices vary in significant ways as the time period examined is changed. Correlations between price changes and informational variables that might be found in the data over some stretch of time eventually change or disappear, and are replaced by new relationships.

Because participants' forecasting is the key factor underpinning the causal process in asset markets, models of these markets are particularly prone to such irregular temporal instability. For example, Fama and MacBeth (1973) and others report favorable estimates of the Capital Asset Pricing Model (CAPM), which is widely used in academia and industry, over a sample that runs until 1965. However, when the sample was updated to include the 1970s and 1980s, and additional variables were added to the analysis, the results implied that the CAPM was "atrocious as an empirical model" (Berg 1992: D1). Commenting in an interview with *Institutional Investor* on the temporal instability of correlations in asset-price data, Nobel laureate William Sharpe quipped that "it's almost true that if you don't like an empirical result, if you can wait until somebody uses a different [time] period . . . you'll get a different answer" (Wallace 1980: 24).

It is not surprising that models that disregard the importance of non-routine change in driving outcomes have repeatedly failed to predict outcomes in real-world markets, let alone predict them "sharply." In examining the widely reported empirical difficulties of REH-based models for price and risk movements in currency markets, Frydman and Goldberg (2007: chapters 7 and 8) trace their failures to the premise that fully predetermined accounts of price and risk movements are within reach of economic analysis.

Although both REH and behavioral economists largely missed the connection between the failure of REH models and the core premise on which they rest, their research has helped to uncover these models' dismal empirical performance. After considering many econometric studies of REH models, Maurice Obstfeld and Kenneth Rogoff concluded in their magisterial book on international macroeconomics that

> the undeniable difficulties that international economists encounter in empirically explaining nominal exchange rate movements are an embarrassment, but one shared with virtually any other field that attempts to explain asset price data. [Obstfeld and Rogoff 1996: 625]

---

25. Even when it comes to past relationships, there are many possible models that might adequately describe the causal processes underpinning outcomes in any selected historical period. For an argument that subjective judgments play a key role in understanding the past, see Frydman and Goldberg (2011: chapter 11).

Drawing on extensive laboratory and psychological studies, behavioral economists also reached the conclusion that microfoundations based on an economist's a priori notion of rationality were inconsistent with empirical evidence, and replaced them with formalizations of their empirical findings on how individuals "actually" behave. But, despite their focus on the "psychological realism" of their representations, behavioral macroeconomists and finance theorists embraced the core premise of the contemporary approach. Consequently, they formalized their empirical findings with mechanical rules, thereby basing their accounts of aggregate outcomes on fully predetermined microfoundations.

4.8 The Irrelevant "Inconsistency" of Behavioral Finance Models

Representing market participants as robots who act according to rules fully prespecified by an economist is odd for an approach that claims the mantle of psychological realism.[26] As we have argued, fully predetermined models are anything but realistic. Indeed, whether they appeal to a priori assumptions about how a rational market participant should behave or to empirical findings about how they actually behave, fully predetermined models disregard by design crucial features of real-world markets.[27]

Although behavioral models have gained a significant following among economists and nonacademic commentators in recent years, a large segment of macroeconomists continue to view behavioral explanations with considerable skepticism. This position seems to be related to Lucas's arguments for REH, which many found so convincing. Because non-REH behavioral models' microfoundations are internally inconsistent with their representations on the aggregate level, Lucas argued that such models are "the wrong theory."

But, as we have argued, fully predetermined models are the wrong theory on both the individual and aggregate levels. Thus, consistency between these levels has no connection to rationality in real-world markets, and inconsistency within these models is not, as Lucas and his followers believe, a symptom of departures from full rationality in those markets. The consistency of participants' fully prespecified forecasting strategies with an economist's representation of aggregate outcomes is, to put it bluntly, beside

---

26. Camerer et al. (2004) argue that greater psychological realism is the main advantage of behavioral models over their "fully rational" counterparts.

27. Another oddity of the behavioral approach is that some behavioral economists continue to rely on REH. For an influential example, see Barberis et al. (2001). Because our critique of REH-based fully predetermined rationality also applies to these models' microfoundations, we focus here on non-REH behavioral models.

the point. Imputing such strategies to market participants merely presumes that every one of them disregards nonroutine change, and that their—and the economist's own—understanding of the causal process underpinning market outcomes is inherently imperfect.

4.9 The Fatal Flaw

We have argued that there is an inherent conflict between the objective of modeling market outcomes on the basis of mathematical, yet plausible, microfoundations and contemporary economists' insistence that their models produce sharp probabilistic predictions of change. Regardless of whether they are "fully rational" or "less-than-fully rational," fully predetermined microfoundations are incompatible—and, indeed, have no connection—with profit seeking in real-world markets. Thus, to open macroeconomic models' foundations to minimally reasonable decision-making, let alone individual rationality, economists must jettison their core premise that nonroutine change is unimportant for understanding market outcomes.

We should emphasize that our critique of contemporary models is not that they are abstract or mathematical. Useful scientific models are those that abstract from features of reality that are irrelevant for an adequate account of the phenomenon that the model seeks to explain. The hope is that the omitted considerations really are relatively unimportant to understanding the phenomenon.

The need to exclude many potentially relevant considerations is particularly acute if one aims to account for outcomes with mathematical models, which ipso facto make use of a few assumptions to explain complex phenomena. So the bolder an abstraction that one seeks, the more important it is to scrutinize the assumptions that are "termed crucial . . . on the grounds [of their] intuitive plausibility or capacity to suggest, if only by implication, some of the considerations that are relevant in judging or applying the model" (Friedman 1953: 26).[28]

The fatal flaw of contemporary macroeconomic and finance models is that they rule out by design the crucial factors—participants' revisions of forecasting strategies and how the diversity of these strategies and the social context unfold over time—that underpin the market outcomes they are

---

28. Contemporary economists brush off criticism that their assumptions are unrealistic by invoking the dictum put forth by Milton Friedman (1953: 23) in his well-known essay on economic methodology: "theory cannot be tested by the 'realism' of its assumptions." In fact, at no point did Friedman suggest that economists should not be concerned about the inadequacy of their models' assumptions. For an argument that Friedman's influential essay has been misinterpreted as legitimizing contemporary models' core assumptions, see Frydman and Goldberg (2011: chapter 1).

attempting to explain. No one can fully specify these factors in advance. Only when we abandon contemporary economists' mechanistic conception of science can we hope to develop models that might account for how market outcomes unfold over time and that are compatible with profit-seeking behavior and individual rationality in the real world. Indeed, we show in Frydman and Goldberg (Chapter 6, this volume) that, by stopping short of fully prespecifying change, IKE can account for movements in asset prices and risk that extant approaches have found so difficult to explain.

4.10 Opening Macroeconomics and Finance Theory to Imperfect Knowledge and Diversity

We make use of our simple example in (1) and (2) to illustrate how, by not fully prespecifying change, economic analysis can escape contemporary models' insurmountable epistemological and empirical difficulties. As before, for the sake of simplicity, we continue to impose the invariance restriction on the parameters and causal variables in (1) and focus on the representations of market participants' forecasting strategies in (2).

We begin by jettisoning fully predetermining restrictions on how participants revise their forecasting strategies in the aggregate. Thus, we rewrite the representation of this aggregate in (10) at time $t + 1$ in terms of the structure of its representation and the realization of the causal variable at t:

$$\hat{P}_{t+1|t+2} - \hat{P}_{t|t+1} = \hat{A}_{(t,t+1)} + \hat{B}_{(t,t+1)}z_t + \left(\beta_t + \beta_{(t,t+1)}\right)\varepsilon^z_{t+1} \qquad (24)$$

where $\hat{A}_{(t,t+1)} = \alpha_{(t,t+1)} + (\beta_t + \beta_{(t,t+1)})\mu_z\left(1 - \rho_z\right)$, $\hat{B}_{(t,t+1)} = \beta_{(t,t+1)} + \left(\beta_t + \beta_{(t,t+1)}\right)\left[\rho_z - 1\right]$, and $\left(\alpha_{(t,t+1)}, \beta_{(t,t+1)}\right)$ represent revisions of forecasting strategies, which, for convenience, we repeat here from (4):

$$\alpha_{(t,t+1)} = \alpha_{t+1} - \alpha_t \quad \text{and} \quad \beta_{(t,t+1)} = \beta_{t+1} - \beta_t \qquad (25)$$

Analogously to (11), we can also write the change in the market price as

$$P_{t+1} - P_t = \left[A_{(t,t+1)} + Bx_t + C_{(t,t+1)}z_t\right] + \eta_{t+1} \qquad (26)$$

where $A_{(t,t+1)} = b\left[\mu_x\left(1 - \rho_x\right) + \left(\rho_x - 1\right)\right] + c\hat{A}_{(t,t+1)}$, $B = b\left(\rho_x - 1\right)$, $C_{(t,t+1)} = c\hat{B}_{(t,t+1)}$, $\hat{A}_{(t,t+1)}$ and $\hat{B}_{(t,t+1)}$ are defined in (24) and (25), and

$$\eta_{t+1} = b\varepsilon^x_{t+1} + c(\beta_t + \beta_{(t,t+1)})\varepsilon^z_{t+1} \qquad (27)$$

Because the unrestricted model in (24) and (26) does not constrain in any way the probability distribution for outcomes at $t + 1$ or beyond, it is trivially compatible with nonroutine change on both the individual and aggregate levels, as well as with the diversity of forecasting strategies and their revisions. Consequently, unless further restrictions are imposed on revisions of forecasting strategies, the unrestricted representation has no empirical content: it is compatible with any time path of outcomes and with any causal process that underpins them.

4.10.1 Methodological Extremes: Animal Spirits versus Fully Predetermined Accounts of Outcomes

The unrestricted model illustrates radical uncertainty, a situation in which individual decisions cannot be adequately represented with a standard probability distribution. Keynes (1921, 1936) and Knight (1921) forcefully argued that most business decisions are fraught with such uncertainty. An extreme version of radical uncertainty is often thought to force participants to act according to their "animal spirits," psychological impulses that are largely disconnected from any fundamental considerations that might drive outcomes. However, unless participants' forecasting strategies could be connected, at least during some periods, to the causal factors observable by economists, no formal economic theory with empirical content would be possible. As Phelps (2008: A19) has recently put it, "animal spirits can't be modeled."

Contemporary models, with their core premise that fully predetermined causal accounts of individual decisionmaking and market outcomes are within reach of economic analysis, occupy the opposite methodological extreme. Searching for such accounts, economists constrain their models in a severe way: they fully prespecify change. Their models represent outcomes at each point in time—and thus how they unfold over time—with a single overarching conditional probability distribution. The relationships between the moments of this distribution and the set of causal variables constitute the empirical content that can be confronted with the time-series evidence on market outcomes.

Like the opposite (animal spirits) extreme of the methodological spectrum, the contemporary approach to macroeconomics and finance theory is inherently in conflict—though for very different reasons—with the objective of developing empirically relevant economic theory. As we have argued, contemporary models' core premise leads to intractable epistemological problems, which inevitably translate into gross inconsistencies between their supposedly sharp predictions of market outcomes and the empirical record.

4.10.2 IKE's Nonstandard Probabilistic Formalism

IKE stakes out an intermediate position between radical uncertainty (which, in its extreme, animal spirits, version, denies that economists can formulate testable mathematical models of any features of the causal process driving change) and the contemporary presumption that a standard conditional probability distribution can fully and adequately represent this process.

Although it stops short of imposing fully predetermining restrictions on change, IKE aims to explain outcomes with mathematical models that can be confronted with empirical evidence. To this end, IKE relies on nonstandard probabilistic formalism to formulate its mathematical representations of forecasting strategies and their revisions.

To illustrate how IKE opens economic models to nonroutine revisions of forecasting strategies and their diversity, and to compare its representations with its fully predetermined counterparts, we formulate an IKE version of the representation of diversity in (17) and (18). This example represents diversity on the micro level with the forecasting strategies of two groups of participants—say, bulls and bears—in an equity market:

$$\hat{P}^{(i)}_{t|t+1} = \alpha^{(i)}_t + \beta^{(i)}_t Z^{(i)}_t, \quad i = 1, 2 \tag{28}$$

where $(\alpha^{(i)}_t, \beta^{(i)}_t)$ are parameters and $Z^{(i)}_t$ denotes the two causal variables appearing in a representation for each of the forecasting strategies for $i = 1, 2$, respectively.

Consequently, the aggregate of forecasting strategies can be written as

$$\hat{P}_{t|t+1} = w\hat{P}^{(1)}_{t|t+1} + (1 - w)\hat{P}^{(2)}_{t|t+1} \tag{29}$$

where, as before, $\hat{P}_{t|t+1}$ denotes the aggregate of participants' forecasting strategies, and w and $(1 - w)$ are the aggregation weights that sum up to unity.

To model how aggregate outcomes unfold over time, we write the updating of forecasts generated by (28) and (29), which drive these movements, as follows:

$$\hat{P}^{(i)}_{t+1|t+2} - \hat{P}^{(i)}_{t|t+1} = \alpha^{(i)}_{(t,t+1)} + \beta^{(i)}_{(t,t+1)} Z^{(i)}_t$$
$$+ \left(\beta^{(i)}_t + \beta^{(i)}_{(t,t+1)}\right)\left(Z^{(i)}_{t+1} - Z^{(i)}_t\right), \quad i = 1, 2 \tag{30}$$

and

$$\hat{P}_{t+1|t+2} - \hat{P}_{t|t+1} = w\left(\hat{P}^{(1)}_{t+1|t+2} - \hat{P}^{(1)}_{t|t+1}\right) + (1 - w)\left(\hat{P}^{(2)}_{t+1|t+2} - \hat{P}^{(2)}_{t|t+1}\right)$$
$$= \alpha_{(t,t+1)} + \beta_{(t,t+1)} Z_t$$
$$+ \left(\beta_t + \beta_{(t,t+1)}\right)\left(Z_{t+1} - Z_t\right) \tag{31}$$

where $\alpha_{(t,t+1)} = w\alpha^{(1)}_{(t,t+1)} + (1 - w)\alpha^{(2)}_{(t,t+1)}$, $\beta_{(t,t+1)} Z_t = w\beta^{(1)}_{(t,t+1)} Z^{(1)}_t$ $+(1 - w)\beta^{(2)}_{(t,t+1)} Z^{(2)}_t$, and $\left(\beta_t + \beta_{(t,t+1)}\right)\left(Z_{t+1} - Z_t\right)$ is defined analogously.

This representation shows that the updating of participants' forecasts stems from two sources: revisions of forecasting strategies, as represented here by $\alpha^{(i)}_{(t,t+1)}$ and $\beta^{(i)}_{(t,t+1)}$, and new information on the causal variables, $\left(Z^{(i)}_{t+1} - Z^{(i)}_t\right)$.

For the sake of simplicity, we continue to maintain the time-invariance restrictions in (1). This enables us to relate the representation of change in the market price to revisions in forecasting strategies and new information on the causal variables $Z^{(i)}_{t+1}$ and X_{t+1}:

$$P_{t+1} - P_t = b\left(X_{t+1} - X_t\right) + c\left(\hat{P}_{t+1|t+2} - \hat{P}_{t|t+1}\right) \tag{32}$$

In contrast to contemporary models, IKE recognizes that our knowledge of the causal process underpinning outcomes is inherently imperfect. Consequently, IKE does not fully prespecify which causal variables may be relevant, or when and how these variables may enter an economist's representation of forecasting behavior. In this way, IKE models remain open to nonroutine changes in the ways that individuals in real-world markets forecast the future.

However, like any scientific theory, IKE must presume that purposeful behavior exhibits regularities, even if these regularities are only qualitative, context-dependent, and relevant at a time that no one can fully specify in advance. IKE explores the possibility that revisions in forecasting strategies and changes in the social context can be characterized with qualitative mathematical conditions. In portraying an individual's forecasting strategy at a given point in time, we use a conditional probability distribution, but we do not fully prespecify how it unfolds over time. Instead, we impose qualitative restrictions on this change.

4.10.3 Partially Predetermined Probability Distributions

In the representation (30), revisions of forecasting strategies and changes in the social context are reflected in $\alpha^{(i)}_{(t,t+1)}$ and $\beta^{(i)}_{(t,t+1)}$, and $\left(Z^{(i)}_{t+1} - Z^{(i)}_t\right)$, $i = 1, 2$, respectively. Thus, for the model to generate empirically relevant implications, we need to specify qualitative conditions for both these components of change.

For example, in Chapter 6 of this volume, we follow this approach in specifying the microfoundations of a model of swings in asset prices and risk. We build on an idea that goes back to Keynes (1936): Faced with imperfect knowledge concerning the causal process driving market outcomes, a participant tends to revise in guardedly moderate ways her thinking about how fundamentals influence the prospects of her investments. There are stretches of time during which she either maintains her forecasting strategy or revises it gradually.

How one would formalize "guardedly moderate revisions" depends on the context. In general, doing so requires a specification of both the formation of forecasting strategies and the baseline against which revisions of these strategies are judged. In our recent work, we have developed a formalization of such revisions in the context of modeling asset-price swings.[29]

To complete the microfoundations of our simple IKE model, we also need to specify qualitative conditions for changes in the fundamental variables. The empirical record suggests that many of these fundamentals tend to trend in particular directions for long stretches of time. Although these trends generally vary in magnitude, for the sake of simplicity, we constrain them to be time invariant and assume that these fundamentals are characterized by processes with fixed drifts in (6) and (8).

Because IKE imposes qualitative restrictions on the structure of its models, it can characterize how an individual revises her forecasting strategy, regardless of whether she is a bull or a bear. Although bulls and bears forecast prices to move in opposite directions, if both revise their strategies in guardedly moderate ways, and fundamentals trend in unchanging directions between two successive periods—say, $t - 1$ and t, and t and $t + 1$—it can be shown that their price forecasts would move in the same direction in each of these periods.

IKE uses nonstandard probabilistic formalism to represent the qualitative conditions making up its models' microfoundations and their predictions for aggregate outcomes. In contrast to fully predetermined models, IKE represents forecast revisions with myriad distributions implied by (30) and constrains these distributions to share common qualitative features. We refer to such representations as "partially predetermined probability distributions."

For example, it can be shown that if fundamentals were to trend in unchanging directions and a participant were to revise her forecasting strategies in guardedly moderate ways over two successive periods, the mean of any of the myriad conditional distributions of change implied by IKE representations of her forecast revisions in (30) would be the same in each period. Consequently, during time periods in which these conditions characterize forecast revisions of "most" market participants—as measured by the relative weight of their positions in the market—the aggregate forecast in (31) will tend to move in one direction over time. In connecting how the aggregate price forecast unfolds over time to individual behavior, we make use of assumptions about diversity in the qualitative way that trends in fundamentals impact bulls' and bears' forecasts (see Frydman and Goldberg, Chapter 6, this volume).

29. In Frydman and Goldberg (Chapter 6, this volume), we present a revised version of the model developed in our earlier work, as well as a more complete formal demonstration of the main assertions sketched in this section.

The qualitative conditions on the micro level, together with our assumptions about diversity, generate empirically relevant implications on the aggregate level. Specifically, price swings in asset markets will occur during stretches of time in which trends in market fundamentals are persistent, and participants, on the whole, interpret the impact of these trends on their price forecasts in a qualitatively similar manner, as well as revise their strategies in guardedly moderate ways.

4.11   The Contingency of IKE's Representations

One would not expect participants to revise their forecasting strategies in guardedly moderate ways or fundamentals to continue to trend in the same direction forever. One would also not expect the way these decisions translate into aggregate outcomes to remain unchanged, even if by qualitative conditions. Indeed, the conditions that make up an IKE model are both qualitative and contingent. Probabilistic representations generated by an IKE model are not only compatible with myriad post-change probability distributions, but their structure also undergoes change at moments that no one can fully prespecify. Thus, IKE models are open to nonroutine change and recognize the importance of the imperfect knowledge and diversity of forecasting strategies that such change engenders.

The contingent and qualitative nature of the conditions that characterize IKE's approach to macroeconomics and finance theory plays a crucial role in its ability to deliver empirically relevant accounts of swings in asset prices and risk. Qualitative regularities, like market participants' tendency to revise their forecasts in guardedly moderate ways for stretches of time, play a key role in an IKE model of protracted upswings and downswings. But because these conditions are also contingent, they are consistent with the irregular structural change in macroeconomic and finance models that, as we discussed earlier, has been pointed out in many studies. The contingency of these conditions also plays a key role in IKE's ability to account for the reversals that occur when markets eventually self-correct.

Asset-price swings end when market participants' tendency toward guardedly moderate revisions of their forecasting strategies—or the qualitative similarity of how trends in fundamentals impact their price forecasts—no longer holds. This contingency is likely to be related to that of the tendency of fundamentals to trend in the same direction. For example, news about how trends in fundamentals change may lead participants to revise their forecasting strategies so substantially as to spell the end of a price swing in one direction and the start of a new one in the opposite direction.

Thus, by specifying qualitative and contingent models, IKE accounts for the irregular duration and magnitude of asset-price swings that we observe in real-world markets. The stretches of time in which fundamentals trend in unchanging directions and revisions are guardedly moderate are irregular. As a result, one of our IKE model's important predictions is irregular swings in asset prices and risk.

4.12 Opening Microfoundations to Genuine Diversity and Individual Rationality

Beyond accounting for the pattern of asset-price swings in real-world markets, the contingency of IKE models renders them compatible with the coexistence of bulls and bears in asset markets and the rationality of both positions, despite their contradictory predictions of price movements.

An IKE model explains the presence of both bulls and bears in the market at every point in time by the fact that no participant can predict with certainty when trends in fundamentals may switch direction; when other participants may cease to revise their forecasting strategies in guardedly moderate ways; or when the qualitative impacts of how trends in fundamentals influence their price forecast will diverge substantially. Because a price swing may continue or end at any time, betting one way or the other does not involve any obvious irrationality on the part of participants who hold either bullish or bearish views.

4.13 Fundamentals and Psychology in IKE's Microfoundations

Behavioral economists have uncovered important insights into the role of psychological factors in individual decisionmaking. However, the contemporary approach's core premise has constrained behavioral theorists either to disregard these insights or to formalize them with mechanical rules that are fully prespecified by an economist. This has led to a widespread belief that the salience of psychological factors should be viewed as a symptom of less than "full rationality."[30]

But once we acknowledge the inherent imperfection of market participants' and economists' knowledge, we should also acknowledge that both fundamental and psychological considerations play a role in rational decisionmaking:

> We are merely reminding ourselves that human decisions affecting the future, whether personal or political or economic, cannot depend on strict

---

30. Many other influential claims in contemporary economics are an artifact of the belief that the litmus test of rationality is the absence of psychological factors in individual decisionmaking. For a critical discussion of this belief in the context of modeling individual decisions in asset markets, swings in asset prices, and thinking about the rationale for and scope of financial regulation, see Frydman and Goldberg (2011).

mathematical expectation, since the basis for making such calculations does not exist; and . . . that our *rational* selves [are] choosing between alternatives as best as we are able, calculating where we can, but often falling back for our motive on whim or sentiment or chance. [Keynes 1936: 162, emphasis added]

For Keynes, unlike for contemporary behavioral economists, reliance on psychological factors in decisionmaking is not a symptom of irrationality. He emphasizes that even though rational individuals in the real world use knowledge of facts, such as information about fundamentals, our understanding of the processes underpinning outcomes is inherently imperfect; thus, calculation alone is insufficient in decisionmaking.

Precisely because IKE models comprise conditions that are *both* qualitative and contingent, they can incorporate both sets of factors in economic analysis. In our IKE model of swings in asset prices and risk, the qualitative and contingent conditions that constrain revisions of forecasting strategies play an important role in accounting for upswings, reversals, and downswings. These conditions are motivated by Keynes's insights into markets, as well as by subsequent psychological research (see Edwards 1968; Shleifer 2000; and references therein). Moreover, their contingent formalization in our IKE model reflects the widely held view that psychologically based conditions, especially in asset markets, are subject to change that no one can fully foresee.

To be sure, to account for the asset-price swings that we actually observe in markets, we must look beyond psychological and other nonfundamental considerations.[31] Indeed, the purely psychological and nonfundamental accounts of asset markets overlook the possibility that in forecasting price movements, participants look to fundamental factors that they think will move the market over whatever time horizon interests them for the purpose of forecasting returns. Any confidence and optimism that might exist in the market would quickly evaporate if, say, earnings and overall economic activity consistently moved in the "wrong" direction.

4.14   Sharp versus Contingent Predictions

The evidence that psychology alone cannot drive asset-price movements is good news for the possibility of empirically relevant economic theory: after all, fundamental considerations are, for the most part, the only tangible

---

31. For example, we make use of Keynes's (1936) insight that price departures from estimates of benchmark values play a key role in how participants assess the riskiness of their speculative positions.

factors that economists can use to develop models that might enable them to distinguish among alternative explanations of outcomes.

However, although predictions in both IKE and REH models are driven by fundamental considerations, IKE's qualitative and contingent predictions are inherently different from contemporary models' requirement of sharp predictions.

The aim of contemporary economists to find a model that can predict the complete set of future market outcomes and probabilities is not the first such endeavor in the social sciences. In his seminal refutation of the claim that "historicism" might one day enable social science to "predict the future course of history," Karl Popper pointed out that any such approach is futile "to the extent to which [historical developments] may be influenced by the growth of our knowledge" (Popper 1957: xi–xii).

Because market outcomes—especially outcomes in financial markets—crucially depend on changing understandings of the process and psychology that underpin those outcomes on both the individual and aggregate levels, our critique of contemporary macroeconomics and finance theory can be viewed as further refutation of the historicist's vain ambition.

Although Popper was strongly critical of attempts to develop fully pre-determined accounts of history, he was quick to point out that his

> argument does not, of course, refute the possibility of every kind of social prediction; on the contrary, it is perfectly compatible with the possibility of testing social theories—for example economic theories—by way of predicting that certain developments will take place *under certain conditions*. It only refutes the possibility of predicting historical developments to the extent to which they may be influenced by the growth of our knowledge. [Popper 1957: xii, emphasis added]

The contingent predictions generated by our IKE model of asset-price swings exemplify what Popper would regard as a feasible goal of economic theory. Although our model predicts that, under certain conditions, an asset price will undergo a sustained movement in one direction, it does not predict when such upswings or downswings will begin or end.

Beyond building on Popper's insights concerning the possibility, scope, and character of predictions in the social sciences, our IKE model of asset-price swings exemplifies Hayek's claim that "our capacity to predict will be confined to . . . general characteristics of the events to be expected and not include the capacity for predicting particular individual events" (Hayek 1978: 33). Although an IKE model, by design, stops short of predicting "particular individual events," such as when the swing will begin and end, it does generate predictions concerning their "general characteristics"—for example, that they tend to be quite persistent. Thus, by examining the persistence and related features of swings in asset prices and risk implied by alternative models, an economist may compare explanations of economic phenomena. Johansen et al. (2010) and Frydman et al. (2012a,b) develop such an approach to econometric testing and conclude that an IKE model provides a significantly better account than standard and REH-based bubble models of swings in currency markets.[32]

These studies show that, despite placing imperfect knowledge and non-routine change at the center of economic analysis and limiting our ambition solely to generating qualitative predictions, IKE models may still yield "predictions which can be falsified and which therefore are of empirical significance" (Hayek 1978: 33).

4.15 Probing the Frontier of Formal Macroeconomic and Finance Theory

In Frydman and Goldberg (2007) and our recent technical studies, we show how IKE models shed new light on salient features of the empirical record on exchange rates that have confounded international macroeconomists for decades. In Frydman and Goldberg (2011), we focus on how recognizing the centrality of nonroutine change and imperfect knowledge enables us to understand better the process by which financial markets, particularly equity markets, help society allocate its capital, and why asset-price swings are an integral part of this process.

IKE also provides a new way to explain why asset-price swings sometimes become excessive and shows how the hitherto neglected relationship between financial risk and price swings can help us to understand how excessive swings come to an end. This analysis provides a conceptual framework for prudential policy aimed at dampening excessive price swings—and thus at reducing the social costs inflicted when they reverse direction.

Although the application of IKE to financial markets appears promising, it is too early to claim broader usefulness for it in macroeconomic and policy modeling. If qualitative regularities can be established in contexts other than asset markets, IKE's nonstandard probabilistic formalism can show how to incorporate them into mathematical models. However, when revisions of forecasting strategies (or more broadly, change on the individual and aggregate levels) cannot be adequately characterized with qualitative and contingent conditions, empirically relevant mathematical models of how market outcomes unfold over time may be beyond

---

32. Our approach to testing the implications of IKE versus REH models of swings makes use of cointegrated vector autoregressive methodology and inference. For book-length treatments, see Johansen (1996) and Juselius (2007).

the reach of economic analysis. In this sense, IKE explores the frontier of what formal macroeconomic and finance theory can deliver. How far, and in which contexts, this boundary can be extended is the crucial open question.

References

Barberis, Nicolas C., Ming Huang, and Tano Santos. (2001) "Prospect Theory and Asset Prices," *Quarterly Journal of Economics,* 116: 1–53.

Berg, Eric N. (1992) "A Study Shakes Confidence in the Volatile Stock Market Theory." *New York Times,* February 18, p. D1.

Cagan, Phillip. (1956) "The Monetary Dynamics of Hyperinflation," in Milton Friedman (ed.), *Studies in the Quantity Theory of Money.* Chicago: University of Chicago Press, pp. 25–117.

Camerer, Colin F., George Loewenstein, and Matthew Rabin. (2004) *Advances in Behavioral Economics.* Princeton, NJ: Princeton University Press.

Cochrane, John H. (2009) "How Did Paul Krugman Get It So Wrong?" Available at: http://faculty.chicagobooth.edu/john.cochrane/research/Papers/krugman_response.htm.

DeLong, Bradford J., Andrei Shleifer, Lawrence H. Summers, and Robert J. Waldman. (1990a) "Noise Trader Risk in Financial Markets," *Journal of Political Economy* 98: 703–738.

———. (1990b) "Positive Feedback Investment Strategies and Destabilizing Rational Speculation," *Journal of Finance* 45: 375–395.

Edwards, Ward. (1968) "Conservatism in Human Information Processing," in Benjamin Kleinmuth (ed.), *Formal Representation of Human Judgement.* New York: John Wiley and Sons, pp. 17–52.

Evans, George W., and Seppo Honkapohja. (2005) "An Interview with Thomas J. Sargent," *Macroeconomic Dynamics* 9: 561–583.

Fama, Eugene F., and James D. MacBeth. (1973) "Risk, Return, and Equilibrium: Empirical Tests," *Journal of Political Economy* 81: 607–636.

Friedman, Milton. (1953) *Essays in Positive Economics.* Chicago: University of Chicago Press.

———. (1956) *A Theory of Consumption Function.* Princeton, NJ: Princeton University Press.

Frydman, Roman. (1982) "Towards an Understanding of Market Processes: Individual Expectations, Learning and Convergence to Rational Expectations Equilibrium," *American Economic Review* 72: 652–668.

———. (1983) "Individual Rationality, Decentralization and the Rational Expectations Hypothesis," in Roman Frydman and Edmund S. Phelps (eds.), *Individual Forecasting and Aggregate Outcomes: "Rational Expectations" Examined.* New York: Cambridge University Press, pp. 97–122.

Frydman, Roman, and Michael D. Goldberg. (2007) *Imperfect Knowledge Economics: Exchange Rates and Risk.* Princeton, NJ: Princeton University Press.

———. (2008) "Macroeconomic Theory for a World of Imperfect Knowledge," *Capitalism and Society* 3: Article 1, available at http://www.bepress.com/cas/vol3/iss3/art1/.

———. (2011) *Beyond Mechanical Markets: Asset Price Swings, Risk, and the Role of the State.* Princeton, NJ: Princeton University Press.

Frydman, Roman, and Edmund S. Phelps. (1983) "Introduction," in Roman Frydman and Edmund S. Phelps (eds.), *Individual Forecasting and Aggregate Outcomes: "Rational Expectations" Examined.* New York: Cambridge University Press, pp. 1–30.

Frydman, Roman, and Andrzej Rapaczynski. (1993) *Markets by Design.* Mimeo, New York University.

———. (1994) *Privatization in Eastern Europe: Is the State Withering Away?* Budapest and Oxford: Central European University Press in cooperation with Oxford University Press.

Frydman, Roman, Michael D. Goldberg, Soren Johansen, and Katarina Juselius. (2010a) "Imperfect Knowledge and Long Swings in Currency Markets." Working paper, New York University.

———. (2010b) "Why REH Bubble Models Do Not Adequately Account for Swings." Working paper, New York University.

Hamilton, James D. (1988) "Rational-Expectations Econometric Analysis of Changes in Regime: An Investigation of the Term Structure of Interest Rates," *Journal of Economic Dynamics and Control* 12: 385–423.

———. (1994) *Time Series Analysis.* Princeton, NJ: Princeton University Press.

Hayek, Friedrich A. (1945) "The Use of Knowledge in Society," *American Economic Review* 35: 519–530.

———. (1948) *Individualism and Economic Order.* Chicago: University of Chicago Press.

———. (1978) "The Pretence of Knowledge," 1974 Nobel Lecture, in *New Studies in Philosophy, Politics, Economics and the History of Ideas.* Chicago: University of Chicago Press, pp. 23–34.

Johansen, Soren. (1996) *Likelihood Based Inference on Cointegration in the Vector Autoregressive Model.* Oxford: Oxford University Press.

Johansen, Soren, Juselius Katarina, Roman Frydman, and Michael D. Goldberg. (2010) "Testing Hypotheses in an *I*(2) Model with Applications to the Persistent Long Swings in the Dmk/$ Rate," *Journal of Econometrics* 158: 117–129.

Juselius, Katarina. (2007) *The Cointegrated VAR Model: Methodology and Applications.* Oxford: Oxford University Press.

Keynes, John M. (1921) *A Treatise on Probability.* London: Macmillan. Reprinted in 1957.

———. (1936) *The General Theory of Employment, Interest and Money.* New York: Harcourt, Brace and World.

Knight, Frank H. (1921) *Risk, Uncertainty and Profit.* Boston: Houghton Mifflin.

Lucas, Robert E., Jr. (1973) "Some International Evidence on Output-Inflation Trade-offs," *American Economic Review* 63: 326–334.

———. (1976) "Econometric Policy Evaluation: A Critique," in Karl Brunner and Allan H. Meltzer (eds.), *The Phillips Curve and Labor Markets*, Carnegie Rochester Conference Series on Public Policy. Amsterdam: North-Holland, pp. 19–46. Reprinted in Robert E. Lucas, Jr. (1981) *Studies in Business-Cycle Theory.* Cambridge, MA: MIT Press, pp. 104–130.

———. (1995) "Monetary Neutrality," *Nobel Lecture.* Stockholm: Nobel Foundation, pp. 246–265.

———. (2001) "Professional Memoir." Mimeo. Available at: http://home.uchicago .edu.

Muth, John F. (1961) "Rational Expectations and the Theory of Price Movements," *Econometrica* 29: 315–335.

Nerlove, Marc. (1958) *The Dynamics of Supply: Estimation of Farmers' Response to Price.* Baltimore: Johns Hopkins University Press.

Obstfeld, Maurice, and Kenneth Rogoff. (1996) *Foundations of International Macroeconomics.* Cambridge, MA: MIT Press.

Phelps, Edmund S. (1983) "The Trouble with 'Rational Expectations' and the Problem of Inflation Stabilization," in Roman Frydman and Edmund S. Phelps (eds.), *Individual Forecasting and Aggregate Outcomes: "Rational Expectations" Examined.* New York: Cambridge University Press.

———. (2008) "Our Uncertain Economy," *Wall Street Journal,* March 14, p. A19.

Phelps, Edmund S., G. C. Archibald, and Armen A. Alchian (eds.). (1970) *Microeconomic Foundations of Employment and Inflation Theory.* New York: W. W. Norton.

Popper, Karl R. (1957) *The Poverty of Historicism.* London and New York: Routledge.

———. (1990) *A World of Propensities.* Bristol, UK: Thoemmes Antiquarian Books.

Sargent, Thomas J. (1987) *Macroeconomic Theory.* New York: Academic Press.

———. (1993) *Bounded Rationality in Macroeconomics.* Oxford: Oxford University Press.

Shleifer, Andrei. (2000) *Inefficient Markets.* Oxford: Oxford University Press.

Simon, Herbert A. (1971) "Theories of Bounded Rationality," in Bruce McGuire and Roy Radner (eds.), *Decision and Organization.* Amsterdam: North-Holland, pp. 161–176.

Stiglitz, Joseph E. (2001) "Information and the Change in the Paradigm in Economics," *Nobel Lecture.* Stockholm: Nobel Foundation, pp. 472–540.

———. (2010) "The Non-Existent Hand," *London Review of Books,* April 22, pp. 17–18.

Von Neumann, John, and Oscar Morgenstern. (1944) *Theory of Games and Economic Behavior.* Princeton, NJ: Princeton University Press.

Wallace, Anise. (1980) "Is Beta Dead?" *Institutional Investor,* July, pp. 23–30.

PART TWO

Autonomous Expectations in Long Swings in Asset Prices

CHAPTER FIVE

Heterogeneous Gain Learning and Long Swings in Asset Prices

Blake LeBaron

5.1 Introduction

Many asset prices exhibit large and highly persistent deviations from their fundamental values, yielding potential long-run predictability.[1] That asset prices can move from simple benchmark rational pricing levels and then stay far from these levels for some time is a major puzzle. The swings can be both short or long in duration, and their time series shows few regular patterns when one analyzes their long-range behavior. Many explanations have been proposed involving varying levels of rationality, knowledge, and learning, but no one explanation has dominated the debate. This chapter explores an underparameterized learning model with heterogeneous gain parameters and traders using differing perspectives on history.[2]

The author is grateful for useful comments and suggestions from George Evans; Roman Frydman, one of the volume editors; Harrison Hong; Mike Woodford; and seminar participants at the fortieth anniversary conference of *Microeconomic Foundations of Employment and Inflation Theory* held at Columbia University.

1. The early evidence is in Shiller (1981) and Campbell and Shiller (1988). For a textbook treatment, see Campbell et al. (1996). A recent survey of this literature is Lettau and Ludvigson (2010).

2. The topic of learning models and asset pricing is extensive. A recent survey by Pastor and Veronesi (2009) is a good starting place. A more general survey covering the broader macroeconomic context is Evans and Honkapohja (2008). All these works are influenced by the early work collected in Phelps et al. (1970) and Frydman and Phelps (1983). Also, Timmerman (1993) and Hong and Stein (1999) are early examples of learning models capable of generating market volatility, which will be a key aspect of the model presented here. Frydman and Goldberg (2007) is another summary of the adaptive learning approach that also presents models displaying persistent deviations in foreign exchange rates from purchasing power parity benchmarks. A recent model with Bayesian learning agents that replicates movements in long-run price-dividend ratios is Adam and Marcet (2010a).

Gain parameters are present in almost all learning models, and they control the weight given to new observations as learners update their parameters. They can be thought of as controlling how much data from the past agents use to estimate new forecast parameters. They also can be interpreted as related to the signal-to-noise ratio in an unobserved state-variable world.[3] Learning models can also entertain both decreasing and constant gain levels. In decreasing-gain models, the weight on new observations approaches zero as time passes, often generating useful convergence results. Constant-gain learners always are forgetting some data from the distant past, and they continue to give new data points the same weight as these data are collected. Committing to a fixed gain level locks agents onto a certain belief about the overall stationarity of the time series they are observing. Entertaining various beliefs about gain parameters would be suggested in a world in which priors about data stationarity, persistence, and long-range dynamic features may be spread over many possibilities. Also, the data series may be short enough, and the features long enough, that the data alone do not lead to much convergence in these beliefs. In other words, the belief that we are in a "new world" and the last 5 years of data are all that is relevant will always hold some appeal in such a world, and statistical evidence firmly rejecting this idea may be very weak.

It is not hard to find candidate time series that appear to be very persistent, but the persistent behavior is often irregular and appears at horizons that are long relative to the sample length. This chapter concentrates specifically on price-dividend ratios (P/Ds) from U.S. stock markets, but there are many other candidates. Inflation rates, interest rates, and real exchange rates are all possible candidates for such persistent behavior. More subtly, the levels of volatility in financial markets also demonstrate this form of extreme persistence. In all cases an argument could be made for some very persistent process that could formally be a long memory or a fractionally integrated system, or there may simply be infrequent changes in regime. In a learning environment agents may be confused among these possibilities both because definitive statistical tests do not exist and because sample sizes may be too short.

This chapter borrows from many parts of the learning literature. Agents use systems derived from adaptive expectations and recursive least-squares algorithms.[4] Agents choose from a set of algorithms all estimated using varying gain levels. Agents also choose from a discrete set of possible forecasting rules designed to span the space of reasonable strategies used

---

3. In the traditional Kalman filter the gain parameter is explicitly defined by the structure of the model.

4. A complete treatment of this topic is in Evans and Honkapohja (2001). An exploration of many forms of heterogeneity in adaptive learning models, including gain parameters, is in Honkapohja and Mitra (2006).

in markets.[5] Finally, the behavior of the market depends on the distribution of wealth across strategies. This is driven both by the active selection of forecast rules by agents and by the passive movement of wealth toward successful strategies.[6]

The importance of heterogeneous gain levels in financial markets was shown in early computational models, such as LeBaron et al. (1999). In that paper, convergence of the market to a rational expectations equilibrium depended critically on how fast agents were updating their forecasting models. Frequent updates, which forced agents to use relatively short time series for decisionmaking, led to a rich pattern in prices and volume that was far from any recognizable equilibrium. However, restricting updates to occur relatively infrequently and forcing agents to use long time series to evaluate rules caused the market to converge to a well-defined homogeneous rational expectations equilibrium.[7]

The macroeconomic environment used here is simple and easily recognizable. It is a form of the Lucas-tree model of asset prices, as in Lucas (1978). A single asset pays a stochastic dividend calibrated to the trend and volatility of real U.S. dividend series. This model is too simple to fit all the facts and puzzles from the macrofinance world. However, it seems to be in a good middle ground, allowing for some quantitative comparisons of the learning model to actual time series but not getting so complex as to hide basic features that are central to the learning dynamics. For example, macro-level shocks should always be viewed as extremely costly in terms of using up modeling degrees of freedom. This model is restricted to only one aggregate shock coming from the movement in aggregate dividends. This restriction is critical and makes it easier to interpret how much of the price volatility from the model can be interpreted as an endogenous feature of learning, as opposed to coming from other poorly specified macro-level shocks.[8]

5. The model shares much basic intuition in this area with the early work in Brock and Hommes (1998), Day and Huang (1990), Frankel and Froot (1988), Kirman (1991), and Lux (1998). Recent surveys of this literature can be found in Chiarella et al. (2009), Hommes and Wagener (2009), and Tesfatsion and Judd (2006).

6. This topic overlaps with the large literature on growth-optimal portfolio strategies, which can be traced back to Kelley (1956); a more recent treatment can be found in Blume and Easley (1990). A recent survey is in Evstigneev et al. (2009).

7. Similar results, but in very different models, can be found in Levy et al. (1994), LeBaron (2006), and Thurner et al. (2002). This chapter directly considers the destabilizing impact of large-gain, or "short-memory," traders on market dynamics. Similar questions about how much data agents should be using from the past are considered in Mitra (2005). A recent model stressing what might happen when agents overweigh shorter run trends, ignoring longer length reversals, is Fuster et al. (2010). Hommes (2010) surveys the growing experimental literature, which often shows people following short-term trends when reporting their expectations in controlled laboratory settings. Finally, Dacorogna et al. (2001) presents a philosophy, and some time-series models, for markets populated by agents with many different time perspectives.

8. The model requires a variety of independent microshocks, but these should be viewed as much more plausible and less costly than adding further aggregate shocks.

A final interesting aspect of learning in this model is the explicit consideration of risk and return. This approach was used in LeBaron et al. (1999). More recently several authors have begun exploring this issue (e.g., Branch and Evans 2011). It allows separation of the dynamics into return and volatility forecasts. The functional form of return forecasts is allowed to vary across forecast families, but the volatility forecasts all follow a common form. Large returns are interpreted as increases in risk by most agents. This common perception seems plausible and is critical to how the market is able to generate fundamental deviations in price.

Section 5.2 gives a short explanation of the basic model. Section 5.3.1 examines some benchmark simulation runs and describes the output of the model compared to actual financial time series. This section cannot report all the results from the model, because this would distract the chapter from its main mission of exploring mostly long-range swings in prices from their fundamentals. Sections 5.3.2 and 5.3.3 look at many internal mechanisms of the agents and forecasts in use and how wealth moves across them over time. Learning algorithms appear to be behaving in a predictable fashion, and interesting dynamics come from how agent wealth selects rules over time. The final section concludes and introduces some questions for researchers working on learning in financial markets.

5.2 Model Description

This section briefly describes the structure of the model. The model combines components from many parts of the learning literature. The goal is to build a heterogeneous-agent asset market that is as parsimonious as possible but can still do a good job of replicating certain features of financial markets. Also, its inner workings should be simple enough for detailed analysis, should meet a general plausibility test, and yet be rich enough to illuminate several aspects of how wealth moves around in a learning investment environment.

5.2.1 Assets

The market consists of only two assets. First, there is a risky asset paying a stochastic dividend:

$$d_{t+1} = d_g + d_t + \epsilon_t \tag{1}$$

where d_t is the logarithm of the dividend paid at time t, and d_g is the dividend growth rate. Time is incremented in units of weeks. Lowercased variables represent logarithms of the corresponding variables, so the actual dividend is given by

$$D_t = e^{d_t} \tag{2}$$

The shocks to dividends are given by ϵ_t, which is independent of time and follows a Gaussian distribution with zero mean and a variance σ_d^2 that will be calibrated to actual long-run dividends from the United States. The dividend growth rate would then be given by $e^{g+(1/2)\sigma_d^2}$, which is approximately $D_g = d_g + (1/2)\sigma_d^2$.

The return on the stock with dividend at date t is given by

$$R_t = \frac{P_t + D_t - P_{t-1}}{P_{t-1}} \tag{3}$$

where P_t is the price of the stock at time t. Timing in the market is critical. Dividends are paid at the beginning of period t. Both P_t and D_t are part of the information set used to forecast future returns R_{t+1}. There are I individual agents in the model indexed by i. The total supply of shares is fixed and is set to unity:

$$\sum_{i=1}^{I} S_{t,i} = 1 \tag{4}$$

There is also a risk-free asset that is available in infinite supply, with agent i holding $B_{t,i}$ units at time t. The risk-free asset pays a rate of R_f, which is assumed to be zero. This is done for two important reasons. It limits the injection of outside resources to the dividend process only. Also, it allows for an interpretation of this model as one with a perfectly storable consumption good along with the risky asset. The standard intertemporal budget constraint holds for each agent i:

$$W_{t,i} = P_t S_{t,i} + B_{t,i} + C_{t,i} = (P_t + D_t)S_{t-1,i} + (1 + R_f)B_{t-1,i} \tag{5}$$

where $W_{t,i}$ and $C_{t,i}$ represent the wealth and consumption of agent i at time t, respectively.

5.2.2 Preferences

Portfolio choices in the model are determined by a simple myopic power utility function in future wealth. The agent's portfolio problem corresponds to

$$\max_{\alpha_{t,i}} \frac{E_t^i W_{t+1,i}^{1-\gamma}}{1-\gamma} \tag{6}$$

such that

$$W_{t+1,i} = (1 + R_{t+1,i}^p)(W_{t,i} - C_{t,i}) \tag{7}$$

$$R_{t+1,i}^p = \alpha_{t,i} R_{t+1} + (1 - \alpha_{t,i})R_f \tag{8}$$

$\alpha_{t,i}$ represents agent i's fraction of savings $(W - C)$ in the risky asset, E_t^i is the expectation of agent i at time t of future wealth, and γ is the coefficient of relative risk aversion. It is well known that the solution to this problem yields an optimal portfolio weight given by

$$\alpha_{t,i} = \frac{E_t^i(r_{t+1}) - r_f + \frac{1}{2}\sigma_{t,i}^2}{\gamma \sigma_{t,i}^2} + \epsilon_{t,i} \tag{9}$$

with $r_t = \log(1 + R_t)$ and $r_f = \log(1 + R_f)$; $\sigma_{t,i}^2$ is agent i's estimate of the conditional variance at time t, and $\epsilon_{t,i}$ is an individual shock designed to make sure that there is some small amount of heterogeneity to keep trade operating.[9] It is distributed normally with variance σ_ϵ^2.

In the current version of the model neither leverage nor short sales are allowed. The fractional demand is restricted to $\alpha_L \leq \alpha_{t,i} \leq \alpha_H$ (see Table 5.1 below for these values). The addition of both these features is important but adds significantly to model complexity. One key problem is that with either of these features, one must address problems of agent bankruptcy and borrowing constraints. Both are nontrivial additions and involve many possible implementation choices.

Consumption is assumed to be a constant fraction of wealth, λ. This fraction is identical for all agents and is constant over time. The intertemporal budget constraint is therefore given by

$$W_{t+1,i} = (1 + R_{t+1}^P)(1 - \lambda)W_{t,i} \tag{10}$$

This result also gives the current period budget constraint:

$$P_t S_{t,i} + B_{t,i} = (1 - \lambda)((P_t + D_t)S_{t-1,i} + (1 + R_f)B_{t-1,i}) \tag{11}$$

This simplified portfolio strategy is used throughout the chapter. It is important to note that the approach of a fixed consumption-wealth ratio and a myopic strategy given here would be optimal in a standard intertemporal model for a consumption portfolio choice subject to two key assumptions. First, the intertemporal elasticity of substitution would have to be unity to fix the consumption-wealth ratio. Second, the correlation between unexpected returns and certain state variables would have to be zero to eliminate the demand for intertemporal hedging.[10]

---

9. The derivation of this solution follows Campbell and Viceira (2002). It involves taking a Taylor series approximation for the logarithm of the portfolio return.

10. See Campbell and Viceira (1999) for the basic framework. Also, see Giovannini and Weil (1989) for early work on determining conditions for myopic portfolio decisions. Hedging demands would only impose a constant shift on the optimal portfolio, so how much of an impact this might have on the results is an interesting question.

5.2.3 Expected-Return Forecasts

The basic problem faced by agents is to forecast both expected returns and the conditional variance one period into the future. This section describes the forecasting tools used for expected returns. A forecast strategy, indexed by j, is a method for generating an expected-return forecast $E^j(r_{t+1})$. Agents, indexed by i, will choose forecast rules, indexed by j, according to an expected utility objective.

All forecasts use long-range forecasts of expected values using constant-gain learning algorithms equipped with the minimum gain level, denoted by g_L:

$$\bar{r}_t = (1 - g_L)\bar{r}_{t-1} + g_L r_t \tag{12}$$

$$\overline{pd}_t = (1 - g_L)\overline{pd}_{t-1} + g_L pd_{t-1} \tag{13}$$

$$\bar{\sigma}_t^2 = (1 - g_L)\bar{\sigma}_{t-1}^2 + g_L (r_t - \bar{r}_t)^2 \tag{14}$$

where pd_t is $\log(P_t/D_t)$, and the overbar indicates a forecast variable.

$$\bar{\sigma}_{pd,t}^2 = (1 - g_L)\bar{\sigma}_{pd,t-1}^2 + g_L (pd_t - \overline{pd}_t)^2 \tag{15}$$

The forecasts used combine four linear forecasts drawn from well-known forecast families. The first of these is a form of adaptive expectations, which corresponds to

$$f_t^j = f_{t-1}^j + g_j(r_t - f_{t-1}^j) \tag{16}$$

Forecasts of expected returns are dynamically adjusted based on the latest forecast error. This forecast format is simple and generic. It has roots connected to adaptive expectations, trend-following technical trading, and Kalman filtering.[11] The critical parameter is the gain level, represented by g_j. This determines the weight that agents put on recent returns and how this weighting impacts their expectations of the future. Forecasts with a large range of gain parameters will compete against one another in the market. Finally, this forecast is trimmed, in that it is restricted to stay in the interval $[-h_j, h_j]$. These interval limits are set to relatively large values and are randomly distributed across rules.

---

11. See Cagan (1956), Friedman (1956), Muth (1960), and Phelps (1967) for original applications. A nice summary of the connections between Kalman filtering, adaptive expectations, and recursive least squares is given in Sargent (1999). A recent paper demonstrating a more general connection to state-space models and expected returns is Pastor and Stambaugh (2009). Empirically, Frankel and Froot (1987) and Taylor and Allen (1992) provide evidence that at least some forecasters do use these rules. Finally, Hommes (2010) surveys some laboratory evidence that experimental subjects also use extrapolative methods for forecasting time series.

The second forecasting rule is based on a classic fundamental strategy. This forecast uses log (P/D) regressions as a basis for forecasting future returns:

$$f_t^j = \bar{r}_t + \beta_t^j (pd_t - \overline{pd_t}) \tag{17}$$

where pd_t is $\log(P_t/D_t)$. Although agents are only interested in the one-period-ahead forecasts, the P/D regressions are estimated using the mean return over the next M_{PD} periods, where $M_{PD} = 52$ weeks.

The third forecast rule is based on simple linear regressions. It is a predictor of returns at time t given by

$$f_t^j = \bar{r}_t + \sum_{i=0}^{M_{AR}-1} \beta_{t,i}^j (r_{t-i} - \bar{r}_t) \tag{18}$$

This strategy works to eliminate short-range autocorrelations in returns series, and $M_{AR} = 3$ for all runs in this chapter. It is referred to as the short-autoregressive (short-AR) forecast.[12]

The previous two rules will be estimated each period using recursive least squares. There are many examples of this approach for financial market learning.[13] The key difference is that this model stresses heterogeneity in the learning algorithms, with wealth shifting across many different rules, and each rule uses a different gain parameter in its updating.[14]

The final rule is a buy and hold strategy using the long-run mean $\bar{r}_t$ for the expected return and the long-run variance $\bar{\sigma}_t^2$ as the variance estimate. This portfolio fraction is then determined by the demand equation used by the other forecasting rules. This rule gives a useful passive benchmark strategy that can be monitored for relative wealth accumulation compared with the other, active, strategies.

5.2.4 Regression Updates

Forecasting rules are continually updated. The adaptive forecast only involves fixed forecast parameters, so its updates are trivial, requiring only the recent return. The two regression forecasts are updated each period using recursive least squares.

All the rules assume a constant gain parameter, but each rule in the family corresponds to a different gain level. This again corresponds to varying

---

12. These simple forecasting agents who use only recent returns in their models, fighting against return correlations, share some features with the momentum traders of Hong and Stein (1999).

13. See Evans and Honkapohja (2001) for many examples and also for extensive descriptions of recursive least-squares learning methods.

14. Another recent model stressing heterogeneity in an ordinary least-squares (OLS) learning environment is Georges (2008), in which OLS learning rules are updated asynchronously.

weights for the forecasts looking at past data. The fundamental regression is run using the long-range return:

$$\tilde{r}_t = \frac{1}{M_{PD}} \sum_{j=1}^{M_{PD}} r_{t-j+1} \tag{19}$$

The fundamental regression is updated according to

$$\beta_{t+1}^j = \beta_t^j + \frac{g_j}{\bar{\sigma}_{pd,t}^2} (pd_{t-M_{PD}} - \overline{pd}_{t-M_{PD}}) u_{t,j} \tag{20}$$

$$u_{t,j} = (\tilde{r}_t - f_{j,t-M_{PD}})$$

Also, β_t^j is restricted to be between 0 and -0.05. The zero upper bound on β makes sure this strategy is mean reverting, with an overall stabilizing impact on the market.

For the lagged return regression the update would be

$$\beta_{t+1,i}^j = \beta_{t,i}^j + \frac{g_j}{\bar{\sigma}_{r,t}^2} (r_{t-i} - \bar{r}_{t-i}) u_{t,j} \tag{21}$$

$$u_{t,j} = (r_t - f_t^j)$$

where g_j is again the critical gain parameter, and it varies across forecast rules.[15] In both forecast regressions the forecast error, $u_{t,j}$, is trimmed. If $u_{t,j} > h_j$, it is set to h_j, and if $u_{t,j} < -h_j$, it is set to $-h_j$. This trimming dampens the impact of large price moves on the forecast estimation process.

5.2.5 Variance Forecasts

The optimal portfolio choice demands a forecast of the conditional variance as well as the conditional mean.[16] The variance forecasts are generated from adaptive expectations, as in

---

15. This format for multivariate updating is only an approximation to the true recursive estimation procedure. It assumes that the variance/covariance matrix of returns is diagonal. Generated returns in the model are close to uncorrelated, so this approximation is probably reasonable. The assumption of diagonal matrices is made to avoid performing many costly matrix inversions. Also, the standard recursive least squares is simplified by using the long-run estimates for the mean in both regressions. Only the linear coefficient is estimated with a heterogeneous learning model, which is done to simplify the learning model and concentrate heterogeneity on the linear parameters β_t^j.

16. Several papers have explored the dynamics of risk and return forecasting, including Branch and Evans (2011) and Gaunersdorfer (2000). In LeBaron (2001b) risk is implicitly considered through the utility function and portfolio returns. Obviously, methods that parameterize risk in the variance may miss other components of the return distribution that agents care about, but the gain in tractability is important.

$$\hat{\sigma}_{t+1,j}^2 = \hat{\sigma}_{t,j}^2 + g_{j,\sigma}(e_{t,j}^2 - \hat{\sigma}_{t,j}^2) \qquad (22)$$

$$e_{t,j}^2 = (r_t - f_{t-1}^j)^2 \qquad (23)$$

where $\hat{\sigma}_{t+1}^2$ is the forecast of the future variance, and $e_{t,j}^2$ is the squared forecast error at time t, for rule j. The above conditional variance estimate is used for all the rules. There is no attempt to develop a wide range of variance forecasting rules, because even though there may be many ways to estimate a conditional variance, they often produce similar results.[17] This forecast method has many useful characteristics as a benchmark forecast. First, it is essentially an adaptive expectations forecast on second moments and therefore has a functional form similar to that for the adaptive expectations family of return forecasts. Second, it is closely related to other familiar conditional variance estimates.[18] Finally, the gain level for the variance in a forecast rule, $g_{j,\sigma}$, is allowed to differ from that used in the mean expectations, g_j. This allows rules to have different time-series perspectives on returns and volatility.

Finally, agents do not update their estimates of the variance each period. They instead update their variance estimates stochastically with probability 0.25 for each period. This is done for several reasons. First, it introduces more heterogeneity into the variance estimation part of the model, as its construction yields a great deal of similarity in variance forecasts. Second, if variance updating occurred simultaneously with return forecasts, the market would be unstable. Spirals of ever-falling prices and increasing variance estimates would be impossible to avoid in this case.

5.2.6 Market Clearing

The market is cleared by setting the individual share demands equal to the aggregate share supply of unity:

$$1 = \sum_{i=1}^{I} Z_{t,i}(P_t) \qquad (24)$$

Writing the demand for shares as its fraction of current wealth and remembering that $\alpha_{t,i}$ is a function of the current price give

$$P_t Z_{t,i} = (1 - \lambda)\alpha_{t,i}(P_t)W_{t,i} \qquad (25)$$

$$Z_{t,i}(P_t) = (1 - \lambda)\alpha_{t,i}(P_t)\frac{(P_t + D_t)S_{t-1,i} + B_{t-1,i}}{P_t} \qquad (26)$$

---

17. See Nelson (1992) for early work on this topic.
18. See Bollerslev et al. (1995) and Andersen et al. (2006) for surveys of the large literature on volatility modeling.

This market is cleared for the current price level P_t. Clearing needs to be done numerically, given the complexities of the various demand functions and forecasts, and also the boundary conditions on $\alpha_{t,i}$.[19] It is important to note that forecasts are conditional on the price at time t, so market clearing involves finding a price that clears the market for all agent demands, allowing these demands to be conditioned on their forecasts of R_{t+1} given the current price and dividend.[20]

5.2.7 Gain Levels

An important design question for the simulation is how to set the range of gain levels for the various forecast rules. These ranges will determine the dynamics of forecasts. Given that this is an entire distribution of values, it will be impossible to accomplish much in terms of sensitivity analysis. Therefore, a reasonable mechanism is used to generate these limits, which is used in all simulations.

Gain levels are thought of as using their half-life equivalents, because the gain numbers themselves do not offer much in the way of economic or forecasting intuition. Think of the simple exponential forecast mechanism:

$$f_{t+1}^j = (1 - g_j)f_t^j + g_j e_{t+1} \tag{27}$$

This mechanism easily maps to the simple exponential forecast rule:

$$f_t = \sum_{k=1}^{\infty} (1 - g_j)^k e_{t-k} \tag{28}$$

The half-life of this forecast corresponds to the number of periods, m_h, which drops the weight to $1/2$:

$$\frac{1}{2} = (1 - g_j)^{m_h} \tag{29}$$

or

$$g_j = 1 - 2^{-1/m_h} \tag{30}$$

The distribution of m_h then is the key object of choice here. It is chosen so that $\log_2(m_h)$ is distributed uniformly between a given minimum and a maximum value. The gain levels are further simplified to use only five discrete values. These are given in Table 5.1, and are 1, 2.5, 7, 18, and 50

---

19. A binary search is used to find the market clearing price, using starting information from P_{t-1}.

20. The current price determines R_t, which is an input into both the adaptive and short-AR forecasts. Also, the price level P_t enters into P_t/D_t, which is required for the fundamental forecasts. All forecasts are updated with this time-t information in the market clearing process.

Table 5.1 Parameter definitions

Parameter	Value
d_g	0.0126
σ_d	0.12
r_f	0
γ	3.5
λ	0.0007
I	16000
J	4000
g_j	$[1, 2.5, 7, 18, 50]$ years
g_L	50 years
g_u	$[1, 2.5, 7, 18, 50]$ years
L	5 percent/year
$[\alpha_L, \alpha_H]$	$[0.05, 0.95]$
σ_ϵ	0.02
M_{PD}	52 weeks
M_{AR}	3
h_j	$[0.025, 0.15]$

Notes: The annual standard deviation of dividend growth is set to the level from real dividends in Shiller's annual long-range dataset. The growth rate of log (dividends), 0.0126, corresponds to an expected percentage change of $D_g = 0.02 = d_g + (1/2)\sigma_d^2$ in annual dividends. This corresponds to the long-range value of 0.021 in the Shiller data.

years, respectively. In the long-memory (low-gain) experiments these five values will be distributed uniformly between 45 and 50 years.

These distributions are used for all forecasting rules. All forecast rules need a gain both for the expected-return forecast and the variance forecast. These are chosen independently of each other, which allows agents to have differing perspectives on the importance of past data for the expected-return and variance processes.

5.2.8 Adaptive Rule Selection

The design of the models used here allows for both passive and active learning. Passive learning corresponds to the long-term evolution of wealth across strategies. Beyond passive learning, the model allows for active learning, or adaptive rule selection. This mechanism addresses the fact that agents will seek out strategies that best optimize their estimated objective functions. In this sense the process is a form of adaptive utility maximization.

Implementing such a learning process opens up a large number of design questions. This chapter stays with a relatively simple implementation. The first question is how to deal with estimating expected utility. Expected utility is estimated using an exponentially weighted average over the recent past:

$$\hat{U}_{t,j} = \hat{U}_{t-1,j} + g_u^i (U_{t,j} - \hat{U}_{t-1,j}) \tag{31}$$

where $U_{t,j}$ is the realized utility for rule j received at time t. This corresponds to

$$U_{t,j} = \frac{1}{1-\gamma}(1 + R_{t,j}^p)^{(1-\gamma)} \tag{32}$$

where $R_{t,j}^p$ is the portfolio holdings of rule j at time t. Each rule reports this value for the five discrete agent gain parameters, g_u^i. Agents choose rules optimally, using the objective that corresponds to their specific perspective on the past, g_u^i, which is a fixed characteristic. The gain parameter g_u^i follows the same discrete distribution as that for the expected-return and variance forecasts.

The final component to the learning dynamic is how the agents make the decision to change rules. The mechanism is simple but is designed to capture a kind of heterogeneous updating that seems plausible. Each period a certain fraction L of agents is chosen at random. Each one randomly chooses a new rule out of the set of all rules. If this rule exceeds the current one in terms of estimated expected utility, then the agent adopts the new forecasting rule.

5.3   Results

5.3.1   Benchmarks

This section presents results from two sets of benchmark parameters for the model. The first restricts gain parameters to low values, corresponding to long learning horizons. It is referred to as the "low-gain" experiment. This is an important test to see whether the model is capable of converging to a reasonable steady state, and whether the learning dynamics will function as long as all gain levels are set low enough and agents are using data over long ranges in the forecasts. The half-life ranges for gain parameters in these experiments are set to 45–50 years. Also, for this run only, the coefficient of relative risk aversion is raised from 3.5 to 8. This increase is necessary, because the model converges to a very low return variance. The convergence in this situation would drive all portfolio holdings to their extreme, α_H, which makes the market difficult to clear. The model is run for 200,000 weeks to make sure it has reached some form of long-run steady state and all early transients have been eliminated. Figure 5.1 displays P/D, returns, and trading volume from the last 100 years of simulated data. Prices do not move far from dividends, as shown in the top panel. Returns appear to be regular, and they can be shown to be uncorrelated and close to Gaussian. Trading volume is nearly constant, reflecting the small amount of noise added to each agent's portfolio demand.

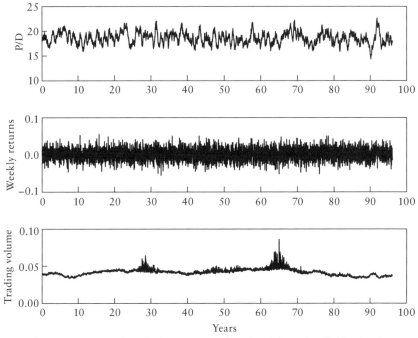

Figure 5.1 Low gain only: long memory learning. P/D, price-dividend ratio.

This simulated set of prices and returns generates an important but relatively uninteresting set of results for the market simulation. Although these features are not close to those of actual markets, they do demonstrate that for a certain set of parameters this market and the agents' learning algorithms are capable of converging to a reasonable approximation to a rational expectations equilibrium. The most important aspect of this set of parameters is that agents use learning algorithms that force them to concentrate on long-range averages as opposed to short-run trends. Also, though the aggregate data look like an equilibrium, they are not quite in equilibrium in the traditional sense. There is still trading and shifts in strategies, which do not appear in the aggregate time series.

Figure 5.2 displays results from a run that is used extensively to demonstrate the features of heterogeneous gain learning in this model. In this case, the five gain levels used vary from 1 to 50 years, as shown in Table 5.1. This case will often be referred to as the "all gain" experiment. The three panels of Figure 5.2 should be compared with those in the previous figure. Now P/D varies erratically through time, which is important for generating reasonable long swings in asset prices. The weekly returns demonstrate two features common to relatively high-frequency returns. First, there are a large number of extreme returns, and second, periods of high volatility appear clumped together. These features are interesting and are important

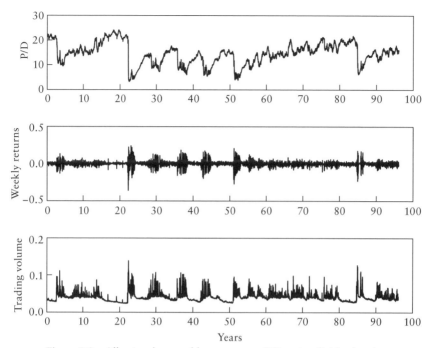

Figure 5.2 All gain: short and long memory. P/D, price-dividend ratio.

to the dynamics that this model generates. However, they are secondary to the main mission of this chapter, which is concerned with the top panel and long swings from fundamentals. Another interesting result is shown in the bottom panel, which presents the trading volume time series. Volume clearly moves with changes in P/D level and return volatility. As with most real financial series, volume appears to be largest when return volatility is high. It also appears to be lowest at the top of a P/D bubble, sharply increasing as the price falls.[21]

The large swings in the P/D are compared to the values from the actual series in Figure 5.3. The persistent, but erratic swings in the actual P/D are clear.[22] This series is not easy to characterize, and it is possible that visual

21. Hong and Sraer (2010) describe different types of bubbles based on volume-price dynamics. In their framework this would be described as a "quiet" bubble. How well it lines up with historical bubbles is an interesting question for the future. It should be noted that these volume comovements are very common in the laboratory, as in Smith et al. (1988). Further evidence on the dynamics of volume and prices for this market structure is presented in LeBaron (2010).

22. The S&P series used here is the Shiller annual series, available at http://www.econ.yale.edu/~shiller/. This series contains both dividend and earnings information. The rough visual features of this series would be similar if P/D ratio were replaced with the annual price-earnings ratio.

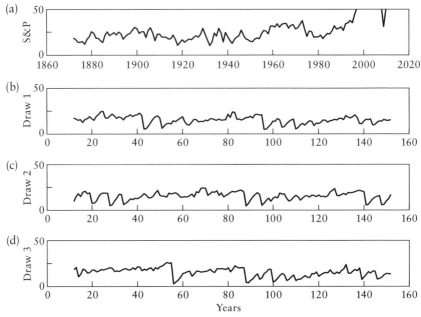

Figure 5.3 Price-dividend ratios (P/Ds): S&P and three simulations. (a) Estimation based on the Shiller annual dataset and represents the real P/D for the S&P from 1872 to 2009. (b–d) Random 140-year snapshots taken from a simulation run of 4,000 years using all gain-level learning. The Shiller series goes to a high of near 90 around 2000.

analysis may be the best that can be done. There appear to be fluctuations occurring at frequencies that are large relative to the length of the series, and one could also question the stationarity of this series as well. The long-gain half-life is set to 50 years in recognition that this length of data (140 years) is probably the best that many investors can do in assessing the long-range dynamics for stock returns. Panels (b–d) represent three random snapshots from runs of the simulations using the long- and short-gain levels. They draw 140-year periods from a simulated time series of 4,000 years, so there is little chance for overlap. Visually, these series show similar patterns to the actual data, with varying levels of persistence and variability. It is interesting to note that all series are capable of long periods of near-constant ratios. Eyeball tests of time series should always be viewed with suspicion, but in this case the special nature of the target series and the sorts of dynamics we are interested in make these tests essential.[23]

---

23. The skeptic could argue that the original series is simply too nonstationary to deal with. However, even this statement makes a big point about learning and long-range financial data. What should investors do in that case?

Table 5.2 Annual statistics

Statistic	Baseline	Shiller earnings	Shiller dividends
Mean(P/D)	15.29	15.37	26.79
Standard deviation(P/D)	4.24	5.97	13.90
Autocorrelation(1)	0.64	0.68	0.91
Mean(log(return))	6.82	—	6.22
Standard deviation(return)	0.25	—	0.17
Annual Sharpe ratio	0.35	—	0.30

Notes: The baseline model uses a sample of 100,000 weeks or about 1,900 years. The Shiller series are annual from 1871 to 2009. P/D refers to the price-dividend ratio for the model and the Shiller dividends column. The earnings column uses the annual price-earnings ratio instead. All returns are real, including dividends. The Sharpe ratio estimated from the Shiller annual data uses the 1-year interest rates from that series. —, not applicable.

Table 5.2 presents summary statistics on annual data comparing the all-gain-level simulations with the annual Shiller data. Simulation results are taken from the final 1,000 years in the 4,000-year all-gain run. Comparisons are made to both the P/D and the P/E, because the model could be viewed as generating either of these series. The table shows that the simulated data generates reasonable levels and variability in the first two rows. It is a little low relative to the mean P/D, but it should be realized that much of that large mean, 26, is driven by observations of the late 1990s or early 2000s. The model does generate a slightly lower level of variability with a standard deviation of only 4.24, which is smaller than the two ratio comparison series. There is some evidence of this smoother dynamics in Figure 5.3, but it should be stressed that all these moments from the data are estimated with very low precision.

Table 5.2 also reports the annual real return and standard deviation for the simulation and the actual data along with the Sharpe ratio. These are comparable, but the simulation generates a slightly higher level of return variability, with an annual standard deviation of 0.25 compared to the historical value of 0.17. This behavior is common for many simulation runs. Two issues should be kept in mind when comparing these values. First, the data moments are again not estimated with great precision, and 0.25 falls within a reasonable range of 0.17. More importantly, the simulation is concerned with generating the dynamics of a single representative asset. Given this, it is not clear whether the variability of its return output should be judged in comparison to the index or to the much higher level of volatility displayed by individual stocks. Table 5.2 shows that the simulations are in a reasonable range when compared with long-range data.

The most demanding and controversial aspect of long-range deviations from fundamentals is that they generate some observed predictability in long-range returns. This trait is explored in Table 5.3, which implements standard long-horizon forecasting regressions of 1 year and 5 years on the current log(P/D). This is done both for the all-gain simulation and the low-gain-only benchmark, which was displayed in Figure 5.1. In all cases the dependent variable is log (return) at either the 1- or 5-year horizon. These returns are regressed on both the log(P/D) ratio and the logarithm of the consumption-dividend ratio. This later ratio is an important consumption ratio for this model, because consumption can only be funded through dividend flows. When this ratio is less (greater) than unity, agents are increasing (decreasing) their savings through changes to their asset positions. Row one shows that the regression is capable of forecasting future returns with a highly significant coefficient and R^2 of nearly 0.19. Relative to actual data this value is large, but it should be remembered that this regression is run on a sample length of 1,000 years.[24] The second row adds the consumption ratio, which is highly significant but does not add significantly to R^2. The third row reports the regression for the 5-year horizon. The coefficient is still highly significant, but R^2 falls to 0.14.

The lower half of Table 5.3 reports the results for the small-gain-only (long half-life) only rules. The results for these simulations are displayed as the important initial benchmark in Figure 5.1. In all cases the predictability is near zero. All regression coefficients are insignificant, with near-zero R^2. This model again displays features consistent with an efficient market driven by well-functioning simple learning algorithms. They have achieved their mission of driving predictability from the market.

The next two figures deal with shorter horizon phenomena generated in the all-gain simulations that have important implications for the longer horizon returns. Figure 5.4 compares the distribution of weekly returns for both the Center for Research in Security Prices (CRSP) value-weighted index for 1926–2009 and the all-gain simulation shown in Figure 5.2. These returns are drawn from the final 50,000 weeks of a 200,000-week simulation. Both distributions show that they are not Gaussian, and are leptokurtic, possessing "fat-tail" features. This result is well known for high-frequency asset returns in most markets. Although this is not a long-range feature, the high frequency of extreme moves in these distributions does impact the learning dynamics of the various strategies.

---

24. It would be interesting to see how well this model works on sample sizes comparable to the real data series. In these series the issue of the usefulness of predictability is still an open question. See Goyal and Welch (2003) for some of the debate on out-of-sample predictability, and Fisher and Statman (2006) for some skeptical views on the usefulness of trading rules based on P/D.

Table 5.3 Long-range return regressions

Simulation	log(P/D)	log(C/D)	R^2
All gain (1 year)	−0.41	—	0.19
	(0.03)		
All gain (1 year)	−0.47	0.15	0.20
	(0.03)	(0.05)	
All gain (5 year)	−0.52	—	0.14
	(0.09)		
Small gain (1 year)	−0.01	—	0.00
	(0.05)		
Small gain (1 year)	−0.02	0.06	0.00
	(0.05)	(0.04)	
Small gain (5 year)	−0.39	—	0.01
	(0.25)		

Notes: Dependent variables are 1- and 5-year log (simulation returns). Simulation runs use 50,000 weeks of data, or approximately 1,000 years of nonoverlapping data for regressions. "All gain" corresponds to runs with both small and large forecast gain levels. "Small gain" corresponds to runs with only small-gain (long-memory) forecasts. P/D, price-dividend ratio; C/D, consumption-dividend ratio; —, not applicable.

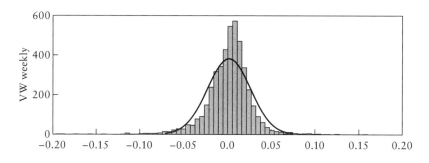

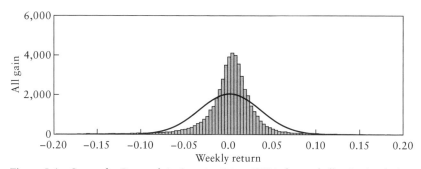

Figure 5.4 Center for Research in Security Prices VW index and all gain simulation weekly return distributions.

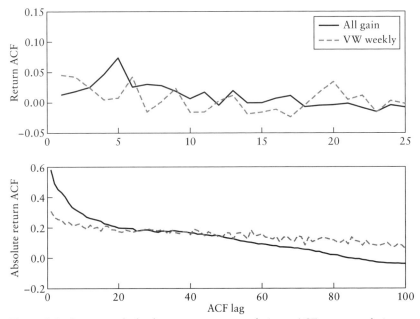

Figure 5.5 Return and absolute return autocorrelations. ACF, autocorrelation function.

Figure 5.5 summarizes two key time-series features of the generated returns and compares them with the CRSP benchmark. The top panel reports return autocorrelations for the CRSP index and the same sample of 50,000 weeks used in the previous figure. Both series show very little evidence for any correlation in returns. The lower panel displays the weekly autocorrelation for absolute returns for the same data. The simulation generates very strong positive autocorrelations, as do the actual returns. However, the correlation pattern is a little high at smaller lags and drops to zero by the lag at 100 weeks.[25] Though this feature is short range in nature, its long correlation pattern demonstrates that it may be important for long-range patterns in financial data. Further evidence in support of this idea is presented in the next section.

25. Modeling the dynamics of volatility at longer horizons is far from settled in finance. For these figures one would see dramatic instability in the autocorrelation pattern, depending on whether the Great Depression was added to the series. Also, several authors have proposed formal fractionally integrated models, such as FIGARCH (Baillie et al. 1996). Models suggesting multiple (but finite) numbers of horizons have also been discussed in LeBaron (2001a) and Corsi (2009). Some authors have also proposed using splines to fit these low-frequency components, as in Engle and Rangel (2008). Given what we know, one could say that the model and the data both generate a form of long-range persistence similar to that observed in the fundamental ratios.

5.3.2 Wealth Distributions

The previous section demonstrated that the benchmark simulation model with forecast rules and agents using small- and large-gain learning algorithms can generate reasonably calibrated time series. These series are not perfect, but they still generate features that are hard to replicate in many traditional theoretical frameworks. Generation of these features is interesting but is only a small part of model construction. Do these models give any insights into what is driving the results? Can one look into their inner workings to better understand the features found in the actual data? This section explores this issue in terms of the initial question about long swings of prices from fundamentals using the all-gain simulation as a test bed.

Beyond prices and returns, the model provides a rich set of information about the dynamics of the forecasting rules, the learning algorithms, and wealth distributions. How wealth endogenously falls across forecasting strategies is the key state variable in the model. This determines the dynamics of prices and trading volume as the market moves, but it is important to remember that these wealth distributions are moving targets as they change through time as well. Figure 5.6 presents the time series of wealth fractions for the four forecast families over the entire 200,000-week (~4,000-year)

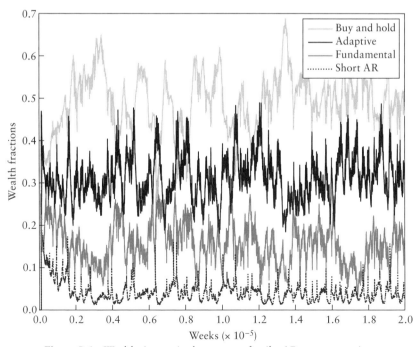

Figure 5.6 Wealth time series by strategy family. AR, autoregression.

period. These fractions vary across runs, but this picture is generally representative of many other simulations. There are many important features in the figure. First, the wealth fractions do vary over time. There is no tendency to settle down to relatively constant wealth fractions. The fractions appear to take swings that can both be short and long lived. Similar to the earlier figures showing long swings in P/Ds this figure shows swings in wealth ratios that can last for almost 100-year periods.

Although the time series are not completely smooth, they do appear to converge to a relatively stable ranking. The simple buy and hold strategy, which invests a constant fraction in stock based on the long-range forecast for the expected return and variance, controls roughly 50 percent of wealth in the market over the entire range. This might be surprising, in that this passive strategy cannot contribute to dramatic fluctuations in prices, but it is important to remember that in a heterogeneous world, this type may not be the marginal investor, critical for pricing.[26] Also, it is interesting that any model generating reasonable financial time series should also generate evidence that is at least roughly consistent with efficient markets at some horizons, and therefore the objective functions of many investors will find the passive strategies optimal. Basically, the gains to dynamic trading strategies do not dramatically dominate the passive strategies, and in a noisy decisionmaking world some investors will go with each type.

The next two strategies by wealth in Figure 5.6 are the adaptive trend-following family and the fundamental family. The battle between these strategies is critical to the overall stability of the market. Throughout the simulation the adaptive types control nearly 30 percent of wealth, compared with 15 percent for the fundamental types. This larger share of wealth in what are essentially destabilizing strategies is important to the behavior of the market at both long and short horizons, and some examples are given in later figures.[27] Finally, the short-AR traders, who use a short-range regression to forecast returns, remain a small part of the market at about 5 percent of wealth. This strategy follows a classic efficient market dynamic. Its presence drives short-range return correlations to zero while putting itself nearly out of business. It always stays in the fringe, soaking up some short-term predictability, and is ready to take action when large short-term correlations appear, but it never takes a large share of wealth.[28]

The strategy families are only one broad distinction among the forecast rules. Each strategy in a family is also characterized by its forecast gain pa-

---

26. See Adam and Marcet (2010b) for some recent theoretical results on heterogeneous agents and pricing.

27. The basic fact that the fundamental strategies may not control enough wealth to mitigate extreme moves in asset prices is related to "limits to arbitrage" ideas, as in Shleifer and Vishny (1997).

28. Simulation experiments without this strategy show that its role is critical. Removing it generates time series with short-range autocorrelations much larger than actual financial series.

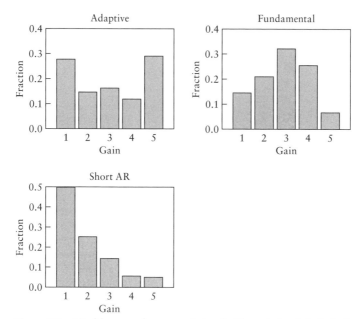

Figure 5.7 Wealth across forecast gain levels. The gain levels 1, 2, 3, 4, and 5 correspond to half-lives of 50, 18, 7, 2.5, and 1 years, respectively. AR, autoregressive.

rameter and its variance forecast gain parameter. As mentioned previously, these are critical in determining how the agents weigh past data in their forecasts. It has already been shown that limiting these two parameters to small values across all forecast rules leads to convergence of the market into a rough approximation of a rational expectations equilibrium. With many gain levels active, more realistic price and returns series are generated. Figure 5.7 shows the distribution of wealth across the five discrete gain levels. These are the same half-lives as shown in Table 5.1. For both the adaptive and fundamental strategies, wealth is not converging to any particular gain level, and, most importantly, there is no strong tendency for wealth to move to the smallest possible gain (largest half-life) strategy. The situation is different for the short-AR strategy, which shows wealth moving to the smaller gain strategies. In this case, almost 75 percent of wealth is using forecasting models with gain half-lives of 18 or 50 years, which seems comfortably long for estimating weekly regression models. The buy and hold strategies only use long half-life forecasts in their rules, so their distributions are not presented.[29]

29. These histograms are generated as a single-period snapshot at the end of the 200,000-week run. They should be viewed with some caution, because sampling variability over time could be important. Specific patterns may not be as strong as they appear, but the basic idea that for two of the forecasts, many gain levels remain active in the market is generally robust.

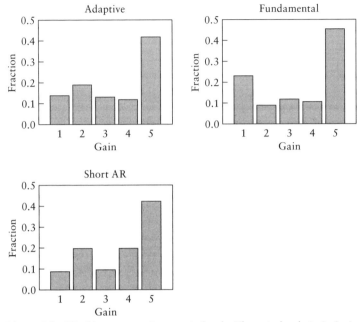

Figure 5.8 Wealth across variance gain levels. The gain levels 1, 2, 3, 4, and 5 correspond to half-lives of 50, 18, 7, 2.5, and 1 years, respectively. AR, autoregressive.

Figure 5.8 reports the results for the variance-forecast gain levels. In this case the figure shows a more distinct pattern, with a large amount of wealth concentrated on the large gain (low half-life) forecasts. The rules still leave a moderate amount of wealth at longer horizons, but in each case there is a distinct concentration of wealth in rules that use a small amount of data in their volatility forecasts.

In the model a key gain parameter is concerned with how agents assess the value of the different available strategies, described in equation (31). Figure 5.9 reports the distribution of wealth across utility gain levels g_u^i. The gain level is considered a fixed component of all agents' beliefs about the world. The figure shows whether there is any tendency for any type, particularly those using longer horizons of data, to dominate the market. This does not appear to be the case, and all types survive. There is some weak evidence for some of the lower gain (longer half-life) strategies to do better, but it appears to be very weak.

Wealth distributions show a few broad features across the model. Buy and hold strategies dominate, but adaptive strategies continue to hold a large amount of wealth as well. Fundamental strategies reveal a significantly smaller fraction of the market relative to these other two strategies, which is important in market dynamics. In terms of gain levels, in most cases there is no strong selection for low-gain learning models that would use large

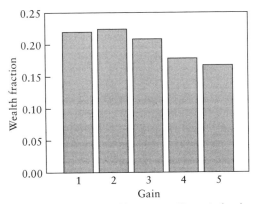

Figure 5.9 Agent wealth across utility gain levels. The gain levels 1, 2, 3, 4, and 5 correspond to half-lives of 50, 18, 7, 2.5, and 1 years, respectively.

amounts of data. This is important, because it is this restriction that allows the learning models to converge as shown in the first benchmark simulation. The next section explores some long-range dynamics for this population of agents and rules.

5.3.3   Mechanisms

Because the model gives full access to the strategies, it is insightful to look inside and see exactly what they are doing. The next few figures produce some snapshots of prices and forecasts showing the general pattern of forecast behavior as it responds to price movements. Figure 5.10 displays the dynamics of the wealth-weighted expected returns across all four forecast families along with the price level. This is done over a 3,000-week (or roughly 60-year) snapshot of data. The middle panel shows the forecast for the two most important strategies, adaptive and fundamental. These move as they should, and they are dominated by their large moves near big price drops. The adaptive forecasts observe the down trend in the market and make low-return forecasts, whereas the fundamental forecasts see the price as being low relative to the fundamentals and respond with a high conditional return forecast. Qualitatively, these behaviors are realistic for these strategies.

The bottom panel reports the results for the buy and hold strategy and the short-AR strategy. The buy and hold is basically a constant, corresponding to its long horizon mean. The short-AR strategy generates a lot of variability around this value with high volatility and large swings. Because this strategy is driven purely as an autoregressive model on lagged returns, it is sensible that the forecast itself picks up much of the return variability. This intense variability in the strategy may be related to its rather poor performance.

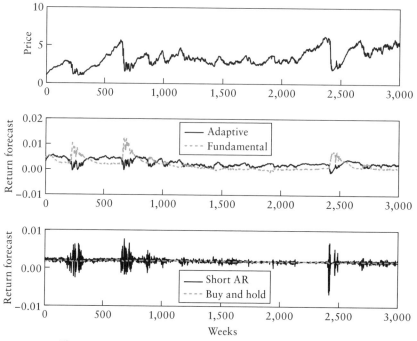

Figure 5.10 Forecasts by strategy family. AR, autoregressive.

Figure 5.11 presents the same time-series snapshot, but now replaces the expected-return forecast with the actual portfolio strategy for each family, as represented by the equity fraction. This involves combining the expected-return forecast along with the variance forecast. This figure shows more interesting dynamics than the last one. The top panel shows the price levels, and the middle and bottom panels are the different forecast family strategies. First, the adaptive forecasts do behave as expected in following general price trends. They appear to be readjusting portfolio weights very quickly in response to small price trends, and they also back off their positions substantially after large price declines. The behavior of the fundamental strategy is also more interesting. During large price increases it actually starts increasing its holding of stock. This behavior is curious, because it does not make sense for this strategy, as the price is moving further out of line with dividends. There are two mechanisms at work here. First, during major price run-ups volatility falls, so the estimated risk levels are falling, pushing agents to a more aggressive portfolio, regardless of the conditional return forecasts. Also, these forecasts are dependent on estimates of P/D regressions. As a price rise continues, evidence in support of reversion to the fundamental diminishes in strength. In other words, agents begin to lose faith in their fundamental models, and this would sweep across their

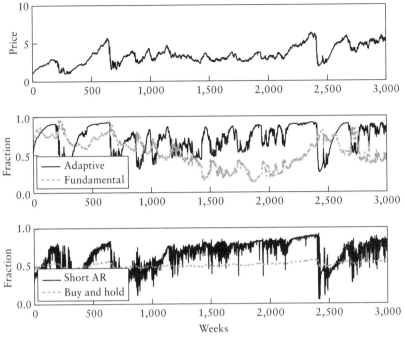

Figure 5.11 Portfolio holdings by strategy family. AR, autoregressive.

populations from small to large half-lives. It is also true that the response to a large price drop seems surprisingly weak. This weakness is also a reminder that agents' behavior is impacted by the conditional variance. While agents' expected returns are high after a fall, these large returns are feeding into their variance models, and the agents believe that risk is high in these states of the world. They are nervous and may not take as aggressive a position as their conditional return models suggest.

The features of the fundamental trading strategies become clearer when they are analyzed over the extreme gain levels, as shown in Figure 5.12. The middle panel in this figure shows the fundamental strategies for the highest and lowest gain levels in the volatility component only. If the low-gain strategies are relatively long term in their assessment of risk, they should respond to a fall in price more aggressively than the short-gain volatility strategies. This difference is very dramatic in the figure. Low-gain strategies come into the market immediately on a price fall and max out their portfolios, whereas the high-gain strategies do not behave as aggressively.[30]

30. This hesitancy on the part of risk-averse rational investors is in the spirit of noise trader models, as in DeLong et al. (1992).

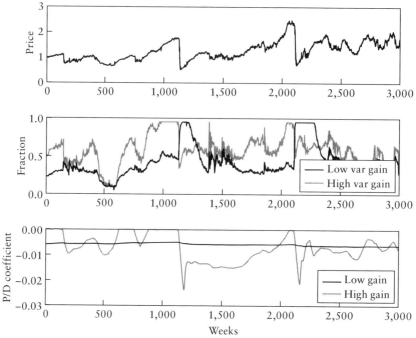

Figure 5.12 Fundamental strategies by gain. The middle panel shows the equity fractions for the high- and low-variance gain levels in the fundamental rule family. The bottom panel shows the estimated log(P/D) coefficient for the high and low gain parameters in the recursive least-squares regression. P/D, price-dividend ratio; var, variance.

The bottom panel presents the estimates of their least-squares coefficient from the return regressions on the value for log(P/D). For the low-gain strategies this coefficient is stable and negative.[31] The high-gain forecasts show a pattern that moves through time in a predictable fashion. It maxes out at 0, which is its maximum allowable value, during significant price run-ups. The short range of data that this regression is relying on shows no strong return to fundamentals, and the regression coefficient simply reflects this belief. After a large price drop, the parameter swings negative, again reflecting that the recent data now strongly support the fact that large negative returns often follow periods when prices are large relative to fundamentals. If these results seem somewhat extreme, it is important to remember that these are the extreme gain levels. There are three others,

31. These regressions are run on the mean weekly return over 52 weeks as opposed to annual returns themselves. This is why the parameter differs from those in Table 5.3. Multiplying by 52 shows that they are indeed consistent with each other in magnitude.

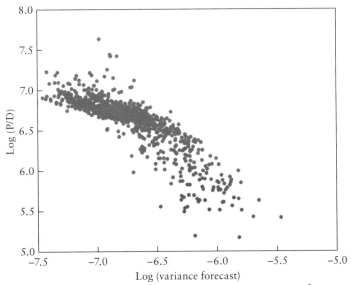

Figure 5.13 Volatility forecast and price-dividend ratio (P/D): $R^2 = 0.71$.

which lie in between these gain levels. The aggregate forecast depends on how wealth falls across these different strategies as given in Figure 5.7.

The next figures explore the mechanism behind the large swings in fundamentals in the model. Specifically, they explore the hypothesis of whether the swings are driven by the common component in agents' forecast models, their prediction of the conditional variance. Figure 5.13 is a simple plot of log(P/D) versus the logarithm of the wealth-weighted variance forecast in the market. The negative correlation is very strong, and a regression of log(P/D) on the logarithm of the variance forecast yields $R^2 = 0.72$.[32]

Further evidence of this connection is given in the time-series results in Figure 5.14. The top panel plots P/D for a 50-year sample of time, and the middle panel displays the wealth-weighted variance forecast. The wealth-weighted variance clearly moves closely with P/D. Large price falls cause a jump in the variance estimates, and these generate a persistent increase in the market average variance forecast.[33] Now the issue of which

32. Obviously, this right-hand-side variable here is endogenous, so the regression should only be viewed as instructive about the comovements.

33. A quick back-of-the-envelope test is useful to understand the impact of this volatility change on prices. A rough representative-agent approximation to the pricing relation would give $P = (\frac{x}{\gamma \sigma^2} + \frac{1}{2\gamma})W$. Ignoring the second term in the sum as being relatively small yields a direct proportionate connection between the price level and the variance for a given wealth level. An increase in σ^2 by a factor of 3 as shown in Figure 5.14 could lead to a reduction in prices by the same factor, which is a similar order of magnitude as shown in the figure. This reduction would be larger if one correctly considered the decrease in wealth as well.

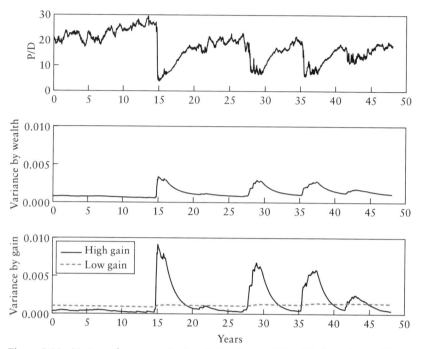

Figure 5.14 Variance forecast and price-dividend ratio (P/D). "Variance by wealth" is the wealth-weighted variance forecast. The bottom panel shows the variance forecast averaged (equal weight) across all small- and large-gain strategies.

variance forecast is being used becomes important. The bottom panel in the figure displays the variance forecasts for the highest and lowest gain levels across all forecast rules. The low-gain (or long half-life) forecast generates a very stable estimate of the conditional variance. It is remarkably stable even after the occurrence of a large price drop. In contrast, the high-gain forecast moves quickly, with the new information coming from the price fall. The middle panel lies somewhere between these two. It also reveals some evidence for a more persistent impact of volatility, as more of the lower gain strategies pick up the increased volatility levels that are usually persistent. Evidence in this figure is consistent with the portfolio strategy results given in Figure 5.11. The low-gain strategies are not changing their risk assessments even after large price declines, and they are therefore very aggressive in their portfolio weights, which other strategies are more cautious about. Higher gain strategies perceive the increase in conditional variance, which moderates their response to their high conditional return forecasts. In other words, they know it is a good time to invest in equity, but they are scared.

Why don't agents choose what appears to be a more desirable variance forecast? This interesting question is addressed in Figure 5.15. The top pan-

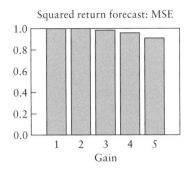

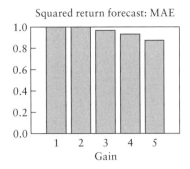

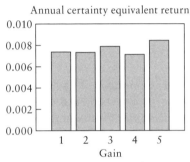

Figure 5.15 Forecasting and variance gain. MSE and MAE are the mean squared and mean absolute errors for the different variance forecasts estimated across gain levels. They are normalized against the value from guessing the unconditional mean squared return in each case. In other words, 1 indicates no forecast improvement. The utility levels are annualized certainty equivalent returns for the portfolios. The gain levels 1, 2, 3, 4, and 5 correspond to half-lives of 50, 18, 7, 2.5, and 1 years, respectively.

els in the figure report the mean squared error (MSE) and mean absolute error (MAE) for the different gain-level variance forecasts evaluated over the last 50,000 weeks of the simulation. They are normalized by the value from the forecast using the unconditional mean over the sample. A value of one would correspond to getting the same prediction error as the unconditional mean. The lowest gain level shows that it is very close to using the unconditional mean squared return, which should be expected. What is interesting is that the higher gain forecasts all generate modest improvements in terms of forecast errors. For the highest gain (lowest half-life) forecast there is an improvement of more than 10 percent for the MSE and MAE forecast measures. This is important, because these are out of sample forecasts at fixed parameter values. They could have gone well above one in value, and did not have to show an improvement. Also, this result is consistent with the results on wealth distributions over forecasting rules shown in Figure 5.8. It is not a direct causal path, but it is an indication of why these higher gain forecasting rules seem to be doing well. They are generating an endogenous pattern in volatility that yields some amount of predictability for higher gain learning forecasts over the more stable low-gain forecasts, causing these same forecasts to thrive in the population.

These forecast measures are not really relevant to how agents are actually selecting rules based on expected-utility estimates. The bottom histogram of Figure 5.15 shows a snapshot of an expected-utility estimate. The histogram rates the overall value of all forecasting rules to agents in certainty-equivalent terms across the different volatility gain levels. The histogram shows relatively equal values, with some indication for higher utilities for the high-gain variance strategy. The dynamic here would be that these strategies more accurately warn agents of the higher volatility periods, allowing them to back off on equity positions during these periods. If this dynamic strategy is effective, then it will be reflected in a higher risk-adjusted return for this strategy, which appears to be the case.[34]

These results make a strong case for the importance of high-gain, short half-life learning rules. The fact that at least some fraction of wealth stays with these rules over time would appear essential to building reasonable market dynamics. However, what about the low-gain, long half-life rules? Do they play any role, or are they superfluous in generating reasonable dynamics? Many of the distributions still show a large fraction of wealth using these rules, so the question remains about their impact. To explore this, a reverse of the first benchmark (low-gain) experiment is performed. Agents with only high-gain (short half-life) rules are used. The set of rules is again concentrated on five different gain levels, but instead of being distributed between 1 and 50 years, they are reduced to a range of 1–5 years only. Figure 5.16 displays a 100-year period of a run with these gain parameters. The market still displays significant instability. However, the dynamics do not appear reasonable for lining up with real data. There are quick bursts in the price level, which suddenly takes off and crashes almost as quickly. After a sharp drop, prices return relatively quickly to a central P/D level. Returns are punctuated by large-tail events, but prolonged periods of high volatility are not evident. The competing dynamics of learning agents of all gain levels would appear essential to spread out some of the market instability, making it less dramatic and more persistent in all dimensions. This is a critical requirement for modeling deviations from fundamentals that are not only large but also persistent.

---

34. The results in this panel should be viewed with some care, because they are a one-period snapshot. They are probably subject to extensive sampling variation, which is not reported in the figure. A cautious interpretation of the figure suggests that utility-based models would view all rules equally. However, it does appear that the slightly higher value of the short-gain rules is being transmitted into real adjustments of agent wealth toward these strategies.

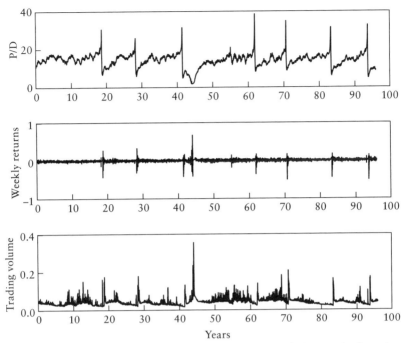

Figure 5.16 High gain only: short-memory learning. Simulation results for gain parameters in the range of [1–5] years only. P/D, price-dividend ratio.

5.4 Conclusion

The model presented in this chapter demonstrates that heterogeneous-gain learning may generate reasonable long-range dynamics for stock prices. In particular, the model generates persistent swings in prices and fundamentals, as well as replicating many other features of asset prices. More importantly, it does so in a framework that uses a simple set of strategies representing behaviors that are probably generic to most financial settings. Finally, when the details of agent behavior are analyzed, they generate patterns consistent with individual objective functions. In other words, they appear individually rational, relative to the environment that their own strategies self-generate.

The model is still highly stylized, and it would be premature to call it a definitive model for financial markets. It therefore can only be viewed as a computational thought experiment.[35] For example, no attempt is made to calibrate the consumption series or to model real interest rates. These

35. The book by Miller and Page (2007) advocates stylized computational experiments, which still may not completely capture reality but influence our intuition about the interactions and dynamics of heterogeneous-agent worlds.

enhancements remain open challenges for the future. The model does quantitatively capture swings in the price-dividend ratio. It does this through the mechanism of the common volatility forecasts and their endogenous structure across gain levels in their variance forecasts. Obviously, this is the component that one should question in terms of the results. As usual in heterogeneous-agent models, questions should be asked about whether these are the types of forecasts used by market participants. Would other variance forecasts change the results? It seems plausible that a wide range of forecasting models will give relatively similar results. One critical issue to consider is whether the models should entertain some convergence to a long-run mean level. The exponential filter is consistent with a world with an unobserved state-variable following a random walk, as in Muth (1960). This persistence in forecasts obviously contributes to the generated large swings in P/Ds. It is not clear that adding some kind of long-run mean reversion would change the situation, because the measured volatility in the simulation generates a lot of persistence, but this experiment would be interesting.

Another learning issue that needs to be further explored is how the rules react to large shocks. The market endogenously generates large returns from distributions that are not normal. These distributions have a dramatic impact as inputs into the learning models, and occasionally they lead to large swings in parameters that can last for some time. Would real investors blindly feed these extreme values into their own learning algorithms, or would some more complicated filtering algorithm be more appropriate? If the latter is the case, it is still not clear which stylized modeling framework would be appropriate in this context. This issue is another one for future consideration, both for learning models in finance and in macroeconomics.[36]

This chapter has made the case for greater consideration of heterogeneity in gain parameters in learning models. When these models are carefully constructed, they are capable of producing price dynamics replicating most empirical financial market features. High-gain learners are a destabilizing force in the market, as some agents put heavy weight on the recent past in assessing risk and return. Low-gain learners are also essential, because their longer term perspective is necessary to generate relatively persistent swings from fundamental values. Finally, when one examines the internals of these models, the micro-level behavior appears sensible, consistent, and capable of generating the macro features. The agents self-generate a time-series world in which their own behavior is reinforced, and a robust range of beliefs survive, which continue to perpetuate these patterns. The generated long swings in prices are large, persistent, and unpredictable. All these features

36. Examples of early research exploring this topic are Benhabib and Dave (2011) and Hansen and Sargent (2008).

make it difficult for learning agents to lock down on the strategies that would be necessary to eliminate such swings.

References

Adam, K., and A. Marcet. (2010a) "Booms and Busts in Asset Prices." Technical report 2010-E-2, Bank of Japan, Tokyo.

———. (2010b) "Internal Rationality, Imperfect Market Knowledge and Asset Prices." Technical report, Mannheim University, Mannheim, Germany.

Andersen, T. G., T. Bollerslev, P. F. Christoffersen, and F. X. Diebold. (2006) "Volatility and Correlation Forecasting," in G. Elliott, C. W. J. Granger, and A. Timmermann (eds.), *Handbook of Economic Forecasting*. Amsterdam: North-Holland, pp. 778–878.

Baillie, R. T., T. Bollerslev, and H.-O. Mikkelsen. (1996) "Fractionally Integrated Generalized Autoregressive Conditional Heteroskedasticity." *Journal of Econometrics* 74: 3–30.

Benhabib, J., and C. Dave. (2011) "Learning, Large Deviations, and Rare Events." Technical report, New York University, New York.

Blume, L., and D. Easley. (1990) "Evolution and Market Behavior." *Journal of Economic Theory* 58: 9–40.

Bollerslev, T., R. F. Engle, and D. B. Nelson. (1995) "ARCH Models," in R. F. Engle and D. McFadden (eds.), *Handbook of Econometrics*, volume 4. New York: North-Holland, pp. 2959–3038.

Branch, W. A., and G. W. Evans. (2011) "Learning about Risk and Return: A Simple Model of Bubbles and Crashes." *American Economic Journal: Macroeconomics* 3: 159–191.

Brock, W. A., and C. H. Hommes. (1998) "Heterogeneous Beliefs and Routes to Chaos in a Simple Asset Pricing Model," *Journal of Economic Dynamics and Control* 22: 1235–1274.

Cagan, P. (1956) "The Monetary Dynamics of Hyperinflation," in M. Friedman (ed.), *Studies in the Quantity Theory of Money*. Chicago: University of Chicago Press, pp. 25–120.

Campbell, J., and R. Shiller. (1988) "Stock Prices, Earnings, and Expected Dividends," *Journal of Finance* 63: 661–676.

Campbell, J. Y., and L. M. Viceira. (1999) "Consumption and Portfolio Decisions when Expected Returns Are Time Varying," *Quarterly Journal of Economics* 114: 433–495.

———. (2002) *Strategic Asset Allocation*. Oxford: Oxford University Press.

Campbell, J. Y., A. W. Lo, and A. C. MacKinlay. (1996) *The Econometrics of Financial Markets*. Princeton, NJ: Princeton University Press.

Chiarella, C., R. Dieci, and X.-Z. He. (2009) "Heterogeneity, Market Mechanisms, and Asset Price Dynamics," in T. Hens and K. R. Schenk-Hoppe (eds.), *Handbook of Financial Markets: Dynamics and Evolution*. New York: Elsevier, pp. 277–344.

Corsi, F. (2009) "A Simple Approximate Long-Memory Model of Realized Volatility," *Journal of Financial Econometrics* 7: 174–196.

Dacorogna, M. M., R. Gencay, U. A. Muller, R. B. Olsen, and O. V. Pictet. (2001) *An Introduction to High-Frequency Finance*. San Diego, CA: Academic Press.

Day, R. H., and W. H. Huang. (1990) "Bulls, Bears, and Market Sheep." *Journal of Economic Behavior and Organization* 14: 299–330.

DeLong, J. B., A. Shleifer, L. Summers, and R. Waldman. (1992) "Noise Trader Risk in Financial Markets." *Journal of Political Economy* 98: 703–738.

Engle, R. F., and J. G. Rangel. (2008) "The Spline-Garch Model for Low-Frequency Volatility and Its Global Macroeconomic Causes." *Review of Financial Studies* 21: 1187–1222.

Evans, G. W., and S. Honkapohja. (2001) *Learning and Expectations in Macroeconomics*. Princeton, NJ: Princeton University Press.

———. (2008) "Learning in Macroeconomics," in S. N. Durlauf and L. E. Blume (eds.), *The New Palgrave Dictionary of Economics*. London: Palgrave Macmillan. Available online.

Evstigneev, I. V., T. Hens, and K. R. Schenk-Hoppe. (2009) "Evolutionary Finance," in T. Hens and K. R. Schenk-Hoppe (eds.), *Handbook of Financial Markets: Dynamics and Evolution*. Amsterdam: North-Holland, pp. 509–564.

Fisher, K. L., and M. Statman. (2006) "Market Timing in Regressions and Reality," *Journal of Financial Research* 29: 293–304.

Frankel, J. A., and K. A. Froot. (1987) "Using Survey Data to Test Standard Propositions Regarding Exchange Rate Expectations," *American Economic Review* 77: 133–153.

———. (1988) "Explaining the Demand for Dollars: International Rates of Return and the Expectations of Chartists and Fundamentalists," in R. Chambers and P. Paarlberg (eds.), *Agriculture, Macroeconomics, and the Exchange Rate*. Boulder: Westview Press, pp. 73–126.

Friedman, M. (1956) *A Theory of the Consumption Function*. Princeton, NJ: Princeton University Press.

Frydman, R., and M. D. Goldberg. (2007) *Imperfect Knowledge Economics*. Princeton, NJ: Princeton University Press.

Frydman, R., and E. S. Phelps (eds.). (1983) *Individual Forecasting and Aggregate Outcomes: Rational Expectations Examined*. Cambridge: Cambridge University Press.

Fuster, A., D. Laison, and B. Mendel. (2010) "Natural Expectations and Macroeconomic Fluctuations," *Journal of Economic Perspectives* 24(4): 67–84.

Gaunersdorfer, A. (2000) "Endogenous Fluctuations in a Simple Asset Pricing Model with Heterogeneous Agents," *Journal of Economic Dynamics and Control* 24: 799–831.

Georges, C. (2008) "Staggered Updating in an Artificial Market," *Journal of Economic Dynamics and Control* 32: 2809–2825.

Giovannini, A. and P. Weil. (1989) "Risk Aversion and Intertemporal Substitution in the Capital Asset Pricing Model." Working paper 2824, National Bureau of Economic Research, Cambridge, MA.

Goyal, A., and I. Welch. (2003) "Predicting the Equity Premium with Dividend Ratios," *Management Science* 49: 639–654.

Hansen, L. P., and T. J. Sargent. (2008) *Robustness*. Princeton, NJ: Princeton University Press.

Hommes, C. H. (2010) "The Heterogeneous Expectations Hypothesis: Some Evidence from the Lab." Technical report, Center for Nonlinear Dynamics in Economics and Finance, University of Amsterdam, Amsterdam.

Hommes, C. H., and F. Wagener. (2009) "Complex Evolutionary Systems in Behavioral Finance," in T. Hens and K. R. Schenk-Hoppe (eds.), *Handbook of Financial Markets: Dynamics and Evolution*. Amsterdam: North-Holland, pp. 217–276.

Hong, H., and D. Sraer. (2010) "A Taxonomy of Bubbles." Technical report, Princeton University, Princeton, NJ.

Hong, H., and J. C. Stein. (1999) "A Unified Theory of Underreaction, Momentum Trading, and Overreaction in Asset Markets," *Journal of Finance* 54: 2143–2184.

Honkapohja, S., and K. Mitra. (2006) "Learning Stability in Economies with Heterogeneous Agents," *Review of Economic Dynamics* 9: 284–309.

Kelley, J. L. (1956) "A New Interpretation of Information Rate," *Bell Systems Technical Journal* 35: 917–926.

Kirman, A. P. (1991) "Epidemics of Opinion and Speculative Bubbles in Financial Markets," in M. Taylor (ed.), *Money and Financial Markets*. London: Macmillan, pp. 354–368.

LeBaron, B. (2001a) "Stochastic Volatility as a Simple Generator of Apparent Financial Power Laws and Long Memory," *Quantitative Finance* 1: 621–631.

———. (2001b) "Evolution and Time Horizons in an Agent Based Stock Market," *Macroeconomic Dynamics* 5: 225–254.

———. (2006) "Agent-Based Financial Markets: Matching Stylized Facts with Style," in D. Colander (ed.), *Post Walrasian Macroeconomics*. Cambridge: Cambridge University Press, pp. 221–235.

———. (2010) "Heterogenous Gain Learning and the Dynamics of Asset Prices." Technical report, International Business School, Brandeis University, Waltham, MA.

LeBaron, B., W. B. Arthur, and R. Palmer. (1999) "Time Series Properties of an Artificial Stock Market," *Journal of Economic Dynamics and Control* 23: 1487–1516.

Lettau, M., and S. Ludvigson. (2010) "Measuring and Modeling Variation in the Risk-Return Trade-off," in Y. Ait-Shalia and L. P. Hansen (eds.), *Handbook of Financial Econometrics*, volume 1. Amsterdam: Elsevier, pp. 617–690.

Levy, M., H. Levy, and S. Solomon. (1994) "A Microscopic Model of the Stock Market: Cycles, Booms, and Crashes," *Economics Letters* 45: 103–111.

Lucas, R. E., Jr. (1978) "Asset Prices in an Exchange Economy," *Econometrica* 46: 1429–1445.

Lux, T. (1998) "The Socio-Economic Dynamics of Speculative Markets: Interacting Agents, Chaos, and the Fat Tails of Return Distributions," *Journal of Economic Behavior and Organization* 33: 143–165.

Miller, J. H., and S. E. Page. (2007) *Complex Adaptive Systems: An Introduction to Computational Models of Social Life*. Princeton, NJ: Princeton University Press.

Mitra, K. (2005) "Is More Data Better?" *Journal of Economic Behavior and Organization* 56: 263–272.

Muth, J. (1960) "Optimal Properties of Exponentially Weighted Forecasts," *Journal of the American Statistical Association* 55: 299–306.

Nelson, D. B. (1992) "Filtering and Forecasting with Misspecified ARCH Models I: Getting the Right Variance with the Wrong Model," *Journal of Econometrics* 52: 61–90.

Pastor, L., and R. F. Stambaugh. (2009) "Predictive Systems: Living with Imperfect Predictors," *Journal of Finance* 64: 1583–1628.

Pastor, L., and P. Veronesi. (2009) "Learning in Financial Markets," *Annual Review of Financial Economics* 1: 361–381.

Phelps, E. S. (1967) "Phillips Curves, Expectations of Inflation and Optimal Unemployment over Time," *Economica* 34: 254–281.

Phelps, E. S., G. C. Archibald, and A. A. Alchian (eds.). (1970) *Microeconomic Foundations of Employment and Inflation Theory*. New York: W. W. Norton.

Sargent, T. (1999) *The Conquest of American Inflation*. Princeton, NJ: Princeton University Press.

Shiller, R. (1981) "Do Stock Prices Move Too Much to Be Justified by Subsequent Changes in Dividends?" *American Economic Review* 71: 421–436.

Shleifer, A., and R. W. Vishny. (1997) "The Limits of Arbitrage," *Journal of Finance* 52: 35–55.

Smith, V. L., G. L. Suchanek, and A. W. Williams. (1988) "Bubbles, Crashes, and Endogenous Expectations in Experimental Spot Asset Markets," *Econometrica* 56: 1119–1151.

Taylor, M., and H. Allen. (1992) "The Use of Technical Analysis in the Foreign Exchange Market," *Journal of International Money and Finance* 11:304–314.

Tesfatsion, L., and K. L. Judd (eds.). (2006) *Handbook of Computational Economics: Agent-Based Computational Economics*. Amsterdam: North-Holland.

Thurner, S., E. J. Dockner, and A. Gaunersdorfer. (2002) "Asset Price Dynamics in a Model of Investors Operating on Different Time Horizons." Technical report, University of Vienna, Vienna.

Timmerman, A. (1993) "How Learning in Financial Markets Generates Excess Volatility and Predictability in Stock Prices," *Quarterly Journal of Economics* 108: 1135–1145.

CHAPTER SIX

Opening Models of Asset Prices and Risk to Nonroutine Change

Roman Frydman and Michael D. Goldberg

6.1 Introduction

Financial markets are, in most respects, prototypes of the markets for which much of contemporary economic analysis was designed. They are characterized by a large number of buyers and sellers; powerful monetary incentives; few, if any, barriers to entry and exit; no impediments to the adjustment of prices; and a plethora of available information that is quickly disseminated around the world. We would expect that financial markets would offer the best opportunity for contemporary economic models to provide explanations of aggregate outcomes. But it is precisely in these markets that contemporary macroeconomic and finance theory has encountered many of its most glaring empirical difficulties.

In Chapter 4 of this volume, we trace contemporary economic theory's empirical and epistemological problems to how it models change in the causal process underpinning market outcomes (see also Frydman and Goldberg 2007, 2011). In financial markets, outcomes are driven primarily by participants' forecasts of prices and risk. As time passes, participants revise their forecasting strategies in ways that they themselves, let alone an economist, cannot fully foresee. Economic policies, institutions, the state of technology, and other features of the social context within which participants make decisions also change in novel ways. Thus, change in financial markets, and in capitalist economies more broadly, is to a significant degree nonroutine, for it cannot be adequately represented in advance with mechanical rules and procedures. Yet the hallmark of contemporary theory is the core premise that an economist can fully specify, in terms of some causal

The authors are grateful to the Institute for New Economic Thinking for supporting the research on which this chapter is based.

factors, how individuals alter the way that they make decisions, and how market outcomes unfold over time.

In sharp contrast, we follow an alternative approach to economic analysis—Imperfect Knowledge Economics (IKE). In this chapter, we develop a model of asset prices and risk that has explicit mathematical microfoundations and yet remains open to nonroutine change.[1] At any given point in time, the general structure of our IKE model is no different from that of other macroeconomic and finance models. It consists of representations of individuals' preferences, forecasting behavior, constraints, and decision rules in terms of a set of causal (often called "informational") variables, which portray the influence of economic policy, institutions, and other features of the social context. It also entails an aggregation rule and processes for the informational variables. That participants revise their forecasting strategies, and that the social context changes, at least intermittently, implies that we will need different structures—different specifications of individuals' decisionmaking and the social context—in different time periods. Like other models, the adequacy of an IKE model in accounting for the time-series data hinges on how it characterizes this change.

Most macroeconomists and finance theorists use mechanical rules and procedures that fully prespecify any change in their models' structures. Indeed, nearly all economists construct models that rely on the same structure to represent individual behavior and aggregate outcomes at every point in time. These time-invariant models presume that economic policy and the ways that individuals forecast market outcomes never change. Their key feature is that they represent outcomes in all time periods with a single conditional probability distribution.

To be sure, economists sometimes portray change in their models. However, when they do, they fully prespecify it with deterministic or probabilistic rules that suppose not only that individual decisionmaking or changes in the social context exhibit regularities, but also that these regularities can be adequately characterized with mechanical rules and procedures. As a result, even if they allow for change, these models specify it fully in advance: conditional on the values of the causal variables at a point in time, they determine *exactly* all potential changes and the probabilities with which they might occur—in the past, present, and future all at once. Fully predetermined models represent change as random deviations from a fully predetermined time path and thus assume away nonroutine change altogether.

It was not always so. Early modern economists like Keynes (1921, 1936) and Knight (1921) argued that most business decisions are fraught with "radical uncertainty," a situation in which individual decisions cannot be adequately represented with a standard probability distribution. An extreme

---

1. The analysis in this chapter builds on Frydman and Goldberg (2007, 2008).

version of such uncertainty is often thought to force participants to act according to their "animal spirits," psychological impulses that are largely disconnected from any fundamental considerations that might drive outcomes. However, unless participants' decisionmaking could be connected, at least during some time periods, to the causal factors observable by economists, no formal economic theory with empirical content would be possible.

At the same time, even if one supposes that economic behavior exhibits some regularities, nonroutine change alters how market outcomes unfold over time in ways that put an overarching probabilistic representation of outcomes out of reach of economic analysis. IKE, therefore, stakes out an intermediate position between radical uncertainty, which in its extreme, "animal spirits" version, denies that economists can formulate testable mathematical models of any features of the causal process driving change, and the contemporary presumption that a single conditional probability distribution can adequately represent this process. Although IKE jettisons the presumption that individual decisionmaking and changes in the social context exhibit regularities that conform to fully prespecified rules, it explores the possibility that such behavior nonetheless exhibits regularities. But, at best, we would expect these regularities to be context dependent and qualitative. We would also expect them to be contingent: they begin and cease to be relevant at moments that no one can fully foresee.

In modeling asset prices and risk, an economist's assumptions concerning market participants' forecasting behavior play a crucial role. In searching for empirically relevant regularities that might characterize such behavior, we are guided by empirical findings from behavioral economics and other social sciences. For example, to portray how market participants sometimes revise their forecasting strategies, we make use of psychological findings that indicate that individuals are often slow to revise their beliefs in the face of new evidence. We also build on Keynes's (1936) insight that social conventions are important for understanding how participants form their expectations in financial markets. But our IKE model formalizes these insights with qualitative and contingent conditions, rather than with the mechanical rules that behavioral finance models use to represent behavior.

We also rely on behavioral findings in modeling market participants' risk preferences, drawing on the prospect theory of Kahneman and Tversky (1979). But we use an extension of their original formulation, which we call "endogenous prospect theory," that recognizes that outcomes cannot be represented with an overarching probability distribution.[2]

---

2. See Frydman and Goldberg (2007). Kahneman and Tversky (1979) developed their theory for experimental conditions that assume away imperfect knowledge on the part of economists. Subsequent applications of the theory were implemented in fully predetermined models. Endogenous prospect theory extends the applications of the theory to IKE models. It also solves several problems in applying prospect theory to modeling asset markets.

We show that opening a mathematical model to nonroutine change and imperfect knowledge on the part of economists enables us to incorporate both fundamental variables (e.g., earnings and interest rates), on which rational expectations theorists focus, and psychological and social considerations (e.g., confidence and conventions), which behavioral economists emphasize, without presuming obvious irrationality on the part of market participants. We also show that, despite its openness to economists' ever-imperfect knowledge about the process driving change, the model generates implications that can be confronted with time-series evidence.

6.2 Irregular Swings in Asset Prices and Risk

In this chapter, we model market outcomes that contemporary macro-economics and finance theory have found difficult to explain. We focus on the tendency of asset prices to undergo prolonged swings away from and toward estimates of common benchmark levels and on the two-way interdependence of this behavior and financial risk.

Two examples of price fluctuations in asset markets are provided in Figures 6.1 and 6.2, which plot the S&P 500 price index relative to underlying earnings and the British pound–U.S. dollar (BP/$) exchange rate, respectively, along with a common benchmark.[3] The figures show that asset prices can move away from benchmark levels for years at a time. But the instability is bounded: eventually these swings undergo sustained countermovements back toward benchmark values. If prices happen to reach these values, they often overshoot them and begin trending away from the other side. Moreover, although such fluctuations are a recurrent feature of market outcomes, the observed swings are irregular: the magnitude and duration of upswings and downswings vary from one episode to the next in ways that do not seem to follow any consistent pattern. The inability of models based on the Rational Expectations Hypothesis (REH) to account for these features of asset price fluctuations is well known.[4]

The other aggregate regularity that we model involves the market risk premium—the anticipated excess return that market participants in the

3. The price-earnings (PE) ratio in Figure 6.1 is based on a trailing 10-year moving average of earnings. The data are from Shiller (2000), which are updated on his web site: www.econ.yale/~shiller. The benchmark in the figure is a 20-year moving average of Shiller's PE ratio. The benchmark exchange rate in Figure 6.2 is a purchasing power parity (PPP) rate, which was calculated using the *Big Mac* PPP exchange rate reported in the April 6, 1990, issue of *The Economist* (which was BP1.96/$1) and consumer price index–inflation rate differentials from the IMF's *International Financial Statistics*. Historical averages of PE ratios and PPP exchange rates have long traditions as benchmark values in stock and currency markets, respectively.

4. For stock and currency markets, see Shiller (2003) and Frydman and Goldberg (2007), respectively, and references therein.

Figure 6.1 S&P 500 stock PE, 1901–2005. MA, moving average; PE, price-earnings ratio.

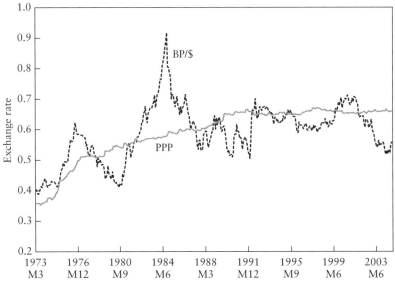

Figure 6.2 British pound (BP)/U.S. dollar exchange rate, 1973–2005. PPP, purchasing power parity.

aggregate require to hold the available supply of the risky asset. REH risk-premium models relate this premium to the second-moment properties of the data. However, since Mehra and Prescott (1985), economists have known that REH models are grossly inconsistent with time-series data on the market risk premium.

There is much evidence that the market risk premium also undergoes swings and that these fluctuations depend on how the asset price moves relative to benchmark values: as participants bid the price farther away from estimates of benchmark values, it becomes increasingly more risky to gamble on a widening gap. Such behavior can be seen in Figure 6.3, which plots the ex ante excess return on holding U.S. dollar long positions in the BP/$ market and the gap between the exchange rate and its PPP value.[5] The tendency for the market risk premium to move positively with the swing in the exchange rate relative to PPP is striking.

Frydman and Goldberg (2007) and Stillwagon (2012) undertake more formal statistical analyses using parametric and nonparametric procedures and find a positive relationship between the premium and the gap in the three largest currency markets.

As for other asset markets, there is widespread understanding in policymaking circles that risks grow as upswings in equity and housing prices continue for prolonged periods.[6] As the financial crisis that erupted in 2008 dramatically showed, long upswings in these prices are eventually followed by sharp and protracted downswings. Zheng (2009), for example, uses regression analysis to examine the relationship between the premium on stocks over bonds and the gap from benchmark values. Her results are broadly consistent with those for currency markets: the equity premium tends to rise and fall in concert with swings in equity prices relative to the benchmark.

In the remainder of this chapter, we develop microfoundations for an IKE model that can account for the long swings that characterized fluctuations in asset prices and risk—and for the connection between the two—without presuming that individuals forgo obvious profit opportunities.

---

5. We use survey data on exchange rate forecasts to measure the market risk premium and the *Big Mac* PPP exchange rate, as in Figure 6.2. The survey data are from Money Market Services International (MMSI), which entail participants' median responses concerning their 4-week-ahead point forecast of the exchange rate. For more details concerning the time plots in Figure 6.3, see Frydman and Goldberg (2007: chapter 12). Other studies that have used MMSI's survey data include Frankel and Froot (1987) and Froot and Frankel (1989).

6. For example, see Borio (2003), Borio and Shim (2007), and Bank for International Settlements (2010). Reinhart and Rogoff (2009) look at data going back as far as eight centuries for 66 countries spanning six continents and find that excessive movements in real exchange rates, real housing prices, and real stock prices are among the top five predictors of subsequent sharp reversals and crises.

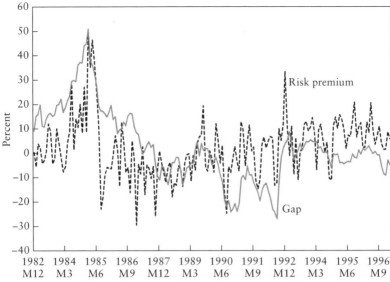

Figure 6.3 British pound (BP) / U.S. dollar risk premium and the gap, 1982–1997.

6.3   Endogenous Prospect Theory of Risk

We portray individual decisionmaking with the usual assumption of utility maximization. But when specifying an individual's preferences and decision rule under uncertainty, we rely on endogenous prospect theory, rather than a standard risk-averse specification and expected utility theory.[7] This alternative specification of preferences and decisionmaking, together with our IKE representation of forecasting, leads to a new model of risk in asset markets: individuals' assessments of the riskiness of holding speculative positions depend on the gap between the asset price and their perceptions of common benchmark levels, rather than on standard measures of volatility.

6.3.1   Individual Preferences

The structure of our model assumes that individuals hold their nonmonetary wealth in a risky and a riskless asset ("stocks" and "bonds," respectively).[8] Individuals can issue bonds and take short positions in stocks without limit,

7. There is much experimental evidence showing that standard specifications are grossly inconsistent with how individuals actually behave. See Kahneman and Tversky (1979) and Barberis and Thaler (2003) and references therein.

8. In Frydman and Goldberg (2007), we develop the model in the context of currency markets.

although in equilibrium, they must, in the aggregate, hold the available supplies of stocks and outside bonds.

We denote the ex post nominal return on holding a long position in stocks for one period by R_{t+1} and express it using a logarithmic approximation:

$$R_{t+1} = P_{t+1} - P_t - i_t \qquad (1)$$

where P_t denotes the logarithm level of the time-t stock price; i_t is the riskless nominal return on bonds; and, for the sake of simplicity, we ignore dividends.[9] Analogously, the one-period return on a short position in stocks is given by $-R_{t+1}$.

An individual's preferences over alternative long and short positions in stocks are specified in terms of gains and losses in wealth relative to some reference level, which Kahneman and Tversky (1979) call "reference dependence." This one-period change in wealth can be written as

$$\Delta^r W^i_{t+1} = W^i_{t+1} - \Gamma^i_t \qquad (2)$$

$$= W^i_t \left[a^i_t R_{t+1} + \left(1 + i^A_t - \pi_t \right) \right] - \Gamma^i_t$$

where W^i_t denotes an individual i's nonmonetary real wealth at time t, a^i_t denotes the share of stocks in her portfolio at time t ($a^i_t < 0$ implies a short position), π_t is the nonstochastic rate of inflation, Γ^i_t denotes an individual's reference level, and Δ^r denotes the one-period change in wealth relative to the reference level.[10] When $\Delta^r W^i_{t+1} > 0$ ($\Delta^r W^i_{t+1} < 0$), an individual is said to experience a gain (a loss).

In the context of financial markets, it is natural to set an individual's reference point to the level of wealth she would obtain were she to stay out of the stock market completely:[11]

$$\Gamma^i_t = W^i_t \left(1 + i^A_t - \pi_t \right) \qquad (3)$$

Substitution of (3) into (2) yields the following expression for the change in an individual's wealth relative to her reference level:

---

9. Alternatively, we could redefine P_t to include dividends without changing the main conclusions of our analysis.

10. The real returns on stocks and bonds are $P_{t+1} - P_t + i_t - \pi_t$ and $i_t - \pi_t$, respectively. As such, next-period's wealth is $W^i_{t+1} = W^i_t \left[1 + a^i_t \left(S_{t+1} - S_t + i^B_t - \pi_t \right) + \left(1 - a^i_t \right) \left(i^A_t - \pi_t \right) \right] = W^i_t [a^i_t R_{t+1} + (1 + i^A_t - \pi_t)]$. The assumption of a nonstochastic inflation rate is common in the portfolio-balance literature, because asset prices are considerably more volatile than are goods prices. See Krugman (1981), Frankel (1982), and Dornbusch (1983).

11. In general, however, each individual chooses her own reference level, and neither prospect theory nor available experimental evidence provides guidance as to how an economist should represent it. Other studies that use this reference level in applying prospect theory to modeling asset prices include Barberis et al. (2001) and Barberis and Huang (2001). See Ang et al. (2005) for an extensive discussion of the difficulties inherent in modeling the reference level in the context of prospect theory.

$$\Delta^r W^i_{t+1} = a^i_t W^i_t R_{t+1} \tag{4}$$

A positive realization of R_{t+1}, which we denote by r^+_{t+1}, leads to a gain for an individual who holds a long position (i.e., $a^i_t > 0$) and a loss if she holds a short position (i.e., $a^i_t < 0$). A negative realization of R_{t+1}, which we denote by r^-_{t+1}, leads to the converse. It is common to refer to individuals who hold long and short positions as bulls and bears, respectively.

6.3.1.1 Original Utility Function

In addition to reference dependence, Kahneman's and Tversky's (1979) experimental findings imply that individuals are "loss averse"—their disutility from losses substantially exceeds the utility from gains of the same magnitude. Moreover, their preferences display diminishing sensitivity: their marginal utility of both gains and losses decreases with their size.[12] Tversky and Kahneman (1992) propose a utility function that embodies these characteristics, which we express as

$$V(\Delta^r W) = \begin{cases} (W\,|ar^g|)^\alpha \\ -\lambda(W\,|ar^l|)^\beta \end{cases} \tag{5}$$

where λ is a constant and r^g and r^l denote a gain and loss, respectively, on an open position in stocks. It is convenient to define gains on *both* long and short positions as positive values and losses as negative values:

$$r^g = r^+_{t+1} \quad \text{and} \quad r^l = r^-_{t+1} \quad \text{if } a > 0 \tag{6}$$

$$r^g = -r^-_{t+1} \quad \text{and} \quad r^l = -r^+_{t+1} \quad \text{if } a < 0$$

The utility function (5) implies that the degree of loss aversion—defined as the ratio of the disutility of losses to the utility of gains of the same magnitude—depends on the size of an individual's stake in the game, a:[13]

$$\Lambda = \lambda(|ar^l|)^{\beta-\alpha} \tag{7}$$

Like expected utility theory, prospect theory portrays an individual's decisionmaking by assuming that she maximizes a weighted sum of the utilities of single outcomes, called "prospective utility." In the context of our model, an individual chooses a^i_t so as to maximize

---

12. Diminishing sensitivity implies the familiar concavity of the utility function in the domain of gains. However, in the domain of losses, the utility function is convex, implying that individuals have a greater willingness to gamble as the magnitude of their potential loss rises.

13. This can be seen by rewriting (5) as $V(\Delta^r W) = (W\,|ar^g|)^\alpha - \lambda(W\,|ar^l|)^{\beta-\alpha}(W\,|ar^l|)^\alpha$.

$$PU_t^i = \left| a_t^i W_t^i \right|^\alpha \sum_k^{K^+} \omega_{t,k}^i \left(\hat{r}_{t+1,k}^{g^i} \right)^\alpha - \lambda \left| a_t^i W_t^i \right|^\beta \sum_k^{K^-} \omega_{t,k}^i \left(-\hat{r}_{t+1,k}^{l^i} \right)^\beta \quad (8)$$

where the $\hat{r}_{t+1,k}^{g^i}$s and $\hat{r}_{t+1,k}^{l^i}$s are the possible single gains and losses, respectively, that an individual forecasts; K^+ and K^- denote the numbers of these single outcomes, respectively; and the $\omega_{t,k}^i$s are an individual's decision weights.[14]

6.3.1.2 From Prospective to Expected Values

To derive implications from models based on prospect theory and confront them with time-series data, we must relate individuals' prospective utilities to observable causal variables. Behavioral finance economists address this problem by equating decision weights with probabilities and setting $\alpha = \beta = 1$, thereby assuming that the utility function is linear over potential gains and losses, which enables them to express prospective utility in terms of expected values (e.g., see Barberis et al. 2001).

In the context of our model, these assumptions would imply that

$$PU_t^i = \left| a_t^i W_t^i \right| \left[\hat{r}_{t|t+1}^{i,j} - (1-\lambda)\, \hat{l}_{t|t+1}^{i,j} \right] \quad (9)$$

where $\hat{r}_{t|t+1}^{i,j} = E_t^i[R_{t+1}|Z_t^i] \geq 0$ denotes a bull's ($j = \mathrm{L}$) or bear's ($j = \mathrm{s}$) point forecast of the excess return on holding an open position for one period, which is implied by her forecasting strategy (which we represent by a conditional probability distribution $\mathcal{P}_t^i(R_{t+1})$) and the values of the informational variables at time t, Z_t^i. An individual's $\hat{l}_{t|t+1}^{i,j}$ is the conditional expected value of the "loss part" of her distribution of R_{t+1}, which for a bull involves the negative realizations of R_{t+1},

$$\hat{l}_{t|t+1}^{i,\mathrm{L}} = E_t^i[R_{t+1}^{\mathrm{L}}|R_{t+1}^{\mathrm{L}} < 0,\ Z_t^i] < 0$$

whereas for a bear, it involves the positive realizations,

$$\hat{l}_{t|t+1}^{i,\mathrm{s}} = E_t^i[R_{t+1}^{\mathrm{s}}|R_{t+1}^{\mathrm{s}} < 0,\ Z_t^i] < 0 \quad (10)$$

where $R_{t+1}^{\mathrm{L}} = P_{t+1} - P_t - i_t$ and $R_{t+1}^{\mathrm{s}} = i_t + P_t - P_{t+1}$ denote returns on a long and short position, respectively. We refer to $\hat{l}_{t|t+1}^{i,j}$ as an individual's expected potential loss on a unit position.

The specification in (9) implies a risk premium that depends on an individual's degree of loss aversion and her forecast of the potential loss, $(1-\lambda)\,\hat{l}_{t|t+1}^{i,j} > 0$.[15] As long as her expected excess return, $\hat{r}_{t|t+1}^{i,j}$, exceeded

---

14. We follow Tversky and Kahneman (1992) in assuming a finite set of outcomes.

15. We recall that $\lambda > 1$ and $\hat{l}_{t|t+1}^{i,j} < 0$.

her risk premium, she would want to take an open position in stocks. However, because (9) is linear in the decision variable, a_t^i, she would want to take a speculative position of unlimited size. As it stands, a well-defined equilibrium in which individuals hold diverse forecasts is ruled out.[16]

6.3.1.3 Limits to Speculation and an Individual Uncertainty Premium

In Frydman and Goldberg (2007), we show that the Tversky and Kahneman (1992) utility function implies limits to speculation if one recognizes diminishing sensitivity and sets $\beta > \alpha > 0$. The expression (7) shows that under this assumption, an individual's loss aversion is endogenous, rising as the size of her open position increases and implying the concavity of PU_t^i in a_t^i.[17] However, this nonlinearity creates several problems, including an inability to express the aggregate demand for stocks, $a_t W_t$, in terms of aggregate forecasts, $\hat{r}_{t|t+1}$ and $\hat{l}_{t|t+1}$.[18]

Endogenous prospect theory addresses these problems by reformulating the utility function (5) as

$$V(\Delta^r W) = \begin{cases} (W\,|a|)^\alpha\,|r^g| \\ -\lambda_1 (W\,|a|)^\alpha\,\left|r^l\right| - \dfrac{\lambda_2}{-\hat{l}_{t|t+1}^{i,\,j}}(W\,|a|)^{\alpha+1}\left|r^l\right| \end{cases} \tag{11}$$

where $\lambda_1 > 1$ and $\lambda_2 > 0$ ensure loss aversion. We show in Frydman and Goldberg (2007) that the specification (11) is consistent with all of the main experimental findings of Kahneman and Tversky (1979).[19] And because it implies endogenous loss aversion, it implies limits to speculation.[20]

---

16. Modeling finite speculative positions, widely called "limits to arbitrage," is viewed as one of the two main pillars of behavioral finance (see Barberis and Thaler 2003). Linearizing the Tversky and Kahneman utility function has led some economists to model finite speculative positions by relying on the assumptions of risk aversion and loss aversion when specifying preferences. The reliance on risk aversion is puzzling, however, given that its rejection in favor of loss aversion has come to be viewed as one of the key findings of behavioral economics. For a review article on modeling limits to arbitrage, see Gromb and Vayanos (2010).

17. We are unaware of any experimental evidence that directly demonstrates a positive relationship between an individual's degree of loss aversion and the size of her stake. But as Myron Scholes emphasized in remarks at the conference "Derivatives 2003: Reports from the Frontiers," held at the Stern School of Business in January 2003, such a relationship accords well with how participants in real-world markets actually behave.

18. Another problem with the specification (5) when $\beta > \alpha > 0$ is that for small position sizes, it violates the basic assumption of loss aversion.

19. This specification implies what we call "endogenous sensitivity": the marginal value of both gains and losses decreases with position size (as it does in Tversky's and Kahneman's original specification), except when the size of the stake becomes large, at which point the marginal value of losses increases with position size. Although Tversky and Kahneman (1992) assume diminishing sensitivity throughout the domain of gains and losses, they recognize in Kahneman and Tversky (1979) that this behavior is typical for smaller gambles, and that increasing sensitivity may characterize individual preferences for larger gambles.

20. The degree of loss aversion is now given by $\Lambda = \lambda_1 + \dfrac{\lambda_2}{-\hat{l}_{t|t+1}^{i,\,j}}\,W\,|a|$.

To portray an individual's portfolio decision at time t, we maximize the prospective utility function (11) with respect to a_t^i, taking as given the individual's point forecasts of the excess return and potential unit loss on open positions in stocks. This yields the following optimal long or short position, depending on whether the individual is a bull or bear:

$$a_t^{i,\text{L}} W_t^i = \frac{\alpha}{\lambda_2(\alpha+1)} \left[\hat{r}_{t|t+1}^{i,\text{L}} - (1-\lambda_1)\hat{l}_{t|t+1}^{i,\text{L}} \right] \tag{12}$$

$$-a_t^{i,\text{S}} W_t^i = \frac{\alpha}{\lambda_2(\alpha+1)} \left[\hat{r}_{t|t+1}^{i,\text{S}} - (1-\lambda_1)\hat{l}_{t|t+1}^{i,\text{S}} \right] \tag{13}$$

where $a^{i,\text{L}}$ and $a^{i,\text{S}}$ are constrained to be nonnegative and nonpositive, respectively,[21] and we ignore differences in all preference parameters.[22] An individual's "flow" demand for or supply of stock (i.e., the value of stock that she wishes to buy or sell, respectively) at time t is thus given by

$$D_t^i = a_t^{i,j} W_t^i - S_t^i \tag{14}$$

where S_t^i denotes the value of stock with which the individual enters period t. The condition $S_t^i < 0$ implies that the individual holds a short position entering the period, whereas $D_t^i < 0$ indicates that she is a seller of stocks at time t.[23]

The expressions (12) and (13) show that endogenous prospect theory leads to a new specification for the minimum expected return that individuals require to take risky positions in stocks, which we call an individual's "uncertainty premium":[24]

$$\widehat{up}_{t+1}^{i,j} = (1-\lambda_1)\,\hat{l}_{t|t+1}^{i,j} > 0 \tag{15}$$

An individual's uncertainty premium depends on her forecast of the potential loss from speculating, rather than on standard measures of volatility.

21. The inequality constraints on $a_t^{i,\text{L}}$ and $a_t^{i,\text{S}}$ reflect the possibility that an individual's optimal position size in stocks would be zero if her expected excess return did not outweigh her concern about potential losses, as represented by the expected unit loss, $(1-\lambda_1)\hat{l}_{t|t+1}^{i,j}$.

22. We consider an IKE model of currency returns with heterogeneity over preferences in Frydman and Goldberg (2007).

23. Although an individual may remain a bear from one period to the next, her trading may nonetheless add to buying in the market. This would be the case if she wanted to reduce the size of her short position, that is, if $0 > a_t^{i,\text{S}} W_t^i > S_t^i$, so that $D_t^i > 0$. Analogously, a bull's trading would add to selling in the market if $0 < a_t^{i,\text{L}} W_t^i < S_t^i$, so that $D_t^i < 0$.

24. We refer to this minimum return as an uncertainty premium to highlight Knight's (1921) distinction between uncertainty and risk, which recognizes that the risk in markets cannot be represented in standard probabilistic terms because it arises from the inherent imperfection of knowledge.

6.3.2 Momentary Equilibrium Price and the Uncertainty Premium

Endogenous prospect theory and portfolio balance lead to a new *momentary* equilibrium condition for the stock market. It is obtained by aggregating individuals' demands and supplies in (14) using wealth shares and assuming that the stock price adjusts instantaneously to balance the total buying and selling in the market at every point in time:

$$\hat{r}_{t|t+1} = \widehat{up}_{t|t+1} + \lambda_2 \frac{S_t}{W_t} \tag{16}$$

where $\hat{r}_{t|t+1} = \hat{P}_{t|t+1} - P_t - i_t$, $\hat{P}_{t|t+1}$ represents the aggregate of participants' conditional point forecasts of P_{t+1}; S_t and W_t are the available supplies of stock and total nonmonetary wealth held by market participants, respectively; and $\widehat{up}_{t|t+1}$ is the aggregate uncertainty premium,

$$\widehat{up}_{t|t+1} = \widehat{up}^{\mathrm{L}}_{t|t+1} - \widehat{up}^{\mathrm{S}}_{t|t+1} = \frac{1}{2}\left(1 - \lambda_1\right)\left(\hat{l}^{\mathrm{L}}_{t|t+1} - \hat{l}^{\mathrm{S}}_{t|t+1}\right) \tag{17}$$

which depends on the uncertainty premium of the bulls minus the uncertainty premium of the bears.[25]

Equation (16) defines momentary equilibrium in the stock market as the situation in which the expected excess return exceeds the uncertainty premium in the aggregate sufficiently for market participants willingly to hold the available supply of stocks (and bonds). The implied market premium—$\widehat{pr}_{t|t+1} = \widehat{up}_{t|t+1} + \lambda_2 \frac{S_t}{W_t}$—depends on both the aggregate uncertainty premium and relative asset supplies. This specification shows that to account for one of the key features of fluctuations of $\widehat{pr}_{t|t+1}$ in asset markets—reversals in its algebraic sign from one time period to another (see Figure 6.3)—we must recognize the coexistence of both bulls and bears in the market.[26]

Endogenous prospect theory and portfolio balance imply that the unfolding of the equilibrium price, P_t, depends on movements in participants' point forecasts of the next period's price and potential unit loss, as well as

---

25. In general, the wealth shares of the bulls and bears vary over time. However, we abstract from such variation and assume that the wealth share of the bulls, ω^{L}, and that of the bears, ω^{S}, are constant and equal to half. More generally, $\widehat{up}_{t|t+1} = (1 - \lambda_1)\left(\omega^{\mathrm{L}}\hat{l}^{\mathrm{L}}_{t|t+1} - \omega^{\mathrm{S}}\hat{l}^{\mathrm{S}}_{t|t+1}\right)$.

26. Sign reversals of $\widehat{pr}_{t|t+1}$ occur when the relative uncertainty premium of the bulls and bears fluctuates sufficiently to offset the influence of $\lambda_2 \frac{S_t}{W_t} > 0$. In sharp contrast, REH risk-premium models have been unable to account for such behavior. See Mark and Wu (1998) and Zheng (2009), who find that consumption capital asset pricing models are grossly inconsistent with sign reversals of $\widehat{pr}_{t|t+1}$ in currency and stock markets, respectively. Frydman and Goldberg (2007) examine the inability of the portfolio-balance approach sketched here under the assumptions of expected utility theory and risk aversion to explain sign reversals in currency markets, regardless of whether we assume diversity in individuals' forecasting strategies.

the interest rate on bonds and relative asset supplies. However, to simplify our discussion, we assume that i_t and $\frac{S_t}{W_t}$ are constant and set $i + \lambda_2 \frac{S}{W} = 0$, yielding the following equilibrium condition:

$$\hat{P}_{t|t+1} - P_t = (1 - \lambda_1)\,\hat{l}_{t|t+1} \tag{18}$$

where $\hat{l}_{t|t+1} = \frac{1}{2}\left(\hat{l}^{\mathrm{L}}_{t|t+1} - \hat{l}^{\mathrm{S}}_{t|t+1}\right)$. This simplification enables us to focus on the main drivers of price—movements in individuals' forecasts, $\hat{P}_{t|t+1}$ and $\hat{l}_{t|t+1}$.[27]

6.3.3 Imperfect Knowledge and Expected Values

As time advances, news becomes available about causal variables, and an individual may decide to revise her forecasting strategy, which we represent with a new conditional probability distribution, $\mathcal{P}^i_{t+1}\left(R_{t+2}\right)$. Both news and a revised forecasting strategy will, in general, lead her to alter her point forecast not only of price but also of the potential unit loss (and thus the riskiness) from holding open positions in stocks. We would not expect such revisions to follow any mechanical rule. But how an individual's $\hat{r}^{i,j}_{t|t+1}$ and $\hat{l}^{i,j}_{t|t+1}$ change from one period to the next may nonetheless exhibit qualitative and contingent regularities. To model this change, therefore, we make use of qualitative and contingent constraints that only partially prespecify it.

This IKE approach enables endogenous prospect theory's specification of risk to address a key concern that other asset market studies applying prospect theory ignore: "[in] the typical situation of choice, where the probabilities of outcomes are not explicitly given[,] . . . the decision weights may be affected by other considerations, such as ambiguity or vagueness" (Kahneman and Tversky 1979: 288–289), which cannot be represented adequately with specific parametric functions of probabilities. These and other considerations arise from the imperfection of knowledge and are what distinguishes decisionmaking in real-world markets from that in experimental settings, where the experimenter fixes the fully prespecified probability distribution that governs the subject's payoffs.

Disregarding the distinction between decision-weighted sums and expected values of outcomes may be unavoidable when applying endogenous prospect theory. However, partially prespecifying change in $\hat{r}^{i,j}_{t|t+1}$ and $\hat{l}^{i,j}_{t|t+1}$ opens the model to the importance of ambiguity and vagueness, and, more generally, to ever-imperfect knowledge in individual decisionmaking.

---

27. The variation in interest rates is an order of magnitude or more lower than the variation in stock and currency prices. Consequently, the variations in R_{t+1} and $P_{t+1} - P_t$ are of roughly equal magnitude.

6.4   An IKE Gap Model of the Market Risk Premium

We turn first to portraying individuals' forecasts of the potential unit loss from speculating with qualitative and contingent constraints and show that the model generates predictions concerning the market risk premium that, although contingent, can be confronted with time-series evidence. We sketch in Section 6.6 how these predictions help explain why protracted price swings away from market participants' estimates of benchmark values are ultimately bounded.

We are guided not only by the empirical record on excess returns discussed in Section 6.2 but also by Keynes's (1936) account of asset markets. Keynes argued that speculators are aware of asset prices' tendency to undergo irregular swings around benchmark levels, and that they take account of this feature of the social context in their attempts to forecast market outcomes. In discussing why an individual might hold cash rather than risky interest-bearing bonds, he observed that "what matters is not the absolute level of [the interest rate] r but the degree of its divergence from what is considered a fairly safe [benchmark] level of r, having regard to those calculations of probability which are being relied on" (Keynes 1936: 201).[28]

Keynes's discussion of the importance of benchmark levels as anchors for asset price swings suggests that market participants look at the gap between the asset price and its benchmark value when forecasting the potential unit loss from speculation. As he put it, "Unless reasons are believed to exist why future experience will be very different from past experience, a . . . rate of interest [much lower than the safe rate] leaves more to fear than to hope, and offers, at the same time, a running yield which is only sufficient to offset a very small measure of fear [of capital loss]" (Keynes 1936: 202).

This insight leads us to relate an individual's expected unit loss on open positions in stocks to her assessment of the gap between the stock price and her perception of the benchmark value:

$$\hat{l}^{i,j}_{t|t+1} = \hat{l}^{i,j}_{t|t+1}\left(\widehat{gap}^i_t\right) \tag{19}$$

where $\widehat{gap}^i_t = P_t - \hat{P}^{i,\text{BM}}_t$, and $\hat{P}^{i,\text{BM}}_t$ denotes an individual's assessment at t of the benchmark stock price.[29]

---

28. A benchmark level is, of course, specific to each asset market. Every individual arrives at her own determination of the benchmark value, which implies that, in general, these assessments will differ among individuals. How individuals come to decide on a benchmark level is an open question. Keynes suggests that conventions and the historical record play an important role.

29. The gap could also be defined in terms of an individual's forecast of the next period's asset price (relative to her benchmark value) rather than the asset price itself, or some weighted average of the two, without affecting the conclusions of our analysis. See Frydman and Goldberg (2007).

6.4.1 The Gap Effect

Over time, movements in $\widehat{gap}^i_t$ lead an individual to alter her forecast of the potential unit loss, which may involve revisions of her forecasting strategy, $\mathcal{P}^i_t\left(R_{t+1}\right)$. But, no matter how she might revise her strategy, we suppose that movements of $\hat{l}^{i,j}_{t|t+1}$ are characterized by a "gap effect" that depends on which side of the market she takes.

Consider, for example, an upswing in stock prices that has already climbed above participants' assessments of benchmark levels. A bull forecasts that the price swing will continue, while a bear forecasts the opposite. Nonetheless, both contemplate the potential loss that they would incur if the price were to move against them. If, for example, bulls were to increase their long positions and bid up the price even more, they would also raise their assessments of the potential loss from being wrong: the greater the gap from their estimate of the benchmark, the more concerned they would tend to be about a reversal. In contrast, bears would respond in the opposite way to a further rise in prices: they would tend to become more confident about an eventual reversal, and thus lower their assessments of the potential loss from their short positions.

Of course, how a market participant interprets the gap from benchmark values when assessing risk changes over time in ways that neither she nor an economist can specify fully in advance. Indeed, we present evidence in Frydman and Goldberg (2007, 2011) that the importance individuals attach to the gap when it is historically large is much greater than when it is historically small. No one can fully foresee the thresholds above or below which individuals might consider the magnitude of the gap to be large or small or how the crossing of these thresholds might impact their values of $\hat{l}^{i,j}_{t|t+1}$.

Consequently, we formalize the influence of movements of $\widehat{gap}^i_t$ on $\hat{l}^{i,j}_{t|t+1}$ with qualitative restrictions:[30]

$$\frac{\Delta\hat{l}^{i,\mathrm{L}}_{t|t+1}}{\Delta\widehat{gap}^i_t} < 0 \quad \text{and} \quad \frac{\Delta\hat{l}^{i,\mathrm{S}}_{t|t+1}}{\Delta\widehat{gap}^i_t} > 0 \tag{20}$$

where Δ is the first-difference operator. These conditions allow for myriad possible nonroutine revisions of an individual's forecasting strategy between

---

Depending on the context, an individual's forecast of the potential unit loss may also depend on factors other than the gap. In Frydman and Goldberg (2007), for example, we include current account imbalances as an additional variable in modeling currency risk.

30. The less-than and greater-than inequalities that are used in specifying the gap conditions for a bull and bear follow from defining $\hat{l}^{i,\mathrm{L}}_{t|t+1}$ and $\hat{l}^{i,\mathrm{S}}_{t|t+1}$ as negative values. As such, greater (smaller) losses imply a fall (rise) in $\hat{l}^{i,j}_{t|t+1}$.

successive points in time as $\widehat{gap}_t^i$ changes. They are thus consistent with myriad possible post-change conditional probability distributions, that is, with many $\mathcal{P}_{t+1}^i(R_{t+2})$. But, conditions (20) constrain the set of possible $\mathcal{P}_{t+1}^i(R_{t+2})$s to share a common qualitative feature: they all imply that if the gap were higher at $t + 1$, a bull would forecast a larger potential unit loss (in size) from holding a long position, whereas a bear would forecast a smaller potential unit loss from holding a short position.

The model does not pick out any one of these post-change distributions, so it does not predetermine the exact size of the gap effect over any period. We thus refer to the post-change distributions that are consistent with the gap conditions as "partially predetermined."[31] Any of these partially predetermined $\mathcal{P}_{t+1}^i(R_{t+2})$ distributions represents an individual's forecasting strategy at $t + 1$.

6.4.2 Contingent Predictions of the Market Premium

Restricting change on the individual level with qualitative restrictions implies that our IKE model generates only qualitative predictions on the aggregate level. Equation (19) and the gap conditions (20) imply a partially predetermined specification for the market premium, which we express as

$$\widehat{pr}_{t|t+1} = \sigma_t \left(P_t - \hat{P}_t^{\text{BM}} \right) \tag{21}$$

where $\sigma_t > 0$, $\hat{P}_t^{\text{BM}}$ is the aggregate of individuals' estimates of the benchmark, and

$$\frac{\Delta \widehat{pr}_{t|t+1}}{\Delta \widehat{gap}_t} > 0 \tag{22}$$

As on the individual level, the specification (21) and (22) is consistent with myriad possible nonroutine ways that the market premium might change from one point in time to the next; there are many post-change conditional probability distributions on the aggregate level, $\mathcal{P}_{t+1}(R_{t+2})$, at each point in time. However, each of these partially predetermined distributions is characterized by an aggregate gap effect: if the aggregate gap were higher at $t + 1$, it would be associated with a higher market premium.

Consequently, our IKE gap model predicts that $\widehat{pr}_{t|t+1}$ and $\widehat{gap}_t$ will co-vary positively over time. It is thus able to account for this qualitative regularity in time-series data on returns in asset markets. However, it renders no predictions about whether the premium will rise or fall or what the exact size of the gap effect might be in the coming months.

31. See Chapter 4 (this volume) and Frydman and Goldberg (2008) for a simple algebraic example of partially predetermined probability distributions.

The unfolding of $\widehat{pr}_{t|.t+1}$ over time depends on how P_t moves relative to $\hat{P}_t^{BM}$, which, as we show in the next section, depends on how individuals' price forecasts unfold in aggregate. The qualitative and contingent restrictions that we use to portray change in $\hat{P}_{t|t+1}$, like the gap restrictions, allow for myriad possible revisions of individuals' forecasting strategies. Partially predetermining change leads to the model's key feature:

- Its predictions concerning whether P_t and $\widehat{pr}_{t|t+1}$ will rise or fall in any one period are contingent on how forecasting strategies unfold.

As we discuss in Section 6.6, this contingency enables the model to recognize the coexistence of both bulls and bears without presuming that either group is obviously irrational.

6.4.3 The Gap Model and Momentary Equilibrium

Portfolio balance and the IKE gap model in (21) and (22) imply the following equilibrium condition for price:

$$P_t = \hat{P}_t^{BM} + \frac{1}{(1 + \sigma_t)} \left(\hat{P}_{t|t+1} - \hat{P}_t^{BM} \right) \tag{23}$$

Like most other asset market models, this specification implies that the main driver of price fluctuations in asset markets is individuals' price forecasts. It shows that P_t would undergo a protracted swing away from benchmark values during periods in which $\hat{P}_{t|t+1}$ moved persistently away from these values.[32] This swing would end when the swing in $\hat{P}_{t|t+1}$ ended.

6.5 Bubbles and Lost Fundamentals: Artifacts of the Contemporary Approach

Standard REH models of asset markets suppose that individuals' price forecasts are based on fundamentals, such as corporate earnings and interest rates. The inability of these models to account for the wide price swings in asset markets, and the belief that they provide the right way to portray the importance of fundamentals for rational forecasting, has led economists to develop so-called bubble models. In these models, individuals' price forecasts are driven over the short term not by market fundamentals, but by speculative manias, crowd psychology and other psychological biases, or

---

32. We are assuming that any changes in σ_t do not outweigh the impact of a change in $\hat{P}_{t|t+1}$. This assumption is consistent with the qualitative and contingent conditions that we impose on how market participants revise their forecasting strategies. See Section 6.6.3.

technical momentum trading. Such forecasting behavior, which behavioral finance portrays with mechanical rules, leads participants to bid an asset price increasingly away from levels that are consistent with fundamental considerations.[33]

Many point to the long upswing in U.S. equity prices during the 1990s as a prime example of such behavior, and widely refer to this upswing as the "dot.com (or Internet) bubble." During this period, there was indeed much confidence and optimism, and even a sense of euphoria, about Internet stocks, with initial public offerings for many companies witnessing remarkable price increases.[34] At its height in August 2000, the broader S&P 500 price index had climbed to roughly 43 times its underlying smoothed earnings. This eclipsed the market's valuation in October 1929 of 33 times smoothed earnings, which had stood as the market's all-time high until the 1990s.

But, beyond their epistemological flaws (see Chapter 4, this volume), many bubble models are simply inconsistent with the basic features of the price swings that we actually observe in asset markets. According to most of these accounts, prices are supposed to rise steadily, save for occasional random movements in the opposite direction, and when the speculative fever dissipates and the bubble bursts, prices are supposed to jump immediately back to their "known true" fundamental values. However, the long swings shown in Figures 6.1 and 6.2 all involve extended periods (sometimes lasting months), during which the asset price undergoes a persistent, but partial, movement back toward the benchmark. Moreover, the sustained reversals that eventually arise do not involve an immediate return to benchmark values; some last for years at a time and eventually shoot through benchmarks.[35]

6.5.1 Technical Trading and Psychology's Inability to Sustain Swings

To be sure, many participants in markets make use of technical rules, and this trading can contribute to price trends. But the bubble notion's assumption that such considerations alone could sustain an upswing lasting

33. See Blanchard and Watson (1982) for an early REH bubble model. For seminal behavioral bubble models, see Frankel and Froot (1987) and De Long et al. (1990). More recent models include Abreu and Brunnermeier (2003) and De Grauwe and Grimaldi (2006).

34. Globe.com and eToys, to name just two, saw price rises on the first day of trading of 606% and 280%, respectively. During October 1999, the six largest technology-related companies—Microsoft, Intel, IBM, Cisco, Lucent, and Dell—had a combined market value of $1.65 trillion, or nearly 20% of U.S. GDP.

35. Some behavioral bubble models imply long upswings and downswings, for example, Frankel and Froot (1987). An open question is whether these and learning models (e.g., Mark 2009) can account for the persistence of asset price fluctuations relative to benchmark values.

an entire decade is implausible. Technical trading mostly takes place over minutes or hours. Schulmeister (2003) points out that the technical rules that are used in markets differ in terms of how quickly they generate a buy or sell signal once a price trend has started. This can lead speculators to prolong an initial price trend. However, the trigger times of most technical market strategies differ only in terms of hours or days. Such speculation simply cannot account for long swings lasting many months or years.

Psychological factors, such as confidence and optimism, also influence decisionmaking and no doubt played a role in leading participants in the aggregate to bid up stock prices in the 1990s. But purely psychological accounts of asset markets overlook the possibility that, when forecasting price movements, participants look to fundamental factors that they think will move the market. Moreover, psychological factors themselves are influenced by fundamental considerations. It is simply implausible to suppose that pure crowd psychology could sustain price swings lasting many years. Indeed, any confidence and optimism that might exist in the stock market would quickly evaporate if, say, earnings and overall economic activity consistently moved in the opposite direction.

6.5.1.1   The Fundamental Underpinnings of Psychological and Other Nonfundamental Considerations

Technical and psychological considerations are difficult to measure and incorporate into formal statistical analysis of the determinants of asset price fluctuations. However, using textual data compiled from Bloomberg News' daily "market-wrap" (end-of-day) stories, Mangee (2011) could measure the influence of these considerations, as well as the influence of a wide range of fundamental factors, on daily stock price fluctuations.[36] In writing market-wrap stories, Bloomberg journalists rely on contacts with 100–200 fund managers and other actors directly involved in the markets. Every one of their wrap stories includes at least one direct quote from one or more of these individuals concerning their views about the key factors driving the market. These stories thus provide a window into the decisionmaking of the professional players whose trading determines prices.

Bloomberg journalists indicate that psychological considerations, such as confidence, optimism, and fear, play an important role in daily price fluctuations, having mentioned them as a main driver of prices on 55% of the days in the sample.[37] However, when Mangee (2011) examines the influence of pure psychology—psychological factors that are mentioned separately

---

36. The study covers January 4, 1993 (Bloomberg's first report) through December 31, 2009.

37. Two excerpts from Bloomberg wrap stories illustrate how psychological factors are reported. In one story (April 21, 2009), a money manager for Pilgrim Investments reports that "IBM earnings are extremely positive . . . this will give confidence and stability to the market."

from fundamentals—he finds that they were mentioned on only 1% of the days.[38]

Bloomberg wrap stories indicate that technical momentum trading also played a relatively minor role in stock price fluctuations. Mangee (2011) finds that this type of trading was mentioned as a main driver of stock prices on only 2% of the days in the sample.[39]

Even when Mangee (2011) combines the influence of pure psychology and momentum trading, there is little support for the bubble view of swings. In virtually no cases do bubble considerations alone move the market. This finding is illustrated in Figure 6.4, which plots the average proportion of days per month that any one of these bubble considerations was mentioned.[40]

The figure shows that bubble considerations had their greatest impact in the second half of the 1990s, providing perhaps some evidence of the bubble view of long upswings. However, these considerations were hardly mentioned at all during much of the 1990s upswing in stock prices. Their importance did rise sharply beginning in 1997. But a high mark of 9% means that they were mentioned on less than 2 of 20 trading days per month on average. Moreover, the importance of bubble considerations began falling rapidly in February 1999. This was a full year before the sharp reversal in equity prices in mid-2000, during the most excessive part of the upswing and exactly when the bubble view would imply that pure psychology and momentum trading should have had their greatest impact. But whatever their impact on prices, these considerations were not the main drivers of the upswing.

Even if one were to view this evidence that psychology and momentum considerations alone do not drive asset price movements as "too soft" to constitute a formal rejection of the bubble view, there is an abundance of

---

In another story (March 2, 2009) titled "US Stocks Tumble Trimming Gains at End of Three Week Rally," a money manager observes that "you have got a lot of fear going into earnings."

38. The reporting of pure psychological factors is illustrated by two excerpts from Bloomberg wrap stories. The market wrap on April 21, 1998, cites a chief investment officer for BankBoston, who remarked that "I do think it's mania . . . anytime stocks appreciate 30 to 50 percent in a day, it's the greater fool theory. People think there will always be someone who will pay a higher price." In another story (August 4, 1998), the same investment officer observes that "the selling is feeding on itself . . . people are indifferent about stock prices and valuations. Now they're fearful."

39. The reporting of technical momentum trading is illustrated by two excerpts from Bloomberg wrap stories. The market wrap on January 11, 2001, reports that "the Nasdaq extended gains after 1 pm surging more than 2 percentage points in an hour, as 'momentum' investors, or those who make short term bets on a stock's direction, rushed to buy shares, traders said." In another story (October 4, 2001), a money manager observes that "so-called momentum investors have been buying technology shares because they have to get their foot back in the door and not get left behind."

40. The time plot in Figure 6.4 is based on a 12-month moving average.

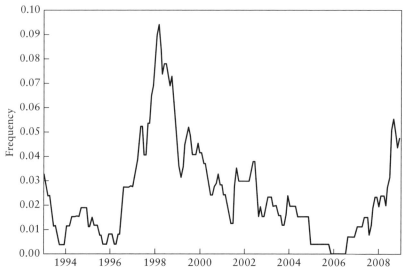

Figure 6.4 Bubble considerations, 1993–2009. The figure shows the average proportion of days per month that Bloomberg wrap stories mentioned a bubble consideration.

evidence showing the central role that fundamental factors play in asset markets.

6.5.2 *Fundamentals Matter, But in Nonroutine Ways*

One only has to watch Bloomberg Television or CNBC for a week or two to recognize that news on a wide range of fundamental factors drives prices in major asset markets. As earnings announcements are made or policy developments in Washington, D.C., become known, one sees the markets react. One also sees that the fundamentals that matter change over time in nonroutine ways.

During much of the 1990s, for example, corporate earnings, GDP, employment, exports, productivity levels, and other economic indicators were rising strongly, while inflation rates were declining or holding at benign levels. Free-trade agreements and other political and institutional changes, together with loose monetary policy, were also conducive to growth. As these developments unfolded, they no doubt reinforced confidence and optimism in the widespread view that the U.S. and other economies were in the midst of an information-technology revolution. The bullish trends in fundamental factors, and the greater confidence that they engendered, led many market participants to raise their price forecasts, thereby bidding up stock prices.

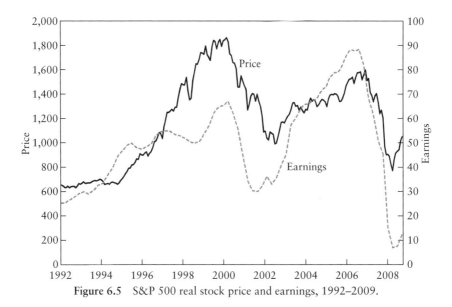

Figure 6.5 S&P 500 real stock price and earnings, 1992–2009.

The importance of fundamental factors in driving asset prices is easily seen in Figure 6.5, which plots the S&P 500 price index along with the basket's underlying earnings. The comovement of the two series is striking. Not only do the broad swings in the series rise and fall together, but their major turning points in 2000, 2003, and 2007 are also closely synchronized. The figure belies the bubble view that long upswings in stock prices away from benchmark levels are unrelated to fundamental factors.

Not surprisingly, Bloomberg wrap stories point to the importance of fundamentals in sustaining swings.[41] Mangee's (2011) data show that at least one fundamental factor was mentioned as a driver of stock prices on virtually every day in his sample. The top four broad categories of fundamental considerations were earnings, the economy, interest rates, and sales. A factor in one of these categories was mentioned on 65%, 47%, 38%, and 23% of the days in the sample, respectively.[42]

---

41. We again illustrate Bloomberg reporting with excerpts from two of its wrap stories. The story of April 18, 2001, reports that "US stocks rallied after the Federal Reserve surprised investors by cutting interest rates for the fourth time this year." In a story on March 1, 2004, the chairman of Walnut Asset Management observes that "the environment is pretty doggone good for stocks . . . earnings appear to be stronger than anticipated."

42. Mangee's measure of the frequency with which earnings considerations are mentioned by Bloomberg wrap stories includes company announcements of earnings and earnings forecasts. It also includes mentions of stock-price movements that are reported to have arisen because other informational variables, for example, interest rates or sales, led participants to revise their earnings predictions.

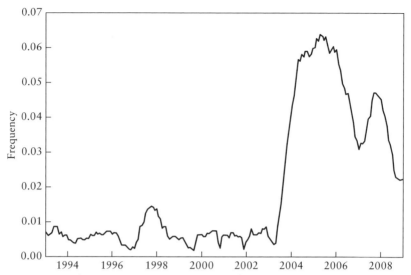

Figure 6.6 Oil price considerations, 1993–2009. The figure shows the average proportion of days per month that Bloomberg wrap stories mentioned oil prices as a major driver of stock prices.

We have argued that the causal process underpinning asset prices changes in nonroutine ways, in part because profit-seeking participants must rely on imperfect knowledge and psychological considerations in revising their forecasting strategies. Bloomberg wrap stories point to this nonroutine change. Indeed, they indicate that the changing nature of the fundamental relationships driving asset markets takes a striking form: different variables matter for prices during different periods. For example, Figure 6.6 plots the average proportion of days per month that oil prices were mentioned as a main driver of stock prices.[43] The figure shows that the market did not pay much attention to the oil price until the end of 2003, when its importance began rising dramatically. By the end of 2004, 60% of each month's wraps mentioned this factor as a driver of the market. No one could have fully foreseen the timing and magnitude of this rise.

Empirical studies that allow for structural change without fully prespecifying it find a similar result. They report that although the causal process driving asset markets changes in non–fully predetermined ways, there are extended periods during which the nonroutine change that does occur is sufficiently moderate that a relatively stable relationship between an asset

---

43. Again, a 12-month moving average is used.

price and a set of fundamental variables can be estimated. They find not only that fundamental factors matter over the short term, but that different sets of fundamentals matter during different periods.[44] Fully foreseeing when such distinct periods might begin or how long they might last—let alone the precise nature of the fundamental relationships during such periods—is simply beyond anyone's reach.

6.6   An IKE Account of Asset Price Swings

The importance of fundamentals for short-term price movements in asset markets and the central role that individual's price forecasts play in the process (portrayed by (23)) indicate that prolonged price swings stem from trends in fundamentals and how individuals revise the ways that they interpret these trends in thinking about the future. The microfoundations of our account of asset price swings recognize the importance of fundamentals for forecasting and, as before, involve qualitative and contingent restrictions to portray revisions of forecasting strategies.

Market participants' imperfect knowledge and the influence of psychological considerations on their decisionmaking imply that when and how they revise their forecasting strategies do not conform to any mechanical rules. Moreover, a key feature of price swings in asset markets is that they are irregular in duration and magnitude: some swings last for months, whereas others last for years; some involve small departures from benchmark values, whereas others involve large departures. No one can predict precisely when a price swing might begin or end.

To build the microfoundations for a model of this aggregate regularity, we look for regularities on the individual level that are similarly contingent. To portray how individuals revise their strategies for forecasting price, we formalize a qualitative regularity that often, but not always, characterizes behavior. Consequently, our representation is not only qualitative, but also contingent: although the qualitative conditions that we use to portray individual forecasting are assumed to hold most of the time, we do not prespecify the points when they do not. This contingency enables us to account for the unpredictable irregularity of asset price swings and the nonroutine way that fundamentals underpin them. It also allows us to recognize that bulls and bears coexist in the market, and that psychological considerations play a role in decisionmaking, without presuming that individuals forgo obvious profit opportunities.

---

44. For stock prices, see Mangee (2011), and for exchange rates, see Goldberg and Frydman (1996a,b) and Beckman et al. (2011).

6.6.1 An Individual's Price Forecast

We portray an individual's point forecast of the next period's stock price as

$$\hat{P}^i_{t|t+1} = \beta^i_t Z^i_t \tag{24}$$

where the vector Z^i_t represents the informational variables that individual i uses in forming her price forecast, and β^i_t represents the vector of weights that she attaches to them in thinking about the future.[45] This representation implies that there are two key factors that underpin the evolution of an individual's price forecast over time: revisions of her forecasting strategy—changes in β^i_t, which could include changes in the composition of the set of causal variables Z^i_t—and movements of the informational variables.

6.6.2 Movements of Fundamentals

To illustrate our model of asset price swings, we begin with the assumption that the informational variables in the model follow random walks with constant drifts:[46]

$$\Delta Z^i_t = \mu^i + \epsilon^i_t \tag{25}$$

where μ^i and ϵ^i_t are the vectors of drifts and white-noise errors, respectively. The processes underpinning the unfolding of these fundamentals, of course, depend on economic policy and other features of the social context. Economic policy does change from time to time as new policymakers take charge or as their understanding of economic and social conditions evolves. These conditions themselves also change at times in nonroutine ways. To represent such change in the model we could allow for time-varying drifts in the Z processes in (25). This would enable us to capture the kind of behavior we have already seen in corporate earnings (Figure 6.5): this variable trends in one direction for extended periods, followed by periods in which it trends in the opposite direction.[47]

---

45. The vector Z^i_t includes expected one-period-ahead changes in informational variables. In this chapter, we simplify by setting these expected changes to constants. A more general IKE model would impose qualitative and contingent constraints on how they unfold over time.

46. To simplify, we assume that the set of information variables does not include the asset price. Recognizing the importance of this variable does not alter the main conclusions of our analysis. See Frydman and Goldberg (2007).

47. In fact, there is much evidence that the processes underpinning many macroeconomic times series are better characterized as involving a persistent drift rather than a constant or no drift, thereby implying near-$I(2)$ behavior. For evidence of such behavior in macroeconomic time series, see Johansen (1997), Kongsted and Nielsen (2004), Juselius (2006), Johansen et al. (2010), and Frydman et al. (2012).

As with market participants' forecasting, we would look for qualitative and contingent regularities in the social context that might help account for the irregular price swings. However, to highlight how IKE representations of forecasting behavior help account for this aggregate regularity, we maintain the assumption of constant drifts for most of this section. We refer to this assumption as a "fixed policy environment."[48]

6.6.3 Nonroutine Revisions of Forecasting Strategies

We recall from the equilibrium condition in (23) that a price swing away from or toward benchmark values arises in the model during any stretch of time in which individuals' price forecasts move persistently away from or toward these values. The swing ends when the swing in $\hat{P}_{t|t+1} - \hat{P}_t^{BM}$ ends. Estimates of common benchmark values, such as those discussed in Section 6.2, move much more slowly than the asset price. Thus, to focus on the central role of price forecasts in driving swings in asset markets, we set the aggregate of individuals' estimates of the benchmark equal to the constant $\hat{P}^{BM}$.[49]

To model revisions of forecasting strategies, we again rely on Keynes's (1936) account of asset markets. This account is often invoked by those who support the view that underlies bubble models, namely, that asset prices are driven by purely psychological considerations. Indeed, Keynes repeatedly alludes to psychological considerations when describing speculation and investment, referring, for example, to the "confidence with which we . . . forecast" (Keynes 1936: 148), "mass psychology" (Keynes 1936: 154), "spontaneous optimism" (Keynes 1936: 161), and "animal spirits" (Keynes 1936: 162).

However, we argue in Frydman and Goldberg (2011) that, although psychological factors undoubtedly played a role in Keynes's thinking about markets, there is much in his *General Theory* to suggest that fundamental considerations were also important to his view of asset price fluctuations. Indeed, he begins his analysis of asset markets by discussing how "expectations of prospective yields" are, in the first place, rooted in individuals' understanding of fundamentals or

> knowledge of the facts which will influence the yield of the investment. . . . [The] existing market valuation . . . will only change in proportion to changes in this knowledge. [Keynes 1936: 152]

---

48. In Section 6.6.6.1, we show how shifts in the policy environment help explain the boundedness of asset price swings.

49. Movements of the imperfectly known benchmark are likely to play a significant role in some markets. However, we focus in this chapter on the fluctuations around benchmark levels.

In using their "knowledge of the facts" to form forecasts, participants

> fall back on what is, in truth, a convention . . . [which] lies in assuming
> that the existing state of affairs will continue indefinitely, except in so far
> as we have specific reasons to expect a change. [Keynes 1936: 152][50]

Keynes's insight that market participants tend to assume that the "existing state of affairs will continue" suggests that they tend to stick with a forecasting strategy for stretches of time. Indeed, it is often unclear whether an individual should alter her strategy. A quarter or two of poor forecasting performance may be the result of random events rather than an indication of a failing strategy. So, unless an individual has "specific reasons to expect a change" in the market, she may leave her current strategy unaltered—even if its performance begins to flag over several periods. Moreover, even armed with "specific reasons to expect a change," it is entirely unclear what new forecasting strategy, if any, she should adopt.

We thus represent how participants tend to alter their thinking about how fundamentals matter with an empirical regularity that we refer to as "guardedly moderate revisions": there are stretches of time during which participants either maintain their strategies or revise them gradually. Such revisions do not generally alter, in substantial ways, the set of fundamentals that participants consider relevant or their interpretation of these fundamentals' influence on future outcomes. As we shall see, all that is needed to sustain a price swing during these time periods is for fundamentals to trend in unchanging ways, which they do quite often.

But, like price swings themselves, the tendency toward guardedly moderate revisions is a qualitative regularity that occurs in contingent ways. There are occasions when news about fundamentals and price movements leads participants to revise their forecasting strategies in nonmoderate ways. Such revisions can have a dramatic impact on price and spell the end of a price swing in one direction and the start of a new swing in the opposite direction.

6.6.3.1 Formalization of Guardedly Moderate Revisions

To formalize the contingent regularity of guardedly moderate revisions, we need to define a baseline against which revisions may be judged to be either moderate or nonmoderate. We note that as trends in fundamentals unfold, an individual would, in general, alter her price forecast even if she were to keep her forecasting strategy unchanged. The drift underpinning this change in the status quo of $\hat{P}^i_{t|t+1}$ serves as our baseline for judging whether revisions are guardedly moderate.

---

50. By "existing state of affairs," Keynes means "knowledge of the facts."

Given the representations in (24) and (25), the total change in an individual's price forecast can be expressed as

$$\hat{P}^i_{t|t+1} - \hat{P}^i_{t-1|t} = T\hat{P}^i_{t|t+1} + \epsilon^i_t \tag{26}$$

where $T\hat{P}^i_{t|t+1}$ is the "trend change" in the individual's forecast between $t-1$ and t:

$$T\hat{P}^i_{t|t+1} = \Delta\beta^i_t Z^i_t + \beta^i_{t-1}\mu^{Z^i} \tag{27}$$

This trend change depends on how an individual revises her forecasting strategy, $\Delta\beta^i_t$, and on what we call the "baseline drift" in her point forecast, $\beta^i_{t-1}\mu^{Z^i}$.[51] The baseline drift represents the change that would result if an individual were to use the same forecasting strategy at $t-1$ and t and if the only change in her price forecast at t resulted from drifts in fundamentals. If she were to refrain from revising her strategy over the next T points in time, $T\hat{P}^i_{t|t+1}$ would again be equal to $\beta^i_{t-1}\mu^{Z^i}$ between each of these points. During this stretch of time, $\hat{P}^i_{t|t+1}$ would tend to move in one direction, which would be determined by the algebraic sign of the baseline drift.

Suppose, for example, that an individual's $\beta^i_{t-1}\mu^{Z^i}$ was positive. In this case, movements in fundamentals would, on average, lead her to raise her price forecast between $t-1$ and $t+T$.

Of course, movements in fundamentals may lead an individual to revise her forecasting strategy at any point during this stretch of time. To see how this works in our model, consider such a revision at t, which is portrayed by a new set of parameters, $\beta^i_t \neq \beta^i_{t-1}$. The impact of the new parameters on the price forecast at t is $\Delta\beta^i_t Z^i_t$. But the revision also gives rise to a new baseline drift, $\beta^i_t \mu^{Z^i}$, which portrays how trends in fundamentals influence the individual's forecast in the next period, $t+1$.

Each of these effects on the price forecast—$\Delta\beta^i_t Z^i_t$ at t and $\beta^i_t \mu^{Z^i}$ at $t+1$—could reinforce or impede the influence of the initial baseline drift, $\beta^i_{t-1}\mu^{Z^i}$, which in our example is positive. The new β^i_t would be reinforcing at t and $t+1$ if $\Delta\beta^i_t Z^i_t > 0$ and $\beta^i_t \mu^{Z^i} > \beta^i_{t-1}\mu^{Z^i}$. In this case, the revision at t would add to the initial influence of fundamentals and contribute to a higher $\hat{P}^i_{t|t+1}$ at t and a faster growing $\hat{P}^i_{t|t+1}$ at $t+1$.

---

51. To portray change in the set of fundamentals that an individual might use to form her price forecast, we suppose that the vector Z^i_t represents at every point in time all possible fundamentals that she might use. If, for example, an individual uses a particular variable Z^i_j to form her forecast at t but not at $t-1$, then $\beta^i_{j,t-1} = 0$ and $\Delta\beta^i_{j,t} = \beta^i_{j,t}$.

If, however, the new β_t^i was impeding at t and $t+1$—$\Delta\beta_t^i Z_t^i < 0$ and $\beta_t^i \mu^{Z^i} < \beta_{t-1}^i \mu^{Z^i}$—it would subtract from the positive influence of fundamentals at t and lead to a lower baseline drift at $t+1$. The size of these effects could be large enough that, although the initial influence of fundamentals was positive, $\hat{P}_{t|t+1}^i$ fell at t and $t+1$.

But, regardless of whether revisions were reinforcing or impeding between $t-1$ and $t+T$, if their effects on an individual's price forecast and baseline drift were moderate enough throughout this period, the trends in fundamentals would still tend to dominate and lead her to raise her price forecast in one direction.

This reasoning underpins our formalization of guardedly moderate revisions, which involves two qualitative conditions,

$$\left|\Delta\beta_t^i Z_t^i\right| < \delta_t^i \tag{28}$$

$$\left|\Delta\beta_t^i \mu^{Z^i}\right| < \delta_t^i \tag{29}$$

where $|\cdot|$ denotes absolute value, and $\delta_t^i = \left|\beta_{t-1}^i \mu^{Z^i}\right|$ is the magnitude of the baseline drift. The first condition constrains revisions at t so that the impact of movements in fundamentals on an individual's price forecast tends to outweigh the impact from revisions. The second condition also constrains revisions at t and implies that the sign of the baseline drift does not change. Consequently, if these conditions were to characterize how an individual revised her forecasting strategy over a stretch of time, and trends in fundamentals remained unchanged over that time, she would tend to alter her price forecast in one direction or the other.

The qualitative constraints (28) and (29) embody the idea that unless an individual has "specific reasons to expect a change" in the "existing state of affairs," she tends to maintain her forecasting strategy or, if she revises it, to do so in ways that would not have a large impact on her price forecast or its baseline drift. Because they restrict neither the causal variables that may enter (24) nor how exactly these variables might matter, these constraints leave room for non–rule based revisions. Moreover, they do not imply that the change in an individual's price forecast must be small: our model's constraints are compatible with large changes in $\hat{P}_{t|t+1}^i$ that result from large movements in fundamentals.

6.6.3.2 Psychological Motivation for Guardedly Moderate Revisions?

Although we find compelling Keynes's insight that individuals fall back on the assumption that the "existing state of affairs will continue," we are unaware of any direct empirical evidence that would support this claim. To be sure, psychologists have uncovered experimental evidence of a regularity that they call "conservatism": when individuals change their forecasts about uncertain outcomes, they tend to do so gradually, relative to some baseline—a finding that is consistent with our characterization of guardedly moderate revisions (see Edwards 1968; Shleifer 2000; and references therein). But it is a finding that pertains to how an individual alters her *forecast* rather than to how she might revise her forecasting *strategy*.

Even if we were to formulate conservatism as a qualitative regularity, it would imply a restriction on an individual's forecasting behavior that was stronger than our guardedly moderate restrictions. For example, suppose that an individual kept her forecasting strategy unchanged between two consecutive points in time, but increased her price forecast nonetheless because of movements in fundamentals. Conservatism would restrict the size of the impact on $\hat{P}^i_{t|t+1}$, whereas our guardedly moderate conditions would not.

Moreover, because behavioral economists insist on sharp predictions, they characterize conservatism not as a qualitative regularity but as a mechanical one. As a result, existing formulations of conservatism imply restrictions on individual behavior that are much stronger than our representation of guardedly moderate revisions. These fully predetermined representations presume that individuals underreact to new information in a fixed way relative to what an economist's overarching probability model would imply. They thus imply that individuals never revise their forecasting strategies (e.g., see Barberis et al. 1998).

6.6.4 Irregular Swings in an Individual's Price Forecast

Market participants' tendency to deal with uncertainty by keeping forecasting strategies unaltered or revising them in guardedly moderate ways is a *contingent* regularity: it characterizes behavior during stretches of time that begin and end at moments that no one can predict. Eventually, the "existing state of affairs" changes or an individual has "specific reasons to expect" such a change. Even if trends in fundamentals continued in the same broad directions, the qualitative regularity of guardedly moderate revisions may cease to hold at unpredictable moments.

Consequently, our IKE representation does not restrict an individual's forecasting behavior to be consistent with conditions (28) and (29) at every point in time. Moreover, it does not prespecify the stretches of time during which they characterize behavior, that is, when these stretches might begin or end. Because of this contingency, our model implies that an individual's price forecast will undergo swings of irregular duration and magnitude.

To see this, consider a stretch of time from $t-1$ to $t+T$, during which trends in fundamentals remained unchanged and an individual's initial interpretations of these trends would, in the absence of any revisions of her strategy, lead her to raise her price forecast. If, during this stretch, revisions of her strategy could be characterized as guardedly moderate, her price forecast would tend to rise over the period. An end to this upswing in $\hat{P}^i_{t|t+1}$

would occur at $t + T + 1$, if her revisions were impeding and nonmoderate—that is, *not* characterized by the conditions (28) and (29). Such drastic revisions would have a greater impact on her price forecast than the impact from the drifts in fundamentals, and so $\hat{P}^i_{t|t+1}$ would tend to fall at $t + T + 1$. Moreover, nonmoderate and impeding revisions would lead to a switch in the sign of the baseline drift, so that the influence of these drifts on the individual's price forecast in the next period, $\beta^i_{t+T+1}\mu^{Z^i}$, would be downward. The fall in $\hat{P}^i_{t|t+1}$ would then tend to continue if revisions of the individual's strategy were once again characterized as guardedly moderate for another stretch of time beyond $t + T + 1$.

The downswing in $\hat{P}^i_{t|t+1}$ would continue until the individual once again decided to revise her strategy in a dramatic and impeding fashion. At such times, her forecast would experience another reversal, which might or might not turn into a sustained countermovement.

6.6.5 Bulls, Bears, and Irregular Swings in the Aggregate Forecast

There are, of course, stark differences in bulls' and bears' strategies; after all, one group forecasts a rise in price, whereas the other forecasts a decline. However, because our characterization of guardedly moderate revisions is qualitative and contingent, it is open to nonroutine changes in bulls' and bears' forecasting strategies and is consistent with the myriad diverse ways in which this change occurs. Regardless of the precise way in which a participant revised her strategy, or whether she was a bull or a bear, her price forecast would tend to move in one direction or the other for as long as her revisions continued to be guardedly moderate and trends in fundamentals remained unchanged.

The equilibrium condition (23) shows that what matters for asset prices is how the aggregate of participants' diverse price forecasts moves over time. Even if all participants were assumed to revise their strategies in guardedly moderate ways over a stretch of time, this would not, in general, imply that the aggregate forecasting strategy was also characterized by guardedly moderate revisions.

To connect the implications of our representation of individual behavior to aggregate outcomes, we rely on assumptions concerning the degree to which qualitative interpretations of movements in fundamentals vary across individuals. This variation implies another layer of contingency to our IKE model's predictions.

6.6.5.1 Moving to the Aggregate Level

To see what assumptions about diversity are needed for our model to generate predictions on the aggregate level, we initially consider a stretch of time, t to $t + T$, during which the drifts in fundamentals remain unchanged and all participants revise their forecasting strategies in guardedly moderate ways. Participants who are bulls at t predict a higher price at $t + 1$,

$$\hat{P}^{i,\mathrm{L}}_{t|t+1} - P_t > 0 \tag{30}$$

whereas those who are bears predict a lower price,

$$\hat{P}^{i,\mathrm{S}}_{t|t+1} - P_t < 0 \tag{31}$$

But, regardless of whether they are bulls or bears at t, we know from Section 6.6.3.1 that all the individual $\hat{P}^{i}_{t|t+1}$ values in our example move in one direction or the other, on average, between t and $t + T$.

Whether an individual's price forecast rises or falls over the period depends on how the trends in fundamentals initially impact her forecast, which we portray by the initial baseline drift. If, for example, the initial impact is positive $(\beta^{i}_{t-1}\mu^{Z^i} > 0)$, all subsequent trend changes in an individual's forecast will be positive $(T\hat{P}^{i}_{t|t+1} > 0)$, and she will tend to raise $\hat{P}^{i}_{t|t+1}$ over the period. We note that such an upswing in $\hat{P}^{i}_{t|t+1}$ could characterize an individual who is a bear throughout the period. Although a bear's interpretation of fundamentals implies $\hat{P}^{i}_{t|t+1} < P_t$, movements in fundamentals—say, a rise in overall economic activity—could well lead her to increase $\hat{P}^{i}_{t|t+1}$, thereby becoming less bearish over time.

In the aggregate, the trend change in $\hat{P}_{t|t+1}$ at each point in time is a weighted average of the individual values of $T\hat{P}^{i}_{t|t+1}$ given by (27):

$$T\hat{P}_{t|t+1} = \sum_i \omega^i \left(\Delta\beta^i_t Z^i_t + \beta^i_{t-1}\mu^{Z^i} \right) \tag{32}$$

where the aggregation weights, as before, are based on wealth shares and are assumed to be constant. It is immediately clear that if trends in fundamentals and guardedly moderate revisions led all individuals to alter their price forecasts in the same direction between t and $t + T$, the aggregate $\hat{P}_{t|t+1}$ would also undergo a swing.

To be sure, knowledge is imperfect, and some market participants will interpret movements in certain fundamentals positively, whereas others will view them negatively. Whether $\hat{P}_{t|t+1}$ tends to move in one direction between t and $t + T$ in our example would then depend on the degree to which participants interpret movements of fundamentals in a qualitatively similar way. This diversity of qualitative interpretations varies over time in ways that no one can fully foresee. However, if it remained sufficiently small, the constant trends in fundamentals and guardedly moderate revisions on the individual level would lead most participants to alter their price forecasts in one direction over the period. Moreover, these swings in individual $\hat{P}^i_{t|t+1}$ values would be associated with a swing in $\hat{P}_{t|t+1}$ in the same direction.

In what follows, we impose this constraint on the variation in diversity as long as asset price departures from estimates of the benchmark value are below a threshold level. Indeed, in most markets, participants tend to interpret many of the fundamentals that drive forecasts in a qualitatively similar way. For example, in the stock market, positive trends in overall economic activity, earnings, sales, and employment are widely viewed by participants as reasons to raise their price forecasts regardless of whether they are bulls or bears, whereas rising interest rates and oil prices have the opposite effect.

However, we would expect diversity in the market to grow if stock prices moved, for example, far above estimates of benchmark values. Participants know that such departures are eventually reversed, although no one knows when the reversal will begin. Even when valuations become high, some participants continue to forecast that the upswing will persist over the next period, while others predict a reversal. Rising earnings and economic activity may lead both bulls and bears to raise their price forecasts, but at some point, even these trends would not be interpreted in qualitatively similar ways as bears began to gain greater confidence in a reversal and stopped raising their forecasts $\hat{P}^i_{t|t+1}$. As we discuss in more detail in the next section, this growth in diversity can spell the end of a price swing.

The assumption that all market participants revise their strategies in guardedly moderate ways is strong. At each point in time we would expect that the forecasting behavior of some participants could be characterized as guardedly moderate, while that of others could not. Whether the aggregate forecast tends to move in one direction between t and $t + T$ in our example depends on the relative weight of the participants in the market whose revisions are guardedly moderate. A swing would arise during the period if this weight remained sufficiently high.

6.6.6 *Irregular Price Swings*

As long as departures of the asset price from estimates of benchmark values remain below some unknown threshold, the model does not prespecify the stretches of time during which market participants, on the whole, revise their forecasting strategies in guardedly moderate ways. Therefore, it does not prespecify when swings in the aggregate price forecast, $\hat{P}_{t|t+1}$, and thus in the asset price, will begin or end.

Participants' decisions to revise their strategies depend on many considerations, including their current strategy's performance, whether they have "specific reasons to expect a change" in how fundamental factors are trending or how they are influencing prices, and the "confidence with which we . . . forecast" (Keynes 1936: 148). Nonmoderate and impeding revisions of forecasting strategies are often proximate to points at which trends in fundamentals also reverse or there is a major change in economic policies or institutions. At such points, the market undergoes a price reversal. But once such changes have occurred and have been interpreted, individuals are likely to resume revising their strategies in guardedly moderate ways: they would tend to keep their forecasting strategies unchanged or revise them only moderately, but they would always be on guard for change. In that case, and if fundamentals trended in persistent directions, the asset price would begin trending in the other direction for another stretch of time.

The new price swing would continue until participants again lost confidence that the new trends in fundamentals would persist, or some other change in the existing state of affairs led them to revise their strategies in a nonmoderate and impeding fashion. At such times, the asset price would experience another reversal, which might or might not turn into a sustained countermovement.

6.6.6.1 Risk and Bounded Instability
Although our model does not fully prespecify when asset price swings begin or end, it does imply that swings away from estimates of benchmark values eventually end and are followed by sustained countermovements back toward these values. This implication follows from our account of risk and assumptions about the unfolding of diversity.

As an asset price rises well above or falls well below most participants' perceptions of benchmark values, those who are betting on further movements away from these levels raise their assessments of the riskiness of doing so. Eventually, these assessments lead them to revise their forecasting strategies in nonmoderate and nonreinforcing ways. When that happens, even the most excessive price swings come to an end and are followed by sustained reversals back toward benchmark levels.

Consider a stretch of time during which market participants revise their forecasting strategies in guardedly moderate ways. A bull forecasts that the price swing will continue over the near term, whereas a bear forecasts the opposite. However, our assumption about diversity implies that as long as the asset price does not depart too far from benchmark values, most bulls and bears would interpret movements in fundamentals in qualitatively similar ways. Suppose, initially, that the mix of forecasting strategies and drifts in fundamentals leads both bulls and bears to raise their price forecasts over time; that is, the baseline drifts for both groups, $\beta_{\tau-1}^{i,\text{L}} \mu^{Z^{i,\text{L}}}$ and $\beta_{\tau-1}^{i,\text{S}} \mu^{Z^{i,\text{S}}}$, are positive. These developments would lead bulls to become more bullish and bears to become less bearish. During this stretch of time, then, $\hat{P}_{t|t+1}$ and P_t, would tend to rise, say, farther above most estimates of benchmark levels.

But, although bulls expect a greater return, they understand that such upswings eventually end, so they increase their assessment of the risk of a reversal and capital losses. The resulting rise in their premiums tempers their desire to increase their speculative positions. If trends in fundamentals continued, thereby prolonging the excessive price swing, a threshold would eventually be reached at which bulls would become so concerned about a reversal that they would no longer revise their forecasting strategies in guardedly moderate ways. At that point, they would either reduce their long positions or abandon them altogether, precipitating a price reversal.

Bears also understand that upswings eventually end, which is why they also change their premiums, but in the opposite direction. If the upswing continued, they would eventually cease to interpret trends in fundamentals as reasons to raise their price forecasts. But this would imply that they revised their forecasting strategies in nonmoderate and impeding ways, likewise contributing to the self-limiting nature of long swings away from benchmark levels.

When, precisely, the gap from benchmark levels is perceived to be too large for bulls and bears to continue to revise their strategies in guardedly moderate ways depends on many factors, including economic, political, and policy considerations that no one can fully prespecify. Thus, no one can foresee when long swings away from benchmark levels will eventually end.

In currency markets, policymakers use such benchmarks as PPP to set economic policy, and their actions play an important role in keeping exchange rate swings bounded. The empirical record shows that policy officials eventually become concerned about large departures in the exchange rate from PPP and alter policy to engender a reversal.[52] As with revisions of forecasting strategies, we would not expect that such policy changes would follow any mechanical rule. But the proximity of major reversals in currency markets to major changes in policy suggests that policymakers play an important role in keeping long swings in currency markets bounded.[53]

---

52. Examples of such behavior include the coordinated interventions by central banks and the changes in monetary and fiscal policies that were aimed at bringing down U.S. dollar exchange rates in 1985 and yen exchange rates in 1995, as well as the interventions by the U.S. Federal Reserve and the European Central Bank to stem the dollar's fall in 2007 and the first half of 2008.

53. For example, the major reversals in U.S. dollar exchange rates in late 1979 and early 1985 were associated with the arrival of Paul Volcker and James Baker, respectively, both of whom quickly engineered major changes in policy. An example of a connection between policy and major reversals in other asset markets is provided by the downturn in U.S. equity markets that began in August 2000, which came on the heels of the Federal Reserve's decision to raise the federal funds rate from 4.74% in July 1999 to 6.5% in May 2000. Beyond the policy channel, departures in asset prices from benchmark values endogenously influence trends in macroeconomic fundamentals in ways that also keep asset price swings bounded. For example, swings in exchange rates eventually lead to changes in current account imbalances and economic growth that tend to limit such swings.

6.7 Contingent Predictions of Long Swings and Their Compatibility with Rationality

Despite its contingent character and openness to nonroutine change, our representation of bulls' and bears' decisionmaking and assumptions about diversity place sufficient structure on the analysis to account for the basic features of asset price swings depicted in Figures 6.1 and 6.2.

The qualitative conditions formalizing guardedly moderate revisions and our assumptions about diversity do not produce sharp predictions about asset price fluctuations. Instead, they are consistent with myriad possible changes in β_t and the composition of Z_t between two consecutive points in time. At any point in time, therefore, they imply myriad post-change probability distributions for price—one for each possible value of β_t—conditional on any of the distributions at time $t-1$ and the processes underpinning fundamentals. However, each of these partially predetermined distributions implies that the price would tend to move in one direction or the other over time if the drifts underpinning fundamentals remained unchanged.

Our IKE model predicts, therefore, that price swings in asset markets will occur during stretches of time in which trends in market fundamentals are persistent, and participants, on the whole, interpret the impact of these trends on their price forecasts in a qualitatively similar manner and revise their strategies in guardedly moderate ways. The uncertainties inherent in forecasting asset prices, as well as findings in psychology, suggest that participants often stick with a strategy for stretches of time and that when they do revise their strategies, they are reluctant to do so in dramatic ways. Moreover, macroeconomic fundamentals often trend in particular directions for years at a time. Given these qualitative regularities in individual forecasting and the social context, our IKE model predicts that asset prices quite often will undergo swings either away from or toward estimates of benchmark values. If a price swing is headed toward benchmark values and the qualitative conditions for a swing endure (which they often do), the asset price will eventually shoot through the benchmark and begin trending away from the other side. Moreover, participants' use of the gap from benchmark levels to assess the riskiness of their speculative positions implies that long swings away from these levels cannot last forever. Eventually, conditions in the market change, and a sustained reversal results.

The contingent nature of its representation on the individual level implies that the model renders no prediction of whether the asset price will rise or fall in any given period. The trends in fundamentals could reverse directions at any time, and participants may cease to interpret these trends in a qualitatively similar manner or decide to revise their strategies in nonguardedly moderate ways at any time. Consequently, at each point in time, the model is consistent with many partially predetermined probability distributions that imply a tendency for the asset price to move in the same direction during some period and with many others that imply a tendency for it to move in the opposite direction during the same period.

The model is thus compatible with the coexistence of both bulls and bears. At each point in time, it is reasonable for some participants to expect the price to rise and for others to expect it to fall. It may even be reasonable for some individuals to remain consistently bullish or bearish during a period in which the asset price moves steadily against them. Indeed, an individual might reasonably decide to increase the size of her long or short position precisely *because* the price has moved farther away from her expected level.

6.8   An Intermediate View of Markets and the Role of the State

Our IKE model enables us to uncover the importance of both fundamentals and psychological considerations for understanding price swings and risk in financial markets without presuming that market participants forgo obvious profit opportunities. In Frydman and Goldberg (2009, 2011), we show how this model leads to an intermediate view of asset price swings away from and back toward benchmark values: they play an integral role in the process by which financial markets evaluate prior investments and foster new companies and projects—the key to modern economies' dynamism. And yet, owing to the imperfection of knowledge, these swings can sometimes become excessive, exacting huge economic and social costs.

This intermediate view contrasts sharply with the polarized positions that are implied by fully predetermined models of macroeconomics and finance: asset price swings are based either on "rational" decisionmaking that enables society to allocate its scarce capital nearly perfectly or on crowd psychology and technical trading that allocates capital haphazardly.

Our intermediate view of markets not only sheds new light on the supposed empirical puzzles implied by fully predetermined models; it also leads to a new way of thinking about the relationship between the market and the state. Because asset price swings away from benchmark values can sometimes become excessive, there is a role for the state to stand guard and dampen this excess. Our IKE model implies new channels for policy officials to accomplish this task and supplies new tools with which regulators can assess systemic and other financial sector risks.

References

Abreu, Dilip, and Markus K. Brunnermeier. (2003) "Bubbles and Crashes," *Econometrica* 71: 173–204.
Ang, Andrew, Geert Bekaert, and Jun Liu. (2005) "Why Stocks May Disappoint," *Journal of Financial Economics* 76: 471–508.

Bank for International Settlements. (2010) "Macroprudential Instruments and Frameworks: A Stocktaking of Issues and Experiences." Paper 38, Committee on the Global Financial System, Bank for International Settlements, Basel, Switzerland.

Barberis, Nicolas C., and Ming Huang. (2001) "Mental Accounting, Loss Aversion, and Individual Stock Returns," *Journal of Finance* 56: 1247–1292.

Barberis, Nicolas C., and Richard H. Thaler. (2003) "A Survey of Behavioral Finance," in George Constantinides, Milton Harris, and Rene Stulz (eds.), *Handbook of the Economics of Finance*. Amsterdam: North-Holland, pp. 1051–1121.

Barberis, Nicolas, Andrei Shleifer, and Robert Vishny. (1998) "A Model of Investor Sentiment," *Journal of Financial Economics* 49: 307–443.

Barberis, Nicolas C., Ming Huang, and Tano Santos. (2001) "Prospect Theory and Asset Prices," *Quarterly Journal of Economics* 116: 1–53.

Beckman, Joscha, Ansgar Belke, and Michael Kuhl. (2011) "How Stable Are Monetary Models of the Dollar-Euro Exchange Rate? A Time-Varying Coefficient Approach," *Review of World Economics* 147: 11–40.

Blanchard, Olivier, and Mark Watson. (1982) "Bubbles, Rational Expectations and Financial Markets," in P. Wachtel (ed.), *Crises in the Economic and Financial Structure*. Lexington, MA: Lexington Books, pp. 295–316.

Borio, Claudio. (2003) "Towards a Macroprudential Framework for Financial Supervision and Regulation." Working Paper 128, Bank for International Settlements, Basel, Switzerland.

Borio, Claudio, and Ilhyock Shim. (2007) "What Can (Macro-) Prudential Policy Do to Support Monetary Policy?" Working Paper 242, Bank for International Settlements, Basel, Switzerland.

De Grauwe, Paul, and Marianna Grimaldi. (2006) *The Exchange Rate in a Behavioral Finance Framework*. Princeton, NJ: Princeton University Press.

De Long, Bradford J., Andrei Shleifer, Lawrence H. Summers, and Robert J. Waldman. (1990) "Positive Feedback Investment Strategies and Destabilizing Rational Speculation," *Journal of Finance* 45: 375–395.

Dornbusch, Rudiger. (1983) "Exchange Rate Risk and the Macroeconomics of Exchange Rate Determination," in R. Hawkins, R. Levich, and C. G. Wihlborg (eds.), *The Internationalization of Financial Markets and National Economic Policy*, volume 3. Greenwich, CT: JAI Press, pp. 3–27.

Edwards, Ward (1968) "Conservatism in Human Information Processing," in Benjamin Kleinmuth (ed.), *Formal Representation of Human Judgement*. New York: John Wiley and Sons, pp. 17–52.

Frankel, Jeffrey A. (1982) "In Search of the Exchange-Rate Risk Premium: A Six Currency Test Assuming Mean Variance Optimization," *Journal of International Money and Finance* 1: 255–274.

Frankel, Jeffrey A., and Kenneth Froot. (1987) "Using Survey Data to Test Standard Propositions Regarding Exchange Rate Expectations," *American Economic Review* 77: 133–153.

Froot, Kenneth, and Jeffrey A. Frankel. (1989) "Forward Discount Bias: Is it an Exchange Risk Premium?" *Quarterly Journal of Economics* 104: 139–161. Reprinted in Jeffrey A. Frankel (ed.), (1995) *On Exchange Rates*. Cambridge, MA: MIT Press, pp. 245–260.

Frydman, Roman, and Michael D. Goldberg. (2007) *Imperfect Knowledge Economics: Exchange Rates and Risk*. Princeton, NJ: Princeton University Press.

———. (2008) "Macroeconomic Theory for a World of Imperfect Knowledge," *Capitalism and Society* 3(3): Article 1. Available at http://www.bepress.com/cas/vol3/iss3/art1/.

———. (2009) "Financial Markets and the State: Price Swings, Risk, and the Scope of Regulation," *Capitalism and Society* 4(2): Article 2. Available at http://www.bepress.com/cas/vol4/iss2/art2/.

———. (2011) *Beyond Mechanical Markets: Asset Price Swings, Risk, and the Role of the State*. Princeton, NJ: Princeton University Press.

Frydman, Roman, Michael D. Goldberg, Søren Johansen, and Katarina Juselius. (2012) "Long Swings in Currency Markets: Imperfect Knowledge and I(2) Trends." Working paper, University of Copenhagen, University of New Hampshire, Durham, and New York University, New York.

Goldberg, Michael D., and Roman Frydman. (1996a) "Imperfect Knowledge and Behavior in the Foreign Exchange Market," *Economic Journal* 106: 869–893.

———. (1996b) "Empirical Exchange Rate Models and Shifts in the Co-Integrating Vector," *Journal of Structural Change and Economic Dynamics* 7: 55–78.

Gromb, Denis, and Dimitri Vayanos. (2010) "Limits to Arbitrage: The State of the Theory," *Annual Review of Financial Economics* 2: 251–275.

Johansen, Søren. (1997) "Likelihood Analysis of the $I(2)$ Model," *Scandinavian Journal of Statistics* 24: 433–462.

Johansen, Søren, Katarina Juselius, Roman Frydman, and Michael D. Goldberg. (2010) "Testing Hypotheses in an $I(2)$ Model with Applications to the Persistent Long Swings in the Dmk/$ Rate," *Journal of Econometrics* 158: 117–129.

Juselius, Katarina. (2006) *The Cointegrated VAR Model: Methodology and Applications*. Oxford: Oxford University Press.

Kahneman, Daniel, and Amos Tversky. (1979) "Prospect Theory: An Analysis of Decision under Risk," *Econometrica* 47: 263–291.

Keynes, John Maynard. (1921) *A Treatise on Probability*. London: Macmillan.

———. (1936) *The General Theory of Employment, Interest and Money*. London: Harcourt, Brace and World.

Knight, Frank H. (1921) *Risk, Uncertainty and Profit*. Boston: Houghton Mifflin.

Kongsted, Hans Christian, and Heino B. Nielsen. (2004) "Analyzing $I(2)$ Systems by Transformed Vector Autoregressions," *Oxford Bulletin of Economics and Statistics* 66: 379–397.

Krugman, Paul. (1981) "Consumption Preferences, Asset Demands, and the Distribution Effects in International Financial Markets." NBER Working Paper 651, National Bureau of Economic Research, Cambridge, MA.

Mangee, Nicholas. (2011) "Long Swings in Stock Prices: Market Fundamentals and Psychology." PhD dissertation, University of New Hampshire, Durham.

Mark, Nelson C. (2009) "Changing Monetary Policy Rules, Learning, and Real Exchange Rate Dynamics," *Journal of Money, Credit, and Banking* 41: 1047–1070.

Mark, Nelson C., and Yangru Wu. (1998) "Rethinking Deviations from Uncovered Interest Parity: The Role of Covariance Risk and Noise," *Economic Journal* 108: 1686–1786.

Mehra, Rajnish, and Edward C. Prescott. (1985) "The Equity Premium Puzzle: A Puzzle," *Journal of Monetary Economics* 15: 145–161.

Phelps, Edmund S. (2008) "Our Uncertain Economy," *Wall Street Journal,* March 14, p. A19.

Reinhart, Carmen M., and Kenneth S. Rogoff. (2009) *This Time Is Different: Eight Centuries of Financial Folly.* Princeton, NJ: Princeton University Press.

Schulmeister, Stephan. (2003) "Technical Trading Systems and Stock Price Dynamics." Österreichisches Institut für Wirtschaftsforschung Studie mit Unterstützung des Jubiläumsfonds der Österreichischen Nationalbank, Vienna.

Shiller, Robert J. (2000) *Irrational Exuberance.* New York: Broadway Books.

———. (2003) "From Efficient Markets to Behavioral Finance," *Journal of Economic Perspectives* 17(1): 83–104.

Shleifer, Andrei. (2000) *Inefficient Markets.* Oxford: Oxford University Press.

Stillwagon, Joshua. (2012) "Imperfect Knowledge and Currency Risk: A CVAR Analysis with Survey Data." Working paper, University of New Hampshire, Durham.

Tversky, Amos, and Daniel Kahneman. (1992) "Advances in Prospect Theory: Cumulative Representation of Uncertainty," *Journal of Risk and Uncertainty* 5: 297–323.

Zheng, Liping. (2009) "The Puzzling Behavior of Equity Returns: The Need to Move Beyond the Consumption Capital Asset Pricing Model." PhD dissertation, University of New Hampshire, Durham.

PART THREE

Rethinking Unemployment-Inflation Trade-offs and the Natural Rate Theory

CHAPTER SEVEN

Animal Spirits, Persistent Unemployment, and the Belief Function

Roger E. A. Farmer

7.1 Introduction

This chapter provides an interpretation of persistence in the unemployment rate that draws from two central ideas in Keynes's *General Theory* (1936). The first is that any unemployment rate can persist as an equilibrium. The second is that the unemployment rate that prevails is determined by animal spirits.

Existing nonclassical approaches to economic policy are grounded in New Keynesian economics, an approach based on the idea that there are frictions that prevent prices from quickly adjusting to their Walrasian levels. In this chapter I present a three-equation monetary model that provides an alternative to the New Keynesian representation of the monetary transmission mechanism. Unlike the New Keynesian representation, this alternative is not based on the assumption of sticky prices. My alternative model adds money to a theory of the real economy that I developed in Farmer (2012a): I refer to it as the "Farmer monetary model."[1]

This chapter was prepared for the Center on Capitalism and Society's 8th Annual Conference. I thank Ned Phelps and Roman Frydman for inviting me to write the chapter and Olivier Blanchard, Guillermo Calvo, and Ned Phelps for their comments on my presentation. Thanks also to Leigh Caldwell, Larry Christiano, Eric Leeper, Dmitry Plotnikov, Frank Smets, Harald Uhlig, Yi Wen, and seminar participants at the Paris School of Economics, Duke University, Greqam, and the European Summer Symposium on Macroeconomics. The National Science Foundation funded this research in part through Grant 0720839.

1. In the working paper version of this chapter (Farmer 2010a), I refer to my work as an "old Keynesian" model. I have dropped that nomenclature in the published version, because it is too easily confused with the textbook investment-saving (IS)/liquidity preference–money supply (LM) version of Keynes's *General Theory*. The model developed in Farmer (2010b, 2012a), on which this chapter is based, is distinct from the IS-LM model. The main difference is that my work provides a theory of labor market failure in which any unemployment rate may persist as a long-run steady state equilibrium.

The Farmer monetary model discards the New Keynesian Phillips curve and replaces it with a *belief function* that describes how agents form expectations of future nominal income. I showed in Farmer (2008a,b, 2010b, 2012a) that any unemployment rate is consistent with a zero profit labor market equilibrium by providing a microfounded theory of aggregate supply, based on costly search and recruiting. The Farmer monetary model shares this property and, in addition, any inflation rate is consistent with any unemployment rate in a steady state equilibrium.

This chapter builds and estimates the Farmer monetary model using U.S. data for the period from 1952:Q1 to 2007:Q4. I compare the Farmer monetary model to a New Keynesian model by computing the posterior odds ratio. I find that the posterior odds favor the Farmer monetary model, and I discuss the implications of this finding for fiscal and monetary policy.

7.2   Genesis of the Natural Rate Hypothesis

In 1970 the "Phelps volume" (Phelps et al. 1970) launched an exciting new approach to the microeconomics of employment and inflation theory that was, in the words of Edmund Phelps, "an economics of disequilibrium." That volume collected a set of papers that provided an intellectual foundation for the *expectations-augmented Phillips curve*: the idea that there is a short-run trade-off between inflation and unemployment, but in the long-run, that trade-off disappears and the Phillips curve is vertical.

The Phelps volume helped solidify an interpretation of Keynesian economics that began with Hansen (1936) and Hicks (1937) and was introduced to generations of undergraduates by the third edition of Samuelson's (1955) introductory textbook. In this interpretation, unemployment may fall and GDP may increase following a monetary shock, because prices are sticky. In the long run, GDP returns to its trend growth path, and unemployment returns to its natural rate.

The papers in the Phelps volume aimed to provide a microfoundation for these characteristics of the monetary transmission mechanism. Alchian (1970) talked of information costs, Holt (1970) discussed the role of unions in wage setting, and Phelps (1970) explored a model of staggered wage setting. These papers, and all the others in this remarkable collection, provided an intellectual foundation that evolved into New Keynesian economics in the 1980s.

The idea that demand-management policies cannot influence unemployment in the long run became known as the Natural Rate Hypothesis (NRH). The papers by Phelps (1968) and Friedman (1968), which formulated that hypothesis, were bold innovative steps that challenged the 1960s Keynesian orthodoxy of an exploitable trade-off between inflation and unemployment.

But although the NRH is intellectually appealing, it soon became apparent that the simple form of the NRH is inconsistent with an unemployment rate that has highly persistent long-run movements. Edmund Phelps himself has addressed this problem in his book on structural slumps (Phelps 1994), where he argues that many determinants of the natural rate of unemployment can be influenced by economic policy. In this chapter, I present an alternative explanation of persistent unemployment based on the two central ideas from Keynes's *General Theory* that I alluded to in Section 7.1: any unemployment rate can persist as an equilibrium, and the unemployment rate that prevails is determined by animal spirits.

7.3   New Keynesian Economics

There is a widely held view among economic policymakers that monetary policy can influence real economic activity in the short run, but in the long run, all changes in the quantity of money are reflected in prices. This view was nicely summarized in Hume's (1987 [1777]) essay "Of Money."

In a large and growing literature, researchers have distilled Hume's view into a theory that has become known as New Keynesian economics.[2] In this chapter I frequently refer to the "canonical New Keynesian model." By this term, I mean a three-equation monetary model, based on dynamic stochastic general equilibrium theory, that encapsulates the main insights of David Hume's essay.

The New Keynesian model is described by

$$ay_t = aE_t\left[y_{t+1}\right] - i_t + E_t\left[\pi_{t+1}\right] + \rho + z_t^d \tag{1}$$

$$i_t = \lambda\pi_t + \mu y_t + b \tag{2}$$

$$\pi_t = \beta E_t\left[\pi_{t+1}\right] + \phi\left(y_t - z_t^s\right) \tag{3}$$

Here, y_t is the logarithm of GDP; π_t is inflation; i_t is the interest rate; and z_t^d and z_t^s are demand and supply shocks, respectively. The expectations operator is $E\left[\cdot\right]$, and I assume that expectations are rational and hence expectations are taken with respect to an equilibrium probability measure. The intertemporal elasticity of substitution is a; ρ is the rate of time preference; λ, μ, and b are policy parameters; and β and ϕ are parameters of the Phillips curve.

Equation (1) is an optimizing IS curve that is derived from a representative agent's Euler equation. Equation (2) is the Taylor rule (Taylor 1999), a description of central bank policy that John Taylor has argued is a good description of how the Federal Reserve behaves in practice, and (3) is the

---

2. As I argue in Farmer (2010c: 78), New Keynesian economics has much more in common with the quantity theory of money than it does with the economics of Keynes's *General Theory*. Because the misnomer is by now well established, I will continue to use the term "New Keynesian economics" in this chapter in the same way that it is used elsewhere in the literature.

New Keynesian Phillips curve. Derivations of the New Keynesian Phillips curve, based on Calvo's (1983) elegant model of sticky prices, can be found in the books by Galí (2008) or Woodford (2003) and in the survey paper by Clarida et al. (1999).

As long as policy is active in the sense that the central bank responds to inflation by raising the expected real interest rate (Leeper 1991), the New Keynesian model has a unique rational expectations equilibrium given by

$$y_t = \alpha_y + \alpha_{yd} z_t^d + \alpha_{ys} z_t^s \tag{4}$$

$$\pi_t = \alpha_\pi + \alpha_{\pi d} z_t^d + \alpha_{\pi s} z_t^s \tag{5}$$

$$i_t = \alpha_i + \alpha_{id} z_t^d + \alpha_{is} z_t^s \tag{6}$$

where the coefficients $\alpha_{i,j}$ are functions of the structural parameters. These equations are derived by

1. assuming that a rational expectations equilibrium is a stationary probability measure that describes how endogenous variables respond to the state variables and to random shocks and

2. using the stationarity assumption and the assumption that shocks are bounded to eliminate the influence of unstable roots from (1)–(3).

7.4   A Preview of an Alternative Approach

In a model of the real economy that I developed in Farmer (2012a), I showed that the absence of a complete set of markets in a labor search model leads to a steady state indeterminacy in the labor market: any unemployment rate can be a steady state equilibrium. Indeterminacy arises because I retain the assumption that firms and workers are price takers, and I drop the assumption of Nash bargaining over wages. That leads to a model with fewer steady state equations than unknowns.

To resolve the indeterminacy of equilibrium, I assume that output is determined by aggregate demand, which, in turn, depends on the value of aggregate wealth. I showed that for every belief about the real value of wealth, there is a self-fulfilling equilibrium. The current chapter extends that idea to a monetary economy.

My work is related to the fundamental contributions of Shell (1977), Azariadis (1981), and Cass and Shell (1983), who showed that, in the presence of market failures, equilibria may exist in which sunspots (non-fundamental shocks to beliefs) can influence economic outcomes. That work inspired Benhabib and Farmer (1994), Farmer and Guo (1994), and many others to construct models in which there are many paths leading to a unique steady state (see the survey by Benhabib and Farmer 1999).

By randomizing over the paths that lead back to the steady state, that literature showed that there may exist business cycle models that replicate the features of a real business cycle economy, but their movements in economic activity are caused, not by fundamental shocks to productivity, but by nonfundamental shocks to beliefs. In a series of books and papers (Farmer 2008a,b, 2010b,d, 2012a) I have taken this agenda one step further by constructing models in which there is not just an indeterminacy of paths: there is also an indeterminacy of the steady state.

When a general equilibrium model has multiple equilibria, the theory must be supplemented by an additional equation that resolves the indeterminacy by explaining how people in the model would behave. In the model that I developed in Farmer (2012a), there are not enough equations to determine a unique labor market equilibrium. Standard search models are closed with the Nash bargaining assumption. My model is closed, instead, by a theory of beliefs. I view the function that determines beliefs as an additional fundamental with the same methodological status as preferences, endowments, and technologies. Because the belief function replaces the Nash bargaining equation and is itself fundamental, I am able to retain the assumption that expectations are rational in the sense that one-step-ahead forecast errors have zero mean.[3]

7.5 Five Problems with New Keynesian Economics

In this section I raise five objections to the canonical New Keynesian model: (1) it assumes that prices are implausibly sticky; (2) it cannot explain inflation persistence in data; (3) there is no unemployment in the model; (4) the welfare costs of business cycles are trivial; and (5) the model cannot explain bubbles and crashes.

7.5.1 Prices Are Implausibly Sticky

The core of New Keynesian economics is the New Keynesian Phillips curve (3). There are two main ways that this equation has been derived in the literature. Both involve variants of the cost of changing nominal prices. Rotemberg (1982) assumes a quadratic cost of price adjustment; Yun

---

3. As Frydman and Goldberg (2011; Chapter 4, this volume) point out, the rational expectations assumption imposes an unrealistic burden on agents who cannot be expected to act rationally in a world in which future events are unforecastable. However, in a model like the one I consider here, in which almost any path for future prices is consistent with equilibrium, it is no longer clear that there is much difference between rational expectations equilibria and nonrational expectations equilibria. Any sample path could conceivably be rationalized as the outcome of some nonstationary sequence of beliefs.

(1996), drawing on work by Calvo (1983), assumes that a fixed fraction of agents reset their prices in each period.

Studies of price change in large micro datasets have been used to evaluate the New Keynesian assumption that prices are sticky. The evidence from this literature suggests that price stickiness at the micro level is not large enough for the New Keynesian model to explain the aggregate data. In their *Handbook* survey, Klenow and Malin (2010: 278) conclude that

> Prices change quite frequently, although much of this flexibility is associated with price movements that are temporary in nature. Even if all short-lived prices are excluded, however, the resulting nominal stickiness, by itself, appears insufficient to account for the sluggish movement of aggregate prices.

Klenow and Malin suggest that a coordination failure may cause agents to act in ways that make aggregate prices more sluggish than individual prices. That is a possible explanation of the disparity between the micro and macro evidence—but it is not an assumption of the canonical New Keynesian model.[4]

7.5.2 *Inflation Is Persistent*

Macroeconomic evidence from vector autoregressions suggests that prices move less than one would expect based on the Walrasian market clearing model. In addition, *inflation* is highly persistent in U.S. data. In vector autoregressions using data from 1950 through 1980, lagged inflation is the only significant predictor of current inflation. For that period, inflation is well described by a random walk. After 1980, inflation is less persistent, but there is still a significant role for lagged inflation in reduced-form representations of the data (Beyer and Farmer 2007).

The New Keynesian model can explain sticky prices, but it cannot explain persistence in the inflation rate. It is possible to modify the model by adding habit persistence to preferences and a lagged interest rate to the policy rule. These modifications imply that the lagged interest rate and lagged GDP should be included in the reduced form of the model as state variables and they help explain persistence in GDP and the interest rate (Beyer et al. 2008). It is much harder to find a plausible modification to the New Keynesian model that gives a role to lagged inflation while maintaining the core assumption of rational agents.

---

4. Some progress has been made on models of rational inattention (Sims 2010) and the related concept of sticky information (Mankiw and Reis 2002), but neither of these ideas has yet been fully incorporated into New Keynesian theory.

Fuhrer and Moore (1995) write down a contracting model that can lead to inflation persistence. Although the Fuhrer-Moore modification can produce a role for lagged inflation in the Phillips curve, it is not clear why the contracts they consider would be signed by rational agents, a point first made by Barro (1977) in his critique of the first generation of contracting papers (Fischer 1977).

7.5.3 There Is No Unemployment

Because the New Keynesian model has a classical core, the canonical model does not explain unemployment. The New Keynesians accepted the arguments of Lucas and Rapping (1970) that the labor market should be modeled as an equilibrium in the classical sense: the supply of labor is equal to the demand for labor at the observed wage.

Gertler and Trigari (2009) have added unemployment to the New Keynesian model, and Gertler et al. (2008) find that the model augmented in this way can explain the data about as well as similar New Keynesian models. The version of the New Keynesian model that they develop is similar to the theory I describe in Section 7.6. Their model is closed with a wage equation based on long-term contracts. Because this equation leads to a unique unemployment rate in the long run, their model preserves the NRH.

In my own work, I drop the wage equation and replace it with a model in which beliefs enter as a fundamental. This leads to a model in which there *is no natural rate of unemployment*. As a consequence, my work can explain the persistence of unemployment without making arbitrary and unrealistic assumptions about the costs of changing money wages.

7.5.4 Welfare Costs of Business Cycles Are Small

According to the New Keynesian model, business cycles are caused by demand and supply shocks that generate autocorrelated movements of output and GDP around a social planning optimum.[5] The equations of the model are derived from an equilibrium business cycle model with added frictions, such as money in the utility function or the Calvo (1983) pricing rule. These frictions prevent the equilibrium of the model from adjusting quickly to the social planning optimum.

Although frictions could potentially explain large welfare losses, calibrated models fail to deliver on this promise. When the canonical model

---

5. This position is sometimes modified to recognize that the steady state of the model may deviate from the social planning optimum because of tax distortions or monopolistic competition. These modifications do not alter the fact that the welfare costs of business cycles in this model are trivial.

is calibrated to realistic parameter values, Galí et al. (2007) have shown that the magnitude of the distortions caused by New Keynesian frictions is comparable to the numbers found by Lucas (1987) in his study of equilibrium business cycle models. These distortions can be responsible for at most one-tenth of 1% of steady state consumption.

That a model based on the equilibrium assumption cannot generate large welfare losses would not have surprised James Tobin. Around the time that Ned Phelps and Milton Friedman formulated the NRH, Tobin quipped that "it takes a lot of Harberger triangles to fill an Okun gap." In other words, the distortions caused by what today we would refer to as "wedges" (Chari et al. 2007) are small relative to large movements in the unemployment rate during major recessions. The New Keynesian model cannot explain why we should care about recessions, because business cycles in this model have trivial effects on people's lives.

7.5.5 The Model Cannot Explain Bubbles and Crashes

In his *General Theory,* Keynes (1936) stressed the importance of animal spirits as an independent driving force in the economy. In his view, the stock market crash of 1929 *caused* the Great Depression. In my own work (Farmer 2012b), I have argued that the stock market crash of 2008 *caused* the Great Recession. New Keynesian economics does not have room for that idea. The 2008 financial crisis is widely thought to have been triggered by the bursting of a bubble—a large inflation in asset prices that was not associated with fundamentals. The New Keynesian model cannot explain an asset price bubble, because equilibria in the model are driven by fundamentals.

The assertion by Keynes that nonfundamental market movements caused the Great Depression is not evidence for or against that proposition. And the assertion by many economists that the 2008 crash was caused by the collapse of a bubble does not make it so. To compare the bubble hypothesis with alternative explanations, we need a theory of bubbles that is consistent with microeconomic principles and can be consistently articulated and compared with the alternatives.

What is needed to advance our understanding is a model of markets that preserves no-arbitrage pricing but allows for independent movements in asset prices. In Farmer (2011), I have shown that the Farmer (2012a) model *can* explain asset price bubbles. The model admits equilibria in which beliefs are driven by an independent fundamental shock, and asset values can take on many different values, including those of explosive bubbles. In this environment, the collapse of an asset bubble is fully consistent with rational behavior on the part of forward-looking agents, and that collapse can have devastating effects on unemployment and economic welfare.

7.5.6 Should My Objections to the New Keynesian Model Be Taken Seriously?

A defender of the New Keynesian approach will object that I am setting up a straw man and will claim that all the problems mentioned are well known and have been addressed in the literature. Although there is a sense in which the latter claim is correct, the defenses necessary to support the theory against my five objections are, in my view, a sign of what Lakatos (1978) referred to as a "degenerative" research program.

In 1543, Copernicus introduced the sun-centered theory of the solar system. Ptolemy's theory, which preceded that of Copernicus, placed the earth at the center of the universe; that theory was initially better at computing the motion of the planets than that of Copernicus. But Ptolemy's theory was successful only through repeated and increasingly implausible modifications to the concentric circles that described the orbits of the planets (Kuhn 1957).

The modifications that allow New Keynesian economics to explain the data are similar to the addition of the concentric circles used to allow Ptolemy's theory to fit new data. When new evidence contradicts a pillar of the New Keynesian theory, a piece is tacked on to the theory to account for the anomaly. A subset of irrational agents accounts for bubbles as in Kyle (1985). A concern for relative wages accounts for inflation persistence as in Fuhrer and Moore (1995). Wage contracting accounts for persistent unemployment as in Gertler and Trigari (2009). These modifications have been relatively successful at explaining data from the 1980s and 1990s. The 2008 financial crisis presents a major new challenge.

The New Keynesian model is not a convincing theory of major recessions. During the Great Depression, unemployment remained above 10% for a decade, and in the 2008 financial crisis it has remained above 8% for 39 months in a row with no sign of a return to more normal levels as of June 2012. We need a more radical departure from classical economics that can explain persistently high unemployment. My model *can* explain why high unemployment persists, and as I demonstrate below, it can also account for variations in output and inflation in more normal times.

7.6 Keynesian Economics without Sticky Prices: A Monetary Version of the Farmer Model

Keynes's *General Theory* (1936) argued that persistent unemployment is a pervasive feature of market economies. In modern language, we would describe that idea as a possibility for the economy to display a continuum of steady state unemployment rates. That idea was replaced by post-war interpreters of Keynes, who appended the Phillips curve to the IS-LM model and created a synthesis of Keynesian and classical ideas that evolved into the current mainstream New Keynesian paradigm. In New Keynesian economics, there is a unique steady state unemployment rate: the natural rate of unemployment.

This section describes an alternative theory of aggregate employment based on the Farmer (2012a) model.[6] There, I introduced the idea that high unemployment can persist as a steady state equilibrium, and I selected a specific equilibrium by introducing beliefs as an independent driving variable. The theory of employment that I developed was based on the economics of costly search that first appeared in papers by Alchian (1970) and Mortensen (1970) in the Phelps volume published more than 40 years ago. Here I sketch the main properties of that theory. In Section 7.7, I use it to present an alternative to the New Keynesian theory of the monetary transmission mechanism.

7.6.1 Technology in the Farmer Model

The Farmer (2012a) model explains unemployment as an equilibrium in an economy in which there are two different technologies: a production technology for producing goods from labor and capital, and a search technology for moving workers between leisure and productive activities.

Aggregate output is produced from the production technology

$$\bar{Y}_t = \bar{K}_t^{\alpha} \bar{X}_t^{1-\alpha} \tag{7}$$

where $\bar{Y}_t$ is output, $\bar{X}_t$ is labor used in production, $\bar{K}_t$ is capital, and a bar over a variable denotes the economywide average.

Workers are moved from home to work using a search technology. This takes the form

$$\bar{L}_t = \bar{H}_t^{1/2} \left(\Gamma \bar{V}_t \right)^{1/2} \tag{8}$$

where Γ is a parameter, $\bar{V}_t$ is the number of workers assigned to the task of recruiting, and $\bar{H}_t$ is the measure of workers searching for a job. The variables $\bar{V}_t$, $\bar{L}_t$, and $\bar{X}_t$ are constrained by the identity

$$\bar{L}_t \equiv \bar{V}_t + \bar{X}_t \tag{9}$$

These assumptions are relatively standard in search theory. The main difference from more mainstream approaches is my assumption that firms

---

6. The theory is explained in more depth in Farmer (2008a,b, 2010b, 2012a), where I referred to it as "old Keynesian economics." The closest precedent to old Keynesian economics is the hysteresis theory of Blanchard and Summers (1986, 1987), in which the unemployment rate is path dependent because of insider-outsider behavior in wage bargaining.

take the wage and the price as given. Howitt and McAfee (1987) pointed out that this assumption leads to a continuum of unemployment rates in a model with costly search and recruiting. I exploit this observation to construct a general equilibrium model with many steady state equilibrium unemployment rates.

7.6.2 Profit Maximization

The production technology is operated by a large number of competitive firms, each of which solves the problem

$$\max_{Y_t, K_t, V_t, X_t, L_t} \Pi_t = P_t Y_t - w_t L_t - r_t K_t \tag{10}$$

$$Y_t \leq K_t^{\alpha} X_t^{1-\alpha} \tag{11}$$

$$L_t = q_t V_t \tag{12}$$

$$L_t = X_t + V_t \tag{13}$$

Here, Π_t is profit, P_t is the price of commodities, w_t is the money wage, and r_t is the rental rate for capital. Firms take P_t, w_t, r_t, and q_t as given, where q_t is the number of workers that can be hired by one worker assigned to the recruiting department.

At the beginning of time, a measure one of workers looks for jobs. Firms put together plans that allocate a fraction V_t/L_t of workers to the recruiting department and the remaining X_t/L_t of workers to production. To keep the dynamics as close as possible to those of the standard model, I assume that the entire workforce is fired at the end of every period, and next period, the process begins again.[7]

Substituting (11)–(13) into (10) and defining

$$\Theta_t \equiv \left(1 - \frac{1}{q_t}\right) \tag{14}$$

leads to the reduced-form problem

$$\max_{K_t, L_t} \Pi_t = P_t K_t^{\alpha} \left(\Theta_t L_t\right)^{1-\alpha} - w_t L_t - r_t K_t \tag{15}$$

---

7. Thus, workers are allowed to recruit themselves. This improbable assumption is a convenient way of reducing the dynamics of the model, and it considerably simplifies the exposition of the theory. More generally, employment should appear as a state variable governed by the equation

$$\bar{L}_{t+1} = (1 - \delta_L)\,\bar{L}_t + B U_t^{\theta} V_t^{1-\theta}$$

where δ_L, B, and θ are parameters, and U_t is the unemployment rate.

which has the same first-order conditions as a standard competitive model. These are represented by

$$(1 - \alpha) \, P_t Y_t = w_t L_t \tag{16}$$

$$\alpha P_t Y_t = r_t K_t \tag{17}$$

7.6.3 Search Theory without the Nash Bargain

In a classical model, firms and households take prices and wages as given. In Farmer's model, they also take the externality Θ_t as given. For every value of Θ_t there is a profit-maximizing labor demand decision in which the firm equates the marginal product of labor to the real wage. When output is produced from a Cobb-Douglas technology by competitive firms, this leads to (16), the first-order condition for choice of labor by firms.

In a standard search model, one appends an additional equation to the model to determine the wage. Typically, this is the Nash bargaining assumption. When a firm and a worker meet, there is a surplus to be split. The firm would be willing to pay any wage up to and including the worker's marginal product. The worker would accept any wage greater than or equal to his reservation wage. Mortensen and Pissarides (1994) assume that the wage is determined by bargaining over the surplus, which is split according to a bargaining weight χ. This weight is a free parameter, which is often chosen to match employment in the search model with the level that maximizes worker utility.

In my model, I do not use the Nash bargaining equation. I assume instead that the externality Θ_t is a variable to be determined by the assumption that the corporate sector produces enough goods to meet aggregate demand. Once Θ_t is determined, the real wage, unemployment, and GDP are determined from profit-maximizing behavior by firms. In my previous work, I showed how to determine Θ_t from the self-fulfilling beliefs of households about the value of wealth. Farmer's model, closed in that way, provides an explanation of aggregate variables in which beliefs are a driving force of business cycles.

7.7 Animal Spirits and the Belief Function

The New Keynesian model is popular, because it provides a tractable explanation of the data, summarized in the three-equation model described in Section 7.3. In this section I develop a counterpart to that model grounded in a search theory of unemployment. The main difference between the two approaches is that my work gives a central role to the idea that animal spirits matter. In the New Keynesian approach, in contrast, expectations are determined by market fundamentals.

In my model, confidence is an independent driving force that selects the long-run steady state unemployment rate. In my previous work (Farmer

2012a), I modeled that idea by assuming that households' beliefs about asset prices are determined by market psychology. Here I model the evolution of beliefs about nominal GDP by introducing a new fundamental equation: the *belief function*.

Models of self-fulfilling beliefs are often criticized as incomplete theories because they are based on general equilibrium models in which equilibrium is indeterminate. I have argued elsewhere (Farmer 1999) that this is a mistaken criticism. When a general equilibrium model has multiple equilibria, the theory must be supplemented by an additional equation that resolves the indeterminacy by explaining how people in the model would behave. Standard search models are closed with the Nash bargaining assumption. I close my model with a theory of beliefs.

$$ay_t = aE_t\left[y_{t+1}\right] - i_t + E_t\left[\pi_{t+1}\right] + \rho + z_t^d \qquad (18)$$

$$i_t = \lambda\pi_t + \mu y_t + b \qquad (19)$$

$$E_t\left[\pi_{t+1}\right] + \left(E_t\left[y_{t+1}\right] - y_t\right) = \pi_t + \left(y_t - y_{t-1}\right) + z_t^s \qquad (20)$$

Equations (18)–(20) represent a three-equation model that is implied by the Farmer monetary theory of aggregate supply. Equations (18) and (19) are identical with (1) and (2) of the New Keynesian model. Equation (20) provides a theory of how agents forecast the future. I call this equation the "belief function."

If we let p_t be the logarithm of the price level, then

$$x_t = p_t + y_t \qquad (21)$$

is the logarithm of nominal GDP. The belief function is equivalent to the assumption that

$$E_t\left[\Delta x_{t+1}\right] = \Delta x_t + z_t^s \qquad (22)$$

where Δ is the difference operator, and z_t^s is a fundamental random variable that represents shocks to beliefs. In words, agents believe that the growth rate of nominal GDP follows a random walk.[8]

The belief function is not an alternative to the rational expectations assumption. It is an addition to it. I still assume that

$$y_t - E_{t-1}\left[y_t\right] = w_t^y \qquad (23)$$

and

$$\pi_t - E_{t-1}\left[\pi_t\right] = w_t^\pi \qquad (24)$$

---

8. Because I have defined y_t as log (deviation of GDP from trend), the drift component of the random walk has been removed in the detrending operation.

where w_t^y and w_t^π are endogenously determined random variables with conditional mean zero.

Agents in the model developed here form expectations of nominal GDP growth based on their observation of current nominal GDP growth. The belief function provides an anchor to their expectations. Given the belief function (20), the IS curve (18) interacts with the policy rule (19) to determine the realization of inflation and output growth in period t.

7.8 Long-Run Properties of the Two Models

If one identifies the long run with the nonstochastic steady state of a model, the steady values of inflation, the interest rate, and the deviation of output from trend for the New Keynesian model are given by

$$\bar\pi = \frac{\phi\,(\rho - b)}{\phi\,(\lambda - 1) + \mu\,(1 - \beta)}, \qquad \bar\imath = \rho + \bar\pi, \qquad \bar y = \bar\pi\frac{(1 - \beta)}{\phi} \qquad (25)$$

When $\beta = 1$, these equations simplify to give the approximate steady state solution[9]

$$\bar\pi = \frac{\rho - b}{\lambda - 1}, \qquad \bar\imath = \rho + \bar\pi, \qquad \bar y = 0 \qquad (26)$$

These expressions demonstrate that, in the New Keynesian model, the central bank can influence inflation through its choice of b; but the steady state deviation of GDP from trend is equal to zero. Thus, demand management policy cannot affect real economic activity in the long run, and it is a direct corollary of the NRH, stated in terms of the output gap y.

The expressions for steady state variables given in (25) are found by solving the steady state versions of (1)–(3). In contrast, the Farmer monetary model has only two steady state equations to determine three steady state variables, because $\bar y$, $\bar\pi$, and $\bar\imath$ all cancel from (20). This leaves the expressions

$$\bar\imath - \rho + \bar\pi = 0 \qquad (27)$$

$$\bar\imath = b + \lambda\bar\pi + \mu\bar y \qquad (28)$$

to determine $\bar y$, $\bar\pi$, and $\bar\imath$.

7.8.1 Why the Farmer Monetary Model Is a Good Description of the Data

The reduced form of the Farmer monetary model is a cointegrated vector autoregression. In the three-dimensional space spanned by inflation, the

---

9. This is a good approximation, because β represents the discount rate, which is close to 1 in practice.

output gap, and the interest rate, the model pins down a one-dimensional manifold that the data cluster around. Fed policy can decide how movements in nominal GDP are divided between movements in real output and inflation, but it cannot stabilize all three variables at the same time. This predicted theoretical behavior describes the data well. The interest rate, inflation, and deviation of GDP from trend are all highly autocorrelated, and one cannot reject the hypothesis that each series is individually nonstationary, but the series are connected by two cointegrating vectors.[10]

7.8.2 *Why the New Keynesian Model Does Not Support Policy Activism*

In the New Keynesian model, the variable z_t^s represents the time-varying value of potential output. A crude form of the NRH would assert that z_t^s is white noise. If this were true, the deviation of GDP from trend would quickly revert to the mean, a property that is strongly contradicted in the data. For the New Keynesian model to fit the facts, z_t^s must be highly autocorrelated. This implies that persistent unemployment is a consequence of permanent shifts in supply-side factors, such as population demographics or industrial composition. In other words, New Keynesian economics implies that there is nothing that demand management policy can do to alleviate the very high unemployment that often follows a major recession like the 2008 financial crisis.

7.9 Data Used in This Study

How well do the two models explain the data? To address this question, I used full-information Bayesian methods to estimate both models on U.S. time-series data from 1952:Q1 through 2007:Q4.

I excluded data from the 2008 financial crisis, because the interest rate for that period was constrained by the zero lower bound.[11] I used the Treasury bill rate, the CPI inflation rate, and a measure of the percentage deviation of real GDP from a linear time trend. These data are graphed in Figure 7.1.

10. The variable y_t represents the deviation of GDP from a linear trend, and although this variable does not have a systematic drift component, it has a root close to or equal to one. The current chapter draws on joint work with Andreas Beyer (Beyer and Farmer 2007). The work shows that the behavior of inflation, the interest rate, and unemployment are well described by a cointegrated vector autoregression.

11. In 1979:Q3, Paul Volcker took over as chairman of the Federal Reserve, and for the period from 1979:Q3 through 1982:Q4, the Fed is known to have used an operating procedure in which it targeted the rate of growth of the money supply. To check for robustness of my estimates, I estimated the two models over the full sample and over two separate subperiods. The first subperiod was from 1952:Q1 through 1979:Q3 and the second from 1983:Q1 through 2007:Q4. The estimates for the subperiods gave similar results to the full sample results reported here.

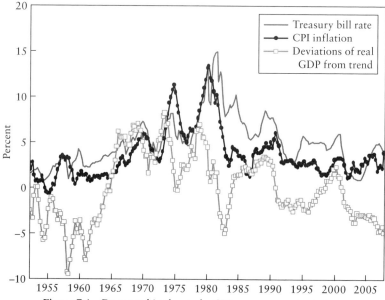

Figure 7.1 Data used in the study. CPI, consumer price index.

For comparison with earlier studies (Lubik and Schorfheide 2004), I allowed for autocorrelated demand and supply shocks in the New Keynesian model, and I allowed for slow adjustment of the policy rule by including the lagged interest rate in this equation. I also added an autocorrelated policy disturbance. This specification of the New Keynesian model leaves residuals that are approximately white noise.[12] For each model, I replaced their respective policy rules (2) and (19) by

$$i_t = b + (1 - \eta)\left(\lambda\pi_t + \mu y_t\right) + \eta i_{t-1} + z_t^i \tag{29}$$

$$z_t^i = \lambda^i z_{t-1}^i + \varepsilon_t^i \tag{30}$$

In practice, I found that the constant b in the policy rule was insignificantly different from zero in both specifications. For both models, I allowed z_t^d and z_t^s to follow the autocorrelated processes

$$z_t^d = \lambda^d z_{t-1}^d + \varepsilon_t^d \tag{31}$$

$$z_t^s = \lambda^s z_{t-1}^s + \varepsilon_t^s \tag{32}$$

---

12. I use the word "approximately" loosely. The correlogram of each series displays little or no autocorrelation, but there is fairly strong evidence of heteroskedasticity. The mean of each series is zero by construction.

and the innovations ε_t^d, ε_t^s, and ε_t^i were allowed to be correlated. For the Farmer monetary model, the parameter η in the policy rule and the autocorrelation parameter λ^s were insignificant, and I set those parameters to zero and left them out of the results reported in the next section.

7.10   Empirical Results

To estimate the two models, I computed the likelihood function from the Kalman filter and used Markov-chain Monte Carlo simulations to draw from the posterior. Table 7.1 reports the log data density and the posterior odds ratio for the two models.

The posterior odds ratio for these models is equal to 0.0058. This is a number that can vary between 0 and ∞, where 0 means that the data overwhelmingly supports the Farmer monetary model over the New Keynesian model, and ∞ means that it overwhelmingly rejects it. The reported value of 0.0058 is evidence in favor of my interpretation of the facts.

The estimates of the smoothed residuals from the Kalman filter, ε_t^d, ε_t^s, and ε_t^i, are graphed in Figure 7.2. Because z_t^s enters the New Keynesian and Farmer monetary models with a different sign, I have graphed the negative of ε_t^s for the Farmer monetary model. The model assumes that these shocks are normal random variables with constant variance. The constant variance assumption appears to be violated for the period from 1979:Q3 to 1982:Q4, when the Fed is known to have followed a different operating procedure. The demand shocks and the policy shocks for this period are much larger than at the beginning and end of the sample.[13]

Graphs of the prior and posterior parameter distributions are reported in Figures 7.A1–7.A4 of the Appendix. The figures suggest that the parameters λ, μ, and λ^d are not identified in the New Keynesian model. The parameter λ is the policy response to inflation, μ is the response to GDP, and λ^d is the autocorrelation of the demand shock. Lack of identification is reflected in the fact that the posterior distributions for these parameters are equal to the priors. In contrast, the parameters of the Farmer monetary model are all identified.[14]

---

13. Histograms of the smoothed residuals are reported in the working paper version of this chapter (Farmer 2010a).

14. I also tested the random walk assumption by modifying (22) as

$$E_t \left[\Delta x_{t+1} \right] = \phi \Delta x_t + z_t^s \tag{33}$$

and by allowing z_t^s to be autocorrelated. The data strongly favored the restriction $\phi = 1$ and $\lambda^s = 0$, and I imposed those restrictions in the reported estimates.

Table 7.1 Model comparison of the New Keynesian and Farmer models

Sample 1952.1:2007.4	Log data density
New Keynesian model	2324.10
Farmer monetary model	2329.25
Posterior odds ratio of New Keynesian model versus Farmer model	0.0058

Note: Results are from 10^5 draws from Markov-chain Monte Carlo simulations.

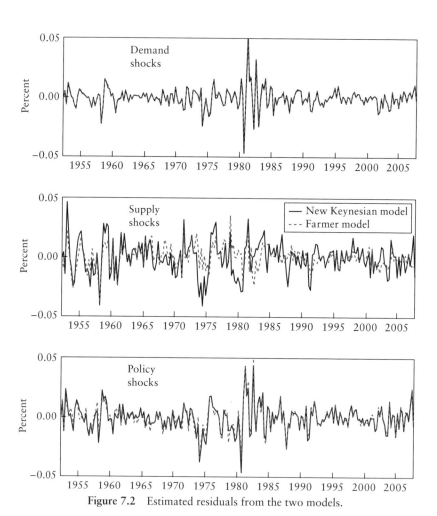

Figure 7.2 Estimated residuals from the two models.

7.11 The Implications of These Results for Economic Policy

What should one take away from these results? I do not want to overstate the evidence in favor of my approach, because one should not read too much into estimates based on a single dataset. As Sims (1980) pointed out, identification in rational expectations models is fragile.[15] An example of just how fragile is provided by Beyer and Farmer (2008), who show that there is an equivalence between New Keynesian rational expectations models with a unique determinate equilibrium and indeterminate monetary models of the kind studied by Benhabib and Farmer (2000) that are driven by self-fulfilling beliefs.[16]

7.11.1 How the New Keynesian Model Explains Persistent Unemployment

Suppose the reader has a strong prior that the New Keynesian model is correct and that the unemployment rate and the output gap really are reverting to unique fundamental values. Suppose further that the Phillips curve is the right way to close a three-equation model, as opposed to the Farmer monetary model's belief function. How does that influence one's beliefs about the role of active policy to combat a recession?

To explain the data, the New Keynesian model must attribute much of the persistence in the unemployment rate to movements in the natural rate of unemployment. In that model, the output gap is persistent because the supply disturbance z_t^s has a root λ^s that is close to one. The median of the posterior of λ^s is 0.985, and 95% of its probability mass is above 0.97.

That z_t^s has a root close to unity is a problem for New Keynesians who favor policy activism. The variable z_t^s does not represent demand disturbances that cause the unemployment rate to be away from its natural rate because of sticky prices. It represents movements of the natural rate itself. A New Keynesian can explain persistence in the unemployment rate only by arguing that the new, higher, unemployment rate following a financial crisis is due to a structural change. It is a short step to arguing that the natural unemployment rate is efficient, and that the market should be left to recover on its own. When λ_t^s is 0.985, as my estimates suggest, the mean time for the rate of unemployment rate to return to its natural rate is 17 years.

---

15. I am certain that a perseverant New Keynesian would be able to find a variant of the New Keynesian model that reverses the conclusion I have presented in this chapter.

16. One way to tell two models apart is to experiment by changing the policy rule. Beyer and Farmer (2003) suggest that evidence can be accumulated by comparing periods over which policy rules changed, but to date, there have not been good examples of conclusive policy experiments of this kind.

7.11.2 How the Farmer Monetary Model Explains Persistent Unemployment

In contrast, if the Farmer monetary model is true, the output gap, inflation, and interest rate are random walks with drift. The unit root in the data arises from drift in the money value of GDP caused by self-fulfilling shifts in expectations of future aggregate demand. The Fed can decide how much of the drift in nominal GDP causes an increase in inflation and how much causes an increase in the output gap. But it cannot independently stabilize both variables.

The Farmer monetary model is eclectic in its implications for fiscal policy (Farmer 2010d). In the three-equation version of the Farmer monetary model presented here, fiscal policy appears as a component of the demand shock z_t^d. It is consistent with the results presented here for z_t^d to be independent of fiscal policy. It is also possible that z_t^d has a nonzero mean that is influenced by tax and expenditure policies. I did not allow for that possibility in this study, because the mean of z_t^d and the rate of time preference ρ cannot be separately identified. What is certain is that if fiscal policy *is* effective, then my model provides support for its use in times of high unemployment to increase aggregate demand.

Although fiscal policy might be effective, I am skeptical that it is the best solution to the current crisis. Farmer and Plotnikov (2012) have shown that a real version of the model developed here can be a correct description of what goes wrong in a financial crisis, but that need not lead one to support fiscal policy as a remedy for inefficiently high unemployment. That depends on the determinants of aggregate demand. If one believes, as I do, that consumption depends on wealth and not on income, then fiscal policy may not be the panacea that its proponents claim. Instead, as I argue in Farmer (2010d), a variant of monetary policy in which the Fed directly stabilizes a stock market index could provide a more effective way of restoring confidence in the markets and moving the economy back toward a full employment equilibrium.

7.12 Conclusion

Forty years ago the Phelps volume gave us a new way of thinking about the relationship between inflation and unemployment. That volume contained the seeds of several important research programs that followed. Lucas and Rapping (1970) provided the genesis of new classical economics by showing how to model employment as an equilibrium phenomenon. Alchian (1970) and Mortensen (1970) laid the foundation for a search theory of unemployment that was rewarded with Nobel prizes for search theory in 2010 to Peter Diamond, Dale Mortensen, and Chris Pissarides. In the same volume Phelps (1970) gave us the NRH.

In this chapter, I hope to have persuaded economists to think about unemployment and inflation in a new way. The relationship we have observed in data between these two variables does not arise from sticky prices adjusting to disequilibrium. It arises from the interaction of demand and supply shocks in a world where the forecasts made by households and firms have real consequences for what happens in the marketplace. Confidence is the new fundamental, and the role of confidence is captured by the belief function—a replacement for the Phillips curve.

My ideas have been hugely influenced by the papers in the Phelps volume. But they have also been hugely influenced by current national and global events. The dominant empirical fact of the 1970s was the emergence of stagflation. Arguably, it was that fact that led Milton Friedman and Edmund Phelps to argue that there is no long-run trade-off between inflation and unemployment. The theory sketched here preserves that idea. But the absence of a Phillips curve does not imply that unemployment is efficient; nor does it imply that we must accept persistently high unemployment as the cost of living in a market economy.

Appendix   Parameter Estimates

Figures 7.A1–7.A4 present prior and posterior distributions for the two models. In each case, I used Markov-chain Monte-Carlo methods to draw

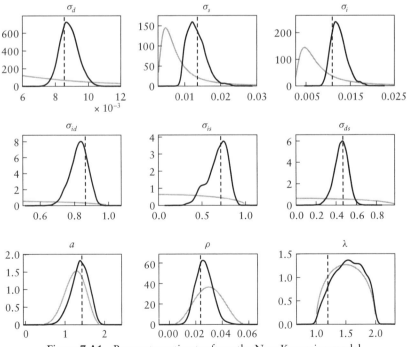

Figure 7.A1   Parameter estimates from the New Keynesian model.

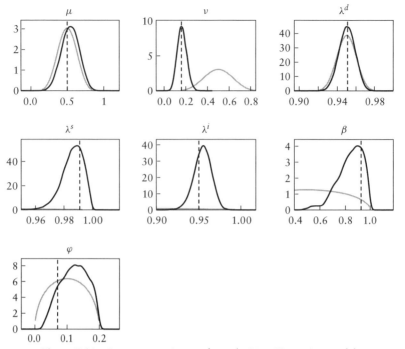

Figure 7.A2   Parameter estimates from the New Keynesian model.

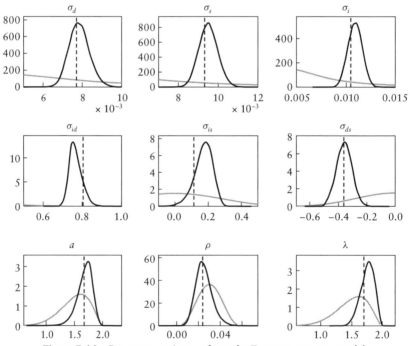

Figure 7.A3   Parameter estimates from the Farmer monetary model.

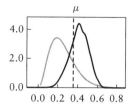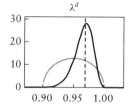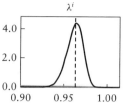

Figure 7.A4 Parameter estimates from the Farmer monetary model.

200,000 times from the posterior, and I discarded the first 100,000 draws. The dashed line in each case is the maximum likelihood estimate. The dark curve is the posterior parameter estimate, and the light curve is the prior.

References

Alchian, A. A. (1970) "Information Costs, Pricing, and Resource Unemployment," in E. S. Phelps, G. C. Archibald, and A. A. Alchian (eds.), *Microeconomic Foundations of Employment and Inflation Theory*. New York: W. W. Norton, pp. 27–52.

Azariadis, C. (1981) "Self-Fulfilling Prophecies," *Journal of Economic Theory* 25: 380–396.

Barro, R. J. (1977) "Long-Term Contracting, Sticky Prices and Monetary Policy," *Journal of Monetary Economics* 3: 5–31.

Benhabib, J., and R. E. A. Farmer. (1994) "Indeterminacy and Increasing Returns," *Journal of Economic Theory* 63: 19–46.

———. (1999) "Indeterminacy and Sunspots in Macroeconomics." in J. B. Taylor and M. Woodford (eds.), *Handbook of Macroeconomics*. Amsterdam: North-Holland, pp. 387–443.

———. (2000) "The Monetary Transmission Mechanism," *Review of Economic Dynamics* 3: 523–550.

Beyer, A., and R. E. A. Farmer. (2003) "Identifying the Monetary Transmission Mechanism Using Structural Breaks." Working Paper 275, *European Central Bank,* Frankfurt, Germany.

———. (2007) "Natural Rate Doubts," *Journal of Economic Dynamics and Control* 31: 797–825.

———. (2008) "What We Don't Know about the Monetary Transmission Mechanism and Why We Don't Know It," *Macroeconomic Dynamics* 12(Supplement 1): 60–74.

Beyer, A., R. E. A. Farmer, J. Henry, and M. Marcellino. (2008) "Factor Analysis in a New Keynesian Model," *Econometrics Journal* 11: 271–286.

Blanchard, O. J., and L. H. Summers. (1986) "Hysteresis and the European Unemployment Problem," *NBER Macroeconomics Annual* vol. 1: 15–90.

———. (1987) "Hysteresis in Unemployment," *European Economic Review* 31: 288–295.

Calvo, G. A. (1983) "Staggered Prices in a Utility Maxmimizing Model," *Journal of Monetary Economics* 12: 383–398.

Cass, D., and K. Shell. (1983) "Do Sunspots Matter?" *Journal of Political Economy* 91: 193–227.

Chari, V. V., P. Kehoe, and E. McGrattan. (2007) "Business Cycle Accounting," *Econometrica* 75: 781–836.

Clarida, R., J. Galí, and M. Gertler. (1999) "The Science of Monetary Policy: A New Keynesian Perspective," *Journal of Economic Literature* 37: 1661–1707.

Farmer, R. E. A. (1999) *The Macroeconomics of Self-Fulfilling Prophecies*, second edition. Cambridge, MA: MIT Press.

———. (2008a) "Aggregate Demand and Supply," *International Journal of Economic Theory* 4: 77–94.

———. (2008b) "Old Keynesian Economics," in R. E. A. Farmer (ed.), *Macroeconomics in the Small and the Large*. Cheltenham, UK: Edward Elgar, pp. 23–43.

———. (2010a) "Animal Spirits, Persistent Unemployment and the Belief Function." NBER Working Paper 16522, National Bureau of Economic Research, Cambridge, MA.

———. (2010b) *Expectations, Employment and Prices*. New York: Oxford University Press.

———. (2010c) *How the Economy Works: Confidence, Crashes and Self-Fulfilling Prophecies*. New York: Oxford University Press.

———. (2010d) "How to Reduce Unemployment: A New Policy Proposal," *Journal of Monetary Economics* 57 (Carnegie Rochester Conference Issue): 557–572.

———. (2011) "Animal Spirits, Financial Crises and Persistent Unemployment." NBER Working Paper 17137. National Bureau of Economic Research, Cambridge, MA.

———. (2012a) "Confidence, Crashes and Animal Spirits," *Economic Journal* 122: 155–172.

———. (2012b) "The Stock Market Crash of 2008 Caused the Great Recession: Theory and Evidence," *Journal of Economic Dynamics and Control* 36: 697–707. Plenary address to the Society for Computational Economics, Federal Reserve Bank of San Francisco, July 1, 2011.

Farmer, R. E. A., and J. T. Guo. (1994) "Real Business Cycles and the Animal Spirits Hypothesis," *Journal of Economic Theory* 63: 42–73.

Farmer, R. E. A., and D. Plotnikov. (2012) "Does Fiscal Policy Matter? Blinder and Solow Revisited," *Macroeconomic Dynamics* 16(Supplement 1): 149–166.

Fischer, S. S. (1977) "Long-Term Contracts, Rational Expectations and the Optimal Money Supply Rule," *Journal of Political Economy* 85: 191–205.

Friedman, M. (1968) "The Role of Monetary Policy," *American Economic Review* 58: 1–17.

Frydman, R., and M. D. Goldberg. (2011) *Beyond Mechanical Markets: Asset Price Swings, Risk, and the Role of the State*. Princeton, NJ: Princeton University Press.

Fuhrer, J. C., and G. R. Moore. (1995) "Inflation Persistence," *Quarterly Journal of Economics* 110: 127–159.

Galí, J. (2008) *Monetary Policy, Inflation and the Business Cycle*. Princeton, NJ: Princeton University Press.

Galí, J., M. Gertler, and D. L. Salido. (2007) "Markups, Gaps and the Welfare Costs of Business Cycle Fluctuations," *Review of Economics and Statistics* 89: 44–59.

Gertler, M., and A. Trigari. (2009) "Unemployent Fluctuations with Staggered Nash Wage Bargaining," *Journal of Political Economy* 117: 38–86.

Gertler, M., L. Sala, and A. Trigari. (2008) "An Estimated DSGE Model with Unemployment and Staggered Wage Bargaining," *Journal of Money, Credit, and Banking* 40: 1713–1764.

Hansen, A. (1936) "Mr. Keynes on Underemployment Equilibrium," *Journal of Political Economy* 44: 667–686.

Hicks, J. R. (1937) "Mr. Keynes and the Classics: A Suggested Interpretation," *Econometrica* 5: 147–159.

Holt, C. (1970) "Job Search, Phillips' Wage Relation, and Union Influence: Theory and Evidence," in E. S. Phelps, G. C. Archibald, and A. A. Alchian (eds.), *Microeconomic Foundations of Employment and Inflation Theory*. New York: W. W. Norton, pp. 53–123.

Howitt, P., and R. P. McAfee. (1987) "Costly Search and Recruiting," *International Economic Review* 28: 89–107.

Hume, D. (1987 [1777]) "Of Money," in E. F. Miller (ed.), *Essays, Moral, Political, and Literary*. Based on the 1777 edition with a foreword and notes by E. F. Miller. Indianapolis, IN: Liberty Fund, pp. 281–294.

Keynes, J. M. (1936) *The General Theory of Employment, Interest and Money*. London: MacMillan. 1973 edition published for the Royal Economic Society, Cambridge.

Klenow, P. J., and B. A. Malin. (2010) "Microeconomic Evidence on Price Setting," in B. M. Friedman and M. Woodford (eds.), *Handbook of Monetary Economics*, volume 3. Amsterdam: Elsevier, pp. 231–284.

Kuhn, T. S. (1957) *The Copernican Revolution*. Cambridge, MA: Harvard University Press.

Kyle, A. S. (1985) "Continuous Auctions and Insider Trading," *Econometrica* 53: 1315–1335.

Lakatos, I. (1978) *The Methodology of Scientific Research Programmes*. Cambridge: Cambridge University Press.

Leeper, E. M. (1991) "Equilibria under 'Active' and 'Passive' Monetary and Fiscal Policies," *Journal of Monetary Economics* 27: 129–147.

Lubik, T. A., and F. Schorfheide. (2004) "Testing for Indeterminacy: An Application to U.S. Monetary Policy," *American Economic Review* 94: 190–219.

Lucas, R. E., Jr. (1987) *Models of Business Cycles*. Oxford: Basil Blackwell.

Lucas, R. E., Jr., and L. Rapping. (1970) "Real Wages, Employment and Inflation," in E. S. Phelps, G. C. Archibald, and A. A. Alchian (eds.), *Microeconomic Foundations of Employment and Inflation Theory*. New York: W. W. Norton, pp. 257–305.

Mankiw, N. G., and R. Reis. (2002) "Sticky Information versus Sticky Prices: A Proposal to Replace the New Keynesian Phillips Curve," *Quarterly Journal of Economics* 117: 1295–1328.

Mortensen, D. T. (1970) "A Theory of Wage and Employment Dynamics," in E. S. Phelps, G. C. Archibald, and A. A. Alchian (eds.), *Microeconomic Foundations of Employment and Inflation Theory*. New York: W. W. Norton, pp. 167–211.

Mortensen, D. T., and C. Pissarides. (1994) "Job Creation and Job Destruction in the Theory of Unemployment," *Review of Economic Studies* 61: 397–415.

Phelps, E. S. (1968) "Money Wage Dynamics and Labor Market Equilibrium," *Journal of Political Economy* 76: 678–711.

———. (1970) "Money Wage Dynamics and Labor Market Equilibrium," in E. S. Phelps, G. C. Archibald, and A. A. Alchian (eds.), *Microeconomic Foundations of Employment and Inflation Theory.* New York: W. W. Norton, pp. 124–166.

———. (1994) *Structural Slumps.* Cambridge, MA: Harvard University Press.

Phelps, E. S., G. C. Archibald, and A. A. Alchian (eds.). (1970) *Microeconomic Foundations of Employment and Inflation Theory.* New York: W. W. Norton.

Rotemberg, J. J. (1982) "Sticky Prices in the United States," *Journal of Political Economy* 90: 1187–1211.

Samuelson, P. A. (1955) *Economics: An Introductory Analysis,* third edition. New York: McGraw-Hill.

Shell, K. (1977) "Monnaie et Allocation Intertemporelle." Mimeo, Malinvaud Seminar, CNRS, Paris.

Sims, C. A. (1980) "Macroeconomics and Reality," *Econometrica* 48: 1–48.

———. (2010) "Rational Inattention and Monetary Economics," in B. M. Friedman and M. Woodford (eds.), *Handbook of Monetary Economics,* volume 3. Amsterdam: Elsevier, pp. 155–181.

Taylor, J. B. (1999) *Monetary Policy Rules.* Chicago: University of Chicago Press.

Woodford, M. (2003) *Interest and Prices: Foundations of a Theory of Monetary Policy.* Princeton, NJ: Princeton University Press.

Yun, T. (1996) "Nominal Price Rigidity, Money Supply Endogeneity, and Business Cycles," *Journal of Monetary Economics* 37: 345–370.

CHAPTER EIGHT

Indeterminacies in Wage and Asset Price Expectations
A Structuralist Model of Employment and Growth

Edmund S. Phelps

8.1   Introduction

When the contributors to the volume *Microeconomic Foundations* (Phelps et al. 1970) met at the University of Pennsylvania in January 1969, we felt we were present at the creation—the creation of a new macroeconomics. I conceived and organized both the conference and the volume—and authored much of it, too—so I take special pride in its seminal contribution to the profession.

My work in this mold, which started in January 1966, grew out of my awareness that Keynesian economics did not have a microeconomics to accompany its macroeconomic story. I had no other quarrel with it at that time. Center stage in Keynesian thinking are shifts in the demand for liquidity, which lead to changes in the velocity of money—shifts that are not observed and are not common knowledge. If consumers tighten their belts to increase their cash balances, the result is cash accumulating in households and decumulating in businesses. One might think, however, that businesses, seeing that daily receipts were down, would lower their prices and wages—or at any rate slow their rise—until real cash balances reached the increased

I thank Roman Frydman for thousands of conversations over the decades on the subject of knowledge and expectations, from which both of us gained much. He has made his own contributions, and he also helped devise much of the vocabulary for the concepts that both he and I have needed. I am also grateful to another collaborator, Hian Teck Hoon, not only for correcting my mistakes and filling in gaps in my analysis here, but also for working with me over the past decade to develop the Austro-Swedish model used here and elsewhere. (The general model is in Hoon and Phelps 2011.) Finally, I am grateful to the Ewing Marion Kauffman Foundation for supporting the research on which this chapter is based.

amount demanded, so that consumer demand would return to its old level—without the pain of laying off experienced and trusted employees.[1] In my 1968 paper, I proposed two reasons why that does not necessarily happen soon enough to avert layoffs and recession. The first was that firms do not initially know that other firms in the industry (and other industries) are having the same experience, so firms do not cut prices as much as they would if they knew. (Objectors assumed that every firm will know—from the data specific to it and from the subsequent release of macro data—how to estimate the new equilibrium price that would be optimal for it to charge if other firms charged their equilibrium price.) My second reason was that the annual price and wage resets of firms or industries come at different times in the year, so firms or industries resetting prices soon will figure that they need to cut their price only a little to regain their old volume of output sold.[2] Firms resetting wages will figure that they had better not get too far out of line. Thus, an economy might need a very long time to achieve full adjustment of the price level, by which time firms may have decumulated quite a lot of employees.

Years later, it occurred to me that if the shock hit just one industry, such as farming, or just one sector, such as the investment goods industries, there could be an indeterminacy in who leaves for a job in the rest of the economy and who stays, which could take years to resolve fully. (Alphonse and Gaston fits here.) So I concluded that Keynes's vision of poor "coordination" (to use the term from his notes) made sense. And I have never lost the visceral feeling that real-life economies are almost always in an expectational disequilibrium of some appreciable magnitude—meaning that expectations of some variables will not be validated, even if there are no new surprises.

Yet I did not see how Keynes's notion of coordination problems could be the key to understanding how an economy might experience decade-long depressions—or booms. If Keynes's theoretical economy is always working out its current coordination problems, then activity will soon turn around and head back toward the *natural* level, even if the emergence of new problems is forever sending activity above or below that level. So there was something missing that lay behind most, if not all, low-frequency movements—something that could cause protracted slumps and protracted booms. Keynes himself contrived a makeshift device by which expectations of future developments might disturb employment. He speaks of the long bond and the long rate of interest. However, he does not explain why, if the

---

1. In fact, it was easier to study a downshift in liquidity demand, so the task was to understand why employment might increase from its initial level.

2. Keynesians at Yale and the Massachusetts Institute of Technology often invoked Irving Fisher's debt-deflation thesis here, but they never showed in their regression equations that reduced levels of money wages, by ultimately raising the real value of company debt, would lead to a decrease in the equilibrium level of employment.

long rate is a real rate of interest, it is necessary or even desirable to model all other prices in nominal terms. (The nominal interest rate can perfectly well be negative, as has been observed in recent years.) Work by John Hicks and Hugh Rose suggested that, as a slump wore on, evaporation of capital would ultimately rekindle investment demand. Gardner Ackley argued that if the government runs deficits in a slump, household wealth will ultimately be large enough to restore "aggregate demand." But what if the prime cause of the slump (or boom) is structural? Or if the outcome of such a full nominal adjustment would be the creation of a nonmonetary effect, such as a reduced supply of labor? Then the economy cannot generally return to where it was. And if the cause is monetary, why not just increase the money supply? As the 1970s progressed, I came to suspect that an undersupply of liquidity relative to the price level, which forced up real rates of interest, or a liquidity trap that prevented real rates from going low enough, was not necessary for low employment—whether or not either was sufficient to bring it about. From this suspicion, I came to believe that it was necessary to rethink macroeconomics.

In the 1970 conference volume, I wrote of my vision of "Pinteresque figures" peering with some apprehension at a world of which they had little understanding. I knew that the task was to get a handle on what I later dubbed the "modern economy," which was the subject of the pioneering economists of the interwar period. I understood that, as Keynes (1936) comments in his masterful *General Theory of Employment, Interest and Money,* companies and investors in such an economy "simply do not know" the outcomes of their actions and those of other companies and investors. I was steeped in the work of Knight, Morgenstern, M. Polanyi, Popper, and latter-day Hayek, as well as such postwar figures as Nelson and Winter. My 1966 paper with Nelson modeled an aspect of the problematic adoption stage in the innovation process, with the understanding that innovative ideas are not predetermined—otherwise, they would not be new ideas—and that innovative success is not determinate, so the future is far from being wholly known. But I did not get around to making a start in that direction until the early 2000s.

The work I set out to do in the 1980s was more mechanical. In the primitive terms I was then using, I sought structuralist models of disturbances to the "natural" level of employment—not swings around a fixed natural rate. I was tinkering with models of employment in nonmonetary terms. (I had always had a fascination with the Keynes-Ramsey model of wealth accumulation and its ramifications for labor supply. And a 1983 paper with Calvo married that model of saving to a Phelps-Winter model of customer markets.) Then, in 1985, when I was at the Bank of Italy and observing up close the disconnect between Keynesian thinking on the slump in Europe and the actual features of the situation, such as rising prices amid high interest rates, I began working in earnest toward an employment theory with non-Keynesian features. *Structural Slumps* (Phelps 1994) and a couple of follow-up papers with Hian Teck Hoon and Gylfi Zoega—who were already de facto co-authors of chunks of the book—provided a full-fledged alternative to Keynesian theory. It abstracted from liquidity and money as the numeraire in which to measure wages and prices and distanced itself from the Keynesian obsession with the short-run effects of what happens to the unemployment rate when an employer lays off someone. I was focused on the big swings—the 1970s slump in the United States and the 1980s slump in Europe. Later, I applied my structuralist models to the 1990s boom in the United States, the disastrous crash and financial crisis of 2008–2009 in several countries, and, most recently, the debt crisis on the southern periphery of Europe.

So I cannot help but deplore the recent retreat in American policy circles to an apparently vulgar Keynesianism: one that denies the existence not only of a fixed natural rate—I, for one, never said it was fixed and I wrote about influences on it as early as the 1970s—but also of any current medium-term natural rate to which the economy tends (in some approximate way, at any rate). It has been appalling that several of the most prominent American economists have adopted a crude version of what is presented in Keynes's profound *General Theory*.

These self-styled Keynesians do not ask how recent events may have shifted the natural unemployment rate, nor do they suggest how their policies would shrink or enlarge it. Of course, the tendency of the economy to home in on the medium-term natural rate is not as dependable as many economists once supposed it to be. (My 1972 book suggested the strong possibility that some amount of disequilibrium is impervious to everyday observations, owing to the economy's complexity, as did Axel Leijonhufvud's 1968 book and a 1970 paper by Dagobert Brito.) But to banish the very concept of paths of expectational equilibrium and disequilibrium smacks of philistinism. It is unsophisticated and ahistorical to suggest that the inflation rate cannot fall when the unemployment rate is at 9% or that no amount of Federal Reserve credit, no matter how large, can spark rising inflation until the unemployment rate is back in the accustomed range.

This Keynesianism Redux would do no harm if it were directed simply at keeping the annual consumer price index marching upward along its 2% trend path. It is very unfortunate that the Fed took its eyes off the ball in the last months of 2009, causing the price level to sag farther below the old trend path. That gave a pretext for the Keynesians to blame the entire slump on a "deficiency of aggregate demand." Monetary policy was, for Keynes, the first line of defense against a slump.

However, it was *consumer* demand that became the new Keynesians' focus of attention. Their apparent reasoning was that consumer spending is much larger than investment purchases or government purchases, so an increase in consumption adds more to GDP than would the same percentage increase in investment or government purchases. Of course, that assumes that a dollar increase in consumer demand matters as much for employment as a dollar increase of investment demand. Ironically, some accredited Keynesians, such as James Tobin, built a model in which consumer demand did not matter at all for employment, as resources just migrate from the capital goods industries. And some other Keynesians built two-sector models in which increased consumer demand, by driving up interest rates, reduces employment in the investment goods sector more than it increases employment in the consumer goods sector. The reasoning further assumes that this dollar increase in consumer demand matters about as much for employment as a dollar increase in investment demand. In the structuralist perspective, it matters much less.

So, by way of a preface, I point out in Section 8.2 what I see to be the fatal flaws in this Keynesianism and explain why I believe that structuralist models of the sort that I prefer—the first wave of such models in the early 1990s and the second wave in the early 2000s—better illuminate the long slump without inflation in the United States. Then, in Section 8.3, I turn to the central subject of this volume: how to think about the formation of expectations in modern economies—economies of the sort that became the lifetime subject of Knight, Keynes, and Hayek.

8.2 Crude Keynesianism versus a Crude Natural Rate

Mention of the term "natural rate" summons up the notion that, following a shock and until the next one, the unemployment rate approaches (approximately, at least) a medium-term rest point at which price and wage expectations are again realized. Unemployment is forced away from that level if people are driven out of expectational equilibrium, so that price and wage expectations are, so to speak, incorrect, or self-falsifying—at least for a time. I built such a model for my 1967 paper but moved on to build a more general one: from each possible starting point, there is a corresponding path of expectational equilibrium along which demand expands (or contracts) so as to deliver the wage and price inflation that are expected. The medium-term rest point to which every such equilibrium path converges is the "natural rate." Although these concepts have been hugely influential in macroeconomics, the crude Keynesianism of late does not use or recognize them.

The hypothesis of crude Keynesianism is that the slump in the United States, the United Kingdom, Spain, and Ireland is driven by a "deficiency" of "aggregate demand"—just as the 2003–2007 boom in those countries is blamed on a supposed excess of aggregate demand. In this view, the great swings of modern economic history (from the early 1800s, if not before) are transmitted by changes in the stock of paper money and in the illiquidity of capital assets, tangible output, and services (in short, "goods"). But key implications of this model do not square with observations:

- The sophisticated New Keynesian model of the textbooks supposes that higher unemployment will prompt employers to reduce average wages, thus lowering the rate of wage inflation, as described by a Phillips curve, which will lead in turn to lower price inflation—or the other way around. But the rates of wage and price inflation in 2011 were not discernibly lower than they were in, say, 2005–2007. There was a whiff of disinflation in 2008–2009, but the Fed nipped it in the bud. Then it allowed some disinflation in 2010, which had to be countered with so-called Quantitative Easing 2 (QE2). As of early 2012, annual inflation, measured by the Personal Consumption Expenditures Implicit Price Deflator, is running at 2.1%.

- A friend who joined the crude Keynesian camp responds that there was no decline in inflation because money wages exhibit "downward rigidity." But even if that were true (which is to be doubted), how can it serve to support the deficiency-of-demand explanation when prices and money wages have been rising steadily?

- Another Keynesian says that quantitative easing cannot remove the assumed deficiency of demand because there is a "liquidity trap": the opportunity cost of holding money is now so low that increasing the stock of money would not lower it more. The Fed cannot re-create the liquidity needed for a return to high employment. But, as just noted, the inflation rate is not subdued, as it would be if there were a deficiency of liquidity. In addition, since the 1980s, banks in the United States have been free to pay interest on deposits. That rate of return on money falls when interest rates fall; so, as interest rates that firms could pay fell, there could not have been a fall in the opportunity cost of holding money that would have caused people to dump risky stocks and bonds to get into cash. (They dumped for other reasons.)

- Keynesians use a rhetorical device to try to deter efforts to use any kind of structuralist model. They introduce a syllogism: All structuralist models portray markets as perfect. We observe that some markets are seriously imperfect. Therefore, all structuralist models are unsatisfactory. But some of Keynes's ideas about the coordination failures in markets could easily be injected into structuralist models. For example, a model could incorporate indeterminacy about *which* unemployed workers are going to pick up and move to another sector. Such additions would not be a defeat for structuralism. Section 8.3 indicates some features of more recent structuralist models that are closer to Keynes's portrait of the modern economy than are any of the standard Keynesian models now in use.

- A fine economist with Washington experience was stunned when asked on TV whether the high unemployment rate—then between 8% and 9% and gently falling—could be the result of structural factors. How could there be evil without the Keynesian devil at work? The gist of the economist's response was that unemployment means excess supply, so, for the current path of the unemployment rate to be an equilibrium one, the job vacancy rate must also be quite large (whether or not between 8% and 9%). But the theory of involuntary unemployment based on labor turnover, shirking, and the rest does not portray labor markets as frictionless auction markets that wages would always clear.

I make these points not to take some passing shots at the Keynesian approach, but because I do not want readers unfamiliar with the pros and cons of that approach to think that it is eccentric of me—or maybe self-important—to represent consequences of incomplete knowledge and information in a *structuralist* model, rather than a Keynesian one.

8.3   The Structuralist Approach

In a structuralist model, nonmonetary forces operate through structural channels to impact the path of employment and its medium-term level (as well as its long-term level). Asset prices, such as housing prices, are expressed in real terms, so the term "housing prices" refers to the *real price* of a house, expressed in units of shelter; a unit of shelter per unit of time serves as the numeraire and therefore has a real rental price of 1—whatever the rental in money might be.

Structuralist models, while abstracting from money and its velocity, can nonetheless accommodate incorrect as well as correct expectations—and do so no less easily than monetary models can. But before I take up some of the issues surrounding equilibrium—interspatial and intertemporal—let me first discuss the familiar features of structuralist models.

Rather typically, structuralist models focus on one or another of several business assets, such as customers, or employees with their specialized know-how, as well as office space or other tangible capital. I have given a structuralist account of the 2007 crisis and the 2008–2009 downswing (Phelps 2010) in which the analogous asset is housing. My longtime collaborator Hian Teck Hoon and I have produced a reworking of the model that clears up an ambiguity in my first formulation (Phelps and Hoon 2010). Stripped to essentials, the analysis sees the run-up of housing prices as a "speculative excess," to use Spiethoff's felicitous term. The level to which housing prices were expected to rise could not be attained, and when expectations of the future price level were lowered in response, actual prices began falling. The amount of construction supplied—and thus demand for construction labor—was therefore falling, too, while the associated decline in wealth was pushing up labor supply. Employment and the real wage do not simply subside to the old and future natural level, however. The overhang of houses directly adds to wealth, which is bad for labor supply.[3] Of course, some complications came into play in the downturn (and economies, like patients, can even die from them). Bad balance sheets at big and small banks impeded financing of investment projects in small and medium-sized firms. The resulting uncertainties operated to depress further the "demand prices" put on various business assets and on houses. (In addition, uncertainties in the housing market may drive up the "supply price" of new housing: if it is not known how long it will take to sell a new house, the construction industry may be deterred from building them.)

This structuralist view of the recent slump (which we have not yet escaped) has clashed with the Keynesian view in recent discussions of measures that government should take to arrest the downturn, speed the economy's recovery, and reduce the medium-term unemployment level. Keynesians have called for tax cuts to encourage consumer spending or stepped-up government purchases of goods and services—both in the name of boosting "aggregate demand." Structuralists, in contrast, have confined their approval to government purchases of capital goods. Although Keynesians see deficit spending as good because it raises consumption, structuralists see it as bad because it raises private saving, which, by swelling private wealth, operates to contract the supply of labor. Furthermore, structuralists view the extra accumulation of public debt as endangering government solvency and the exchange rate.

Now let me offer a broader and more formal discussion of expectations in such a theoretical framework.

8.4   The Structure of a Structuralist Model

Even in the simplest models that we can bear, expectations must be formed about at least two variables: the *future of wages* (real wages in our context) and the *future of profits* (rents) on which the present value of the business asset(s) depends—the capital good in the Austro-Swedish models of wine

---

3. The question then becomes whether the construction industry shuts down, thus minimizing the time the housing level takes to shrink, as required for employment at the natural level, or promptly cuts back a bit before gradually shrinking, always producing less housing than is being retired for reasons of age and use, until the steady state is reached. Hoon's analysis shows that a perfect market will opt for the former option—thus going "cold turkey."

and firewood. (An open economy model requires expectations to be formed about the future of overseas prices and interest rates expressed in domestic terms.)

I would point out that the next wave of papers following those associated with *Structural Slumps* (Phelps 1994)—the Phelps-Zoega papers of 1999–2001 and the Hoon-Phelps papers of 2002–2006 on "structural booms"—handle the arbitrariness in valuations at least as naturally as Keynes's "marginal efficiency" did. His allusion to Plato's "animal spirits" brilliantly conveyed his message: the "extreme precariousness" of the "basis of knowledge" on which expectations of the future (Keynes 1936: 149) are based and the resulting "flimsiness" of current beliefs (Keynes 1937: 214). To be sure, asset valuations are affected by the intuitions, instincts, and emotional needs of the entrepreneurs. But the papers just cited specify some future unexpected structural shifts that, owing to the uncertainty that results, might well excite a speculative jump to *new levels of business asset prices* or a *new level of wages*. The stationary locus relating the demand price for an asset to the stock of the asset does not have to be "solved out" by supposing perfect understanding of the working of the economy—as I was driven to do in *Structural Slumps* to minimize the complexity of the models and the themes. A downward shift of this valuation curve in the (asset stock, asset price) plane will lead also to a drop in observed valuations of, say, real estate prices and share prices. A nonmonetary approach is not inherently yoked to perfect knowledge and infinite experience or to their illegitimate offspring, rational expectations.

My 1968 paper centers around wage expectations—money wages in that context. But it did not have to be couched in monetary terms, as Salop (1979) was the first to point out. What would a firm do if it suddenly expected other firms to step up the rate at which they increased their wages? The answer was that such a firm would defend itself from declining competitiveness in the labor market by stepping up the pace of its own wage increases. (It is a common error to deduce at this point that the firm cuts the rate at which it adds to employment. It is the worrying expectation of wage increases elsewhere that will cause the firm to slow its expansion or quicken its contraction. Because its wage level was optimal, a small increase has no first-order effect on its employment decisions.) What is at issue here is interspatial disequilibrium in the labor market—an employer's not getting right what is currently going on in another, unseen "space."

We come now to intertemporal equilibrium and disequilibrium. When analyzing the effects of expectations of the future, it helps to have exactly one model for purposes of discussion. It is also natural to talk about the effects of expectations in the context of what has prompted the shift in expectations. The model proposed here has the Austro-Swedish feature that the consumer good is produced with capital alone, whereas the capital good is produced with labor alone.

The full model is laid out in the Appendix. Here I present it in what is perhaps the most natural expression of its reduced form. It consists of (20), (22), (23), (24), (25), and (26) in the Appendix.

The first of these equations denotes that the price of capital (and ownership claims to capital), $q(t)$, is such as to make the expected rate of return on capital, which is given on the right-hand side, equal to the real rate of interest, $r(t)$:

$$r(t) = \frac{\Lambda_C(t)}{q(t)} - \delta + \frac{\dot{q}(t)}{q(t)} \tag{22}$$

The next two equations suppose that there is market clearing in the nondurable market consumption good sector and the capital good-producing sector, so that consumption, $C(t)$, and gross investment, $\dot{K}(t) + \delta K(t)$, are given by current capacity in their respective sectors. Here $K(t)$ denotes the capital stock, and $L^s(t) = \bar{L} - C^L(t)$ denotes the number of people currently employed. For simplicity, it is assumed that the real wage clears the labor market at all times, so that $L(t)$ is given by the total number in the working age population, less the number choosing leisure, $C^L(t)$. (Workers whose wealth has reached a high level go in and out of employment.) These two equations are:

$$C(t) = \Lambda_C(t) K(t) \tag{23}$$

$$\dot{K}(t) + \delta K(t) = \Lambda_K(t) L(t) \tag{24}$$

In this Austro-Swedish model, there is no net wealth other than the market value of the capital stock. So, in intertemporal equilibrium, nonhuman wealth, $W(t)$, is equal to $q(t)K(t)$. As a result, the Euler-Blanchard-Yaari differential equation can be written as

$$\frac{\dot{C}(t)}{C(t)} = [r(t) - \rho] - \theta(\theta + \rho) \left(\frac{A+1}{A} \right) \left[\frac{q(t)K(t)}{C(t)} \right] \tag{25}$$

The analogous differential equation in the demand for leisure is

$$\frac{\dot{C}^L(t)}{C^L(t)} = \left[r(t) - \rho - \frac{\dot{q}(t)}{q(t)} - \lambda_K(t) \right] - \frac{\theta(\theta + \rho)}{A+1} \left[\frac{K(t)}{\Lambda_K(t)C^L(t)} \right] \tag{26}$$

The above system, (20), (22), (23), (24), (25), and (26), together with the initial capital stock, $K(0)$, comprises five equations in just five variables, $C(t)$, $C^L(t)$, $r(t)$, $q(t)$, and $K(t)$, upon substituting $L^s(t) = \bar{L} - C^L(t)$ for $L(t)$.

One can derive from the full equilibrium model another reduced-form system of the same size that is more convenient for some or all purposes.

This system replaces (25) with what is (17) in the full model, here labeled (25alt) to remind us of what it replaces:

$$C(t) = Av(t)C^L(t) \qquad \text{(25alt)}$$

This demand-for-leisure equation expresses the idea that, with all markets clearing, an individual may trade consumption for more leisure and will do so up to the point where the ratio of the marginal utilities is equal to the real wage, $v(t)$. Leisure is pushed up until its marginal utility has fallen to equality with the marginal utility of consumption multiplied by the wage. (Here A is a parameter of the utility function.)

There are several areas in which the actors' knowledge may be deficient. A very basic source of deficient understanding is that, even if this model is the true one, or true enough, the actors do not know that. And, even if they thought it was true, there is no compelling reason to believe that they all would understand it well enough to use it to form correct expectations, make correct valuations, and anticipate the consequences of other actors' behavior. However, to understand the consequences of a particular deficiency of knowledge, we want to see how the model's economy would behave if it were understood and its quantitative features correctly estimated.

In the extreme case of full information and perfect knowledge, a couple of features of the model are obvious. For one thing, the equilibrium (or self-fulfilling) expectation of the value, q, of capital per unit would be correctly understood to be proportional to Λ_C, the Hicks-neutral parameter in the consumer good production function. (Scanning the equations, we see that q always appears as a ratio of Λ_C.) So if Λ_C doubled, q would immediately double also. It is a well-known property of the standard two-sector model that such a technological advance generates a proportional increase in the real wage and the rent per unit of capital, as well as in q. But an increase in Λ_K or in the working-age population would cause q immediately to drop and, with it, the wage. Another "intuitive" property is that an increase in K drives down the relative price of the capital-using product, which is the consumer good, so it drives up the real price of the capital good, q.

A formal analysis can start with the Euler-type equation (25) giving the growth rate of consumption. (To simplify, we set the time rate of change of Λ_C and Λ_K to zero.) For that rate, we may, by (23), substitute the growth rate of capital, in turn given by (24), which obviously involves C^L as well as K. One can use (17) to express C^L in terms of C and q. Thus, we obtain

$$\Lambda_K \left[\frac{\bar{L}}{K} - \frac{\Lambda_C}{Aq\Lambda_K} \right] = r - \rho - \theta(\theta + \rho) \left(\frac{A+1}{A} \right) \left(\frac{q}{\Lambda_C} \right)$$

This result, and the use of the Fisher condition in (22) to substitute for $r - p$, gives a differential equation for q in terms of K and q/Λ_C. The corresponding stationary locus in the (K, q) plane is upward sloping. The companion stationary locus for K is also upward sloping and steeper, which delivers saddle-path stability. The saddle-path solution for q as a function of K can be seen to be upward sloping as well and is flatter than the two stationary loci. This phase diagram suffices to determine the motion of K and q, a motion that is conveniently independent of C^L. The three properties of the model noted in the previous paragraph can be derived with the use of this phase diagram.

To go from these results to the consequences for employment, one may turn to another phase diagram, this one in the (K, C^L) plane. Equations (26) and (22) give a differential equation for C^L. Using (24) and the relation between L and C^L gives the differential equation for K. The stationary locus for C^L is upward sloping: when K is larger, C^L must be higher if C^L is to be stationary. The stationary locus for the latter differential equation is downward sloping: the larger K is, the less room there is for leisure if K is to be stationary. It follows that a sudden step-increase in Λ_C is neutral for employment, because such an increase requires an equiproportionate increase in q to reestablish intertemporal equilibrium. In contrast, an increase in Λ_K may cause employment to rise or fall, depending on its effect on $q\Lambda_K$, which gives v. Finally, an increase in K unambiguously increases leisure—the operation of the wealth effect—because, in increasing q, it causes qK to increase both indirectly and directly.

In this model, two sorts of expectational shifts suggest themselves. One such shift is a sudden expectation of a medium-term improvement in the technology with which capital produces the consumer good, Λ_C. That may have consequences for business activity in the present. Participants will understand that this quantum increase in productivity in the consumer goods sector entails a lower relative price for the consumer good, which means a higher price for the capital good. So, in the case of perfect knowledge, it will be calculated that at the time the productivity of capital finally increases, the price of the capital good, or unit valuation, will already have reached an elevated level in anticipation of the technological improvement. This expectation of the increased price of the capital good in the future operates to increase the demand-price in the present—by enough that the rate at which it will rise further just offsets the reduced yield per dollar in the present. This anticipatory jump in the price of the capital good will provoke an equiproportionate jump in the wage rate of workers, who alone can produce capital. To infer the results for C^L in the (K, C^L) plane, it is useful to note that using (19) and (23) in (17), we obtain the demand for leisure in terms of K and q:

$$C^L(t) = \Lambda_C K(t)/(Aq(t)\Lambda_K) \tag{25alt'}$$

It follows immediately that the upward jump of q sparks an instantaneous drop in C^L. At that point, according to the perfect-knowledge story, q continues to rise; hence C^L continues to decline as the relative price effect on work more than offsets the wealth effect of higher capital accumulation. This motion can be seen from an inspection of the phase diagram in the (K, C^L) plane discussed above.[4]

The other expectational shift is a sudden anticipation of improvement in the not-too-distant future in the technology with which labor produces the capital good. That expectation has a complex array of effects on business activity in the present. Other things being equal, the expectation of reduced costs of producing the capital good would induce buyers to postpone some of their purchases to the time when the price will be lower—an effect that, taken alone, would cut capital goods output and thus total employment. In technical terms, the sudden expectation of the reduced price of the capital good in the future operates to reduce the demand price in the present. If future wages are expected to be reduced by the lower price more than they are increased by the productivity gain, workers may respond by supplying more labor to make up for the anticipated loss of future wage income. The worker with some accumulation of wealth may increase his labor supply to the extent that his wealth has been reduced by the prospective fall in the relative price of the capital good. For these two reasons, the supply price in the capital goods industry falls as well. The fall in the demand price may be the stronger, causing a net decline in employment. If future wages are expected to be increased because of expectations that higher productivity will outweigh the lower price that it causes, the supply price is increased. In that case, employment falls even more than in the previous case: it falls for supply-price reasons as well as demand-price reasons. In both cases, we see that what matters is not only the expectation of the future price of the capital good (and thus the present valuation of a unit of that good) but also the expectation of the future wage.

Let me digress to make two brief comments of a personal sort. It comes as a relief that the Austro-Swedish model has the property that expectations of increased productivity in consumer goods production stimulate an increase

---

4. It may be added that at future time t_1, if the anticipated technological improvement affecting the consumer good, Λ_C, occurs, we find C^L jumping up to a point on the saddle path that passes through the original steady state. Hence, C^L overshoots the steady state level as the excess capital stock is gradually reduced and returned to its original level before the anticipatory shock occurred. So the immediate employment effect is positive. In the stripped-down model, the unit cost is increased equiproportionately to the increase in unit valuation. In a larger model with public debt, entitlements, and foreign investments, however, it is possible to argue that the supply price is pushed up less than the demand price is pulled up—a force operating to increase employment.

in employment. My papers in the years from 1999 to 2001 unambiguously stated that expectations of higher values placed on customers or on employees stimulated efforts to acquire more of these assets, with the result that wages are sharply increased and employment rises (Phelps 1999, 2000a–c, 2001a,b). But this is yet another model, and the property that expectations of increased productivity in the capital goods sector could weigh down employment (i.e., it would do so under certain conditions) is interesting and perhaps of some considerable importance for understanding employment problems in today's global economy. Second, it is interesting that the model portrays expectations of future wage increases to be contractionary in the theoretical setting here, which was also a feature of the models in *Microeconomic Foundations,* though the mechanisms are quite different.[5] When structural slumps of a certain kind occur, it may be that underestimation of the reduction of future wages operates to protract the slump.

8.5   Conclusion

The message of this chapter is now easy to grasp and is supported by the analysis above. In a world that is importantly indeterminate—a world in which even some central things, such as the "rate and direction" of innovation, and thus of productivity advances, are not predetermined (because they depend on new ideas as yet unborn, undeveloped, and untested)—some models are better than others in outlining the structure of relationships. But even our models cannot offer forecasts of the future levels of the real price, q, of capital and the real wage, v, in relation to present levels. The models cannot even forecast that the structure (two-sector, three-sector, . . .) will long remain. Given this, there is a substantial element of indeterminacy in the present levels of the two prices, especially the general price level of capital goods (because the substitutability of future leisure for present leisure appears to be small). As Keynes, when writing on this very point, put it, "we simply do not know." Knight (1921) argued much the same thing, invoking uncertainty originating in unforeseen external events. The methodological lesson is that we must view the present valuation of each capital good and, strictly speaking, the present valuation of leisure, as having a large exogenous component. The current level of the qs put on each of the capital goods will reflect the cost of capital, and thus real interest rates, which are observable, but the future yields of current investments, which will depend

---

5. It is a familiar idea that expectations of a wage increase demanded by workers could hasten orders of the capital goods before the inevitable price increase. But in the extreme Austrian case, as in the model unveiled below, when production of the consumer good requires no labor, that effect would not be operative.

on productivity levels and labor costs, cannot be closely predicted. We can assume that the past is a reliable guide to the future, and most of the time it may be, but new configurations of the parameters and even new structures may emerge.

Does this finding mean that the "natural" level of (un)employment no longer exists? That depends on what we mean by "natural." If we mean some immutable central tendency, then it never existed. I never said that the mean unemployment rate over the past century was a good estimate of what we may call the "natural rate." The structure is always changing and, with it, the unemployment rate to which the system may—or may not—tend. If the natural rate refers to the current medium-term tendency, the term "natural" is obviously inappropriate once we recognize that the unemployment rate to which the economy tends is contingent on the market's guesses about the future—that is, future prices of capital goods and labor. The "contingent equilibrium" rate would be a better term than "natural" for that conception of the homing tendency. It is ironic that the originators of models of the natural rate, whose formulations did not explicitly exclude the possibility that background expectations of future capital goods prices and future wages might be quite wrong, stand accused of not appreciating that any sort of economic equilibrium is to some extent a social phenomenon— a creature of beliefs, optimism, the policy climate, and so forth—while today's crude Keynesians, despite their mechanical deterministic approach, wrap themselves in the mantle of Keynes, who, with his profound sense of indeterminacy and, consequently, radical uncertainty, was worlds away from their thinking.

The revivalists of crude Keynesianism, in contrast to Keynes himself, spare little time for recognizing indeterminacies, which they do not invoke in their dismissal of the natural rate. They suppose that the underlying structure is fixed, so that it can safely be abstracted from, and that the only elements that go "wrong" pertain to the monetary system. And, fortunately, this fault can be addressed through monetary policy or, failing that, through fiscal stimulus of consumer demand. It is obvious how the model in this chapter undercuts any such possibility. As long as economists restrict themselves to simplistic monetary models of employment and unemployment, they will have no chance of understanding many of the most powerful forces operating in the global economy.

Embracing a structuralist view of the indeterminacies in modern economies, however, does not mean that economic policy should not take an activist stance against structural slumps. Structuralists can be active in proposing adjustments of the structure—subsidies, for example. Crude Keynesians must not be allowed to portray structuralists as passive, a tactic aimed at ensuring that if the public wants activism, it will have to place its trust in the Keynesians' monetary models and their policy prescriptions.

Appendix   Anatomy of the Austro-Swedish Model

8.A.1   A Formal Model Carefully Interpreted

I now lay out the Austro-Swedish model that underlies the foregoing discussion. I have recently added it to the quiver of models I use when attempting to puzzle out what is unfolding in the American economy. This model evolved unexpectedly out of related models that Hian Teck Hoon and I have built and analyzed over the past decade.

We proceed by first setting out the labor supply decisions of individuals and aggregating to obtain the economywide supply of labor and then identify the economywide sources of labor demand. For simplicity, we take the case of a neoclassical labor market, so there is market clearing in labor market equilibrium. In the closed economy, the whole path of the instantaneous real rate of interest, to which the equity rate of return must be equal in capital market equilibrium, is endogenously determined.

8.A.2   Supply of Labor

The economy comprises individuals who all face a constant and equal probability of death per unit of time, denoted by θ (see Blanchard 1985; Weil 1989). A new cohort is born at each instant of time with individuals facing the same probability of death, θ. The cohort size is sufficiently large that the size of each cohort declines deterministically through time. By normalizing the size of each new cohort to equal θ, total population (also equal to the total size of the labor force) at time t is given by $\int_{-\infty}^{t} \theta \exp^{-\theta(t-s)} ds = 1$. With this normalization, aggregate variables are also interpretable as per capita variables.

Individuals purchase insurance policies whereby they receive payments from the insurance company when alive and turn over their estates to the company upon death. With an actuarially fair scheme, an individual who is alive receives payment θ in exchange for the insurance company's claim of one unit of good contingent on death.

Let the period-t utility function of an individual born at time s be given by $A^{-1}\log(\bar{L} - l(s, t)) + \log c(s, t) + B$. Here, A and B are positive parameters, $\bar{L}$ is total time endowment, $l(s, t)$ is individual labor supply, and $c(s, t)$ is consumption of a homogeneous nondurable final market good produced with physical capital alone. We note that individuals in this model are not bequeathed with nonhuman wealth at birth and thus start life with a positive supply of labor. As worker-savers, they accumulate nonhuman wealth throughout their lives, leading to the possibility that there could exist individuals who become so wealthy that they use their entire time endowment for leisure. This would make it difficult to derive an aggregate labor supply schedule. To avoid this aggregation problem, we assume that, although additional hours spent at market work lead directly to a loss of utility as time available for leisure declines in the traditional way, spending a positive amount of time in market work also gives a positive fixed amount of utility, subsumed in the term B, that the activity of home production does not provide. This positive fixed utility from being in the workforce captures the value obtainable from social interaction with colleagues at the workplace, as well as from the mental stimulus of solving problems not normally found in home-based work.

To facilitate aggregation, we ensure that every living person in the economy spends a positive amount of time in market work by means of the following premise:

$$B > A^{-1}[\log \bar{L} - \log(\bar{L} - 0^+)]$$

Under this assumption, a very wealthy individual who might have chosen to retire in a model (at least one lacking a positive utility value from market work) will spend a very small positive amount of time working in the market ($l_m = 0^+ > 0$), given the positive utility value of market work compared to housework in our model.

At time 0, the individual's intertemporal optimization problem can be written as

$$\text{Maximize} \int_0^\infty \{A^{-1}[\log(\bar{L} - l(s,t))] + \log c(s,t) + B\} \exp^{-(\theta+\rho)T} dt$$

subject to $\dot{w}(s,t) = [r(t) + \theta]w(s,t) + v(t)l(s,t) - c(s,t)$

given $w(s,0)$

Here $w(s,t)$ is the individual's nonhuman wealth, $r(t)$ is the interest rate, θ is the actuarially fair premium rate, ρ is the subjective rate of time preference, and v is the real wage. We choose the homogeneous nondurable market consumption good as the numeraire.

Solving the individual's intertemporal problem gives the following optimal conditions:

$$\frac{A^{-1}}{\bar{L} - l(s,t)} = v(t)\mu(s,t) \tag{1}$$

$$\frac{1}{c(s,t)} = \mu(s,t) \tag{2}$$

$$\frac{\dot{\mu}(s,t)}{\mu(s,t)} = -[f(t) - \rho] \tag{3}$$

$$\lim_{T \to \infty} \mu(s,T)w(s,T) \exp^{-(\theta+\rho)T} = 0 \tag{4}$$

where $\mu(s, t)$ is the costate variable. Combining (1) and (2), and eliminating $\mu(s, t)$, we obtain

$$c(s, t) = Av(t)[\bar{L} - l(s, t)] \tag{5}$$

Using (5) in the individual's dynamic budget constraint, we obtain

$$\dot{w}(s, t) = [r(t) + \theta]w(s, t) + v(t)\bar{L} - \left(\frac{A + 1}{A}\right)c(s, t) \tag{6}$$

Using a no-Ponzi-game condition that, conditional on being alive at time T, requires

$$\lim_{T \to \infty} \exp^{-\int_t^T [r(\kappa) + \theta]d\kappa} w(s, T) = 0$$

we can integrate (6) forward in time to obtain

$$\int_0^\infty \left(\frac{A + 1}{A}\right) c(s, t) \exp^{-\int_0^t [r(\kappa) + \theta]d\kappa} dt$$

$$= w(s, 0) + \int_0^\infty v(t)\bar{L} \exp^{-\int_0^t [r(\kappa) + \theta]d\kappa} dt \tag{7}$$

The right-hand side of (7) gives the sum of nonhuman wealth and what may be called "full human wealth."

From (2) and (3), we obtain

$$\dot{c}(s, t) = [r(t) - \rho]c(s, t) \tag{8}$$

Integrating (8) to obtain

$$c(s, t) = c(s, 0) \exp^{\int_0^t [r(\kappa) - \rho]d\kappa}$$

and substituting into (7) gives an individual consumption function:

$$c(s, t) = (\theta + \rho) \left(\frac{A + 1}{A}\right) \left[w(s, t) + \int_t^\infty v(\kappa)\bar{L} \exp^{-\int_t^\kappa [r(v) + \theta]dv} d\kappa\right] \tag{9}$$

Denoting aggregate consumption by $C(t)$ and aggregate nonhuman wealth by $W(t)$, we obtain the aggregates by integrating over generations:

$$C(t) = \int_{-\infty}^t c(s, t)\theta \exp^{-\theta(t-s)} ds \tag{10}$$

$$W(t) = \int_{-\infty}^t w(s, t)\theta \exp^{-\theta(t-s)} ds \tag{11}$$

Because the wage rate paid is independent of the cohort, aggregate full human wealth, denoted by W^{fh}, is

$$W^{fh}(t) = \int_t^\infty v(\kappa)\bar{L}\, \exp^{-\int_t^\kappa [r(v)+\theta]dv} d\kappa \tag{12}$$

Then, from (9), we obtain the aggregate consumption function:

$$C(t) = (\theta + \rho)\left(\frac{A+1}{A}\right)[W(t) + W^{fh}(t)] \tag{13}$$

Differentiating $W(t)$ in (11) with respect to time, we obtain

$$\dot{W}(t) = \theta w(t,t) + \int_{-\infty}^t [\theta \exp^{-\theta(t-s)} w(s,t) - \theta^2 \dot{w}(s,t) \exp^{-\theta(t-s)}]ds$$

Noting that $w(t,t) = 0$ and using (6), this equation can be simplified to give

$$\dot{W}(t) = r(t)W(t) + v(t)\bar{L} - \left(\frac{A+1}{A}\right)C(t) \tag{14}$$

Differentiating W^{fh} in (12) with respect to time, we obtain

$$\dot{W}^{fh}(t) = -v(t)\bar{L} + [r(t) + \theta]W^{fh}(t) \tag{15}$$

and

$$\lim_{T \to \infty} W^{fh}(T) \exp^{-\int_t^T [r(\kappa)+\theta]d\kappa} = 0$$

Using (13), (14), and (15), we obtain

$$\frac{\dot{C}(t)}{C(t)} = [r(t) - \rho] - \theta(\theta + \rho)\left(\frac{A+1}{A}\right)\left[\frac{W(t)}{C(t)}\right] \tag{16}$$

We also note that aggregating across generations in (5) gives

$$C(t) = Av(t)C^L(t) \tag{17}$$

where $C^L(t)$ is the aggregate demand for leisure. Using (16) and (17), we obtain

$$\frac{\dot{C}^L(t)}{C^L(t)} = \left[r(t) - \rho - \frac{\dot{v}(t)}{v(t)}\right] - \frac{\theta(\theta + \rho)}{A+1}\left[\frac{W(t)}{v(t)C^L(t)}\right] \tag{18}$$

Aggregate labor supply, $L^s(t)$, is given by $L^s(t) \equiv \bar{L} - C^L(t)$.

8.A.3 Sources of Labor Demand and Labor Market Equilibrium

As noted before, the nondurable market consumption good is produced with capital alone. In particular, $Z_C(t) = \Lambda_C(t)K(t)$. In contrast, the capital good is produced with labor alone, that is, $Z_K(t) = \Lambda_K(t)L(t)$. Therefore, labor demand derives entirely from capital good firms.

The optimal choice of employment requires that the following first-order condition be satisfied:

$$v(t) = q(t)\Lambda_K(t) \tag{19}$$

The clearing of the labor market requires that the aggregate supply of labor be equal to the aggregate demand for labor:

$$\bar{L} - C^L(t) = L(t) \tag{20}$$

8.A.4 Capital Market Equilibrium and Goods Market Clearing

The rate of return to holding equity is given by

$$\frac{R(t)}{q(t)} - \delta + \frac{\dot{q}(t)}{q(t)}$$

where $R(t)$ is the rental rate, and δ is the capital rate of depreciation. Profit maximization in the capital-good-using sector gives

$$R(t) = \Lambda_C(t) \tag{21}$$

Using (21) and requiring that the equity rate of return be equal to the instantaneous real rate of interest gives

$$r(t) = \frac{\Lambda_C(t)}{q(t)} - \delta + \frac{\dot{q}(t)}{q(t)} \tag{22}$$

Market clearing in the nondurable market consumption-goods sector and capital-goods-producing sector, respectively, gives

$$C(t) = \Lambda_C(t)K(t) \tag{23}$$

$$\dot{K}(t) + \delta K(t) = \Lambda_K(t)L(t) \tag{24}$$

8.A.5 The General Equilibrium System of Equations

Noting that nonhuman wealth, $W(t)$, is equal to $q(t)K(t)$, we can write (16) as

$$\frac{\dot{C}(t)}{C(t)} = [r(t) - \rho] - \theta(\theta + \rho)\left(\frac{A+1}{A}\right)\left[\frac{q(t)K(t)}{C(t)}\right] \tag{25}$$

Using $W(t) \equiv q(t)K(t)$ and (19) in (18), we obtain

$$\frac{\dot{C}^L(t)}{C^L(t)} = \left[r(t) - \rho - \frac{\dot{q}(t)}{q(t)} - \lambda_K(t) \right] - \frac{\theta(\theta + \rho)}{A + 1} \left[\frac{K(t)}{\Lambda_K(t)C^L(t)} \right] \quad (26)$$

The general equilibrium system in the variables $C(t)$, $C^L(t)$, $L(t)$, $r(t)$, $q(t)$, and $K(t)$ is represented by (20), (22), (23), (24), (25), and (26), given an initial capital stock, $K(0)$.

It may be wondered how the potential shift in pseudoparameters can be congruent with a model that seems to be deterministic—a model in which expectations of future profits and future wages, having been "solved out," play no role in determining the wage and capital goods price. But the above system of equations does not determine q and v, because future values of both will depend on future parameter values, which are unknown. That point could be underlined by explicitly regarding the future parameters as unknown functions of time. The trouble began when economists took models of a stationary state in a medieval economy—models in which the parameters could indeed be regarded as known—and applied them to a modern economy in which innovation changes the parameters in unpredictable ways.

This chapter differs from the literature on anticipated regime change in insisting that future productivity levels are unknown, so that the capital goods price and wage have to be figured out on the basis of expectations, or assumptions, regarding productivity at a horizon that is a distance h into the future and the price and wage at that future time. (The wage will depend on expectations of subsequent productivity and subsequent price and wage expectations.) Thus, the solution for the price and the wage—the belief concerning the right price and the right wage—has to be indexed by the set of expectations of the two future productivity parameters. If it is expected that, at the future time, there will be expectations of subsequent productivity increases, that belief also must be indexed by expectations of the future price and wage. Incidentally, even after a short time, it may well be that expectations of the productivity levels at the old horizon need to be revised; also, people may be able to form expectations for the same distance h into the future or for some new distance, greater or smaller. Expectations are capable of shifting with the passage of time, during which economic actors generate new ideas. To tie the parameters to time would be to turn the model into one that really is deterministic.

So the natural rate is not known in the sense of being determined by parameters, and is dependent on autonomous and private expectations about the future, which are unknown, if not knowable. But, conditional on expectations about events on the horizon, there is an associated equilibrium path of employment running from its current level to its medium-term rest point. And that medium-term rest point is the corresponding natural rate— the natural rate contingent on the maintenance of current expectations of future productivity levels, future wages, and future asset valuations.

References and Suggested Readings

Abramovitz, Moses (ed.). (1962) *The Rate and Direction of Inventive Activity.* Princeton, NJ: Princeton University Press.

Blanchard, Olivier J. (1985) "Debt, Deficits, and Finite Horizons," *Journal of Political Economy* 93: 223–247.

Brito, Dagobert. (1970) "On the Limits of Economic Control," in Edmund S. Phelps (ed.), *Recent Developments in Macroeconomics,* 3 volumes. Aldershot, UK: Edward Elgar.

Calvo, Guillermo. (2010) "To Spend or Not to Spend: Is That the Main Question?" Working Paper 64, Center on Capitalism and Society, Columbia University, New York.

Calvo, Guillermo A., and Edmund S. Phelps. (1983) "A Model of Non-Walrasian General Equilibrium: Its Pareto Inoptimality and Pareto Improvement," in J. Tobin (ed.), *Macroeconomics, Prices and Quantities: Essays in Memory of Arthur M. Okun.* Washington, DC: Brookings Institution Press, pp. 135–157.

Fleming, J. Marcus. (1962) "Domestic Financial Policies under Fixed and Floating Exchange Rates," *IMF Staff Papers* 9: 369–379.

Hoon, Hian Teck, and Edmund S. Phelps. (2011) "Innovation and Employment." Working Paper 69, Center on Capitalism and Society, Columbia University, New York.

Keynes, John Maynard. (1936) *The General Theory of Employment, Interest and Money.* London: Palgrave Macmillan.

———. (1937) "The General Theory of Unemployment," *Quarterly Journal of Economics* 51: 209–233.

Knight, Frank H. (1921) *Risk, Uncertainty, and Profit.* New York: Houghton Mifflin.

Leijonhufvud, Axel. (1968) *On Keynesian Economics and the Economics of Keynes.* Chicago: University of Chicago Press.

Metzler, Lloyd A. (1951) "Wealth, Saving, and the Rate of Interest," *Journal of Political Economy* 59: 93–116.

Mortensen, Dale. (1970) "A Theory of Wage and Employment Dynamics," in Edmund S. Phelps, G. C. Archibald, and Armen A. Alchian (eds.), *Microeconomic Foundations of Employment and Inflation Theory.* New York: W. W. Norton, pp. 167–211.

Mundell, Robert A. (1963) "Capital Mobility and Stabilization Policy under Fixed and Flexible Exchange Rates." *Canadian Journal of Economic and Political Science* 29: 475–485. doi:10.2307/139336. Reprinted in Mundell, Robert A. (1968) *International Economics.* New York: Macmillan, pp. 250–271.

Nelson, Richard R., and Sidney Winter. (1985) *An Evolutionary Theory of Economic Change.* Cambridge, MA: Belknap Press of Harvard University Press.

Phelps, Edmund S. (1967) "Phillips Curves, Expectations of Inflation and Optimal Unemployment over Time," *Economica* 34: 254–281.

———. (1968) "Money-Wage Dynamics and Labor-Market Equilibrium," *Journal of Political Economy* 76: 678–711. An altered version is in Edmund S. Phelps, G. C. Archibald, and Armen A. Alchian (eds.). (1970) *Microeconomic Foundations of Employment and Inflation Theory*. New York: W. W. Norton, pp. 124–166. Reprinted in Panayotis G. Korliras and Richard S. Thorn (eds.). (1979) *Modern Macroeconomics*. New York: Harper and Row, pp. 213–241.

———. (1972) *Inflation Policy and Unemployment Theory*. New York and London: W. W. Norton and Macmillan.

———. (1992) "Consumer Demand and Equilibrium Unemployment in a Customer-Market Incentive-Wage Economy," *Quarterly Journal of Economics* 106: 1003–1032.

———. (1994) *Structural Slumps: The Modern Equilibrium Theory of Employment, Interest and Assets*. Cambridge, MA: Harvard University Press.

———. (1997) "The Rise and Downward Trend of the Natural Rate," with Gylfi Zoega, *American Economic Review* 87(Papers and Proceedings): 283–289.

———. (1999) "Behind This Structural Boom: The Role of Asset Valuations," *American Economic Review* 89(Papers and Proceedings): 63–68.

———. (2000a) "Roots of the Recent Recoveries: Labor Reforms or Private Sector Forces?" with Jean-Paul Fitoussi, David Jestaz, and Gylfi Zoega, *Brookings Papers on Economic Activity* 2000 (1): 237–311.

———. (2000b) "Education and the Natural Rate of Unemployment," with J. Michael Orszag and Gylfi Zoega, *Oxford Economic Papers* 52: 204–223.

———. (2000c) "Lessons in Natural-Rate Dynamics," *Oxford Economic Papers* 52: 51–71.

———. (2001a) "Structural Booms: Productivity Expectations and Asset Valuations," *Economic Policy* 32: 85–126.

———. (2001b) "Balanced-Budget Restraint in Taxing Income from Wealth in the Ramsey Model," in Kevin A. Hassett (ed.), *Inequality and Tax Policy*. Washington, DC: American Enterprise Institute, pp. 166–186.

———. (2010) "The Slump, the Recovery and the 'New Normal.'" Working Paper 61, Center on Capitalism and Society, Columbia University, New York.

Phelps, Edmund S., and Hian Teck Hoon. (2005) "Channels and Mechanisms Linking Future Budgetary Shocks to Present Asset Prices and Economic Activity." Paper presented at the 2nd Annual Conference, Center on Capitalism and Society, Reykjavik, June 16–17.

———. (2006) "Future Fiscal and Budgetary Shocks," *Journal of Economic Theory* 143: 499–518.

———. (2007) "A Structuralist Model of the Small Open Economy in the Short, Medium and Long Run," *Journal of Macroeconomics* 29: 227–254.

———. (2010) "Macroeconomic Effects of Over-Investment in Housing in an Aggregative Model of Economic Activity." Working Paper 63, Center on Capitalism and Society, Columbia University, New York.

Phelps, Edmund S., and Sidney Winter. (1970) "Optimal Price Policy under Atomistic Competition," in E. S. Phelps, et al. (eds.), *Microeconomic Foundations of Employment and Inflation Theory*. New York: W. W. Norton, pp. 309–337.

Phelps, Edmund S., and Gylfi Zoega. (1998) "Natural-Rate Theory and OECD Unemployment," *Economic Journal* 108: 782–801.

Phelps, Edmund S., G. C. Archibald, and Armen A. Alchian (eds.). (1970) *Microeconomic Foundations of Employment and Inflation Theory.* New York: W. W. Norton.

Phelps, Edmund S., Hian Teck Hoon, and Gylfi Zoega. (2005) "The Structuralist Perspective on Real Exchange Rate, Share Price Level and Employment Path: What Room Is Left for Money?" in Willi Semmler (ed.), *Monetary Policy and Unemployment.* London: Routledge, pp. 107–132.

Salop, Steven C. (1979) "A Model of the Natural Rate of Unemployment," *American Economic Review* 69: 117–125.

Shapiro, Carl, and Joseph Stiglitz. (1984) "Equilibrium Unemployment as a Worker Discipline Device," *American Economic Review* 74: 433–444.

Weil, Philippe. (1989) "Overlapping Families of Infinitely-Lived Agents," *Journal of Public Economics* 38: 183–198.

Zoega, Gylfi. (2010) "The Financial Crisis: Joblessness and Investmentlessness." Working Paper 62, Center on Capitalism and Society, Columbia University, New York.

CHAPTER NINE

The Long Swings of Employment, Investment, and Asset Prices

Gylfi Zoega

9.1 Introduction

Several papers published in *Microeconomic Foundations of Employment and Inflation Theory* in 1970 (Phelps et al. 1970) show why monetary policy cannot attain an arbitrary unemployment rate other than the natural rate of unemployment without generating rising inflation or deflation. However, even though the natural rate itself was never assumed to be a constant of nature in the volume—the Phelps (1970) paper in the volume makes it a function of the rate of growth of the labor force[1]—modeling of the determinants of the natural unemployment rate only took off when economists were faced with a persistent elevation of unemployment in the 1970s and 1980s.

The objective of this chapter is to map one stylized fact that a model of the natural rate should be able to account for: the relationship among unemployment, investment, and share prices that is observed in the data. Although this relationship is often ignored, it provides a justification for some recent models of the natural rate. The intuition behind these models is quite simple. For example, when the value of a trained employee increases compared to the cost of training him, firms increase their rate of hiring, which lowers equilibrium unemployment when real wages are rigid.[2] Similarly, when the value of a vacancy increases, firms respond by posting more vacancies, which lowers equilibrium unemployment in a search model of the labor market. In both cases firms are investing in the employment of new

The author thanks Olafur G. Halldorsson for research assistance.

1. See also Phelps (1972) on the effect of monetary and fiscal policy on the natural rate.

2. This may cause output to fall initially as workers are diverted from production to the training of new employees.

workers because of an increase in the expected future profits from employing a worker.

9.2 A Moving Natural Rate of Unemployment

Initial attempts to explain persistently high unemployment in the 1980s were founded on the idea that a transitory recession could leave permanent scars in the labor market—there was hysteresis in the labor market (see Lindbeck and Snower 1989; Layard et al. 1991). However, as the period of high unemployment turned from years to decades, this explanation lost credence. Theories that explained changes in the labor market equilibrium not related to the past performance of this market turned out to be more convincing, and they could potentially explain infrequent shifts in mean unemployment.[3] There are basically two variants of the theory, one based on flow models and the other on stock models. Phelps (1994), Blanchard (1997), and Nickell et al. (2005) provide good examples of the stock approach, whereas Mortensen and Pissarides (1994) and Pissarides (2000) are good examples of the flow approach.

A distinction can also be made between models in which changes in equilibrium unemployment are caused by changing macroeconomic factors and those in which changes in the equilibrium are brought about by changing labor market institutions. Phelps (1994) presented three basic models in which the demand for labor had an investment dimension, which opened the way for expectations about future profits and interest rates to affect current labor demand and the equilibrium in the labor market when real wages are rigid. He then went on to attribute the elevation of unemployment in Europe and elsewhere in OECD countries to a rise in the world real interest rate. The related idea that productivity growth may affect equilibrium unemployment is due to Pissarides (2000), who made firms discount future profits from vacancies by the difference between the real interest rate and the expected rate of productivity growth.[4] Greenwald and Stiglitz (1993) linked labor demand and equilibrium unemployment to the state of balance sheets. In their model lower levels of equity raise expected bankruptcy costs, which makes firms lower their labor demand when future output prices are uncertain. Their model is supported by the empirical results of Nickell and

3. See Bianchi and Zoega (1998) and Papell et al. (2000) on the importance of infrequent shifts in mean unemployment.

4. The importance of the rate of productivity growth for unemployment has been emphasized by, among others, Manning (1992), Hoon and Phelps (1997), Pissarides (2000), and Ball and Moffitt (2001). Hatton (2006) explores the empirical relationship between productivity growth and unemployment using long-run historical data for the United Kingdom and finds that high productivity growth brings low unemployment.

Wadhwani (1991) and Nickell and Nicolitsas (1999), who analyzed firm-level data and found that various financial factors have a significant effect on employment. In particular they find that employment increases with firms' market capitalization and decreases with their leverage ratio and that increased financial pressure—measured as the ratio of interest payments to cash flow—has a large negative effect on employment, a negative impact on pay increases, and a small positive effect on productivity.

An alternative approach is to attribute changes in equilibrium unemployment to changes in labor market institutions. An early synthesis of this work is found in Layard et al. (1991), and later contributions include Nickell et al. (2005), to name just one of a very large number of papers. In these models, the level of unemployment in equilibrium depends on the level and duration of unemployment benefits, the level of firing restrictions, the coverage of labor unions, and the centralization of bargaining, to mention a few of the variables included in the analysis. Belot and van Ours (2000) explain changes in unemployment in OECD countries by changes in these institutions while allowing for interactions among institutions. Coe and Snower (1997) analyze complementarities among a variety of labor market institutions and find complementary effects for a wide range of institutions, which implies that partial labor market reform is less likely to have a significant effect on unemployment than a coordinated change in a number of policies.

The two approaches—the one emphasizing macroeconomic developments and the other emphasizing labor market institutions—are not mutually exclusive. Phelps (1994), Blanchard and Wolfers (2000), and Fitoussi et al. (2000) combine them by letting the effect of shocks depend on institutions. In addition, Ljungqvist and Sargent (1998) allow institutions to interact with shocks. They show that an increase in labor market turbulence may lead to greater skill losses and unemployment in countries where the level of benefits is high and their duration long, such as in many European countries. However, the relative importance of macroeconomic variables, on one hand, and labor market institutions, on the other, does matter. In one view, unemployment should be tackled through institutional changes in the labor market without paying too much attention to other parts of the economy. In contrast, a moving equilibrium model of unemployment—in which the equilibrium depends on expectations about future profits and interest rates—implies that the level of unemployment depends on economic performance in a wider sense: productivity, expected productivity growth, innovations, entrepreneurship, and the functioning of global capital markets (see Phelps 2006).

In the following sections a relationship between equilibrium unemployment and asset prices is explained and shown to hold for the data. The labor market implications of the current financial crisis are then discussed.

9.3   Employment and Asset Prices

Any theory that assumes adjustment costs of labor gives a relationship between employment and the implicit shadow price of labor. Oi (1962) pioneered the idea that labor is a quasi-fixed factor of production, because part of the cost of labor consists of variable wages, whereas other parts are fixed (i.e., the cost of hiring and training workers). Phelps (1994) built on Salop (1979), Calvo (1979), and his own work in the 1960s (Phelps 1968), including that published in the *Microeconomic Foundations* volume (Phelps et al. 1970), to obtain three models linking unemployment to different asset prices where there is real wage rigidity stemming from the effects of efficiency wages (see also Hoon and Phelps 1992). There is the customer market model first formulated by Phelps and Winter (1970) and extended to a general equilibrium framework, where changes in the shadow price of customers lead firms to change their price mark-up over marginal cost and hence also their demand wage. Intuitively, the more firms value their customers, the harder they will try to expand their market share by cutting prices. When the shadow price goes up—because of lower interest rates or higher expected profits—firms respond by lowering prices to invest in a larger market share and acquire more customers, making the demand wage increase and unemployment fall.[5] In Phelps's turnover-training model, an increase in the shadow price of trained workers makes firms decide to train more workers, and this lowers unemployment in a steady state. Finally, in a two-sector model of a labor-intensive capital goods sector and a capital-intensive consumer goods sector, an increase in the shadow price of capital will make firms increase wages, which will also lower unemployment, as in the Stolper-Samuelson effect (see Hoon and Phelps 2007). One application of a two-sector model is to analyze the relationship between house prices and employment, where labor-intensive construction is one of the two sectors. An increase in the relative price of the labor-intensive construction sector then triggers a construction boom, which raises the real demand wage and employment.

Intertemporal considerations also affect unemployment in matching models. Pissarides (2000) develops the matching framework and shows how an increase in the shadow price of a vacancy will make firms offer more vacancies, creating more matches between employers with vacancies and unemployed workers and causing equilibrium unemployment to fall. The increased supply of vacancies moves the economy along a Beveridge curve toward a point of lower unemployment and higher vacancy rate, as long as workers do not succeed in capturing an increased share of the now-higher value of a match between a worker and a firm.

---

5. In a symmetric equilibrium all firms cut prices, which makes their attempts to expand market share futile, the only effect being to lower mark-ups and raise the real demand wage.

Empirically, the shadow price of customers can be proxied by an index of stock prices. In Fitoussi et al. (2000) and Phelps and Zoega (2001) we document the empirical relationship between unemployment and share prices normalized by labor productivity. We find that both variables are subject to discrete changes in their mean values and that these changes are related, so that when a country experiences an upward shift in mean unemployment, the mean level of share prices drops from one plateau to another. To mention one example, the transition from a regime of low unemployment to one of high unemployment that took place in many continental European economies in the 1970s and 1980s coincided with a similar transition in the stock market toward lower share prices.

Phelps and Zoega (2004) find that stock market capitalization and unemployment are inversely related and that market capitalization and productivity growth are positively related in a sample of OECD countries. In related work, Smith and Zoega (2006, 2008) use principal components analysis to compare global changes in employment and investment and find that the two variables are closely related, mirroring the movement of the world real interest rate. Taken together, the results suggest that the long swings of unemployment may reflect changes in the investment outlook—expected profits and interest rates. Finally, Gatti et al. (2009) estimate a dynamic panel model for 18 OECD countries for 1980–2004 and find that increased market capitalization lowers unemployment in a flexible labor market, where the level of regulation, union density, and coordination in wage bargaining is low.

The next section discusses a stripped-down natural rate model that generates a relationship among the natural rate of unemployment, investment, and asset prices. Section 9.5 takes a look at the data.

9.4   Modeling Structural Unemployment

The modeling of a moving natural rate of unemployment requires adding a variety of market imperfections and rigidities to the standard classical labor supply/demand framework. The labor market is no longer described by conventional labor demand and labor supply curves. Instead it is given by a wage curve that defines wages as a function of the unemployment rate—there is real wage rigidity—and a price-setting curve, which replaces the labor demand curve when there is imperfect competition in the goods market. In equilibrium at the intersection of the price-setting curve and the wage curve, there is excess supply of labor in the market under conditions of correct expectations.

The price-setting curve can be derived by assuming that customers have imperfect information about prices (as in Phelps and Winter 1970); they only know the price at the firms they patronize and then switch to other firms when they learn by word of mouth about lower prices elsewhere. The flow of customers is described by an equation that relates the change in the market share x^i of representative firm i to the ratio of the price charged p^i and the average price in the industry p, in addition to the number of existing customers (because existing customers inform potential customers about lower prices). The equation for customer flows can be written as[6]

$$\dot{x} = \left(\gamma - \gamma \left(\frac{p^i}{p} \right)^{\mu} \right) x^i \tag{1}$$

where the dot denotes the time derivative, $\gamma, \mu \geq 0$, and $0 \leq x \leq 1$. The parameter μ measures the effectiveness of prices at affecting customer flows; γ can be interpreted as measuring the level of habit persistence—the lower its value is, the greater habit formation will be.[7]

The demand for output by each of the x^i customers is denoted by y^i and is a function of the firm's relative price p^i / p:

$$y^i = A \left(\frac{p^i}{p} \right)^{-\eta}, \eta > 1 \tag{2}$$

where η is the elasticity of demand. Current profits can then be written as

$$\left(p^i - c(1 - u) \right) y^i x^i \tag{3}$$

where $c(1 - u)$ is the unit cost of production, which each firm takes as given but is a function of the rate of employment $1 - u$ in the economy. In particular, unit labor costs can be written as

$$c(1 - u) = \frac{w}{e \left(\frac{w}{z} \right)}, \quad e' \left(\frac{w}{z} \right) > 0 \tag{4}$$

where w denotes the nominal wage; e is an effort function that makes effort an increasing function of the ratio of wages to the expected income if not employed at that firm; $z = (1 - u)w + ub$, where b is the level of unemployment benefits. The unit labor costs are increasing in the employment rate $1 - u$, because workers lower their effort when expected income elsewhere rises due to improved job prospects.

The representative firm maximizes the present value of future profits,

$$\max \int_0^\infty e^{-\rho t} \left[\left(p^i - c(1 - u) \right) y^i x^i \right] dt \tag{5}$$

---

6. The functional firm is as in Choudhary and Orszag (2007).

7. This can be seen most clearly by letting p^i go to zero, in which case the equation will converge to γ. It follows that lower values of γ signify greater habit persistence.

where ρ is the real interest rate, subject to

$$\dot{x}^i = \left(\gamma - \gamma \left(\frac{p^i}{p} \right)^\mu \right) x^i$$

This yields a present-value Hamiltonian

$$H = \left(p^i - c(1 - u) \right) x^i y^i + q \left(\gamma - \gamma \left(\frac{p^i}{p} \right)^\mu \right) x^i \tag{6}$$

where q denotes the costate variables for customers.

The Pontryagin condition for optimal prices (p^i) is

$$A \left(\frac{p^i}{p} \right)^{-\eta} - A\eta \left(\frac{p^i}{p} \right)^{-\eta} + A\eta \left(\frac{p^i}{p} \right)^{-\eta} \frac{c(1 - u)}{p^i} = q \frac{\mu\gamma}{p^i} \left(\frac{p^i}{p} \right)^\mu \tag{7}$$

The sum of the terms on the left-hand side denotes the current benefit from raising prices in the form of higher current profits; the right-hand side denotes the cost in terms of the discounted fall in future profits due to a smaller market share. Clearly, the marginal cost is rising in the value of q, which is the shadow price of customers. Also, the higher the value of μ and the higher the value of γ, implying less habit persistence, the greater will be the marginal cost of raising current prices in terms of future profits.

Finally, there is a differential equation for the costate variable q:

$$\dot{q} - \rho q = -A \left(\frac{p^i}{p} \right)^{-\eta} p^i + A \left(\frac{p^i}{p} \right)^{-\eta} c(1 - u) - q \left(\gamma - \gamma \left(\frac{p^i}{p} \right)^\mu \right) \tag{8}$$

One can rewrite (7) and (8) in a symmetric equilibrium where $p^i = p$ and $\dot{x} = 0$ as

$$p^i = \frac{\eta}{\eta - 1} c(1 - u) - q \frac{\mu\gamma}{A(\eta - 1)} \tag{9}$$

$$\dot{q} - \rho q = \frac{-A\eta c(1 - u)}{\eta - 1} + q \frac{\mu\gamma}{\eta - 1} + Ac(1 - u) \tag{10}$$

In (9) prices p^i are written as a mark-up over marginal costs $c(1 - u)$ and a term that captures the customer market model $q\gamma\mu/(A(\eta - 1))$. When $q = 0$ we find that the firm charges the monopoly price $\eta\, c(1 - u)/(\eta - 1)$, whereas when $q > 0$ it will charge a lower price. The more sensitive customers are to prices (as measured by μ and γ) and the more valuable customers are to the firm (as measured by q), the lower prices will be.[8] A phase diagram for the system of equations (9) and (10) is shown in Appendix 9.A.

Equations (9) and (10) can then be solved for a steady state symmetric equilibrium. We first solve (10) for the steady state $\dot{q} = 0$:

$$q = \frac{Ac(1-u)}{\rho(\eta-1) + \mu\gamma + \gamma\beta(\eta-1)} \tag{11}$$

Substituting the optimal value for q into (9) and simplifying gives

$$p^i = \frac{\eta}{\eta-1}c(1-u) - \frac{\mu\gamma c(1-u)}{(\rho(\eta-1) + \mu\gamma)(\eta-1)} \tag{12}$$

As explained earlier, the first term in the price-setting equation is the monopoly mark-up of price p^i over marginal cost $c(1-\mu)$. The second term is the Phelps-Winter effect, which shows how concerns about the impact of prices on future market share depress prices. Note that a rise in interest rates reduces the future value of customers and motivates firms to raise prices.

Equation (12) defines a labor demand curve—or price-setting curve in symmetric equilibrium $p^i = p$, which gives the real demand wage v:

$$v^d = \frac{w}{p} = v^d(q, 1-u; \eta, \mu, \gamma) \tag{13}$$

Given the state of technology, the real demand wage depends on the shadow price q of a customer, the employment rate, and various parameters. The real demand wage is declining in the employment rate.[9]

The labor market is also plagued by information imperfections. Phelps (1970) provides microeconomic foundations for real wage rigidity by showing how firms can use their wage settings to affect workers' propensities to quit. A wage curve can be obtained from the efficiency wage story, such as in Shapiro and Stiglitz (1984); as the outcome of union bargaining, as in Layard et al. (1991); or from matching frictions, as in Pissarides (2000). In all three setups, equilibrium necessarily entails a positive rate of unemployment.

Following Solow (1979), one can derive a wage curve by minimizing unit labor costs $c(1-u)$. Taking the derivative of (4) and setting it equal to zero gives an optimal solution for w/z and hence also for the ratio of the real wage v to the real value of expected income if not employed at the firm:

---

8. Bagwell (2004) correlates current and future growth in demand, which makes mark-ups countercyclical in the true business cycle sense.

9. In addition, various other factors not included in this optimization exercise may influence the mark-up decision. Financial pressure—defined as the requirement to service debt and pay other fixed costs—can make firms raise mark-ups over the value that maximizes the value of the firm, as shown by Nickell and Nicolitsas (1999).

$$\frac{e'\left(\frac{w}{z}\right)\frac{w}{z}}{e\left(\frac{w}{z}\right)} = 1 \qquad (14)$$

Assuming that the effort function takes the functional form

$$e\left(\frac{w}{z}\right) = \left(\frac{w-z}{z}\right)^{\theta}, \quad \theta > 1 \qquad (15)$$

gives a solution for wages $w = z/(1-\theta)$, where z is the expected income if not employed at that firm: $z = (1-u)w + ub$. This condition defines a wage curve in the real wage-output space that is increasing in employment $1-u$, because taking the total differential of the equation results in

$$\frac{dw}{d(1-u)} = \frac{(w-b)/(1-\theta)}{1-(1-\theta)^{-1}(1-u)} > 0 \qquad (16)$$

which gives an upward-sloping wage curve for $1-u < 1-\theta$, which then becomes vertical when $u = \theta$.

The equilibrium in the labor market is described by a (real) wage curve that reflects these information imperfections:

$$v^s = \frac{w}{p} = v^s(1-u, b, I) \qquad (17)$$

Various labor market institutions I can then be added to the equation. Labor unions will affect the position of the wage curve, so that a higher density of unions will shift the wage curve upward, generating higher equilibrium unemployment.[10]

Equilibrium in the labor market is defined by the intersection of a downward-sloping price-setting curve (13) and an upward-sloping wage curve (17):

$$v^d(q, 1-u^*; \eta, \mu, \gamma) = v^s(1-u^*, I) \qquad (18)$$

The equation shows the equilibrium unemployment rate u^* as a function of the shadow price of customers q. Expectations about future increases in demand per customer, y^i, or a fall in the real interest rate r will make the shadow price q of customers jump. The higher shadow price of customers will make the representative firm cut mark-ups of price over marginal cost, which shifts the v^d curve upward in a symmetric equilibrium and lowers the equilibrium unemployment rate. The supply side of the economy is thus described by an upward-sloping curve in the shadow price q-employment $(1-u)$ space.

---

10. Honkapohja and Koskela (1999) drew attention to the importance of household and business debt for equilibrium unemployment in their account of Finland's financial crisis in the early 1990s.

9.5 The Supply of Jobs

We would like to test for an upward-sloping curve in the shadow price q-employment $(1 - u)$ space. Such a relationship implies that employment and asset prices move together in the medium term—the long swings of employment coincide with the long swings of asset prices.

Share prices normalized by labor productivity[11] can be used as a measure of the variable q. The normalization by productivity is done in the tradition of the Tobin q model of investment. In the turnover-training model output per worker is meant to capture the cost of training new workers, because established workers will not be producing when teaching newly hired recruits. In the customer market model output per worker is a proxy for consumption per worker, which affects the sacrificed profits from cutting prices; clearly, cutting prices is more costly in rich economies. In Section 9.6 we also explore the relationship between employment and house prices as well as some of the variables that may affect these prices, such as real interest rates and the real price of oil.

Figure 9.1 relates share prices—normalized by labor productivity—to the employment rate (100 minus the rate of unemployment) for six countries during 1960–2009. The share price variable is measured by its average level for the first 3 years of each half-decade, whereas the employment rate $(1 - u)$ is measured by the last 3 years of each half-decade, the rationale being that price setting and hiring decisions do not have an instantaneous effect on the level of employment. Three of the countries (Belgium, Italy, and Spain) suffered an elevation of mean unemployment over this period. In the other three countries (the Netherlands, the United Kingdom, and the United States) unemployment reverted back to its earlier mean following recessions. The plots for the remaining 10 countries are shown in Appendix 9.B. A clear upward-sloping relationship is apparent for each of the countries. Note that the movement to a level of lower average employment in the 1970s and 1980s in Belgium, Italy, and Spain coincides with a move toward lower share prices. Similarly, the partial recovery in the first years of the new century coincides with rising share prices. In contrast, there is a more complete recovery of both employment and share prices in the Netherlands, the United Kingdom, and the United States.

The relationship can be estimated by a pooled cross-section time-series regression for 16 OECD countries:[12]

---

11. Labor productivity is measured by GDP per employed worker.

12. The 16 countries are Australia, Austria, Belgium, Canada, Finland, France, Ireland, Italy, Japan, Netherlands, New Zealand, Norway, Spain, Sweden, the United Kingdom, and the United States. Denmark, Greece, and Portugal are omitted, because these countries did not have a sufficiently long time series for share prices. Germany is omitted because of its unification in 1990: unemployment has been very high in the eastern regions for structural reasons not captured by the variables included in this chapter.

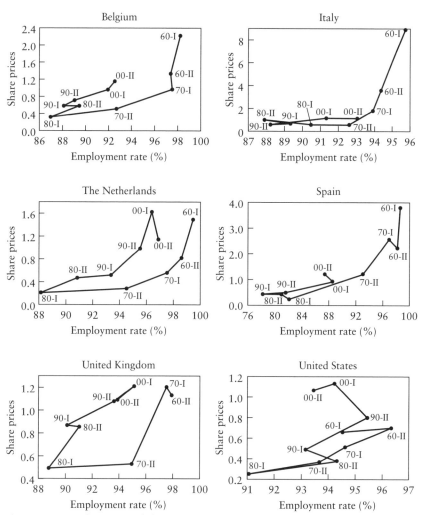

Figure 9.1 Employment and share prices. Shown are share prices (normalized by labor productivity) versus employment rate $(1 - u)$ for half-decades from 1960 to 2010. Share prices are calculated for the first 3 years of the half-decade (e.g., 1960–1962), whereas the employment rate is calculated as the average of the last 3 years (e.g., 1962–1964). The designators in the art denote the year (e.g., "60" for 1960) and the first or second half-decade for that year ("I" and "II," respectively).

$$100 - u_{it} = a_i + bq_{it} + \varepsilon_{it} \tag{19}$$

where q is the normalized share price; it proxies for the shadow price of customers and capital. The index i denotes countries and the index t half-decades, starting with 1960–1964 and ending with 2005–2009. The results for b are reported in Table 9.1. The first column uses half-decades starting with 1960–1964; the next four columns (columns 2–5) test for

Table 9.1 Employment and share prices

	Level					First difference				
	(1)	(2)	(3)	(4)	(5)	(6)	(7)	(8)	(9)	(10)
Half-decade start	1960	1961	1962	1963	1964	1960	1961	1962	1963	1964
b (%)	1.32	1.29	1.42	2.00	2.07	0.95	0.95	1.37	2.45	2.35
t-ratio	3.7	3.4	3.5	6.4	5.1	1.7	2.0	1.9	2.8	2.90

Notes: The estimation method is pooled cross-section time-series weighted least squares. The parameter b is from equation (9).

the robustness of the results by starting with the half-decades 1961–1965, 1962–1966, 1963–1967, and 1964–1968, respectively.

It is difficult to determine whether the series have unit roots, given the small size of the sample, especially because both the employment rate and the normalized share price series are subject to infrequently shifting means.

Therefore, finding similar results using first-difference data would be evidence that the association is not the result of a spurious regression of $I(1)$ data. The first five columns show the estimation results for the equation in terms of levels, whereas columns 6–10 in the table show the results in terms of first differences.

The variable q has the value one in 2005, which is its base year. The coefficients b of q in Table 9.1 indicate that a doubling of q, from its base year value of 1 to 2, will generate a fall in unemployment of between 0.95% and 2.45%. One cannot reject the hypothesis that the five estimates in columns 1–5 are statistically equivalent.[13] Overall, the estimates confirm a robust relationship between share prices and unemployment.[14]

Price setting has been modeled as investment in market share, which depends on the shadow price of customers. A closely related variable is the shadow price of physical capital, which suggests that there should be a relationship between employment and gross capital formation. Table 9.2 shows the results when share prices are replaced by gross capital formation as a share of GDP in (19).

The results indicate that a 10% increase of investment as a share of GDP (e.g., from 10% to 20% of GDP) is associated with a 2.1–5.6% fall in unemployment. When both share prices and investment are included, both variables remain significant, as shown in Table 9.3.

---

13. A Wald test using the estimation results in columns 1 and 6 was used to test whether the estimated coefficient of q could take the values reported in columns 2–5 and 7–10, respectively. The hypothesis of equality could not be rejected at the 5% level of significance.

14. These results are consistent with Nickell and Wadhwani (1991), who used firm-level data to study what determines employment level. They found that a 1% fall in market capitalization was associated with a 0.17% decline in employment.

Table 9.2 Employment and gross capital formation

	Level					First difference				
	(1)	(2)	(3)	(4)	(5)	(6)	(7)	(8)	(9)	(10)
Half-decade start	1960	1961	1962	1963	1964	1960	1961	1962	1963	1964
b (%)	0.44	0.53	0.51	0.56	0.42	0.22	0.35	0.43	0.43	0.21
t-ratio	6.2	7.8	7.6	5.7	4.6	4.3	4.9	3.5	4.1	2.6

Notes: The estimation method is pooled cross-section time-series weighted least squares. The parameter b is from equation (9).

Table 9.3 Employment, share prices, and gross capital formation

Indicator	Level (1960)		First difference (1960)	
	Coefficient	t-ratio	Coefficient	t-ratio
Share price	2.68	5.1	2.10	4.9
Investment	0.46	9.2	0.21	5.5
Number of observations	125		109	

Note: Estimation is done using data for the half-decade starting in 1960.

The results so far appear to suggest that employment and investment are related and that changes in the level of share prices precede changes in the rate of employment. A test of Granger causality can be applied to verify this result. Granger causality tests were performed using annual data for the same variables, and the results are reported in Table 9.4. The null hypothesis of changes in share prices not Granger-causing employment can be rejected for 14 of the 16 countries studied at a 5% level of significance and for 1 more at a 10% significance level.[15] The alternative hypothesis of changes in employment not Granger-causing changes in share prices can only be rejected for two countries, Norway and Sweden.

The medium-term relationship between average share prices and employment for all 16 countries in the sample is shown in Figure 9.2a, which plots the average value of employment rate $(1 - u)$ versus share prices for the 16 countries in the sample. Figure 9.2b plots the relationship between average investment (gross capital formation as a proportion of GDP) and the employment rate.

15. The hypothesis cannot be rejected for Austria, for which the probability is 13.5% that the hypothesis of no relationship is true.

Table 9.4 Granger causality tests of employment and share prices

Country	Number of observations	*F* test	Probability	Lags
Australia	46	7.50	0.0002**	4
Austria	46	1.88	0.1349	4
Belgium	46	6.96	0.0003**	4
Canada	25	3.22	0.0865*	4
Finland	48	6.93	0.0025**	2
France	17	4.53	0.0032**	4
Ireland	48	3.38	0.0432**	2
Italy	49	8.72	0.0049**	1
Japan	46	5.19	0.0020**	4
Netherlands	46	5.28	0.0018**	4
New Zealand	46	2.78	0.0410**	4
Norway	47	3.12	0.0366**	3
Spain	46	3.29	0.0210**	4
Sweden	46	4.62	0.0040**	4
United Kingdom	43	3.00	0.0321**	4
United States	46	4.11	0.0074**	4

Notes: The table reports Granger causality tests for changes in normalized share prices q not causing changes in employment $1 - u$. ** denotes rejection of the null hypothesis of no Granger causality at the 5% level; * denotes rejection at the 10% level.

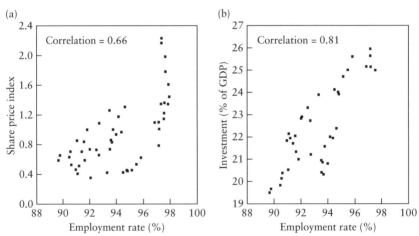

Figure 9.2 Average share prices, investment, and employment. Shown are (a) average values of the share price index for 16 OECD countries versus the average rate of employment and (b) average share of gross capital formation in GDP versus the employment rate.

9.6   Other Factors

Macroeconomic variables other than q and labor market variables are added to the regression equation (19) in Tables 9.5 and 9.6. The macroeconomic variables include an index of house prices (normalized by productivity), the world real interest rate, and real oil prices. The labor market variables include a measure of coordination in wage bargaining, the union density, the unemployment benefit replacement ratio, the duration of benefits, and employment protection (see Appendix 9.C for sources and definitions).

Clearly, it is difficult to determine whether the series have unit roots, given the small size of the sample, especially because both the employment rate and the share price series are subject to infrequently shifting means (see Bianchi and Zoega 1998). Moreover, time averaging using half-decades removes the high-frequency annual component. Finding similar results using first-difference data would be evidence that the association is not the result of spurious regression of the $I(1)$ data. For this reason the same equation is estimated in Table 9.6 using first differences to test for robustness.

Consistent with the results in Table 9.1, share prices have a statistically significant positive coefficient that is robust to the inclusion of the other variables. The numerical value of the coefficient implies that a doubling of share prices from its base value of one to two makes employment rise by about 2%. Estimating using first differences does not make the coefficient insignificant. When house prices (column 2) are added, many observations are lost: only 91 observations remain to cover the most recent periods. A doubling of house prices from their base value of one to two will raise employment by 3.7%. Taken together, a doubling of both share prices and house prices (relative to labor productivity)—that is, from a value of one to two—will raise employment by about 6%. In contrast to share prices, the coefficient of house prices loses its significance when first-difference data are used, probably because of the limited number of observations.

Turning to the other macroeconomic variables, the world real interest rate has a negative and significant coefficient that remains significant for first-difference data. The rate of productivity growth has a positive and significant coefficient in the levels regression, which, in contrast, becomes insignificant when estimating with first differences. The one remaining macroeconomic variable, the real price of oil, has a predicted negative coefficient when estimating in levels; it remains statistically significant when using first differences. The numerical values of the estimated coefficients imply that a 100-basis-point increase in real interest rate lowers employment between 0.5 and 1%, and a US\$10 increase in the price of a barrel of crude oil has a slightly smaller effect on the employment rate.

Labor market variables are included in columns 6–11 of Tables 9.5 and 9.6. More coordination in wage bargaining raises employment, and

Table 9.5 Multiple regressions: Fixed-effects estimation of employment equation (19)

Dependent variable: employment rate: 100 − u

Regressor	(1)	(2)	(3)	(4)	(5)	(6)	(7)	(8)	(9)	(10)	(11)
Stock prices (normalized)	1.32* (3.7)	2.56* (12.3)		2.02* (5.2)	2.04* (4.7)	2.33* (5.5)	2.03* (4.7)	2.07* (5.0)	2.09* (5.0)	2.14* (4.5)	2.14* (4.1)
House prices (normalized)		3.66* (11.2)									
World real interest rate (%)			−0.79* (4.3)	−0.67* (8.6)	−0.81* (5.5)	−0.83* (6.0)	−0.81* (5.0)	−0.79* (5.2)	−0.79* (5.4)	−0.83* (5.3)	−0.74* (5.2)
Productivity growth				0.68* (7.1)	0.45* (5.0)	0.46* (4.8)	0.55* (4.9)	0.48* (3.7)	0.48* (3.5)	0.42* (3.1)	0.54* (3.6)
Real oil prices					−0.03* (4.0)	−0.03* (3.8)	−0.02* (2.7)	−0.02* (2.5)	−0.02* (2.4)	−0.02* (2.9)	−0.02* (2.2)
Coordination						2.19* (6.2)	2.10* (6.3)	2.04* (6.1)	2.04* (6.2)	2.41* (6.3)	2.31* (5.5)
Union density							−0.07* (3.4)	−0.07* (3.3)	−0.07* (3.3)	−0.07* (3.1)	−0.07* (2.6)
Replacement ratio								−1.88 (1.3)	−1.79 (1.3)	−2.19 (1.6)	−1.46 (1.2)
Duration of benefits									−0.33 (1.3)	−0.52 (0.6)	−0.09 (0.1)
Employment protection										2.14* (2.2)	2.01 (1.7)
Inflation (change)											0.03 (1.2)
R^2	0.67	0.98	0.75	0.83	0.80	0.83	0.82	0.83	0.83	0.82	0.83
Number of observations	148	91	148	144	144	144	144	144	144	144	134

Notes: Linear estimations with White cross-section standard errors and covariance. The t-statistics are reported in parentheses. Units for dimensional variables are given in Appendix 9.C. * denotes significance at the 5% level.

Table 9.6 Multiple regressions: Fixed-effects estimation of employment equation (19), first differences

Dependent variable: employment rate: $d(100 - u)$

Regressor (first differences)	(1)	(2)	(3)	(4)	(5)	(6)	(7)	(8)	(9)	(10)	(11)
Stock prices (normalized)	0.95	2.10*	1.29	2.41*	2.04*	2.03*	1.89*	1.84*	1.89*	2.00*	2.65*
	(1.7)	(2.5)	(1.7)	(3.0)	(2.6)	(2.6)	(2.4)	(2.3)	(2.3)	(2.4)	(2.8)
House prices (normalized)		−1.29									
		(0.9)									
World real interest rate (%)			−0.49	−0.52*	−0.55*	−0.55*	−0.55*	−0.55*	−0.56*	−0.58*	−0.49*
			(1.4)	(2.0)	(3.5)	(3.3)	(3.1)	(3.10)	(3.0)	(3.5)	(2.5)
Productivity growth				0.57	0.18	0.17	0.11	0.12	0.05	0.10	0.17
				(1.1)	(0.3)	(0.3)	(0.2)	(0.2)	(0.1)	(0.2)	(0.3)
Real oil prices					−0.03	−0.02*	−0.03*	−0.03*	−0.03*	−0.03*	−0.02*
					(3.5)	(3.2)	(2.7)	(2.6)	(2.7)	(2.8)	(2.4)
Coordination						−0.23	−0.16	−0.19	−0.26	−0.15	−0.14
						(0.4)	(0.2)	(0.3)	(0.4)	(0.20)	(0.1)
Union density							−0.10*	−0.09*	−0.09*	−0.11*	−0.10*
							(2.9)	(2.8)	(2.7)	(4.0)	(2.8)
Replacement ratio								−1.60	−1.53	−2.64	−3.88
								(1.0)	(0.9)	(1.0)	(1.5)
Duration of benefits									−1.83	−1.82	−2.19
									(0.8)	(0.8)	(1.0)
Employment protection										1.85	2.09
										(0.7)	(0.7)
Inflation (change of a change)											0.03*
											(9.6)
R^2	0.13	0.19	0.17	0.25	0.29	0.29	0.31	0.31	0.31	0.32	0.35
Number of observations	132	75	132	128	128	128	128	128	128	128	118

Notes: Linear estimations with White cross-section standard errors and covariance. The t-statistics are reported in parentheses. Units for dimensional variables are given in Appendix 9.C. * denotes significance at the 5% level.

increased union density lowers it. Only union density survives first differencing of the data. There only remains to include an inflation shock variable—the first difference of the inflation rate—to control for nominal shocks (column 11). This term has a statistically significant and positive effect on employment while not changing the signs or the significance of the other variables.

To summarize these results, the normalized share price variable, the world real interest rate, oil prices, and the union density variables appear to be the most robust determinants of equilibrium unemployment.

Finally (and not reported in Tables 9.5 and 9.6 because of the limited number of observations), measures of debt—household, nonfinancial business, and consolidated general government—and the countries' net foreign assets (data are from OECD financial balance sheets and IMF International Financial Statistics) were added to the estimation equation. These variables turned out to be insignificant in both the levels and the first-difference estimations.

9.7 Financial Crises

The economic models that describe the observed relationship among employment, investment, and asset prices capture some of the employment dynamics that take place during a financial crisis. Financial crises follow a pattern that consists of changes in asset prices, investment, and employment (see Reinhart and Rogoff 2009). A noteworthy feature is the "jobless recoveries" that often follow such crises. This was the case in Finland and Sweden in the aftermath of their financial crises in the early 1990s, where the behavior of employment mirrored that of investment, as shown in Figure 9.3.

During the economic boom that preceded the crises, there was a strong house price boom in Finland and Norway, followed by a decline; the movement of house prices was less pronounced in Sweden, where the stock market boom was stronger. Before the crises stock prices increased steeply in Sweden and Finland in the late 1980s and the early 1990s. These changes in asset prices coincided with an investment boom and a bust. In contrast, there was little stock price movement in Norway before and after the crises.

The crises started in 1991, and both investment and employment fell significantly from 1991 to 1994 in Finland and Sweden. A recovery of investment and employment only started 4 years after the onset of the crises. Table 9.7 shows unemployment, investment, share prices, house prices, real wages, unit labor costs, and the labor share for Finland and Sweden in the years before and after their respective financial crises. Before the

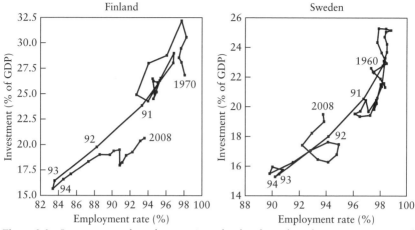

Figure 9.3 Investment and employment in Finland and Sweden. Shown are gross capital formation as a share of GDP for Finland and Sweden versus the employment rate $(1 - u)$ using annual data from 1970 to 2008.

onset of these crises, unemployment was low, the share of labor in national income was high, unit labor costs were high, asset prices were rising, and investment as a share of GDP was high. During the crises these trends were reversed: unemployment increased, and real wages, asset prices, and investment fell.

Note that for Finland share prices started to recover 2 years after the start of its crisis, house prices 3 years after the crisis hit, whereas unemployment, investment, and real wages began recovering 1–2 years later. The pattern for Sweden is similar. Moreover, employment did not recover until asset prices started to increase and investment began to recover.

This pattern is consistent with a changing natural rate of unemployment, where seismic shifts in asset prices coincide with changes in mean unemployment. The crisis is preceded by a period when banks are expanding credit at a rapid rate, and both business and household debt is building up. Firms can expect demand to remain robust, which makes the shadow price of a customer (or a vacancy, a trained worker, or new capital equipment) high. Firms respond by investing in an expanded market share, cutting mark-ups of price over marginal costs (i.e., the price-setting curve shifts upward), and real wages and employment increase, while profits and the share of profits in GDP fall. The investment boom is followed by an investment collapse. When the financial crisis hits, banks stop lending, and consumers face debt problems, making them less attractive customers for firms. Firms, anticipating weaker demand, raise mark-ups of price over marginal costs, which

Table 9.7 The labor market during the financial crises in Finland and Sweden

Country	Indicator	1989	1990	1991	1992	1993	1994	1995	2000
Finland	Unemployment (%)	3.1	3.2	6.7	11.7	16.4	16.6	15.5	9.8
	Investment (%)	29.8	28.7	24.4	20.1	16.7	15.8	16.6	19.4
	Share prices	100.0	68.6	47.7	37.4	58.5	86.4	88.6	639.4
	House prices	100.0	89.1	73.7	59.5	53.2	55.8	53.2	77.7
	Real wages	100.0	102.7	98.9	91.4	84.6	85.3	89.5	107.1
	Unit labor cost	1.07	1.09	1.12	1.08	1.00	0.97	0.98	0.92
	Labor share (%)	71.5	72.9	76.5	74.7	69.7	67.7	65.8	61.7
Sweden	Unemployment (%)	1.6	1.8	3.3	5.8	9.5	9.8	9.2	5.9
	Investment (%)	23.7	23.4	20.9	18.3	15.4	15.3	15.7	17.6
	Share prices	100.0	86.0	72.1	60.1	75.2	93.8	101.9	352.3
	House prices	100.0	101.5	99.3	88.1	74.8	76.5	75.0	104.8
	Real wages	100.0	101.8	98.0	94.5	88.7	91.2	92.8	117.9
	Unit labor cost	—	—	—	—	1.00	0.99	0.96	1.02
	Labor share (%)	70.8	72.6	73.1	72.3	69.6	68.3	65.5	67.9

Sources: Labor share, OECD; share prices (real), OECD; house prices (real), Statistics Finland and Statistics Sweden; real wages, OECD (compensation of employees) and International Financial Statistics (consumer price index). Unit labor cost (real), OECD. Data are available online.

Notes: Unit labor cost is normalized to 1 in 1993; share prices, house prices, and real wages are normalized to 100 in 1989. — indicates data not available. Units for dimensional variables are given in Appendix 9.C.

shifts the price-setting curve back down. The effect of this shift is that real wages and employment fall, and the share of labor in GDP also declines.

It follows that the pre-crisis period, which is characterized by expectations of robust demand, is good for labor, but the crisis and its aftermath hits labor badly, both in terms of employment and real wages. Workers benefit when firms invest but lose when firms become more focused on the present.

Figure 9.4 shows employment versus investment and normalized share prices for three countries currently facing a financial crisis: Ireland, Spain, and the United States, using quarterly data for the past two decades (one decade for Ireland). Note that the fall of employment coincides with falling share prices and investment. Based on the experience in Scandinavia in the 1990s, one can expect employment to remain low until investment starts to recover. Note that the recent recovery in the U.S. stock market is not matched by a recovery in the labor market. This is one anomaly in the data that requires an explanation.

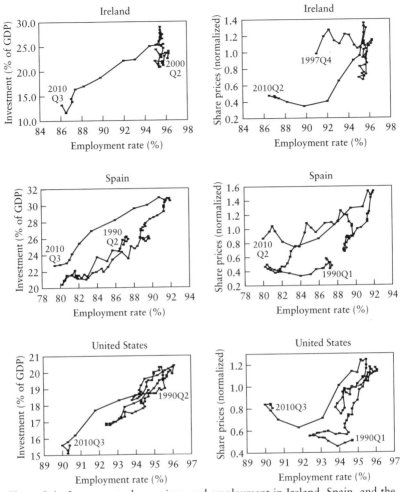

Figure 9.4 Investment, share prices, and employment in Ireland, Spain, and the United States.

9.8   Conclusion

The papers on customer markets and labor market equilibrium in the *Microeconomic Foundations* volume (Phelps et al. 1970) provided important insights into the determinants of unemployment in the medium term. A model with information imperfections in goods and labor markets of the kind proposed in these papers can explain changes in the natural rate of unemployment by changes in an economy's current and expected performance as captured by stock prices. The observed positive relationship between share prices, investment, and employment found in this chapter supports such a model.

A model of the natural rate of unemployment—in which expectations about future profits and productivity affect employment through decisions on mark-ups, training, and investment—implies that the current state of the labor market reflects an economy's future prospects, such as innovations and productivity growth, no less than the institutions of the labor market. Policies designed to increase a country's long-term growth performance will therefore also tend to raise employment in the medium term.

Appendix 9.A   Phase Diagram for a Saddle Path

Figure 9.A1 shows the phase diagram for the system of differential equations (9) and (10) in q and x. Assume a linear production function so that $n^i = y^i x^i$, where n^i is employment at firm i. We can define unemployment in a symmetric equilibrium as $u = 1 - yx/n^s$, where n^s is the labor force divided by the number of firms. Now normalizing $n^s = 1$, we have that $1 - u = yx$. Using the optimal solutions for p^i and assuming symmetric equilibrium, $p^i = \bar{p}$, gives an expression for the horizontal $\dot{x} = 0$ demarcation curve:

$$\frac{dq}{dx} = \frac{\eta A^2 ca''(yx)}{\gamma \mu} > 0 \tag{A1}$$

which has a positive slope. The $\dot{q} = o$ demarcation curve has a negative slope:

$$\frac{dq}{dx} = \frac{H_{xx} - H_{xp}^2/H_{pp}}{r + H_{xp}H_{pq}/H_{pp} - H_{xq}} < 0 \tag{A2}$$

where

$$H = p^i y^i x^i - c(yx) + q\left[\gamma - \gamma\left(\frac{p^i}{p}\right)^\mu\right]x^i \tag{A3}$$

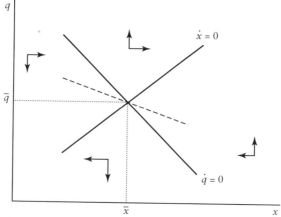

Figure 9.A1   Phase diagram for a saddle-path stable equilibrium.

and

$$y_i = A \left(\frac{p_i}{\bar{p}} \right)^{-\eta}$$ (A4)

The resultant phase diagram shows a saddle-path stable equilibrium.

Appendix 9.B   Normalized Share Prices and Employment Rates in 10 OECD Countries

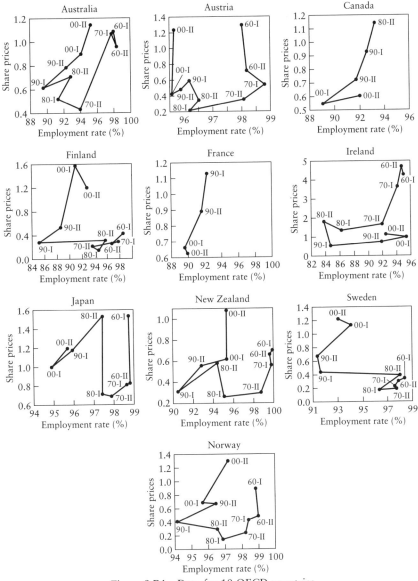

Figure 9.B1   Data for 10 OECD countries.

Appendix 9.C The Data and Their Sources

Variable	Definition	Unit	Source
World real interest rate	Weighted average of real rates of interest in the G7 countries where their relative GDP, taken from the Summers-Heston dataset, is used as weights	Percentage	IMF: International Financial Statistics and the Penn-World tables
Real oil prices	Average crude price, constant prices	U.S. dollars per barrel, 2005 prices	IMF: International Financial Statistics
Share prices	An index of share prices, normalized by GDP per employed worker	Index: base = 1 in 2005	IMF: International Financial Statistics
House prices	House prices, normalized by GDP per employed worker	Index: base = 1 in 2005	See Section C.1
Productivity growth	Rate of growth of real GDP per employed worker	Percentage	IMF: International Financial Statistics
Coordination	An index of the coordination of unions and employers in wage negotiations	Index: 1–3	Database of Nickell et al. (2005)
Density	Share of labor force that belongs to a labor union	Percentage	Database of Nickell et al. (2005)
Replacement ratio	The ratio of unemployment benefits and average wages	Decimals	Database of Nickell et al. (2005)
Duration of benefits	Maximum duration of unemployment benefits	Index[a]	Database of Nickell et al. (2005)
Employment protection	An index of employment protection	Index: 0–2	Database of Nickell et al. (2005)

a. See Nickell et al. (2005) for the formula for this index.

9.C.1 House Prices: National Sources

Australia: Australian Bureau of Statistics
Austria: Oesterreichische (Austrian) National Bank
Belgium: OECD-IMF Workshop on Real Estate Price Indexes
Canada: Mortgage and Housing Corporation
Finland: StatFin Online Service
France: National Institute for Statistics and Economic Studies
Ireland: Environment, Heritage and Local Government of Ireland
Italy: Housing Prices and Housing Wealth in Italy (Cannari and Faiella 2008)
Japan: Japan Real Estate Institute
Netherlands: OECD-IMF Workshop on Real Estate Price Indexes
New Zealand: Reserve Bank of New Zealand
Norway: Statistics Norway
Spain: OECD-IMF Workshop on Real Estate Price Indexes
Sweden: http://www.scb.se/
United Kingdom: Nationwide
United States: S&P online

References

Bagwell, K. (2004) "Countercyclical Pricing in Customer Markets," *Economica* 71: 519–542.

Ball, Laurence M., and Robert A. Moffitt. (2001) "Productivity Growth and the Phillips Curve," NBER Working Paper W8421, National Bureau of Economic Research, Cambridge, MA.

Belot, Michèl, and Jan C. van Ours. (2004) "Does the Recent Success of Some OECD Countries in Lowering Their Unemployment Rates Lie in the Clever Design of Their Labor Market Reforms?" *Oxford Economic Papers* 56: 621–642.

Bianchi, Marco, and Gylfi Zoega. (1998) "Unemployment Persistence: Does the Size of the Shock Matter?" *Journal of Applied Econometrics* 13: 283–304.

Blanchard, Olivier J. (1997) "The Medium Run," *Brookings Papers on Economic Activity* 1997(2): 89–158.

Blanchard, Olivier J., and Justin Wolfers. (2000) "The Role of Shocks and Institutions in the Rise of European Unemployment: The Aggregate Evidence," *Economic Journal* 110(Conference Papers): C1–C33.

Calvo, Guillermo. (1979) "Quasi-Walrasian Models of Unemployment," *American Economic Review* 69: 102–107.

Cannari, Luigi, and Ivan Faiella. (2008) "Housing Prices and Housing Wealth in Italy." Working Paper A4, Bank of Italy, Rome.

Choudhary, Ali, and J. Michael Orszag. (2007) "Costly Customer Relations and Pricing," *Oxford Economic Papers* 59: 641–661.

Coe, David T., and Dennis J. Snower. (1997) "Policy Complementarities: The Case for Fundamental Labor Market Reforms," CEPR Discussion Paper 1585, Center for Economic and Policy Research, Washington, DC.

Fitoussi, Jean-Paul, David Jestaz, Edmund Phelps, and Gylfi Zoega. (2000) "Roots of the Recent Recoveries: Labor Reforms or Private Sector Forces?" *Brookings Papers on Economic Activity* 2000(1): 237–311.

Gatti, Donatella, Christophe Rault, and Anne-Gael Vaubourg. (2009) "Unemployment and Finance: How Do Financial and Labor Market Factors Interact?" CESifo Working Paper 2901, Center for Economic Studies, Ifo Institute, Munich.

Greenwald, Bruce C. N., and Joseph E. Stiglitz. (1993) "Financial Market Imperfections and Business Cycles," *Quarterly Journal of Economics* 108: 77–114.

Hatton, Timothy. (2006) "Can Productivity Growth Explain the NAIRU? Long-Run Evidence from Britain, 1871–1999," *Economica* 74: 475–491.

Honkapohja, Seppo, and Erkki Koskela. (1999) "The Economic Crisis of the 1990s in Finland," *Economic Policy* 29: 399–436.

Hoon, Hian Teck, and Edmund S. Phelps. (1992) "Macroeconomic Shocks in a Dynamized Model of the Natural Rate of Unemployment," *American Economic Review* 82: 889–900.

———. (1997) "Growth, Wealth and the Natural Rate: Is Europe's Jobs Crisis a Growth Crisis?" *European Economic Review* 41: 549–557.

———. (2007) "Overinvestment and Employment Dynamics in a Non-Monetary Incentive-Wage Economy." Mimeo, Columbia University, New York.

Layard, Richard, Stephen Nickell, and Richard Jackman. (1991) *Unemployment: Macroeconomic Performance and the Labor Market.* Oxford: Oxford University Press.

Lindbeck, Assar, and Dennis Snower. (1989) *The Insider-Outsider Theory of Employment and Unemployment.* Cambridge, MA: MIT Press.

Ljungqvist, Lars, and Thomas J. Sargent. (1998) "The European Unemployment Dilemma," *Journal of Political Economy* 106: 514–550.

Manning, Alan. (1992) "Productivity Growth, Wage Setting and the Equilibrium Rate of Unemployment." Discussion Paper 63, Centre for Economic Performance, London.

Mortensen, Dale T., and Christopher A. Pissarides. (1994) "Job Creation and Job Destruction in the Theory of Unemployment," *Review of Economic Studies* 61: 397–415.

Nickell, Stephen, and Daphne Nicolitsas. (1999) "How Does Financial Pressure Affect Firms?" *European Economic Review* 43: 1435–1456.

Nickell, Stephen, and Sushil Wadhwani. (1991) "Employment Determination in British Industry: Investigation Using Micro-Data," *Review of Economic Studies* 58: 955–969.

Nickell, Stephen, Luca Nunziata, and Wolfgang Ochel. (2005) "Unemployment in the OECD Since the 1960s: What Do We Know?" *Economic Journal* 115: 1–27.

Oi, Walter. (1962) "Labor as a Quasi-Fixed Factor of Production," *Journal of Political Economy* 70: 538–555.

Papell, David H., Christian J. Murray, and Hala Ghiblawi. (2000) "The Structure of Unemployment," *Review of Economics and Statistics* 82: 309–315.

Phelps, Edmund S. (1968) "Money-Wage Dynamics and Labor-Market Equilibrium," *Journal of Political Economy* 76: 678–711.

———. (1970) "Money-Wage Dynamics and Labor-Market Equilibrium," in Edmund S. Phelps, G. C. Archibald, and Armen A. Alchian (eds.), *Microeconomic Foundations of Employment and Inflation Theory*. New York: W. W. Norton, pp. 124–166.

———. (1972) "Money, Public Expenditure and the Labor Supply," *Journal of Economic Theory* 5: 69–78.

———. (1994) *Structural Slumps: The Modern Equilibrium Theory of Unemployment, Interest and Assets*. Cambridge, MA: Harvard University Press.

———. (2006) "Further Steps to a Theory of Innovation and Growth—On the Path Begun by Knight, Hayek and Polanyi." Paper presented at the Allied Social Science Association 2006 Conference, Boston, January 7.

Phelps, Edmund S., and Sidney G. Winter, Jr. (1970) "Optimal Price Policy under Atomistic Competition," in Edmund S. Phelps, G. C. Archibald, and Armen A. Alchian (eds.), *Microeconomic Foundations of Employment and Inflation Theory*. New York: W. W. Norton, pp. 309–339.

Phelps, Edmund S., and Gylfi Zoega. (2001) "Structural Booms: Productivity Explanations and Asset Valuations," *Economic Policy* 16: 85–126.

———. (2004) "The Search for Routes to Better Economic Performance in Continental Europe," *CESifo Forum*, April, pp. 3–11.

Phelps, Edmund S., G. C. Archibald, and Armen A. Alchian (eds.). (1970) *Microeconomic Foundations of Employment and Inflation Theory*. New York: W. W. Norton.

Pissarides, Christopher A. (2000) *Equilibrium Unemployment Theory*, second edition. Cambridge, MA: MIT Press.

Reinhart, Carmen M., and Kenneth S. Rogoff. (2009) *This Time Is Different: Eight Centuries of Financial Folly*. Princeton and Oxford: Princeton University Press.

Salop, Steven C. (1979) "A Model of the Natural Rate of Unemployment," *American Economic Review* 69: 117–125.

Shapiro, Carl, and Joseph Stiglitz. (1984) "Equilibrium Unemployment as a Worker Discipline Device," *American Economic Review* 74: 433–444.

Smith, Ron, and Gylfi Zoega. (2006) "Global Unemployment Shocks," *Economics Letters* 94: 433–438.

———. (2008) "Global Factors, Unemployment Adjustment and the Natural Rate," *Economics: The Open-Access, Open-Assessment E-Journal* 2: 1–27.

Solow, Robert M. (1979) "Another Possible Source of Wage Stickiness," *Journal of Macroeconomics* 1: 79–82.

CHAPTER TEN

Imperfect Knowledge, Asset Price Swings, and Structural Slumps

A Cointegrated Vector Autoregressive Analysis of Their Interdependence

Katarina Juselius

10.1 Introduction

The aim of this chapter is to discuss interactions between speculative be-havior in the currency markets and aggregate activity in the real economy, inspired by the Structural Slumps theory in Phelps (1994) and the recent theory of Imperfect Knowledge Economics (IKE) in Frydman and Gold-berg (2007). The former provides a coherent theoretical framework for how nonmonetary mechanisms can generate unemployment slumps in open economies connected by the world real interest rate and the real exchange rate, whereas the latter gives a rationale for why real exchange rates tend to fluctuate persistently around long-run benchmark values and why this is likely to be compensated by similar movements in the real interest dif-ferential. To combine the two theories is, therefore, likely to improve our understanding of the two-way interdependence between persistent swings in asset markets and persistent fluctuations in the real economy. In particular, it may shed new light on the mechanisms behind the long recurrent spells of unemployment that continue to mar our economies.

The main arguments, presented in Section 10.7, rely heavily on a number of estimated empirical regularities describing the foreign exchange market and wage, price, and unemployment dynamics. The findings that (1) the natural rate of the Phillips curve is a function of a nonstationary real interest rate and (2) "profit share" is a function of a nonstationary real exchange

The views in this chapter are strongly influenced by previous and ongoing research with Roman Frydman, Michael Goldberg, and Søren Johansen. I am deeply grateful to Roman and Michael for sharing with me their profound insight into international macroeconomics and how Imperfect Knowledge Economics can resolve its many empirical puzzles and to my son, Mikael Juselius, for numerous valuable comments on an early version of this chapter.

rate are particularly important for understanding the mechanisms by which the Structural Slumps and IKE theories interact. These regularities have been found in several countries' data by applying the Cointegrated Vector Autoregressive (CVAR) model (Johansen 1995; Juselius 2006). Because the CVAR model offers a precise way of handling unit-root nonstationarity and breaks—features that are typical of macroeconomic data—it has been my favored methodology.

To set the scene, Section 10.2 discusses exchange rate determination in two models, one based on the Rational Expectations Hypothesis (REH) and the other on the theory of IKE. The discussion focuses on their different implications for basic international parity conditions in terms of time-series persistence. Section 10.3 discusses some general principles for how to structure the observed persistence in the data, and Section 10.4 is a brief discussion of how these principles can be used in the CVAR model. Section 10.5 lists a set of testable hypotheses that can be used to discriminate between REH- and IKE-based explanations of real exchange rate persistence, and Section 10.6 gives some arguments for why multivariate tests are more reliable than univariate tests. Section 10.7 discusses how foreign currency speculation under IKE interacts with a customer market economy where profit shares are adjusting to fluctuations in the real exchange rate and where the natural rate is a function of a nonstationary real long-term interest rate. Section 10.8 summarizes the chapter's conclusions.

10.2 Expectations Formation and Real Exchange Rate Persistence

Frydman et al. (2011) show how REH versus IKE assumptions about expectations formation lead to different hypotheses about the persistence of the real exchange rate and the real interest rate differential. Juselius (2011) discusses persistence in terms of $I(0)$, $I(1)$, and $I(2)$, defining processes integrated of order 0, 1, and 2, respectively. This section builds heavily on these two papers.

10.2.1 REH-Based Models

The REH-based monetary model assumes that purchasing power parity (PPP) holds as an equilibrium condition so that the real exchange rate, q_t, is stationary, that is,

$$q_t = \rho q_{t-1} + \varepsilon_{1,t} \qquad (1)$$

where $\rho < 1.0$, and $\varepsilon_{1,t}$ is a random noise. The stationarity of the real exchange rate is consistent with uncovered interest rate parity as a market clearing mechanism:

$$i_{1,t} - i_{2,t} = \Delta s_{t+1}^e + rp_t \qquad (2)$$

where Δs^e_{t+1} is the expected change in the nominal exchange rate, and rp_t is a stationary risk premium. Provided (1) and (2) hold, the Fisher parity holds as a stationary condition:

$$i_t = \bar{r} + \Delta p^e \tag{3}$$

where $\bar{r}$ is an average real interest rate, and Δp^e is the expected inflation rate. Similarly, under the above conditions the term spread is stationary, and the term structure of interest rates is well described by the expectations hypothesis.

10.2.2 IKE-Based Models

The theory of IKE (Frydman and Goldberg 2007) assumes that individuals (bulls and bears) in the foreign currency market recognize their imperfect knowledge about the processes driving outcomes and, therefore, use a multitude of forecasting strategies, which they revise over time in a way that cannot be fully prespecified in advance. Under certain conditions on revisions of individuals' forecasting strategies, and assuming that their forecasting variables are persistent, nominal exchange rates will show a tendency to move persistently (away from or toward) benchmark values. Figure 10.1a illustrates the persistent movements of the nominal U.S. dollar/Deutsche Mark rate around relative prices as the natural benchmark values. Thus, IKE revisions of forecasts will generate an additional persistence in nominal exchange rates that is different from the persistence implied by REH-based models.

Frydman et al. (2011) showed that under the above conditions, the change in real exchange rate, Δq_t, can be approximated with the following model:

$$\Delta q_t = \zeta_t + \varepsilon_{1,t} \tag{4}$$

where

$$\zeta_t = \bar{\rho}\zeta_{t-1} + \varepsilon_{2,t}$$

ζ_t is a drift term measuring the change in the real exchange rate due to a change in individuals' forecasting strategies; and $\bar{\rho}$ is an average of ρ_t, $t = 1, \ldots, T$, such that $\rho_t \approx 1.0$ when q_t is in the neighborhood of long-run benchmark values and $\rho_t < 1.0$ when q_t is far away from such values. Thus, $\bar{\rho}$ may vary over different sample periods but is generally within a small band close to the unit circle.

As long as the nonconstant drift term, ζ_t, is well approximated by a near-$I(1)$ process, the real exchange rate behaves like a near-$I(2)$ process; that is, it exhibits pronounced persistence. Figure 10.1b illustrates the long swings

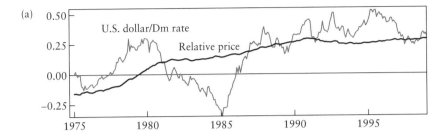

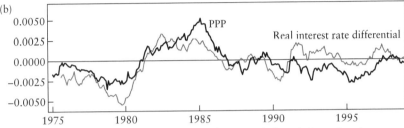

Figure 10.1 The U.S. dollar/Deutsche Mark rate and the relative prices between the United States and Germany (a) and the U.S.-German real exchange rate (purchasing power parity [PPP]) together with the U.S.-German real long-term interest rate differential (b).

in the real U.S. dollar/Deutsche Mark rate. Modeling the real exchange rate as a near-$I(2)$ process is consistent with swings of both shorter and longer durations and implies that the length of these swings is not predictable (Frydman and Goldberg 2007). That the near-$I(2)$ process is a good approximation has been shown empirically in Johansen et al. (2010), thus confirming the theoretically expected results in Frydman and Goldberg (2007; Chapter 6, this volume) and Frydman et al. (2011).

When the real exchange rate is moving away from its benchmark value, the real interest rate differential has to move in a compensating manner to restore equilibrium in the product market (see Frydman and Goldberg 2007). Thus, the IKE equilibrium relation is a cointegration relation between the real exchange rate, the nominal interest rate differential, and the inflation rate differential:

$$(p_{1,t} - p_{2,t} - s_{12,t}) = \omega\{(i_{1,t} - i_{2,t}) - (\Delta p_{1,t} - \Delta p_{2,t})\} + e_t \qquad (5)$$

where e_t is a stationary equilibrium error. In (5), the real exchange rate and the nominal interest rate differential are both near $I(2)$, whereas the inflation rate differential is near $I(1)$. Stationarity of e_t is then achieved if the real exchange rate and the nominal interest rate differential cointegrate

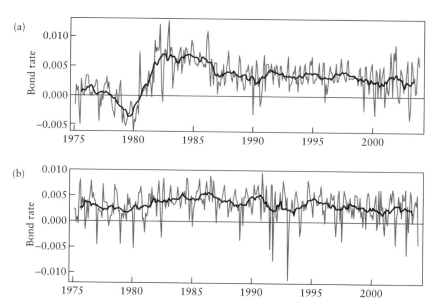

Figure 10.2 Real long-term bond rates together with a 12-month moving average in the United States (a) and in Germany (b).

from near $I(2)$ to near $I(1)$ and the latter is identical to the near-$I(1)$ trend in the inflation rate differential.

Under IKE, the standard uncovered interest rate parity needs to be replaced by the uncertainty-adjusted uncovered interest rate parity (Frydman and Goldberg 2007) as a market clearing mechanism:

$$i_{1,t} - i_{2,t} = \Delta s^e_{t+1} + up_t \tag{6}$$

where $up_t = f(p_{1,t} - p_{2,t} - s_{12,t})$ is an uncertainty premium measuring how far the market has moved away from PPP benchmark values. The nominal interest rate differential and the uncertainty premium, both near $I(2)$, cointegrate to near $I(1)$, and the interest rate differential corrected for the uncertainty premium cointegrates with Δs^e_{t+1} to produce a stationary market clearing mechanism.

In an IKE model, the nominal interest rate and inflation rate are integrated of different orders, and the Fisher parity does not hold as a stationary condition. Figure 10.2 illustrates the persistence in U.S. and German real long-term interest rates. Similarly, the term spreads are not stationary, implying that the term structure of interest rates is not adequately described by REH. Figure 10.3 illustrates the pronounced persistence in the U.S. and German short-long interest rate spreads.

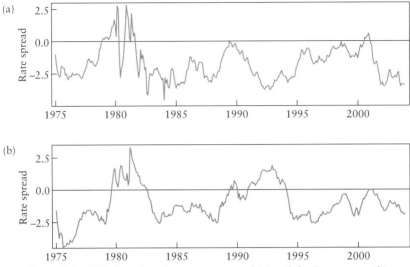

Figure 10.3   U.S. short-long interest rate spread (a) and the German one (b).

10.3   Persistence as a Structuring Device

As discussed above, REH-based models differ from IKE-based models in a very important aspect: the former imply no persistence in the changes of the real exchange rate, whereas the latter are consistent with a marked persistence. To distinguish empirically between the two model classes, we need an econometric methodology that can discriminate between different degrees of persistence. Therefore, the purpose of this section is to discuss such a methodology and give the intuition for how it works. A reader not interested in the empirical/econometric methodology can jump to Section 10.4 without losing track of the narrative.

10.3.1   Time-Series Persistence

The notion of persistence is typically associated with the strength of the time dependence of a shock to a variable. If the effect of a shock dies out quickly, it is transitory and the corresponding variable is considered to be stationary, whereas if the shock has a lasting effect, it is considered permanent and the variable is considered to be unit-root nonstationary. Distinguishing exclusively between transitory (stationary) and persistent (nonstationary) behavior is often too crude for empirical modeling. For example, stationary processes can be divided into highly erratic $I(-1)$ processes and $I(0)$ processes, both of which describe transitory behavior. Nonstationary unit-root processes can be generated from shocks that cumulate once, dubbed $I(1)$; or from shocks that cumulate twice, dubbed $I(2)$.[1] The latter is particularly important for describing speculative behavior under IKE, whereas the former is generally consistent with REH behavior.

Although a classification in $I(0)$, $I(1)$, and $I(2)$ is mathematically unambiguous, it can be more problematic in empirical modeling. This is so because depending on the sample size, the degree of permanence, and the relative noise ratio of the $I(1)$ and $I(2)$ components, there are gray zones where data could be said to be near $I(1)$ rather than $I(1)$ or $I(0)$, and near $I(2)$ rather than $I(1)$ or $I(2)$. For example, a random walk process, $x_t = x_{t-1} + \varepsilon_t$ (an $I(1)$ process), and a strongly autoregressive AR(1) process, $x_t = 0.95x_{t-1} + \varepsilon_t$ (mathematically an $I(0)$ process), would often be difficult to distinguish from each other, even based on relatively long samples. This is illustrated in Figure 10.4, where an AR(1) with $\rho = 0.95$ and a random walk are simulated in 200 steps. Both series look similar in terms of persistence. For a short time series, it is even more difficult to discriminate between near-unit roots and unit roots. This is illustrated in Figure 10.5 for a stationary AR(1) process with autoregressive parameter $\rho = 0.80$ and a random walk process simulated in 50 steps. In contrast, an AR(1) process with $\rho = 0.99$ would often be found to be significantly different from 1.0 in a large sample of, say, 5,000 observations, even though such a variable would be highly persistent. If we characterize such a process as type $I(0)$, we would give up cointegration as a tool for identifying similar persistency profiles between variables.

Hence, statistical significance alone does not seem to work well as an organizing principle for classifying data into different persistence profiles. See Hendry and Juselius (2000) for a discussion.

10.3.2 Different Levels of Persistence

Another possibility is to define persistence in terms of the modulus of the characteristic roots of the autoregressive polynomial. For nonexplosive models, the roots are defined over the interval $(-1, 1)$, and they can, therefore, be given a convenient interpretation as a measure of the speed of adjustment. For example, consider the simple AR(1) model, $x_t = \rho_1 x_{t-1} + \varepsilon_t$ or equivalently, $\Delta x_t = -(1 - \rho_1)x_{t-1} + \varepsilon_t$, with $\rho_1 = 0.9$. This corresponds roughly to an adjustment coefficient $\alpha_1 \simeq -(1 - \rho_1) = -0.10$. An adjustment coefficient of -0.10 corresponds to an average adjustment time of $ln(2)/(1 - 0.10) = 7$ periods. Using annual data this adjustment coefficient would imply an average adjustment period of 7 years, for quarterly data it would be almost 2 years, for monthly data slightly more than half a year, for weekly data less than 2 months, and so forth. Whether a characteristic root

---

1. See Johansen (1995) for a mathematically precise definition of the order of integration of stochastic processes.

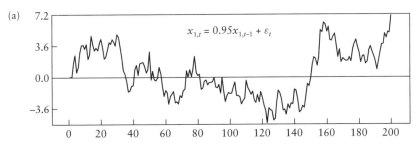

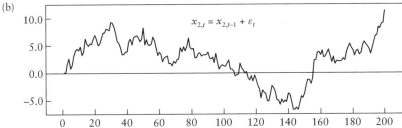

Figure 10.4 Simulated series of an autoregressive AR(1) process with $\rho = 0.95$ (a) and a random walk (b).

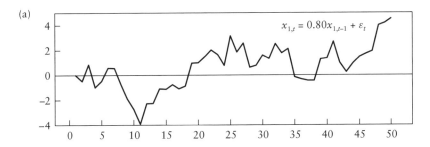

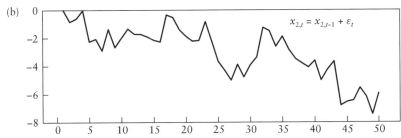

Figure 10.5 Simulated autoregressive AR(1) process with $\rho = 0.8$ (a) and a random walk (b).

can be interpreted as evidence of persistent behavior depends, therefore, both on the sample period and the observational frequency.

To illustrate the idea, consider a variable x_t with the autoregressive representation $(1 - \varphi_1 L - \cdots - \varphi_p L^p)x_t = \varepsilon_t$, where ε_t is N independent identically distributed, and define a threshold parameter ρ^* above which the process is considered persistent. The choice of ρ^* is to some extent subject to judgement. For high-frequency data its value would generally be closer to the unit circle than for low-frequency data. In the context of a specific theory, ρ^* could in some cases be thought of as defining the longest adjustment time for which the policy implications of the model are still useful.

The persistence of x_t could, for example, be defined as:

- $I(0)$ type when the modulus of the largest root, ρ_1, satisfies $\rho_1 < \rho^*$.
- $I(1)$ type when the modulus of the largest root, ρ_1, satisfies $\rho^* < \rho_1 \leq 1.0$, and the next root satisfies $\rho_2 < \rho^*$.
- $I(2)$ type when the modulus of the largest root, ρ_1, satisfies $\rho_1 = 1.0$, and the next one satisfies $\rho^* < \rho_2 \leq 1.0$.

Although the above classification is directly applicable in a univariate model, it needs some modification in a multivariate model like the CVAR. For example, in a univariate model a large characteristic root can be directly associated with the variable in question, $x_{i,t}$, whereas in a p-dimensional VAR model of $x_t' = [x_{1,t}, \ldots, x_{p,t}]$, the number of large roots in the characteristic polynomial is a function of the number of exogenous (common) stochastic trends, $p - r$, in the system (where r is the number of cointegration relations) and of the number of the stochastic trends that are of first order, s_1, or second order, s_2, where $s_1 + s_2 = p - r$. Consider, for example, a five-dimensional VAR model for which three of the characteristic roots are greater than ρ^*. This model could be consistent with three stochastic trends of first order ($p - r = 3$; $s_1 = 3$), or, alternatively, with two stochastic trends of first order and one of second order ($p - r = 2$; $s_1 = 1$, $s_2 = 1$).

To determine the number of stochastic trends and their division into types $I(1)$ and $I(2)$, the following simple procedure can be used. Start with the unrestricted VAR model ($r = p$), and determine the number, m^*, of characteristic roots that are greater than ρ^*.[2] Next, use the $I(2)$ trace test (Nielsen and Rahbek 2007) to test the cases (r, s_1, s_2) for which $s_1 + 2s_2 =$

---

2. Note, however that if a large-modulus root corresponds to a complex pair with a significant imaginary part, it is not possible to force it to become a unit root on the real line. In this case, it will be considered a stationary, albeit persistent, cyclical component. Also, Nielsen and Nielsen (2012) and Pantula and Fuller (1993) have shown that if the VAR model is estimated with too many lags (e.g., adding lags to compensate for a structural break), the number of large, but insignificant, roots will increase. In such a case, the number becomes uninformative.

m^*. An empirically relevant candidate is found when the trace test is not rejected, all unrestricted characteristic roots $\rho_i < \rho^*$, and the number of restricted unit roots is m^*.

10.3.3 Near-Unit-Root Inference

Another issue is how the asymptotic $I(2)$ inference is affected when data are near $I(2)$ rather than being exactly $I(2)$. It is useful to distinguish between the cases when a near-unit root is treated as (1) stationary or (2) nonstationary. In the first case, Johansen (2006) showed by simulation that some inferences (on steady state values) became very fragile when a near-unit root was treated as stationary. For example, up to 5,000 observations were needed for the empirical distribution to converge to Student's t when the near-unit root was 0.998. Following the rule that the characteristic roots have to be smaller than ρ^* in the preferred model with rank r^* is likely to work as a safeguard against this problem.

In the second case, Elliot (1998) showed both analytically and by simulations that the asymptotic distribution is no longer mixed Gaussian and that standard asymptotic inference can be misleading. However, corollary 1 in Johansen (1997) can be used to show that inference on β and α in the $I(2)$ model is also efficient and unbiased in the near-$I(2)$ case.[3] Because all results discussed in the subsequent sections have been obtained by cointegration analysis in the $I(2)$ model, the corollary result allows us to attach a fair degree of confidence to our empirical findings. Nonetheless, robustness is an important issue that needs to be further studied.

10.4 Structuring Persistence Using CVAR

The CVAR model is inherently consistent with a world where unanticipated shocks accumulate over time to generate stochastic trends that move economic equilibria (the pushing forces) and where deviations from these equilibria are corrected by the dynamics of the adjustment mechanism (the pulling forces). Thus, the CVAR model has a good chance of nesting a multivariate, path-dependent data-generating process and relevant dynamic macroeconomic theories (see Hoover et al. 2008).

In line with the above, Juselius (2006) and Juselius and Franchi (2007) asked the question: Which empirical regularities would we see in the data, if the assumptions of exogenous shocks, equilibrium relations, steady state behavior, and dynamic adjustment were correct in the theoretical model?

---

3. This is because the second reduced-rank condition (which is associated with the $I(2)$ model property) does not affect the asymptotic efficiency of the maximum likelihood estimator of β and α.

The answer was formalized in what was called a theory-consistent CVAR scenario, which essentially translates all basic assumptions about the theoretical model's shock structure, equilibrium relations, and steady state behavior into testable hypotheses on common stochastic trends, cointegration, steady state values, and dynamic adjustment (for a comprehensive treatment, see Juselius 2006). Because of its ability to structure the relevant data into economically meaningful directions *without subjecting them to prior restrictions,* CVAR can be thought of as providing broadly defined "confidence intervals" within which empirically relevant models should fall.

The CVAR approach starts from an unrestricted VAR model, which is essentially just a representation of the covariances of the data. By imposing (testable) reduced-rank restrictions on the VAR model, it is formulated as a vector equilibrium-error-correcting model of first order (the $I(1)$ model) or of second order (the $I(2)$ model). The former is appropriate for describing an economy where growth rates and deviations from equilibria are stationary, the latter where they are unit-root nonstationary. See the Appendix for a definition of the $I(1)$ and $I(2)$ models and an interpretation of their structure.

In the $I(1)$ model, the deviation from a static equilibrium is assumed to be stationary. For example, REH-based models would allow real exchange rates to move away from PPP values albeit in a stationary manner, and the α coefficients in (7) in the Appendix would describe the speed of adjustment back to equilibrium.

In the $I(2)$ model, the deviations from equilibrium values can exhibit a pronounced persistence, implying that the nominal exchange rate, say, can move away from equilibrium values for extended periods of time, provided they are compensated by something else.

10.5 Testable Empirical Regularities under REH and IKE

Juselius (2011) used the concept of a CVAR scenario to translate the assumptions about expectations formation and forecasting behavior in an REH-contra IKE-based model for nominal exchange rate determination into testable hypotheses on the CVAR model, the most important of which are:

1. Under IKE, speculative behavior in the currency markets tends to drive nominal exchange rates away from PPP benchmark values for extended periods of time. These persistent movements have the property of a near-$I(2)$ process, so that the real exchange rate is near $I(2)$. Under REH, the movements around PPP are stationary or at most near $I(1)$.

2. Under IKE, the real exchange rate is comoving with the real interest rate differential. Hence, the latter is empirically near $I(2)$. Under

REH, the real interest rate differential is stationary or at most near $I(1)$.

3. Under IKE, the real exchange rate and the real interest rate differential cointegrate to a stationary equilibrium relation. Under REH, they are individually stationary albeit allowed to exhibit some persistence.

4. Under IKE, the nominal interest rate and the inflation rate are not cointegrated, so that the Fisher parity does not hold as a stationary condition. Under REH, the Fisher parity is stationary.

5. Under IKE, the term structure of interest rates is driven by two stochastic trends, one typically associated with the short end (monetary policy shocks), the other with the long end (financial market shocks). Thus, the standard expectations hypothesis does not hold, and the interest rate spreads are nonstationary but cointegrated. Under REH, the expectations hypothesis implies one stochastic trend and stationary spreads.

These hypotheses (and many more) were tested within a five-dimensional CVAR model based on the principles discussed in Section 10.3. The test results showed that the IKE-based scenario obtained a remarkable support for every single testable hypothesis, whereas the REH-based scenario was empirically rejected on all counts.[4] Detailed results are reported in Frydman et al. (2011) and Juselius (2011).[5]

10.6   Are Near-$I(2)$ Results Credible?

Many economists would feel uncomfortable treating real exchange rate and interest rate differentials as (near) $I(2)$, arguing that economic variables or relations cannot be $I(2)$, as this would have implausible consequences for the economic model. Although, in my view, this is confusing economic properties with statistical properties, it is, nevertheless, the case that finding economic data to be (near) $I(2)$ by statistical testing can be interpreted as evidence in favor of an IKE-based model. Therefore, the question asked by Ricardo Rice, in the discussion of an earlier version of this chapter, "How come you find real exchange rates to be near $I(2)$ when others find them to be near $I(1)$?" is of considerable interest.

---

4. For an argument detailing how the empirical difficulties of the REH models discussed here can be traced to their epistemologically flawed microfoundation, see Frydman and Goldberg (2011; Chapters 4 and 6, this volume).

5. Previously Juselius (1995) and Juselius and MacDonald (2004, 2007) reported empirical support for these hypotheses based on data for Danish-German, U.S.-Japanese, and U.S.-German exchange rates, prices, and interest rates in the post–Bretton Woods period of currency floats. IKE has now provided the missing theoretical background.

A first answer to the question is that most empirical studies find real exchange rates to be (near) $I(1)$ because they use univariate testing, whereas I find near $I(2)$ because I use multivariate testing. For example, based on a CVAR model for U.S. and German prices and the nominal exchange rate, Juselius (2009) explored the consequences of assuming the variables to be $I(1)$ versus $I(2)$. In the former case, any choice of rank left one or two near-unit roots (of magnitude 0.99) in the model, rendering any Gaussian-based inference completely unreliable. In the latter case, it was possible to account for all large roots in the model, but the estimated relationship between relative prices and nominal exchange rates was not economically plausible. By including nominal interest rates in the empirical model, Juselius (2011) found a completely plausible relationship between the real exchange rate and the real interest rate differential, but only in the $I(2)$ model. Treating the variables (and the real exchange rate) as $I(1)$ invariably left two large characteristic roots (0.96, 0.96) in the model. But a univariate Dickey-Fuller test would not have detected these large roots because of the small variance of the $I(2)$ component.

A simulation exercise can illustrate why this is the case. I have generated two time series, the first one, $x_{1,t}$, being a random walk process (consistent with an REH-based model for which the real exchange rate is at most $I(1)$). The second one, $x_{2,t}$, is a random walk augmented with a small, but very persistent, drift term ζ_t (consistent with an IKE-based model). The former is defined as:

$$x_{1,t} - x_{1,t-1} = \varepsilon_t, \qquad \varepsilon_t \sim N(0, 1), \quad t = 1, \ldots, 500$$

and the latter as:

$$x_{2,t} - x_{2,t-1} = \zeta_t + \varepsilon_{1,t}, \qquad \varepsilon_{1,t} \sim N(0, 1) \quad t = 1, \ldots, 500$$

$$\zeta_t = 0.95\zeta_{t-1} + \varepsilon_{2,t}, \qquad \varepsilon_{2,t} \sim N(0, 0.15^2)$$

Because the variance of the ζ_t process is small compared to the variance of $\Delta x_{2,t}$, the fact that $\Delta x_{1,t}$ is $I(0)$ whereas $\Delta x_{2,t}$ is near $I(1)$ can be difficult to detect visually, as Figure 10.6 illustrates. One way of spotting an underlying persistent movement in a noisy series is to plot the series together with a suitable (12-period) moving average, as has been done in Figure 10.6. It is now obvious that $\Delta x_{2,t}$ has an underlying persistent trend, whereas the moving average trend in $\Delta x_{1,t}$ is much less persistent.[6]

When it comes to unit-root testing, the large root associated with $\varepsilon_{2,t}$ in $x_{2,t}$ would not be easily detected based on a univariate test. This is because the estimated residual is the sum of $\varepsilon_{1,t}$ with a large variance and ζ_t with

---

6. As a moving average is time dependent by construction, one should also expect some persistence for the random walk case.

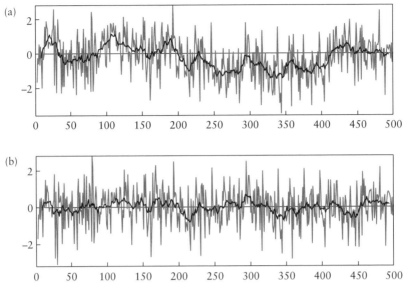

Figure 10.6 A differenced near-$I(2)$ process (a) and a random walk (b), together with a 12-period moving average.

a much smaller variance. For example, when subjecting simulated versions of the variable, $x_{2,t}$, to a Dickey-Fuller unit-root test, the results suggested $I(1)$ or even $I(0)$, whereas $I(2)$ was strongly rejected. Based on multivariate testing the second near-unit root was detected both by the $I(2)$ trace tests and by checking the roots of the characteristic polynomial.

This result was confirmed in a more comprehensive simulation study by Juselius and Jensen (2012): for a small signal-to-noise ratio, the Dickey-Fuller unit-root test completely failed to detect the second near-unit root, whereas the multivariate trace test was able to spot it in almost all cases.

10.7 Currency Speculation and Structural Slumps

The discussion here is based on many years of systematic investigation by myself and my students of how the persistency of the real exchange rates, real interest rates, and the term spreads has influenced aggregate activities in the real economy, in particular, how they have affected wage, price, and unemployment dynamics. Phelps's (1994) Structural Slumps theory was a frequent reference in my early papers, subsequently to be combined with the Frydman and Goldberg (2007) IKE theory.

This section is a first attempt to put the bits and pieces together into something that eventually may have the potential of becoming a coherent theoretical and empirical framework for understanding persistent fluctuations in the macroeconomy. Although the main results are given in Section 10.7.4, the logic of the arguments first requires a discussion of the role of a non-stationary long-term interest rate and a nonstationary Fisher parity, what initiates swings, and what allows them to be so long lasting.

10.7.1 Preliminaries

The Structural Slumps theory explains how open economies connected by the world real interest rate (set in the global capital market) and by the real exchange rate (determined in a global customer market for tradables) can be hit by long episodes of unemployment. The theory predicts that an exogenous shock to the world level of public debt and/or capital stock will change the world level of interest rates, whereas an exogenous shock to the public debt of an individual open economy increases its interest rate relative to the world interest rate.

The empirical analyses in Johansen et al. (2010), Frydman et al. (2011), and Juselius (2011), find that shocks to the long-term U.S. bond rate (a proxy for the world interest rate) and to the U.S.-German interest rate differential (measuring relative debt levels between the two countries) are the main exogenous forces in a system comprising U.S.-German prices, nominal exchange rates, and long-term interest rates.

IKE theory predicts that the real exchange rate is primarily determined in a speculative market for foreign currency (rather than in a customer market for tradables) and that speculation under some plausible conditions drives the nominal exchange rate away from long-term PPP values together with a compensating movement in the real interest rate differential.

Assuming that prices of tradable goods are primarily determined in very competitive customer markets, as in Phelps (1994), means that they are not in general much affected by speculation (energy, precious metals, and, recently, grain may be exceptions in this respect) and, therefore, do not exhibit persistent swings around benchmark values. If nominal interest rates exhibit persistent swings but consumer price inflation does not, then the real interest rate will also exhibit persistent swings. This might give an incentive for speculation in currency markets. For example, such an incentive would not exist if the Fisher parity is stationary. In this case, an increase in the long-term interest rate would be associated with an expected increase in the inflation rate, and speculators would have no specific incentive to invest their long-term capital in such an economy.

10.7.2 What Initiates a Long Swing?

Johansen et al. (2010) and Juselius (2011) find that shocks to the interest rate differential and to the level of long-term U.S. interest rate have been pushing the system. A shock to the former can be interpreted as a shock to the expected change in nominal exchange rate, whereas one to the latter as a shock shifting the world interest rate level. In this sense, a long swing can be initiated by changes in exchange rate expectations or by pure interest rate shocks. The interdependence between the two makes it difficult to discriminate between them.

For instance, a shock to the long-term interest rate (e.g., as a result of a domestic increase in sovereign debt) without a corresponding increase in the inflation rate is likely to increase the amount of speculative capital moving into the economy. The exchange rate would appreciate, jeopardizing competitiveness in the tradable sector, the trade balance would worsen, and the pressure on the interest rate would increase. Under this scenario, the interest rate is likely to keep increasing as long as the structural imbalances are growing, thus generating persistent movements in real interest rates and real exchange rates. Figure 10.1 illustrates such historical comovements.

Thus, persistent shocks to the domestic interest rate relative to the world interest rate are likely to hit the economy as a result of structural imbalances in the domestic economy. In Europe, such imbalances have typically been associated with a political reluctance to adequately address painful structural reforms in the labor market. In the United States, they are typically associated with trade balance problems.

This circle of increasing/decreasing real interest rates and real appreciation/depreciation rates is empirically manifested as an equilibrium-error-increasing behavior of the δ adjustment in (8) in the Appendix. Risk-averse individuals will require increasingly large risk premiums for holding the domestic currency as the macroeconomic imbalances grow, which will sooner or later cause a reversal in the exchange rate movement (Frydman and Goldberg 2007). In the empirical analysis this was manifested in the equilibrium-error-correcting behavior of the α adjustment in (8) in the Appendix.

10.7.3 Why Are Swings So Long Lasting?

A persistent deviation away from benchmark values is likely to trigger a compensating reaction in other sectors of the economy. In the currency market, nonstationary movements in the real exchange rate are compensated by nonstationary movements in the nominal interest rate differential corrected for the inflation rate differential. As long as this interactive (reflexive) process is at work, the deviations from benchmark PPP values can be long lasting. Such an interactive process between speculative markets and the real economy may explain the pronounced persistence of real exchange swings that have puzzled economists for such a long time. It also provides a rationale for why the $I(2)$ model is a good description of IKE behavior: it is tailor made to describe an economy where persistent deviations from long-run static equilibrium values are compensated by similar persistent movements in other variables. Thus, an IKE economy is still characterized by equilibrating forces but in a dynamic rather than static set up.

10.7.4 *Persistent Fluctuations in the Real Economy*

The tendency of the domestic real interest rate to increase and the real exchange rate to appreciate at the same time is likely to aggravate domestic competitiveness in the tradable sector. In an IKE economy where the nominal exchange rate is determined by speculation, firms cannot in general count on exchange rates to restore competitiveness after a permanent shock to relative costs. Unless firms are prepared to lose market shares, they cannot use constant mark-up pricing as their pricing strategy. To preserve market shares, they would have to adjust productivity or profits rather than increasing their product price. Therefore, in an IKE economy, we would expect customer-market pricing (Phelps 1994) to replace constant mark-up pricing. Profits would then be squeezed in periods of persistent appreciation and increased during periods of depreciation. Evidence of a nonstationary profit share comoving with the real exchange rate has, for instance, been found in Juselius (2006).

In addition, a customer-market firm, facing an increase in the domestic wage cost in excess of the foreign one, would improve labor productivity rather than increase its price. Labor productivity can be achieved by new technology or by producing the same output with less labor (i.e., by laying off the least-productive part of the labor force). In the latter case, the increase in productivity would be achieved at the cost of a rising unemployment rate. Therefore, in a customer-market economy with the nominal exchange rate determined by speculation, labor productivity and unemployment would rise in periods of real currency appreciation and increasing real interest rates. Evidence of unemployment comoving with trend-adjusted productivity and the real interest rate has been found, among others, in Juselius (2006).

Increasing unemployment generally exerts a downward pressure on nominal or real wage claims and, thus, on wage inflation, Δw. Thus, wage inflation is negatively associated with unemployment, u, in an augmented Phillips curve relation with a nonstationary natural rate, u^*: $\Delta w = -b_1(u - u^*)$, where $u^* = f(r)$ is a function of the real interest rate level, r. In Phelps (1994), the latter is a function of domestic government debt and the world real interest rate level. Evidence of a nonstationary natural rate as a function of the long-term real interest rate is found, among others, in Juselius (2006) and Juselius and Ordóñez (2009).

Thus, there seems to be a direct link from financial market behavior causing long persistent swings in real exchange rates and real interest rates to the recurring unemployment slumps discussed in Phelps (1994).

10.7.5   Further Remarks

Frydman and Goldberg (2007) suggest that the uncertainty premium increases with deviations from the fundamental PPP value. But as discussed above, one can also think of the unemployment rate and the profit share as alternative, but related, measures of deviations from benchmark values that eventually will put an end to long swings in nominal exchange rates.

The structural slumps mechanism seems to work well in periods when the major driver underlying the fluctuations in aggregate activity is the long swings in real exchange rates. It is, however, not likely to work well in the aftermath of a fundamental financial crisis, such as the present one, as discussed in Koo (2010) and Miller and Stiglitz (2010). This is because when numerous balance sheets in the economy are "under water," savings will primarily be used for financial consolidation rather than for investment. As the Japanese experience after the collapse of the housing bubble in the 1990s showed, not even a zero interest rate will have the intended effect in such a situation.

10.8   Conclusion

Macroeconomic data have a reputation for not being sufficiently informative, thereby justifying the use of mild force to make them tell an economically relevant story. Based on my long experience of analyzing macroeconomic data,[7] my claim is that macroeconomic data are surprisingly informative, but only if you let them tell the story they want to tell.

So, what do the data tell if they are allowed to speak freely? Some robust findings typical of the past three decades of capital deregulation and globalization can be summarized as follows. First, there is more persistence in the data than standard REH-based theories can explain. In particular, basic parity conditions—such as PPP, real interest rates, uncovered interest rate parity, and the term spread—seem to exhibit a pronounced persistence untenable with $I(0)$-type stationarity. Second, this persistence seems to originate from complex interactions between speculative financial markets and the real economy that tend to drive prices away from benchmark values.

---

7. This includes supervising hundreds and hundreds of seminar papers and BS, MS, and PhD theses.

To summarize, the stories data tell seem consistent with speculative be-havior, imperfect knowledge, long swings, and strong reflexivity between the financial and the real economy. Further research along these lines is likely to result in a fruitful synthesis between the theoretical framework of Phelps (1994) and the Frydman and Goldberg (2007) IKE theory, thereby improv-ing our understanding of the long recurrent spells of high unemployment that continue to mar our economies.

Appendix   The $I(1)$ and $I(2)$ Models

10.A.1   The $I(1)$ Model

To introduce notation and the idea of structuring the data into pulling and pushing forces, I use a simple three-dimensional VAR model for $x'_t = [p_1, p_2, s_{12}]$, where the three variables describe domestic and foreign prices and the nominal exchange rate. The model is structured around $p - r$ stochastic trends (the pushing or exogenous forces) and r cointegration relations (the pulling or equilibrating forces). I consider the case $r = 1$, and $p - r = 2$.

The pulling force is formulated as the vector equilibrium-error-correction model, $\Delta x_t = \alpha \beta' x_{t-1} + \varepsilon_t$:

$$
\begin{bmatrix} \Delta p_{1,t} \\ \Delta p_{2,t} \\ \Delta s_{12,t} \end{bmatrix} = \begin{bmatrix} \alpha_1 \\ \alpha_2 \\ \alpha_3 \end{bmatrix} \beta' x_{t-1} + \cdots + \begin{bmatrix} \varepsilon_{1,t} \\ \varepsilon_{2,t} \\ \varepsilon_{3,t} \end{bmatrix} \tag{7}
$$

where $\beta' x_t$ is an equilibrium error, and α_i is an adjustment coefficient describing how the system adjusts back to equilibrium when it has been pushed away. For example, $\beta' x_t = p_{1,t} - p_{2,t} - s_{12,t}$ would describe an economy where PPP holds as a stationary condition. The α_i coefficients tell us whether it is prices or exchange rates or all three variables that take the adjustment when unanticipated shocks, $\varepsilon_{i,t}$, have pushed the system out of equilibrium.

The pushing forces are analyzed in the moving average form of the CVAR model, describing the cumulated effects of the exogenous shocks, $u_{i,t}$, on the variables:

$$
\begin{bmatrix} p_{1,t} \\ p_{2,t} \\ s_{12,t} \end{bmatrix} = \begin{bmatrix} \beta_{\perp,11} & \beta_{\perp,21} \\ \beta_{\perp,12} & \beta_{\perp,21} \\ \beta_{\perp,13} & \beta_{\perp,21} \end{bmatrix} \begin{bmatrix} \sum_{i=1}^{t} u_{1,i} \\ \sum_{i=1}^{t} u_{2,i} \end{bmatrix} + \cdots + \begin{bmatrix} \varepsilon_{1,t} \\ \varepsilon_{2,t} \\ \varepsilon_{3,t} \end{bmatrix}
$$

where $u_{1,t} = \alpha'_{\perp,1} \varepsilon_t$ and $u_{2,t} = \alpha'_{\perp,2} \varepsilon_t$ are two autonomous common shocks that have a permanent effect on the system; $\alpha_\perp = [\alpha_{\perp,1}, \alpha_{\perp,2}]$, is a $3 \times$

2 matrix, orthogonal to α, defining the two common shocks as linear combination of the VAR residuals $\hat{\varepsilon}_t$; and $\beta_\perp = [\beta_{\perp,1}, \beta_{\perp,2}]$, is a 3×2 matrix orthogonal to β, describing the long-run effect of a structural shock to the system.

For example, $\alpha'_{\perp,1} = [1, -1, 0]$ and $\alpha'_{\perp,2} = [0, 0, 1]$ would describe an economy where shocks to relative prices and shocks to the nominal exchange rate are the main exogenous driving forces, respectively. The case $\beta'_{\perp,1} = [a, a, 0]$ and $\beta'_{\perp,2} = [b, c, b - c]$ would define a stationary real exchange rate:

$$
\begin{bmatrix} p_{1,t} \\ p_{2,t} \\ s_{12,t} \end{bmatrix} = \begin{bmatrix} a & b \\ a & c \\ 0 & b-c \end{bmatrix} \begin{bmatrix} \sum_{i=1}^{t} u_{1,i} \\ \sum_{i=1}^{t} u_{2,i} \end{bmatrix} + \cdots + \begin{bmatrix} \varepsilon_{1,t} \\ \varepsilon_{2,t} \\ \varepsilon_{3,t} \end{bmatrix}
$$

10.A.2 The I(2) Model

The $I(2)$ model is useful to describe an economy where the persistency in the data is one degree higher than in the $I(1)$ world. To account for this, the $I(2)$ model is formulated in acceleration rates, medium-run relations between growth rates, and dynamic relations. It has a richer but also more complicated structure. The vector x_t is now integrated of order 2, and the $p - r$ stochastic trends are divided into s_1 first-order and s_2 second-order stochastic trends (i.e., $p - r = s_1 + s_2$). The r cointegration relations, $\beta' x_t$, are generally integrated of order 1 (i.e., they cointegrate from $I(2)$ to $I(1)$) and become stationary by adding a linear combination of the growth rates, $\delta' \Delta x_t$. In addition, there are s_1 linear combinations, $\beta'_{\perp 1} x_t \sim I(1)$, which can become stationary exclusively by differencing: $\beta'_{\perp 1} \Delta x_t \sim I(0)$. Thus, the $I(2)$ model contains $p - s_2$ relations, $\tau' x_t$, which cointegrate from $I(2)$ to $I(1)$, where $\tau = (\beta, \beta_{\perp 1})$.[8]

I consider here the case, $r = 1$, $s_1 = 1$, and $s_2 = 1$, implying as before one equilibrium relation and two stochastic trends. The differences are that the equilibrium relation needs to be combined with a growth rate to become stationary, and one of the common stochastic trends is an $I(2)$ trend, whereas the other is an $I(1)$ trend. The former could, for example, describe price shocks and the latter exchange rate shocks.

Under this assumption, the vector equilibrium-error-correcting model for $I(2)$ data can be formulated as $\Delta^2 x_t = \alpha(\beta' x_{t-1} + \delta' \Delta x_{t-1}) + \zeta \tau' \Delta x_{t-1} + \varepsilon_t$, where $\tau = [\beta, \beta_{\perp 1}]$. The system of prices and exchange rates would look like:

---

8. If $r - s_2 > 0$, then it is possible to find $r - s_2$ relations $\beta' x$ that are stationary without adding the growth rates.

$$\begin{bmatrix} \Delta^2 p_{1,t} \\ \Delta^2 p_{2,t} \\ \Delta^2 s_{12,t} \end{bmatrix} = \begin{bmatrix} \alpha_1 \\ \alpha_2 \\ \alpha_3 \end{bmatrix} (\beta' x_{t-1} + \delta' \Delta x_{t-1})$$

$$+ \begin{bmatrix} \zeta_{11} & \zeta_{21} \\ \zeta_{12} & \zeta_{22} \\ \zeta_{13} & \zeta_{23} \end{bmatrix} \begin{bmatrix} \beta' \Delta x_{t-1} \\ \beta'_{\perp 1} \Delta x_{t-1} \end{bmatrix} + \begin{bmatrix} \varepsilon_{1,t} \\ \varepsilon_{2,t} \\ \varepsilon_{3,t} \end{bmatrix} \qquad (8)$$

where $\beta' x_{t-1} + \delta' \Delta x_{t-1}$ describes a deviation from a dynamic equilibrium relation, and $\beta' \Delta x_{t-1}$ and $\beta'_{\perp 1} \Delta x_{t-1}$ describe deviations from two medium-run equilibrium relations among growth rates. For example, if $\beta' x_{t-1} + \delta' \Delta x_{t-1} = (p_{1,t} - p_{2,t} - s_{12,t}) + \delta_1 \Delta p_{1,t}$, then this would describe an economy where deviations from PPP exhibit $I(1)$-type persistence that is compensated by a similar persistence in country 1's inflation rate.

The common stochastic trends are analyzed in the moving-average form of the CVAR model, $x_t = \beta_{\perp 2} \Sigma \Sigma u_s + B \Sigma u_i + \cdots + \varepsilon_t$. For the price and exchange rate system, it can be formulated as:

$$\begin{bmatrix} p_{1,t} \\ p_{2,t} \\ s_{12,t} \end{bmatrix} = \begin{bmatrix} \beta_{\perp 2,1} \\ \beta_{\perp 2,2} \\ \beta_{\perp 2,3} \end{bmatrix} \begin{bmatrix} \sum_{i=1}^{t} \sum_{s=1}^{i} u_{1,s} \end{bmatrix} + \begin{bmatrix} b_{11} & b_{21} \\ b_{12} & b_{22} \\ b_{13} & b_{23} \end{bmatrix} \begin{bmatrix} \sum_{i=1}^{t} u_{1,i} \\ \sum_{i=1}^{t} u_{2,i} \end{bmatrix} + \cdots$$

where $u_{1,t} = \alpha'_{\perp 2} \varepsilon_t$ is an autonomous shock that cumulates twice over time; $u_{2,t} = \alpha'_{\perp 1} \varepsilon_t$ is an autonomous shock that cumulates once over time; $\alpha_\perp = [\alpha_{\perp,1}, \alpha_{\perp,2}]$ is a 3×2 matrix orthogonal to α, defining the two shocks as a linear combination of the VAR residuals $\hat{\varepsilon}_t$; and $\beta_{\perp 2}$ is a 3×1 vector orthogonal to $\{\beta, \beta_{\perp 1}\}$ and describing the long-run effect of a structural $I(2)$ shock to the system. If $u_{1,t}$ is a relative price shock, then $\alpha'_{\perp 2} = [1, -1, 0]$, and if $u_{2,t}$ is a nominal exchange rate shock, then $\alpha'_{\perp 1} = [0, 0, 1]$. Assuming that only the two prices are affected by the $I(2)$ trend, the system can be described by:

$$\begin{bmatrix} p_{1,t} \\ p_{2,t} \\ s_{12,t} \end{bmatrix} = \begin{bmatrix} 1 \\ 1 \\ 0 \end{bmatrix} \begin{bmatrix} \sum_{i=1}^{t} \sum_{s=1}^{i} u_{1,s} \end{bmatrix} + \begin{bmatrix} b_{11} & b_{21} \\ b_{12} & b_{22} \\ b_{13} & b_{23} \end{bmatrix} \begin{bmatrix} \sum_{i=1}^{t} u_{1,i} \\ \sum_{i=1}^{t} u_{2,i} \end{bmatrix} + \cdots$$

Thus, prices would be type $I(2)$, but relative prices and the nominal exchange rate would be type $I(1)$. The real exchange rate would generally be $I(1)$ unless $b_{13} = b_{11} - b_{12}$ and $b_{23} = b_{21} - b_{22}$.

References

Elliot, G. (1998) "The Robustness of Cointegration Methods When Regressors Almost Have Unit Roots," *Econometrica* 66: 149–158.

Frydman, R., and M. Goldberg. (2007) *Imperfect Knowledge Economics: Exchange Rates and Risk*. Princeton, NJ: Princeton University Press.

———. (2011) *Beyond Mechanical Markets: Risk and the Role of Asset Price Swings*. Princeton, NJ: Princeton University Press.

Frydman, R., M. Goldberg, K. Juselius, and S. Johansen. (2011) "Imperfect Knowledge and Long Swings in Currency Markets." Manuscript under preparation, New York University, New York, and University of New Hampshire, Durham.

Hendry, D. F., and K. Juselius. (2000) "Explaining Cointegration Analysis. Part 2," *Energy Journal* 22: 1–52.

Hoover, K., S. Johansen, and K. Juselius. (2008) "Allowing the Data to Speak Freely: The Macroeconometrics of the Cointegrated VAR," *American Economic Review* 98: 251–255.

Johansen, S. (1995) *Likelihood-Based Inference in Cointegrated Vector Autoregressive Models*. Oxford: Oxford University Press.

———. (1997) "Likelihood Analysis of the $I(2)$ Model," *Scandinavian Journal of Statistics* 24: 433–462.

———. (2006) "Confronting the Economic Model with the Data," in D. Colander (ed.), *Post Walrasian Macroeconomics: Beyond the Dynamic Stochastic General Equilibrium Model*. Cambridge: Cambridge University Press, pp. 287–300.

Johansen, S., K. Juselius, R. Frydman, and M. Goldberg. (2010) "Testing Hypotheses in an $I(2)$ Model with Piecewise Linear Trends. An Analysis of the Persistent Long Swings in the Dmk/\$ Rate," *Journal of Econometrics* 158: 117–129.

Juselius, K. (1995) "Do Purchasing Power Parity and Uncovered Interest Rate Parity Hold in the Long Run? An Example of Likelihood Inference in a Multivariate Time-Series Model," *Journal of Econometrics* 69: 211–240.

———. (2006) *The Cointegrated VAR Model: Methodology and Applications*. Oxford: Oxford University Press.

———. (2009) "The Long Swings Puzzle: What the Data Tell When Allowed to Speak Freely," in K. Patterson and T. C. Mills (eds.), *Handbook of Empirical Econometrics*. London: MacMillan, pp. 367–384.

———. (2011) "Testing Exchange Rate Models Based on Rational Expectations versus Imperfect Knowledge Economics: A Scenario Analysis." Working paper, University of Copenhagen.

Juselius, K., and M. Franchi. (2007) "Taking a DSGE Model to the Data Meaningfully," *Economics: The Open-Access, Open-Assessment E-Journal* 4: 1–38.

Juselius, K., and A. N. Jensen. (2012) "Testing for Near $I(2)$ Trends When the Signal to Noise Ratio Is Small." Working paper, University of Copenhagen.

Juselius, K., and R. MacDonald. (2004) "The International Parities between the USA and Japan," *Japan and the World Economy* 16: 17–34.

———. (2007) "International Parity Relationships between Germany and the United States: A Joint Modelling Approach," in A. Morales-Zumaquero (ed.), *International Macroeconomics: Recent Development*. Hauppauge, NY: Nova Science Publishers, pp. 79–103.

Juselius, K., and J. Ordóñez. (2009) "Balassa-Samuelson and Wage, Price and Unemployment Dynamics in the Spanish Transition to EMU Membership," *Economics: The Open-Access, Open-Assessment E-Journal* 3: 2009-4.

Koo, R. (2010) *The Holy Grail of Macroeconomics: Lessons from Japan's Great Recession.* Hoboken, NJ: John Wiley & Sons.

Miller, M., and J. Stiglitz. (2010) "Leverage and Asset Bubbles: Averting Armageddon with Chapter 11?" *Economic Journal* 120: 500–518.

Nielsen, B., and H. B. Nielsen. (2009) "The Asymptotic Distribution of the Estimated Characteristic Roots in a Second Order Autoregression." Manuscript in preparation, University of Copenhagen.

Nielsen, H. B., and A. Rahbek. (2007) "The Likelihood Ratio Test for Cointegration Ranks in the *I*(2) Model," *Econometric Theory* 23: 615–637.

Pantula, S. G., and W. A. Fuller. (1993) "The Large Sample Distribution of the Roots of the Second Order Autoregressive Polynomial," *Biometrika* 80: 919–923.

Phelps, E. (1994) *Structural Slumps.* Princeton, NJ: Princetion University Press.

CHAPTER ELEVEN

Stabilization Policies and Economic Growth

Philippe Aghion and Enisse Kharroubi

11.1 Introduction

Macroeconomic textbooks generally tend to present the analysis of long-term growth and the study of macroeconomic policies (e.g., fiscal and monetary policies) aimed at achieving short-run stabilization as distinct bodies of research. Indeed, the common wisdom among economists sees no connection between the way stabilization policies are implemented and the average speed at which the affected economy grows. If anything, growth theories tend to highlight the importance of stable and consistent policies as exemplified by recommendations to run prudent fiscal and monetary policies through balanced fiscal accounts or moderate inflation.

Yet the view that policy recommendations to foster long-term growth should stop at calls for prudent fiscal and monetary policies has recently been challenged. In particular a growing literature has highlighted the *negative* link between the volatility of the business cycle and the growth performance of an economy. For example, Ramey and Ramey (1995) were among the first to provide empirical evidence of a negative correlation between growth volatility and long-run average growth based on cross-country regressions. More recently, Aghion et al. (2010) claim that greater business cycle volatility can be detrimental to growth, because firms are forced to cut productivity-enhancing investments during downturns, when they lack the ability to levy capital to finance these investments. This mechanism is indeed confirmed by empirical evidence: higher macroeconomic volatility encourages more pronounced procyclical investments in research and development in firms that are more credit constrained.

The views expressed here are those of the authors and do not necessarily represent those of the Bank for International Settlements.

A natural implication of such observations is that the cyclical pattern of stabilization could be a significant determinant of growth. More precisely, that fiscal and/or monetary policies are run in a procyclical or countercyclical manner may have implications for long-term growth. For instance, if monetary policy reduces the cost of short-term refinancing in downturns—a typical example of countercyclical monetary policy—that should help firms go through downturns without having to cut productivity-enhancing investments. Moreover, it should also help raise firm incentives to engage in such investments, as the likelihood of cuts being necessary during downturns is reduced.

This chapter provides an empirical test of this view, namely, looking at the effect of the cyclical pattern of fiscal and monetary policies on growth. To do so, we rely on cross-industry, cross-country panel data regressions to investigate whether industry that faces tighter financial constraints did effectively benefit in a disproportionate manner from countercyclical fiscal or monetary policies. Indeed, the empirical evidence presented later in the chapter seems to confirm this view: industries with greater financial constraints tend to grow faster in countries with more stabilizing fiscal or monetary policies.

We build on the methodology developed in the seminal paper by Rajan and Zingales (1998). Using cross-industry, cross-country panel data, we test whether industry growth is positively affected by the interaction between fiscal or monetary policy cyclicality (computed at the country level) and industry-level measures of financial constraints (computed for each corresponding industry in the United States). The main reason we favor such an approach is because it provides a clear way to deal with causality issues. As noted above, the negative relationship between business cycle volatility and long-run growth is only indicative of a negative comovement: it does not determine whether high volatility tends to reduce growth or whether low growth contributes to raising business cycle volatility. By looking at the effect of macroeconomic policies conducted at the country level on long-term growth at the industry level and recognizing that all industries are small compared to the total economy, we can confidently rule out the possibility that growth at the industry level affects the cyclical pattern of macroeconomic policy. Instead, we focus on the causality link from macroeconomic policy to industry growth. In other words, to the extent that the cyclical pattern of macroeconomic policy can affect industry growth, the opposite (industry growth affecting macroeconomic policy) is much less likely to hold. A significant interaction coefficient in our growth regressions is therefore indicative that the cyclical pattern of stabilization policies indeed has a causal impact on long-run growth.

Our main empirical finding is that the interaction between financial constraints in an industry and fiscal or monetary policy countercyclicality in a country has a positive, significant, and robust impact on industry growth. More specifically, the higher the extent to which the corresponding industry in the United States relies on external finance (or the lower the asset tangibility of the corresponding sector in the United States), the more such an industry will benefit from a more countercyclical fiscal policy. Put differently, industries with tighter borrowing constraints do benefit more from countercyclical fiscal policy. Besides, a similar type of result applies to monetary policy and extends beyond measures of borrowing constraints (e.g., financial dependence or asset tangibility), because the interaction between monetary policy countercyclicality and an industry's dependence on *liquidity* also has a significant and positive effect on industry growth. Based on the regression coefficients, we can assess the magnitude of the corresponding difference-in-difference effects. The figures we obtain happen to be relatively large for both fiscal and monetary policies, especially compared with the equivalent figures in Rajan and Zingales (1998). This suggests that the effect of countercyclical fiscal or monetary policy is economically significant and cannot be discarded as being of second-order importance.

Overall, our results suggest a role for countercyclical fiscal and monetary policies to foster economic growth in economies where firms face credit or liquidity constraints. However, it is important to bear in mind that our approach departs substantially from alternative (more short-term) justifications based on the Keynesian multiplier for fiscal policy or price distortions for monetary policy.

The chapter is organized as follows. Section 11.2 describes the methodology and the data used. Section 11.3 presents our main empirical results. Section 11.4 presents our conclusions. Appendixes 11.A and 11.B supply details on the sample and estimation results.

11.2 Methodology and Data

Our dependent variable is the average annual growth rate of real value added in industry j in country k for a given period of time, say, $[\tau; \tau + n]$. As explanatory variables, we introduce industry and country fixed effects $\{\alpha_j; \beta_k\}$ to control for unobserved heterogeneity across industries and across countries. The variable of interest, $(ic)_j \times (spc)_k$, is the interaction between industry j's intrinsic characteristic and the degree of (counter) cyclicality of stabilization policies in country k over the same period during which the industry growth rates were computed, here $[\tau; \tau + n]$. Finally, we control for initial conditions by including the ratio of real value added in industry j in country k to the total real value added in the manufacturing sector in country k at the beginning of the period, here τ. Denoting the real value added in industry j (in manufacturing) in country k at time t by y_{jk}^t (y_{jk}) and the error term by ε_{jk}, our main estimation equation can then be expressed as

$$\frac{\ln\left(y_{jk}^{\tau+n}\right) - \ln\left(y_{jk}^{\tau}\right)}{n} = \alpha_j + \beta_k + \gamma(ic)_j \times (spc)_k - \delta \ln\left(\frac{y_{jk}^{\tau}}{y_k^{\tau}}\right) + \varepsilon_{jk} \quad (1)$$

The stabilization policy cyclicality measure in country k, $(spc)_k$, is estimated as the marginal change in the stabilization policy considered (fiscal or monetary) following a change in the domestic output gap. We use country-level data to estimate the following country-by-country "auxiliary" equation over the period $[\tau; \tau + n]$:

$$sp_{kt} = \eta_k + (spc)_k z_{kt} + u_{kt} \qquad (2)$$

where sp_{kt} is a measure of fiscal policy in country k in year t (e.g., total fiscal balance or primary fiscal balance to GDP for fiscal policy, or real short-term interest rate for monetary policy); z_{kt} measures the output gap in country k in year t (i.e., the percentage difference between actual and potential GDP) and therefore represents the country's current position in the cycle; η_k is a constant; and u_{kt} is an error term. For example, if the dependent variable in (2) is total fiscal balance to GDP, a positive (negative) regression coefficient $(spc)_k$ reflects a countercyclical (procyclical) fiscal policy as the country's fiscal balance improves (deteriorates) in upturns. Similarly, if the dependent variable in (2) is the real short-term interest rate, a positive (negative) regression coefficient $(spc)_k$ reflects a countercyclical (procyclical) monetary policy as the central bank tends to make short-term credit more (less) costly in upturns.[1]

Turning now to industry-specific characteristics, we follow Rajan and Zingales (1998) in using firm-level data pertaining to the United States. In our case, these characteristics should capture two sets of constraints affecting firms: borrowing constraints on the one hand and liquidity constraints on the other. There are two different proxies for borrowing constraints: external financial dependence and asset tangibility. External financial dependence is measured as the median ratio, across firms belonging to a given industry, of capital expenditures minus current cash flow to total capital expenditures. Asset tangibility is measured as the median ratio, across firms in a given industry, of the value of net property, plant, and equipment to total assets. As for liquidity constraints, there are three different measures available. The first is the median ratio, across firms belonging to a given industry, of inventories to total sales. The second is a cash conversion cycle variable that measures the median time elapsed between the moment a firm pays for its inputs and the moment it is paid for its output. The last measure for liquidity constraints is the median ratio, across firms in a given industry, of labor costs to total sales. The first two measures give an indication of an industry's need to raise (or difficulty of raising) external finance and as such can be considered as proxies for industry borrowing constraints.

---

1. Figures 11.B1 and 11.B2 in Appendix 11.B show the estimation results of the country-by-country auxiliary regression (2).

The last three measures give an indication of an industry's need for short-term financing. For example, industries with a larger ratio of labor costs to sales have larger payments to make on a regular basis and should therefore have greater needs for short-term refinancing. Similarly, industries are supposed to maintain larger inventories when they face greater refinancing needs, because inventories are the most liquid physical assets that firms can hold. Confirming this view, the data show a very high correlation across industries between the inventories to sales ratio and the cash conversion cycle variable.

This methodology, which consists in using U.S. firm data to compute industry characteristics, is predicated on the assumptions that (1) differences across industries are driven largely by differences in technology; (2) technological differences persist over time across countries; and (3) countries are relatively similar in terms of the overall institutional environment faced by firms. Under these three conditions, the U.S.-based industry-specific measure is likely to be a valid measure for industries in countries other than the United States. We believe that these assumptions are satisfied, especially given our restriction to a set of rich countries that all belong to the Organisation for Economic Co-operation and Development (OECD). For example, if pharmaceuticals require proportionally more external finance or have lower labor costs than do textiles in the United States, this is likely to be the case in other OECD countries as well. Moreover, because little convergence has occurred among OECD countries over the past 20 years, cross-country differences are likely to persist over time. Finally, to the extent that the United States is more financially developed than other countries worldwide, U.S.-based measures are likely to provide the least noisy measures of industry borrowing or liquidity constraints.

Following Rajan and Zingales (1998), we estimate our main equation (1) with a simple ordinary least squares (OLS) procedure, correcting for heteroskedasticity bias when needed, without worrying much about endogeneity issues. In particular, the interaction term between industry-specific characteristics and stabilization policy cyclicality is likely to be largely exogenous to the dependent variable. Our reasons for assuming this are as follows. First, our variable for industry-specific characteristics pertains to industries in the United States, whereas the dependent variable involves other countries. Hence, reverse causality, whereby industry growth outside the United States could affect industry-specific characteristics in the United States, seems quite implausible. Second, stabilization policy cyclicality is measured at a macro level, whereas the dependent variable is measured at the industry level, which again reduces the scope for reverse causality as long as each individual industry represents a small share of the total output in the domestic economy.

Our data sample focuses on 15 industrial OECD countries. The sample does not include the United States, as to do so would be a source of reverse causality problems.[2] Our data come from various sources. Industry-level real value added data are drawn from the European Union (EU) KLEMS dataset (O'Mahony and Timmer 2009) and are restricted to manufacturing industries.[3] The primary source of data for measuring industry-specific characteristics is Compustat, which gathers balance sheets and income statements for U.S. listed firms. We draw on Rajan and Zingales (1998), Braun (2003), Braun and Larrain (2005), and Raddatz (2006) to compute the industry-level indicators for borrowing and liquidity constraints. Finally, macroeconomic variables used to compute stabilization policy cyclicality are drawn from the OECD (2008) Economic Outlook dataset. Fiscal policy data exist only on an annual frequency for our set of countries. Hence we use a relatively long time span—beginning in 1980 and ending in 2005—to obtain precise estimates of fiscal policy cyclicality. In contrast, there is quarterly data for monetary policy variables. We hence choose to concentrate on the most recent period (1995–2005) during which monetary policy was essentially conducted through short-term interest rates to make sure that our auxiliary regression does capture the bulk of monetary policy decisions.[4]

11.3   Results

11.3.1   Fiscal Policy

We first investigate the effect of fiscal policy countercyclicality. To this end, we estimate our main regression equation (1) using financial dependence or asset tangibility as industry-specific characteristics and two sets of fiscal policy indicators. The first set is built around the total fiscal balance variable, which we consider as either cyclically adjusted or not and which we compute as a ratio of GDP or of potential GDP.[5] The second set of fis-

---

2. The sample consists of the following countries: Australia, Austria, Belgium, Denmark, Spain, Finland, France, Great Britain, Greece, Ireland, Italy, Japan, The Netherlands, Portugal, and Sweden.

3. See Appendix 11.A for the list of industries in the sample.

4. Yet it is fair to say that even during this period, some countries (e.g., Japan) did conduct monetary policy mainly though other means than short-term interest rates. Japan went through a long period of "unconventional" monetary policy, during which the central bank was monetizing fiscal deficits. Under these circumstances, (2) may give a biased picture of monetary policy cyclicality.

5. The cyclically adjusted balance represents the underlying fiscal position when movements stemming from automatic stabilizers are removed. Put differently, changes in cyclically adjusted fiscal balance represent changes in discretionary fiscal policy. The reason fiscal indicators are considered as a ratio of potential GDP is to make sure that changes in fiscal policy indicators come from fiscal policy itself and not from changes in GDP. Otherwise, there could be fluctuations in fiscal policy indicators even if the fiscal balance is constant simply because of fluctuations in GDP.

cal policy indicators is built around the primary fiscal balance variable.[6] As in the previous case, we consider it either as cyclically adjusted or not. Moreover, we compute it as a ratio of GDP or of potential GDP. The empirical results show that growth in industry real value added is significantly and positively correlated with the interaction of financial dependence and fiscal policy countercyclicality (see Table 11.1): increased sensitivity to the output gap of total fiscal balance to GDP tends to raise industry real value added growth disproportionately for industries with higher financial dependence. This result holds irrespective of whether total fiscal balance is cyclically adjusted or not and irrespective of whether fiscal balance is considered as a ratio of actual or potential GDP. Table 11.2 provides a similar picture: increased sensitivity of total fiscal balance to GDP to the output gap raises industry real value added growth disproportionately for industries with lower asset tangibilities. As in the previous case, this result holds independent of the precise measure of fiscal policy countercyclicality.

Three remarks are worth making at this point. First, the estimated coefficients are highly significant, in spite of the relatively conservative standard error estimates, which we cluster at the country level. Second, the pairwise correlation between industry financial dependence and industry asset tangibility is about -0.6, which is significantly below -1. In other words, these two variables are far from being perfectly correlated, which, in turn, implies that Tables 11.1 and 11.2 do not just mirror each other, but instead convey complementary information. Finally, the estimated coefficients remain essentially the same whether the fiscal balance is considered as a ratio of actual or of potential GDP. This insensitivity suggests that we are capturing the effect of fiscal policy rather than just the effect of changes in actual GDP. Similarly, the estimated coefficients remain essentially the same whether the fiscal balance is considered as cyclically adjusted or not, which suggests that the effect we capture is not exclusively related to automatic stabilizers.

We now repeat the same estimation exercise, but taking primary fiscal balance, not total fiscal balance, as our fiscal policy indicator (Tables 11.3 and 11.4). The difference between these two indicators is that the primary fiscal balance does not include net interest repayments to or from the government. The results are qualitatively similar in both cases: industries with greater financial dependence or lower asset tangibility tend to benefit disproportionately from a more countercyclical fiscal policy in the sense of increased sensitivity of the primary fiscal balance to variations in the output gap.

---

6. The primary fiscal balance excludes net interest payments to or from the government as opposed to total fiscal balance which includes all government revenues and expenditures.

Table 11.1 Correlation between growth in real value added and the interaction between financial dependence and fiscal policy cyclicality: Total fiscal balance

Independent variable	Fiscal balance to GDP (1)	Fiscal balance to potential GDP (2)	Cyclically adjusted fiscal balance to GDP (3)	Cyclically adjusted fiscal balance to potential GDP (4)
Logarithm of initial share in manufacturing value added	−0.784** (0.284)	−0.795** (0.282)	−0.772** (0.286)	−0.780** (0.285)
Interaction (financial dependence and fiscal policy countercyclicality)	6.724*** (1.526)	6.742*** (1.434)	7.847*** (1.604)	7.799*** (1.537)
Number of observations	521	521	521	521
R^2	0.569	0.571	0.573	0.575

Notes: The dependent variable is the average annual growth rate of real value added for 1980–2005 for each industry in each country. Initial share in manufacturing value added is the ratio of beginning-of-period industry real value added to beginning-of-period total manufacturing real value added. Financial dependence is the fraction of capital expenditures not financed with internal funds for U.S. firms in the same industry for 1980–1990. Fiscal policy countercyclicality is the coefficient of the output gap when the variable indicated in the column is regressed on a constant and the output gap for each country over 1980–2005. The interaction variable is the product of variables in parentheses. Estimated coefficients are in percentages. Standard errors—clustered at the country level—are in parentheses. All estimations include country and industry dummies. *** denotes significance at the 1% level; ** denotes significance at the 5% level.

Table 11.2 Correlation between growth in real value added and the interaction between asset tangibility and fiscal policy cyclicality: Total fiscal balance

Independent variable	Fiscal balance to GDP (1)	Fiscal balance to potential GDP (2)	Cyclically adjusted fiscal balance to GDP (3)	Cyclically adjusted fiscal balance to potential GDP (4)
Logarithm of initial share in manufacturing value added	−0.515 (0.350)	−0.517 (0.351)	−0.508 (0.351)	−0.508 (0.352)
Interaction (financial dependence and fiscal policy countercyclicality)	−13.77*** (4.544)	−13.74*** (4.388)	−16.19*** (5.214)	−15.98*** (5.093)
Number of observations	521	521	521	521
R^2	0.550	0.550	0.551	0.552

Notes: The dependent variable is the average annual growth rate of real value added for 1980–2005 for each industry in each country. Initial share in manufacturing value added is the ratio of beginning-of-period industry real value added to beginning-of-period total manufacturing real value added. Asset tangibility is the fraction of assets represented by net property, plant, and equipment for U.S. firms in the same industry for 1980–1990. Fiscal policy countercyclicality is the coefficient of the output gap when the variable indicated in the column is regressed on a constant and the output gap for each country over 1980–2005. The interaction variable is the product of variables in parentheses. Estimated coefficients are in percentages. Standard errors—clustered at the country level—are in parentheses. All estimations include country and industry dummies. *** denotes significance at the 1% level.

Table 11.3 Correlation between growth in real value added and the interaction between financial dependence and fiscal policy cyclicality: Primary fiscal balance

Independent variable	Primary fiscal balance to GDP (1)	Primary fiscal balance to potential GDP (2)	Cyclically adjusted primary fiscal balance to GDP (3)	Cyclically adjusted primary fiscal balance to potential GDP (4)
Logarithm of initial share in manufacturing value added	−0.794*** (0.250)	−0.796*** (0.250)	−0.786*** (0.247)	−0.784*** (0.248)
Interaction (financial dependence and fiscal policy countercyclicality)	4.679*** (0.864)	4.700*** (0.846)	5.170*** (0.893)	5.183*** (0.872)
Number of observations	521	521	521	521
R^2	0.569	0.569	0.571	0.572

Notes: The dependent variable is the average annual growth rate of real value added for 1980–2005 for each industry in each country. Initial share in manufacturing value added is the ratio of beginning-of-period industry real value added to beginning-of-period total manufacturing real value added. Financial dependence is the fraction of capital expenditures not financed with internal funds for U.S. firms in the same industry for 1980–1990. Fiscal policy countercyclicality is the coefficient of the output gap when the variable indicated in the column is regressed on a constant and the output gap for each country over 1980–2005. The interaction variable is the product of variables in parentheses. Estimated coefficients are in percentages. Standard errors—clustered at the country level—are in parentheses. All estimations include country and industry dummies. *** denotes significance at the 1% level.

Table 11.4 Correlation between growth in real value added and the interaction between asset tangibility and fiscal policy cyclicality: Primary fiscal balance

Independent variable	Primary fiscal balance to GDP (1)	Primary fiscal balance to potential GDP (2)	Cyclically adjusted primary fiscal balance to GDP (3)	Cyclically adjusted primary fiscal balance to potential GDP (4)
Logarithm of initial share in manufacturing value added	−0.492 (0.351)	−0.494 (0.351)	−0.485 (0.352)	−0.485 (0.352)
Interaction (financial dependence and fiscal policy countercyclicality)	−9.228*** (2.878)	−9.336*** (2.812)	−10.230*** (3.136)	−10.330*** (3.072)
Number of observations	521	521	521	521
R^2	0.549	0.549	0.550	0.550

Notes: The dependent variable is the average annual growth rate of real value added for 1980–2005 for each industry in each country. Initial share in manufacturing value added is the ratio of beginning-of-period industry real value added to beginning-of-period total manufacturing real value added. Asset tangibility is the fraction of assets represented by net property, plant, and equipment for U.S. firms in the same industry for 1980–1990. Fiscal policy countercyclicality is the coefficient of the output gap when the variable indicated in the column is regressed on a constant and the output gap for each country over 1980–2005. The interaction variable is the product of variables in parentheses. Standard errors—clustered at the country level—are in parentheses. All estimations include country and industry dummies. *** denotes significance at the 1% level.

11.3.2 Monetary Policy

We now investigate the effect of monetary policy countercyclicality. To this end, we estimate our main regression equation (1) using either industry measures of borrowing constraints or of liquidity constraints. Moreover, as a measure of monetary policy cyclicality, we use the sensitivity to the output gap of the real short-term interest rate (measured as the difference between the 3-month short-term policy interest rate set by the central bank and the 3-month annualized inflation rate).[7] As a robustness check, we also consider as a measure of monetary policy cyclicality the sensitivity to the output gap of the real short term interest rate, controlling for the one-quarter-lagged real short-term interest rate to take into account some possible persistence in monetary policy decisions.

The empirical results show that growth in industry real value added is significantly and positively correlated with the interaction of financial dependence and monetary policy countercyclicality (Table 11.5): increased sensitivity to the output gap of the real short-term interest rate tends to raise industry real value added growth disproportionately for industries with greater financial dependence. A similar result holds for the interaction between monetary policy cyclicality and industry asset tangibility: enhanced sensitivity of real short-term interest rate to the output gap raises industry real value added growth disproportionately for industries with lower asset tangibilities. Finally, these two results extend to the case where monetary policy cyclicality is estimated with a control for persistence over time in the real short-term interest rate.[8]

We now repeat the same estimation exercise for measures of industry liquidity constraints (Table 11.6). As noted above, a countercyclical monetary policy should help raise growth in the sectors that are most dependent on liquidity by easing the process of refinancing. Indeed, the empirical evidence shows that for each of our three measures of liquidity constraints, the interaction of countercyclical monetary policy and liquidity constraints does have a positive effect on industry growth. And as in the case of borrowing constraints, these results extend pretty much the same way to the case where monetary policy countercyclicality is estimated by taking into account possible time persistence in the real short-term interest rate. Two remarks are in order. First, the correlations between the three different measures of liquidity constraints show that the inventories to sales variable and the

---

7. Ideally, we would like to measure monetary policy countercyclicality by estimating a Taylor rule. However, the problem with such an estimate is that short-term nominal interest rates and inflation rates are not stationary over the period (1995–2005) used for our estimation.

8. In this case, the cyclicality measure of monetary policy is obtained by estimating the equation $sp_{kt} = \eta_k + \theta_k sp_{kt-1} + (spc)_k z_{kt} + u_{kt}$, where sp_{kt-1} is the one-quarter-lagged real short-term interest rate.

Table 11.5 Correlation between growth in real value added and the interaction between credit constraints and monetary policy countercyclicality

Independent variable	Real short-term interest rate sensitivity to output gap		Real short-term interest rate sensitivity to output gap, controlling for time persistence	
Monetary policy countercyclicality variable	(1)	(2)	(3)	(4)
Logarithm of initial share in manufacturing value added	−0.781 (0.478)	−0.775 (0.475)	−0.764 (0.477)	−0.760 (0.475)
Interaction (financial dependence and fiscal policy countercyclicality)	2.372** (0.925)		3.235** (1.467)	
Interaction (financial asset tangibility and fiscal policy countercyclicality)		−7.915** (3.062)		−11.180** (4.547)
Number of observations	720	720	720	720
R^2	0.432	0.431	0.432	0.431

Notes: The dependent variable is the average annual growth rate of real value added for 1995–2005 for each industry in each country. Initial share in manufacturing value added is the ratio of beginning-of-period industry real value added to beginning-of-period total manufacturing real value added. Asset tangibility is the fraction of assets represented by net property, plant, and equipment for U.S. firms in the same industry for 1980–1990. Financial dependence is the fraction of capital expenditures not financed with internal funds for U.S. firms in the same industry for 1980–1990. The interaction variable is the product of variables in parentheses. Standard errors—clustered at the industry level—are in parentheses. All estimations include country and industry dummies. ** denotes significance at the 5% level.

Table 11.6 Correlation between growth in real value added and the interaction between liquidity constraints and monetary policy countercyclicality

Independent variable	Real short-term interest rate sensitivity to output gap		Real short-term interest rate sensitivity to output gap, controlling for time persistence	
Monetary policy countercyclicality variable	(1)	(2)	(3)	(4)
Logarithm of initial share in manufacturing value added	−0.769 (0.478)	−0.771 (0.479)	−0.764 (0.477)	−0.768 (0.480)
Interaction (financial dependence and fiscal policy countercyclicality)	14.010** (6.918)		22.270** (10.180)	
Interaction (financial asset tangibility and fiscal policy countercyclicality)		7.658** (3.788)		12.930** (5.304)
Number of observations	720	720	720	720
R^2	0.430	0.431	0.431	0.431

Notes: The dependent variable is the average annual growth rate of real value added for 1995–2005 for each industry in each country. Initial share in manufacturing value added is the ratio of beginning-of-period industry real value added to beginning-of-period total manufacturing real value added. Inventories to sales is the ratio of total inventories over annual sales for U.S. firms in the same industry for 1980–1990. Labor costs to sales is the ratio of labor costs to shipments for U.S. firms in the same industry for 1980–1990. The interaction variable is the product of variables in parentheses. Standard errors—clustered at the industry level—are in parentheses. All estimations include country and industry dummies. ** denotes significance at the 5% level.

cash conversion cycle variable are very highly correlated (0.9), which means these two variables are simply replicating a unique result. However, this is not the case for the correlation between the inventories to sales variable and the labor cost to sales variable, because the correlation is much lower (0.6). Second, the correlation between indicators of borrowing constraint and liquidity constraint is also far from being one. It ranges between 0.4 and 0.7 (when borrowing constraints are measured with external financial dependence, correlations being opposite when using asset tangibility). Liquidity and borrowing constraints are therefore two distinct channels through which monetary policy countercyclicality can affect industry growth.

11.3.3 *Magnitude of the Effects*

How large are the effects implied by the regressions? To get a sense of the magnitudes involved, we compute the difference in growth between (1) an industry in the third quartile (seventy-fifth percentile) in terms of borrowing or liquidity constraint located in a country in the third quartile in terms of fiscal or monetary policy countercyclicality and (2) an industry in the first quartile (twenty-fifth percentile) located in a country in the first quartile of the same respective measures. We then carry out a similar exercise, replacing financial dependence with asset tangibility.[9]

For fiscal policy countercyclicality, the approximate gain in real value added growth is between 1.7 and 2.4 percentage points a year when the industry characteristic considered is external financial dependence. In contrast, the approximate gain in real value added growth is between 2.1 and 2.7 percentage points a year when the industry characteristic considered is asset tangibility. For monetary policy, the gain in real value added growth ranges between 0.9 and 2.3 percentage points a year. Yet it is important to note that growth gains are larger when the industry characteristics considered relate to liquidity constraints (the range is from 1.5 to 2.3 percentage points a year) than when they relate to borrowing constraints (the range is from 0.9 to 1.5 percentage points a year).

These magnitudes are fairly large, especially compared to the corresponding figures in Rajan and Zingales (1998). According to their results, the

---

9. In this case, we compute the difference in growth between (1) an industry in the first quartile in terms of asset tangibility located in a country in the third quartile in terms of fiscal policy countercyclicality and (2) an industry in the third quartile located in a country in the first quartile of the same respective measures.

Given our difference-in-difference specification, it is impossible to infer the economic magnitudes of the estimated coefficients differently. In particular, the presence of industry and country fixed effects precludes investigating the impact of a change in the cyclical pattern of fiscal policy for a given industry, or conversely, the effect of a change in industry characteristics (financial dependence or asset tangibility) in a country with a given cyclical pattern of fiscal policy. Both these effects are absorbed in our country and industry dummies.

gain in real value added growth from moving from the twenty-fifth to the seventy-fifth percentile, both in a country's level of financial development and in an industry's level of external financial dependence, is roughly equal to 1 percentage point a year.

However, the following considerations are worth pointing out here. First, these are difference-in-difference (cross-country or cross-industry) effects, which are not directly interpretable as countrywide effects. Second, we are just looking at manufacturing sectors, which represent no more than 40% of total GDP for the countries in our sample. Third, irrespective of the indicator for countercyclicality considered, there is a high degree of dispersion across the countries in our sample. Hence, moving from the twenty-fifth to the seventy-fifth percentile in policy countercyclicality corresponds to a radical change in the design of stabilization policies along the cycle, which, in turn, is unlikely to take place in a country over a short time. Fourth, this simple computation does not take into account the possible costs associated with the transition from a steady state with low policy countercyclicality to one with high policy countercyclicality. Yet the above exercise suggests that differences in the cyclicality of fiscal and monetary policy are an important driver of the observed cross-country, cross-industry differences in growth performance.

11.4 Conclusion

We have analyzed the extent to which macroeconomic policy over the business cycle can affect industry growth. Following the Rajan and Zingales (1998) methodology, we have interacted

1. industry-level financial constraints (measured with financial dependence or asset tangibility in U.S. industries) or liquidity constraints (measured by the average inventory to sales ratio, the cash conversion cycle, or the labor costs to sales ratio in U.S. industries) and
2. monetary or fiscal policy cyclicality at the country level

to assess the impact of this interaction on output growth at the industry level. Empirical evidence shows that a more countercyclical fiscal policy significantly enhances output growth in more financially constrained industries, that is, in industries whose U.S. counterparts are more dependent on external finance or display lower asset tangibility. Similarly, a more countercyclical monetary policy enhances output growth more in industries that are either more financially or more liquidity constrained. This investigation also suggests that the effect on growth of the cyclical pattern of fiscal and monetary policies is of comparable (or even greater) importance than that of more structural features, a conclusion at odds with previous work on policy, institutions, and growth (e.g., see Easterly 2005).

More generally, our analysis in this chapter has far-reaching implications for how to conduct macroeconomic policy over the business cycle. For example, it sheds light on the recent debate on the role of stimulus packages during recessions. A common justification for such policies relies on the Keynesian multiplier (i.e., on short-term induced-demand effects stemming from public spending). However, recent work (e.g., Taylor 2009; Barro and Redlick 2011) has questioned the magnitude of the multiplier. Our analysis suggests a rationale based more on long-term and supply-side considerations for a stimulus package during recessions: namely, to help (credit constrained) firms maintain innovative investments over the cycle. Clearly, a major difficulty in designing such policies is to make sure that innovative firms will benefit the most from them, rather than have such policies help inefficient firms survive without engaging in necessary restructuring.

Appendix 11.A   Industries in the Sample

The first column provides the industry code based on the International Standard Industrial Classification (ISIC) revision 3 at the two-digit level. The second column provides a brief description of the industry.

Industry code	Industry description
15	Food products and beverages
16	Tobacco products
17	Textiles
18	Wearing apparel, dressing and dyeing of fur
19	Leather, leather products, and footwear
20	Wood and products of wood and cork
21	Pulp, paper, and paper products
22	Printing and publishing
23	Coke, refined petroleum products, and nuclear fuel
24	Chemicals and chemical products
25	Rubber and plastics products
26	Other nonmetallic mineral products
27	Basic metals
28	Fabricated metal products, except machinery and equipment
29	Machinery and equipment, not elsewhere classified
30	Office, accounting, and computing machinery
31	Electrical machinery and apparatus, not elsewhere classified
32	Radio, television, and communication equipment
33	Medical, precision, and optical instruments
34	Motor vehicles, trailers, and semi-trailers
35	Other transport equipment
36	Manufacturing not elsewhere classified
37	Recycling

Appendix 11.B Estimation Results

Figures 11.B1–11.B3 show the country-by-country results of fiscal policy regression (2). Bars represent the coefficient *spc* estimated in (2) for each country. Figures 11.B1 and 11.B2 apply to fiscal policy. Figure 11.B3 applies to monetary policy. Error bars indicate the confidence interval at the 10% level around the mean estimate of *spc*, based on the standard errors estimated in (2). The country abbreviations used in the figures are: AUS, Australia; AUT, Austria; BEL, Belgium; CAN, Canada; DEU, Germany; DNK, Denmark; ESP, Spain; FIN, Finland; FRA, France; GBR, Great Britain; GRC, Greece; IRL, Ireland; ITA, Italy; JPN, Japan; LUX, Luxembourg; NLD, The Netherlands; PRT, Portugal; SWE, Sweden.

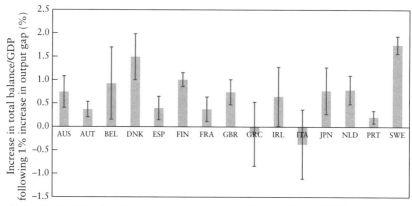

Figure 11.B1   Fiscal policy countercyclicality: total fiscal balance / GDP sensitivity to the output gap.

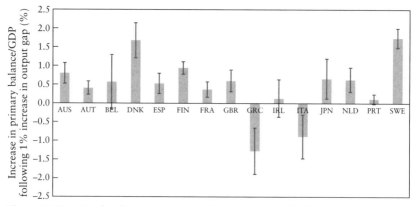

Figure 11.B2   Fiscal policy countercyclicality: primary fiscal balance / GDP sensitivity to the output gap.

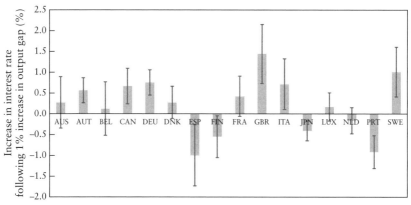

Figure 11.B3 Monetary policy countercyclicality: real short-term interest rate sensitivity to the output gap.

References

Aghion, Philippe, George-Marios Angeletos, Abhijit Banerjee, and Kalina Manova. (2010) "Volatility and Growth: Credit Constraints and Productivity-Enhancing Investment," *Journal of Monetary Economics* 57: 246–265.

Barro, Robert J., and Charles J. Redlick. (2011) "Macroeconomic Effects from Government Purchases and Taxes," *Quarterly Journal of Economics* 126: 51–102.

Braun, Matías. (2003) "Financial Contractibility and Asset Hardness." Mimeo, Harvard University, Cambridge, MA.

Braun, Matías, and Borja Larrain. (2005) "Finance and the Business Cycle: International, Inter-Industry Evidence," *Journal of Finance* 60: 1097–1128.

Easterly, William. (2005) "National Policies and Economic Growth: A Reappraisal," in Philippe Aghion and Steven Durlauf (eds.), *Handbook of Economic Growth,* volume 1. Amsterdam: Elsevier, pp. 1015–1059.

OECD (Organisation for Economic Co-operation and Development). (2008) *Economic Outlook,* volume 84, December.

O'Mahony, Mary, and Marcel P. Timmer. (2009) "Output, Input and Productivity Measures at the Industry Level: the EU KLEMS Database," *Economic Journal* 119: 374–403.

Raddatz, Claudio. (2006) "Liquidity Needs and Vulnerability to Financial Underdevelopment," *Journal of Financial Economics* 80: 677–722.

Rajan, Raghuram, and Luigi Zingales. (1998) "Financial Dependence and Growth," *American Economic Review* 88: 559–586.

Ramey, Garey, and Valerie Ramey. (1995) "Cross-Country Evidence on the Link between Volatility and Growth," *American Economic Review* 85: 1138–1151.

Taylor, John B. (2009) "The Lack of an Empirical Rationale for a Revival of Discretionary Fiscal Policy," *American Economic Review* 99: 550–555.

PART FOUR

Policymaking after "Rational Expectations"

CHAPTER TWELVE

Swings and the Rules-Discretion Balance

John B. Taylor

12.1 Introduction

I am honored to join in this fortieth anniversary of the Ned Phelps *Microeconomic Foundations* volume and to participate in this panel on rules versus discretion in economic policy during the past 40 years. Though I did not attend the January 1969 conference, my research on policy rules began around that time, so perhaps I can provide some historical perspective.

Looking back at actual U.S. macroeconomic policy during this period, I see major swings in the balance between rules and discretion, first away from discretion toward rules-based policies and then back again toward discretion. I use the word "balance" to emphasize that the ideal of a pure rule, without any discretion, is a theoretical abstraction. Evidence of the swing away from discretion is seen in actual fiscal policy and in the wide consensus among economists against the use of discretionary countercyclical fiscal policy in the 1980s and 1990s; it is also seen in the efforts to make monetary policy predictable and transparent, including through the use of inflation targets and actual policy rules for the instruments. The swing back toward discretion is found in the recent large discretionary fiscal stimulus packages and in deviations of monetary policy from the simple rules that described policy well in the 1980s and 1990s.

In this chapter I examine these swings and their causes and effects. I begin with a short summary of the economic and the political rationale for rules versus discretion, because I think that changes in people's attitudes toward those rationales are key factors in explaining shifts in the rules-discretion balance.

12.2 The Economic Rationale for Policy Rules

The easiest way for me to review the economic rationale for rules-based macroeconomic policy is to start by explaining the reasons for my own interest in policy rules, which stems from the way I first learned macroeconomics. It was in an undergraduate course at Princeton taught by Phil Howrey. It was my first macro course, but it was not the typical 1960s macro course. We did not study the static ISLM model[1] or other textbook Keynesian models. Instead, we studied dynamic models using stochastic difference or differential equations and even a little spectral analysis. I had no idea at the time how unusual this introduction to macroeconomics was, but it ingrained in me a way of thinking about the economy as an evolving dynamic stochastic structure in which the impact of policy changes occurred with lags as people adjusted their behavior to these changes. The only way one could evaluate monetary and fiscal policy in such a model was with a policy rule. It was not enough to show that a one-time increase in the money supply or a one-time fiscal stimulus package would shift the LM curve or the IS curve and thereby fill a gap in aggregate demand.

So I focused on rules in my undergraduate thesis on monetary and fiscal policy, building on the work of A. W. Phillips (1954). The economic motivation continued in graduate school, where I worked with my adviser, statistician Ted Anderson, to determine how much "experimentation" should be built into policy rules and found that "very little" was the right answer.

Then I moved to Columbia, where my work on policy rules continued with Ned Phelps (Phelps and Taylor 1977). We examined the properties of policy rules in a sticky-price model with rational expectations, which had recently been introduced to macro policy evaluation by Lucas (1976) and reinforced the economic rationale for rules. From then on I concentrated virtually all of my research on policy rules as I worked with colleagues and students, moving back to Princeton and then to Stanford, incorporating staggered wages and prices; multicountry spillovers; numerical solution techniques; and, most importantly, empirically estimated parameters, which brought the technical work closer to practical application as in my 1993 paper "Discretion versus Policy Rules in Practice," where the so-called Taylor rule was proposed (Taylor 1993).

At their most basic level these policy rules are statements about how government policy actions will react in a predictable way to different circumstances. They can be stated algebraically as for many monetary policy rules, such as the Taylor rule, which says that the short-term interest rate

---

1. The ISLM model refers to the diagram with an IS curve (standing for "investment equals saving") and an LM curve ("liquidity preference equals money").

should be set by the central bank to equal one-and-a-half times the inflation rate plus one-half times the GDP gap plus one. So if the inflation rate is 1.5% and the GDP gap is –5%, then the federal funds rate should be 1.5 times 1.5, plus 0.5 times (–5), plus 1, which equals 0.75%. But, of course, a rule does not have to be viewed as mechanical formula to be used rigidly.

This brief review demonstrates that, from my perspective, the rationale for using rules over discretion in formulating macroeconomic policy is an economic one. The same is true of Ben McCallum's (1999) survey in the *Handbook of Macroeconomics*, which carefully reviews rules versus discretion issues from Friedman (1960) to Kydland and Prescott (1977). More recently, in our *Handbook of Monetary Economics* survey, John Williams and I (Taylor and Williams 2011) show that this economic focus is true of the vast modern literature on monetary policy rules. There is no mention of political factors in these surveys.

12.3 The Political Rationale for Policy Rules

There is another strand of writing on policy rules that has focused mainly on political factors, perhaps best exemplified by F. A. Hayek's work. For example, Hayek (1944) wrote in *The Road to Serfdom* in favor of rules rather than discretion as essential to limiting government and protecting individual freedom. His concept of a policy rule is quite similar to what I just described, but the motivation for that concept is much different: political rather than economic. Hayek himself stressed this in *The Road to Serfdom*, stating that it "is a political book."

Chapter 6 of *The Road to Serfdom* (1944: 112–123), titled "Planning and the Rule of Law," makes the case clear:

> Nothing distinguishes more clearly conditions in a free country from those in a country under arbitrary government than the observance in the former of the great principles known as the Rule of Law. Stripped of all technicalities, this means that government in all its actions is bound by rules fixed and announced beforehand—rules which make it possible to foresee with fair certainty how the authority will use its coercive powers in given circumstances and to plan one's individual affairs on the basis of this knowledge. [Hayek 1944: 112]

Hayek (1944: 112) adds that "though this ideal can never be achieved perfectly . . . the essential point, that the discretion left to the executive organs wielding coercive power should be reduced as much as possible, is clear enough." He also indicated that rules did not necessarily have to be written down formally in a "bill of rights or in a constitutional code," arguing that "firmly established tradition" could work just as well. To

Hayek, predictability was an important characteristic of policy rules: "If actions of the state are to be predictable, they must be determined by rules fixed independently of the concrete circumstances which can be neither foreseen nor taken into account beforehand" (Hayek 1944: 114).

By emphasizing Hayek's political views I do not mean to imply that he did not have economic views about how government policy rules should operate; of course he did, but these are not the point of his political writings. In fact, he argues that the exact form of the rule is less important than just having some rule, because it will still limit government action. Similarly, Milton Friedman, whose economic writings on monetary and fiscal policy rules have influenced generations of economists, sometimes wrote about these political rationales for policy rules, as, for example, in *Capitalism and Freedom* (Friedman 1962). In the chapter on monetary policy rules he emphasizes that "the objective is to preserve the maximum degree of freedom" in a way that is compatible with not interfering with others, and "that this objective requires that government power be dispersed" (Friedman 1962: 39).

Though I and many others have favored rules over discretion for economic reasons, when it comes to explaining shifts in the balance between rules and discretion over time, these political factors must also be considered. Because policy rules are viewed as a way of limiting government and protecting individual freedom, changes in attitudes about these political issues will shift the balance between rules and discretion.

12.4   The Swing in Balance in Favor of Rules

The general shift toward rules-based macro policy in the 1980s and 1990s is evidenced in various ways. Consider monetary policy. One indication is the increased popularity of inflation targets, either informally, as with the Federal Reserve, or more formally, as with the Bank of England. The shift of Fed policy to a focus on inflation under the leadership of Paul Volcker was a dramatic change from the 1970s. Volcker and his successor Alan Greenspan were very clearly committed to the goal of price stability. Meltzer (2009) describes these changes in detail in volume 2 of his history of the Fed. The use of numerical inflation targets at other central banks reinforced the idea of price stability as the primary goal of monetary policy.

Additional evidence of a rules-based policy was the move toward a more predictable and transparent decisionmaking process with a focus on expectations of future policy actions. The Fed started announcing its interest rate decisions immediately after making them. It also started explaining its intentions about the future. Prior to the 1980s, decisions about interest rates were hidden in decisions about borrowed reserves. Other central banks also clarified their decisionmaking process by publishing reports on their inflation and output forecasts. The aim was to be more predictable and systematic with the instruments of policy.

Evidence is also found in the transcripts of the Federal Open Market Committee in the 1990s. They show a large number of references to policy rules and related developments, as Kahn (2012) has shown. Meyer (2004) emphasizes a systematic framework for policy, which contrasts with Maisel's (1973) emphasis on the lack of a strategy in earlier periods.

Moreover, if you compare actual U.S. monetary policy with policy rules at the time, you see a much tighter correspondence between the two, as Judd and Trehan (1995) at the San Francisco Fed and Poole (2006) at the St. Louis Fed point out. Judd and Rudebusch (1998) and Clarida et al. (2000) show that the Fed's interest rate moves were less responsive to changes in inflation and to real GDP in the 1970s than in the 1980s and 1990s. Levin and Taylor (2010) show that responses of the Fed to inflation were unstable over time in the 1970s and were not very rule-like compared with the 1980s and 1990s.

Next consider fiscal policy. Although in the 1960s and 1970s Keynesian countercyclical policy was viewed very favorably in much of academia and in policy circles, actual fiscal policy shifted away from discretion in the 1980s and 1990s. Early signs of the shift are found in the economic and statistical analyses of the stimulus packages during the Carter Administration, which transferred funds to state and local governments for infrastructure and other government spending. Ned Gramlich (1979: 180) concluded that "the general idea of stimulating the economy through state and local governments is probably not a very good one."

By the early 1990s cyclical movements in the budget deficit were dominated by the automatic stabilizers, not by discretionary policy. For example, in the early 1990s the Bush Administration proposed a stimulus package, but it was very small, including such items as moving US\$10 billion in government purchases from the future to the present. None of the items in the package that required legislation actually passed the Congress. Similarly, the Clinton Administration proposed a stimulus that would have added US\$16 billion to government purchases, but this too did not pass the Congress.

By the late 1990s there was about as much a consensus among economists as there ever was about an issue. In an assessment of fiscal policy in 1997, Eichenbaum (1997: 236) concluded that "there is now widespread agreement that countercyclical discretionary fiscal policy is neither desirable nor politically feasible." In a paper in 2000, I concluded that "in the current context of the U.S. economy, it seems best to let fiscal policy have its main countercyclical impact through the automatic stabilizers. . . . It would be appropriate in the present American context for discretionary fiscal policy to be saved explicitly for longer-term issues, requiring less frequent changes" (Taylor 2000: 34–35). And Feldstein (2002: 1) wrote that "there is now widespread agreement in the economics profession that deliberate 'counter-cyclical' discretionary fiscal policy has not contributed to economic stability and may have actually been destabilizing at particular times in the past."

Did the shift from discretion to rules have a beneficial effect? It is impossible to know for sure what caused what, but the shift was closely correlated with the Great Moderation in the United States, which began in the early 1980s. Not only did inflation and interest rates and their volatilities diminish compared with the experience of the 1970s, but the volatility of real GDP was also very low. Economic expansions became longer and stronger, while recessions became shorter and shallower. The variance of real GDP growth, the variance of the real GDP gap, the frequency of recessions, and the duration of recessions were all lower. There was also an improvement in price stability, with the inflation rate much lower and less volatile than the period from the late 1960s, through the 1970s, and into the early 1980s. Statistical techniques can help assess causality. Stock and Watson (2002) found that the change in monetary policy had an effect on performance, but they also found a reduction in shocks to the economy stemming from supply factors.

Another measure of the benefit of the more predictable behavior was the response of the private sector. Recognizing that the central bank's interest rate settings followed more rule-like responses to inflation and real GDP, the private sector took these responses into account in projecting future variables and in developing their own rules of thumb for making decisions. An important example is the formation of expectations of future short-term interest rates, which affect long-term interest rates. The private sector and other public sector institutions developed rules of thumb that depended on the rule-like behavior of the monetary authorities. These rules of thumb improved the operation of the economy.

12.5   The Swing in the Balance in Favor of Discretion

In the past few years, there has been a dramatic shift back toward discretionary macroeconomic policy. Examples[2] of such policy actions in the fiscal and monetary policy areas include the deviation from monetary policy rules followed during the Great Moderation in 2003–2005, the U.S. discretionary fiscal stimulus of 2008, the on-again/off-again interventions in financial firms by the Fed in 2008, the money market–mutual fund liquidity

---

2. Although the first fiscal policy example in this list occurs in 2008, the shift may have started earlier, perhaps in 2001 with the tax rebates in the 2001 recession at the start of the Bush administration. Indeed, Milton Friedman was quite critical of those rebates. When asked about them, he said "Keynesianism has risen from the dead" and called the move toward discretion "a serious mistake." See Pine (2001).

facility of 2008, the commercial paper funding facility of 2008, the discretionary fiscal stimulus of 2009, the Cash for Clunkers program of 2009, Quantitative Easing 1 (QE1; the large-scale asset purchase program of the Fed) in 2009, and QE2 in 2010. During the past 3 years I have empirically examined the impact of many of these programs and can briefly summarize them and their effects.[3]

First consider the decision by the Fed during 2003–2005 to hold its target interest rate below the level implied by monetary rules that had described policy well for the previous 20 years. One can characterize this decision as a deviation from a policy rule, such as the Taylor rule. Without this deviation, interest rates would not have reached such a low level, and they would have returned much sooner to a neutral level. The deviation was large—on the order of magnitude seen in the unstable decade of the 1970s. One does not need to rely on the Taylor rule to conclude that rates were held too low for too long: The real interest rate was negative for a very long period, similar to what happened in the 1970s. The Fed's statements that interest rates would be low for a "prolonged period" and that interest rates would rise at a "measured pace" is evidence that this was an intentional departure from a policy that was followed in the 1980s and 1990s. The low interest rates added to the housing boom and led to risk taking and eventually a sharp increase in delinquencies, foreclosures, and toxic assets at financial institutions. My research shows that a higher rules-based federal funds rate would have prevented much of the boom and bust.[4]

Next consider the discretionary countercyclical fiscal package—the Economic Stimulus Act of 2008—passed in February 2008, in which checks were sent to people on a one-time basis. The objective was to jump-start consumption demand and thereby jump-start the economy. However, aggregate personal consumption expenditures did not increase much at all when disposable income rose at around the time of the stimulus payments. Of course, this is what the permanent income theory or the life cycle theory predicts.

Continuing down the list, next consider the on-again/off-again rescues of financial firms and their creditors. These interventions started when the Fed used its balance sheet to rescue the creditors of Bear Stearns in March 2008. The Fed's interventions were then turned off for Lehman, turned on again for AIG, and then turned off again when the Troubled Asset Relief Program (TARP) was proposed. These interventions clearly did not prevent

---

3. For a more detailed summary, see Taylor (2010a) and the references there.

4. Borio and Lowe (2004) argued early on that the Fed and other central banks did not tighten enough during this period. Though not part of the macroeconomic focus of this chapter, the problem was greatly exacerbated by the failure to follow rules-based regulations of banks, which were allowed to have large off–balance sheet operations containing many of the toxic assets.

the panic that began in September 2008, and in my view were a likely cause of the panic, or at least made the panic worse. Could the unpredictable nature of these interventions have been avoided? In my view, the Fed and the Treasury could have stated more clearly the reasons behind the Bear Stearns intervention as well as the intentions of policy going forward. If they had done so, people would have had some sense of what was to come. But no such description was provided. Uncertainty was heightened and probably reached a peak when the TARP was rolled out. Panic ensued, with the S&P 500 falling by 30%.

The original purpose of the TARP was to buy up toxic assets on banks' balance sheets, but there was criticism and confusion about how that would work. After the TARP was changed to inject equity into the banks rather than to buy toxic assets, uncertainty was reduced, and conditions began to improve. The panic stopped when uncertainty about the TARP was removed on October 13, 2008.

Two other monetary policy interventions taken during the panic in late September and October 2008 were the Fed's programs to assist money market mutual funds and the commercial paper market. In my view these interventions were helpful in rebuilding confidence. So not every discretionary intervention was harmful, but these would not have been necessary had the earlier interventions been avoided.

The end of the panic did not end the interventions. The American Recovery and Reinvestment Act of 2009 was enacted into law in February 2009. The amount paid in checks was smaller and more drawn out than the 2008 stimulus, but the impact was about the same: no noticeable effect on consumption. In addition, my analysis of the parts of the stimulus aimed at infrastructure spending suggests they were ineffective, as described in my paper with Cogan (Cogan and Taylor 2010).

Cash for Clunkers was an attempt to bring purchases of automobiles forward and thus increase consumption demand. Mian and Sufi (2010) have examined the impacts using regional data. In Figure 12.1 I have scaled up their results to show the impact on total consumption, which is very small. There was a shift forward, but the negative offsetting effects occurred while the economy was almost as weak as when the positive effects took place.

Other interventions were introduced by the Fed in the period following the panic, most significantly the large quantitative easing, now called QE1, which involved large-scale asset purchases, including the US$1.25 trillion mortgage-backed securities (MBS) purchase program and the Treasury securities purchase program. My view is that the MBS program had at most a small effect on mortgage rates once prepayment risk and default risk are controlled for.

Following QE1 the Fed embarked on QE2, in which the Fed purchased another $600 billion in Treasury securities and also reinvested maturing MBS securities, hoping to drive interest rates down. It is difficult to evaluate the effect of QE2, but Figures 12.2 and 12.3 show that neither government

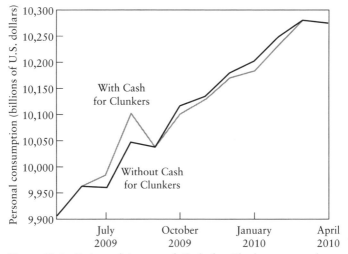

Figure 12.1 Estimated impact of Cash for Clunkers on total consumption.

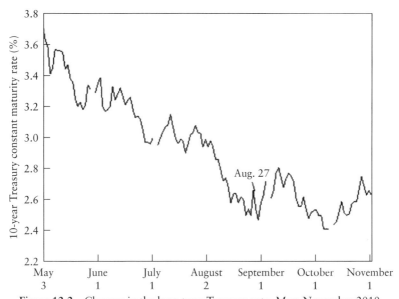

Figure 12.2 Changes in the long-term Treasury rate, May–November 2010.

nor private sector long-term interest rates came down after strong hints that the purchases would occur were given on August 27, 2010, in a speech by Ben Bernanke.

Other possible impacts of these programs may occur over the longer term. Many have helped increase government debt and monetary overhang. The Fed interventions raise questions about central bank independence, because

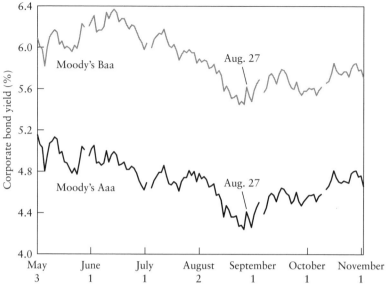

Figure 12.3 Changes in corporate bond rates, May–November 2010.

many of the interventions are not monetary policy as conventionally defined, but rather fiscal policy or credit allocation policy. Unwinding the programs creates uncertainty, and there is a risk of inflation if they are not unwound.

Others have different views of the impact of the programs. Bernanke (2010), for example, argues that the low interest rates in 2003–2005 were not a deviation from rules-based policies if you use a modified policy rule with *forecasts* of inflation rather than actual inflation. But the Fed's forecasts of inflation were too low in this period, which suggests that such a modified rule is not such a good one.

12.6   Explaining the Swings

Although some may disagree with my assessment of the impacts of these swings in the rules-discretion balance, it is hard to deny that the swings occurred. But what caused them?

12.6.1   Was It Simply an Emergency?

One explanation for the shift back to discretion is that the financial panic of 2008 and the Great Recession were so large that they required the large discretionary packages; the unprecedented actions were necessary because of the emergency. But the first three items on the list of discretionary interventions were taken before the panic in the fall of 2008.

Moreover, if the emergency were the explanation, one would expect to see a return to rules-based policies once the panic was over. But instead, another large discretionary stimulus program, QE2, was undertaken. During the debate over QE1, I worried that the emergency argument would be replaced by another excuse once the unprecedented actions were undertaken. Early in 2009 I wrote that

> the danger I see is that as the recovery begins, or after we are a couple of years into it, people may feel that it's not fast enough, or there is an unpleasant pause. Either could generate heavy pressure on the Fed to intervene. . . . Why would such interventions only take place in times of crisis? Why wouldn't future Fed officials use them to try to make economic expansions stronger or to assist certain sectors and industries for other reasons? [Taylor 2009: 98]

Fed officials dismissed concerns about such a scenario, saying that it was an emergency. Yet this is exactly the scenario that has played out. The recovery paused, and then there was a QE2.

A closely related explanation for the shift back toward discretion is that policymakers tried to do more than the underlying economics suggested was possible. After two decades of the Great Moderation, policymakers wanted to do even better. So they kept interest rates extra low and intervened in other ways, trying to reduce downside risks.

This problem is common in decisionmaking, as Milton Friedman pointed out many years ago in a debate with Walter Heller (1969) over rules versus discretion:

> The available evidence . . . casts grave doubts on the possibility of producing any fine adjustments in economic activity by fine adjustments in monetary policy—at least in the present state of knowledge. . . . There are thus serious limitations to the possibility of a discretionary monetary policy and much danger that such a policy may make matters worse rather than better. . . . The basic difficulties and limitations of monetary policy apply with equal force to fiscal policy. . . . Political pressures to 'do something' . . . are clearly very strong indeed in the existing state of public attitudes. The main moral to be drawn from the two preceding points is that yielding to these pressures may frequently do more harm than good. There is a saying that the best is often the enemy of the good, which seems highly relevant. . . . The attempt to do more than we can will itself be a disturbance that may increase rather than reduce instability. [Friedman and Heller 1969: 48]

12.6.2 Was There a Great Awakening?

Another explanation for the shifts lies in the economic analysis of policy rules. I argued in Taylor (2010b) that improvements in our understanding of rules-based policies, through study and experience with particular rules, could have been a reason for the shift toward rules-based policy, at least in the case of monetary policy. Reviewing the academic and policy literature, I argued that there was a "great awakening" in monetary theory closely associated in time with the shift toward an actual monetary policy in a rules-based direction.

One problem with this explanation is that it does not provide such a straightforward explanation of the shift back toward discretionary policy. Although there was no major reversal in economic theory, there were some new ideas that could have taken policy away from rules, or at least away from the relatively simple rules that characterize rules-based policy in practice. In fact, the idea that a fully optimal policy conducted in real time could do better than simple rules seemed to gain some favor even in the context of modern rational expectations modeling. For example, Giannoni and Woodford (2005) show that the optimal policy can be characterized by an equation with leads and lags of target variables, such as the inflation rate. They argue that the optimal policy takes into account all relevant information for monetary policy and is thereby superior to simple policy rules. There is debate about how great this informational advantage is, but a disadvantage is that the optimal rules are very complicated and difficult to explain and communicate compared with simple rules. In a sense they verge on a more discretionary approach.

For example, Mishkin (2007) uses optimal control methods to find paths for the federal funds rate and then contrasts these paths with simple policy rules. He argues that for the optimal policy "the federal funds rate is lowered more aggressively and substantially faster than with the Taylor-rule. . . . This difference is exactly what we would expect because the monetary authorities would not wait to react until output had already fallen" (Mishkin 2007: 393). The implication is that simple policy rules are inadequate for real-world policy situations and that policymakers should deviate from them as needed.

Such doubts about the practical relevance of research supporting policy rules were expressed earlier, but they did not take account of developments in research on active policy rules. For example, in 1992, the same year I presented the first paper that contained the Taylor rule, I commented on a paper by Bernanke and Mishkin (1992). Their paper raised doubts about the use of rules for the policy instruments and made the case for using a considerable amount of discretion in monetary policymaking. They said that "monetary policy rules do not allow the monetary authorities to respond to unforeseen circumstances" (Bernanke and Mishkin 1992: 184).

12.6.3 *Did Political Swings Change the Rules-Discretion Balance?*

Finally, let me consider the possibility that changes in political attitudes about the roles of the individual, the market, and the state (to use the words of the title of this session) were a factor in the swings in the rules-discretion balance. Without taking a position one way or the other, there was clearly a political change in the 1980s in the United States and the United Kingdom in which attitudes favoring more limited government and a corresponding encouragement of free markets were on the rise. This shift was maintained through the 1980s and into the 1990s as Reagan was followed by Bush 41 and then Clinton, while Thatcher was followed by Major and then Blair. That the swing toward more limited government coincided with a swing toward more rules-based policy is what one would expect, given the stress placed on the role of rules in limiting government and preserving individual freedom and free markets. That the economics was moving in the same direction meant that economics and politics were reinforcing one another.

Does this political explanation fare any better than the economic ones in explaining the swing back in favor of discretion over the past few years? There were political changes in the U.S. presidency in 2009 that would appear to place less emphasis on limiting the role of government, but many of the examples of increased discretion mentioned in this chapter occurred before 2009, though they continued into 2009 and 2010 with increased intensity. Although much more research is needed, a conjecture is that factors like the 9/11 attacks in the United States and the policy responses tended to reduce the sentiments for limited government and, in the presence of terrorist threats, place less emphasis on individual freedom. The rise of government spending as a share of GDP from 2000 onward is some evidence in favor of this view.

One question about this explanation is how the politics can cut through the economics. In other words, if the economic case for rules-based policies was so strong and convincing, how did it lose out to political pressure? One way is through what I call "discretion in rule's clothing." One interested in a discretionary policy move might argue that the traditional policy rule has become outdated, or was wrong in the first place, and needs to be changed. One can justify just about any discretionary intervention in this way. An example of how this may have happened recently is the argument that the parameters of policy rules should be replaced with recently estimated parameters. In fact, some have argued that a statistically estimated policy rule is an improvement over the rule I proposed in 1992. Such estimated rules frequently have a larger coefficient for the output gap and therefore give interest rate settings in the current slump lower than the 75 basis points suggested at the start of this chapter—indeed, some have suggested minus 6 percent! This then justifies discretionary actions, such as QE2, or suggests that the interest rate should remain at zero for a very long period, which may be what advocates of discretion actually want. But curve fitting without theory is dangerous. In the case of policy rules, it can perpetuate mistakes: the large coefficient for the gap may be due to periods when the federal funds rate was too low for too long.

If advocates of higher coefficients for the output gap can show why the higher coefficient improves performance, then they may have a case for such a change. But studies show that a higher coefficient is not robust, and some argue that the coefficient should be lower, not higher, than in the Taylor rule because of uncertainty in measuring the output gap.

12.7 Conclusion

This chapter documents two major swings in the balance between rules and discretion in actual U.S. economic policymaking in the past four decades. One swing was in favor of rules and the other in favor of discretion. In my view, the swing toward rules improved macroeconomic performance, and the swing back toward discretion worsened it. If so, the policy implication is clear: we should go back toward more rules-based policies.

The chapter also examines several possible reasons for these swings. It rejects the explanation that the recent move toward discretion was due to the emergency of the recent crisis, because the swing started before the crisis. Instead the chapter focuses on two other explanations: economic and political.

According to the economic explanation, the swing toward rules was the result of extensive theoretical and empirical research on policy rules—especially in the monetary area—that began in the 1970s and is continuing today. This research showed the benefits of simple and robust rules through model simulations and historical studies of actual policy. This explanation is less straightforward as an explanation of the swing back toward discretion. However, recent research on optimal policy, which suggested that much more complex rules for the instruments were necessary, may have encouraged the swing back: when policy rules become highly complex and hard to explain, they are likely to shift the rules-discretion balance toward discretion. But more research is needed on this possibility.

The political explanation is based on the rationale for rules as a way to limit government and protect individual freedom. Though not a factor in the research on policy rules described in the previous paragraph, including my own research, it may have been a force moving toward rules in the 1980s as attitudes toward government changed. It too is less straightforward as an explanation of the swing back toward discretion, because the swing started before the obvious political realignments in early 2009. It requires that some other event—perhaps 9/11—changed attitudes about the roles of the individual, the market, and the state. More research is needed on this possibility too.

References

Bernanke, Ben. (2010) "Monetary Policy and the Housing Bubble." Speech at the Annual Meeting of the American Economic Association, Atlanta, GA, January 3.

Bernanke, Ben, and Frederic Mishkin. (1992) "Central Bank Behavior and the Strategy of Monetary Policy: Observations from Six Industrialized Countries," in Oliver Blanchard and Stanley Fischer (eds.), *NBER Macroeconomics Annual,* volume 7. Cambridge, MA: MIT Press, pp. 183–227.

Borio, Claudio, and Philip Lowe. (2004) "Securing Sustainable Price Stability: Should Credit Come Back from the Wilderness?" BIS Working Paper 157, Bank for International Settlements, Basel, Switzerland.

Clarida, Richard, Jordi Gali, and Mark Gertler. (2000) "Monetary Policy Rules and Macroeconomic Stability: Evidence and Some Theory," *Quarterly Journal of Economics* 115: 147–180.

Cogan, John F., and John B. Taylor. (2010) "What the Government Purchases Multiplier Actually Multiplied in the 2009 Stimulus Package." NBER Working Paper 16505, National Bureau of Economic Research, Cambridge, MA.

Eichenbaum, Martin. (1997) "Some Thoughts on Practical Stabilization Policy," *American Economic Review* 87: 236–239.

Feldstein, Martin. (2002) "The Role for Discretionary Fiscal Policy in a Low Interest Rate Environment." NBER Working Paper 9203, National Bureau of Economic Research, Cambridge, MA.

Friedman, Milton. (1960) *A Program for Monetary Stability.* New York: Fordham University Press.

———. (1962) *Capitalism and Freedom.* Chicago: University of Chicago Press.

Friedman, Milton, and Walter Heller. (1969) *Monetary vs. Fiscal Policy: A Dialogue.* New York: W. W. Norton.

Giannoni, Marc P., and Michael Woodford. (2005) "Optimal Inflation Targeting Rules," in Ben Bernanke and Michael Woodford (eds.), *The Inflation Targeting Debate.* Chicago: University of Chicago Press, pp. 93–162.

Gramlich, Edward M. (1979) "Stimulating the Macro Economy through State and Local Governments," *American Economic Review* 69: 180–185.

Hayek, Friedrich A. (1944) *The Road to Serfdom.* Chicago: University of Chicago Press. Reprinted in *The Collected Works of F. A. Hayek,* Bruce Caldwell (ed.), University of Chicago Press, 2007.

Judd, John P., and Glenn D. Rudebusch. (1998) "Taylor's Rule and the Fed: 1970–1997," *Federal Reserve Bank of San Francisco Economic Review* 3: 1–16.

Judd, John P., and Bharat Trehan. (1995) "Has the Fed Gotten Tougher on Inflation?" *FRBSF Weekly Letter,* March 31.

Kahn, George A. (2012) "The Taylor Rule and the Practice of Central Banking," in Evan F. Koenig, Robert Leeson, and George A. Kahn, *The Taylor Rule and the Transformation of Monetary Policy.* Stanford, CA: Hoover Institution Press, pp. 63–102.

Kydland, Finn, and Edward Prescott. (1977) "Rules Rather than Discretion: The Inconsistency of Optimal Plans," *Journal of Political Economy* 85: 473–491.

Levin, Andrew T., and John B. Taylor. (2010) "Falling behind the Curve: A Positive Analysis of Stop-Start Monetary Policies and the Great Inflation." NBER Working Paper 15630, National Bureau of Economic Research, Cambridge, MA.

Lucas, Robert E., Jr. (1976) "Econometric Policy Evaluation: A Critique," *Carnegie-Rochester Conference Series on Public Policy* 1: 19–46.

Maisel, Sherman J. (1973) *Managing the Dollar.* New York: W. W. Norton.

McCallum, Bennett. (1999) "Issues in the Design of Monetary Policy Rules," in John B. Taylor and Michael Woodford (eds.), *Handbook of Macroeconomics.* Amsterdam: Elsevier, pp. 1483–1530.

Meltzer, Allan H. (2009) *A History of the Federal Reserve,* volume 2. Chicago: University of Chicago Press.

Meyer, Laurence. (2004) *A Term at the Fed: An Insider's View.* New York: Harper-Collins.

Mian, Atif, and Amir Sufi. (2010) "The Effects of Fiscal Stimulus: Evidence from the 2009 'Cash for Clunkers' Program." NBER Working Paper 16351, National Bureau of Economic Research, Cambridge, MA.

Mishkin, Frederick. (2007) "Housing and the Monetary Policy Transmission Mechanism." Paper presented at the Federal Reserve Bank of Kansas City, Jackson Hole Conference, Jackson Hole, WY, August.

Phelps, Edmund, and John B. Taylor. (1977) "Stabilizing Powers of Monetary Policy under Rational Expectations," *Journal of Political Economy* 85: 163–190.

Phillips, A. W. (1954) "Stabilization Policy in a Closed Economy," *Economic Journal* 64: 290–323.

Pine, Art. (2001) "Friedman Boos, Stiglitz Cheers and Keynes Returns to Washington," *Bloomberg News,* October 18. Available online.

Poole, William. (2006) "The Fed's Monetary Policy Rule," *Federal Reserve Bank of St. Louis Review,* January/February, pp. 1–12.

Stock, James, and Mark Watson. (2002) "Has the Business Cycle Changed?" in *Monetary Policy and Uncertainty: Adapting to a Changing Economy.* Kansas City, MO: Federal Reserve Bank of Kansas City, pp. 9–56.

Taylor, John B. (1993) "Discretion versus Policy Rules in Practice," *Carnegie-Rochester Conference Series on Public Policy* 39: 195–214.

———. (2000) "Reassessing Discretionary Fiscal Policy," *Journal of Economic Perspectives* 14(3): 21–36.

———. (2009) "The Need for a Clear and Credible Exit Strategy," in John Ciorciari and John B. Taylor (eds.), *The Road Ahead for the Fed.* Stanford, CA: Hoover Institution Press, pp. 85–100.

———. (2010a) "Assessing the Federal Policy Response to the Economic Crisis." Testimony before the Committee on the Budget, United States Senate, September 22.

———. (2010b) "Better Living through Monetary Economics," in John Siegfried (ed.) *Better Living through Economics.* Cambridge, MA: Harvard University Press, pp. 146–163.

Taylor, John B., and John C. Williams. (2011) "Simple and Robust Rules for Monetary Policy," in Benjamin Friedman and Michael Woodford (eds.), *Handbook of Monetary Economics,* volume 3B. Amsterdam: Elsevier, pp. 829–859.

CHAPTER THIRTEEN

Principled Policymaking in an Uncertain World

Michael Woodford

13.1 Introduction

A crucial legacy of Phelps et al. (1970) has been recognition of the importance of economic agents' anticipations as a determinant of macroeconomic outcomes. This has had many profound consequences for macroeconomic analysis. Among them is that the subsequent theoretical literature on monetary policy has focused on the analysis of monetary policy rules rather than on decisions about individual policy actions. The present chapter considers the reasons for this development and the extent to which such a focus continues to be appropriate in the light of subsequent events—changes in central banks' approach to monetary policy in the decades since the publication of the Phelps volume, and even more crucially the reconsideration of macroeconomic theory and policy that is necessary in the wake of the global financial crisis.

13.2 Rule-Based Policy or Discretion?

13.2.1 Policy Rules as an Object of Study

There are at least two important reasons why recognition of the importance of expectations led to an emphasis on policy rules in the theoretical literature (for further discussion, see Woodford 2003: 14–24). First, if one is to specify agents' anticipations in an economic model using the common hypothesis of rational expectations (RE), one cannot answer questions about

I thank Amar Bhidé, Roman Frydman, and Andy Haldane for helpful comments, and the Institute for New Economic Thinking for research support.

the predicted effect of a given policy action, even in the context of a particular economic model, unless one also specifies expected future policy over an indefinite future and for all potential future contingencies. One cannot solve for the consequences of a given action (say, purchases of a certain quantity of Treasury securities by the Fed this month) without specifying what people expect about future outcomes (e.g., future inflation), both with and without the action in question. Under the hypothesis of "rational" (or, more properly, model-consistent) expectations, what people expect in either case should be what the model predicts will occur; but that will depend on what is assumed about future policy, and in what respects it does or does not change as a result of the policy change that one wishes to analyze.

Hence the object of analysis must always be a complete specification of current and future policy, including how policy can be expected to respond to all possible future developments. In other words, the only possible object of analysis is a complete policy strategy (e.g., see Sargent 1993). This does not mean that such an approach cannot be used to analyze the consequences of approaches to policy other than ones for which policymakers consciously follow a rule; the analyst might postulate a systematic pattern of conduct— which it is furthermore assumed that the public should also be able to predict—even if it is neither announced nor consciously formulated by policymakers themselves. But once the object of study is defined as the comparative advantages of alternative systematic patterns of conduct, the only goal of normative policy analysis must be to propose a systematic pattern of conduct that it would be desirable for the policy authority to follow, in a sufficiently faithful way for the pattern to be predictable. In other words, even if positive analyses of policy in particular times and places do not necessarily assume that policymakers consciously follow a rule, a normative analysis must recommend a rule that should be followed systematically, rather than an individual action that is appropriate to some particular situation.

There is a second reason for the recent literature's focus on policy rules. In this case "rule" has a more specific meaning, namely, a prescription that constrains the policymaker to behave in a way other than what would be judged desirable using a sequential optimization procedure of the kind criticized by Kydland and Prescott (1977). Kydland and Prescott criticize "discretionary" policy, by which they mean sequential optimization each time an action must be taken, with no constraints resulting from prior commitments. This sequence of optimizing decisions—in which no more is decided at any one time than is necessary to determine the action that must be taken at that time—can be contrasted with an alternative form of optimization, in which an overall pattern of conduct that will be followed forever after is chosen once and for all. Note that the complaint about discretionary policy is not that it is unsystematic or unpredictable—as conceived by Kydland and Prescott, it involves a clear objective that is pursued consistently over time, and in their analysis of the consequences of such behavior, they assume (following RE methodology) that it is completely predictable.

The Kydland-Prescott critique of such a sequential approach to decision-making is rather that it fails to internalize the consequences of people's anticipation of systematic patterns in the policymaker's conduct. Each time that a decision must be made about a specific action (say, the level at which the federal funds rate should be maintained for the next six weeks), people's prior expectations about that action are a fact about the past that can no longer be affected. Thus, an analysis of the consequences of the action for the policymaker's objectives assumes no possibility of influencing those expectations, even though a different systematic approach to choice regarding this action could have given people a reason to have had different expectations, and shaping expectations is relevant to the achievement of the policymaker's objectives. In general, a superior outcome can be achieved (according to the RE analysis) through commitment by the policy authority to behave in a systematically different way than a discretionary policymaker would wish to behave ex post; this requires commitment to follow a rule. The key feature of the Kydland-Prescott conception of a policy rule is thus the element of advance commitment, which is contrasted with ad hoc decisionmaking at the time when action is necessary.

Even a brief review of these familiar arguments raises an important question. Does not a recognition of the possibility (indeed, the inevitability, eventually) of nonroutine change undermine the desirability of commitment to a policy rule? In a theoretical exposition of the advantages of policy commitment—such as the examples presented by Kydland and Prescott—it is easy to assume that possible future states in which the policymaker may find herself can be enumerated in advance, and that a commitment can be chosen ex ante that specifies what will be done in each state if it is reached. In practice, this will not be possible, for reasons that go beyond a mere assertion that the number of possible future states is very large (the elements of some infinite-dimensional space). There are often developments that are not simply elements in a large space of possibilities *the dimensions of which* were conceptualized in advance, but that instead were inconceivable previously. Policymakers are then confronted not simply with the question of whether it is now desirable to behave differently than they were expected to behave in such a situation, but with a need to think afresh about a type of situation to which they have given little prior thought.[1] The experience of policymakers after the unexpected eruption of the global financial crisis in the summer of 2007 underlines the relevance of this possibility, if further proof were needed.

---

1. On the importance for policy analysis of confronting the occurrence of nonroutine change, see Frydman and Goldberg (2011).

It is fairly obvious that the existence of nonroutine change of this sort undermines the desirability of a certain conception of a policy rule: one where a rule is understood to mean a fully explicit formula that prescribes a precise action for any possible circumstance. Nonetheless, it does little to reduce the relevance of the abovementioned reasons that the recent literature on monetary policy has focused on the evaluation of policy rules. It does not eliminate the need to assess policy strategies, rather than individual decisions considered in isolation, even if such strategies cannot realistically be supposed to represent complete specifications of behavior in all possible circumstances. Nor does it eliminate the potential benefits from requiring policy decisions to be based on general principles, rather than making an ad hoc decision about what will achieve the best outcome under current circumstances.

13.2.2 Policy Analysis without RE

Strategies and principles would be irrelevant only if one were to view decisionmakers as responding mechanically to the current economic environment and not on the basis of anticipations that can be influenced by the announced policy commitments of a central bank; that is, only if one were to deny the relevance of the "modern" turn advocated by Phelps et al. (1970). In fact, a variety of approaches to dynamic economic analysis has been proposed that still allow a role for anticipations that should take into account what is known about central bank policy commitments, without imposing the strong form of expectational coordination implied by the postulate of RE.

One example is the concept of "calculation equilibrium" proposed by Evans and Ramey (1992). Evans and Ramey propose that individuals make decisions that are optimal for a particular anticipated future evolution of the economy (extending, in principle, indefinitely into the future); they also propose that individuals possess a correct model of the economy, in the sense that they are able to correctly predict the evolution of the variables they wish to forecast under a particular conjecture about the way that others expect the economy to evolve. People's expectations can then be disciplined by requiring them to result from a calculation using the economic model, starting from an expectation about others' expectations. Evans and Ramey relax, however, the RE assumption that everyone must forecast a future evolution that is predicted by the commonly agreed-on model under the assumption that others predict precisely that same evolution. Instead, they propose that individuals start with some initial conjecture about the future path of economic variables and progressively refine this forecast by calculating (at each stage in an iterative process) the evolution that should be predicted if others are expected to forecast using the output of the previous stage's calculation. (The thought process that this involves is like the one described by Keynes [1936] in his famous analysis of the "beauty contest.")

If this iterative calculation were pursued to the point of convergence[2]— so that a forecast were eventually obtained with the property that expecting others to forecast that way would lead to the same forecast—the resulting forecast would correspond to an RE equilibrium (REE) of the model used by decisionmakers.[3] But Evans and Ramey assume instead (like Keynes) that in practice decisionmakers will truncate such calculations after a finite number of iterations; they propose that calculation costs limit the number of iterations that it is reasonable for a decisionmaker to undertake (and propose a particular stopping rule that need not concern us). Given the truncation of the expectation calculations, dynamic phenomena are possible—even assuming that people's model of the economy is actually correct—that would not occur in an RE analysis. These include asset "bubbles" that last for some time (though not indefinitely) and are sustained by beliefs that are consistent with the economic model, based on a belief about others' beliefs that is also consistent with others' understanding the model, and so on for a finite number of iterations. But ultimately the asset bubble depends on higher-order beliefs that will be disconfirmed.

The eductive stability analysis proposed by Guesnerie (2005) similarly assumes that individuals make decisions that are optimal for a particular anticipated future evolution of the economy, and that they each possess a correct model of the economy. It further imposes the stronger restriction that both of these things are "common knowledge" in the sense that that term is used in game theory: each individual's beliefs are consistent with knowledge that all others know that all others know [and so on ad infinitum] that these things are true. Nonetheless, as Guesnerie stresses, only under rather special circumstances are RE beliefs the only ones consistent with such a postulate. (It is in this case that Guesnerie refers to the REE as eductively stable and hence is a reasonable prediction of one's model.) Under more general circumstances, he proposes that one should consider the entire set of possible paths for the economy that can be supported by beliefs consistent with common knowledge of rationality (the analog of the "rationalizable" outcomes considered by Bernheim [1984] and Pearce [1984]). This includes paths along which fluctuations in asset prices occur that are sustained purely by changing conjectures about how others will value the assets in the

---

2. This assumes that the process would converge, if pursued far enough. In the examples considered by Evans and Ramey (1992), this is the case, and their interest is in the alternative forecasts that remain possible when the calculation is instead truncated after a finite number of iterations. But such an algorithm need not converge at all, nor need there be a unique limiting forecast independent of the initial conjecture, as Guesnerie (2005) emphasizes.

3. Of course, this would still only be an equilibrium relative to the model that they happen to believe in, because the iterative calculation is merely a check on the internal consistency of their forecasting and is not a proof that it must correctly describe how the world will actually evolve. Thus, such a conception of how people forecast could still allow for surprises, at which times there might be an abrupt change in the model that people believe and hence in the way that they forecast.

future—conjectures that must be consistent with similar rationalizability of the conjectured future beliefs. Guesnerie proposes that policies should be selected with an eye on the entire set of rationalizable outcomes associated with a given policy; for example, it may be desirable to eliminate the risk of fluctuations due to arbitrary changes in expectations by choosing a policy for which a unique REE is eductively stable—but this is a criterion for policy design, rather than something that can be taken for granted.

In the approach proposed by Woodford (2010), a given policy is again associated with an entire set of possible outcomes, rather than with a unique prediction, and it is argued that one should seek a policy that ensures the greatest possible lower bound for the average level of welfare, over the set of outcomes associated with the policy. The set of possible outcomes corresponds to a set of possible (not perfectly model-consistent) beliefs about the economy's future evolution that people may entertain. In this approach, however, the set of possible beliefs is disciplined not by a requirement that the evolution in question be rationalizable using a theory of others' behavior (more generally, be consistent with knowledge of the correct model of the economy), but rather by a requirement that subjective beliefs not be grossly out of line with actual probabilities—an assumption of "near-rational expectations." For example, events that occur with complete certainty (according to the policy analyst's model) are assumed to be correctly anticipated, though events that occur with probabilities strictly between zero and one may be assigned somewhat incorrect probabilities. A parameter (which indexes the analyst's degree of concern for robustness of policy to departures from model-consistent expectations) determines how large of a discrepancy between subjective and model-implied probabilities is to be contemplated.[4] This approach requires policymakers to contemplate equilibrium outcomes that differ from the REE prediction to a greater or lesser extent, depending on policy and other aspects of the economic structure. For example, for a given value of the robustness parameter, equilibrium valuations of long-lived risky assets can depart to a greater extent from their "fundamental" (REE) values when the short-term riskless rate of return is lower, so that the anticipated future sale price of the asset accounts for a larger share of its current valuation.

Each of these concepts assumes less-perfect coordination of expectations than does the hypothesis of RE, and so they may provide a more plausible basis for policy analysis following structural change. Yet in each case, the central bank's commitments regarding future policy will influence the set of possible subjective forecasts consistent with the hypothesis. In the proposals

---

4. Note that what is relevant is the discrepancy between the subjective beliefs and what the model predicts should happen *if people hold those beliefs*, and not the discrepancy between subjective and REE beliefs. These may be quite different, if the model's prediction for the economy's evolution is highly sensitive to subjective beliefs.

of Evans and Ramey (1992) or of Guesnerie (2005), this is because the mapping from given conjectures about others' forecasts to what one should oneself forecast (using the model of the economy) is influenced by the central bank's public commitments regarding its conduct of policy. In the Woodford (2010) proposal, it is because the degree of discrepancy between given subjective beliefs and model-consistent beliefs will depend on policy commitments. Hence in any of these approaches, a comparative evaluation of alternative monetary policies will require a specification of the entire (state-contingent) future path of policy, and not simply a current action, just as in the case of REE analysis. Similarly, there will be potential benefits from commitment relative to the outcome under discretionary policy. Indeed, Woodford (2010) finds that when the policymaker wishes to choose a policy that is robust to departures from fully model-consistent expectations, the advantages of commitment over discretionary policy are even greater than when one assumes that agents in the economy will necessarily have RE.

Regardless of the degree of expectational coordination that is assumed, is it still reasonable for a central bank to commit itself in advance to a rule, chosen based on one view of what possible future contingencies may arise, even though future situations may well arise that were not contemplated at all?

I believe that the argument that rule-based policymaking is necessarily foolhardy in a world where nonroutine change occurs depends on too narrow a conception of what is involved in following a rule. In particular, it is important to recognize that there are different levels at which it is possible to describe the process through which policy decisions are to be made. Judgment may be exercised in the application of policy to particular circumstances (at a more concrete level of description of the policy) even though the judgment is used to determine the implications of a rule (at a more general level of description) that has been stated explicitly in advance. At a general level of description, it may be possible to state in advance a rule that is to be applied; but at a more concrete level of description of the policy, the application of the rule to specific circumstances may require an exercise of judgment.

I illustrate this idea with a more detailed discussion of possible types of commitments in the case of monetary policy.

13.3 Alternative Levels of Policy Commitment: The Case of Monetary Policy

One might imagine a rule for the conduct of monetary policy being specified at any of four distinct levels of description of the policy in question.[5] These

---

5. The first three levels are distinguished in Woodford (2007: 5–9), which also discusses the possible specification of policy rules at the different levels.

involve increasing degrees of abstraction as one proceeds to higher level descriptions.

The lowest level is what I call the "operational" level. At the most concrete level of description, monetary policy (under routine conditions, rather than those during the recent crisis) involves a decision about a quantity of bank reserves to inject or withdraw each day, typically through open-market purchases or repo transactions. One might imagine that a monetary policy rule should be a specific formula that would tell the Trading Desk of the Federal Reserve Bank of New York (or the corresponding branch of another central bank) which trades to execute each day, as a function of various observable conditions. McCallum (1988, 1999) argues for a policy rule that is operational in this sense, and so proposes rules that specify equations for the adjustment of the monetary base.

The literature on monetary policy rules has instead often discussed specifications at a second, somewhat higher level, which I call the "instrument" level. At most central banks, the key decision of the policy committee (again, under routine conditions) is the choice of an operating target for a particular overnight interest rate—the federal funds rate, under the operating procedures of the Federal Reserve since at least the mid-1980s. The decision about how to achieve this target through market trades is then delegated to staff members with these operational responsibilities, or is at any rate determined without having to convene the central's policy committee (i.e., the committee that chooses the operating target for the instrument of policy: the Federal Open Market Committee, in the case of the United States).[6] One might imagine that a monetary policy rule should be a specific formula that determines what the correct target for the federal funds rate should be at each point in time, as a function of observable variables. The celebrated Taylor rule (Taylor 1993) is of this form, and so are most empirical characterizations of policy through estimation of a central bank reaction function and most of the normative proposals considered in the theoretical literature.

A still higher level description of policy is possible, however, at least in the case of those central banks basing their policy decisions on a clear intellectual framework that remains constant over the course of many meetings of the policy committee and is articulated with some degree of explicitness in the bank's public communications. This level can be referred to as the "policy-targets" level.[7] A central bank may determine the correct instrument setting (i.e., the operating target for the policy rate) at each meeting of the policy committee on the basis of previously specified targets for other

6. For the distinction between instrument choice and the decisions involved in implementation of that decision, see, for example, Friedman and Kuttner (2011).

7. The distinction between policy prescriptions that are specified at the instrument level (instrument rules) and those specified at the policy-targets level (targeting rules) has been stressed in particular by Svensson (2003).

macroeconomic variables that are expected to be indirectly influenced by the path of the policy rate.

In particular, a forecast-targeting regime (Svensson 1999, 2005; Woodford 2007) involves choosing a target for the policy rate at each meeting that is consistent with the anticipated path for the policy rate required (according to the policy committee's analysis) for the economy's projected evolution to satisfy a quantitative target criterion. A policy rule might be specified by announcing the particular target criterion that will guide such deliberations; Svensson calls such a prescription a "targeting rule" (as opposed to an "instrument rule," e.g., the Taylor rule). This is in fact the level at which central banks have most been willing to commit themselves to explicit criteria for the conduct of policy. Many central banks now have explicit quantitative targets for some measure of medium-run inflation; a few have also been fairly explicit about the criteria used to judge whether near-term economic projections are acceptable, and about the way in which projections for variables other than inflation are taken into account (Qvigstad 2006).[8]

Finally, it is possible, at least in principle, for a central bank's policy commitments to be formulated at a still higher level, which I call the "policy-design" level. At this level, one would specify the principles on which policy targets are chosen, given a particular model of the way that monetary policy affects the economy. A commitment to specified principles at this level could be maintained in the face of a change in either the structure of the economy or policymakers' understanding of that structure, even though it might well be appropriate to modify a central bank's policy targets in light of such change. I do not think that any central banks have yet made explicit statements committing themselves to principles of policy design at this level of abstraction. But the formulation of useful principles at this level has been a goal of at least a part of the research literature on normative monetary policy. I believe that the quest for useful principles at this level becomes more important the more seriously one takes the likelihood of nonroutine change.

13.3.1 At Which Level of Specification Is Policy Commitment Appropriate?

Note that these four distinct levels are mutually compatible ways of describing a central bank's policy; the same policy might simultaneously be correctly described at each of these levels. Hence, when contrasting possible specifications of monetary policy "rules" of these four distinct types, one is not necessarily talking about policies that are different, in terms of the actions that they would require a central bank to take under particular

---

8. See Woodford (2007: 21–25) for further discussion of the Norges Bank procedures as a particularly explicit example of a forecast-targeting approach.

circumstances. But the levels of description differ in the degree to which it is useful to imagine specifying a rule for policy in advance.

At each successively lower level of the specification, one comes closer to saying precisely what the central bank ultimately must do. At each lower level, finer institutional details about the precise mechanism through which monetary policy affects the economy become relevant. And finally, at each lower level, it is appropriate for the central bank to be prepared to adjust course more frequently on the basis of more recent information. In practice, decisions will be reviewed more frequently, the lower the level is. For example, in the case of the Federal Reserve, decisions at the operational level are adjusted daily, and sometimes more often, during periods of market turmoil. In contrast, decisions at the instrument level are scheduled for review only 8 times a year, though occasionally intermeeting changes in the funds rate target are judged necessary. The policy committees of inflation-targeting central banks reconsider the appropriateness of the planned path for the policy rate 8 or 12 times a year, but the inflation target itself remains unchanged for years. Yet even inflation targets change from time to time; for example, the Bank of England's official target was changed at the end of 2003, and the European Central Bank slightly changed its definition of price stability after a review of its monetary policy strategy in 2003. The Bank of Canada's inflation target has been modified several times since its introduction in 1991 and is reviewed at 5-year intervals. And surely the possibility of such changes in the light of changing knowledge is entirely appropriate.

The degree to which it is either possible or useful to articulate the principles on which decisions are made also differs greatly depending on the level of specification. I think that few monetary economists or central bankers—even among those who are strong proponents of rule-based policy and central bank transparency—would argue that there is a need for explicit policy commitments at the operational level. The literature on the consequences of alternative policy rules generally assumes that any nonnegative target for the policy rate can be implemented with a high degree of accuracy over time scales (a day or two) that are quite short compared to those that matter for the effects of interest rate policy on economic activity and inflation. It is similarly assumed that the open-market operations required to implement the policy have few if any consequences for the objectives of policy, other than through their effects on interest rates. Moreover, although in principle the same policy prescription (say, adherence to the Taylor rule) should have an equivalent formulation at the operational level, it would be complex to describe this in detail (i.e., to give a precise algorithm that would allow the correct operational decision to be computed under all possible circumstances). A simplified description at the operational level might instead be practical. However, if this is regarded as an actual commitment about how policy will be conducted, it would be less successful at achieving the desired outcome with regard to the state-contingent evolution of the policy instrument, and hence less successful at achieving the central bank's higher level stabilization objectives. Hence insistence on an operational policy commitment would have clear costs.

Deviations from a bank's routine approach to the implementation of its interest rate target are often necessary at times of crisis, as increased uncertainty leads to a sudden increase in demands for liquidity. For example, Sundaresan and Wang (2009) describe the special measures introduced by the Fed to deal with unusual liquidity needs around the time of the millennium date change (the so-called Y2K scare), in such a way as to minimize the consequences of this unusual behavior for money market interest rates. An inability to respond in this way, owing to the existence of a rigid policy commitment at the operational level, would likely have meant greater disruption of financial markets. At the same time, the benefits of such a low-level commitment seem minimal. The most important argument for the desirability of a lower level commitment is that accountability of the central bank to the public is increased by specifying exactly what must be done in terms that can be verified by outside observers. But one cannot really say that a commitment at the instrument level, without specifying in advance the precise operational decisions required, reduces accountability to any significant extent, given central banks' degree of success at achieving their interest rate targets over short time horizons in practice.

It is less obvious that a description of policy at a level of abstraction higher than the instrument level should suffice. Indeed, the literature on the quantitative evaluation of policy rules has almost exclusively focused on rules specified as formulas to determine the value of a policy instrument that is under relatively direct control of the central bank (see, for example, the review of this literature by Taylor and Williams 2011). Nonetheless, I think there are important advantages to considering rules specified by target criteria that need not involve any variable directly controlled by the central bank.

A first question is whether a mere specification of a target criterion suffices to fully determine outcomes under the policy, so that one can compare the outcomes associated with alternative policies. This issue is undoubtedly of practical relevance. For example, a criterion that only involves projected outcomes 2 or more years in the future (as is true of the explicit commitments of many inflation-targeting central banks) is one that is unlikely to imply a determinate solution; there will be alternative paths by which the economy could reach a situation consistent with the criterion, and in such a case the target criterion fails to fully determine policy. In my view, it is important to adopt a target criterion that does fully determine (but not overdetermine) a particular equilibrium. But this is a property that one can analyze given a specification of the target criterion alone; one need not specify the policy at a lower level. Giannoni and Woodford (2010) illustrate how this kind of calculation can be undertaken assuming RE and using a structural model of the economy that specifies the constraints on feasible equilibrium paths of the target variables. The model need not even include the additional model equations required to determine the evolution of the central bank's policy instrument. Giannoni and Woodford also describe a general approach to the derivation of target criteria that guarantees, among other desiderata, that the target criterion necessarily determines a unique bounded REE. There is also a question whether a given interest rate feedback rule determines a unique REE; one argument for the importance of choosing a rule that conforms to the Taylor Principle is that in many models, rules with weaker feedback from inflation to the interest rate operating target have been found to result in indeterminacy of equilibrium (e.g.,Woodford 2003: 252–261).

It is true that the literature on this topic typically assumes RE, and one might wonder instead how precisely the predicted evolution of variables (e.g., inflation and real activity) is pinned down if one admits that people in the economy may not all anticipate the evolution that the policy analyst's own model predicts. I believe that a consideration of this issue is another important part of an analysis of the desirability of a proposed target criterion. But this question can also be analyzed without any need to specify the associated evolution of the central bank's interest rate instrument, as illustrated by Woodford (2010). Moreover, specification of a policy commitment at the level of an instrument rule (or central bank reaction function), rather than through a target criterion, only increases the degree of uncertainty about the equilibrium outcome that results from doubts about whether people in the economy will have model-consistent expectations. This is because the relation between the interest rate reaction function and the evolution of the variables of interest (the "target variables" in terms of which the central bank's stabilization objectives are expressed) is more indirect than the relation between the target criterion and the paths of these variables. In addition, the number of ways in which departures from model-consistent expectations can skew the outcome implied by the policy is correspondingly larger.

The analysis by Evans and Honkapohja (2003) illustrates this point, though they do not express the matter in quite this way. They analyze a standard New Keynesian model (the one analyzed by Clarida et al. [1999] under the RE assumption) under a particular hypothesized alternative to RE, namely least-squares learning dynamics. They compare predicted outcomes under the learning dynamics in the case of two different policy specifications that would be regarded as equivalent under the assumption of RE. (Both imply a determinate REE, and the REE evolution of the endogenous variables that each determines is the same.) The two rules are each described in their paper as interest rate reaction functions. However, the one they call the "expectations-based policy rule" is the equation determining the instrument-level interest rate; they obtain this equation by inverting their model's structural equations to determine the interest rate as a function of *observed private sector expectations,* whether those correspond to the model-consistent expectations or not. This derivation implies that the evolution of inflation and the output gap satisfy a particular target criterion (a type of flexible inflation target) that can be expressed in terms of those two variables alone. Systematic adherence to this rule is equivalent to commitment to the target criterion, rather than to any particular equation specifying the instrument as a function of "objective" factors without reference to people's expectations. The alternative rule that they consider (the "fundamentals-based policy rule") is instead a formula for the instrument-level setting as a function of the exogenous state of the world at each point in time. The two rules are chosen so that they would both determine precisely the same equilibrium evolution for the economy, under the assumption of RE. Yet Evans and Honkapohja show that under least-squares learning dynamics, a commitment to the target criterion (i.e., expectations-based policy) leads to convergence to the REE, whereas commitment to the instrument rule results in unstable dynamics.

A second question is whether specification of a target criterion, rather than a reaction function for the instrument, is a useful way of providing a guideline for policymakers in their deliberations. Of course, a monetary policy committee has to decide on the level of overnight interest rates, so the target criterion alone does not provide them with sufficient information to discharge their duty. Nonetheless, a target criterion relating the paths of some of the variables that the policy committee wishes to stabilize seems to be the appropriate level of detail for a prescription that a policy committee can agree to use to structure its discussions, that can be explained to new members of the committee, and that can ensure some degree of continuity in policy over time. Special factors are likely to be important at each meeting when deciding on the level of interest rates consistent with fulfillment of the target criterion; hence it is difficult to impose too much structure on this kind of deliberation without the committee members feeling that their procedures are grossly inadequate to dealing with the complexity of the situation. The considerations involved in deciding whether a particular target criterion is sensible are instead less likely to constantly change.

Indeed, there are important theoretical reasons to expect that a desirable target criterion will depend on fewer details about the current economic environment than would a desirable specification of a reaction function. Giannoni and Woodford (2010) show how to construct robustly optimal target criteria that implement an optimal response to shocks, regardless of which types of shocks are more important or of the degree of persistence, forecastability, and so on of the shocks that occur. The coefficients of an optimal reaction function will instead depend on the statistical properties of the shocks.[9] Because each shock to the economy is always somewhat

---

9. This behavior is illustrated in Woodford (2003: 529–530) in the context of a simple example.

different from any other, there will always be new information about the particular types of disturbances that have most recently occurred, making advance commitment to a particular reaction function inconvenient. The types of structural change that imply a change in the form or coefficients of the desirable target criterion instead occur more infrequently, though they certainly also occur.

As an example of the undesirability of strict commitment to an instrument rule, consider the consequences of the disruption of financial markets during the global financial crisis of 2007–2009. Prior to the crisis, other U.S. dollar money market interest rates moved closely with changes in the federal funds rate, so that adjustment of the Federal Open Market Committee's target for the funds rate (which in turn resulted in actions that kept the effective funds rate very close to that target, on virtually a daily basis) had direct implications for other rates as well. But during the crisis, many other short-term rates departed substantially from the path of the funds rate. For example, one closely monitored indicator, the London Interbank Offered Rate (LIBOR) for the U.S. dollar—to which the lending terms available to many nonfinancial borrowers are automatically linked—had always remained close to the market forecast of the average funds rate over the corresponding horizon (as indicated by the overnight interest rate swap rate). But after the summer of 2007, a spread that had previously been extremely stable and of 10 basis points or less became highly volatile and at certain times reached several percentage points.

The same kind of Taylor rule for the federal funds rate as a function of general macroeconomic conditions (inflation and real activity) that might be appropriate at other times should not be expected to remain a reliable indicator when the relation between the funds rate and other market interest rates changes. For example, in the simulations of Cúrdia and Woodford (2010a), an inflexible commitment to the standard Taylor rule leads to overly tight policy when a financial disturbance increases spreads between the funds rate and the rates faced by other borrowers. Yet commitment to a target criterion is not subject to the same critique. Even if the central bank's target criterion involves only the projections for inflation and some measure of aggregate real activity, if the bank correctly accounts for the consequences of financial disruptions on the monetary transmission mechanism in the forecast-targeting exercise, it will necessarily be sensitive to changing financial conditions when choosing a path for its policy rate. Likewise, it will modify its implementation procedures, if necessary, the more effectively to keep the policy rate close to that path.

One might counter that such an example shows only that a central bank must be willing to consider modifications of its commitment to an instrument rule occasionally, under sufficiently unusual circumstances. Indeed, John Taylor himself (Taylor 2008) proposed a modification of his celebrated rule during the crisis, under which the funds rate target (given specific values for the current inflation rate and output gap) should be adjusted downward one-for-one with any increase in the LIBOR–Overnight Indexed Swap rate (OIS) spread. However, even this proposed modification is unlikely to provide as accurate a guideline as would be provided by commitment instead to a target criterion and the use of many indicators to determine the instrument setting required to implement it. Taylor's quest for a simple reaction function that can be stated publicly in advance of the decisions made when using it requires him to choose a single indicator of financial conditions—the LIBOR-OIS spread at one particular term. But in fact there are many market rates and asset prices that influence economic decisions, and the different possible spreads and other indicators of financial conditions behave differently, especially during periods of financial instability (e.g., see Hatzius et al. 2010). Commitment to a target criterion rather than to a specific reaction function automatically allows a large number of indicators to be taken into account when judging the instrument setting that is required for consistency with the target criterion. In addition, the indicators that are considered and the weights given to them can easily be changed when economic conditions change.

Hence I would argue that the level at which it is most valuable for a central bank to make an explicit commitment—one that can be expected to guide policy for at least some years into the future—is that of a target criterion (for a detailed discussion, see Woodford 2007). This criterion can then be used to guide policy decisions at the instrument level through commitment to a forecast-targeting procedure for making instrument decisions. In turn these can be used to guide policy decisions at the operational level by making the staff in charge of operations responsible for achieving the operating target over a fairly short time horizon, without any need to specify the requisite market interventions. Note that the process used to derive the instrument path and the concrete market transactions required to implement it should take into account changes in market conditions, including ones that may not have been foreseeable when the target criterion was adopted.

Although I believe it is useful for policymakers to articulate a policy commitment at the level of a target criterion, the kind of commitment that I have in mind does not preclude reevaluation of the target criterion, if there is a significant change in the policy authority's view of the relevant conditions. For example, there may be progress in understanding how the economy works. The benefits obtained from an explicit policy commitment are not vitiated by allowing for occasional reconsideration of the target criterion, if the authority remains committed to choosing the new target criterion in accordance with its higher level commitment to particular principles of policy design.

These highest level principles will include, of course, a specification of the ultimate goals that the policy targets are intended to serve. (In the theory of monetary policy expounded in Woodford [2003], for example, the ultimate goal is assumed to be the maximization of the expected utility of a representative household.) But there are other important principles that deserve to be articulated. For example, I have proposed that when policy targets are reconsidered, they should be chosen from what I have called a "timeless perspective" (Woodford 1999).

13.3.2   Policy Design from a Timeless Perspective

By "choice from a timeless perspective" I mean that the rule of conduct that is chosen is the one that the policy authority would have wished to commit itself to—had it then had the knowledge of the economy's structure that it has now—at a time far enough in the past for all possible consequences of the public's anticipation of the bank's systematic pattern of conduct to be taken into account.[10] I argue that this is a desirable criterion for choice even though, at the time that the new target criterion is actually adopted, the public has already anticipated whatever it has anticipated up until that point, and these past expectations can no longer be affected by the current decision. They can only be fulfilled or disappointed.

This proposal is somewhat in the spirit of John Rawls's (1971) interpretation of social contract theory, according to which citizens should accept as binding the principles of justice to which they have not actually voluntarily submitted themselves, on the grounds that these principles are ones that they should have been willing to choose in a hypothetical "original position," from which—not yet knowing anything about the actual situation that they will occupy in society—they would not make choices that seek to take advantage of the particular circumstances of the individual that they actually become. The doctrine of the timeless perspective similarly argues that a central bank should accept to be bound by principles that it would have accepted before reaching its current situation by having previously considered the possibility of reaching that situation, among others.

A commitment to always choose new policy targets from a timeless perspective means that the occasion of a reconsideration of the policy targets can never be used as an excuse for reneging on previous policy commitments simply because the policymaker's incentives are different ex post (when the effects of the anticipation of her actions need no longer be taken into account) than they were ex ante (when such effects were internalized). In the absence of a commitment to this principle—if, instead, the policy authority simply chooses the new target criterion associated with the best possible equilibrium from the current date—the need to reconsider policy targets from time to time raises difficulties similar to those discussed in the critique of discretionary policy by Kydland and Prescott (1977). In fact, this approach would reduce precisely to discretionary policy in the sense

---

10. See Woodford (2008, 2011: 743–748) for further discussion of this issue in general terms.

of Kydland and Prescott, if the policy target were reconsidered each time a policy action must be taken. The problem is less severe if reconsiderations are less frequent, but the question of why frequent reconsiderations should not be justifiable would itself have to be faced. Strictly speaking, the state of knowledge will constantly be changing, so that if reconsideration is justified when the policy authority's model of the economy changes, there is no obvious limit to the frequency of possible reconsiderations. Moreover, a policy authority that is not committed to the choice of targets from a timeless perspective would have a constant incentive to use any pretext, however minor, to call for reconsideration of the policy targets that it has previously announced but does not wish to adhere to.

With a commitment to choose the target criterion from a timeless perspective, it is no longer essential to prespecify the kinds of situations in which it will be legitimate to reconsider the target criterion. When this principle is followed, a reconsideration will always lead the policy authority to reaffirm precisely the same target criterion as it chose on the previous occasion *if there has been no change in its model of the economy*.[11] In this case it will, as a practical matter, not make sense to go through the necessarily laborious process of debating the appropriateness of the target criterion except when there has been a substantial change in the authority's view of the economy's functioning. Hence reconsiderations of the target criterion should occur much less frequently than reconsiderations of the operating target for the policy rate, as stated above.

13.4   The Theory of Monetary Policy after the Global Financial Crisis

A thorough discussion of the kind of target criterion appropriate for a central bank to adopt is beyond the scope of this chapter. However, some brief remarks may nonetheless be appropriate about an issue that is likely to be on the minds of many at present: To what extent have the dramatic complications facing central banks during the recent global financial crisis shown that ideas about rule-based policymaking that were popular (in academic circles and at some central banks) prior to the crisis must be thoroughly reconsidered? And should such reconsideration cast doubt on the very wisdom of proposing that central banks articulate policy commitments on the basis of economic models that must always be regarded as (at best) provisional attempts to comprehend a complex and ever-changing reality?[12]

---

11. A general method for deriving an optimal target criterion given the policy authority's stabilization objective and its economic model, in a way that conforms to this principle, is explained in Giannoni and Woodford (2010).

12. See Woodford (2010) for further discussion of these issues.

Although reassessments of the theory of monetary policy in the light of the crisis have only begun, a few conclusions are already clear. Disruption of the normal functioning of financial markets, of the kind observed during the crisis, certainly affects the connection between central bank market interventions and the bank's policy rate, the connection between that policy rate and other equilibrium rates of return, and hence the bank's stabilization objectives. It follows that the appropriate policy decisions, at least at the operational and instrument levels, will surely be affected.

Commitment to a mechanical rule specified at one of these lower levels is unwise under such circumstances. For example, an inflexible commitment to the standard Taylor rule will lead to policy that is too tight in the case of financial disturbances, as illustrated by the simulations of Cúrdia and Woodford (2010a). But as argued in the previous section, monetary policy recommendations that are expressed in the form of a target criterion are not so obviously problematic. In fact, except in quite special circumstances, taking account of financial market imperfections should also have consequences for the form of a desirable target criterion. For example, in the presence of financial distortions, there are additional appropriate stabilization goals for policy that could safely be neglected if the financial system could be relied on to function efficiently. (The minimization of financial distortions becomes an additional stabilization goal, in addition to the traditional concerns for price stability and an efficient aggregate level of resource utilization, because of the implications of financial intermediation for the efficiency of the *composition* of expenditure and of production, and not just for their aggregate levels.) These additional concerns almost certainly imply that an ideal target criterion should involve additional variables beyond those that would suffice in a world with efficient financial intermediation. Nonetheless, the severity of the distortions resulting from the neglect of such refinements is probably not as great in the case of commitment to a target criterion as in the case of commitment to an instrument rule for the federal funds rate. At any rate, this is what the simulations reported in Cúrdia and Woodford (2010a) suggest.

Another special problem for many central banks raised by the crisis is that the zero lower bound on short-term nominal interest rates became a binding constraint on the use of traditional interest rate policy to achieve the desired degree of monetary stimulus. A situation in which the constraint binds is theoretically possible, but practically unlikely, in the absence of substantial disruption of the financial system; hence the issue was ignored in many analyses of optimal monetary policy rules prior to the crisis.

This constraint certainly changes what can be achieved by interest rate policy and must be taken into account when choosing an appropriate state-contingent path for the policy rate. However, it does not mean that an appropriate criterion for choosing the path for the policy rate is necessarily much different from the kind that would have been recommended by the standard literature.[13] Eggertsson and Woodford (2003) show that even when the zero lower bound is expected sometimes to bind, an optimal policy commitment can still be characterized by commitment to a particular target criterion. Although the optimal target criterion in this case is slightly more complex than those recommended in the literature (which assumed the bound would never be a binding constraint), Eggertsson and Woodford also show that a particular type of simpler target criterion already advocated in the theoretical literature continues to provide a fairly good approximation to optimal policy (at least in the numerical example that they analyze) even in the case of a crisis that causes the zero lower bound to bind for a substantial number of quarters.[14]

The key feature that is required for a targeting regime to have desirable properties when the zero lower bound binds is for the target criterion to involve a price-level target path, rather than only a target for the rate of inflation looking forward. A purely forward-looking approach to inflation targeting can lead to a very bad outcome when the zero lower bound constrains policy, as shown by Eggertsson and Woodford (2003), because the central bank may be unable to prevent undershooting of its target while the constraint binds. Yet it will permanently lock in any unwanted price declines that occur by continuing to target inflation in a purely forward-looking way once it regains control of aggregate expenditure. An expectation that this will occur leads to expectations of a deflationary bias to policy (to the extent that people correctly understand how the regime will work), which make the zero lower bound on nominal interest rates an even tighter constraint; in such a regime, expectations of deflation and contraction become self-fulfilling, amplifying the effects of the original disturbance. In contrast, in the case of commitment to a price-level target path, any undershooting of the path implies a greater degree of future inflation that will be required to "catch up" to the target path. Hence (again, to the extent that people correctly understand how the regime will work) undershooting should create inflationary expectations that, by lowering the anticipated real rate of return associated with a zero nominal interest rate, will tend to automatically limit the degree of undershooting that occurs.[15]

---

13. This issue had not been neglected in the theoretical literature on optimal monetary policy prior to the crisis. Thanks to Japan's experience since the late 1990s, the consequences of a binding zero lower bound had already been the topic of fairly extensive analysis prior to 2008.

14. Eggertsson and Woodford (2003) analyze the issue in the context of a dynamic stochastic general equilibrium model with perfectly functioning financial markets, but Cúrdia and Woodford (2010b) show how the same analysis applies to a model with credit frictions in which the zero lower bound comes to bind as a result of a disruption of financial intermediation.

15. Although no central bank has yet adopted a target of this kind, there has recently been some discussion in the Federal Reserve System of the advantages of doing so, at least as a temporary measure when the zero lower bound constrains policy, as it has in recent years. In particular, see Evans (2010).

The simple target criterion proposed by Eggertsson and Woodford is actually one that has already been recommended as an optimal target criterion in a variety of simple New Keynesian models that abstracted from the zero lower bound. In fact, target criteria that involve a target path for the price level, and not simply a target for the rate of inflation going forward, have been found to be more robust in the sense of reducing the extent to which economic stabilization suffers as a result of errors in achieving the target.[16] The greater robustness of this form of target criterion to difficulties caused by a failure to achieve the target owing to the zero lower bound is closely related to the other robustness results.

Financial disruptions also require reconsideration of the traditional doctrine that interest rate policy is the sole tool that a central bank should use for macroeconomic stabilization, and policy can be conducted while maintaining a balance sheet made up solely of short-term Treasury securities. I would argue that the traditional doctrine is a sound one, as long as financial markets operate with a high degree of efficiency. But disruption of the ability of private parties to effectively arbitrage between different markets, as during the recent crisis, creates a situation in which targeted asset purchases by the central bank and/or special credit facilities serving particular classes of institutions become additional relevant dimensions of central bank policy.

Cúrdia and Woodford (2011) analyze the effects and illustrate the potential usefulness of these additional dimensions of policy in the context of a dynamic stochastic general equilibrium model with credit frictions. They find, however, that the existence of potential additional dimensions of policy does not greatly change the principles for choosing an appropriate target path for the policy rate. Hence these dimensions do not call into question the desirability of a forecast-targeting framework for addressing that issue or even justify departure from a conventional form of target criterion. The extent to which the central bank is able to limit anomalous behavior of credit spreads through unconventional policies will matter, of course, for the appropriate path of the policy rate, as Cúrdia and Woodford show through numerical examples. But this kind of modification of interest rate policy will automatically occur under the forecast-targeting procedure; it does not require a change in the target criterion.

The effective use of unconventional dimensions of policy also requires that policy be conducted within a systematic framework that involves some degree of advance commitment of policy actions, rather than in a purely discretionary fashion. The reasons are similar to those advanced in discussions

---

16. These errors may arise from imperfect knowledge on the part of the central bank, stemming either from poor estimates of parameters of the bank's structural model or from mistaken judgments of the economy's current state. See Woodford (2007, 2011: 741–742) for further discussion of this topic.

of conventional interest rate policy. Once again, the effects of policy depend not only on current actions (e.g., the quantity and type of assets that the Fed purchases this month) but also on expectations about future policy (whether this month's purchases are only the start of an intended sequence of further purchases, how long it intends to hold these assets on its balance sheet, etc.). Given this, a purely discretionary approach to policy, which chooses a current action to achieve some immediate effect without internalizing the consequences of having been anticipated to act in that way, is likely to be quite suboptimal. In particular, the introduction of unconventional measures ought to be accompanied by an explanation of the anticipated exit strategy from these measures.

The crisis has also led to much discussion of the extent to which monetary policy (of the Fed in particular) during the real estate boom contributed to the occurrence or severity of the crisis. This issue raises the question of whether, even during times when financial markets appear to be functioning well, monetary policy decisions need to take into account their potential consequences for financial stability. This is not a topic that is yet well understood, but it is surely an important topic for central bankers to study. In Woodford (2012), I consider some standard arguments for trying to separate this issue from monetary policy deliberations and conclude that the arguments do not justify avoiding this inquiry.

To the extent that the risk of financial crisis is endogenous and is influenced by monetary policy, this is a concern that has not been addressed in traditional analyses of optimal monetary policy rules (e.g., Woodford 2003; Cúrdia and Woodford 2010a,b, 2011). Hence the target criteria for setting monetary policy proposed in the traditional literature are not necessarily appropriate when one takes this additional consideration into account.[17] This is an example of a circumstance under which it might be justifiable for a central bank to modify its existing policy commitment at the policy-targets level, though in a way that is consistent with its existing higher level commitments at the policy-design level.

In Woodford (2012), I give an example of how this might be done. In the simple model proposed there, the optimal target criterion for interest rate policy involves not only the projected path of the price level and of the output gap but also the projected path of a "marginal crisis risk" variable. This variable measures the degree to which marginal adjustments of the policy rate are expected to affect the risk of occurrence of a financial crisis (weighted by the expected welfare loss in the event of such a crisis). In

17. Of course, the significance of the problem will depend on both the degree to which the risk of financial crisis is predictably influenced by monetary policy and the extent to which such risk cannot be adequately controlled using other policy tools (improved regulation, macroprudential supervision, etc.). But I do not believe that we can confidently conclude at this time that the problem is negligible.

periods when the marginal crisis risk is judged to be negligible, the recommended procedure would reduce to flexible price-level targeting of the kind discussed in Woodford (2007). But when the risk is not negligible, the target criterion would require the central bank to tolerate some undershooting of the price-level target path or output relative to the natural rate (or both) to prevent a greater increase in the marginal crisis risk.

Although the adoption of such a procedure would require a departure from recent conventional wisdom, in that it would allow some sacrifice of conventional policy targets to reduce crisis risk, it would maintain many salient characteristics of the kind of policy regime advocated in the precrisis literature. It would still be a form of inflation-targeting regime (more precisely, a form of price-level targeting regime). Such a procedure would not only ensure relative constancy of the inflation rate that people would expect in the medium run (i.e., a few years in the future), but it would also in fact ensure constancy of the long-run price-level path, regardless of the occurrence either of occasional financial crises or of (possibly more frequent) episodes of nontrivial marginal crisis risk.

13.5   Conclusion

I am not suggesting that the recent crisis provides no grounds for reconsideration of previously popular doctrines about central banking. On the contrary, it raises many new issues, some of which are already the topics of an active literature. However, I will be surprised if confronting these issues requires wholesale abandonment of the lessons for policy emphasized by the literature on policy rules. Among the insights that I think most likely to be of continuing relevance is the recognition that suitably chosen policy commitments can substantially improve on the macroeconomic outcomes that could be expected from purely discretionary policy, even when those chosen to exercise the discretion are policymakers of superb intelligence and insight into current economic conditions.

There is an important respect, however, in which prior thinking about the advantages of policy rules should be modified in the light of recent events. It has been common in the theoretical literature to draw a sharp distinction between policy rules—understood as completely specified prescriptions for action under all possible contingencies—and purely discretionary policy, as if these two poles represent the only intellectually coherent positions. I have argued instead for both the possibility and the desirability of an intermediate position, in which there are multiple levels of description of policy; policy can and should be specified in advance at the level of the general principles in accordance with which decisions will be made, whereas judgment that cannot be reduced to a mechanical formula will necessarily be involved in the application of those principles to concrete situations. I have shown in detail how multiple levels of description are possible in the case of monetary policy decisions. I believe that this reformulation of what is understood by a policy rule can increase both the practical relevance of theoretical prescriptions for monetary policy and the political legitimacy of decisionmaking by central banks.

References

Bernheim, Douglas. (1984) "Rationalizable Strategic Behavior," *Econometrica* 52: 1007–1028.

Clarida, Richard, Jordi Gali, and Mark Gertler. (1999) "The Science of Monetary Policy: A New Keynesian Perspective," *Journal of Economic Literature* 37: 1661–1707.

Cúrdia, Vasco, and Michael Woodford. (2010a) "Credit Spreads and Monetary Policy," *Journal of Money, Credit and Banking* 42(s1): 3–35.

———. (2010b) "Conventional and Unconventional Monetary Policy," *Federal Reserve Bank of St. Louis Review* 92: 229–264.

———. (2011) "The Central-Bank Balance Sheet as an Instrument of Monetary Policy," *Journal of Monetary Economics* 58: 54–79.

Eggertsson, Gauti, and Michael Woodford. (2003) "The Zero Interest-Rate Bound and Optimal Monetary Policy," *Brookings Papers on Economic Activity* 2003(1): 271–333.

Evans, Charles. (2010) "Monetary Policy in a Low-Inflation Environment: Developing a State-Contingent Price-Level Target." Speech given at the *55th Economic Conference*, Federal Reserve Bank of Boston, October 16. Available at: http://www.chicagofed.org/webpages/publications/speeches/2010/10_16_boston_speech.cfm.

Evans, George W., and Seppo Honkapohja. (2003) "Expectations and the Stability Problem for Optimal Monetary Policy," *Review of Economic Studies* 70: 807–824.

Evans, George W., and Garey Ramey. (1992) "Expectation Calculation and Macroeconomic Dynamics," *American Economic Review* 82: 207–224.

Friedman, Benjamin M., and Kenneth N. Kuttner. (2011) "Implementation of Monetary Policy: How Do Central Banks Set Interest Rates?" in Benjamin M. Friedman and Michael Woodford (eds.), *Handbook of Monetary Economics,* volume 3B. Amsterdam: Elsevier, pp. 1345–1438.

Frydman, Roman, and Michael D. Goldberg. (2011) *Beyond Mechanical Markets: Asset Price Swings, Risk, and the Role of the State.* Princeton, NJ: Princeton University Press.

Giannoni, Marc P., and Michael Woodford. (2010) "Optimal Target Criteria for Stabilization Policy." NBER Working Paper 15757, National Bureau of Economic Research, Cambridge, MA.

Guesnerie, Roger. (2005) *Assessing Rational Expectations 2: Eductive Stability in Economics.* Cambridge, MA: MIT Press.

Hatzius, Jan, Peter Hooper, Frederic S. Mishkin, Kermit L. Schoenholtz, and Mark W. Watson. (2010) "Financial Conditions Indexes: A Fresh Look after the Financial Crisis." NBER Working Paper 16150, National Bureau of Economic Research, Cambridge, MA.

Keynes, John Maynard. (1936) *The General Theory of Employment, Interest and Money.* New York: Macmillan.

Kydland, Finn E., and Edward C. Prescott. (1977) "Rules Rather Than Discretion: The Inconsistency of Optimal Plans," *Journal of Political Economy* 85: 473–491.

McCallum, Bennett T. (1988) "Robustness Properties of a Rule for Monetary Policy," *Carnegie-Rochester Conference Series on Public Policy* 29: 173–203.

———. (1999) "Issues in the Design of Monetary Policy Rules," in John B. Taylor and Michael Woodford (eds.), *Handbook of Macroeconomics,* volume 1C. Amsterdam: Elsevier, pp. 1483–1530.

Pearce, David. (1984) "Rationalizable Strategic Behavior and the Problem of Perfection," *Econometrica* 52: 1029–1050.

Phelps, Edmund S., G. C. Archibald, and Armen A. Alchian (eds.). (1970) *Microeconomic Foundations of Employment and Inflation Theory.* New York: W. W. Norton.

Qvigstad, Jan F. (2006) "When Does an Interest Rate Path 'Look Good'? Criteria for an Appropriate Future Interest Rate Path: A Practitioner's Approach." Staff Memo 2006/5, Norges Bank, Oslo, Norway.

Rawls, John. (1971) *A Theory of Justice.* Cambridge, MA: Harvard University Press.

Sargent, Thomas J. (1993) "Rational Expectations and the Reconstruction of Macroeconomics," in *Rational Expectations and Inflation,* second edition. New York: HarperCollins, pp. 1–18.

Sundaresan, Suresh, and Zhenyu Wang. (2009) "Y2K Options and the Liquidity Premium in Treasury Markets," *Review of Financial Studies* 22: 1021–1056.

Svensson, Lars E. O. (1999) "Inflation Targeting as a Monetary Policy Rule," *Journal of Monetary Economics* 43: 607–654.

———. (2003) "What Is Wrong with Taylor Rules? Using Judgment in Monetary Policy through Targeting Rules," *Journal of Economic Literature* 41: 426–477.

———. (2005) "Monetary Policy with Judgment: Forecast Targeting," *International Journal of Central Banking* 1: 1–54.

Taylor, John B. (1993) "Discretion versus Policy Rules in Practice," *Carnegie-Rochester Conference Series on Public Policy* 39: 195–214.

———. (2008) "Monetary Policy and the State of the Economy." Testimony before the Committee on Financial Services, U.S. House of Representatives, February 26. Available at: http://www.stanford.edu/~johntayl/Onlinepaperscombinedbyyear/2008/Monetary_Policy_and_the_State_of_the_Economy.pdf.

Taylor, John B., and John C. Williams. (2011) "Simple and Robust Rules for Monetary Policy," in Benjamin M. Friedman and Michael Woodford (eds.), *Handbook of Monetary Economics,* volume 3B. Amsterdam: Elsevier, pp. 829–860.

Woodford, Michael. (1999) "Commentary: How Should Monetary Policy Be Conducted in an Era of Price Stability?" in *New Challenges for Monetary Policy.* Kansas City, MO: Federal Reserve Bank of Kansas City, pp. 277–316.

———. (2003) *Interest and Prices: Foundations of a Theory of Monetary Policy.* Princeton, NJ: Princeton University Press.

———. (2007) "Forecast Targeting as a Monetary Policy Strategy: Policy Rules in Practice." NBER Working Paper 13716, National Bureau of Economic Research, Cambridge, MA.

———. (2008) "Principles and Public Policy Decisions: The Case of Monetary Policy." Paper presented at the *Yale Law School Legal and Economic Organization* seminar, New Haven, CT, March 6. Available at: www.columbia.edu/~mw2230/ Principles and Policy_YLS.pdf.

———. (2010) "Robustly Optimal Monetary Policy with Near-Rational Expectations," *American Economic Review* 100: 274–303.

———. (2011) "Optimal Monetary Stabilization Policy," in Benjamin M. Friedman and Michael Woodford (eds.), *Handbook of Monetary Economics,* volume 3B. Amsterdam: Elsevier, pp. 723–828.

———. (2012) "Inflation Targeting and Financial Stability," *Sveriges Riksbank Economic Review* 2012: 7–32.

Philippe Aghion studied at the French École Normale Superieure de Cachan and received his PhD in economics from Harvard University in 1987. He is currently the Robert C. Waggoner Professor of Economics at Harvard University, after holding positions at CNRS in France, Oxford University, and University College London. His research focuses on growth economics and contract theory. With Peter Howitt, he introduced the so-called Schumpeterian growth paradigm, which he subsequently used to analyze growth policy design, in particular, how growth interacts with competition, macroeconomic policy, education, and the environment. Philippe Aghion is a fellow of the Econometric Society and of the American Academy of Arts and Sciences. In 2001 he received the Yrjö Jahnsson Award, which recognizes a European economist under the age of 45.

Sheila Dow is Emeritus Professor of Economics at the University of Stirling, Scotland; co-Convenor of the Scottish Centre for Economic Methodology; and a Foreign Member of the Center on Capitalism and Society. Before serving on the faculty at Stirling she worked with the Bank of England and the Government of Manitoba, and has served as a special adviser on monetary policy to the UK Treasury Select Committee and as Chair of the International Network for Economic Method. She has published in the areas of methodology, the history of economic thought (especially Hume, Smith, and Keynes), money and banking, and regional finance. Recent books include *Economic Methodology: An Inquiry* (Oxford University Press, 2002), *A History of Scottish Economic Thought* (Routledge, 2006, co-edited with Alexander Dow), and *Open Economics* (Routledge, 2009, co-edited with Richard Arena and Matthias Klaes). Her latest book, *Foundations for New Economic Thinking: A Collection of Essays*, was published by Palgrave Macmillan in 2012.

George W. Evans is the John B. Hamacher Professor of Economics and the College of Arts and Sciences Distinguished Professor at the University of Oregon, and he is also Professor of Economics and Finance at the University of St. Andrews. He has previously held appointments at the University of Stirling, Stanford University, the London School of Economics, and the University of Edinburgh. He is best known for his research on expectational stability and learning in stochastic, dynamic macroeconomic models. He is co-author of *Learning and Expectations in Macroeconomics* (Princeton University Press, 2001, with Seppo Honkapohja) and has published numerous articles in leading economic journals. Recent applications include monetary policy design, asset price bubbles and crashes, macroeconomic policy in deep recession, and the impact of anticipated fiscal policy changes.

Roger E. A. Farmer is Distinguished Professor and Chair of the Department of Economics at the University of California at Los Angeles. He is a Fellow of the Econometric Society, a Research Associate of the National Bureau of Economic Research, a Research Associate of the European Centre for Economic Policy Research, a Fellow Commoner of Cambridge University, and Co-editor of the *International Journal of Economic Theory*. He has served as a consultant to several American Federal Reserve Banks and the Reserve Bank of Australia, the European Central Bank, and the Bank of England. In 2000, he received the University of Helsinki Medal in recognition of his work on self-fulfilling prophecies and multiple equilibria. His most recent academic works on the Great Recession, including two books, *How the Economy Works* (Oxford University Press, 2010) and *Expectations, Employment and Prices* (Oxford University Press, 2010), provide a new paradigm for macroeconomics and a new fiscal and monetary framework for economic stability in the twenty-first century. He will be an Houblon Norman Senior Fellow at the Bank of England in 2013.

Roman Frydman is Professor of Economics at New York University and a founding member of the Center on Capitalism and Society. He was one of the early critics of the Rational Expectations Hypothesis (REH). In recent years, he has worked with Michael Goldberg on a new approach to macroeconomic analysis that jettisons REH models and places rational individuals' need to cope with nonroutine change and imperfect knowledge at the center of the research agenda. They presented their approach in their book *Imperfect Knowledge Economics: Exchange Rates and Risk* (Princeton University Press, 2007). In their latest book, *Beyond Mechanical Markets: Asset Price Swings, Risk, and the Role of the State* (Princeton University Press, 2011), Frydman and Goldberg apply and extend Imperfect Knowledge Economics to assess the causes of the global financial crisis, as well as to propose a new policy framework aimed at rectifying systemic failures. Since October 2011, Frydman has been Chair of the Institute for New Economic Thinking (INET) Program on Imperfect Knowledge Economics.

Michael D. Goldberg is the Todd H. Crockett Professor of Economics at the Peter T. Paul College of Business and Economics, University of New Hampshire, and a Senior Research Associate at the Institute for New Economic Thinking (INET). He has written extensively in the fields of international finance and macroeconomics, and his columns on asset price fluctuations and policy reform have been published by leading newspapers in more than 50 countries. His best-selling books, *Imperfect Knowledge Economics: Exchange Rates and Risk* (2007) and *Beyond Mechanical Markets: Asset Price Swings, Risk, and the Role of the State* (2011), both co-authored with Roman Frydman and published by Princeton University Press, propose a much-needed new approach to economics that places the imperfection of knowledge at the center of analysis. *Beyond Mechanical Markets* was a *Financial Times* nonfiction favorite of 2011, commended by its chief economics commentator, Martin Wolf. James Pressley of Bloomberg News also selected it as a top business book of 2011. *Beyond Mechanical Markets* was a finalist for the 2011 TIAA-CREF Paul A. Samuelson Award and will soon be translated into German, French, Italian, Chinese, and Polish.

Roger Guesnerie is currently holder of the chair "Théorie économique et organisation sociale" at the Collège de France, Director of Studies at École des Hautes Études en Sciences Sociales, and President of the Paris School of Economics. A graduate of the École Polytechnique, he has taught throughout the world. His work in public economics, on the theory of mechanisms, and on general equilibrium has made him one of the best-known French economists. Roger Guesnerie has been a member of the editorial boards of several leading journals in economics, the co-editor of *Econometrica* from 1984 to 1989, the President of the European Economic Association in 1994, the President of the Econometric Society in 1996, and the President of the Association Française de Science Economique in 2003. He was awarded the Medaille d'Argent (Silver Medal) of CNRS in 1993 and has been an Honorary Foreign Member of the American Economic Association since 1997 and a member of the American Academy of Arts and Sciences since 2000.

Seppo Honkapohja has been a Member of the (Governing) Board of the Bank of Finland since 2008. Previously he was Professor of International Macroeconomics at the University of Cambridge and before that was Professor of Economics at the University of Helsinki and at the Turku School of Economics and Business Administration. He is a member of Academia Europaea and of the Finnish Academy of Science and Letters, and a Fellow of the Econometric Society and of the European Economic Association. Major publications include the books *Economic Prosperity Recaptured: The*

Finnish Path from Crisis to Prosperity (MIT Press, 2009, co-authored with Erkki Koskela, Willi Leibfrietz, and Roope Uusitalo), *The Nordic Model: Embracing Globalization and Sharing Risks* (Taloustieto OY, 2009, co-authored with Torben M. Andersen, Bengt Holmström, Sixten Korkman, Hans Tson Söderstrom, and Juhana Vartiainen), *Learning and Expectations in Macroeconomics* (Princeton University Press, 2001, co-authored with George W. Evans), *The Swedish Model under Stress: A View from the Stands* (SNS Förlag, 1997, co-authored with Thorvaldur Gylfason, Torben Andersen, Arne Jon Isachsen, and John Williamson); several edited books; and numerous articles in international refereed journals and collected volumes.

Katarina Juselius is Professor in the Economics Department at the University of Copenhagen and is one of Denmark's leading scientists specializing in the methodology and applications of cointegrated vector autoregressive models. She has written the book *The Cointegrated VAR Model: Methodology and Applications* (Oxford University Press, 2006), has published extensively in international peer-reviewed journals, has been invited to write handbook chapters, and is one of the most frequently cited economists in the world. She is also an active member of the scientific community and has been a member of several scientific councils and advisory committees in Denmark and abroad. She is a former Chair of the EuroCore and Forward Look Programmes at the European Science Foundation and has been a member of the Danish Independent Research Council for the Social Sciences. She is presently the director of the Institute for New Economic Thinking (INET) Center for Imperfect Knowledge Economics at the University of Copenhagen.

Enisse Kharroubi is an economist in the Monetary Policy Division of the Bank for International Settlements (BIS), which he joined in August 2010. Prior to that, he served as a senior economist in the International Affairs Department of the Bank of France. He holds an MS in economics from the French National School for Statistics (ENSAE) and a PhD in economics from the Paris School of Economics (2004). He joined the Bank of France just after obtaining his PhD and first served in the Economic Studies Department on financial integration before moving to the Macro Analysis and Forecast Department, where he specialized in emerging market economies. In 2008, he joined the International Affairs Department to work on liquidity and global imbalances. His main areas of research are financial economics, international macroeconomics and finance, and fiscal and monetary policy.

Blake LeBaron has a PhD in economics from the University of Chicago. He is the Abram L. and Thelma Sachar Chair of International Economics at the International Business School at Brandeis University. He is a Research Associate at the National Bureau of Economic Research, and he was a Sloan Fellow. He also served as Director of the Economics Program at the

Santa Fe Institute in 1993. His current research interests are focused on understanding the quantitative dynamics of interacting systems of adaptive agents and how these systems replicate observed real-world phenomena.

Edmund S. Phelps was born in 1933 near Chicago and received his BA from Amherst College in 1955 and his PhD from Yale University in 1958. After appointments at Yale and the University of Pennsylvania he joined Columbia University in 1971. He founded the Center on Capitalism and Society in 2001 and won the 2006 Nobel Prize in Economics. In 2008 he was named Chevalier of the Legion of Honor, received the Premio Pico della Mirandola and the Kiel Global Economy Prize, and was honored by the establishment of a Phelps Chair at the Universidad de Buenos Aires. In 2010 he was appointed President-Dean of the New Huadu Business School and awarded an honorary doctoral degree from the Université libre de Bruxelles. In 2011 he was given the Louise Blouin Award for Creative Leadership and appointed Full Foreign Member of the Russian Academy of Sciences.

John B. Taylor is the Mary and Robert Raymond Professor of Economics at Stanford University and the George P. Shultz Senior Fellow in Economics at Stanford's Hoover Institution. He served as senior economist on the President's Council of Economic Advisers from 1976 to 1977, as a member of the Council from 1989 to 1991, as a member of the Congressional Budget Office's Panel of Economic Advisers from 1995 to 2001, and as Under Secretary of the Treasury for International Affairs from 2001 to 2005. Among many awards for his contributions to research and policy, he has received the Bradley Prize, the Adam Smith Award from the National Association for Business Economics, the Alexander Hamilton Award, and the United States Treasury Distinguished Service Award. He was awarded the Hoagland Prize and the Rhodes Prizes for excellence in undergraduate teaching. He received a BA summa cum laude from Princeton University and a PhD from Stanford University. His latest book is *First Principles: Five Keys for Restoring America's Prosperity* (W. W. Norton, 2012), which won the Hayek Prize in 2012.

Michael Woodford is the John Bates Clark Professor of Political Economy at Columbia University. He is also a Fellow of the American Academy of Arts and Sciences, as well as a Fellow of the Econometric Society, a Research Associate of the National Bureau of Economic Research, and a Research Fellow of the Centre for Economic Policy Research. In 2007 he was awarded the Deutsche Bank Prize in Financial Economics. His work includes the treatise *Interest and Prices: Foundations of a Theory of Monetary Policy* (Princeton University Press, 2003). He is also co-editor of a three-volume *Handbook of Macroeconomics* (Elsevier, 1999, with John B. Taylor), a two-volume *Handbook of Monetary Economics* (Elsevier, 2011, with Benjamin M. Friedman), and *The Inflation Targeting Debate* (University of Chicago

Press, 2005, with Ben S. Bernanke). He is a member of the Economic Advisory Panel of the Federal Reserve Bank of New York and a Scientific Advisor for Sveriges Riksbank, the central bank of Sweden.

Gylfi Zoega is Professor of Economics at the University of Iceland and Birkbeck College, London, an external member on the Central Bank of Iceland Monetary Policy Committee, and a Foreign Member of the Center on Capitalism and Society. He has published numerous articles on macroeconomics and labor economics. His work on unemployment dynamics and economic growth has contributed to the understanding of structural booms and slumps. His most recent work is focused on the labor market effects of financial crises.

Page numbers for entries occurring in figures are followed by an *f;* those for entries in notes, by an *n;* and those for entries in tables, by a *t.*